THE VEST-POCKET REAL ESTATE ADVISOR

Martin J. Miles

PRENTICE HALL
Englewood Cliffs, New Jersey 07632

Prentice-Hall International (UK) Limited, *London*
Prentice-Hall of Australia Pty. Limited, *Sydney*
Prentice-Hall Canada Inc., *Toronto*
Prentice-Hall Hispanoamericana, S.A., *Mexico*
Prentice-Hall of India Private Limited, *New Delhi*
Prentice-Hall of Japan, Inc., *Tokyo*
Simon & Schuster Asia Pte. Ltd., *Singapore*
Editora Prentice-Hall do Brasil, Ltda., *Rio de Janeiro*

©1989 by

PRENTICE-HALL, Inc.
Englewood Cliffs, NJ

10 9 8 7 6 5 4 3 2

Library of Congress Cataloging-in-Publication Data

Miles, Martin J., 1933-
   The vest-pocket real estate advisor/by Martin J.
   Miles. p.   cm.
   Includes index.
   ISBN 0-13-945064-5
   1. Real estate business. 2. Business mathe-
matics-Real estate business   I. Title.
HD1375.M477   1989
333.33'01'5121--dc20   89-8476
                                               CIP

ISBN 0-13-945064-5

ISBN 0-13-964941-7 PBK

PRENTICE HALL
BUSINESS & PROFESSIONAL DIVISION
A division of Simon & Schuster
Englewood Cliffs, New Jersey 07632

Printed in the United States of America

To my parents
Mrs. Mary L. and the late Dr. Martin B. Miles,
my children,
Barbara and Martin
and
my granddaughter,
Kelly

ACKNOWLEDGMENTS

The author would like to express his indebtedness to Dr. Edwin L. Crow, mathematical statistician with the National Center for Atmospheric Research; Mr. Robert G. Good and Mr. Paul A. Morris, attorneys at law; Mr. Thomas F. Hagerty, formerly with the Internal Revenue Service; Ms. Patricia Melvin, closings officer with First American Title Company of Colorado; Mr. Werner A. Meuller, assistant vice-president of Alexander & Alexander; and Mr. J. Tom Miles, president of Financial Planning Company. Their review and suggestions were essential.

The author is equally indebted to Ms. Patricia Sanchez for the excellent preparation of this lengthy and difficult manuscript, and to E. Dean Eicher for his excellent illustrations.

WHAT THIS BOOK WILL DO FOR YOU

How soon will this book pay for itself? Just as soon as you put it to work. Consider these three examples:

- You can estimate the monthly payment on a loan at a glance! Consider a $200,000 loan at 12% for 20 years. From page 155 the monthly payment on a $1,000 loan of 12% for 20 years is estimated to be $11. Therefore, the payment on this loan is estimated to be 200 × $11 = $2,200. (The actual payment is $2,202.20.)

- You can salvage a deal by adjusting any two of the following three quantities to suit the parties while preserving the (present) value of the investment:
  - asking price
  - down payment
  - balloon payment due date.

- You can determine the area of any lot— regardless of its shape.

These three features and many, many others can be found here—and nowhere else.

This handy pocket problem-solver is tailored for today's busy real estate professional or investor. It's a working guide to help you quickly solve problems in the complex world of real estate. You'll find formulas, tables, guidelines, rules of thumb, and countless examples to help you analyze and evaluate almost any real estate problem. Throughout, you'll find this book practical, quick, and useful.

Part I introduces you to extraordinary tools to help you optimize your decisions, make projections, and save deals that would otherwise seem hopeless. . .

- You are in the midst of negotiating and need to alter the asking price, the down payment, or the due date of a balloon payment, while maintaining the value of the investment. Simply turn to Chapter 2, and you'll find the answers to solve the problem.

- You have available investment dollars. Should they be used to improve a present property, or buy a new property? A handy technique helps you find the solution.

One formula illustrates how frequently you should "turn over" your property for maximum profitability. Another shows you how to forecast the value of a property, given the rate of inflation, the age, and so on. All of this information will help you quickly increase your profits.

Part II is about "value." It shows you how to estimate the value of real estate—the way appraisers do it. It shows you how to dissect a real estate investment, how to determine the value and rates of return for investors, and how to determine its present value.

Part III shows you how to finance property. It pinpoints the pros and cons of 14 types of mortgages, where to obtain financing for different types of property, how to figure the math of finance, and the legal aspects of mortgages such as default, priority, assignment, and so forth.

Part IV is about property management. You will learn the ins and outs of leases, liens, and tips on day-to-day operations.

Table 1 is one of the most extensive annuity tables to be found. Using this table, you can determine value over time for either annual or monthly compounding. The benefit of having this table at your finger tips is worth the price of the book.

CONTENTS

PART I

IMPORTANT NEW INVESTMENT TOOLS

CHAPTER 1

TOOLS FOR INVESTING SUCCESS

1.1 HOW TO FORECAST PROPERTY VALUE

The future property value can be forecast if the annual rate of change of reproduction cost, the rate of depreciation, and the maintenance are estimated. The change in reproduction cost can be somewhat difficult to estimate because it depends on economic forces external to the property. On the other hand, the rate of depreciation (Section 3.1) can usually be predicted more accurately. The effects of physical deterioration and functional obsolescence can be at least partially offset by the judicious application of maintenance. The effect of economic obsolescence is ignored in the following formulation.

Figure 1.1-1 shows a surface that describes the forecast property value through time and for different amounts of maintenance. Straight line depreciation is assumed for a building with a 20-year economic life. The figure shows the surface for four different annual rates of increase in replacement cost and land value (i.e. 0, 2, 4, and 6%).

The figure for 6% shows that if no maintenance is applied to the building, the property value becomes the value of the land plus salvage value (both have inflated by 6% annually) at the end of the 20-year economic life of the building. Then, the property value is simply the salvage value plus land value. If 50% of the maintenance required to keep the building in new condition is judiciously applied, the building has a value that exceeds salvage value until the 31st year.

3

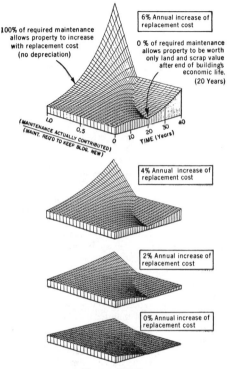

Figure 1.1-1

If 100% of the maintenance required to keep the building in new condition is judiciously applied, the building doesn't depreciate at all, and the entire property value increases at the rate of 6% annually.

The following formula forecasts the future property value based on certain assumptions of reproduction cost, depreciation, and maintenance.

$$V_p = \begin{cases} \left[v_p - A_n \left(v_b - s - \dfrac{m_0}{a_0} \right) \right] \cdot R_n & \text{if } A_n \leq \dfrac{1}{1 - \dfrac{m_0}{a_0(v_b - s)}} \\ \left[v_p - (v_b - s) \right] \cdot R_n & \text{otherwise} \end{cases}$$

where

V_p = forecast property value after n years

v_p, v_b = present value of the property and building, respectively

$m_0 = a_0(v_b - s)$

$$a_0 = \begin{cases} 1/k \\ 2/k \\ w/(k - w) & \text{where } w = 1.25, 1.50, \text{ or } 2.00 \\ t/(1 - e^{-kt}) & \text{where } 0 < t < 0.1 \end{cases}$$

A_n = fraction of accrued depreciation after n years (Section 3.1)

k = remaining economic life of building (Section 13.3)

s = estimated salvage value (Section 13.3)

r_i = annual rate of change of reproduction cost in the ith year,

R_n = cumulative change in reproduction cost

$$= \begin{cases} (1 + r_1) \cdot \ldots \cdot (1 + r_i) \cdot \ldots \cdot (1 + r_n) \\ \qquad\qquad\qquad\qquad \text{if } r_i \text{ is variable} \\ c(r_n, n, 1) & \text{if } r_i \text{ is constant} \end{cases}$$

EXAMPLE

A property owner wants to predict the value of his property three years hence by the reproduction cost approach.

The present value of the property is $200,000, and the building is thought to represent $160,000 of this value. The owner is contributing $1,000 annually to maintenance $\left(\text{a rate of } \dfrac{m_0}{v_p} = \dfrac{\$1,000}{\$200,000} = .005 \right)$ and plans to continue at this rate $\left(\text{i.e., } \dfrac{m_0}{v_p} \right)$. Assume the building is actually depreciating according to the straight line rate. The remaining economic life of the building is 36 years at which time its scrap value is estimated to be $16,000 (i.e., 10% of its present value). If, over the next three years, the change in reproduction cost is −1%, 3%, and 8%, what is the forecast value of the building?

SOLUTION

In this example, $v_p = \$200,000$, $v_b = \$160,000$, $m_0 = \$1,000$, $k = 36$ years (therefore $a_0 = 1/36 = .027778$ and $A_3 = .083333$), $s = \$16,000$, $n = 3$ years, $r_1 = -.01$, $r_2 = .03$, and $r_3 = .08$.

Determine $R_3 = (1 - .01) \cdot (1 + .03) \cdot (1 + .08) = 1.10$. Now the forecast property value by the replacement cost method is

$$V_p = \left[\$200,000 - .083333 \times \left(\$160,000 - \$16,000 - \frac{\$1,000}{.027778}\right)\right] \times 1.10$$

$$= (\$200,000 - .083333 \times \$108,000) \times 1.10$$

$$= \$191,000 \times 1.10$$

$$= \$210,100.$$

1.2 HOW TO DETERMINE THE OPTIMUM HOLDING PERIOD FOR YOUR INVESTMENTS

Due to the costs incurred when buying and selling properties, even good investments must be held for a minimum period of time before these costs are offset. Conversely, a good investment can be held so long that, due to appreciation, there is almost no leverage remaining to the equity investor. That is, the value has increased to the point that nearly all of the value is the investor's equity. There is some holding period between these extreme cases that, theoretically, is optimal in the following sense: If, over a given number of years, an investor repeatedly turned over a certain type of property investment after this optimal period of time, his yield would be greater than if he repeatedly turned over the same property after any other holding period.

Suppose there is a type of investment that one would typically seek and could regularly obtain. The typical investment could be characterized by its yields, $z_1, z_2, \ldots, z_n$ after $1, 2, \ldots, n$ years. Suppose that over n years, this type of investment is acquired and disposed of:

- every year for n years. Let w_1 describe the compound yield resulting at the end of n years.
- every 2 years for n years. Let w_2 describe the compound yield resulting at the end of n years.

. . .

- once at the end of the nth year. Let w_n describe the resulting compound yield.

The above concept not only indicates (theoretically) the optimum holding period for a single investment program, but by comparing the maximum compound yields resulting from two different investment programs, it indicates the more profitable of the two. See Example 2.

FORMULA

$$w_i = (1 + z_i)^{n/i} - 1$$

where

w_i = compound yield after n years if each holding period is i years $(i = 1, \ldots, n)$

z_i = yield on investment if property is held for i years, expressed as a decimal

n = number of years in projection period

i = holding period, expressed in years

n/i = number of turnovers in n years

EXAMPLE 1 (Evaluate an Investment Plan)

Directors of the Eagle Corporation seek a certain type of investment and feel that it will generally be available to them (for example, surburban apartment complexes). They believe the yields over 5 years will be as shown in the table. What is the optimal holding period if this type of investment will be repeatedly turned over?

SOLUTION

Yield	Yield	Compound Yield
i	z_i	w_i
1	14%	92.5%
2	60	224
3	110	244
4	150	214
5	170	170

The w_i's are determine in the following way:

$$w_1 = (1 + .14)^{5/1} - 1 = .925$$
$$w_2 = (1 + .60)^{5/2} - 1 = 2.24,$$
$$w_3 = (1 + 1.10)^{5/3} - 1 = 2.44,$$
$$w_4 = (1 + 1.50)^{5/4} - 1 = 2.14, \text{ and}$$
$$w_5 = (1 + 1.70)^{5/5} - 1 = 1.70.$$

Figure 1.2-1 shows both z_i and w_i over the five-year period. The optimal holding period is about

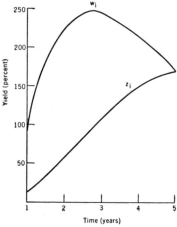

Figure 1.2-1

2.7 years. That is, if this type of investment is continually acquired and disposed of every 2.7 years, it will yield about 245% on equity after five years.

EXAMPLE 2 (Compare Two Investment Plans)

An investor believes that two types of investments might be desirable. Both have essentially the same risk, liquidity, and management burden. The five yields for each are listed in the table. Which type of investment, if optimally traded, will provide the greater return (compound yield) over the five-year period?

Year	Case 1		Case 2	
i	z_i	w_i	z_i	w_i
1	4%	21.7%	8%	46.9%
2	60	224	50	176
3	97.5	211	90	194
4	110	153	112	156
5	115	115	125	125

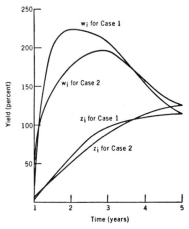

Figure 1.2-2

SOLUTION

As in Example 1, compute the five w_i values for each case.

Case 1 would provide the more profitable investment program because the maximum compound yield is 225%, better than the 197% for Case 2.

1.3 HOW TO DETERMINE IF YOU SHOULD USE YOUR INVESTMENT DOLLARS TO UPGRADE YOUR PROPERTY OR BUY ANOTHER

Most properties are not put to their "highest and best use." Even if the property is occupied by the proper type of tenant, usually the rent could be increased if the property were judiciously improved. Every owner must address the question of whether to spend money to improve the property or to invest it in another way. In other words, which investment results in the higher rate of return.

The answer to the question begins with these two estimates:

- What is the owner's usual rate of return on investments?
- How much will the monthly income be increased by a given expenditure to improve the property?

It it assumed that the property value increases in proportion to the increased gross income. This is a realistic assumption unless the improvement is very extensive or the use is changed.

If z is the rate of return on the expenditures to improve, and if y is the usual rate of return, improvement makes financial sense if z exceeds y.

FORMULA

$$z = \frac{x}{w} \cdot \left[a(y,i,q) + \frac{qu(d + ef)}{c(y,i,q)} \right] - 1$$

where

z = rate of return on expenditure to improve, expressed as a decimal

x = increase in rental income per rental period after expenditure to improve. If this is computed on a per-unit basis, w must also be computed on a per-unit basis

w = amount of expenditure

y = owner's usual rate of return

i = number of rental periods between improvement and sale

q = number of rental periods per year = number of mortgage periods per year. (They don't have to be equal, but they are assumed to be here so that the formula will be concise.)

u = gross income multiplier for the property = the value of the property divided by the annual gross income. The improvement won't change the multiplier unless the improvement is very substantial or the use is changed.

d = fraction of the selling price that the owner receives as a down payment

e = fraction of the selling price that the owner takes as a mortgage

r = interest rate on the mortgage taken by the owner

m = total number of payment periods on the mortgage

j = number of payment periods after which the owner receives a balloon payment. If there is no balloon payment, set $j = m$.

$a(y,i,q)$, etc. = present value of an annuity of 1 (note: $a(y,0,q) = 0$)

$c(y,i,q)$, etc. = amount of 1 at compound interest (note: $c(y,0,q) = 1$)

$s(y,j,q)$ = amount of an annuity of 1 (note: $s(y,0,q) = 0$)

$f = \left[\dfrac{s(y,j,q) + a(r,m - j,q)}{c(y,j,q) \cdot a(r,m,q)} \right]$ = present value of a mortgage of amount 1 that yields y, and has the balance due in one balloon payment after j periods. This value is listed in Table 2.1-1 for a good variety of parameter values.

EXAMPLE

John Simonsen owns an apartment building with a gross multiplier estimated to be 7. He also estimates that he can increase the monthly rent by $10 a unit for each $200 he spends on improvements. His usual rate of return on investments is 30%. After 12 months, he plans to sell the property. He will require a down payment that is 20% of the asking price and take a mortgage for 30% of the asking price (the remaining 50% of the asking price is an existing third-party mortgage that doesn't affect the result). The mortgage will have an interest rate of 10% and call for monthly payments amortized over 30 years with a balloon payment after 15 years.

Will Mr. Simonsen have a greater rate of return by spending money to improve the property, or by investing it in the usual way? That is, will z exceed y?

SOLUTION

In this example,

$$u = 7, q = 12, x = \$10, w = \$200, y = 30\%,$$
$$i = 12, d = 0.20, e = 0.30, r = 10\%$$
$$m = 30 \times 12 = 360, \text{ and } j = 15 \times 12 = 180.$$

From Table 1 or the annuity formulas (Appendix A.4),

$$c(y,i,q) = c(30,12,12) = 1.3448888,$$
$$a(y,i,q) = a(30,12,12) = 10.257764,$$
$$s(y,j,q) = s(30,180,12) = 3366.87156,$$
$$c(y,j,q) = c(30,180,12) = 85.1717892$$
$$a(r,m - j,q) = a(10,180,12)$$
$$= 93.057439, \text{ and}$$
$$a(r,m,q) = a(10,360,12) = 113.95082.$$

⎫
⎬ needed to
⎭ determine f

Now,

$$f = \frac{3366.87156 + 93.057439}{85.1717892 \times 113.95082}$$
$$= \frac{3459.929000}{9705.39522} = 0.356495.$$

From the formula,

$$z = \frac{\$10}{\$200} \cdot \left[10.257764 + \frac{12 \times 7}{1.34489}(0.20 + \right.$$
$$\left. 0.30 \times 0.356495) \right] - 1$$

$$= 0.05 \times \left(10.25776 + \frac{84}{1.34489} \times 0.306949 \right) - 1$$

$$= 0.05 \times (10.257764 + 19.17162) - 1$$

$$= 0.05 \times 29.4294 - 1$$

$$= .4715 = 47.15\%$$

In this case, improvement is quite profitable. Also, if rents are raised $8.83 for every $200 of expenditure Mr. Simonsen would achieve his usual rate of return of 30%.

1.4 EFFECTIVE TRADING REGION

The value of commercial property depends on the income it can generate. In turn, the potential income is affected by the accessibility of the property by customers. Although many factors affect the accessibility between two geographic locations, the following formulation assumes that accessibility depends only on the straight line distance between them and the propensity to gravitate from one to the other.[1]

Consider two commercial sites a and b (e.g., retail stores, shopping centers, towns, etc.). We ask: From which locations is a customer equally likely to gravitate to either site? In the narrowest sense, this question is answered by Reilly's Principle of Gravitation which determines a point on the straight line between a and b from which customers are equally likely to gravitate. In the broadest sense, this question is answered by the second formula, below, which defines a circle.[2]

[1] Here the propensity to gravitate concerns a customer's willingness to travel to a commercial site because of its size, selection of goods, bargains, etc.

[2] This circle is the locus of points in the plane for which the ratio of the distances (from the point to site a and from the point to site b) is a constant.

Customers located inside the circle will tend to gravitate to the site within the circle (call it b), and those located outside the circle will tend to gravitate to site a.

To be sure, this formulation portrays idealized situations. Rarely are two commercial sites unaffected by other such sites or by other aspects of accessibility. Nonetheless, these formulas do provide an estimate of the effective trading region about a site.

FORMULAS

$$d_a = \frac{d}{1 + \sqrt{q}} \quad \left(\begin{array}{l} \text{Effective Trading Distance,} \\ \text{Reilly's Formula} \end{array} \right.$$

$$\left. \begin{array}{l} \text{Center} = \dfrac{d}{1 - q} \\[3mm] \text{Radius} = \dfrac{d\sqrt{q}}{1 - q} \end{array} \right\} \text{(Effective Trading Circle)}$$

where

  a,b = designation of two sites (designate the larger site as a)

  d_a = effective trading distance (or travel time) from site a to site b

  d = actual distance (or travel time) between sites a and b

S_a, S_b = size of sites a and b, respectively (i.e., population, retail floor area, etc.) Take $S_a > S_b$

  $q = \dfrac{S_b}{S_a}$ = ratio of sizes of the two sites

EXAMPLE 1 (Towns)

Towns a and b are 30 miles apart and have populations of 20,000 and 10,000, respectively. Determine the circle that defines the locations from which customers are equally likely to visit either town. This example is depicted in Figure 1.4-1.

SOLUTION

In this example,

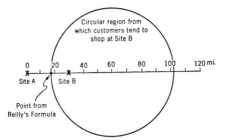

Figure 1.4-1

$d = 30$ mi, $S_a = 20,000$, and $S_b = 10,000$

Now,

$$q = \frac{10,000}{20,000} = 0.5.$$

The center of the circle is

$$\frac{d}{1 - q} = \frac{30 \text{ miles}}{1 - .5}$$
$$= 60 \text{ miles from town a toward town b.}$$

The radius of the circle is

$$\frac{d\sqrt{q}}{1 - q} = \frac{30 \times \sqrt{.5}}{1 - .5}$$
$$= \frac{21.213}{.5}$$
$$= 42.43 \text{ miles.}$$

EXAMPLE 2 (Retail Centers)

Department stores a and b have 250,000 ft^2 and 50,000 ft^2 of sales area, respectively. They are relatively isolated from other stores, and the travel time between them averages 10 minutes. Determine the circle that defines the locations from which customers are equally likely to visit either shopping center.

SOLUTION

In this example,

S_a = 250,000 ft^2, S_b = 50,000 ft^2, and d = 10 min.

Now,

$$q = \frac{50,000}{250,000} = .2.$$

The center of the circle is

$$\frac{d}{1-q} = \frac{10 \text{ min.}}{1-.2} = 12.5 \text{ min.}$$

from shopping center a toward center b. The radius of the circle is

$$\frac{d\sqrt{q}}{1-q} = \frac{10 \text{ min.} \times .4472}{1-.2} = 5.59 \text{ min.}$$

CHAPTER 2

TOOLS TO HELP YOU BUY OR SELL A PROPERTY

2.1 VARYING THE ASKING PRICE AND THE BALLOON PAYMENT DATE

In an effort to sell his property, the seller will frequently take a mortgage. If he does, and if a prospective buyer wants the asking price reduced, the seller can advance the due date of the balance due in a balloon payment. In this way the balloon payment that he receives early can counter the reduced asking price and preserve the present value of his investment.[1]

The following two formulas can be used to determine either the new loan amount or the new due date that preserves value. Notice that f and f' can be either determined by the formula or found in Table 2.1-1 (for certain values).

FORMULA

$$p' = p \cdot \frac{f}{f'}, \text{ or } f' = f \cdot \frac{p^{1a}}{p'}$$

[1] Of course, the buyer may want the due date pushed back. In this case, value is preserved by increasing the asking price.

[1a] Note that the new due date (denoted by j' in the list of parameters) cannot be determined explicitly. Rather, one must choose various values of j', and, by trial and error, see which renders f' reasonably close to $f \cdot \frac{p}{p'}$ (the right side of the equation). In many cases j' can be determined accurately enough by searching Table 2.1-1 for f'.

where

p,p' = original and adjusted amount of mortgage taken by the seller, respectively

y = seller's usual rate of return

r = mortgage interest rate

j,j' = original and adjusted mortgage period in which the balloon payment is due, respectively

q = number of payment periods per year

n = number of years in mortgage

$m = nq$ = total number of periods in mortgage

$f = \left[\dfrac{s(y,j,q) + a(r,m - j,q)}{c(y,j,q) \cdot a(r,m,q)} \right]$ = present value of a mortgage of amount 1 that yields y and has the balance due in one balloon payment after j periods

f' = same formula as f with j' replacing j

EXAMPLE

Mr. Grant is asking $500,000 for his property. As part of the price, he will take a junior mortgage for $200,000 at 10% interest, and amortized with monthly payments over 30 years. He also wants to receive the balance in a single balloon payment after 20 years. A prospective buyer offers $480,000. Consequently, the junior mortgage would be reduced to $180,000. Mr. Grant's usual rate of return is 20%. What new due date on the balloon payment will preserve the present value of the investment (at this rate of return)?

SOLUTION

In this example,

$p = \$200{,}000, r = 10\%, q = 12, n = 30$ years,
$m = nq = 360, j = 20 \times 12 = 240, p' = \$180{,}000,$
and $y = 20\%$.

From Table 1 or the formulas preceding Table 1,

$s(y,j,q) = s(20,240,12) = 3109.6518,$
$c(y,j,q) = c(20,240,12) = 53.827531,$

$a(r, m - j, q) = a(10, 120, 12) = 75.671163$, and
$a(r, m, q) = a(10, 360, 12) = 113.95082$.

Now,

$$f = \frac{3109.6518 + 75.671163}{52.827531 \times 113.95082} = \frac{3185.3230}{6019.7405}$$
$$= 0.529146.$$

(For these values, f can also be found in Table 2.1-1 at $m = 360$, $r = 10\%$, $y = 20\%$, and $j = 240$.)
Now, from the formula,

$$f' = 0.529146 \times \frac{\$200{,}000}{\$180{,}000} = 0.587940.$$

From Table 2.1-1, a good estimate of 0.587940 is 0.593, which is found at 108 periods (9 years). Hence, a balloon payment at 9 years instead of 20 years will preserve the present value Mr. Grant would have achieved with his original asking price of $500,000.

2.2 VARYING THE DOWN PAYMENT AND THE BALLOON PAYMENT DATE

A prospective buyer might propose a smaller down payment than that specified by the seller. If the seller is taking a mortgage for part of the asking price, he may agree to the reduced down payment if the present value of his investment can be preserved by advancing the due date on the balance due in one balloon payment.

In the following formulas it should be noted that the down payment is expressed as a fraction of the total amount due to the seller from the buyer (i.e., down payment plus amount of mortgage taken by the seller). Also, in the first formula, the new due date for the balloon payment (denoted by j') cannot be determined explicitly. Rather, one must choose various values of j', and, by trial and error, see which value renders f' reasonably close to the value on the right side of the equation. The correct value of j' can often be estimated simply by searching Table 2.1-1 for f'.

FORMULAS

$$f' = f - \left(\frac{d' - d}{1 - d}\right), \text{ or } d' = d + (1 - d)(f - f')$$

where

d,d' = original and adjusted down payment, respectively, expressed as a fraction of the total payment due to the seller from the buyer (i.e., down payment + amount of mortgage taken by the seller)

y = seller's usual rate of return

r = mortgage interest rate

j,j' = original and adjusted mortgage period in which the balloon payment is due, respectively

q = number of payment periods per year

n = number of years in mortgage

$m = nq$ = total number of periods in mortgage

$f = \left[\dfrac{s(y,j,q) + a(r,m - j,q)}{c(y,j,q) \cdot a(r,m,q)}\right]$ = present value of a mortgage of amount 1 that yields y and has the balance due in one balloon payment after j periods

f' = same formula as f with j' replacing j

$s(y,j,q)$ = amount of an annuity of 1

$c(y,j,q)$ = amount of 1 at compound interest

$a(r,m,q), a(r,m - j,q)$ = present value of an annuity of 1

EXAMPLE

When Mark Meredith sells his property he wants a $100,000 down payment and will take a $300,000 mortgage[2] at 10% interest with monthly payments for 30 years and the balance due in 20 years. In this case, a prospective buyer suggests a down payment of $60,000 and asks Mr. Meredith to take a mortgage of $340,000. (The asking price is still

_____

[2] A third-party loan may exist, but it would not affect the problem.

$400,000). Since Mr. Meredith usually makes 30% on his investments, when must the balloon payment be due to compensate him for the smaller down payment and preserve the present value of his investment?

SOLUTION

In this example,

$$d = \frac{\$100,000}{\$400,000} = .25, r = 10\%, q = 12,$$

$$n = 30 \text{ years}, m = nq = 360, d' = \frac{\$60,000}{\$400,000} = 0.15,$$
$$\text{and } y = 30\%.$$

From Table 1 or the formulas preceding Table 1,

$s(y,j,q) = s(30,240,12) = 14949.519,$
$c(y,j,q) = c(30,240,12) = 374.73797,$
$a(r,m - j,q) = a(10,120,12) = 75.671163,$ and
$a(r,m,q) = a(10,360,12) = 113.95082.$

Now,

$$f = \frac{14949.519 + 75.671163}{374.73797 \times 113.95082} = \frac{15025.1902}{42701.6990}$$
$$= 0.351864.$$

(This value can also be found in Table 2.1-1 at m = 360, r = 10%, y = 30%, and j = 240.)
From the formula,

$$f' = f - \left(\frac{d' - d}{1 - d}\right)$$
$$= 0.351864 - \left(\frac{0.15 - 0.25}{1 - 0.25}\right)$$
$$= 0.351864 + 0.13333$$
$$= 0.485197.$$

By trial and error (or from Table 2.1-1), we find that when j' = 60, f' = 0.491; this value is reasonably close to f' = 0.485197. It is close particularly since y = 30% is probably a rough estimate. Hence, the present value of Mr. Meredith's investment is preserved if the due date of the balloon payment is advanced to 5 years (i.e., 60 periods) instead of the originally proposed 20 years.

2.3 VARYING THE ASKING PRICE AND THE DOWN PAYMENT

Often the prospective buyer of a property will want to make a smaller down payment than that specified by the seller. The seller is interested in preserving the present value of his investment, and he can be equally compensated for the smaller down payment either by calling for a balloon payment on a mortgage he is taking (Section 2.2) or by increasing the asking price.[3]

If the asking price is increased, the seller will be taking a mortgage.[4] The following formulas determine the adjusted asking price or adjusted down payment that preserve the present value of the investment.

FORMULAS

$$v' = v + (d - d') \cdot \left[\frac{a(r,m,q)}{a(y,m,q)} - 1 \right],$$

or

$$d' = d - \frac{v' - v}{\left[\dfrac{a(r,m,q)}{a(y,m,q)} - 1 \right]}$$

where

v,v' = original and adjusted asking price, respectively

d,d' = original and adjusted down payment, respectively

y = seller's usual rate of return

r = mortgage interest rate

q = number of payment periods per year

[3] Some other techniques, such as adjusting the interest rate, can also be used.

[4] This is necessary because third-party financing (either new or existing) will not be sufficient to cover both a small down payment and an asking price that exceeds appraised value. Furthermore, the result of this technique is independent of third-party financing since it depends only upon payments to the seller.

n = number of years in mortgage

m = nq = total number of periods in mortgage

a(r,m,q), a(y,m,q) = present value of an annuity of 1

EXAMPLE

Stan Nicholas is asking $100,000 for his property and wants a $25,000 down payment. A third party has agreed to take a mortgage of $75,000, the balance of the asking price. However, a prospective buyer is willing to put only $20,000 down. To preserve the present value of his investment, Mr. Nicholas will increase the asking price and take a junior mortgage for the difference (i.e., asking price less amount of third-party mortgage less down payment). The junior mortgage will have an interest rate of 10% and call for monthly payments for 10 years. If Mr. Nicholas's usual rate of return is 30%, what must the new asking price be to preserve the present value of his investment?

SOLUTION

In this example,

$$v = \$100,000, d = \$25,000, d' = \$20,000,$$
$$r = 10\%, q = 12, n = 10 \text{ years}, m = nq = 120,$$
$$\text{and } y = 30\%.$$

From Table 1 or the formulas preceding Table 1,

$$a(r,m,q) = a(10,120,12) = 75.67116, \text{ and}$$
$$a(y,m,q) = a(30,120,12) = 37.93369.$$

Now, from the formula,

$$v' = \$100,000$$
$$+ (\$25,000 - \$20,000) \cdot \left[\frac{75.67116}{37.93369} - 1 \right]$$
$$= \$100,000 + \$5,000 \times (1.994827 - 1)$$
$$= \$100,000 + \$5,000 \times 0.994827$$
$$= \$100,000 + \$4,974.14$$
$$= \$104,974.14 \text{ (say } \$105,000).$$

Hence, Mr. Nicholas will preserve the present value of his investment if he asks $105,000 for his property and takes a second mortgage for $10,000 (i.e., $105,000 = $75,000 + $10,000 + 20,000).

Table 2.1-1. The values listed in this table are those of f (or f′), the present value of a mortgage of amount 1 that yields y and has a balance due in one balloon payment after j (or j′) periods.

					$r = 8\%$					
j\y	10	20	30	40	50	60	70	80	90	100
m = 120										
2	.982	.895	.817	.747	.684	.626	.575	.528	.485	.447
24	.966	.816	.691	.589	.504	.434	.375	.326	.285	.250
36	.953	.756	.606	.491	.403	.335	.282	.240	.207	.181
48	.943	.712	.548	.432	.348	.286	.240	.205	.178	.157
60	.935	.680	.511	.397	.318	.262	.221	.191	.167	.149
72	.928	.658	.487	.377	.302	.250	.213	.185	.164	.147
84	.924	.643	.473	.365	.294	.245	.210	.183	.162	.146
96	.921	.634	.465	.360	.291	.243	.208	.182	.162	.146
108	.919	.629	.461	.357	.289	.242	.208	.182	.162	.146
120	.918	.628	.460	.357	.289	.242	.208	.182	.162	.146
m = 240										
12	.981	.893	.814	.742	.678	.619	.567	.519	.476	.437
24	.965	.807	.678	.572	.484	.412	.352	.302	.260	.226
36	.950	.739	.580	.460	.369	.299	.246	.204	.172	.147
48	.937	.684	.509	.386	.300	.238	.193	.161	.136	.118
60	.926	.640	.457	.338	.259	.205	.168	.141	.121	.107
72	.916	.606	.421	.307	.235	.187	.155	.132	.116	.103
84	.907	.579	.394	.286	.220	.178	.149	.128	.113	.101
96	.900	.557	.376	.273	.212	.173	.146	.127	.112	.101
108	.893	.541	.362	.265	.207	.170	.145	.126	.112	.100
120	.888	.528	.353	.260	.204	.169	.144	.126	.112	.100
180	.871	.497	.335	.251	.201	.167	.143	.125	.112	.100
240	.867	.492	.334	.251	.201	.167	.143	.125	.112	.100
m = 360										
12	.981	.892	.813	.741	.676	.617	.564	.516	.473	.434
24	.964	.805	.674	.567	.479	.406	.346	.295	.254	.219
36	.949	.734	.573	.451	.356	.289	.236	.195	.163	.138
48	.935	.676	.498	.374	.287	.225	.181	.149	.125	.107
60	.923	.630	.443	.322	.243	.190	.153	.128	.109	.095
72	.912	.592	.402	.288	.218	.170	.139	.118	.102	.091
84	.903	.561	.373	.265	.200	.160	.133	.114	.100	.089
96	.894	.536	.351	.250	.191	.154	.129	.112	.099	.088
108	.886	.516	.335	.240	.185	.151	.127	.111	.098	.088
120	.879	.500	.324	.233	.181	.149	.127	.110	.098	.088
180	.855	.457	.299	.222	.176	.147	.126	.110	.098	.088
240	.843	.443	.294	.220	.176	.147	.126	.110	.098	.088
300	.838	.440	.294	.220	.176	.147	.126	.110	.098	.088
360	.836	.439	.293	.220	.176	.147	.126	.110	.098	.088

*m = ∞ results in an interest-only loan.

				r = 9%					
10	*20*	*30*	*40*	*50*	*60*	*70*	*80*	*90*	*100*

m = 120

.991	.904	.825	.755	.691	.633	.581	.534	.491	.452
.983	.830	.705	.601	.514	.443	.383	.333	.292	.256
.977	.775	.622	.505	.415	.346	.291	.249	.215	.188
.971	.734	.567	.447	.360	.297	.249	.213	.185	.164
.967	.704	.530	.412	.330	.272	.230	.199	.175	.156
.964	.684	.507	.392	.315	.261	.222	.193	.171	.153
.961	.670	.493	.381	.307	.256	.219	.191	.169	.152
.960	.661	.485	.376	.303	.254	.217	.190	.169	.152
.959	.657	.482	.373	.302	.253	.217	.190	.169	.152
.959	.655	.481	.373	.302	.253	.217	.190	.169	.152

m = 240

.991	.902	.822	.750	.685	.626	.573	.525	.482	.442
.982	.823	.692	.584	.496	.422	.361	.310	.268	.233
.975	.760	.598	.475	.382	.311	.256	.214	.181	.155
.968	.709	.529	.403	.314	.251	.204	.170	.145	.125
.963	.669	.480	.356	.274	.218	.179	.151	.130	.114
.958	.637	.444	.325	.250	.200	.166	.142	.124	.110
.953	.611	.418	.305	.236	.191	.160	.138	.122	.109
.949	.591	.400	.292	.227	.186	.157	.136	.121	.108
.946	.575	.387	.284	.222	.183	.156	.136	.120	.108
.943	.563	.378	.279	.220	.181	.155	.135	.120	.108
.935	.534	.361	.270	.216	.180	.154	.135	.120	.108
.932	.530	.359	.270	.216	.180	.154	.135	.120	.108

m = 360

.991	.901	.821	.749	.683	.624	.571	.523	.479	.440
.982	.821	.689	.580	.491	.417	.355	.304	.262	.227
.974	.756	.591	.467	.374	.302	.247	.205	.172	.146
.968	.703	.520	.382	.302	.239	.193	.159	.134	.115
.961	.659	.467	.342	.259	.204	.165	.138	.118	.104
.956	.624	.428	.308	.233	.184	.152	.129	.112	.099
.951	.596	.399	.286	.217	.174	.145	.124	.109	.098
.947	.573	.378	.271	.208	.168	.141	.122	.108	.097
.943	.554	.363	.261	.202	.165	.140	.121	.108	.097
.939	.539	.351	.254	.198	.163	.139	.121	.107	.097
.927	.499	.327	.243	.193	.161	.138	.121	.107	.097
.920	.486	.323	.242	.193	.161	.138	.121	.107	.097
.918	.482	.322	.241	.193	.161	.138	.121	.107	.097
.917	.482	.322	.241	.193	.161	.138	.121	.107	.097

Table 2.1-1 (continued)

				r = 8%					
j\y	10	20	30	40	50	60	70	80	90	100

m = 480

j\y	10	20	30	40	50	60	70	80	90	100
12	.981	.892	.812	.740	.675	.616	.563	.516	.472	.433
24	.964	.804	.673	.565	.477	.404	.343	.293	.251	.217
36	.949	.732	.570	.448	.356	.286	.232	.191	.159	.134
48	.935	.673	.494	.369	.282	.220	.176	.144	.120	.103
60	.922	.626	.437	.316	.237	.184	.148	.122	.104	.091
72	.911	.586	.396	.281	.210	.164	.134	.113	.098	.086
84	.901	.555	.365	.257	.193	.153	.126	.108	.095	.085
96	.892	.529	.342	.241	.183	.147	.123	.106	.094	.084
108	.884	.507	.325	.230	.176	.143	.121	.105	.093	.084
120	.876	.490	.313	.223	.173	.141	.120	.105	.093	.083
180	.849	.442	.285	.210	.167	.139	.119	.104	.093	.083
240	.834	.425	.280	.209	.167	.139	.119	.104	.093	.083
300	.826	.419	.278	.209	.167	.139	.119	.104	.093	.083
360	.821	.418	.278	.209	.167	.139	.119	.104	.093	.083
420	.819	.417	.278	.209	.167	.139	.119	.104	.093	.083
480	.819	.417	.278	.209	.167	.139	.119	.104	.093	.083

m = ∞

j\y	10	20	30	40	50	60	70	80	90	100
12	.082	.077	.073	.070	.066	.063	.060	.057	.054	.052
24	.150	.135	.123	.112	.102	.094	.087	.080	.074	.069
36	.212	.183	.160	.141	.125	.111	.100	.091	.083	.076
48	.267	.222	.187	.160	.138	.121	.107	.096	.086	.078
60	.318	.254	.208	.173	.147	.127	.111	.098	.088	.079
72	.364	.280	.223	.182	.152	.130	.112	.099	.088	.080
84	.405	.302	.234	.188	.155	.131	.133	.100	.089	.080
96	.442	.320	.242	.192	.157	.132	.114	.100	.089	.080
108	.476	.334	.249	.194	.158	.133	.114	.100	.089	.080
120	.507	.346	.253	.196	.159	.133	.114	.100	.089	.080
180	.622	.380	.264	.199	.160	.133	.114	.100	.089	.080
240	.692	.393	.266	.200	.160	.133	.114	.100	.089	.080
300	.734	.397	.267	.200	.160	.133	.114	.100	.089	.080
360	.760	.399	.267	.200	.160	.133	.114	.100	.089	.080
420	.776	.400	.267	.200	.160	.133	.114	.100	.089	.080
480	.785	.400	.267	.200	.160	.133	.114	.100	.089	.080

				r = 10%					
j\y	10	20	30	40	50	60	70	80	90	100

m = 120

j\y	10	20	30	40	50	60	70	80	90	100
12	1.000	.912	.834	.762	.698	.640	.587	.540	.496	.457
24	1.000	.845	.718	.612	.525	.452	.392	.341	.299	.263
36	1.000	.795	.639	.519	.427	.356	.301	.257	.222	.194
48	1.000	.757	.585	.462	.373	.307	.259	.221	.193	.170
60	1.000	.730	.550	.428	.343	.283	.240	.207	.182	.162
72	1.000	.710	.527	.408	.328	.272	.232	.201	.178	.160
84	1.000	.697	.514	.397	.320	.267	.228	.199	.177	.159

r = 9%									
10	20	30	40	50	60	70	80	90	100

m = 480

10	20	30	40	50	60	70	80	90	100
.991	.901	.821	.748	.683	.624	.570	.522	.478	.439
.982	.820	.688	.579	.489	.415	.353	.302	.260	.225
.974	.754	.589	.465	.371	.299	.244	.201	.169	.143
.967	.700	.516	.388	.298	.234	.189	.155	.130	.112
.961	.656	.462	.337	.254	.199	.161	.134	.114	.100
.955	.620	.422	.302	.227	.179	.147	.124	.108	.095
.950	.591	.392	.279	.211	.168	.139	.120	.105	.094
.946	.567	.370	.263	.201	.162	.136	.117	.104	.093
.942	.547	.354	.253	.195	.158	.134	.117	.103	.093
.938	.531	.342	.246	.191	.157	.133	.116	.103	.093
.924	.486	.316	.233	.186	.154	.132	.116	.103	.093
.916	.470	.310	.232	.185	.154	.132	.116	.103	.093
.912	.465	.309	.231	.185	.154	.132	.116	.103	.093
.910	.463	.309	.231	.185	.154	.132	.116	.103	.093
.909	.463	.309	.231	.185	.154	.132	.116	.103	.093
.908	.463	.309	.231	.185	.154	.132	.116	.103	.093

m = ∞

10	20	30	40	50	60	70	80	90	100
.092	.087	.083	.078	.074	.071	.067	.064	.061	.058
.169	.152	.138	.126	.115	.106	.098	.090	.084	.078
.238	.206	.180	.158	.140	.125	.113	.102	.093	.085
.301	.250	.211	.180	.156	.136	.121	.108	.097	.088
.358	.286	.234	.195	.165	.142	.125	.110	.099	.089
.409	.315	.251	.204	.171	.146	.127	.111	.099	.090
.456	.340	.263	.211	.174	.148	.128	.112	.100	.090
.498	.359	.273	.216	.177	.149	.128	.112	.100	.090
.536	.376	.280	.219	.178	.149	.128	.112	.100	.090
.570	.389	.285	.221	.179	.150	.128	.112	.100	.090
.700	.427	.297	.224	.180	.150	.129	.112	.100	.090
.778	.442	.299	.225	.180	.150	.129	.112	.100	.090
.826	.447	.300	.225	.180	.150	.129	.112	.100	.090
.855	.449	.300	.225	.180	.150	.129	.112	.100	.090
.873	.450	.300	.225	.180	.150	.129	.112	.100	.090
.883	.450	.300	.225	.180	.150	.129	.112	.100	.090

r = 11%									
10	20	30	40	50	60	70	80	90	100

m = 120

10	20	30	40	50	60	70	80	90	100
1.000	.921	.842	.770	.705	.647	.594	.546	.502	.462
1.000	.860	.731	.624	.536	.462	.400	.349	.306	.270
1.000	.814	.655	.533	.440	.367	.310	.265	.230	.201
1.000	.780	.604	.478	.386	.319	.268	.230	.200	.177
1.000	.755	.570	.444	.357	.295	.249	.216	.190	.169
1.000	.737	.548	.425	.341	.293	.241	.210	.186	.166
1.000	.725	.535	.414	.334	.278	.238	.208	.184	.166

Table 2.1-1 (continued)

					r = 10%					
j\y	10	20	30	40	50	60	70	80	90	100
96	1.000	.689	.506	.392	.317	.265	.227	.198	.176	.159
108	1.000	.685	.502	.389	.315	.264	.226	.198	.176	.159
120	1.000	.684	.501	.389	.315	.264	.226	.198	.176	.159

m = 240

j\y	10	20	30	40	50	60	70	80	90	100
12	1.000	.911	.830	.758	.692	.633	.580	.531	.488	.448
24	1.000	.839	.706	.597	.507	.432	.371	.319	.276	.240
36	1.000	.781	.616	.491	.396	.323	.267	.223	.189	.162
48	1.000	.734	.550	.421	.329	.263	.215	.180	.153	.133
60	1.000	.697	.502	.375	.289	.231	.190	.160	.139	.122
72	1.000	.668	.468	.344	.265	.213	.177	.152	.133	.118
84	1.000	.644	.443	.325	.251	.204	.171	.148	.130	.117
96	1.000	.626	.425	.312	.243	.199	.168	.146	.129	.116
108	1.000	.611	.413	.303	.238	.196	.167	.145	.129	.116
120	1.000	.600	.404	.298	.235	.195	.166	.145	.129	.116
180	1.000	.573	.387	.290	.232	.193	.165	.145	.129	.116
240	1.000	.568	.385	.289	.232	.193	.165	.145	.129	.116

m = 360

j\y	10	20	30	40	50	60	70	80	90	100
12	1.000	.910	.829	.757	.691	.632	.578	.529	.485	.446
24	1.000	.837	.703	.593	.503	.428	.365	.314	.271	.235
36	1.000	.777	.610	.484	.388	.315	.258	.215	.181	.154
48	1.000	.729	.541	.411	.318	.252	.205	.170	.144	.124
60	1.000	.689	.491	.361	.276	.218	.178	.149	.128	.112
72	1.000	.657	.453	.329	.250	.199	.164	.140	.122	.108
84	1.000	.631	.426	.307	.234	.188	.157	.135	.119	.106
96	1.000	.610	.406	.292	.225	.183	.154	.133	.118	.106
108	1.000	.593	.391	.282	.219	.179	.152	.132	.117	.105
120	1.000	.579	.380	.276	.216	.178	.151	.132	.117	.105
180	1.000	.541	.356	.265	.211	.176	.150	.132	.117	.105
240	1.000	.529	.352	.263	.211	.176	.150	.132	.117	.105
300	1.000	.526	.351	.263	.211	.176	.150	.132	.117	.105
360	1.000	.525	.351	.263	.211	.176	.150	.132	.117	.105

m = 480

j\y	10	20	30	40	50	60	70	80	90	100
12	1.000	.910	.829	.756	.690	.631	.577	.529	.485	.445
24	1.000	.837	.702	.592	.501	.426	.364	.312	.269	.233
36	1.000	.776	.608	.482	.385	.312	.256	.212	.178	.152
48	1.000	.727	.539	.407	.315	.249	.201	.166	.140	.121
60	1.000	.687	.487	.357	.271	.214	.174	.145	.125	.109
72	1.000	.654	.449	.324	.245	.194	.160	.136	.118	.105
84	1.000	.627	.420	.301	.229	.183	.153	.131	.115	.103
96	1.000	.605	.399	.286	.219	.177	.149	.129	.114	.102
108	1.000	.587	.384	.276	.213	.174	.147	.128	.114	.102
120	1.000	.573	.372	.269	.209	.172	.146	.128	.113	.102
180	1.000	.531	.347	.257	.204	.170	.146	.127	.113	.102
240	1.000	.516	.341	.255	.204	.170	.146	.127	.113	.102
300	1.000	.511	.340	.255	.204	.170	.146	.127	.113	.102
360	1.000	.510	.340	.255	.204	.170	.146	.127	.113	.102
420	1.000	.509	.340	.255	.204	.170	.146	.127	.113	.102
480	1.000	.509	.340	.255	.204	.170	.146	.127	.113	.102

				r =	11%				
10	*20*	*30*	*40*	*50*	*60*	*70*	*80*	*90*	*100*
1.000	.718	.527	.408	.330	.276	.236	.207	.184	.165
1.000	.714	.524	.406	.328	.275	.236	.207	.184	.165
1.000	.713	.523	.405	.328	.275	.236	.207	.184	.165

m = 240

10	*20*	*30*	*40*	*50*	*60*	*70*	*80*	*90*	*100*
1.000	.920	.839	.766	.700	.640	.586	.538	.494	.454
1.000	.855	.720	.610	.519	.443	.380	.328	.284	.248
1.000	.802	.634	.507	.409	.335	.277	.233	.198	.170
1.000	.760	.571	.438	.344	.276	.227	.190	.162	.141
1.000	.726	.525	.393	.305	.244	.201	.171	.148	.130
1.000	.700	.492	.364	.281	.227	.189	.162	.142	.126
1.000	.678	.468	.344	.267	.217	.183	.158	.139	.125
1.000	.661	.451	.332	.259	.212	.180	.156	.138	.124
1.000	.648	.439	.324	.254	.209	.178	.155	.138	.124
1.000	.637	.430	.318	.251	.208	.178	.155	.138	.124
1.000	.612	.414	.310	.248	.206	.177	.155	.138	.124
1.000	.608	.412	.310	.248	.206	.177	.155	.138	.124

m = 360

10	*20*	*30*	*40*	*50*	*60*	*70*	*80*	*90*	*100*
1.000	.919	.838	.765	.698	.639	.585	.536	.492	.452
1.000	.853	.718	.607	.515	.439	.375	.323	.279	.243
1.000	.799	.629	.500	.403	.328	.270	.225	.190	.163
1.000	.756	.564	.429	.334	.266	.217	.181	.153	.133
1.000	.720	.515	.382	.293	.232	.190	.160	.138	.121
1.000	.691	.479	.350	.267	.214	.177	.151	.132	.117
1.000	.667	.453	.328	.252	.203	.170	.146	.129	.115
1.000	.648	.434	.314	.243	.197	.167	.144	.128	.115
1.000	.632	.419	.305	.237	.194	.165	.144	.127	.114
1.000	.620	.409	.298	.234	.193	.164	.143	.127	.114
1.000	.585	.386	.287	.229	.191	.163	.143	.127	.114
1.000	.574	.382	.286	.229	.190	.163	.143	.127	.114
1.000	.570	.381	.286	.229	.190	.163	.143	.127	.114
1.000	.570	.381	.286	.229	.190	.163	.143	.127	.114

m = 480

10	*20*	*30*	*40*	*50*	*60*	*70*	*80*	*90*	*100*
1.000	.919	.838	.764	.698	.638	.584	.535	.491	.451
1.000	.853	.717	.606	.513	.437	.374	.321	.278	.241
1.000	.799	.628	.499	.400	.325	.268	.223	.188	.161
1.000	.754	.561	.427	.331	.263	.214	.178	.151	.130
1.000	.718	.512	.378	.289	.229	.187	.157	.135	.119
1.000	.688	.476	.345	.263	.210	.173	.147	.129	.114
1.000	.664	.448	.323	.248	.199	.166	.143	.126	.112
1.000	.644	.428	.309	.238	.193	.163	.141	.125	.112
1.000	.628	.414	.299	.232	.190	.161	.140	.124	.112
1.000	.614	.402	.292	.228	.188	.160	.140	.124	.111
1.000	.577	.378	.280	.223	.186	.159	.139	.124	.111
1.000	.563	.373	.279	.223	.186	.159	.139	.124	.111
1.000	.559	.372	.279	.223	.186	.159	.139	.124	.111
1.000	.557	.371	.278	.223	.186	.159	.139	.124	.111
1.000	.557	.371	.278	.223	.186	.159	.139	.124	.111
1.000	.557	.371	.278	.223	.186	.159	.139	.124	.111

Table 2.1-1 (continued)

					r = 10%					
j\y	10	20	30	40	50	60	70	80	90	100
m = ∞										
12	1.000	.097	.092	.087	.083	.079	.075	.071	.068	.065
24	1.000	.169	.154	.140	.128	.118	.108	.100	.093	.087
36	1.000	.229	.200	.176	.156	.139	.125	.114	.104	.095
48	1.000	.278	.234	.200	.173	.151	.134	.120	.108	.098
60	1.000	.318	.259	.216	.183	.158	.138	.123	.110	.099
72	1.000	.350	.278	.227	.190	.162	.141	.124	.111	.100
84	1.000	.377	.292	.235	.194	.164	.142	.124	.111	.100
96	1.000	.399	.303	.240	.196	.165	.142	.125	.111	.100
108	1.000	.418	.311	.243	.198	.166	.143	.125	.111	.100
120	1.000	.432	.317	.245	.199	.166	.143	.125	.111	.100
180	1.000	.475	.330	.249	.200	.167	.143	.125	.111	.100
240	1.000	.491	.332	.250	.200	.167	.143	.125	.111	.100
300	1.000	.497	.333	.250	.200	.167	.143	.125	.111	.100
360	1.000	.499	.333	.250	.200	.167	.143	.125	.111	.100
420	1.000	.500	.333	.250	.200	.167	.143	.125	.111	.100
480	1.000	.500	.333	.250	.200	.167	.143	.125	.111	.100

					r = 12%					
j\y	10	20	30	40	50	60	70	80	90	100
m = 120										
12	1.018	.930	.850	.778	.712	.653	.600	.552	.508	.468
24	1.034	.876	.745	.636	.546	.472	.409	.357	.313	.276
36	1.047	.834	.672	.548	.452	.378	.320	.274	.237	.208
48	1.058	.803	.623	.493	.399	.330	.278	.239	.208	.184
60	1.067	.781	.590	.460	.370	.306	.259	.224	.197	.176
72	1.074	.765	.569	.441	.355	.295	.251	.218	.193	.173
84	1.079	.754	.556	.431	.347	.289	.248	.216	.192	.172
96	1.083	.747	.549	.425	.344	.287	.246	.215	.191	.172
108	1.085	.743	.545	.423	.342	.286	.246	.215	.191	.172
120	1.086	.742	.544	.422	.342	.286	.246	.215	.191	.172
m = 240										
12	1.019	.928	.847	.774	.707	.647	.593	.544	.500	.459
24	1.036	.871	.735	.623	.530	.454	.390	.337	.292	.255
36	1.051	.824	.653	.523	.423	.347	.288	.243	.207	.178
48	1.064	.786	.593	.456	.359	.289	.238	.200	.171	.149
60	1.076	.756	.549	.412	.321	.258	.213	.181	.157	.139
72	1.086	.732	.517	.384	.298	.240	.201	.172	.151	.135
84	1.096	.712	.494	.365	.284	.231	.195	.168	.148	.133
96	1.104	.697	.478	.352	.276	.226	.192	.167	.147	.132
108	1.111	.685	.466	.344	.271	.223	.190	.166	.147	.132
120	1.117	.675	.457	.339	.268	.222	.189	.165	.147	.132
180	1.136	.652	.441	.331	.264	.220	.189	.165	.147	.132
240	1.141	.648	.439	.330	.264	.220	.189	.165	.147	.132

				r = 11%					
10	20	30	40	50	60	70	80	90	100

m = ∞

10	20	30	40	50	60	70	80	90	100
1.000	.106	.101	.096	.091	.086	.082	.078	.075	.071
1.000	.186	.169	.154	.141	.129	.119	.110	.102	.095
1.000	.252	.220	.193	.172	.153	.138	.125	.114	.104
1.000	.305	.257	.220	.190	.167	.147	.132	.119	.108
1.000	.349	.285	.238	.202	.174	.152	.135	.121	.109
1.000	.385	.306	.250	.209	.178	.155	.136	.122	.110
1.000	.415	.322	.258	.213	.180	.156	.137	.122	.110
1.000	.439	.333	.264	.216	.182	.157	.137	.122	.110
1.000	.459	.342	.267	.217	.182	.157	.137	.122	.110
1.000	.476	.348	.270	.218	.183	.157	.137	.122	.110
1.000	.522	.362	.274	.220	.183	.157	.137	.122	.110
1.000	.540	.366	.275	.220	.183	.157	.137	.122	.110
1.000	.546	.366	.275	.220	.183	.157	.137	.122	.110
1.000	.549	.367	.275	.220	.183	.157	.137	.122	.110
1.000	.549	.367	.275	.220	.183	.157	.137	.122	.110
1.000	.550	.367	.275	.220	.183	.157	.137	.122	.110

				r = 13%					
10	20	30	40	50	60	70	80	90	100

m = 120

10	20	30	40	50	60	70	80	90	100
1.028	.938	.858	.785	.720	.660	.606	.558	.513	.473
1.052	.891	.758	.648	.557	.481	.418	.365	.321	.283
1.072	.854	.689	.562	.465	.389	.329	.282	.245	.215
1.088	.827	.642	.509	.413	.341	.288	.247	.216	.191
1.102	.807	.611	.477	.384	.318	.269	.233	.205	.183
1.112	.793	.590	.458	.369	.306	.261	.227	.201	.180
1.120	.783	.578	.448	.361	.301	.258	.225	.200	.179
1.126	.777	.571	.442	.357	.299	.256	.224	.199	.179
1.129	.774	.567	.440	.356	.298	.256	.224	.199	.179
1.130	.773	.566	.439	.356	.298	.256	.224	.199	.179

m = 240

10	20	30	40	50	60	70	80	90	100
1.028	.937	.855	.781	.715	.654	.600	.550	.506	.465
1.054	.887	.749	.636	.542	.464	.400	.346	.301	.263
1.076	.845	.671	.539	.438	.360	.300	.253	.216	.187
1.096	.812	.614	.474	.375	.303	.250	.210	.181	.158
1.114	.786	.573	.432	.337	.271	.225	.191	.166	.147
1.130	.764	.542	.404	.314	.254	.213	.183	.160	.143
1.144	.747	.520	.385	.301	.245	.207	.179	.158	.141
1.156	.733	.504	.373	.293	.240	.204	.177	.157	.141
1.167	.723	.493	.365	.288	.237	.202	.176	.156	.141
1.176	.714	.485	.360	.285	.236	.201	.176	.156	.141
1.206	.693	.469	.352	.281	.234	.201	.176	.156	.141
1.214	.690	.467	.351	.281	.234	.201	.176	.156	.141

Table 2.1-1 (continued)

					$r = 12\%$					
$j\backslash y$	10	20	30	40	50	60	70	80	90	100
m = 360										
12	1.019	.928	.846	.773	.706	.646	.592	.542	.498	.458
24	1.036	.869	.733	.620	.527	.450	.386	.332	.288	.251
36	1.051	.822	.648	.517	.417	.341	.282	.236	.200	.172
48	1.065	.782	.586	.448	.351	.280	.229	.192	.163	.142
60	1.078	.751	.540	.402	.310	.247	.203	.171	.148	.130
72	1.089	.725	.506	.371	.285	.229	.190	.162	.142	.126
84	1.099	.703	.481	.350	.270	.218	.183	.158	.139	.124
96	1.108	.686	.462	.336	.261	.213	.180	.156	.138	.124
108	1.116	.672	.448	.327	.255	.210	.178	.155	.137	.124
120	1.123	.661	.438	.321	.252	.208	.177	.155	.137	.123
180	1.150	.629	.417	.310	.247	.206	.176	.154	.137	.123
240	1.164	.619	.412	.309	.247	.206	.176	.154	.137	.123
300	1.170	.616	.411	.309	.247	.206	.176	.154	.137	.123
360	1.172	.616	.411	.309	.247	.206	.176	.154	.137	.123
m = 480										
12	1.019	.928	.846	.772	.706	.646	.591	.542	.497	.457
24	1.036	.869	.732	.619	.526	.449	.384	.331	.287	.249
36	1.052	.821	.647	.516	.416	.339	.280	.234	.198	.170
48	1.066	.781	.584	.446	.348	.278	.227	.189	.161	.140
60	1.078	.749	.537	.399	.307	.244	.200	.169	.146	.128
72	1.090	.723	.503	.368	.282	.225	.187	.159	.139	.124
84	1.100	.701	.477	.346	.266	.215	.180	.155	.136	.122
96	1.109	.683	.458	.332	.257	.209	.176	.153	.135	.121
108	1.118	.669	.444	.322	.251	.206	.175	.152	.135	.121
120	1.125	.657	.433	.316	.248	.204	.174	.152	.135	.121
180	1.153	.623	.410	.304	.243	.202	.173	.151	.134	.121
240	1.170	.611	.405	.303	.242	.202	.173	.151	.134	.121
300	1.180	.607	.404	.303	.242	.202	.173	.151	.134	.121
360	1.185	.605	.403	.303	.242	.202	.173	.151	.134	.121
420	1.187	.605	.403	.303	.242	.202	.173	.151	.134	.121
480	1.188	.605	.403	.303	.242	.202	.173	.151	.134	.121
m = ∞										
12	.123	.116	.110	.104	.099	.094	.090	.085	.082	.078
24	.225	.203	.184	.168	.154	.141	.130	.120	.112	.104
36	.317	.275	.240	.211	.187	.167	.150	.136	.124	.114
48	.401	.333	.281	.240	.208	.182	.161	.144	.130	.118
60	.477	.381	.311	.259	.220	.190	.166	.147	.132	.119
72	.545	.421	.334	.273	.228	.194	.169	.149	.133	.120
84	.607	.453	.351	.282	.233	.197	.170	.149	.133	.120
96	.664	.479	.364	.288	.235	.198	.171	.150	.133	.120
108	.714	.501	.373	.292	.237	.199	.171	.150	.133	.120
120	.760	.519	.380	.294	.238	.199	.171	.150	.133	.120
180	.933	.570	.395	.299	.240	.200	.171	.150	.133	.120
240	1.038	.589	.399	.300	.240	.200	.171	.150	.133	.120
300	1.101	.596	.400	.300	.240	.200	.171	.150	.133	.120
360	1.140	.598	.400	.300	.240	.200	.171	.150	.133	.120
420	1.164	.599	.400	.300	.240	.200	.171	.150	.133	.120
480	1.178	.600	.400	.300	.240	.200	.171	.150	.133	.120

				r = 13%					
10	20	30	40	50	60	70	80	90	100

m = 360

1.028	.937	.855	.781	.714	.653	.599	.549	.504	.464
1.054	.886	.747	.633	.539	.461	.396	.342	.297	.259
1.077	.844	.668	.534	.432	.354	.294	.247	.210	.181
1.098	.809	.609	.467	.367	.295	.242	.203	.174	.151
1.117	.781	.565	.423	.327	.262	.216	.183	.158	.140
1.134	.758	.533	.393	.303	.244	.203	.174	.152	.135
1.149	.740	.509	.372	.288	.234	.196	.169	.149	.134
1.163	.725	.491	.359	.279	.228	.193	.168	.148	.133
1.175	.712	.478	.350	.274	.225	.191	.167	.148	.133
1.186	.702	.468	.344	.271	.223	.190	.166	.148	.133
1.226	.674	.448	.333	.266	.221	.190	.166	.147	.133
1.247	.665	.443	.332	.266	.221	.190	.166	.147	.133
1.258	.662	.443	.332	.265	.221	.190	.166	.147	.133
1.261	.662	.442	.332	.265	.221	.190	.166	.147	.133

m = 480

1.028	.937	.855	.780	.713	.653	.598	.549	.504	.463
1.054	.885	.747	.633	.538	.460	.395	.341	.296	.258
1.077	.843	.667	.533	.431	.352	.292	.245	.208	.179
1.098	.809	.607	.466	.365	.293	.240	.201	.172	.149
1.117	.780	.563	.420	.325	.259	.214	.181	.156	.138
1.135	.757	.530	.390	.300	.241	.200	.171	.150	.133
1.150	.738	.506	.369	.285	.231	.194	.167	.147	.132
1.164	.722	.488	.355	.276	.225	.190	.165	.146	.131
1.177	.710	.474	.346	.270	.222	.189	.164	.146	.131
1.188	.699	.464	.340	.267	.220	.188	.164	.145	.131
1.231	.670	.442	.329	.262	.218	.187	.163	.145	.131
1.256	.659	.437	.327	.262	.218	.187	.163	.145	.131
1.270	.655	.436	.327	.261	.218	.187	.163	.145	.131
1.278	.654	.436	.327	.261	.218	.187	.163	.145	.131
1.282	.654	.436	.327	.261	.218	.187	.163	.145	.131
1.283	.653	.436	.327	.261	.218	.187	.163	.145	.131

m = ∞

.133	.126	.119	.113	.107	.102	.097	.093	.088	.084
.244	.220	.200	.182	.166	.153	.141	.130	.121	.113
.344	.297	.260	.229	.203	.181	.163	.148	.135	.123
.434	.361	.304	.260	.225	.197	.174	.156	.140	.127
.516	.413	.337	.281	.238	.206	.180	.159	.143	.129
.591	.456	.362	.295	.247	.211	.183	.161	.144	.130
.658	.491	.380	.305	.252	.213	.184	.162	.144	.130
.719	.519	.394	.312	.255	.215	.185	.162	.144	.130
.774	.543	.404	.316	.257	.216	.185	.162	.144	.130
.824	.562	.412	.319	.258	.216	.186	.162	.144	.130
1.011	.617	.428	.324	.260	.217	.186	.162	.144	.130
1.124	.638	.432	.325	.260	.217	.186	.162	.144	.130
1.193	.646	.433	.325	.260	.217	.186	.162	.144	.130
1.235	.648	.433	.325	.260	.217	.186	.162	.144	.130
1.261	.649	.433	.325	.260	.217	.186	.162	.144	.130
1.276	.650	.433	.325	.260	.217	.186	.162	.144	.130

PART II

HOW TO VALUE REAL ESTATE

CHAPTER 3

HOW TO MAKE A QUICK APPRAISAL

3.0 DECIDING WHICH APPROACH TO VALUE IS BEST FOR YOU

The following three sections discuss the three approaches to value used by professional appraisers: the cost, income, and market approaches.

The cost approach (Section 3.1) uses the current reproduction cost of an improvement and subtracts its estimated accrued depreciation. The estimated value of the land is then added to this value to estimate the property value.

The income approach (Section 3.2) uses the annual net operating income of the property and the estimated current capitalization rate of similar properties. Then, depending on the judgment of the appraiser, one of several possible formulas is used to estimate property value.

The market approach (Section 3.3), the most fundamental of the three, uses a sample of recent comparable sales to estimate the average property value.

This section includes some very useful statistical techniques that refine the average value. The market approach doesn't use the other two approaches; the cost and income approaches do use the other two.[1] Figure 3.0-1 is a schematic diagram depicting the dependence among the three approaches.

[1] It is rare, but sometimes the income approach (the land residual technique in particular) is used to estimate the land value in the cost approach.

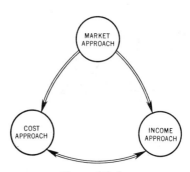

Figure 3.0-1

Table 3.0-1 lists the approaches to value that are generally appropriate for properties with certain characteristics.

An appraiser will use as many of the three approaches as are applicable to the subject property. Then, he will use his judgment to assign weights to each approach to obtain a single estimate of fair market value.[2] This process is called reconciliation or correlation, but it is simply a weighted average.

EXAMPLE

Suppose a property has been appraised at $50,000, $52,000, and $49,000 by the cost, income, and market approaches, respectively. Also suppose that, because of the peculiarities of the subject property, the appraiser feels the respective approaches should be weighted by 60%, 10%, and

[2] Fair market value, as defined by the courts, is "the price that a property will bring in a competitive market under all conditions requisite to a fair sale which would result from negotiations between a buyer and a seller, each acting prudently, with knowledge and without undue pressure." Value can be distorted by legal aspects of property, by need for a quick sale, etc.

The importance of judgment in all aspects of appraisal can't be overemphasized; appraising is not an exact science, and there are many conceivable ways in which a property can fail to fit guidelines.

Table 3.0-1. Approaches to Value that are Appropriate for Some Properties

Property Characteristics	Approaches to value that are appropriate		
	Cost	Income	Market*
Newer improvement without income potential	X		X
Newer improvement with income potential	X	X	X
Older improvement without income potential			X
Older improvement with income potential		X	X
No improvement without income potential			X
No improvement with income potential		X	X

*The market method can't be used when there are no recent comparable sales.

30%.[3] Then, if v_p is the final estimate of property value, we have:

$$v_p = 0.60 \times \$50,000 + 0.10 \times \$52,000$$
$$+ 0.30 \times \$49,000$$
$$= \$30,000 + \$5,200 + \$14,700$$
$$= \$49,900.$$

3.1 THE COST APPROACH: THE FORMULAS AND HOW TO USE THEM

The cost approach to value estimates the value of property by estimating the reproduction cost (new) of the improvement, subtracting the estimated accrued depreciation, and then adding the estimated value of the land (as if vacant):

$$\text{property value} = \begin{pmatrix} \text{reproduction cost} \\ \text{of improvement} \end{pmatrix}$$
$$- \begin{pmatrix} \text{accrued depreciation} \\ \text{of improvement} \end{pmatrix} + (\text{value of land}).$$

This approach to value is used most often to appraise newer properties (because accrued depreciation is difficult to estimate in older properties), and properties for which the other two approaches to value cannot be used. For example, the income approach cannot be used for properties without income potential, and the market approach cannot be used for properties that are rarely sold. The cost approach is also used whenever the value of the improvement must be separated from the value of the land such as required for *ad valorem* taxations, accounting, feasibility studies, the land residual technique (for the income approach), and so on.

Since the cost approach to value utilizes three distinct components, it is useful to examine them separately.

I. Reproduction Cost

The reproduction cost (new) is the cost to substitute the improvement with a new *replica*.[4] Theo-

---

[3] Of course, each weight must be non-negative, and the three must sum to 1.
[4] Replacement cost, on the other hand, is the cost to sub-

retically, the reproduction cost is the upper limit on the value of an improvement because no intelligent buyer would pay more than the cost new to reproduce the improvement.

Three methods are used to estimate the direct costs of reproduction.[5] The three methods are presented in order of decreasing detail (and increasing utility). For example, the first method (quantity survey method) estimates cost by adding the cost of every component such as nails and labor. The second method (unit-in-place) estimates cost by comparing the total improvement with a similar improvement of known cost.

A. Quantity Survey Method. This method considers every unit (component) used in construction (e.g., the number of nails, the amount of each type of pipe, the cubic yards of concrete, etc.), its price, and the labor cost to complete each unit of the improvement. This method is quite accurate but very time-consuming.

B. Unit-in-Place Method. This method is a modified quantity survey method. The components and labor are still accounted for, but in an aggregate way. That is, the reproduction cost of a roof is estimated after it is completed and in place.

C. Comparison Method. This method uses the area or volume of the subject improvement. Then a standard improvement, similar to the subject property, is found in cost estimating manuals. The standard improvement is a certain size (area or volume), and the cost per unit size of the subject property increases or decreases as it is smaller or larger, respectively, than the standard.

---

stitute the improvement with a new one of *like utility.* This concept is used when the reproduction cost cannot be used (i.e., when materials and building techniques are no longer available to construct a *replica*).

[5] Regardless of which is used to estimate direct costs, always include indirect costs: fees (accountant, architect, contractor, engineer, lawyer, surveyor, etc.), financial costs (commissions, insurance, interest on loans, taxes, etc.), equipment that becomes part of the property, and contractor's profit.

EXAMPLE

The subject improvement has an area of 70,000 sq. ft. The cost of a comparable standard improvement is listed in a cost estimating manual at $50.00/sq. ft. However, about 3% should be added to the standard cost because of the quality of the finished work in the subject property. Since the cost manual was compiled there has been a 9% increase in construction costs. Also, the construction costs locally are 3% less than the cost for the standard improvement. Estimate the reproduction cost of this improvement by the comparison method.

SOLUTION

Using the above corrections to the standard, the estimated reproduction cost is:

$$(70,000 \text{ sq. ft.}) \times (\$13.00/\text{sq. ft.}) \times 1.03 \times 1.09$$
$$\times 0.97 = \$991,007.$$

Since quality and time have caused increases to the standard, these factors are represented by $1 + .03 = 1.03$ and $1 + .09 = 1.09$. Similarly, location results in a 3% subtraction from the standard and is represented by $1 - .03 = 0.97$.

II. Accrued Depreciation

Accrued depreciation is the loss of value that an improvement has suffered from all sources since its inception.

A. Sources of Accrued Depreciation. Real estate appraisers generally agree that accrued depreciation or diminished utility can come from three sources:

1. Physical Deterioration. Accrued depreciation due to the damages of use and time. This form of depreciation begins the instant an improvement is constructed and continues forever.

2. Functional Obsolescence. Accrued depreciation due to the loss of appeal and utility. Value is lost in a rather unpredictable manner.

3. Economic Obsolescence. Accrued depreciation due to either unfavorable zoning or unfavorable supply and demand. Diminished utility results from causes external to the property and can be considered as "locational obsolescence." It is thought to be incurable since the property owner cannot solve the problem.

B. Measures of Accrued Depreciation. Three methods are used to measure accrued depreciation:

1. Comparable Sales Method. Assume the reproduction cost new for a building is known. Then the accrued depreciation can be estimated by a market survey of the sale price of similar properties.

2. Comparable Income Method. Assume the reproduction cost new for a building is known. Then the accrued depreciation can be estimated by a market survey of the income from similar properties.

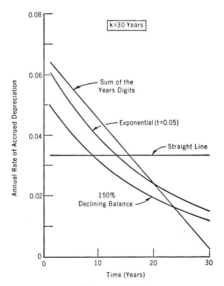

Figure 3.1-1

3. Formula Method. This method utilizes the life of an object as a basis to measure the accrued depreciation. The object can be the building itself or components of the building, such as walls, floors and so on. The life can be the estimated physical life or the economic life. For instance, the physical life would describe physical depreciation only, whereas economic life would describe physical, functional, and economic depreciation. Three of the formulas are straight line, sum of the years digits, and declining balance. The fourth formula describes exponential depreciation. According to this concept, the rate of decay is proportional to the amount of undecayed material. That is, newness vanishes in proportion to the amount present. Hence, the rate of exponential depreciation is highest when the building is new. See Figures 3.1-1 and 3.1-2 on pages 43 and 44.

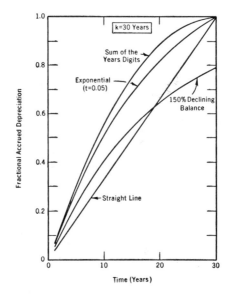

Figure 3.1-2

FORMULAS

$$a_n = \frac{1}{k}$$
$$A_n = \frac{n}{k}$$
$\left.\vphantom{\begin{matrix}a\\A\end{matrix}}\right\}$ Straight Line

$$a_n = \frac{2(k + 1 - n)}{k(k + 1)}$$
$$A_n = \frac{n(2k + 1 - n)}{k(k + 1)}$$
$\left.\vphantom{\begin{matrix}a\\A\end{matrix}}\right\}$ Sum of the Years Digits

$$a_n = 1(1 - q)^{n-1}$$
$$A_n = 1 - (1 - q)^n$$
$\left.\vphantom{\begin{matrix}a\\A\end{matrix}}\right\}$ Declining Balance

$$a_n = \frac{te^{-nt}}{1 - e^{-kt}}$$
$$A_n = \frac{1 - e^{-nt}}{1 - e^{-kt}}$$
$\left.\vphantom{\begin{matrix}a\\A\end{matrix}}\right\}$ Exponential

$$A_n = \frac{v'_b + v_l - v_p}{v'_b}$$
Comparable Sales
and Comparable Income
Method

$\Bigg\}$ Formula Method

where

a_n = annual rate of accrued depreciation in the nth year

A_n = fraction of accrued depreciation after n years

n = age of building

k = remaining economic life of depreciable asset

$q = w/k$ = a parameter for the declining balance method. The values $w = 1.25, 1.50$, and 2.00 are used in depreciation for tax purposes

t = parameter for the exponential method. The value of t is at the user's discretion (probably $0 < t < .10$)

v_p = present value of the property

v'_b = reproduction cost new of the building

v_l = present value of the land, as if vacant and put to its highest and best use

EXAMPLE

(Formula Method). The subject property had an economic life of 40 years when constructed. Since it is now five years old, what is the amount of accrued depreciation by the straight-line method?

SOLUTION

In the example,

$$k = 40 \text{ years}, \ n = 5 \text{ years}, \text{ and } A_5 = \frac{5}{40} = 0.125.$$

From the comparison method, the reproduction cost new was determined to be $991,007. Hence, the amount of accrued depreciation is

$$0.125 \times \$991,007 = \$123,876.$$

III. Land Value

The value of the land (as if vacant) is determined by the market approach. That is, the value is based on recent sales of comparable sites (Section 3.3).

EXAMPLE

Suppose six appraisers, using their experience of recent comparable sales, estimate the value of the subject site to be $230,000, $220,000, $225,000, $215,000, $220,000, and $227,500. The average value is $222,917. However, using a statistical technique introduced in Section 3.3, we can be 95% confident that the true value is between $217,067 and $228,767.

Now that all three components of the cost approach are known (reproduction cost, accrued depreciation, and land value), they can be assembled to estimate the value of the property: Using the same property discussed in the examples from this section, recall that the reproduction cost is $991,007, the accrued depreciation is $123,876, and the land value is $222,917. Now the estimated property value is

$$\$991,007 - \$123,876 + \$222,917 = \$1,090,048.$$

3.2 THE INCOME APPROACH: THE FORMULAS AND HOW TO USE THEM

Industrial, residential rental, and commercial properties can be appraised by several formulas that depend on the actual or potential net operating income and the capitalization rate.

The selection of the most appropriate formula for appraisal depends on assumptions about the future income, the estimated holding period, the relative certainty of values of the physical components (i.e., land and buildings), the judgment of the appraiser, and so on.

The selection of the proper capitalization rate also depends on some of the above factors; the resultant property value is very sensitive to the capitalization rate. The capitalization rate and the appraisal formulas are discussed separately.

I. Capitalization Rate

Capitalization is the process of converting income into a capital value (the original investment). The rate at which this occurs is called the capitalization rate.

A real estate investment is usually comprised of two investments, a mortgage loan and the investor's equity. Not only does the property have a capitalization rate, but also each investment component has its own capitalization rate. Conceptually, the capitalization rate for these or any investment is the sum of two rates: the interest rate (the rate of return *on* invested capital) and the recapture rate (the rate of return *of* invested capital).

If the invested capital is a mortgage loan, the lender's investment is the loan amount. Each payment of an amortized loan consists of an amount of interest and an amount of principal. The interest is the return on his investment, and the principal is the return of his investment. The mortgage capitalization rate is the sum of these two rates. It is also expressible as the ratio of annual payment-to-loan amount (called the annual mortgage constant).

If the invested capital is the original equity (down payment) in an income property, the return on the investment consists of some or all of the cash flow. Any cash flow in excess of the return on capital can be regarded as a return of capital. The equity capitalization rate is the sum of these rates, and is also expressible as the ratio of annual cash flow-to-down payment.

The property value is the sum of the mortgage

amount and the property investor's equity. Hence, the property interest rate can be thought of as the weighted average of the mortgage interest rate and the equity interest rate. The property recapture rate can be thought of as the weighted average of the mortgage recapture rate and the equity recapture rate. The property capitalization rate is the sum of the property interest rate and the property recapture rate. It is also expressible as the ratio of annual net operating income-to-property value or as the reciprocal of the net income multiplier (i.e., if property is valued at "eight times net," its capitalization rate is 12.5%).

Table 3.2-1 lists formulas for interest rates, recapture rates, and capitalization rates for investments of mortgage, equity, and property. The interest, recapture, and capitalization rates are discussed in greater depth in Sections 4.4, 4.5 and 4.6, respectively.

DEFINITION OF PARAMETERS FOR TABLE 3.2-1

r_m, r_e, r_p = interest rate for mortgage, equity, and property, respectively

r_1 = safe rate (such as that paid on government bonds)

r_2 = risk rate (for possible declining income)

r_3 = non-liquidity rate

r_4 = management rate (for burden of clerical duties associated with ownership)

r'_m, r'_e, r'_p = recapture rate for mortgage, equity, and property, respectively

z_m, z_e, z_p = capitalization rate for mortgage, equity, and property, respectively

x_m, x_e, x_p = annual mortgage payment, cash flow, and net operating income, respectively

v_m, v_e, v_p = loan amount, present value of equity, and present value of property, respectively

$t = \dfrac{v_m}{v_p}$ = loan-to-value ratio

h = forecast-to-present property value ratio

n = number of years in income projection period (for Ellwood rate)

q = number of mortgage interest periods per year

m = total number of mortgage interest periods

$j = nq$ = number of mortgage interest periods until end of income projection period

$s(r_m, m, q)$, etc. = amount of an annuity of 1

$a(r_m, m, q)$ = present value of an annuity of 1

The three important property capitalization rates are the comparison rate, the band of investment rate, and the Ellwood rate.

A. Comparison Rate. The property capitalization rate $z_p = \dfrac{x_p}{v_p}$ is the ratio of annual net operating income-to-present value of the property. This ratio is the reciprocal for the commonly used net income multiplier.

B. Band of Investment Rate. The financial components of the property (mortgage and equity) each have their own capitalization rate. The band of investment rate is the weighted average of these rates.

EXAMPLE 1

Consider a property for which the mortgage capitalization rate (annual mortgage constant) is 9.26%, and the equity capitalization rate is 12%. If the loan-to-value ratio is 75%, what is the property capitalization rate by the band of investment method?

SOLUTION

In this example, $z_m = 0.0926$, $z_e = 0.12$, and $t = 0.75$. Then the property capitalization rate is

$$z_p = 0.75 \times .0926 + 0.25 \times 0.12$$
$$= 0.0695 + 0.03 = 0.0995$$
$$= 9.95\%.$$

Table 3.2-1. Interest, Recapture, and Capitalization Rates for Investments of Mortgage, Equity, and Property

Rates		Investment		
		Mortgage	Equity	Property
	Interest	r_m = (specified by contract)	$r_e = \dfrac{r_p - tr_m}{1 - t}$ (if t < 1)	$r_p = \begin{cases} tr_m + (1-t)r_e & \text{(band of investment rate)} \\ r_1 + r_2 + r_3 + r_4 & \text{(component rate)} \end{cases}$
	Recapture	$r'_m = \dfrac{q}{s(r_m, m, q)}$	$r'_e = \dfrac{r'_p - tr'_m}{1 - t}$ (if t < 1)	$r'_p = \begin{cases} tr'_m + (1-t)r'_e & \text{(band of investment rate)} \\ \dfrac{1}{s(r,k,1)} \end{cases}$ *

Rates	$\left\{ \begin{array}{l} r_m + r'_m \\ z_m = \dfrac{x_m}{v_m} \text{ (reciprocal of net income multiplier)} \end{array} \right.$	$\left\{ \begin{array}{l} r_e + r'_e \\ z_e = \dfrac{x_e}{v_e} \text{ (comparison rate)} \end{array} \right.$	$\left\{ \begin{array}{l} r_p + r'_p \text{ (comparison rate)} \\ \dfrac{x_p}{v_p} \end{array} \right.$
Capitalization	$\dfrac{q}{a(r_m,m,q)}$	$\dfrac{z_p - tz_m}{1-t} \text{ (if t < 1)}$	$z_p = tz_m + (1-t)z_e \text{ (band of investment rate)}$ $\quad tz_m + (1-t)z_e + \dfrac{\left[1 - h - t\dfrac{s(r_m,i,q)}{s(r_m,m,q)}\right]}{s(z_e,n,1)} \text{ (Ellwood rate)}$

*It is conventional to assume that deposits in a sinking fund are made annually. However, they are probably made q times a year (e.g., q = 12). In this case, $r'_p = q/s(r,kq,q)$. If $r = 0$, recapture is according to the straight line method; if $r = r_1$, recapture is according to the Hoskold method; if $r = r_p$, recapture is according to the Inwood method.

C. Ellwood Rate. The Ellwood rate is the band of investment rate plus an additional term. This term depends on the mortgage amortization and the changed property value that occurs during the estimated holding period. The bracketed portion of the additional term is the fraction of property value that must be replaced. This fraction is the *change* in investor's equity (through loan amortization and changed property value) during the holding period, divided by the original property value. Replacement is accomplished by depositing an amount annually in a sinking fund at interest equal to the investor's equity capitalization rate, z_e.

If, during the holding period, the property value has decreased by an amount equal to the loan amortization, there has been no change in the investor's equity, and the Ellwood capitalization rate is equal to the band of investment rate. If the property value has decreased more than the loan amortization, the Ellwood rate exceeds the band of investment rate, and the property will then be appraised lower.

EXAMPLE 2

An apartment investor obtains a first mortgage at 8% interest that is amortized with constant monthly payments for 25 years. The loan amount is 75% of the purchase price. A market survey indicates that the equity capitalization rate for similar properties is 12%. (These are exactly the same conditions as given in the example for the band of investment rate.) It is assumed that the property will be held for 10 years, and at that time, its value will be only 80% of its current value. Determine Ellwood's version of the capitalization rate.

SOLUTION

In this example,

r_m = 8%, m = nq = 25 × 12 = 300 periods,
z = 0.0926, t = 0.75, z_e = 12%, n = 10 years,
j = 10 × 12 = 120 periods, and h = 0.80.

From Table 1,

$$s(r_m,j,q) = s(8,120,12) = 182.9460,$$
$$s(r_m,m,q) = s(8,300,12) = 951.0264, \text{ and}$$
$$s(z_e,n,1) = s(12,10,1) = 17.5487.$$

Now,

$$z_p = tz_m + (1-t)z_e + \frac{\left[1 - h - t\dfrac{s(r_m,j,q)}{s(r_m,m,q)}\right]}{s(z_e,n,1)}$$

$$= 0.75 \times 0.0926 + 0.25 \times 0.12$$

$$+ \frac{\left(1 - 0.80 - 0.75 \times \dfrac{182.9460}{951.0264}\right)}{17.5487}$$

$$= 0.0995 + \frac{0.20 - 0.75 \times 0.1923669}{17.5487}$$

$$= 0.0995 + \frac{0.0557248}{17.5487} = 0.0995 + 0.0032 = 0.1027$$

$$= 10.27\%$$

II. Appraisal Formulas

Two types of formulas are used to estimate value by the income approach: direct capitalization and the formulas of the residual techniques.

A. Direct Capitalization. Direct capitalization is the ratio of annual net operating income to the capitalization rate. In this way income is converted to a capital value. Generally, direct capitalization is used for properties for which one of the residual techniques is not applicable.

FORMULA

$$v_p = \frac{x_p}{z_p}$$

where

v_p = present value of property
x_p = annual net operating income
z_p = property capitalization rate

EXAMPLE

Suppose a commercial property has an annual net operating income of $100,000, and five appraisers independently estimate the property capitalization rate to be 0.105, 0.092, 0.100, 0.098, and 0.110. Determine the property value by direct capitalization.

SOLUTION

The average capitalization rate is $0.101 = 10.1\%$. Moreover, using the technique of Section 3.3, we are 95% confident that the true capitalization rate is between 9.25% and 10.95%.

Using these two limits, we are therefore 95% confident that the property value is between

$$\frac{\$100,000}{.0925} = \$1,081,081, \text{ and } \frac{\$100,000}{.1095} = \$913,242.$$

B. Residual Techniques. Residual techniques are often used when the value of one of the physical components (land or building) is well known, and the other is not. In such cases, the value of the better-known component is determined by the cost or market approach; then the income attributable to the lesser-known component is considered residual. There are three residual techniques: building, land, and property.

The building residual technique assumes that the value of the land is reasonably well known, but the value of the building is not. The value of the land is determined by the market approach. The annual net operating income attributable to the land is subtracted from the annual net operating income from the property. The value of the building is determined by capitalizing the residual amount (due to the building) at the property capitalization rate. The value of the property is the sum of the value of the land and the building.

The land residual technique assumes that the value of the building is reasonably well known, but the value of the land is not. The value of the building is determined by the cost approach. The annual net operating income attributable to the building is subtracted from the annual net operating income from the property. The value of the land is determined by capitalizing this residual amount (due to the land) at the property interest rate. The value of the property is the sum of the value of the building and the land.

The property residual technique assumes that the two property components, land and building, can't be separated. All net operating income is attributed to the property as a whole and capitalized at the property capitalization rate. The land value is assumed to be known and is discounted at the property interest rate over a period that is the estimated useful life of the building, the remaining term of the lease, etc.

Table 3.2-2 lists the type(s) of residual techniques that are appropriate, given certain assumptions about the value of the land and buildings. Formulas and examples for each technique follow the table.

FORMULAS:

$$v_p = \begin{cases} \dfrac{x_p - r_p v_l}{z_p} + v_l & \text{(building residual technique)} \\[2ex] v_b + \dfrac{x_p - z_p v_b}{r_p} & \text{(land residual technique)} \\[2ex] \dfrac{x_p}{z_p} + \dfrac{v_l}{c(r_p,k,1)} & \text{(property residual technique)} \end{cases}$$

where

v_p = present value of the property

v_b = present value of the building

v_l = present value of the land

x_p = annual net operating income from the property

r_p = property interest rate

$z_p = 1/a(r_p,k,1)$ = property capitalization rate

k = remaining useful life of the building or the remaining term of a long-term lease

$c(r_p,k,1)$ = amount of 1 at component interest (Table 1)

Table 3.2-2. Residual Technique(s) Appropriate to Estimate Property Value

Building		
	Building Value Well Known (By Cost Approach)	Building does not exist*
		Building new and represents highest and best use
		Building old, but accrued depreciation known
		Building old, but represents highest and best use
	Building Value Not Well Known	Building new, but doesn't represent highest and best use
		Building old, and accrued depreciation not well known
		Building old, but has stable long-term lease

*Determine a hypothetical value for the land by assuming it is put to its highest and best use.

EXAMPLE 1: (Building Residual Technique)

Consider an older apartment building located in a transitional neighborhood. Because the building is older, there has been considerable accrued depreciation, and its value is difficult to determine by the cost approach. However, since it is located in a transitional neighborhood, there are enough recent comparable sales of lots to estimate the land value by the market approach at $150,000. The annual net operating income from the building is $50,500. The interest rate for similar properties is

Land	
Land Value Well Known (By Market Approach)	*Land Value Not Well Known*
Land residual Building residual	Land residual
Land residual Building residual	Land residual
Building residual	Property residual
Property residual Building residual	Property residual
Building residual	Property residual
Building residual	Property residual
Property residual Building residual	Property residual

8%, and the property capitalization rate is 11%; the method of recapture is not specified here, but the rate is included implicitly as 3%. Determine the property value by the building residual technique.

SOLUTION

In this example,

$v_l = \$150{,}000$, $x_p = \$50{,}500$, $r_p = 0.08$, and $z_p = 0.11$.

Now, the property value by the building residual technique is

$$v_p = \frac{x_p - r_p v_l}{z_p} + v_l$$

$$= \frac{\$50,500 - 0.08 \times \$150,000}{0.11} + \$150,000$$

$$= \frac{\$50,500 - \$12,000}{0.11} + \$150,000$$

$$= \frac{\$38,500}{0.11} + \$150,000$$

$$= \$350,000 + \$150,000$$

$$= \$500,000.$$

EXAMPLE 2: (Land Residual Technique)

A three-year-old building is estimated by the cost approach to have a value of \$350,000 (e.g., the reproduction cost new could be \$385,000 and the accrued depreciation could be \$35,000). The annual net operating income is \$50,000, the property interest rate is 8%, and the property capitalization rate is 11%. Determine the property value by the land residual technique.

SOLUTION

In this example,

$v_b = \$350,000, \quad x_p = \$50,000, \quad r_p = 0.80,$
$$\text{and } z_p = 0.11.$$

Now

$$v_p = v_b + \frac{x_p - z_p v_b}{r_p}$$

$$= \$350,000 + \frac{\$50,000 - 0.11 \times \$350,000}{0.08}$$

$$= \$350,000 + \frac{\$50,000 - \$38,500}{0.08}$$

$$= \$350,000 + \frac{\$11,500}{.08}$$

$$= \$350,000 + \$143,750$$

$$= \$493,750.$$

EXAMPLE 3: (Property Residual Technique)

Consider an older apartment building in a neighborhood in which there has been neither recent sales nor new construction. The annual net operating income is $50,000, and the land value is estimated to be $140,000. The property capitalization rate is 13%, and the property interest rate is 8%. It is estimated that the building has a remaining useful life of 20 years. Determine the property value by the property residual technique.

SOLUTION

In this example,

$x_p = \$50,000$, $v_l = \$140,000$, $z_p = 0.13$, $r_p = 0.08$, and $k = 20$ years.

From Table 1, $c(r_p,k,1) = c(8,20,1) = 4.66096$. Now,

$$\begin{aligned} v_p &= \frac{x_p}{z_p} + \frac{v_l}{c(r_p,k,l)} \\ &= \frac{\$50,000}{0.13} = \frac{\$140,000}{4.66096} \\ &= \$384,615 + \$30,037 \\ &= \$414,652. \end{aligned}$$

3.3 THE MARKET APPROACH: THE FORMULAS AND HOW TO USE THEM

The market approach to value requires collecting data from recent sales of comparable properties and analyzing the data to estimate the value of the subject property.

Time is measured by change, and change will be noticed not only in fashion, but also in prices. Fashion in real estate (measured by functional obsolescence) changes relatively slowly.

EXAMPLE

Suppose a property sold two years ago for $100,000. After one year, comparable properties were selling 2% lower, but during the second year they increased by 4%. If the same property were sold today, the sale price would probably be

$$\$100,000(1 - .02)(1 + .04) = \$100,000(0.98)(1.04)$$
$$= \$101,920.$$

We shall examine three techniques of analysis that have a great deal of utility in the market approach.[6]

The first technique (confidence limits) measures the precision of the average value.

The second technique (single regression analysis) is used to estimate value when it seems to depend on one important measurable characteristic.

The third technique (multiple regression analysis) is a generalization of the second. This technique is used when value is thought to depend on more than one characteristic.

I. Confidence Limits

Suppose the market value of a property is estimated *independently* by several appraisers. For example, suppose n appraisers independently estimate the value, and then the estimates are averaged. We might ask: How confident are we that the true value is within a given range of the true market value? The two formulas below give an upper and a lower value within which we can be, say, 95% confident that the true value lies.

Figure 3.3-1 illustrates the 90% and 95% confidence limits for the example in this section. Notice that the confidence interval becomes smaller as more appraisers are used.

FORMULA

$$V_l = \bar{v} - q_n s_v \quad \text{and} \quad V_u = \bar{v} + q_n s_v$$

where

V_l, V_u = lower and upper estimate of market value, respectively

---

[6] These techniques assume the data comes from a population that is approximately normally distributed, an assumption that is usually quite realistic.

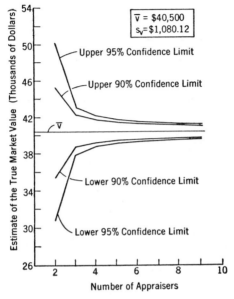

Figure 3.3-1

v_i = the ith independent estimate of market value

n = number of independent estimates

$\bar{v} = \dfrac{1}{n}\sum\limits_{i=i}^{n} v_i$ = average of n independent estimates of market value

$s_v = \sqrt{\dfrac{1}{n-1}\sum\limits_{i=1}^{n}(v_i - \bar{v})^2}$ = standard deviation of n independent estimates of market value

q_n = factor that depends on n and the desired confidence level (e.g., 95%)

VALUES OF q_n

n	2	3	4	5
90%	4.465	1.686	1.177	.9534
95%	8.987	2.484	1.591	1.242

n	6	7	8	9	10
90%	.8226	.7345	.6698	.6198	.5797
95%	1.050	.9248	.8360	.7687	.7153

EXAMPLE

Four brokers independently (i.e., without commu-
nication) estimate the market value of a house at
$41,000, $39,000, $41,500, and $40,500. To estimate the true market value, they will average
their estimates. Both the brokers and the owner
would like to know how precise the estimate is
likely to be. Specifically, they would like to be 95%
confident that the true market value lies within a
certain range of values. Determine these values.

SOLUTION

In this example,

$$n = 4, v_1 = \$41,000, v_2 = \$39,000, v_3 = \$41,500,$$
$$\text{and } v_4 = \$40,500.$$

a. Determine the average of the estimates:

$$\bar{v} = \frac{1}{n} \sum_{i=1}^{n} v_i = \frac{1}{4}(\$41,000 + \$39,000 + \$41,500$$
$$+ \$40,500) = \$40,500.$$

b. Determine the standard deviation of the estimates:

$$s_v = \sqrt{\frac{1}{n-1} \sum_{i=1}^{n} (v_i - \bar{v})^2}$$
$$= \sqrt{\frac{1}{3}[(v_1 - \bar{v})^2 + (v_2 - \bar{v})^2 + (v_3 - \bar{v})^2 + (v_4 - \bar{v})^2]}$$

$$= \sqrt{\frac{1}{3}[(41,000 - 40,500)^2 + (39,000 - 40,500)^2}$$
$$\overline{+ (41,500 - 40,500)^2 + (40,500 - 40,500)^2]}$$

$$= \sqrt{\frac{1}{3}[(500)^2 + (-1,500)^2 + (1,000)^2 + (0)^2]}$$

$$= \sqrt{\frac{1}{3}(250,000 + 2,250,000 + 1,000,000 + 0)}$$

$$= \sqrt{\frac{1}{3} \times 3,500,000} = \sqrt{1,166,666.67} = \$1,080.12.$$

c. Go to the table to find q_4. Corresponding to the 95% confidence level and $n = 4$ estimates find $q_4 = 1.591$.

d. Use the formulas to determine V_l and V_u, the lower and upper 95% confidence limits:

$V_l = \$40,500 - 1.591 \times \$1,080.12 = \$38,781$, and
$V_u = \$40,500 + 1.591 \times \$1,080.12 = \$42,218.$

Hence, if the four brokers arrive at their estimates independently, they can be 95% confident that the true market value of the house is between $38,781 and $42,218.

II. Single Regression Analysis

Single regression analysis can be used to statistically estimate value as it depends on a single characteristic. For example, if it is suspected that the value of single family residences depends largely on floor area, several values of sale price and floor area can be obtained from recent comparable sales. This data can then be used in the formula, below, to estimate the sale price of a single family residence with a known floor area.

The estimate is more accurate as more comparable values are used. Although floor area is the characteristic used in this example, any measurable characteristic can be used.

The floor area and its associated sale price are two numbers that define a point in the plane (two dimensions). The formula, below, is the formula for the straight line that best fits the scattering of

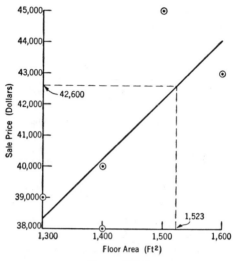

Figure 3.3-2

points.[7] (See Figure 3.3-2 which depicts the following example.)

FORMULA

$$v = b_1 + b_2x$$

where

v = estimated value

x = value of the characteristic of the property to be tested

n = number of observations

v_i = value of the ith observation

$\bar{v} = \dfrac{1}{n} \sum\limits_{i=1}^{n} v_i$ = average value of the observations

[7] The best fitting straight line is the one that renders a minimum the sum of the squares of the vertical distance between the points and the line.

x_i = value of the characteristic of the ith sample

$\bar{x} = \dfrac{1}{n} \sum\limits_{i=1}^{n} x_i$ = average value of the characteristic

$s_x^2 = \dfrac{1}{n-1} \sum\limits_{i=1}^{n} (x_i - \bar{x})^2$ = variance of the characteristic

$b_2 = \dfrac{\dfrac{1}{n-1} \sum\limits_{i=1}^{n} (v_i - \bar{v}) \cdot (x_i - \bar{x})}{s_x^2}$

$b_1 = \bar{v} - b_2 \cdot \bar{x}$

EXAMPLE

Brokers at the MJM Realty Co. know there is a relationship between recent sales price and floor area for comparable single family residences.

The company would like to estimate the sale price of other comparable residences based on the known floor area. They have collected five observations (this small sample size is used to provide a concise example).[8] The values are listed in the table.

(a) Determine the single regression formula for this data, and (b) using the formula, estimate the sale price of a comparable residence with a floor area of 1,523 ft².

Observation	1	2	3
Sale Price, v_i	$40,000	$45,000	$43,000
Floor Area, x_i	1,400 ft²	1,500 ft²	1,600 ft²

Observation	4	5
Sale Price, v_i	$38,000	$39,000
Floor Area, x_i	1,400 ft²	1,300 ft²

[8] To apply regression analysis in practice, the sample size should be at least 10 more than the number of characteristics (i.e., $n \geq 11$). Furthermore, the sale price should be plotted against the characteristic to see if some correlation exists.

SOLUTION

(a) To determine the formula for v, we must first determine $\bar{v}$, $\bar{x}$, and s_x^2:

$$\therefore \bar{v} = \frac{1}{5} \sum_{i=1}^{5} v_i = \frac{1}{5}(\$40,000 + \$45,000$$
$$+ \$43,000 + \$38,000 + \$39,000)$$
$$= \$41,000,$$

$$\bar{x} = \frac{1}{5} \sum_{i=1}^{5} x_i = \frac{1}{5}(1,400 + 1,500 + 1,600 + 1,400$$
$$+ 1,300)\text{ft}^2$$

$$= 1,400 \text{ ft}^2, \text{ and}$$

$$s_x^2 = \frac{1}{4} \sum_{i=1}^{5} (x_i - \bar{x})^2$$

$$= \frac{1}{4}[(-40)^2 + (60)^2 + (160)^2 + (-40)^2$$
$$+ (-140)^2]$$

$$= 13,000.56 \text{ ft}^2.$$

ii. Now we can evaluate the coefficients, b_2 and b_1.

$$b_2 = \frac{\dfrac{1}{4} \sum_{i=1}^{5} (v_i - \bar{v})(x_i - \bar{x})}{s_x^2}$$

$$= \frac{1}{4s_x^2}[(40,000 - 41,000)(1,400 - 1,440)$$
$$+ (45,000 - 41,000)(1,500 - 1,440)$$
$$+ (43,000 - 41,000)(1,600 - 1,440)$$
$$+ (38,000 - 41,000)(1,400 - 1,440)$$
$$+ (39,000 - 41,000)(1,300 - 1,440)]$$

$$= \frac{1}{4s_x^2}[(-1,000)(-40) + (4,000)(60)$$
$$+ (2,000)(160) + (-3,000)(-40)$$
$$+ (-2,000)(-140)]$$

$$= \frac{1,000,000}{4 \times 13,000.56}$$

$$= \$19,22994/\text{ft}^2, \text{ and}$$

$$b_1 = \bar{v} - b_2\bar{x} = \$41,000 - \$19.22994/\text{ft}^2 \times 1,440 \text{ ft}^2$$
$$= \$13,308.89.$$

iii. The regression formula for this example is

$$v = \$13,308.89 + (\$19.22994/\text{ft}^2)x.$$

(b) To determine the sale price, v, for a residence with a floor area of $x = 1,523$ ft^2, we merely substitute this value in the above formula:

$$v = \$13,308.89 + (\$19.22994/\text{ft}^2)(1,523 \text{ ft}^2)$$
$$= \$42,596.09 \text{ (say, \$42,600)}.$$

III. Multiple Regression Analysis

Single regression analysis shows how to determine the statistical relationship between value and one characteristic of the property. Multiple regression analysis shows how to determine the statistical relationship between value and more than one characteristic. The estimate is more accurate as more comparable observations are used.

FORMULA

$$v = b_1 + \sum_{k=2}^{m} b_k x_k$$

where

v = estimated value of the sample

m = number of characteristics

x_k = value of the kth characteristic of the sample to be tested

n = number of samples

x_{ki} = value of the kth characteristic of the ith sample

$\bar{x}_k = \dfrac{1}{n} \sum_{i=1}^{n} x_{ki}$ = average value of the kth characteristic

$c_{kj} = \dfrac{1}{n-1} \sum_{i=1}^{n} (x_{ki} - \bar{x}_k)(x_{ji} - \bar{x}_j)$ = covariance of x_k and x_j

$$C = \begin{vmatrix} c_{22} & \cdots & c_{2m} \\ \vdots & & \vdots \\ c_{m2} & \cdots & c_{mm} \end{vmatrix} = \text{determinant of covariances}$$

$C^{kj} = \dfrac{A_{kj}}{C}$

A_{kj} = cofactor of c_{kj}. That is, $A_{kj} = (-1)^{k+j} \times$ (determinant with the kth row and jth column deleted)

$$b_k = \sum_{j=2}^{m} c_{1j}C^{kj}(k = 2,3,\ldots,m)$$

$$b_1 = \bar{x}_1 - \sum_{k=2}^{m} \bar{x}_k b_k$$

EXAMPLE

We suspect that floor area and age are two characteristics that significantly affect the sale price of single family residences. We sample five comparable single family residences, and gather the following data. (This small sample size is used only to provide a concise example).[9]

Sample (i)	Sale Price (x_{1i})	Floor Area (x_{2i})	Age (x_{3i})
1	$40,000	1,400 ft^2	10 yrs
2	45,000	1,500	6
3	43,000	1,600	9
4	38,000	1,300	7
5	46,000	1,500	4

(a) Determine the multiple regression formula for this data, and (b) using this formula, estimate the sale price for an eight-year-old house with a floor area of 1,435 ft^2.

SOLUTION

For convenience, all units (such as dollars, ft^2, and years) shall be omitted until the end.

(a) To determine the multiple regression formula,

i. first, find the average value of each characteristic:

[9]To apply regression analysis in practice, the sample size should be at least 10 more than the number of characteristics (i.e., $n \geq m + 10$). Furthermore, the sale price should be plotted against each characteristic to see if some correlation exists.

$$\bar{x}_1 = \frac{1}{5} \sum_{i=1}^{5} x_{1i}$$

$$= \frac{1}{5}(40,000 + 45,000 + 43,000 + 38,000 \\ + 46,000)$$

$$= 42,400,$$

$$\bar{x}_2 = \frac{1}{5} \sum_{i=1}^{5} x_{2i}$$

$$= \frac{1}{5}(1,400 + 1,500 + 1,600 + 1,300 + 1,500)$$

$$= 1,460, \text{ and}$$

$$\bar{x}_3 = \frac{1}{5} \sum_{i=1}^{5} x_{3i} = \frac{1}{5}(10 + 6 + 9 + 7 + 4)$$

$$= 7.2.$$

ii. Next, determine the c_{kj} values. These are the $m \times m = 9$ covariances:

$$c_{11} = \frac{1}{4} \sum_{i=1}^{5} (x_{1i} - \bar{x}_1)(x_{1i} - \bar{x}_1)$$

$$= \frac{1}{4}[(40,000 - 42,400)(40,000 - 42,000) \\ + (45,000 - 42,400)(45,000 - 42,400) \\ + (43,000 - 42,400)(43,000 - 42,400) \\ + (38,000 - 42,400)(38,000 - 42,400) \\ + (46,000 - 42,400)(46,000 - 42,400)]$$

$$= \frac{1}{4}[(-2,400)(-2,400) + (2,600)(2,600) \\ + (600)(600) + (-4,400)(-4,400) \\ + (3,600)(3,600)]$$

$$= 11,300,000,$$

$$c_{12} = \frac{1}{4} \sum_{i=1}^{5} (x_{1i} - x_{1i})(\bar{x}_{2i} - \bar{x}_2)$$

$$= \frac{1}{4}[(40,000 - 42,400)(1,400 - 1,460) \\ + (45,000 - 42,400)(1,500 - 1,460) \\ + (43,000 - 42,400)(1,600 - 1,460) \\ + (38,000 - 42,400)(1,300 - 1,460) \\ + (46,000 - 42,400)(1,500 - 1,460)]$$

$$= \frac{1}{4}[(-2,400)(-60) + (2,600)(40) + (600)(140)$$

$$+ (-4{,}400)(-160) + (3{,}600)(40)]$$
$$= 295{,}000,$$

$$c_{13} = \frac{1}{4} \sum_{i=1}^{5} (x_{1i} - \bar{x})(x_{3i} - \bar{x}_3) = -4{,}850,$$

$$c_{21} = c_{12} = 295{,}000^{10},$$

$$c_{22} = \frac{1}{4} \sum_{i=1}^{5} (x_{2i} - \bar{x}_2)(x_{2i} - \bar{x}_2) = 13{,}000,$$

$$c_{23} = \frac{1}{4} \sum_{i=1}^{5} (x_{2i} - \bar{x}_2)(x_{3i} - \bar{x}_3) = -15,$$

$$c_{31} = c_{13} = -4{,}850,$$

$$c_{32} = c_{23} = -15, \text{ and}$$

$$c_{33} = \frac{1}{4} \sum_{i=1}^{5} (x_{3i} - \bar{x}_3)(x_{3i} - \bar{x}_3) = 5.7.$$

iii. We have evaluated each covariance. Hence,

$$C = \begin{vmatrix} c_{22} & c_{23} \\ c_{32} & c_{33} \end{vmatrix} = \begin{vmatrix} 13{,}000 & -15 \\ -15 & 5.7 \end{vmatrix}$$
$$= 13{,}000 \times 5.7 - (-15) \times (-15) = 73{,}875.$$

iv. The cofactors of the c_{kj} are

$$A_{22} = (-1)^{2+2} c_{33} = 5.7, \quad A_{23} = (-1)^{2+3} c_{32} = 15,$$
$$A_{32} = A_{23} = 15, \text{ and } A_{33} = (-1)^{3+3} c_{22} = 13{,}000.$$

v. The C^{kj} are now,

$$C^{22} = \frac{A_{22}}{C} = \frac{5.7}{73{,}875} = .00007715736,$$

$$C^{23} = \frac{A_{23}}{C} = \frac{15}{73{,}875} = .0002030457,$$

$$C^{32} = C^{32} = .0002030457, \text{ and}$$

$$C^{33} = \frac{A_{33}}{C} = \frac{13{,}000}{73{,}875} = .1759729.$$

vi. We are now able to evaluate the coefficients, b_k:

$$b_2 = \sum_{j=2}^{3} c_{1j} C^{2j} = c_{12} C^{22} + c_{13} C^{23}$$
$$= 295{,}000 \times .00007715736$$
$$- 4{,}850 \times .0002030457$$

---

[10] The equation for c_{kj} is symmetric. Hence, $c_{kj} = c_{jk}$ for all k and j. (Likewise the A_{kj} and C_{kj}.)

$$\approx 22.7614 - .9847716$$
$$\approx 21.77663,$$
$$b_3 = \sum_{j=2}^{3} c_{1j} C^{3j} = c_{12} C^{32} + c_{13} C^{33}$$
$$= 295,000 \times .0002030457 - 4,850 \times .1759729$$
$$\approx 59.898481 - 853.4685$$
$$\approx -793.5700, \text{ and}$$
$$b_1 = \bar{x}_1 - \sum_{k=2}^{3} \bar{x}_k b_k$$
$$= 42,400 - (1,460 \times 21.77663$$
$$- 7.2 \times 793.5700)$$
$$\approx 16,319.80.$$

vii. We can now write the multiple regression formula:

$$v = b_1 + b_2 x_2 + b_3 x_3$$
$$= \$16,319.80 + (\$21.77663/\text{ft}^2) \cdot x_2$$
$$- (\$793.5700/\text{yrs}) \cdot x_3.$$

(b) Using this formula, we can estimate the sale price of a single family residence with floor area $x_2 = 1,435$ ft^2 and age $x_3 = 8$ yrs:

$$v = \$16,319.80 + (\$21.77663/\text{ft}^2)(1,435 \text{ ft}^2)$$
$$- (\$793.5700/\text{yrs})(8 \text{ yrs})$$
$$= \$41,200.7 \text{ (say, } \$41,200\text{)}.$$

3.4 HOW PROPERTY IS DESCRIBED AND LOCATED

The realty to be conveyed must be uniquely described in the deed. The land is usually described in one of three ways: lot and block number, metes and bounds, and government survey.

I. Lot and Block Number

Subdivisions are divided into lot and block numbers, and a plat (map) of the subdivision is filed with the county clerk and recorder. For example, the description in a deed might read:

"Lot 4, Block 6, Grandview Heights, a subdivision of the City of Boulder . . ."

The exact size of the lot may be obtained from a

subdivision map filed in the office of the county
clerk. Street name and street numbers are not considered an adequate description of the property.

II. Metes and Bounds

Metes and bounds are properly expressed by
bearing and distance. A monument (landmark) is
chosen as the beginning point. A natural monument could be a tree, a body of water, etc. An
artifical monument could be a concrete block,
fence, wall, building, etc. However, it is usually a
monument set for corners in a legal subdivision or
set by the government in its surveys. Then, from
the monument, a series of connecting straight line
segments is defined by bearing and distance. Finally, the land is defined as the area enclosed by
the connecting line segments. Bearing is measured
from either north or south and toward east or
west, depending upon which angle is smallest.

EXAMPLE 1: (Bearing)

Figure 3.4-1 shows two lines "a" and "b". Line a
has a bearing "N88°55′W". That is, it is measured
from north and is 88°55′ toward west (measuring
from south toward west would have resulted in

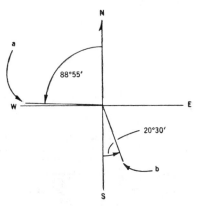

Figure 3.4-1

the larger angle, 91°05'). Line b has the bearing "S20°31'E". It is measured from south and is 20°31' toward east; again, because this is the smallest angle measured from either north or south.

The metes and bounds description in the deed is a narrative of the connected line segment. For clarity, the following example separates and numbers the narrative according to line segments. Each segment is correspondingly numbered in Figure 3.4-2.

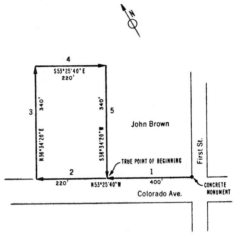

Figure 3.4-2

EXAMPLE 2: (Land Description)

Commencing at a concrete monument located at the NW corner of the intersection of Colorado Avenue and First St., Boulder, Colorado.

(1) Thence, north 53°25'40"W along the northerly ROW line of Colorado Avenue 400 feet to the True Point of Beginning, which point is the southwesterly corner of the John Brown tract;

(2) Thence N53°25'40"W along the northerly ROW line of Colorado Avenue 220 feet;

(3) Thence N36°34'20"E feet;

(4) Thence S53°25'40"E 220 feet to a point on the westerly property line of John Brown tract;

(5) Thence S36°34'20"W 340 feet to the True Point of Beginning.

III. Government Survey

Government survey is used outside the thirteen original states. This method of land description utilizes the latitudes and longitudes of the earth to develop a system of square grids that are further divided. In fact, there are three levels of square grids: quadrangles (that are divided into townships), townships (that are divided into sections), and sections (that are further divided). See Figure 3.4-3.

A. Quadrangles. The United States is partitioned into squares called quadrangles. Each quadrangle is a square area of land measuring 24 miles on each side. The borders are defined by east-west lines called parallels (i.e., parallel to parallel latitudes) and north-south lines called me-

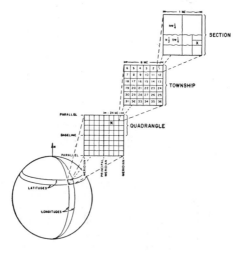

Figure 3.4-3

ridians (i.e., parallel to longitudes). Some of the parallels are designated as baselines, and some of the meridians are designated as principal meridians; these designations are used to identify subsequent subdivisions. Since longitudes meet at the poles, the quadrangles are really not squares, but trapezoids whose deviation from square becomes pronounced near the poles. (They are adjusted to preserve the square.)

B. Townships. Each quadrangle is partitioned into 16 equal squares called townships. The townships are six miles on each side and are identified by two coordinates: townships numbered in the vertical direction are called a tier of townships, and those numbered in the horizontal direction are called a range of townships. The tier and range numbers together define a certain township. For example, the township in the third tier north of the baseline and in the second range east of a particular principal meridian is labeled:

T.3N., R.2E. of the _____ principal meridian
It is identified in Figure 3.4-3 by "*" in the quadrangle.

C. Sections. Each township is partitioned into 36 equal squares called sections. Each section is one mile on a side (containing 640 acres). The sections are identified by the numbers 1 through 36. The numbering begins in the most upper right section and proceeds first to the left, continuing as one would repeatedly draw the letter "s" without lifting the pen. A survey monument is located at each corner of each section.

D. Further Division of Sections. Sections can be divided by repeatedly partitioning them into halves and fourths. For example, the south ½ of a section is a parcel labeled

S½.

Each ¼ of the section is labeled by its location in the section such as

SE¼.

Each ¼ may be further divided into halves or fourths, such as

N½ of SE¼ or NE¼ of SE¼.

Again,

$$S\tfrac{1}{2} \text{ of } NE\tfrac{1}{4} \text{ of } SE\tfrac{1}{4}.$$

The description would then properly read the S½ of the NE¼ of the SE¼ of Section 1, Township 3 North, Range 2 East of the _____ principal meridian. This particular parcel is identified in Figure 3.4-3 by the "X" in the section.

3.5 HOW TO DETERMINE THE AREA OF ANY LOT

Many lots have unusual shapes and, consequently, their size is difficult to determine. The formulas listed here show how to determine the area of any triangular lot, a quadrilateral lot having two parallel sides, and any polygonal lot whose plot plan is available.

I. Area of a Triangular Lot

The area of any triangular lot can be determined by the following formula. Figure 3.5-1a is a schematic drawing of a triangular lot.

FORMULA

$$A = \sqrt{s(s - a)(s - b)(s - c)}$$

where

A = area of lot
a, b, c = length of each side
$$s = \frac{a + b + c}{2}$$

EXAMPLE

Determine the area of the triangular lot whose sides are 120′, 180′, and 100′. This lot is shown in Figure 3.5-1a.
Solution: Let $a = 120′$, $b = 180′$, and $c = 100′$. Then

$$s = \frac{120 + 180 + 100}{2} = \frac{400}{2} = 200′,$$

and

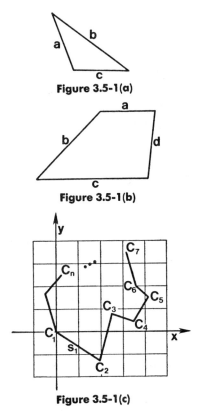

Figure 3.5-1(a)

Figure 3.5-1(b)

Figure 3.5-1(c)

$$A = \sqrt{200(200 - 120)(200 - 180)(200 - 100)}$$
$$= \sqrt{200 \times 80 \times 20 \times 100}$$
$$= \sqrt{32,000,000} = 5,656.85 \text{ sq. ft.}$$

II. Area of a Quadrilateral Lot Having Two Parallel Sides

The area of a quadrilateral lot having two parallel sides can be determined from the following formula. Let a and c be the parallel sides, then

choose c > a, and b ≥ d. Figure 3.5-1b is a schematic drawing of such a lot.

FORMULA

$$A = \frac{c + a}{2}\left\{b^2 - \left[\frac{(c - a)^2 + b^2 - d^2}{2(c - a)}\right]^2\right\}^{1/2}$$

EXAMPLE

Determine the area of the quadrilateral shown in
Figure 3.5-1b whose sides are a = 100', b = 164',
c = 200', and d = 120'.

SOLUTION

$$A = \frac{200 + 100}{2}$$
$$\cdot\left\{164^2 - \left[\frac{(200 - 100)^2 + 164^2 - 120^2}{2(200 - 100)}\right]^2\right\}^{1/2}$$
$$= 150\left[26{,}896 - \left(\frac{10{,}000 + 26{,}896 - 14{,}400}{200}\right)^2\right]^{1/2}$$
$$= 150\left[26{,}896 - \left(\frac{51{,}296}{200}\right)^2\right]^{1/2}$$
$$= 150(26896 - 256.48)^{1/2}$$
$$= 150(26{,}639.52)^{1/2}$$
$$= 150 \times 163.22$$
$$= 24{,}483 \text{ sq. ft.}$$

III. Area of Any Polygonal Lot—If a Plot Plan Is Available

The area of any polygonal lot can be determined if there is a plot plan. Suppose the lot has n
corners. Label the corners C_1, C_2, C_3, . . . , C_n in either a clockwise or a counter-clockwise manner.
Let s_1 represent the stated length of the side between C_1 and C_2. Lay the drawing over a rectangu-
lar grid whose horizontal and vertical directions
we will call x and y, respectively. Position the
drawing so that C_1 is at the origin of the grid i.e.
$C_1 = (0,0)$. Determine the (x,y) coordinates of the
remaining corners (by noticing their locations relative to the grid). Figure 3.5-1c is a schematic
drawing of a polygonal lot.

FORMULA

$$A = \begin{cases} \dfrac{s_1^2(x_2y_3 - x_3y_2)}{2(x_2^2 + y_2^2)} & n = 3 \\[2em] \dfrac{s_1^2[(x_2y_3 - x_3y_2) + (x_3y_4 - x_4y_3)]}{2(x_2^2 + y_2^2)} & n = 4 \\[2em] \dfrac{s_1^2[(x_2y_3 - x_3y_2) + (x_3y_4 - x_4y_3) + (x_4y_5 - x_5y_4)]}{2(x_2^2 + y_2^2)} & n = 5 \\[1em] \qquad\qquad \cdots \\[1em] \dfrac{s_1^2 \displaystyle\sum_{i=1}^{n-1}(x_iy_{i+1} - x_{i+1}y_i)}{2(x_2^2 + y_2^2)} & i = 2, 3, \ldots, n-1 \end{cases}$$

where

A = area of the lot

x_i = x coordinate of the ith corner

y_i = y coordinate of the ith corner

s_1 = stated length of the side between the first and second corner

EXAMPLE

Determine the area of the following pentagonal lot. The coordinates of the corners are $C_1 = (0,0)$, $C_2 = (5,-2)$, $C_3 = (7,1)$, $C_4 = (2,7)$, and $C_5 = (-1,4)$. The length of the side between C_1 and C_2 is stated on the plot plan as $s_1 = 210$ ft.

SOLUTION

The area of this lot is

$$A = \frac{210^2[(5 \times 1 - 7 \times (-2)) + (7 \times 7 - 2 \times 1) + (2 \times 4 - (-1) \times 7)]}{2[5^2 + (-2)^2]}$$

$$= \frac{210^2[(5 + 14) + (49 - 2) + (8 + 7)]}{2(25 + 4)}$$

$$= \frac{210^2(19 + 47 + 15)}{2 \times 29} = \frac{44,100 \times 81}{58} = \frac{3,572,100}{58}$$

$$= 61,587.93 \text{ sq. ft.}$$

CHAPTER 4

MEASURES OF VALUE—FOR THE PROPERTY, THE EQUITY INVESTOR, AND THE MORTGAGE

4.1 EVALUATING CASH FLOW

Cash flow is the amount of money that an investor is free to use for himself. On an annual basis, it is the difference between the annual net operating income and the annual debt service.

$$x_e = x_p - x_m$$

where

x_e = annual cash flow (before taxes)
x_p = annual net operating income
x_m = annual debt service.

Gross income must first serve land and labor (operating expenses), then capital (debt service), and finally entrepreneurship (cash flow). See Figure 4.3-1. Because the equity investor is the last to be served, cash flow is very sensitive to change in either gross income or operating expenses. For example, increased operating expenses can reduce cash flow significantly and even require the contribution of additional equity.

Cash flow is used in Section 4.7 to determine the rate of return for the equity investor. Also the ratio of cash flow-to-equity (down payment) is the equity capitalization rate. If cash flow is computed before income tax, it is called cash throw-off, and if it is computed after income tax, it is called net spendable income.

4.2 USING NET OPERATING INCOME AND NET INCOME MULTIPLIER

Net operating income is the effective gross income less operating expenses (expenses for land and labor). From net operating income the debt service (capital) is paid, and the cash flow is paid to the equity investor (entrepreneur). See Figure 4.3-1.

The property capitalization rate is the ratio of the net operating expenses-to-property value. The reciprocal is called the net income multiplier. For example, a property selling at $480,000 with annual net operating income of $60,000 is said to be "selling at 8 times net."

4.3 USING GROSS INCOME AND GROSS INCOME MULTIPLIER

Scheduled gross income is the maximum income a property can generate. Effective gross income is the income actually received. Therefore, the effective gross income is the scheduled gross income less vacancies and collection losses.

Vacancies and collection losses tend to increase when there is a surplus of comparable properties, when scheduled rent exceeds the economic rent, or when the tenant fails to pay because he lacks either financial means or integrity.

Effective gross income is often used as a measure of property value. The gross income multiplier is the ratio of the property value-to-annual effective gross income. For instance, a property offered for $480,000 with an annual effective gross income of $80,000 is said to be "offered at six times gross."

Scheduled gross income first goes to "others" (appearing in the form of vacancies and collection losses). The resulting effective gross income first serves labor and management (operating expenses). Then the resulting net operating income serves capital (debt service). Finally, the remainder serves entrepreneurship (cash flow). Figure 4.3-1 schematically depicts these demands on schedule gross income.

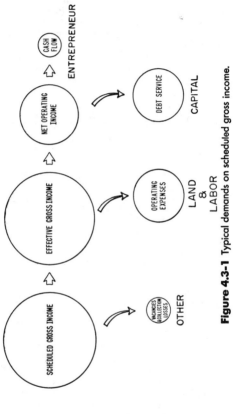

Figure 4.3-1 Typical demands on scheduled gross income.

4.4 HOW TO DETERMINE THE INTEREST RATE FOR AN INVESTMENT

The interest rate is the rate of return on an investment; it exists because time has value.

I. Property Interest Rate

The property interest rate is usually viewed either as the sum of the safe rate plus other rates or as the weighted average of the interest rates of the capital contributions:

A. Component rate. Certainly the property interest rate must exceed the rate expected on safe investments such as government bonds. The extent to which it exceeds the safe rate depends on the uncertainty of income, the lack of liquidity associated with real property, and the burden of managing the investment. Specifically,

$$r_p = r_1 + r_2 + r_3 + r_4$$

where

r_p = property interest rate

r_1 = safe rate (minimum risk, such as for government bonds)

r_2 = rate for uncertainty of income (vacancies, declining income due to depreciation, etc.)

r_3 = rate for non-liquidity of real property

r_4 = rate for burden of property management.

B. Band of Investment rate. This is a commonly used name that refers to a weighted average. Specifically,

$$r_p = tr_m + (1 - t)r_e$$

where

r_p = property interest rate

r_m = mortgage interest rate

r_e = equity interest rate

t = loan-to-value ratio, expressed as a decimal.

II. Mortgage Interest Rate

The mortgage interest rate is similar to long-term lending rates and is correlated with the prime rate, the rate at which member banks can borrow from the Federal Reserve. As with the property interest rate, the mortgage interest rate can be viewed as the sum of other rates:

$$r_m = r_1 + r_2 + r_3 + r_4$$

where

r_m = mortgage interest rate

r_1 = safe rate (minimum risk, such as for government bonds)

r_2 = rate for uncertainty of income, due to default on mortgage payments (about 1%)

r_3 = rate for non-liquidity (1-2%, but should be zero for variable rate mortgages),

r_4 = rate for burden of mortgage management (about 0.5%).

III. Equity Interest Rate

The equity interest rate should be the highest interest rate of all because the equity investor's risk is greatest. Similarly,

$$r_e = r_1 + r_2 + r_3 + r_4$$

where

r_e = equity interest rate

r_1 = safe rate (minimum risk, such as for government bonds)

r_2 = rate for uncertainty of income (5-10% and near 10% for some industrial and farm properties)

r_3 = rate for non-liquidity (from 1% to a very significant percent if property is undesirable or has a questionable title)

r_4 = rate for burden of equity management (depends on desirability of property and the quality of leases).

4.5 HOW THE RECAPTURE RATE IS DETERMINED

The recapture rate is the rate of return *of* invested capital (the interest rate is the rate of return *on* invested capital).

If the invested capital is a mortgage loan, the capital is recaptured through the principal portion of the payments.

The equity investor in income property is generally concerned that depreciation of the improvement will cause a loss of his investment. Hence, he should provide for recapture of this portion of his investment through cash flow that exceeds that which provides the interest on equity, through loan amortization, and possibly through appreciation of the property value.

Generally, the period of recapture is taken to be the remaining ecomonic life of the improvement. Then it is assumed that recapture comes from the excess cash flow which is periodically deposited in an interest-bearing account (a sinking fund). The rate, at which these deposits draw interest varies widely.

- If they are not deposited ($r = 0$), recapture is constant (called straight-line).

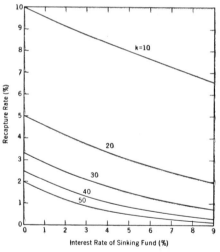

Figure 4.5-1 Recapture rate for various remaining economic lives as it depends upon the interest rate.

- If they are deposited at the safe rate ($r = r_1$ from Section 4.4), recapture is said to be according to the Hoskold method.
- If they are deposited at the property interest rate ($r = r_p$, from Section 4.4), recapture is said to be according to the Inwood method.

Figure 4.5-1 shows the recapture rate as it depends on the interest rate of the sinking fund. Deposits are made annually, and there is one curve for each of several different remaining years of recapture: $k = 10, 20, 30, 40$ and 50 years.

FORMULAS

$$r'_m = \frac{q}{s(r_m,m,q)}$$

$$r'_p = \begin{cases} \dfrac{1}{s(r,k,1)} & {}^1 \\[2ex] \dfrac{x_p}{v_p} - r_p \\[2ex] t \cdot r'_m = (1 - t) \cdot r'_e \end{cases} \quad \textbf{(Band of Investment Rate)}$$

$$r'_e = \frac{r'_p - t \cdot r'_m}{1 - t} \qquad \text{(if t < 1)}$$

where

$\qquad r'_m, r'_e, r'_p =$ recapture rate of the mortgage, equity, and depreciable portion of the property, respectively

$\qquad r_m, r_e, r_p =$ interest rate on the mortgage, equity, and property, respectively

$\qquad t =$ loan-to-value ratio, expressed as a decimal

$\qquad v_p =$ present value of the property

$\qquad x_p =$ annual net operating income

$\qquad r =$ interest rate of sinking fund

[1] It is conventional to assume that deposits in a sinking fund are made annually. However, they are probably made q times a year. In that case,

$$r'_p = \frac{q}{s(r, k \cdot q, q)}$$

> (recapture is straight-line when $r = 0$, Hoskold when $r = r_1$, and Inwood when $r = r_p$)[2]
>
> q = number of mortgage interest periods per year
>
> m = total number of mortgage interest period
>
> k = number of remaining years of recapture (usually the remaining economic life of the improvement)

$s(r_m,m,q)$, $s(r,k,1)$ = amount of an annuity of 1

EXAMPLE

An apartment investor obtains a 70% first mortgage. It bears 8% interest and is to be amortized with constant monthly payments for 25 years. A market survey indicates the property interest rate is 10%. The building has a remaining economic life of 25 years. Determine (a) the mortgage recapture rate, (b) the property recapture rate using the Inwood sinking fund method, and (c) the resulting equity recapture rate.

SOLUTION

In this example,

$$t = .7, r_m = 8\%, q = 12, m = 12 \times 25 = 300,$$
$$r_p = 10\%, \text{ and } k = 25 \text{ years:}$$

(a) From Table 1,

$$s(r_m,m,q) = s(8,300,12) = 951.0264.$$

Now, the mortgage recapture rate is

$$r'_m = \frac{12}{951.0264} = .0126 = 1.26\%.$$

(b) Since the Inwood method of recapture is specified, $r = r_p = 10\%$. From Table 1,

$$s(r,k,1) = s(10,25,1) = 98.3471.$$

---

[2] For straight-line recapture, note that when $r = 0$, $s(r,k,1) = k$.

Now, the property recapture rate is

$$r'_p = \frac{1}{98.3471} = .01017 = 1.017\%.$$

(c) The equity recapture rate is

$$r'_e = \frac{.01017 - .7 \times .0126}{1 - .7}$$
$$= \frac{.00135}{.3}$$
$$= .0045 = .45\%.$$

4.6 HOW THE CAPITALIZATION RATE IS DETERMINED

The capitalization rate is the rate at which income is converted to a capital value—the ratio of annual net income-to-amount of investment. It can also be viewed as the rate of return *on* investment (interest rate, Section 4.4) plus the rate of return *of* the investment (recapture rate, Section 4.5).

Figure 4.6-1 is a schematic diagram of the capitalization rate over a short period of time. The interest rate will fluctuate with supply and demand. The recapture rate is nearly constant because it is determined mostly by the useful life of the property. However some variation could occur due to changes in the interest rate at which the recaptured income is deposited. (See Figure 4.5-1.)

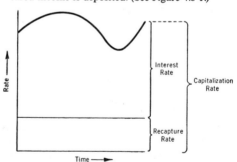

Figure 4.6-1 Schematic diagram of the capitalization rate as the interest rate varies with supply and demand.

Each investment (or financial component of the investment) has its own capitalization rate. Therefore, the following discussion of capitalization rates separates property and its investment components, mortgage and equity.

I. Property Capitalization Rate

The property capitalization rate is the annual rate at which the property earns money. It is the ratio of annual net operating income-to-property value[3] as well as the sum of the two rates.

$$z_p = \frac{x_p}{v_p} = r_p + r_p'$$

where

z_p = property capitalization rate

x_p = annual net operating income

v_p = present value of property

r_p = property interest rate

r_p' = property recapture rate

The property capitalization rate is determined in the following way:

- Observe as many recent comparable sales as is practical.
- Determine the property capitalization rate for each (i.e., the ratio of annual net operating income-to-sale price).
- Average the property capitalization rates. This is your estimate of the property capitalization rate for the subject property. The next step indicates the precision of your estimate of the average.
- Use the method of Section 3.3 to determine the confidence limits for this average value— the values within which you can be, say, 95%, confident the true property capitalization rate lies. The limits tend to draw closer as more properties are observed.

[3] Notice that the property capitalization rate is the reciprocal of the "net income multiple," see Section 4.2.

EXAMPLE

Estimate the property capitalization rate for a subject property by determining the average of several properties, and then determine the 95% confidence limits for this estimate. The following data was compiled from the recent sale of six comparable properties:

Sale Price (v_p)	Annual Net Operating Income (x_p)
$210,000	$20,160
195,000	18,330
190,000	18,620
205,000	19,885
220,000	22,220
195,000	19,305

SOLUTION

From the ratios, the six property capitalization rates are: z_p = 9.6, 9.4, 9.8, 9.7, 10.1, and 9.9%. The average is 9.75%. Using the method of Section 2.3, you can be 95% certain that the true property capitalization rate is between 9.495% and 10.005%. In terms of sale price, these limits mean that if the subject property has an annual net operating income of $20,000, we can be 95% confident that the sale price will be between

$$\frac{\$20,000}{.10005} = \$199,900, \text{ and } \frac{\$20,000}{.09495} = \$210,637.$$

II. Mortgage Capitalization Rate

The mortgage capitalization rate is the annual rate at which the mortgage loan earns money. It is the annual mortgage payment divided by the loan amount (lender's investment):

$$z_m = \frac{x_m}{v_m} = r_m + r_m{'}$$

where

z_m = mortgage capitalization rate

x_m = annual mortgage payment[4]

v_m = loan amount

r_m = mortgage interest rate

r_m' = mortage recapture rate

The mortgage capitalization rate is determined by supply and demand, the security (i.e., the subject property), and the borrower. This rate is readily obtainable from lending institutions and can usually be determined with more certainty than can the property capitalization rate.

Figure 4.6-1 shows how the mortgage capitalization rate varies with the mortgage interest rate and the term. Two observations should be made:

- For longer term loans (e.g., 20 years or more), the mortgage capitalization rate is virtually independent of the number of periodic payments per year (designated by q).
- As the term increases, the mortgage capitalization rate draws closer to the interest rate.

III. Equity Capitalization Rate

The equity capitalization rate is the annual rate at which the investor's down payment earns money. It is the annual cash flow divided by the down payment.

$$z_e = \frac{x_e}{v_e} = r_e + r_e'$$

where

z_e = equity capitalization rate

x_e = annual cash flow(before tax)[5]

v_e = investor's initial investment

r_e = equity interest rate

r_e' = equity recapture rate.

[4] The interest portion of each mortgage payment is the return on the investment, and the principal portion of each payment is the return of the investment (recapture).

[5] During periods of property speculation, property is sometimes purchased even though it has zero or negative cash flow. The purchaser anticipates future positive cash flow and appreciation. If the cash flow is negative, the equity capitalization rate is negative.

The equity capitalization rate can be determined from recent sales of comparable properties. Since the gross income serves all other contributions to property (land, and capital) before cash flow is available to the equity investor (entrepreneur), one would expect it to vary widely as compared to either gross income or net income (which is used to determine the property capitalization rate). Note that cash flow and the down payment are not independent: the larger the down payment, the less the debt service, and, hence, the larger the cash flow. That is, cash flow and down payment tend to be proportional.

4.7 HOW TO USE THE RATE OF RETURN AND PRESENT VALUE CONCEPTS

I. Concept

The present value concept is based upon the idea that time has value. That is, money that is received in the future is not worth as much as money received immediately. This lesser value is referred to as the present value. Money to be received in the future has diminished value because investors believe they could be earning more money by using this money. The rate at which an investor earns money is called the rate of return. If he ordinarily receives 10% on his investment, he is being penalized 10% each year he must wait to receive return *on* his investment.

The rate of return formula can be used for many different purposes. Any one formula can be solved if it contains only one unknown quantity. As the unknown quantity, we can choose the present value of the investment, the rate of return, or the reversion required to achieve a given rate of return. Since we frequently want to know any one of these values let us examine each unknown separately.

II. Example

Consider the following investment that will be used in all examples of this section.

EXAMPLE

The property value is $500,000. It is purchased with a down payment of $100,000 and a $400,000 mortgage at 9% with equal monthly payments of $3,356.79 for 25 years (the annual payment is $40,281.48). The net operating income for the first three years is forecast to be $50,000, $53,000, and $54,000. The cash flow in these three years would be $9,718.52, $12,718.52, and $13,718.52. After three years the property value is forecast to be $600,000, and the loan balance will be $385,317.83. For all investment components (property, mortgage, and equity), determine (a) the rate of return, (b) the present value of the investment, (c) and the reversion necessary to achieve a given rate of return.

SOLUTION

In this example,

$v_p = \$500,000$, $v_e = \$100,000$, $v_m = \$400,000$,
$r_m = 9\%$, $n = 25$ years, $q = 12$, $m = nq = 300$,
$x_m = \$40,281.48$, $x_{p1} = \$50,000$, $x_{p2} = \$53,000$,
$x_{p3} = \$54,000$, $x_{e1} = \$9,718.52$, $x_{e2} = \$12,718.52$,
$x_{e3} = \$13,718.52$, $V_p = \$600,000$, and $V_m = \$385,317.83$.

A. Find the rate of return. We assume the present value and the reversion are know. Since the rate of return, r, cannot be expressed explicitly in the formula, it must be determined by trial and error. That is, one can choose a rate that is obviously too small, and gradually increase it until the right side of the formula equals the left side. The rate that renders the right side equal to the left side is the rate of return on the investment.

1. Property. The equation is

$$v_p = \sum_{i=1}^{3} \frac{x_{pi}}{(1+r)^i} + \frac{V_p}{(1+r)^3}$$

$$\$500,000 = \frac{\$50,000}{(1+r)^1} + \frac{\$53,000}{(1+r)^2} + \frac{\$54,000}{(1+r)^3} + \frac{\$600,000}{(1+r)^3}$$

It has been determined that this equation is satisfied by a rate of return of $r = 16^1/_8\%$.

2. Mortgage.   The equation is

$$V_m = \sum_{i=1}^{3} \frac{x_m}{(1 + r)^1} + \frac{V_m}{(1 + r)^3}^{\,6}$$

$$\$400{,}000 = \sum_{i=1}^{3} \frac{\$40{,}281.48}{(1 + r)^i} + \frac{\$385{,}317.83}{(1 + r)^3}.$$

For the mortgage, there is no reason to search for the value of r that renders the right side equal to the left: The payments and the balance are determined by the conditions of the loan, which include the interest rate on the mortgage (i.e., r_m is the rate of return). The equation is satisfied when $r = r_m = .09$.

3. Equity.   The equation is

$$V_e = \sum_{i=1}^{3} \frac{x_{ei}}{(1 + r)^i} + \frac{V_e}{(1 + r)^3}.$$

The reversion of equity is the difference between the reversion of property and the reversion of mortgage:

$$V_e = V_p - V_m = \$600{,}000 - \$385{,}317.83$$
$$= \$214{,}682.17.$$

Now

$$\$100{,}000 = \frac{\$9{,}718.52}{(1 + r)^1} + \frac{\$12{,}718.52}{(1 + r)^2}$$
$$+ \frac{\$13{,}718.52}{(1 + r)^3} + \frac{\$214{,}682.17}{(1 + r)^3}.$$

By trial and error, the rate of return on equity is found to be about 38.3%.

B. Find the Present Value.   We assume the reversion and the interest rate are known.

1. Property.   Even though the property value is thought to be $v_p = \$500{,}000$, it is worth more or less than that depending on the current property interest rate, the forecast net operating income, and the forecast property value after three years (the reversion). Let us assume the current property interest rate is 10%.

_____

[6] Since all x_m's are equal, they need not be identified by the subscript i.

$$v_p = \frac{\$50,000}{(1.10)^1} + \frac{\$53,000}{(1.10)^2} + \frac{\$54,000}{(1.10)^3} + \frac{\$600,000}{(1.10)^3}$$

$$= \$45,454.55 + \$43,801.65 + \$40,571.00 + \$450,788.88$$

$$= \$580,616.08.$$

Therefore, due to the assumptions about the current property interest rate and the forecast values, the property value is more than the $500,000 that was paid.

2. Mortgage. The present value of the mortgage will be more or less than the $400,000 depending upon whether the current (economic) mortgage interest rate is less than or greater than the contract interest rate. The contract rate is 9%, but determine the mortgage value if, just after making the mortgage, the economic rate becomes $9\frac{1}{4}\%$.

$$v_m = \frac{\$40,281.43}{(1.0925)^1} + \frac{\$40,281.43}{(1.0925)^2} + \frac{\$40,281.43}{(1.0925)^3} + \frac{\$385,317.83}{(1.0925)^3}$$

$$= \$36,870.87 + \$33,749.98 + \$30,891.61 + \$295,498.15$$

$$= \$397,009.71.$$

As expected, the mortgage has lost value because rates are now higher.

3. Equity. The initial equity investment is $100,000. Given the cash flow and equity reversion stated earlier, what is the present value of the equity if equity investors normally achieve a rate of return of 15% on similar investments?

$$v_e = \sum_{j=1}^{3} \frac{x_{ei}}{(1+r)^i} + \frac{V_e}{(1+r)^3}$$

$$= \frac{\$9,718.52}{(1.15)^1} + \frac{\$12,718.52}{(1.15)^2} + \frac{\$13,718.52}{(1.15)^3} + \frac{\$214,682.17}{(1.15)^3}$$

$$= \$8,450.89 + \$9,617.03 + \$9,020.15 + \$141,157.01$$

$$= \$168,245.08.$$

C. Find the Reversion Necessary to Achieve a Given Rate of Return. To determine the reversion for each investment, we must solve the rate of return formula for V_p, V_m, and V_e:

1. Property. For property, the formula is

$$V_p = (1 + r)^3\left[v_p - \sum_{i=1}^{3} \frac{x_{pi}}{(1 + r)^i}\right].$$

Suppose the expected rate of return on the property is 30%. Then after three years the property value must be:

$$V_p = (1.30)^3\left\{\$500,000\right.$$
$$\left. - \left[\frac{\$50,000}{(1.30)^1} + \frac{\$53,000}{(1.30)^2} + \frac{\$54,000}{(1.30)^3}\right]\right\}$$
$$= 2,197 \times \left[\$500,000\right.$$
$$\left. - \left(\frac{\$50,000}{1.3} + \frac{\$53,000}{1.69} + \frac{\$54,000}{2.197}\right)\right]$$
$$= 2.197 \times (\$500,000 - \$38,461.54$$
$$- \$31,360.95 - \$24,578.97)$$
$$= 2.197 \times \$405,598.54$$
$$= \$891,100.00.$$

2. Mortgage. In the case of a \$400,000 mortgage, the rate of return on the mortgage is the interest rate of the mortgage, 9%. The reversion after three years necessary to achieve a 9% return is obviously the loan balance after three years: V_m = \$385,317.83. However, it will not be computed here since it uses 12 periods per year (36 terms would be required). It can be determined easily from the formulas in Section 7.2.

3. Equity. Suppose the investor expects 60% on his equity. Then after three years, the value of his equity would be

$$V_e = (1.60)^3\left\{\$100,000 - \left[\frac{\$9,718.52}{(1.60)^1} + \frac{\$12,718.52}{(1.60)^2}\right.\right.$$
$$\left.\left. + \frac{\$13,718.52}{(1.60)^3}\right]\right\}$$

$$= 4.096\left[\$100,000 - \left(\frac{\$9,718.52}{1.60} + \frac{\$12,718.52}{2.56} + \frac{\$13,718.52}{4.096}\right)\right]$$

$$= 4.096[\$100,000 - (\$6,074.08 + \$4,968.17 + \$3,349.25)]$$

$$= 4.096 \times \$85,608.50$$

$$= \$350,652.42$$

III. Present Value of Equity Forecast by the Cost Approach

Thus far, the method used to forecast the annual net operating income and reversion has not been specified. A plausible model is provided by the future property value forecast by the reproduction cost (See Sec. 1.1). It can be utilized in the following way:

Step 1. Use the model to forecast the property value, V_p. (Call it V_{pi}, for each of the $i = 1, \ldots, n$ years of the projection.)

Step 2. Forecast the property capitalization rate, z_p. (Call it z_{pi}, for each of the $i = 1, \ldots, n$ years.) Recall that $z_{pi} = x_{pi}/V_{pi}$, which implies that $x_{pi} = z_{pi} \cdot V_{pi}$ (see Section 4.6). Now,

$$V_p = \sum_{i=1}^{n} \frac{z_{pi} \cdot V_{pi}}{(1 + r)^i} + \frac{V_{pn}}{(1 + r)^n}.$$

Step 3. However, since most investors are interested in the rate of return on equity, it is necessary to separate property into its two financial components, mortgage and equity, and solve the equation for the equity component:

$$V_e = \sum_{i=1}^{n} \frac{(z_{pi} \cdot V_{pi} - z_{ei} V_{ei})}{(1 + r)^i} + \frac{V_{pn} - V_{mn}}{(1 + r)^n}$$

where V_{mn} is the loan balance after n years of the forecast period (V_{mn} is labeled B_j in Section 7.2, where j is the number of payment periods since the loan was made.).

Obviously, net operating income and property value will not always follow the cost approach model. However, on the average they will.

PART III

HOW TO FINANCE YOUR PROPERTY

CHAPTER 5

THE PROS AND CONS OF 14 TYPES OF MORTGAGES

5.0 SPECIFIC TYPES OF MORTGAGES THAT ARE AVAILABLE TO YOU

By far the most widely used type of real estate financing is the mortgage: a conditional conveyance of property as security for the payment of a debt or the performance of an obligation.

Actually, the mortgage can take many forms, depending upon goals of the parties and the tolerance of the mortgage market. The following sections include the personal property mortgage (Section 5.2), and 13 variations of the real property mortgage. Table 5.0–1 is a list of these instruments and some of their more important characteristics.

5.1 HOW THE BLANKET MORTGAGE COVERS MANY PARCELS OF LAND

A blanket mortgage is a mortgage that covers more than one parcel of real property.

Developers often use blanket mortgages to finance the purchase and development of land. When a parcel is sold, the borrower pays the lender a designated sum (usually more than the value of the parcel, e.g., 125% of its value), and the lender releases that parcel from the mortgage agreement. For example, without partial releases, home purchasers in housing developments could not obtain first mortgages.

The partial release clause states:

Table 5.0-1. Summary of Types of Financing*

Section	Type	Purpose	Security	Priority	Lender	Payment Terms
5.1	Blanket Mortage	One mortgage covering several properties	Subject properties	First	—	Individual releases granted as conditions for each property are satisfied
5.2	Chattel Mortgage	Purchase Personal property	Subject Personal property	—	—	Short-term
5.3	Construction Mortgage	Finance construction of improvements	Subject land, lease or contractor's record	Usually first	Institutions	Depends upon whether financing is temporary or permanent

5.4	Crop Mortgage	Short-term farm loans	Crops	First	—	Short-term
5.5	Installment Land Contract	Purchase subject property with seller financing	Subject property	—	Seller	Deed delivered to buyer when payment conditions met
5.6	Leasehold Mortgage	Usually to construct improvements	Lease and sometimes improvement	Usually first as to leasehold	Institutions	Partly determined by lease conditions. Term shorter than lease term
5.7	Open-End Mortgage	Additional funds with same agreement	Fixtures and subject real property	Additional funds have lower priority	—	Balance of original loan to be reduced before additional funds releases

*"—" means not pertinent to this type of financing

Table 5.0-1. (Continued)

5.8	Package Mortgage	Finance fixtures as well as real property	Fixtures and subject property	—	—	—
5.9	Participation Mortgage	Lender obtains return from property as well from mortgage	Lease or subject property	—	—	Usual mortgage payments as well as profits from property
5.10	Pooled Financing	Finance unusually large projects	Subject property	—	More than one	—
5.11	Purchase Money Mortgage	Purchase subject property	Subject property	High priority compared to other liens	Usually seller	—

			Leasehold and subject property	First	Institutions	
5.12	Sale-Leaseback	*Seller:* Lease instead of borrow. *Buyer:* High loan-to-value ratio and secure income				—
5.13	Variable Rate Mortgage	Mortgage will retain value	Subject property	—	—	Interest rate varies with a standard rate
5.14	Wraparound Mortgage	Purchase subject property with high loan-to-value ratio	Subject property	Junior	—	Payments exceed payments on existing mortgage(s)

The mortgagee agrees to release any lot from the lien of this mortgage upon payment to him by the mortgagor or his assigns of the sum of _____ per lot upon the lands so released.

5.2 HOW TO USE THE CHATTEL MORTGAGE FOR YOUR PERSONAL PROPERTY

A chattel mortgage is a mortgage that creates an interest in personal property as security for the payment of a debt or the fullfulment of an obligation.

Personal property is property that is not real property. An automobile and a fixture such as a heating system are examples of personal property. The automobile is clearly personal property, but the heating system can become real property. That is, sometimes personal property is so firmly attached to real property as to be considered real property. Several tests have been developed (from the law of fixtures) to determine the nature of such property, but the intent of the parties governs most court decisions.

If the real property is purchased with a real property mortgage and fixtures are purchased with a chattel mortgage[1], the fixtures remain personal property until the final payment of the real property mortgage; then they become real property. However, if default occurs on the real property mortgage, the vendor has the right to reclaim the fixtures as personal property.

5.3 FEATURES OF THE CONSTRUCTION MORTGAGE

The construction mortgage is a mortgage that secures advances of money that will be disbursed at various stages of construction. Because the subject land is used as security, the loan amount exceeds the value of the security; hence, disbursements are made only upon completion of predetermined

[1]Or with a conditional sale contract (i.e., a contract in which the property is delivered to the buyer, but title remains with the seller until the conditions of the contract are met).

phases of construction. The construction loan can be either temporary or permanent.

I. Temporary and Permanent Loans

The temporary construction loan is a series of short-term notes that are disbursed at predetermined intervals during construction. The lender is usually a commercial bank, but for some large projects, it is a life insurance company. The maturity date of the loan is set sufficiently past the completion date so the borrower has time to sell the property or to refinance and repay the loan. Permanent financing must then be arranged for the property: the permanent loan pays the temporary loan, and the buyer pays the permanent loan. The temporary loan commitment and the advance permanent loan commitment may each cost 1 to 3 points (paid in advance). Moreover, the builder must pay interest on the temporary loan.

The permanent construction loan is a single long-term note with disbursements at predetermined intervals during construction. Usually the lender is a savings and loan association, mutual savings bank or life insurance company. The note is secured by a mortgage on the property. The mortgage payments begin after the building is occupied.

From the borrower's point of view, permanent financing permits the lower interest rates associated with long-term financing and eliminates the extra fees, commissions, and charges of obtaining two loans (temporary and permanent). From the lender's point of view, permanent financing is risky because the improvement doesn't exist when the loan is executed.

In both types of construction loans, disbursements are made after a specified amount of work has been completed and inspected by the lender; hence, material and labor have been supplied only on the contractor's personal credit.

II. Security

If the loan is granted to an established contractor, his personal credit might be adequate security for the temporary loan. On the other hand, if the loan is granted directly to an individual or to a company for which the building is to be constructed, the subject property will probably be required as security.

III. Lenders

Commercial banks will grant temporary financing, but generally not permanent financing. Savings and loan associations and life insurance companies are the best sources of permanent loans.

IV. Disbursements

Disbursements might be made to the contractor by either the property owner or the lender. In either case, it is essential to obtain proof that materials and labor have been paid before disbursements are made. Disbursements can be made according to a variety of completion schedules:

A. After certain phases of construction are complete.

B. After certain expenditures have been made.

C. After bills are received by the lender. In this case, the lender pays the bills and gives the contractor the balance when construction is complete.

D. After inspections are made. FHA and VA require three inspections for residences.

V. Lender's Precautions

The lender should consider the following precautions:

A. Designate a single agent. Plans, appraisals, and specifications are submitted to the agent who should:

• analyze preliminary costs and planning;

• conduct field inspections;

• fund the disbursements, and

• monitor the project (danger signs are bids by subcontractors that are unusually high or low; requested variances; loan increases; and failure to market the property).

B. Designate an engineer. Before the loan is granted, the engineer should analyze cost estimates and approve design. If the lender is providing temporary financing, he should at least examine the basic elements of construction such as site, soil, and structural aspects. If the lender is providing permanent financing, the engineer should also provide a thorough evaluation of the livability and permanence of the project. After the loan has been granted, the engineer should conduct field inspections with the agent.

C. Withhold funds. Lenders of temporary financing can withhold some funds until after the deadline for filing mechanics' liens. Sometimes the lenders of permanent financing protect themselves by withholding some (15–25%) of the first mortgage loan. After the builder has used all of the disbursed funds he will try to rent his uncompleted project. If he has achieved the required rental, the withheld funds are disbursed to him. If he has not achieved the required rental, he must obtain financing for the amount withheld. This secondary financing is called gap financing. The construction lender will require the borrower to cover the difference (gap) with a letter of credit or apply for a standby commitment for a second mortgage. The commitment might cost 5% of the difference, the interest rate might be 5%–10% higher than that of the construction loan, and the term as short as 6–36 months. Obviously, it is difficult for the builder to meet the obligations of both the construction loan and the gap loan.

D. Obtain:

• Title insurance against mechanics' liens,

• A fixed price contract,

• A guarantee of completion, a guarantee of performance and payment or a general contract,

• Early equity investment from the contractor (to maintain a positive balance prior to disbursements), and

• A certificate of work performed from an independent architect.

5.4 HOW TO USE THE CROP MORTGAGE

A crop mortgage is a short-term mortgage in which crops are used as security. The mortgage specifies the crop, its location, when it is to be grown, that it is free of encumbrances, and how it is to be maintained and harvested.

Usually crops are considered to be personal property, but sometimes they are considered to be real property. Table 5.4-1 lists vegetation that generally belongs to each category.

Table 5.4-1. Vegetation Generally Classified as Personal and Real Property

Personal Property (vegetation which is produced by labor of man and is annual)	Real Property (vegetation which is a natural product of soil and is perennial)

Fruit and Berries
All Nursery Stock
Trees to be Cut
  Within a Short
  Period of Time
Severed or Mature
  Crops on Land
  That is Transferred
	Trees and Shrubs
	
	Trees Standing on
	  Land That is
	  Transferred
	Crops Growing on
	  Land That is Trans-
	  ferred Without
	  Reservation

5.5 WHAT TO WATCH FOR IN THE INSTALLMENT LAND CONTRACT

An installment land contract is a contract between a buyer and a seller of real property whereby the buyer makes a small down payment (often about 10%) and takes possession of the property while making payments toward the balance of the purchase price. The seller retains the deed as security until a certain amount has been paid (usually the balance of the purchase price).[2]

Although the buyer merely possesses the property and does not own it (until he possesses the deed), he assumes all risks of ownership, and his interest in the property passes to his heirs and as-

---

[2]The installment land contract for real property is analogous to the conditional sale contract for personal property. The rules of contract law apply. See footnote 1 of Section 5.2.

signs.[3] He retains the obligations of the contract unless the seller expressly releases him.

The installment land contract is a contract for the deed. That is, satisfaction of the contract should result in a marketable deed being executed and delivered to the buyer.[4] Since the buyer must adhere to the contract in order to acquire the deed, the installment land contract is inferior to the deed of trust (at least from the buyer's point of view). However, if he adheres to the contract, he will not lose his equity, and, perhaps the most serious drawback of the installment land contract vis-a-vis the deed of trust, is the buyer's ability to offer the property as security for subsequent loans.

I. Possession and Assignment

If it is not obvious that the buyer is in possession of the property, he should have the contract recorded. Otherwise another buyer could, in good faith, take possession.[5]

If the contract expressly denies the buyer's right to assign the contract, his assignment gives the seller the right to declare forfeiture. If the contract has been recorded, each assignment should also be recorded (failure to do so could result in a defective record if the deed subsequently rests with an assignee that is not an assignee of record).

II. Default

The rules of contract law apply to installment land contracts (instead of the equitable rules that

[3] The buyer in possession is in essentially the same position as is the mortgagor of real property in a title-theory state: The mortgagor has possession, but he has passed title to the morgagee; upon payment of debt, title reverts to the mortgagor.

[4] Herein is one of the serious pitfalls of the installment land contract: After the buyer satisfies the contract, the seller might fail to deliver a marketable deed (due to an adverse judgement, divorce, liens, etc.). The buyer can sue for damages but still fail to claim the property.

[5] This buyer must give up possession, but he could (1) hold the seller in damages; (2) rescind the contract and recover all payments, or (3) require the seller to account for full consideration.

apply to mortgages). The following are the consequences of default by either party:

A. Buyer's default. In most states, if the buyer defaults, the seller is required to foreclose on the property through the courts:

1. The seller can repossess the property. The buyer might prevent this if he tenders the balance within a reasonable time. Depending upon the contract and the state, the seller must do the following before bringing a possessory action:

    a. give notice to quit   ⎫ (usually depends
    b. give notice of forfeiture ⎭ on the state)

    c. make demand for possession
    d. make tender of deed   ⎫ (only if specified
    e. make a return of payments ⎭ in the contract)

2. In some states the courts of equity will require the buyer to pay the indebtedness within a reasonable time or lose the right of redemption (strict foreclosure); title remains permanently with the seller.

3. The seller has the right to keep the payments, any improvements made by the buyer, and liquidated (determined) damages.

4. Most states allow the seller to bring action to recover a judgement of past-due payments. A few states allow the seller to bring action for damages of breach of contract, but not for the loan balance.

5. Most states permit a clause in which the seller can declare the balance due and payable (an acceleration clause).

B. Seller's Default. Unless stated otherwise in the contract, it is implied that the seller is contracting to convey a marketable title (a title free of mortgages, liens, and encumbrances).[6] If, at the time the title is to be executed and delivered, he does not, the buyer can

1. Rescind the contract and recover his pay-

---

[6] The seller needn't have marketable title when the contract is executed, but he must when the deed is to be executed and delivered.

ments (less a reasonable amount that is considered to be rent),

2. Cancel any non-negotiated note he has given as evidence of the debt, and

3. Recover the value of improvements he has made.

4. Bring an action to recover damages, usually the amount of loss he suffers.

III. Checklist for the Contract

The installment land contract should include the usual provisions for any contract to sell. The following additional provisions should also be considered.

A. Buyer's Considerations:

1. Deed. The seller should execute and deliver a marketable deed. The seller should verify its marketability by supplying an abstract, certificate of title, or title insurance. The deed should be escrowed so that if the seller dies, it is not involved in estate proceedings.

2. Possession. The buyer's right to possession and time of possession should be stated.

3. Liability. The buyer should not be personally liable for a mortgage on the property.

B. Seller's considerations:

1. Title. Title is to remain with seller (or escrowed) until the contract is satisfied.

2. Taxes, insurance, and assessments. If the seller pays taxes, insurance premiums or assessments, this amount is to be added to the loan balance. The insurance carried by the buyer should be specified and approved by the seller and the policy deposited with him.

3. Assignment and lease. The buyer should not be permitted to assign or sell the contract without written permission of the seller. The buyer should not lease or permit occupation of the property without written permission of the seller.

4. Default. The buyer is in default if he fails to pay taxes, insurance premiums, assessments or in-

stallment payments within a specified time. In case of default, the seller may

a. declare the contract void,

b. take possession without court action,

c. retain all payments (considered to be rent), improvements, and liquidated damages,

d. declare all subsequent payments due and payable, and compel performance of the contract,

e. be relieved of all liability to the buyer,

f. foreclose the contract, and

g. make the buyer waive right of notice to quit, of forfeiture, and of demand for possession.

5. Mortgage. The seller should state his right to place a mortgage on the property in an amount not to exceed the loan balance. Such mortgage should have priority over the buyer's equity. The buyer should sign a waiver of priority.

C. Considerations for Both Parties

1. Payment. State all payment conditions.

2. Taxes, insurance, and assessments. State who pays (usually the buyer).

3. All agreements and covenants should apply to heirs, assigns, successors, administrators, and executors.

4. If the contract is to be recorded, it must be executed according to the recording laws of the state. (See Table 5.5-1)

5.6 HOW TO GET THE MOST FROM YOUR LEASEHOLD MORTGAGE

A leasehold mortgage is a mortgage in which the lessee is the mortgagor, and he offers his leasehold interest as security for the loan.[7]

Developers sometimes lease the ground and need financing to construct improvements that they can lease. Lessors usually want to increase the profitability of their property by leasing, and

---

[7] This is permitted by leases unless expressly forbidden. Only the leasehold is offered as security unless the fee is subordinated to it. However, due to profitable subleases, this security can be substantial.

Table 5.5-1. Possible Advantages and Disadvantages of the Installment Land Contract

	Advantages
Buyer	• Small down payment • No qualifying for financing • Owner financing is quick
Seller	• Seller doesn't relinquish deed until buyer satisfies contract • Seller needn't have marketable title at time of sale (he must, however, when it is to be executed and delivered) • No third party financing required

	Disadvantages
Buyer	• Buyer doesn't receive deed until contract is satisfied • Buyer can lose property quickly and easily • Buyer can lose all equity • Buyer can't secure a loan with this property
Seller	• If the buyer records the contract and subsequently defaults, the "cloud" on the title makes the property difficult to resell • Upon default, repossession can be more difficult through the courts than through a simple foreclosure on a deed of trust • Due to liens, the seller may lose the ability to convey title when the contract is satisfied

are often reluctant to sell because of capital gain tax. These leases often run 75 years or more, and all lenders require the remaining term of the lease to exceed the term of the mortgage by 10 years or so.

Leasehold mortgagees are usually life insurance companies, large mutual savings banks, and large commercial banks. Except for a very small percentage of their assets, these institutions are prohibited from making junior mortgages. Hence, the owner of the fee is asked to subordinate the fee interest to the leasehold mortgage.[8] Moreover, if the fee is subordinated, higher ratio financing should be possible.

EXAMPLE

A lessee has a 25-year lease with renewals on land valued at $600,000. The lessee wishes to construct a $900,000 building, resulting in a $1,500,000 property value. A lender is willing to lend 50% of the property value. (Since he will lend $750,000, the lessee must supply the remaining $150,000 to construct the building.) If the landowner were willing to subordinate the fee to the leasehold mortgage, the lender might have lent up to 60% of the property value (i.e., the full value of the building).

The lender should give careful consideration to subordination, condemnation, rents, and construction.

I. Subordination

The lender's security is the leasehold. It can be lost if the lessee defaults on the lease and the fee interest has priority over the mortgage.

Owners are usually willing to subordinate their fee interest to the leasehold mortgage. If they do, development is more likely, and they can increase their income through rent from well-conceived improvements, obtain some participation in the profits, and own the improvement upon expiration of the lease. The owner who subordinates must sign the leasehold mortgage, but he needn't sign

---

[8] If the owner subordinates the fee, the lease is elevated to fee status. If the owner does not subordinate, and, if there is also a mortgage on the fee interest, the priority of the leasehold would be quite low (below both the fee and the mortgage on the fee).

the promissory note because his liability is limited to the loss of the land.

Whether or not the owners subordinates, lenders are more willing to lend if:

- The mortgagee should be given prompt notice of default by the lessee and the right to cure the deficiency.
- The lease should be assignable. (The lender certainly wants the right to sell the lease in the event of default).
- The lessee should prepay a portion of the ground rent (particularly important in the absence of subordination).
- The mortgagor should have an option to purchase the lease (thereby correcting his junior position).
- Rent is insured. Some private mortgage companies do this.

II. Condemnation

If some of the land can be condemned by local government, the lessee's earning potential can be damaged. The mortgagee should:

- Specify that the condemnation award be given to him.
- Prohibit the lessee from cancelling his lease after a relatively minor condemnation.

III. Rent Requirements

If the lessee subleases space, the mortgagee should disburse the loan contingent upon the amount of contracted rent.

IV. Construction Agreements

If a building is to be constructed, the permanent lender will require an agreement among himself, the temporary lender, and the borrower. The agreement should require that:

- A portion of the rental is escrowed so that funds are available for completion of the project.

- The loan documents can be used by both lenders.
- The temporary lender is prohibited from accepting payment from the borrower.
- The loan is assigned to the permanent lender (and to the permanent lender only) after conditions of the commitment are met.

5.7 THE OPEN-END MORTGAGE PROVIDES ADDITIONAL FUNDS

An open-end mortgage is a mortgage that permits additional funds to be loaned after the loan balance has been reduced to a predetermined amount. The additional funds are loaned on the terms of the original agreement and usually include an amount for taxes, assessments, and insurance premiums considered necessary to protect the secured property.

The open-end mortgage is used by the borrower to acquire appliances, make repairs, add improvements, etc.

Lenders might be inclined to grant these mortgages in order to:

- discourage the borrower from obtaining short-term loans to improve the property. Such short-term obligations could impair the borrower's ability to meet those of their mortgage.
- encourage maintenance of and additions to the improvements.

Notice that the package mortgage (Section 5.8) expressly includes fixtures whereas the open-end mortgage is more general.

A question of lien priority can arise concerning the future advances. Generally the priority of advances over intervening liens depends upon whether such advances are required or optional. If required, they usually have priority over intervening liens. However, state laws vary considerably in this regard.

5.8 THE PACKAGE MORTGAGE PROVIDES LOW PAYMENTS FOR PERSONAL PROPERTY

A package mortgage is a mortgage that expressly includes personal property such as appliances and fixtures in addition to the real property. Use of the package mortgage allows houses to be sold more easily because the single long-term mortgage requires smaller payments than would an additional short-term chattel mortgage.

The mortgage agreement should specify the items to be included and should recite the intention of the parties that these items are to be considered fixtures (i.e., real property).[9]

Package mortgages can be FHA-insured. A list of FHA-approved equipment includes such durable items as plumbing accessories, air conditioning, awnings, blinds, cabinets, dishwashers, fireplace accessories, floor coverings, garbage disposals, laundry equipment, ranges, refrigerators, screens, storm doors, etc. Although usually ignored, it is a violation of the package mortgage to sell or dispose of mortgaged items without consent of the mortgagee.

5.9 INCREASE YOUR LEVERAGE WITH THE PARTICIPATION MORTGAGE

The participation mortgage is a mortgage in which the lender participates in some of the financial benefits of owning the secured property, usually in addition to receiving mortgage payments. During periods of "tight money" sometimes supply and demand can so favor the lender that he can obtain some equity participation.

I. Forms of Participation by a Lender

It can occur in many different ways; the only limitations would be legal and the willingness of the parties:

[9] The clause is " . . . and all the estate and rights of the party of the first part in and to said premises, together with all fixtures and articles of personal property attached to, or used in connection with the premises . . .".

A. Income. The lender may obtain a percentage of the annual income (e.g., 2–3% of effective gross income, 20–30% of effective gross income that exceeds a certain level, a percentage of the net operating income, cash flow, etc.).

B. Capital Gain. The lender may obtain a part of the reversion (either upon disposition or pursuant to refinancing).

C. Corporate Ownership. The corporate borrower might issue stock to the lender as participation and even to satisfy some of the loan balance.

II. Participation in Exchange for High-Ratio Financing

Borrowers are sometimes willing to allow participation if they can achieve leverage.

A. Joint Venture. The borrower does not make payments on the loan, but instead, enters a joint venture with the lender. They share profits according to their relative contribution, capital or other. For example, they may agree to share the profits in proportion to their capital contribution. Or the borrower may be a developer or an architect who contributes skill in place of capital.

B. Development. A developer might sell land to the lender who then leases it to the developer for his project. The lender then grants a loan for 75% of the value of the improvements. The developer has obtained a high loan-to-value ratio (i.e., if the land value is 20% of the total value, the loan-to-value ratio for the property is $0.20 \times 1.00 + 0.80 \times 0.75 = 0.80$). In return for the high-ratio financing, the lender will probably participate in the profits. This arrangement is similar to the sale-leaseback (Section 5.12), but the motivation is not.

5.10 CONSIDER POOLED FINANCING FOR LARGE PROJECTS

Pooled financing describes a loan in which several lenders contribute. There is one mortgage, but several promissory notes, (one for each lender).

This form of lending occurs most often with

temporary financing used to construct very large projects. However, after construction the lenders participate separately in the permanent financing. For example, several savings and loan associations might pool their capital for the temporary loan, and, after construction, each would have permanent financing on a predetermined portion of the project.

Pooled financing requires a participation agreement. It specifies the share of each lender, their rights in the event of foreclosure, who collects the payments, and how they are to be distributed.

5.11 HOW TO USE THE PURCHASE MONEY MORTGAGE

A purchase money mortgage is a mortgage that is given by a purchaser to a seller to secure the balance of the purchase price. The seller, instead of a third party, provides the financing. At any rate, property often sells quicker and at a higher price in the absence of third-party financing.

To qualify as a purchase money mortgage,

- the mortgage must be executed and delivered when the property is acquired (considered to be simultaneous events),
- the mortgage must be part of the transaction, and
- the entire amount must be loaned expressly to pay the balance of the purchase price and it must be used for that purpose.

I. Significance of the Purchase Money Mortgage

What is the significance of a purchase money mortgage relative to other mortgages? If recorded immediately, it has priority over any existing and subsequent liens against the purchaser.[10] It is customary to designate the mortgage as a purchase money mortgage; however, this is not necessary to obtain priority.

---

[10] The mortgage is a limitation on the purchaser's title rather than a limitation on the property.

II. How to Phrase a Purchase Money Mortgage

The wording of a purchase money mortgage is essentially the same as that of any other mortgage except:

- After the description of the property, add: "Said property is the same premises conveyed to the mortgagee by the mortgagor by a deed bearing even date with these presents, which is given to secure the (payment) (part payment) of the purchase money mortgage of the said property."

- The "warranty of title" clause found in most other mortgages should be replaced by one that states that the mortgagor warrants only such title as was conveyed to him. Why? Because the purchase money mortgagee and the seller are one, and the mortgagor may have, in fact, received a defective title from the seller.

5.12 ADVANTAGES AND DISADVANTAGES OF THE SALE-LEASEBACK

The term "sale-leaseback" refers to two transactions: a property owner sells his property and then leases it from the new owner. These transactions can replace financing as far as the seller-lessee is concerned, but can be considered financing by the IRS under certain conditions.

Usually the type of owner that is motivated to conduct a sale-leaseback is a corporation that has built the specific improvement it wants to occupy. However, since it doesn't want its capital tied-up as equity in real estate or drained by mortgage payments, it will free the capital by selling the property. The buyer can be motivated to buy the property if he has a very reliable tenant: by virtue of this reliability he may obtain financing with an unusually high loan-to-value ratio.

Table 5.12-1 lists some features of a sale-leaseback not found in the separate sale and lease transactions. The consequences of a repurchase option and the term of the lease are discussed below.

Table 5.12-1. Advantages and Disadvantages for Each Party in a Sale-Leaseback (In Addition to Those Found in Separate Sale and Lease Transactions)

	Advantages

Seller-Lessee	• Capital not tied-up
	  (a) Favorable balance sheet permits easier borrowing
	  (b) Capital can be used for expansion, debt service, or other investment
	• Improvement is chosen by seller

Buyer-Lessor	• If lessee has a very high credit rating, buyer can obtain high leverage financing • Lessee is usually a reliable long-term tenant

	Disadvantages
Seller-Lessee	• The usual deductions of owership are not available to reduce taxable income
Buyer-Lessor	• Lease is always long-term so terms must be negotiated carefully • Seller may require a repurchase option • If the seller-lessee becomes bankrupt, the claim to rental is limited*

*The Chandler Act limits the lessor's claim to 1 year's rental in general bankruptcy and 3 years' rental in case of reorganization.

I. Repurchase of the Property

Sometimes the seller includes a provision in the lease giving him the option to repurchase the property at the term of the lease. In this case the sale-leaseback is, in fact, a method of financing. The question arises, what price should the seller pay for the property? For each party, the answer involves not only investment consequences, but tax consequences.

To understand the repurchase provision of an investment, it should be observed that the result of this provision is analogous to the mortgage that is only partially amortized at its term (Section 7.5). For example, if the seller repurchases the property for essentially nothing, the rent he paid can be thought of as payment sufficient to completely amortize a loan in the amount of the original property value. On the other hand, if he pays full value (the value when the lease was executed), the rent he paid can be thought of as payments of interest only (i.e., containing no principal), and there is no amortization of the imaginary loan.

Concerning taxes, if a repurchase provision allows the seller to repurchase the property at a price below fair market value, the IRS will consider the seller to have been the owner all along. (The IRS considers no sale to have occurred, but only a loan to have been granted to the seller from the buyer.)[11] The rent he has deducted will be disallowed as rent, but will be viewed as interest; this and the other deductions attendant to ownership will be allowed. Similarly, the buyer will be viewed as the lender.

II. Term of the Lease

If the lease has a term of 30 years or more, the lease is considered to be real property. Hence, the sale-leaseback is considered to be an exchange of property of "like-kind"[12]. A shorter-term lease with

[11] Also the IRS may declare there to have been no sale if the lease contains provisions whereby the seller retains the risks, responsibilities, and duties of ownership.

[12] For further information on the exchange of real property, see William T. Tappan, Jr.'s *Real Estate Exchange and Acquisition Techniques*, 2nd edition, Prentice Hall, 1989.

renewal options seemingly structured to avoid the 30-year provision, will be viewed by the IRS as a lease whose term is the sum of the original and renewal terms.

5.13 ADVANTAGES AND DISADVANTAGES OF THE VARIABLE RATE MORTGAGE

A variable rate mortgage is one whose interest rate is adjusted in response to the change in a certain standard interest rate. The variable rate can be viewed as a protective measure for either the lender or the borrower depending on the projected interest rate.

At first glance, the variable rate mortgage is attractive to borrowers only if lower interest rates are anticipated, and attractive to lender only if higher interest rates are anticipated. However, Table 5.13-1 lists other less obvious advantages and disadvantages of the variable rate mortgage for both parties.

I. Provisions.

The following provisions should be considered in a variable rate mortgage.

A. *Rate.* The interest rate is specified to be a fixed percentage above or below a standard rate such as one of the following:

- Federal Reserve discount rate
- prime rate (for bank borrowers)
- Federal Home Loan Bank Board mortgage rate
- bond rate
- intermediate-term yield on government securities
- FHA or VA interest rate
- average of some of the above rates

B. *Period.* The standard rate is to be examined after certain periods of time, say every 6 months, and the interest rate adjusted if necessary.

Table 5.13-1. Advantages and Disadvantages of the Variable Rate Mortgage For Lenders and Borrowers

	Advantages
Borrower	• Prepayment penalty is usually omitted • Loan is easily assumable • Amount borrowed is easily expanded • Term is easily extended • Initial interest rate might be lower than on a fixed rate mortgage • More funds may be available (such as from commerical banks which otherwise prefer short-term loans)
Lender	• Mortgage retains value (because contract interest rate is tied to standard economic interest rate)*

	Disadvantages
Borrower	• Total amount of payments is uncertain • Either the term or the monthly payment is uncertain • Profit projections are difficult to make due to uncertainty of payment amounts
Lender	• Income projections are difficult to make due to uncertainty of payment amounts • More time and paper work is required • Loans are difficult to market because of current lack of acceptance • Customer relations are strained when rate increases

*If the standard is poorly selected, value will not be retained.

C. *Maximum Change.* The maximum interest rate change each period, say 1/4% might be specified.

D. *Notice.* Advance notice of a rate increase, say 45 days, might be specified

E. *Prepayment.* Specify the prepayment penalty, if any

F. *Assumability.* Specify conditions of assumability.

G. *Expandability.* Specify the expandability of the loan amount, if any.

H. *Extendability.* Specify the extendability of the term, if any.[13]

I. *Conditions.* Specify how the changed rate will affect the conditions of the loan: Assuming that the number of payment periods per year is fixed (e.g., 12), a change in the interest rate can cause a change in either the payment or the remaining term.

II. Example.

The following example shows how the payments and remaining term can be altered by the changed interest rate.

EXAMPLE

Suppose a 25-year mortgage loan of $100,000 has an initial interest rate of 8% and monthly payments of $771.85. After 18 months the interest rate becomes $8\frac{1}{4}\%$. Now determine (a) the new remaining term if the monthly payment is to stay $771.85, and (b) the new monthly payment if the total term is to stay 25 years.

SOLUTION

After 18 months, the loan balance is $B_{18} =$ $98,000.43 (see Section 7.2).
(a) The formulas of Section 7.2 and Table 1 can be solved for the remaining term, n years.

$$n = -\frac{1}{q} \cdot \frac{\log[1 - (B_j/q) \cdot (r/q)]}{\log(1 + r/q)}$$

$$= -\frac{1}{12} \cdot \frac{\log\left[1 - \left(\frac{\$98,000.43}{\$771.85}\right)\left(\frac{.0825}{12}\right)\right]}{\log\left(1 + \frac{.0825}{12}\right)}$$

[13] See advantages to the borrower in Table 5.13–1

$$= -\frac{1}{12} \cdot \frac{\log(1 - 126.96823 \times .006875)}{\log(1 + .006875)}$$

$$= -\frac{1}{12} \times \frac{\log(.1270934)_{14}}{\log(1.006875)}$$

$$= -\frac{1}{12} \times \left(\frac{-2.062833}{.00685147}\right)$$

$$= \frac{301.0789}{12} = 25.09 \text{ years.}$$

This is the term remaining after the loan is 18 months old so that the payment remains constant. (b) Again, from Section 7.2 and Table I, if the term remains constant the new monthly payment is

$$\begin{aligned}
g &= \$98,000.43/a(8.25,282,12) \\
&= \$98,000.43/124.38671 \\
&= \$787.87.
\end{aligned}$$

5.14 HOW TO EVALUATE THE WRAPAROUND MORTGAGE

A wraparound mortgage is a junior mortgage whose payments are structured to be at least as large as those of the existing mortgage. The wraparound mortgagee assumes the existing mortgage and uses some of his payments to make payments on the existing mortgage; the remainder pays the lender of the wraparound mortgage.

When structuring the wraparound mortgage, the parties should watch for variable payments in the existing mortgage such as balloon payments, acceleration clauses,[15] graduated payments, vari-

---

[14] Although any positive base can be chosen for the logarithms, the base e has been used here.

[15] Some mortgages contain an acceleration clause which allows the mortgagee to declare the balance immediately due and payable when the title is conveyed. In some states acceleration clauses are automatic, but in most states their execution is at the option of the mortgagee (but subject to the doctrine of estoppel and the statute of limitations). Mortgagees are more likely to enforce this clause when the current interest rate exceeds that of the existing mortgage.

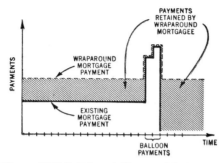

Figure 5.14-1 Schematic Diagram of the Payments for Wraparound and Existing Mortgages

able interest rates, etc. Many investors believe the wraparound interest rate must be higher than that of the existing loan. This is not true; only the payments must be larger. The payments are shown schematically in Figure 5.14-1.

Although the buyer can obtain a wraparound mortgage loan from a third party (e.g., an institutional lender), usually the seller finances the sale by taking the wraparound mortgage.

EXAMPLE (Seller Financing)

Suppose the seller of an $800,000 property wants to take a wraparound mortgage of $600,000 at 8%. The loan is to be amortized over 23 years by monthly payments of $4,760.72. There is an existing loan at 7% with 23 years remaining. The balance is $410,163.19, and the monthly payments are $2,993.86. This is, indeed, a wraparound mortgage since the existing mortgage remains, and its payments can be made from those of the wraparound mortgage. What does the wraparound mortgage mean to the two parties? The borrower simply borrows $600,000 at 8% and makes monthly payments until the loan is amortized in 23 years. The situation is not so clear for the seller, however. For the seller, we should determine (1) the effective monthly payment, (2) the effective loan amount, and (3) the effective interest rate.

SOLUTION

1. The effective monthly payment is the difference between the monthly payments on the two loans:

$$\$4,760.72 - \$2,993.86 = \$1,766.86.$$

2. The effective loan amount is the difference between the balances of the two loans:

$$\$600,000 - \$410,163.19 = \$189,836.81.$$

3. The effective interest rate is obtained from the following formula (from Section 7.5):

$$\begin{aligned} a(r,m,q) &= \frac{\text{Effective Loan Amount}}{\text{Effective Monthly Payment}} \\ &= \frac{\$189,836.81}{\$1,766.86} \\ &= 107.44304. \end{aligned}$$

where

r = effective wraparound mortgage interest rate

q = number of payments per year (12 in this case)

m = total number of payments ($12 \times 23 = 276$ in this case)

$a(r,m,q)$ = present value of an annuity of 1.

Now, all parameters of the formula are known except r, the effective wraparound mortgage interest rate. It can be estimated from Table 1 by finding the value of r that renders $a(r,276,12)$ nearest to 107.44304. In this case, r is approximately 10%.

CHAPTER 6

WHERE TO OBTAIN FINANCING

Although this chapter discusses several institutional lenders, it should be noted that the individual is the only real lender; these institutions merely act as intermediaries for the individual and invest his money in a way that balances risk and reward, either in a prudent way or according to government regulations.

To understand the propensity of these lenders to make real estate loans, it is helpful to know the nature of funds deposited with them.

For example, life insurance companies have a flow of funds that is relatively predictable and unaffected by the money markets. Therefore, they are able to make long-term real estate loans. On the other hand, commercial banks have a high percentage of demand deposits (i.e., checking accounts), so they tend to make short-term, high-interest loans (e.g., construction loans).

Mortgage brokers and mortgage bankers are at the other end of the spectrum from individuals; they act as intermediaries for intermediaries such as commercial banks.

Finally, the supply and demand of the money markets affects almost all lenders (except life insurance companies and pension funds who acquire funds through planned annuity deposits).

6.1 COMMERCIAL BANKS

Commercial banks are private enterprises that are organized under either state or national charter. State-chartered banks can invest under more liberal regulations that can national banks. However,

Table 6.1-1. General Real Estate Lending Policies of Commerical Banks

Purpose	Maximum Loan-to-Value Ratio (%)	Maximum Term (Years)	Comments
Existing real estate	50	5	Simple interest loans
	90	30	Amortized loans
Temporary construction loan (multiple residential, commercial and industrial)	—	3	Permanent loan commitment required
Temporary construction loan (single-family residential and farm)	—	3	Permanent loan commitment not required. High risk, therefore high interest rate.

Leasehold mortgage	75	First mortgage only (i.e., lessor must subordinate fee interest)
Warehousing for mortgage bankers	Few months	Unsold mortgages used as security. Interest rate is about 1% over prime.
Funds for savings and loan associations	—	To purchase notes from Federal Home Loan Bank Board

they have the option to become members of the Federal Reserve System and to insure their deposits with the Federal Deposit Insurance Corporation; those that do are subject to both state and federal regulations.

Commercial banks receive funds from time deposits, demand deposits, and trusts. Time deposits are usually savings accounts. Only 40-50% of a commercial bank's assets are time deposits. Short-term loans are made from demand deposits. Trust deposits must be invested according to the specifications of the trustee. If there are none, the bank can invest these funds as it wishes (e.g., in real estate mortgages).

Since commercial banks are under pressure to maintain liquidity, it is usually only the larger banks that invest directly in long-term real estate mortgages.

Commercial banks make direct short-term real estate loans in two ways. They make interim construction loans for one-half to three years at interest rates that are 1-5% above the prime rate and they make indirect short-term real estate loans to mortgage banks to cover mortgages until they are sold (i.e., warehousing). They sometimes lend on land for development at high interest rates.

Of all the assets of commercial banks, only 10-15% are in real estate loans. Of these, about 60% are in 1-4-family residences, 4% in larger residential properties, and 36% in other properties. Table 6.1-1 lists the general real estate lending policies of commercial banks.

6.2 LIFE INSURANCE COMPANIES

Life insurance companies have a great supply of funds for investment and are a good source of financing for large real estate projects. They are the most important lenders for shopping centers, office buildings, and large residential projects (amounting to about 60% of this financing).

They are regulated by both the state in which they are chartered and the states in which they operate. Regulation usually concerns the type of investments they can make, the maximum percent of assets used for each investment, the percent of liquidity, and the extent of equity participation in their projects.

Long-term mortgage funds are available from life insurance companies on a regular basis because their cash flow is well known and not subject to the supply and demand that affect thrift institutions. Their funds come primarily from premiums paid by their policy holders rather than from savings that can be reduced when interest rates are high.

Life insurance funds are generally not available to individual borrowers with small projects (although the funds of small insurance companies may be). They acquire their mortgages from three sources:

• Correspondents. A local mortgage banker or broker may be designated a correspondent. He completes the loan package and presents it to the insurance company for approval.

• Branch offices. Branch offices of the insurance company can be supervised closely and are sometimes established expressly to originate loans. Their functions are similar to those of the correspondent.

• Home offices. Small insurance companies tend to originate loans through the home office. The smaller companies must make smaller loans, and they tend to be more responsive to small borrowers.

Of all their assets, about 30-40% are invested in real estate loans. Of these, 20% are in 1-4-family residences, 20% in larger residences, and 60% in other properties. Their loans usually bear a low-interest rate, and the amount is about two-thirds of the property value. They rarely make temporary construction loans. In periods of tight money, life insurance companies may seek equity participation in the project, such as cash flow and capital gain. A small percentage (3-5%) of their assets is allowed to be invested in junior mortgages; hence life insurance companies can be a good source of wraparound mortgages for large projects. Table 6.2-1 summarizes the real estate mortgage policies of life insurance companies.

Table 6.2-1. General Real Estate Lending Policies of Life Insurance Companies

Purpose	Maximum Loan-to-Value Ratio (%)†	Maximum Term (Years)	Comments
Single-family Residential	90–100	30	60% are FHA-insured or VA-guaranteed loans (and thereby exempt from state loan-to-value limitation), 40% are conventional loans.
Multi-family Residential	66-2/3–75	—	Largest holders of multi-family residential debt.

	Leasehold Mortgage	66-2/3-75*	35 years or remaining term of lease (whichever is longer)	Largest holders of multi-family residential debt.
			—	—
Land contracts, farms, joint ventures, sale-leasebacks		66-2/3-75	—	—

† Subject to state law: the maximum loan-to-value ratio is subject to laws of both the state of charter (usually New York) and the state of business. This maximum is usually 66-2/3 to 75%. In New York not more than 50% of the companies' assets can be invested in real estate loans.

* Same ratio as on the fee except in Ohio and Minnesota where the maximum is 60 and 50%, respectively.

6.3 MUTUAL SAVINGS BANKS

Mutual savings banks are savings institutions that are mutually owned by their depositors and chartered, generally, in the eastern seaboard states (75% of their assets are in Massachusetts and New York). They are similar to savings and loan associations, but they can invest in a wider variety of investments such as bonds and consumer loans.

About 75% of their assets are invested in real estate mortgages. Most of these assets are invested in FHA-insured and VA-guaranteed loans, particularly out-of-state. They lend about 60-90% of value on conventional loans. The larger mutual savings banks make multi-family residential and commercial mortgage loans. A small percent (3-5%) of their assets can be invested in land, joint ventures, junior mortgages, and so on. Table 6.3-1 lists the general mortgage investment policies of mutual savings banks.

6.4 SAVINGS AND LOAN ASSOCIATIONS

Savings and loan associations are institutions that invest their member's savings in local real estate mortgages. They may be governed by either state charter or federal charter.

State-chartered savings and loan associations are governed by state laws, and, if they are members of the Federal Savings and Loan Insurance Corporation (FSLIC), they are not only governed by that corporation but also by its supervising Federal Home Loan Bank System (FHLBS). Generally, the states regulate the type of loan and the federal government regulates the loan amount.

The Federal Home Loan Bank Board (FHLBB) serves the same function for its member savings and loan associations as does the Federal Reserve Board for its member banks; it serves as a pool from which member associations can borrow. Funds are deposited in the pool from several sources, and when interest rates are high, the associations may find that deposits have slowed or been withdrawn, and they can lend only by borrowing from the pool.

Savings and Loan Associations are the largest

source of mortgage money. Generally their loan policies are determined by a board of directors made up of local business and professional persons elected by the shareholders. However, there are some overriding regulations and inducements:

- Type of Security. At least 80% of their assets must be held in residential (1-4-family residences) mortgages. If no more than 18% of their assets are in larger residential and commercial mortgages, the IRS permits their earnings to be transferred to a non-taxable surplus account.

- Loan-to-Value Ratio. The loan-to-value ratio can be 90-95% for lower-valued residences. (Value is considered to be the lesser of the appraised value and the sale price.) Because there is more risk in high loan-to-value ratios, the interest rate is usually higher also. The ratio is usually smaller for large projects.

- Geography. Some state-chartered associations can lend only within a 50-mile radius. Federal-chartered associations are limited to a 100-mile radius of an agent, and only 10% of their conventional loans can be out-of-state; FHA-insured and VA-guaranteed loans are not limited by state boundaries.

Table 6.4-1 lists some general real estate lending policies of savings and loan associations.

Table 6.3-1. General Real Estate Lending Policies of Mutual Savings Banks

Purpose	Maximum Loan-to-Value Ratio (%)	Maximum Term (Years)	Comments
1-4 family residences	90	20-30 yrs. or 3/4 of the remaining useful life	Conventional loans are limited to state or region of charter, but FHA-insured or VA-guaranteed loans are not
Larger residential rentals	66-2/3 to 90	25	Only larger mutual savings will lend
Leasehold mortgage	Subject to state law	*Subject to state law	Lease term must be at least 21 years and loan amortized within (less than) 80% of term of lease

Construction mortgage	Subject to state law	Subject to state law	Lending permitted on projects for which permanent loans are permitted. High risks, therefore high interest rate.
Wraparound mortgage	—	—	Basket provision allows 3-5% of assets to be invested in otherwise unlawful projects (i.e., wraparound mortgages are junior mortgages)

Table 6.4-1. General Real Estate Lending Policies of Savings and Loan Associations

Purpose	Maximum Loan-to-Value Ratio (%)	Maximum Term (Years)	Comments
1-4 family Residential	80 60 50	1-1/2 3 5	Simple interest*
	80–90	30	Amortized†
Larger residential rental	75	25	—
Commercial	50	5	Simple interest
	75	25	Amortized
Land (intended for home of borrower with low income)		Short	Simple interest 40% of loan to be amortized after 5 years

Leasehold mortgage	—	10 years less than lease	—
Construction mortgage	75	3	High risk, therefore high interest rate
Mobile homes	—	8 if old 12 if new	Chattel mortgage
Unsecured loans	—	5	Loan is discounted (borrower receives the loan amount less the interest). Loan is repaid over the term. Used to alter or improve existing property, for equipment, vacation homes, etc.

*Interest paid semi-annually.

†Must be insured if loan-to-value ratio is greater than 90%. Also, they can accept interest-only payments for the first five years.

CHAPTER 7

QUICK WAYS TO FIGURE YOUR MORTGAGE MATH

7.1 HOW TO DETERMINE THE RATE OF REPAYMENT (THE ANNUAL MORTGAGE CONSTANT)

The annual mortgage constant is the annual loan payment divided by the loan amount. Therefore, it measures the rate of repayment.

From the lender's point of view, the annual mortgage constant is the mortgage capitalization rate. The capitalization rate is the sum of the interest rate (the rate of return *on* investment) and the recapture rate (the rate of return *of* investment).

Each payment of an amortized loan contains an amount of interest (return on investment) and an amount of principal (return of investment), so the annual payment divided by the amount loaned is clearly the mortgage capitalization rate. See Section 4.6.

On the other hand, each payment of a nonamortized loan consists of interest only (with the entire principal amount due at the term); hence, for these loans, there is no rate of recapture and the capitalization rate is equal to the interest rate.

Figure 7.1-1 shows how the annual mortgage constant varies with the interest rate for amortized loans. Notice that it is relatively independent of q, the number of payment periods per year; this is particularly true for loans whose terms are 10 years or longer. Notice, also, that the annual mortgage constant always exceeds the interest rate, but approaches it as the term increases; this is under-

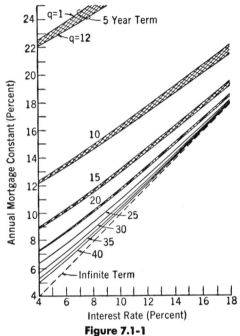

Figure 7.1-1

standable since it is the interest rate plus the recapture rate and the recapture rate approaches
zero as the term increases.

FORMULA

$$z_m = \begin{cases} r + r' = \dfrac{gq}{p} = \dfrac{q}{a(r,m,q)} & \text{(amortized loans)} \\ r & \text{(non-amortized loans)} \end{cases}$$

where

z_m = annual mortgage constant
r = annual interest rate
r' = annual recapture rate (Section 4.5)

g = amount of periodic payment

p = amount of loan

q = number of payment periods per year

n = number of years

m = nq = total number of periods

a(r,m,q) = present value of an annuity of 1.

EXAMPLE

A \$100,000 amortized loan at 10% has monthly payments of \$908.70 for 25 years. What is the annual mortgage constant?

SOLUTION

In this example,

p = \$100,000, r = 10%, q = 12, g = \$908.70,
$$n = 25, \text{ and } m = nq = 300.$$

From this information, we can use either the second or third formula for an amortized loan. The second formula doesn't require using Table 1, so the annual mortgage constant is

$$z_m = \frac{\$908.70 \times 12}{\$100,000} = 0.1090 = 10.90\%$$

7.2 FINDING THE MORTGAGE BALANCE AT A GLANCE

The balance is the amount of the loan that has not been repaid. Each payment of an amortized loan is constant and consists of an amount of interest and an amount of principal. The amount of interest is the interest on the balance. The amount of principal directly reduces the loan balance.[1] With each succeeding payment, the amount of interest decreases and the amount of principal increases equally.

For amortized loans with monthly payments, the loan balance can be quickly estimated from Figure 7.2-1.

[1]The balance is not reduced when payments contain interest only.

LOAN BALANCE

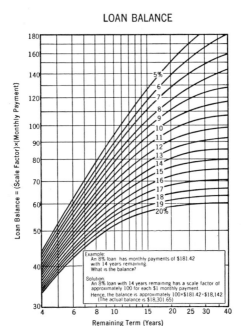

Figure 7.2-1

The following formulas can be used to determine the exact loan balance.

FORMULAS

$$B_j = \begin{cases} g \cdot a(r,k,q) = p \cdot \dfrac{a(r,k,q)}{a(r,m,q)} & \text{number of remaining payments known} \\[2ex] p \cdot c(r,j,q) - g \cdot s(r,j,q) & \text{number of remaining payments not known} \end{cases}$$

where

B_j = balance after j payments

g = periodic payment

p = amount of the loan

r = annual interest rate

n = number of years

q = number of periods per year

$m = nq$ = total number of periods

j = number of periods used

k = number of periods remaining
    (note: $m = j + k$)

$a(r,k,q)$,

$a(r,m,q)$ = present value of an annuity of 1

$c(r,j,q)$ = amount of 1 at compound interest

$s(r,j,q)$ = amount of an annuity of 1

EXAMPLE

A loan at 9% interest has monthly payments of $419.60. If there are 97 remaining payments, what is the balance?

SOLUTION

In this example,

$r = 9\%$, $q = 12$, $g = \$419.60$, and $k = 97$.

We must use the first formula. From Table 1,

$a(r,k,q) = a(9,97,12) = 68.74287$.

Now, the balance is

$B_j = \$419.60 \times 68.74287 = \$28,844.51$

7.3 HOW TO COMPUTE BALLOON PAYMENTS

In the case of amortized loans, a balloon payment is a payment that is larger than is necessary to amortize the loan at its term.

Balloon payments allow the borrower low early payments and the lender the present value of his investment.

EXAMPLE

An amortized loan at 9% interest for 30 years calls for monthly payments of $804.62 with a single balloon payment at 10 years. How large is the balloon payment?

SOLUTION

Since the single balloon payment is simply payment of the loan balance, it can be determined from the methods of the previous section. In this example,

$r = 9\%$, $n = 30$ years, $q = 12$, $m = nq = 360$,
$g = \$804.62$, and $j = 10 \times 12 = 120$

(consequently, $k = m - j = 240$).

Use the first formula:

$$B_j = g \cdot a(r,k,q).$$

From Table 1,

$$a(r,k,q) = a(9,240,12) = 111.144954.$$

The balloon payment is

$$B_{120} = \$804.62 \times 111.144954$$
$$= \$89,429.45.$$

7.4 HOW TO BUY AND SELL MORTGAGES

New and existing mortgages are often traded. Their value depends upon the difference between economic and contract interest rates, the remaining term, the risk, etc. The formulas of this section show how to determine the yield, the purchase price, and the discount.[2]

If there is no prepayment, the mortgage yield, y, can be determined from the first formula if either the purchase price or the discount (from the loan balance) is known. If there is prepayment the yield can be determined from the formula for the purchase price. In either case, the yield cannot be determined explicitly. However, it can be determined by the method shown in the following example. Also, Figure 7.4-1 can be used to estimate the yield or the purchase price for mortgages with monthly payments and no prepayment.

The purchase price that will provide the de-

---

[2]The requirements for transfer are discussed in Section 8.7.

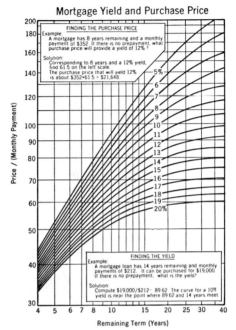

Mortgage Yield and Purchase Price

Figure 7.4-1

sired yield, y, can be determined from the second formula. Notice that this formula can be used either when there is prepayment or when there is not. (If not, set k = 0, in which case a(r,k,q) = 0.)

After the purchase price that provides the required yield has been determined, the discount, r′, can be determined from the third formula.

All of these formulas are for amortized loans. However, they can be used for non-amortized loans (loans whose payments consist of interest only) simply by replacing both a(r,m,q) and a(r,k,q) with q/r.

FORMULAS

$$a(y,kq) = \frac{p'}{g} = \frac{p'}{p} \cdot a(r,m,q)$$

$$= (1 - r') \cdot a(r,k,q) \qquad \text{(yield)}$$

$$p' = p \cdot \frac{s(y,j - i,q) + a(r,k,q)}{c(y,j - i,q) \cdot a(r,m,q)} \qquad \text{(purchase price)}$$

$$r' = 1 - \frac{p'}{B_i} \qquad \text{(discount)}$$

where

y = yield from mortgage

p' = purchase price that guarantees the required yield

g = amount of each periodic payment

p = original amount of mortgage

r = mortgage interest rate

q = number of periods per year

n = number of years (term of mortgage)

$m = nq$ = total number of payment periods

k = number of payment periods remaining after balloon

j = number of payment periods from inception until ballon (note: $m = j + k$)

i = number of payment periods from inception until purchase of mortgage (note: if $i = 0$, use Table 2.1-1)

r' = discount rate on mortgage balance, expressed as a decimal

$.a(y,k,q)$, etc. = present value of an annuity of 1

$s(y,j - i,q)$ = amount of an annuity of 1

$c(y,j - i,q)$ = amount of 1 at compound interest

EXAMPLE

An amortized loan has 84 remaining monthly payments of \$324.43. If it can be purchased for \$17,840.00, what is the yield?

SOLUTION

In this example,

k = 84, q = 12, g = $324.43, and p' = $17,840.00.

From the first formula,

$$a(y,84,12) = \frac{\$17,840.00}{\$324.43} = 54.9887.$$

From Table 1, locate the section with monthly payments (i.e., q = 12) and the row corresponding to 84 periods (i.e., m = 84). Find two consecutive values of a(y,84,12) that bracket 54.9887. The yield is between these two interest rates. Interpolation, would show that the yield is y = 12.99%.

7.5 FINDING MORTGAGE PAYMENTS AT A GLANCE

The payments on an amortized loan are usually constant and are made at equal intervals of time.

Since the payments constitute an annuity to the lender, the size of the payment is determined from the formula for the present value of an annuity. The payment must be such that the present value of the annuity equals the amount loaned. Of course, the rate of return on the investment is the interest rate on the loan. The formula for the pressent value of an annuity with constant payments and constant interest rate (see Table A.4.2-1 on page 276) is

$$p = g \cdot \sum_{i=1}^{m} = \frac{1}{(1 + r/q)^i} = g \cdot a(r,m,q).$$

Rearranging this formula, we have the formula for the periodic payment of an amortized loan:

$$g = p/a(r,m,q).$$

The constant payment can be determined from one of the following formulas. If the payments are monthly, they can be estimated quickly from Figure 7.5-1.

QUICK WAYS TO FIGURE YOUR MORTGAGE MATH 153

MONTHLY PAYMENT

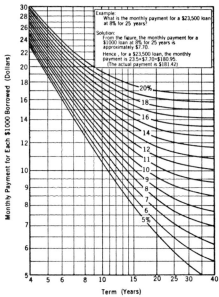

Figure 7.5-1

FORMULAS

$$g = \begin{cases} p/a(r,m,q) & \text{(complete amortization)} \\ p/a(r,j,q) - B_1/s(r,j,q) & \text{(partial amortization)} \end{cases}$$

where

g = amount of periodic payment

p = amount of loan

r = annual interest rate

q = number of periods per year

$m = nq$ = total number of payments

B_j = loan balance after the jth period

j = number of payment periods after which the balance, B_j, remains

a(r,m,q),

$a(r,j,q)$ = present value of an annuity of 1.

$s(r,j,q)$ = amount of an annuity of 1.

EXAMPLE 1: (complete amortization)

Mark Meredith obtained a \$35,300 loan at 10% interest with monthly payments for 25 years. How much must each payment be in order to completely amortize the loan at its term?

SOLUTION

In this example,

p = \$35,300, r = 10%, q = 12, n = 25,

and $m = nq = 300$.

From Table 1,

$a(r,m,q) = a(10,300,12) = 110.04723$.

Now, from the formula, the monthly payment is

g = \$35,300/110.04723 = \$320.77.

EXAMPLE 2: (partial amortization)

Mark Meredith wants to lend \$16,000 at 8% with monthly payments for three years. At the end of three years he wants to receive a single balloon payment of \$5,000. (In the 36th period he will receive the regular payment plus the balloon.) What monthly payment with accomplish this?

SOLUTION

In this example,

p = \$16,000, r = 8%, q = 12, j = 36,

and B_j = \$5,000.

From Table 1,

$a(r,j,q) = a(8,36,12) = 31.91181$, and
$s(r,j,q) = s(8,36,12) = 40.53556$.

Now, from the formula, the monthly payment is

$$g = \$16{,}000/31.91181 - \$5{,}000/40.53556$$
$$= \$501.38 - \$123.35$$
$$= \$378.03.$$

7.6 UNDERSTANDING SIMPLE AND COMPOUND INTEREST

Interest is the cost of renting money. This section shows how to compute the parameters of simple and compound interest loans.

I. Simple Interest

Simple interest is interest paid on a principal amount at a stated rate: the loan balance is not reduced. Since this leaves the lender's investment at risk, nonamortized loans are usually short-term loans with a high interest rate.

Table 7.6-1 lists several formulas for simple interest.

where

I = amount of interest

p = amount of principal

r = annual interest rate, expressed as a decimal

t = interest period, expressed as a fraction of a year.

Table 7.6-1. Formulas for Simple Interest

Amount of Interest	$I = prt$
Amount of Principal	$p = \dfrac{I}{rt}$
Annual Interest Rate	$r = \dfrac{I}{pt}$
Interest Period	$t = \dfrac{I}{pr}$

EXAMPLE

If $10,000 is borrowed for 18 months at simple interest of 12% how much interest must be paid?

SOLUTION

In this example,

$$p = \$10{,}000, \ t = \frac{18}{12} = \frac{3}{2}, \text{ and } r = 0.12.$$

Now the amount of interest is

$$I = \$10{,}000 \times 0.12 \times \frac{3}{2} = \$1{,}800.$$

II. Compound Interest

Compound interest is interest paid on a principal amount that is periodically increased by the amount of interest paid in the previous period (i.e., interest paid on interest). Hence, the amount grows in proportion to itself, a phenomenon occurring frequently in nature and called exponential growth.[3]

The frequency of compounding is surprisingly unimportant. Even if interest is compounded every instant, the amount accumulated is increased very little over that resulting from, say, quarterly compounding.

The following formula is used to compute the accumulated amount of 1 deposited at an interest rate r and compounded q times a year for m periods:

$$(1 + r/q)^m.$$

It is tabulated in Table 1 and labeled c(r,m,q). For example, consider an amount of 1 deposited at $r = 10\%$ and compounded $q = 12$ times a year for 5 years (i.e., $m = 5 \times 12 = 60$ periods). The

---

[3]For example, inflation, population growth, etc.

amount accumulated is

$c(r,m,q) = c(10,60,12) = (1 + 0.10/12)^{60} = 1.6453.$

Table 7.6-2 permits you to determine the value of the different parameters of the compound interest formula.

where

> S = amount accumulated (principal + interest)
>
> p = amount of principal
>
> I = amount of interest accumulated
>
> r = interest rate, expressed as a decimal
>
> q = number of interest periods per year
>
> n = number of years

$m = nq$ = total number of interest periods

Table 7.6-2. Formulas for Compound Interest

Amount Accumulated	$S = p \cdot (1 + r/q)^m = p \cdot c(r,m,q)$
Amount of Principal	$p = \dfrac{S}{(1 + r/q)^m} = \dfrac{S}{c(r,m,q)}$
Amount of Interest	$I = p \cdot [(1 + r/q)^m - 1]$ $= p \cdot [c(r,m,q) - 1]$
Amount of Time	$n = \dfrac{1}{q} \cdot \dfrac{\log(S/p)^\star}{\log(1 + r/q)}$
Number of Interest Periods Per Year	$q = \dfrac{1}{n} \cdot \dfrac{\log(S/p)^\star}{\log(1 + r/q)}$
Rate of Interest	$r = q \cdot \left[\left(\dfrac{S}{p}\right)^{1/m} - 1\right]$

$\star$ The logarithms in this formula can have any base since logarithms are used in a ratio.

EXAMPLE 1: (amount accumulated)

If \$1,000 is deposited at 8% interest and compounded quarterly, how much is accumulated after five years?

SOLUTION

In this example,

$p = \$1,000, r = 8\%, q = 4, n = 5,$
$$\text{and } m = nq = 20.$$

Then

$$S = \$1,000 \times (1 + .08/4)^{20} = \$1,000 \times (1.02)^{20}$$
$$= \$1,485.95.$$

EXAMPLE 2: (rate of interest)

If a deposit has increased from \$200 to \$300 over the last 4 years, what annual rate of increase (interest) is this?

SOLUTION

In this example,

$p = \$200, S = \$300, n = 4, q = 1,$
$$\text{and } m = nq = 4.$$

Then

$$r = 1 \cdot \left[\left(\frac{\$300}{\$200} \right)^{1/4} - 1 \right] = (1.5)^{1/4} - 1 = 1.1067 - 1$$
$$= .1067 = 10.67\%$$

7.7 COMPUTING THE INTEREST PAID EACH YEAR

Since investment interest is a tax deduction, it is necessary to determine the amount of interest paid during the year. The amount of interest can be determined from the following formulas. Also, Table 7.7-1 lists the amount of interest paid through each month for the first 50 months of an \$1,000 amortized loan. It includes terms of 5,10, ..., 40 years and interest rates from 9% through

14.75%. Of course, the interest paid between any two periods can be determined by subtracting one value from the other.

FORMULAS

$$i = p \cdot (r/q)$$
$$I = prt$$ $\Big\}$ non-amortized loans

$$i_j = \begin{cases} (r/q) \cdot B_{j-1} = g - p_j \\ (r/q) \cdot g \cdot a(r, m+1-j, q) \end{cases}$$ $\Bigg\}$ amortized loans

$$I_j = g \cdot [j + a(r, m-j, q) - a(r, m, q)]$$

where

> i, I = amount of interest in each period and from the beginning, respectively
>
> i_j, I_j = amount of interest in the jth period and through the jth period, respectively
>
> p = amount of principal
>
> t = time from the beginning, expressed as a fraction of a year.
>
> p_j = amount of the jth payment that is principal
>
> g = amount of each periodic payment
>
> n = number of years
>
> q = number of periods per year
>
> $m = nq$ = total number of periods
>
> r = interest rate, expressed as a decimal
>
> B_j = balance after j payments

$a(r, m, q)$,

$a(r, m - j)$,

$a(r, m + 1 - j, q)$ = present value of an annuity of 1 (note: $a(r, 0, q) = 0$)

EXAMPLE 1: (interest per period)

A five-year amortized loan at 8% interest has monthly payments of $324.43. How much interest is paid in the 16th period?

SOLUTION

In this example,

$n = 5$ years, $r = 8\%$, $q = 12$, $m = nq = 60$,
$$g = \$324.43, \text{ and } j = 16.$$

From the information given, we must use the third part of the first formula for amortized loans. From Table 1,

$$a(r, m + 1 - j, q) = a(8, 45, 12) = 38.766581.$$

Now,

$$i_{16} = (.08/12) \times \$324.43 \times 38.766581$$
$$= \$83.847.$$

EXAMPLE 2: (interest between two periods)

A five-year amortized loan at 8% interest has monthly payments of $324.43. How much interest is paid between the 23rd and 40th payments?

SOLUTION

To find the interest paid between the 23rd and 40th payments, it is necessary to first determine I_{23} and I_{40}, and then the difference, $I_{40} - I_{23}$. In this example,

$n = 5$ years, $r = 8\%$, $q = 12$, $m = nq = 60$,
$$\text{and } g = \$324.43.$$

From Table 1,

$$a(r, m, q) = a(8, 60, 12) = 49.318433.$$

When $j = 23$,

$$a(r, m - j, q) = a(8, 37, 12) = 32.693847.$$

Now, from the formula, the interest paid through the 23rd payment is

$$I_{23} = \$324.43 \times (23 + 32.693847 - 49.318433)$$
$$= \$324.43 \times 6.375414$$
$$= \$2,068.38.$$

Proceeding in the same way, we find

$$I_{40} = \$3,032.60.$$

Therefore, the amount of interest paid between the 23rd and 40th payment is

$$L_{40} - I_{23} = \$3,032.60 - \$2,068.38$$
$$= \$964.22.$$

EXAMPLE 3: (Using Table 7.7-1)

How much interest has been paid after the first 15 monthly payments of an $80,000 loan at 10% amortized over 30 years?

SOLUTION

From the page listing 30-year loans, the interest paid on $1,000 is $124.5986. Therefore, 80 × $124.5986 = $9,967.89 interest has been paid on $80,000.

Table 7.7-1. 5-YEAR TERM Interest Rate

J	9.00	9.25	9.50	9.75	10.00	10.25	10.50	10.75	11.00	11.25	11.50	11.75
1	7.5000	7.7088	7.9167	8.1250	8.3333	8.5417	8.7500	8.9583	9.1667	9.3750	9.5833	9.7917
2	14.9006	15.3151	15.7297	16.1444	16.5591	16.9738	17.3885	17.8033	18.2181	18.6328	19.0477	19.4626
3	22.2009	22.8196	23.4384	24.0573	24.6763	25.2953	25.9145	26.5338	27.1531	27.7726	28.3921	29.0117
4	29.4004	30.2210	31.0418	31.8628	32.6841	33.5054	34.3270	35.1488	35.9708	36.7929	37.6152	38.4377
5	36.4981	37.5185	38.5392	39.5602	40.5815	41.6032	42.6251	43.6474	44.6699	45.6928	46.7160	47.7395
6	43.4340	44.7113	45.9896	47.1484	48.3677	49.5875	50.8077	52.0284	53.2496	54.4711	55.6932	56.9157
7	50.3855	51.7996	53.2123	54.6267	56.0418	57.4575	58.8739	60.2909	61.7085	63.1268	64.5457	65.9652
8	57.1738	58.7790	60.3964	62.0005	63.6094	65.2183	66.8272	68.4361	70.0457	71.6596	73.2722	74.8868
9	63.8568	65.6534	67.4510	69.2497	71.0488	72.8506	74.6528	76.4558	78.2600	80.0653	81.8717	83.6791
10	70.4346	72.4192	74.4058	76.3927	78.3815	80.3717	82.3632	84.3561	86.3503	88.3459	90.3427	92.3409
11	76.9060	79.0763	81.2483	83.4220	85.5974	87.7745	89.9531	92.1335	94.3155	96.4990	98.6842	100.8710
12	83.2702	85.6238	87.9798	90.3369	92.6964	95.0578	97.4214	99.7869	102.1543	104.5237	106.8949	109.2681
13	89.5265	92.0607	94.5973	97.1362	99.6775	102.2211	104.7670	107.3152	109.8657	112.4186	114.9735	117.5307
14	95.6740	98.3363	101.1014	103.8192	106.5397	109.2629	111.9888	114.7173	117.4485	120.1822	122.9188	125.6578
15	101.7119	104.5896	107.4908	110.3849	113.2821	116.1824	119.0857	121.9921	124.9015	127.8140	130.7294	133.6478
16	107.6395	110.7002	113.7644	116.8322	119.9035	122.9783	126.0566	129.1384	132.2235	135.3121	138.4041	141.4994
17	113.4558	116.6866	119.9215	123.1603	126.4031	129.6498	132.9005	136.1550	139.4134	142.6756	145.9416	149.2114
18	119.1600	122.5583	125.9610	129.3692	132.7798	136.1568	139.6161	143.0408	146.4698	149.9031	153.3406	156.7823
19	124.7513	128.3142	131.8821	135.4549	139.0326	142.6151	146.2025	149.7947	153.3916	156.9933	160.5997	164.2108
20	130.2289	133.9636	137.6838	141.4194	145.1604	148.9067	152.6584	156.4154	160.1776	163.9450	167.7176	171.4964

21	135.5918	139.4755	143.3652	147.2608	151.1622	155.0698	158.9827	162.9017	166.8264	170.7569	174.6330	178.6348
22	140.8393	144.8791	148.9253	152.9779	157.0370	161.1025	165.1743	169.2585	173.3368	177.4276	181.5245	185.6278
23	145.9705	150.1633	154.3631	158.5699	162.7837	167.0044	171.2320	175.4665	179.7078	183.9658	188.2106	192.4722
24	150.9845	155.3273	159.6677	164.0357	168.4012	172.7742	177.1547	181.5425	185.9377	190.3403	194.7501	199.1672
25	155.6804	160.3702	164.8692	169.3743	173.8885	178.4108	182.9410	187.4798	192.0255	196.5796	201.1415	205.7113
26	160.6573	165.2900	169.9334	174.5846	179.2444	183.9129	188.5900	193.2756	197.9697	202.6723	207.3834	212.1028
27	165.3143	170.0887	174.8725	179.6656	184.4679	189.2796	194.1003	198.9302	203.7692	208.6172	213.4743	218.3404
28	169.8506	174.7625	179.6844	184.6162	189.5579	194.5094	199.4707	204.4418	209.4225	214.4129	219.4129	224.4224
29	174.2652	179.3114	184.3692	189.4355	194.5133	199.6015	204.7001	209.8091	214.9283	220.0578	225.1976	230.3474
30	178.5573	183.7344	188.9228	194.1222	199.3328	204.5545	209.7871	215.0308	220.2853	225.5607	230.8269	236.1139
31	182.7258	188.0306	193.3471	198.6754	204.0155	209.3673	214.7306	220.1056	225.4921	230.8900	236.2995	241.7203
32	186.7700	192.1989	197.6402	203.0940	208.5602	214.0386	219.5293	225.0322	230.5473	236.0744	241.6137	247.1649
33	190.6887	196.2384	201.8011	207.3769	212.9656	218.5673	224.1819	229.8093	235.4496	241.1025	246.7681	252.4464
34	194.4812	200.1480	205.8286	211.5228	217.2307	222.9524	228.6871	234.4355	240.1974	245.9726	251.7611	257.5629
35	198.1464	203.9269	209.7218	215.5309	221.3543	227.1919	233.0437	238.9096	244.7895	250.6834	256.5912	262.5130
36	201.6835	207.5740	213.4794	219.3999	225.3352	231.2854	237.2503	243.2300	249.2243	255.2333	261.2566	267.2950
37	205.0093	211.0882	217.1006	223.1287	229.1722	235.2312	241.3057	247.3965	253.5006	259.6209	265.7565	271.9072
38	208.3691	214.4685	220.5844	226.7161	232.8642	239.0283	245.2084	251.4046	257.6167	263.8446	270.0884	276.3480
39	211.5157	217.7140	223.9291	230.1811	236.4098	242.6752	248.9673	255.2560	261.5712	267.9030	274.2512	280.6157
40	214.5302	220.8235	227.1342	233.4624	239.8079	246.1708	252.5509	258.9482	265.3627	271.7943	278.2430	284.7086
41	217.4417	223.7360	230.1965	236.6189	243.0573	249.5136	255.9978	262.4799	268.9897	275.5171	282.0623	288.6251
42	220.1591	226.6306	233.1207	239.6294	246.1567	252.7025	259.2668	265.8495	272.4505	279.0699	285.7075	292.3633
43	222.2714	229.3260	235.8996	242.4827	249.1049	255.7361	262.3064	269.0556	275.7438	282.4509	289.1768	295.9215
44	225.2476	231.8812	238.5346	245.2077	251.9006	258.6131	265.3452	272.2068	278.8690	285.6586	292.4686	299.2980
45	227.5867	234.2952	241.0240	247.7731	254.5425	261.3321	268.1418	274.9716	281.8215	288.6914	295.5813	302.4910
46	229.7877	236.5668	243.3669	250.1877	257.0294	263.8917	270.7748	277.6785	284.6028	291.5476	298.5129	305.4987
47	231.8495	238.6950	245.5620	252.4503	259.3599	266.2908	273.2428	280.2160	287.2103	294.2256	301.2619	308.3192
48	233.7710	240.6787	247.6083	254.5598	261.5328	268.5277	275.5443	282.5825	289.6423	296.7237	303.8265	310.9608
49	235.5513	242.5167	249.5044	256.5145	263.5668	270.6012	277.6079	284.7768	291.8974	299.0402	306.2049	313.3916
50	237.1892	244.2079	251.2494	258.3136	265.4005	272.5100	279.6420	286.7867	293.9738	301.1734	308.3954	315.6397

Table 7.7-1. (continued) 5-YEAR TERM Interest Rate

J	12.00	12.25	12.50	12.75	13.00	13.25	13.50	13.75	14.00	14.25	14.50	14.75
1	10.0000	10.2083	10.4167	10.6250	10.8333	11.0417	11.2500	11.4583	11.6667	11.8750	12.0833	12.2917
2	19.8776	20.2925	20.7075	21.1225	21.5375	21.9528	22.3677	22.7828	23.1980	23.6132	24.0284	24.4436
3	29.6314	30.2513	30.8711	31.4911	32.1112	32.7314	33.3516	33.9719	34.5924	35.2129	35.8334	36.4541
4	39.2604	40.0833	40.9063	41.7295	42.5529	43.3765	44.2002	45.0241	45.8482	46.6725	47.4969	48.3214
5	48.7632	49.7873	50.8117	51.8363	52.8613	53.8865	54.9120	55.9378	56.9639	57.9903	59.0169	60.0438
6	58.1387	59.3620	60.5859	61.8101	63.0348	64.2600	65.4855	66.7115	67.9379	69.1647	70.3919	71.6195
7	67.3854	68.8061	70.2275	71.6495	73.0721	74.4953	75.9190	77.3434	78.7684	80.1939	81.6200	83.0466
8	76.5021	78.1183	79.7352	81.3530	82.9716	84.5910	86.2111	87.8320	89.4537	91.0762	92.6994	94.3234
9	85.4876	87.2971	89.1077	90.9192	92.7319	94.5455	96.3601	98.1757	99.9923	101.8099	103.6285	105.4490
10	94.3405	96.3413	98.3434	100.3467	102.3514	104.3573	106.3644	108.3728	110.3824	112.3932	114.4053	116.4186
11	103.0594	105.2494	107.4409	109.6340	111.8296	114.0247	116.2224	118.4216	120.6222	122.8244	125.0280	127.2331
12	111.6431	114.0201	116.3988	118.7795	121.1620	123.5463	125.9324	128.3204	130.7101	133.1016	135.4948	137.8898
13	120.0902	122.6519	125.2158	127.7818	130.3500	132.9204	135.4928	138.0674	140.6441	143.2229	145.8038	148.3867
14	128.3993	131.1435	133.8902	136.6394	139.3391	142.1453	144.9019	147.6611	150.4226	153.1866	155.9530	158.7218
15	136.5691	139.4934	142.4206	145.3506	148.2836	151.2194	154.1580	157.0995	160.0437	162.9908	165.9406	168.8931
16	144.5991	147.7002	150.8055	153.9141	157.0260	160.1411	163.2594	166.3809	169.5056	172.6335	175.7645	178.8996
17	152.4850	155.7623	159.0434	162.3281	165.6165	168.9086	172.2043	175.5036	178.8065	182.1129	185.4229	188.7364
18	160.2283	163.6764	167.1327	170.5591	174.0537	177.5203	180.9910	184.4657	187.9443	191.4270	194.9136	198.4042
19	167.8266	171.4470	175.0720	178.7016	182.3358	185.9744	189.6176	193.2653	196.9174	200.5739	204.2348	207.9000
20	175.2784	179.0665	182.8596	186.6578	190.4611	194.2693	198.0825	201.9006	205.7236	209.5515	213.3842	217.2218

21	182.5823	186.5354	190.4940	194.4582	198.4279	202.4031	206.3887	210.3697	214.3611	218.3579	222.3600	226.3673
22	189.7368	193.8521	197.9736	202.1010	206.2345	210.3740	214.5194	218.6707	222.8279	226.9910	231.1596	235.3345
23	196.7404	201.0152	205.2967	209.5847	213.8793	218.1903	222.4878	226.8018	231.1221	235.4488	239.7817	244.1210
24	203.5915	208.0231	212.4617	216.9075	221.3603	225.8202	230.2870	234.7608	239.2445	243.7291	248.2235	252.7248
25	210.2888	214.8741	219.4670	224.0676	228.6759	233.2917	237.9151	242.5459	247.1842	251.8299	256.4830	261.1435
26	216.8306	221.5667	226.3110	231.0635	235.8243	240.5931	245.3701	250.1551	254.9481	259.7491	264.6566	269.3749
27	223.2153	228.0992	232.9919	237.8933	242.9036	247.7225	252.6501	257.5864	262.5312	267.4845	272.4463	277.4166
28	229.4415	234.4700	239.5080	244.5553	249.6120	254.8780	259.7532	264.8376	269.9312	275.0339	280.1456	285.2664
29	235.5074	240.6775	245.8576	251.0477	256.2477	261.4576	266.6773	271.9068	277.1461	282.3950	287.6536	292.9218
30	241.4116	246.7200	252.0391	257.3686	262.7088	268.0594	273.4205	278.7919	284.1737	289.5658	294.9681	300.3806
31	247.1524	252.5959	258.0505	263.5164	268.9934	274.4815	279.9906	285.4908	291.0118	296.5438	302.0866	307.6402
32	252.7282	258.3033	263.8903	269.4890	275.0996	280.7218	286.3557	292.0012	297.6583	303.3268	309.0068	314.6983
33	258.1372	263.8406	269.5565	275.2847	281.0254	286.7784	292.5437	298.3212	304.1108	309.9126	315.7264	321.5523
34	263.3779	269.2061	275.0473	280.9016	286.7690	292.6483	298.5424	304.4484	310.3672	316.2987	322.2429	328.1997
35	268.4486	274.3980	280.3611	286.3378	292.3283	298.3323	304.3457	310.3807	316.4251	322.4828	328.5538	334.6390
36	273.3475	279.4145	285.4968	291.5940	297.7013	303.8254	309.9636	316.1158	322.2821	328.4624	334.6566	340.8647
37	278.0730	284.2638	290.4436	296.6604	302.8860	309.1265	315.3817	321.6516	327.9361	334.2352	340.5489	346.8771
38	282.6233	288.9742	295.2208	301.5428	307.8804	314.2335	320.6019	326.9856	333.3846	339.7988	346.2281	352.6726
39	286.9966	293.3338	299.8072	306.2367	312.6825	319.1442	325.6219	332.1156	338.6251	345.1505	351.6916	358.2485
40	291.1912	297.6907	304.2071	310.7402	317.2900	323.8565	330.4396	337.0392	343.6554	350.2879	356.9369	363.6022
41	295.2054	301.8032	308.4184	315.0510	321.7010	328.3682	335.0528	341.7542	348.4728	355.2085	361.9612	368.7308
42	299.0372	305.7292	312.4393	319.1673	325.9133	332.6771	339.4587	346.2580	353.0750	359.9097	366.7619	373.6317
43	302.6849	309.4670	316.2677	323.0869	329.9247	336.7808	343.6554	350.5483	357.4595	364.3888	371.3364	378.3020
44	306.1466	313.0145	319.9016	326.8078	333.7330	340.6773	347.6405	354.6226	361.6236	368.6433	375.6818	382.7389
45	309.4206	316.3699	323.3362	330.3278	337.3362	344.3641	351.4116	358.4785	365.5648	372.6705	379.7954	386.9396
46	312.5048	319.5312	326.5779	333.6448	340.7319	347.8390	354.9663	362.1135	369.2806	376.4676	383.6744	390.9010
47	315.3974	322.4964	329.6161	336.7566	343.9190	351.0997	358.3020	365.5249	372.7682	380.0320	387.3160	394.6204
48	318.0964	325.2634	332.4517	339.6612	346.8919	354.1436	361.4165	368.7103	376.0251	383.3608	390.7173	398.0947
49	320.6001	327.8804	335.0824	342.3562	349.6516	356.9686	364.3071	371.6661	379.0484	386.4513	393.8754	401.3208
50	322.9063	330.1952	337.5062	344.6394	352.1947	359.5721	366.9714	374.3926	381.6357	389.3007	396.7874	404.2958

Table 7.7-1. (continued) 10-YEAR TERM Interest Rate

J	9.00	9.25	9.50	9.75	10.00	10.25	10.50	10.75	11.00	11.25	11.50	11.75
1	7.5000	7.7083	7.9167	8.1250	8.3333	8.5417	8.7500	8.9583	9.1667	9.3750	9.5833	9.7917
2	14.9612	15.3774	15.7836	16.2098	16.6260	17.0422	17.4585	17.8748	18.2911	18.7074	19.1238	19.5401
3	22.3834	23.0069	23.6304	24.2540	24.8776	25.5013	26.1251	26.7490	27.3728	27.9969	28.6209	29.2450
4	29.7663	30.5965	31.4268	32.2573	33.0878	33.9186	34.7495	35.5805	36.4117	37.2429	38.0743	38.9058
5	37.1095	38.1459	39.1825	40.2194	41.2564	42.2938	43.3313	44.3690	45.4070	46.4452	47.4836	48.5221
6	44.4128	45.6548	46.8972	48.1399	49.3830	50.6264	51.8701	53.1142	54.3596	55.6033	56.8483	58.0936
7	51.6759	53.1229	54.5705	56.0185	57.4671	58.9161	60.3656	61.8155	63.2659	64.7167	66.1680	67.6199
8	58.8984	60.5499	62.2021	63.8549	65.5084	67.1625	68.8173	70.4728	72.1286	73.7851	75.4442	77.0999
9	66.0801	67.9354	69.7917	71.6487	73.5066	75.3654	77.2249	79.0852	80.9483	82.8081	84.6707	86.5340
10	73.2206	75.2792	77.3389	79.3996	81.4614	83.5242	85.5880	87.6528	89.7185	91.7852	93.8528	95.9213
11	80.3197	82.5809	84.8434	87.1072	89.3723	91.6386	93.9062	96.1750	98.4449	100.7160	102.9882	105.2615
12	87.3770	89.8402	92.3048	94.7712	97.2390	99.7083	102.1791	104.6513	107.1250	109.6000	112.0764	114.5541
13	94.3922	97.0567	99.7231	102.3912	105.0612	107.7329	110.4064	113.0815	115.7584	118.4368	121.1168	123.7996
14	101.3651	104.2302	107.0975	109.9669	112.8384	115.7120	118.5875	121.4651	124.3446	127.2261	130.1094	132.9945
15	108.2952	111.3603	114.4278	117.4979	120.5703	123.6451	126.7222	129.8017	132.8633	135.9672	139.0533	142.1414
16	115.1824	118.4466	121.7138	124.9838	128.2565	131.5319	134.8100	138.0908	141.3740	144.6598	147.9481	151.2398
17	122.0261	125.4889	128.9650	132.4242	135.8966	139.3721	142.8605	146.3320	149.8163	153.3035	156.7935	160.2863
18	128.8262	132.4868	136.1511	139.8169	143.4903	147.1651	150.8433	154.5249	158.2097	161.6977	165.5889	169.2832
19	135.5823	139.4400	143.3017	147.1674	151.0371	154.9106	158.7880	162.6690	166.5537	170.4420	174.3339	178.2292
20	142.2940	146.3490	150.4065	154.4694	158.5387	162.6083	166.6841	170.7640	174.8490	178.9360	183.0278	187.1236

n												
21	148.9611	153.2106	157.4651	161.7245	165.9887	170.2576	174.5312	178.8094	183.0920	187.3791	191.8705	196.9662
22	155.5831	160.0274	164.4771	168.9322	173.3926	177.8582	182.3289	186.8046	191.2853	195.7709	200.2612	204.7562
23	162.1599	166.7990	171.4422	176.0923	180.7481	185.4096	190.0768	194.7494	199.4275	204.1109	208.7996	213.4932
24	168.6909	173.5222	178.3600	183.2042	188.0548	192.9115	197.7744	202.6432	207.5180	212.3986	217.2848	222.1767
25	175.1759	180.1290	185.0877	190.2677	195.3122	200.3634	205.4213	210.4856	215.5564	220.6335	225.7168	230.6061
26	181.6146	186.8296	192.0522	197.2824	202.5200	207.7649	213.0170	218.2762	223.5422	228.8152	234.0948	239.3810
27	188.0065	193.4120	198.8259	204.2478	209.6778	215.1156	220.5611	226.0143	231.4750	236.9431	242.4184	247.9008
28	194.3514	199.9466	205.5507	211.1635	216.7850	222.4149	228.0532	233.6997	239.3542	245.0187	250.6870	256.3649
29	200.6488	206.4328	212.2263	218.0292	223.8414	229.6626	235.4928	241.3317	247.1794	253.0355	258.9001	264.7729
30	206.8965	212.8703	218.8524	224.8444	230.8464	236.8581	242.8799	248.9100	254.9600	260.9991	267.0572	273.1240
31	213.1000	219.2588	225.4284	231.6088	237.7997	244.0010	250.2125	256.4341	262.6656	268.9068	275.1577	281.4179
32	219.2530	225.5978	231.9641	238.3218	244.7008	251.0908	257.4917	263.9034	270.3256	276.7582	283.2011	289.6540
33	225.3572	231.8870	238.4290	244.9831	251.5493	258.1271	264.7166	271.3175	277.9696	284.5528	291.1968	297.8316
34	231.4122	238.1259	244.8527	251.5924	258.3447	265.1095	271.8866	278.6759	285.4770	292.2899	299.1144	305.9502
35	237.4175	244.3143	251.2248	258.1490	265.0966	272.0375	279.0790	285.9790	292.9674	299.9691	306.9831	314.0092
36	243.3729	250.4517	257.5450	264.6527	271.7746	278.9105	286.0602	293.2235	300.4001	307.5898	314.7926	322.0081
37	249.2760	256.5376	263.8127	271.1030	278.4082	285.7282	293.0628	300.4117	307.7747	315.1516	322.5421	329.9462
38	255.1323	262.5719	270.0276	277.4994	284.9870	292.4901	300.0096	307.5421	315.0906	322.6537	330.2312	337.8230
39	260.9355	268.5539	276.1893	283.8416	291.5104	299.1957	306.8970	314.6143	322.3473	330.0967	337.8593	345.6378
40	266.6873	274.4833	282.2973	290.1230	297.9781	305.8444	313.7277	321.6278	329.5442	337.4769	345.4257	353.3901
41	272.3672	280.3596	288.3512	296.3612	304.3896	312.4360	320.5001	328.5819	336.6809	344.7969	352.9298	361.0792
42	278.0348	286.1829	294.3507	302.5379	310.7443	318.9597	327.2137	335.4761	343.7567	352.0551	360.3712	368.7046
43	283.6298	291.9621	300.2951	308.6585	317.0419	325.4042	333.8680	342.3100	350.7711	359.2509	367.7491	376.2655
44	289.1717	297.6672	306.1842	314.7286	323.2819	331.8619	340.4624	349.0830	357.7235	366.3836	375.0630	383.7614
45	294.6602	303.3276	312.0175	320.7296	329.4637	338.2194	346.9964	355.7945	364.6134	373.4527	382.3122	391.1916
46	300.0948	308.9329	317.7945	326.6759	335.5869	344.5171	353.4636	362.4440	371.4402	380.4576	389.4962	398.5555
47	305.4752	314.4828	323.5148	332.5710	341.6510	350.7546	359.8813	368.9310	378.2032	387.3978	396.6143	405.8525
48	310.8010	319.9768	329.1780	338.4044	347.6556	356.9312	366.2311	375.5548	384.9030	394.2725	403.6659	413.1018
49	316.0717	325.4144	334.7835	344.1789	353.6000	363.0466	372.5183	382.0149	391.5360	401.0812	410.6503	420.2429
50	321.2869	330.7952	340.3310	349.8940	359.4838	369.1001	378.7425	388.4108	398.1044	407.8233	417.5669	427.3350

Table 7.7-1. (continued) 10-YEAR TERM Interest Rate

j	12.00	12.25	12.50	12.75	13.00	13.25	13.50	13.75	14.00	14.25	14.50	14.75
1	10.0000	10.2083	10.4167	10.6250	10.8333	11.0417	11.2500	11.4583	11.6667	11.8750	12.0833	12.2917
2	19.9665	20.3729	20.7894	21.2058	21.6223	22.0388	22.4553	22.8718	23.2883	23.7048	24.1214	24.5380
3	29.8691	30.4934	31.1176	31.7420	32.3663	32.9908	33.6153	34.2398	34.8644	35.4890	36.1137	36.7384
4	39.7374	40.5692	41.4010	42.2330	43.0650	43.8972	44.7296	45.5619	46.3944	47.2269	48.0596	48.8924
5	49.5609	50.5999	51.6390	52.6784	53.7719	54.7576	55.7975	56.8375	57.8877	58.9181	59.9686	60.9933
6	59.3392	60.5851	61.8312	63.0777	64.3244	65.5714	66.8187	68.0662	69.3139	70.5619	71.8101	73.0598
7	69.0717	70.5242	71.9771	73.4304	74.8841	76.3381	77.7925	79.2473	80.7024	82.1578	83.6136	85.0697
8	78.7582	80.4169	82.0762	83.7360	85.3964	87.0572	88.7185	90.3903	92.0425	93.7052	95.3684	97.0320
9	88.3990	90.2627	92.1281	93.9941	95.9608	97.7282	99.5961	101.4647	103.3339	105.2036	107.0740	108.9449
10	97.9907	100.0610	102.1321	104.2041	106.2768	108.3504	110.4248	112.4999	114.5758	116.6524	118.7298	120.8078
11	107.5359	109.8114	112.0879	114.3654	116.6440	118.9235	121.2040	123.4854	125.7678	128.0510	130.3351	132.6201
12	117.0331	119.5134	121.9949	124.4777	126.9517	129.4468	131.9331	134.4206	136.9091	139.3987	141.8894	144.3812
13	126.4818	129.1685	131.8527	134.5403	137.2294	139.9199	142.6117	145.3049	147.9993	150.6951	153.3921	156.0903
14	135.8815	138.7702	141.6606	144.5528	147.4466	150.3420	153.2391	156.1377	159.0378	161.9394	164.8425	167.7470
15	145.2317	148.3240	151.4188	154.5145	157.6127	160.7128	163.8147	166.9184	170.0239	173.1311	176.2400	179.3506
16	154.5319	157.8274	161.1251	164.4250	167.7272	171.0315	174.3390	177.6465	180.9670	184.2695	187.5839	190.9003
17	163.7817	167.2799	170.7805	174.2838	177.7996	181.2977	184.9083	188.3213	191.8365	195.3540	198.8737	202.3966
18	172.9805	176.6808	180.3841	184.0932	187.7991	191.5108	195.2252	198.9422	202.6618	206.3840	210.1086	213.8357
19	182.1278	186.0299	189.9352	193.8437	197.7554	201.6701	205.5879	209.5086	213.4283	217.3588	221.2880	225.2200
20	191.2232	195.3264	199.4333	203.5438	207.6578	211.7751	215.8858	220.0200	224.1472	228.2777	232.4113	236.5478

21	200.2660	204.5700	208.8779	213.1898	217.5057	221.8252	226.1496	230.4755	234.8061	239.1401	243.4776	247.8195
22	209.2558	213.7599	218.2684	222.7813	227.2995	231.8196	236.3453	240.8747	245.4081	249.9454	254.4464	259.0312
23	218.1900	222.8957	227.6043	232.3176	237.0356	241.7582	246.4853	251.2169	255.9527	260.6928	265.4370	270.1854
24	227.0740	231.9768	236.8849	241.7981	246.7165	251.6399	256.5682	261.5013	266.4392	271.3817	276.3287	281.2802
25	235.9015	241.0027	246.1097	251.2223	256.3405	261.4642	266.5932	271.7274	276.8668	282.0113	287.1607	292.3149
26	244.6737	249.9728	255.2781	260.5896	265.9071	271.2305	276.5597	281.8945	287.2350	292.5810	297.9323	303.2889
27	253.3302	258.8965	264.3896	269.8992	275.4155	280.9081	286.4669	292.0019	297.5430	303.0900	308.6428	314.2013
28	262.0504	267.7433	273.4435	279.1508	284.9651	290.5864	296.3144	302.0490	307.7901	313.5376	319.2914	325.0514
29	270.6537	276.5426	282.4392	288.3435	294.2554	300.1747	306.1012	312.0349	317.9756	323.9232	329.8775	335.8386
30	279.1996	285.2837	291.3762	297.4788	303.5857	309.7024	315.8269	321.9591	328.0986	334.2459	340.4002	346.5617
31	287.6875	293.9661	300.2537	306.5501	312.9552	319.1696	325.4307	331.8208	338.1590	344.5050	350.9598	357.2203
32	296.1167	302.5893	309.0713	315.5628	322.0635	328.5733	335.0919	341.6194	348.1554	354.6998	361.2525	367.8134
33	304.4088	311.1525	317.8283	324.5141	331.2097	337.9150	344.8298	351.3540	358.0872	364.8236	371.5906	378.3404
34	312.7972	319.6552	326.5240	333.4034	340.2933	347.1385	354.1037	361.0239	367.9638	374.8833	381.8422	388.8003
35	321.0471	328.0967	335.1578	342.2301	349.3136	356.4079	363.5129	370.6285	377.7544	384.8905	392.0365	399.1923
36	329.2361	336.4765	343.7290	350.9935	358.2698	365.5575	372.8566	380.1669	387.4881	394.8201	402.1627	409.5157
37	337.3635	344.7939	352.2371	359.6929	367.1612	374.6417	382.1342	389.6384	397.1543	404.6816	412.2200	419.7696
38	345.4287	353.0483	360.6813	368.3277	375.9873	383.6587	391.3448	399.0423	406.7521	414.4740	422.2076	429.9629
39	353.4311	361.2389	369.0610	376.8972	384.7472	392.6107	400.4877	408.3777	416.2907	424.1964	432.1246	440.0651
40	361.3701	369.3653	377.3756	385.4006	393.4402	401.4941	409.5621	417.6440	425.7394	433.8482	441.9702	450.1051
41	369.2449	377.4267	385.6242	393.8373	402.0657	410.3091	418.5673	426.8401	435.1273	443.4284	451.7435	460.0721
42	377.0551	385.4224	393.8063	402.2065	410.6228	419.0549	427.5026	435.9655	444.4435	452.9363	461.4436	469.9652
43	384.7998	393.3518	401.9212	410.5076	419.1110	427.7308	436.3670	445.0193	453.6873	462.3708	471.0698	479.7835
44	392.4796	401.2142	409.9681	418.7398	427.5238	436.3360	445.1599	454.0006	462.8578	471.7313	480.6207	489.5260
45	400.0906	409.0090	417.9463	426.9024	435.8770	444.8697	453.8804	462.9086	471.9541	481.0167	490.0960	499.1919
46	407.6354	416.7354	425.8652	435.0158	444.1535	453.3312	462.5276	471.7425	480.9754	490.2862	499.4945	508.7801
47	415.1120	424.3927	433.6940	443.0156	452.3578	461.7196	471.1009	480.5014	489.9208	499.3589	508.8153	518.2897
48	422.5200	431.9902	441.4620	450.9851	460.4893	470.0341	479.5592	489.1845	498.7895	508.4139	518.0574	527.7198
49	429.9696	439.4973	449.1584	458.8418	468.5471	478.2739	488.0219	497.7909	507.5804	517.3902	527.2200	537.0694
50	437.1271	446.9431	456.7826	466.6451	476.5304	486.4392	496.3680	506.3187	516.2928	526.2870	536.3020	546.3375

Table 7.7-1. (continued) 15-YEAR TERM Interest Rate

j	9.00	9.25	9.50	9.75	10.00	10.25	10.50	10.75	11.00	11.25	11.50	11.75
1	7.5000	7.7083	7.9167	8.1250	8.3333	8.5417	8.7500	8.9583	9.1667	9.3750	9.5833	9.7917
2	14.9902	15.3368	15.8133	16.2299	16.6466	17.0632	17.4798	17.8965	18.3132	18.7299	19.1466	19.5633
3	22.4404	23.0651	23.6899	24.3147	24.9395	25.5644	26.1893	26.8143	27.4393	28.0644	28.6895	29.3146
4	29.8805	30.7132	31.5461	32.3790	33.2120	34.0451	34.8783	35.7116	36.5450	37.3784	38.2219	39.0455
5	37.3003	38.3410	39.3818	40.4228	41.4639	42.5052	43.5466	44.5882	45.6299	46.6717	47.7944	48.7557
6	44.6997	45.9492	47.1969	48.4459	49.6950	50.9300	52.1940	53.4439	54.6939	55.9441	57.1944	58.4450
7	52.0786	53.5347	54.9912	56.4480	57.9052	59.3627	60.8204	62.2796	63.7368	65.1963	66.6542	68.1133
8	59.4366	61.1004	62.7645	64.4292	66.0942	67.7597	69.4255	71.0918	72.7584	74.4253	76.0926	77.7602
9	66.7738	68.6450	70.5167	72.3891	74.2819	76.1353	78.0092	79.8836	81.7585	83.6338	85.5096	87.3857
10	74.0900	76.1685	78.2477	80.3276	82.4082	84.4894	86.5713	88.6538	90.7368	92.6206	94.9048	96.9895
11	81.3850	83.8706	86.0571	88.2445	90.5327	92.8218	95.1116	97.4022	99.8935	101.9654	104.2781	106.5714
12	88.6586	91.1512	93.6449	96.1397	98.6354	101.1322	103.6299	106.1284	108.6279	111.1282	113.6293	116.1312
13	95.9107	98.6102	101.3109	104.0129	106.7161	109.4205	112.1259	114.8325	117.5401	120.2496	122.9582	125.6686
14	103.1411	106.0473	108.9550	111.8641	114.7746	117.6865	120.5997	123.5141	126.4297	129.3466	132.2645	135.1835
15	110.3497	113.4624	116.5768	119.6929	122.8107	125.9300	129.0508	132.1731	135.2367	138.4217	141.5490	144.6756
16	117.5363	120.8553	124.1764	127.4994	130.8242	134.1508	137.4791	140.8092	144.1408	147.4739	150.9096	154.1447
17	124.7007	128.2259	131.7534	135.2831	138.8149	142.3487	145.8845	149.4222	152.9617	156.5030	160.0460	163.5905
18	131.8428	135.5740	139.3078	143.0440	146.7827	150.5236	154.2667	158.0120	161.7593	165.5087	169.2599	173.0130
19	138.9623	142.8994	146.8939	150.7820	154.7273	158.6752	162.6256	166.5783	170.5334	174.4307	178.4502	182.4117
20	146.0592	150.2019	154.3477	158.4967	162.6486	166.8033	170.9608	175.1210	179.2837	183.4490	187.6166	191.7865

21	153.1332	157.4814	161.8330	166.1880	170.5463	174.9078	179.2723	183.6399	188.0101	192.3891	196.7589	201.1371
22	160.1843	164.7376	169.2948	173.8557	178.4203	182.9883	187.5557	192.1344	196.7122	201.2391	205.8768	210.4634
23	167.2121	171.9705	176.7330	181.4997	186.2703	191.0448	195.8230	200.6047	205.3899	210.1795	214.9708	219.7650
24	174.2166	179.1797	184.1475	189.1197	194.0965	199.0770	204.0618	209.0505	214.0430	219.0388	224.0388	229.0418
25	181.1975	186.3652	191.5379	196.7155	201.8979	207.0847	212.2760	217.4716	222.6712	227.8749	233.0823	238.2935
26	188.1548	193.5268	198.9043	204.2870	209.6749	215.0678	220.4654	225.8547	231.2747	236.6854	242.1006	247.5198
27	195.0081	200.6642	206.2462	211.8339	217.4272	223.0259	228.6297	234.2385	239.8522	245.4705	251.0333	256.7205
28	201.9974	207.7773	213.5636	219.3561	225.1546	230.9588	236.7687	242.5839	248.4044	254.2299	260.0603	265.8953
29	208.8824	214.8659	220.8563	226.8533	232.8568	238.8665	244.8822	250.9037	256.9308	262.9634	269.0012	275.0440
30	215.7430	221.9299	228.1241	234.3254	240.5336	246.7486	252.9699	259.1976	265.4312	271.6707	277.9159	284.1664
31	222.5780	228.9689	235.3667	241.7721	248.1849	254.6049	261.0318	267.4653	273.9054	280.3517	286.8040	293.2621
32	229.3901	235.9828	242.5840	249.1932	255.8104	262.4352	269.0674	275.7068	282.3530	289.0060	295.6654	302.3310
33	236.1763	242.9715	249.7757	256.5886	263.4099	270.2393	277.0766	283.9216	290.7739	297.6334	304.4997	311.3727
34	242.9373	249.9348	256.9417	263.9579	270.9831	278.0170	285.0592	292.1096	299.1678	306.2336	313.3068	320.3870
35	249.6730	256.8723	264.0818	271.3011	278.5299	285.7679	293.0149	300.2705	307.5344	314.8064	322.0863	329.3736
36	256.3831	263.7841	271.1968	278.6179	286.0501	293.4920	300.9435	308.4041	315.8736	323.3516	330.8380	338.3323
37	263.0674	270.6697	278.2834	285.9080	293.5433	301.1690	308.8447	316.5102	324.1850	331.8689	339.5616	347.2627
38	269.7259	277.5281	285.3444	293.1713	301.0096	308.8587	316.7184	324.5884	332.4044	340.3580	348.2568	356.1647
39	276.3581	284.3621	292.3787	300.4075	308.4483	316.5007	324.5642	332.6366	340.7235	348.8186	356.9235	365.0378
40	282.9641	291.1683	299.3859	307.6165	315.8596	324.1149	332.3820	340.6606	348.9602	357.2505	365.5612	373.8819
41	289.5435	297.9478	306.3660	314.7979	323.2485	331.7010	340.1714	348.6539	357.1490	365.6534	374.1698	382.6967
42	296.0962	304.7001	313.3167	321.9617	330.5985	339.2569	347.5323	356.6185	365.3168	374.0271	382.7489	391.4818
43	302.6220	311.4252	320.2438	329.0774	337.9257	346.7882	355.6644	364.5539	373.4563	382.3713	391.2983	400.2370
44	309.1207	318.1227	327.1410	336.1751	345.2245	354.2887	363.3674	372.4601	381.5663	390.6856	399.8176	408.9619
45	315.5920	324.7926	334.0101	343.2443	352.4944	361.7602	371.0411	380.3366	389.6464	398.9699	408.3067	417.6564
46	322.0358	331.4345	340.8510	350.2848	359.7393	369.2004	378.6852	388.1833	397.6963	407.2660	416.7651	426.3200
47	328.4518	338.0483	347.6634	357.2965	366.9473	376.6151	386.2994	395.9999	405.7159	415.4470	425.1927	434.9525
48	334.8399	344.6337	354.4470	364.2791	374.1296	383.9890	393.8836	403.7881	413.7048	423.6393	433.5891	443.5536
49	341.1999	351.1906	361.2016	371.2324	381.2823	391.3508	401.4674	411.5416	421.6627	431.8003	441.9640	452.1230
50	347.5314	357.7187	367.9271	378.1560	388.4050	398.6734	408.9606	419.2661	429.5894	439.9299	450.2871	460.6604

Table 7.7-1. (continued) 15-YEAR TERM Interest Rate

j	12.00	12.25	12.50	12.75	13.00	13.25	13.50	13.75	14.00	14.25	14.50	14.75
1	10.0000	10.2083	10.4167	10.6250	10.8333	11.0417	11.2500	11.4583	11.6667	11.8750	12.0833	12.2917
2	19.9600	20.3567	20.8135	21.2302	21.6470	22.0637	22.4805	22.8973	23.3141	23.7309	24.1477	24.5645
3	29.8397	30.5649	31.1301	31.8154	32.4407	33.0660	33.6913	34.3166	34.9420	35.5674	36.1928	36.8182
4	39.8791	40.7128	41.5465	42.3804	43.2142	44.0482	44.8821	45.7161	46.5502	47.3843	48.2185	49.0526
5	49.7978	50.8401	51.8824	52.9249	53.9675	55.0101	56.0528	57.0956	58.1385	59.1814	60.2244	61.2675
6	59.6957	60.9466	62.1976	63.4488	64.7001	65.9515	67.2031	68.4548	69.7066	70.9585	72.2105	73.4626
7	69.5728	71.0321	72.4918	73.9518	75.4119	76.8723	78.3328	79.7934	81.2543	82.7153	84.1764	85.6377
8	79.4282	81.0364	82.7649	84.4337	86.1028	87.7720	89.4416	91.1113	92.7813	94.4515	96.1219	97.7924
9	89.2623	91.1193	93.0166	94.8943	96.7723	98.6507	100.5293	102.4083	104.2875	106.1669	108.0467	109.9267
10	99.0748	101.1605	103.2467	105.3333	107.4204	109.5079	111.5957	113.6839	115.7725	117.8614	119.9506	122.0401
11	108.8654	111.1599	113.4550	115.7506	118.0468	120.3434	122.6406	124.9381	127.2361	129.5345	131.8333	134.1325
12	118.6338	121.1372	123.6412	126.1459	128.6512	131.1571	133.6636	136.1706	138.6782	141.1862	143.6947	146.2036
13	128.3800	131.0922	133.8052	136.5189	139.2335	141.9487	144.6646	147.3811	150.0983	152.8160	155.5344	158.2532
14	138.1036	141.0246	143.9466	146.8696	149.7933	152.7179	155.6433	158.5694	161.4963	164.4239	167.3521	170.2809
15	147.8044	150.9343	154.0653	157.1973	160.3304	163.4644	166.5994	169.7352	172.8719	176.0094	179.1476	182.2866
16	157.4821	160.8209	164.1610	167.5022	170.8446	174.1882	177.5327	180.8783	184.2249	187.5723	190.9207	194.2699
17	167.1367	170.6844	174.2334	177.7839	181.3357	184.8887	188.4430	191.9984	195.5549	199.1125	202.6710	206.2305
18	176.7678	180.5243	184.2824	188.0421	191.8033	195.5660	199.3300	203.0952	206.8618	210.6295	214.3983	218.1682
19	186.3752	190.3405	194.3077	198.2767	202.2473	206.2196	210.1933	214.1685	218.1452	222.1231	226.1023	230.0828
20	195.9596	200.1328	204.3091	208.4873	212.6674	216.8493	221.0328	225.2180	229.4048	233.5931	237.7828	241.9738

21	205.5178	209.9009	214.2862	218.6737	223.0693	227.4548	231.8482	236.2435	240.6405	245.0391	249.4393	253.8411
22	215.0527	219.6445	224.2389	228.8356	233.4347	238.0359	242.6393	247.2446	251.8519	256.4609	261.0718	265.6843
23	224.5628	229.3635	234.1668	238.9728	243.7814	248.5923	253.4096	258.2211	263.0387	267.8582	272.6798	277.5031
24	234.0481	239.0574	244.0698	249.0851	254.1031	259.1238	264.1470	269.1727	274.2006	279.2308	284.2630	289.2973
25	243.5081	248.7262	253.9476	259.1721	264.3996	269.6309	274.8632	280.0990	285.3374	290.5782	295.8212	301.0665
26	252.9428	258.3696	263.7996	269.2335	274.6706	280.1107	285.5539	290.9999	296.4488	301.9002	307.3541	312.8105
27	262.3518	267.9871	273.6263	279.2692	284.9158	290.5656	296.2188	301.8751	307.5344	313.1565	318.8614	324.5289
28	271.7348	277.5788	283.4258	289.2789	295.1348	300.9945	306.8576	312.7242	318.5940	324.4668	330.3427	336.2214
29	281.0917	287.1441	293.2010	299.2622	305.3276	311.3969	317.4701	323.5469	329.6272	335.7109	341.7907	347.8876
30	290.4221	296.6830	302.9496	309.2189	315.4936	321.7727	328.0558	334.3429	340.6338	346.9282	353.2261	359.5274
31	299.7259	306.1960	312.6693	319.1486	325.6328	332.1215	338.6146	345.1120	351.6134	358.1187	364.6277	371.1402
32	309.0026	315.6800	322.3630	329.0512	335.7447	342.4431	349.1462	355.8538	362.5658	369.2819	376.0020	382.7259
33	318.2521	325.1377	332.0292	338.9264	345.8291	352.7371	359.6501	366.5690	373.4965	380.4175	387.3488	394.2841
34	327.4741	334.5677	341.6677	348.7737	355.8857	363.0032	370.1262	377.2543	384.3874	391.5252	398.6676	405.8144
35	336.6682	343.9699	351.2782	358.5930	365.9141	373.2412	380.5740	387.9124	395.2642	402.6047	409.9682	417.3165
36	345.8343	353.3438	360.8604	368.3839	375.9142	383.4507	390.9933	398.5419	406.0360	413.6556	421.2203	428.7900
37	354.9721	362.6893	370.4141	378.1462	385.8854	393.6314	401.3838	409.1425	416.9072	424.6776	432.4535	440.2346
38	364.0812	372.0060	379.9389	387.8795	395.8277	403.7830	411.7451	419.7139	427.6891	435.6703	443.6573	451.6500
39	373.1613	381.2937	389.4345	397.5836	405.7406	413.9051	422.0770	430.2558	438.4414	446.6334	454.8316	463.0358
40	382.2123	390.5520	398.9007	407.2580	415.6238	423.9975	432.3730	440.7678	449.1638	457.5666	465.9759	474.3915
41	391.2337	399.7807	408.3371	416.9026	425.4770	434.0598	442.6508	451.2496	459.8559	468.4694	477.0899	485.7169
42	400.2254	408.9794	417.7434	426.5169	435.2899	444.0917	452.8921	461.7008	470.5174	479.3416	488.1731	497.0116
43	409.1669	418.1478	427.1192	436.1007	445.0921	454.0928	463.1026	472.1211	481.1479	490.1827	499.2253	508.2752
44	418.1181	427.2857	436.4644	445.6537	454.8533	464.0629	473.2819	482.5101	491.7479	500.9925	510.2460	519.5073
45	427.0185	436.3927	445.7786	455.1754	464.5833	474.0014	483.4236	492.8674	502.3145	511.7704	521.2349	530.7076
46	435.8879	445.4686	455.0612	464.6657	474.2815	483.9083	493.5455	503.1928	512.8499	522.5162	532.1916	541.8756
47	444.7261	454.5128	464.3123	474.1241	483.9478	493.7829	503.6291	513.4858	523.3528	533.2295	543.1156	553.0109
48	453.5325	463.5253	473.5313	483.5502	493.5817	503.6800	513.6800	523.7461	533.8099	543.9098	554.0067	564.1131
49	462.3070	472.5065	482.7180	492.9439	503.1829	513.4344	523.7038	533.9732	544.2587	554.5569	564.8644	575.1819
50	471.0493	481.4533	491.6720	502.3047	512.7511	523.2105	533.6826	544.1669	554.6629	565.1702	575.6883	586.2168

Table 7.7-1. (continued) 20-YEAR TERM Interest Rate

J	9.00	9.25	9.50	9.75	10.00	10.25	10.50	10.75	11.00	11.25	11.50	11.75
1	7.5000	7.7083	7.9167	8.1250	8.3333	8.5417	8.7500	8.9583	9.1667	9.3750	9.5833	9.7917
2	14.9888	15.4055	15.8222	16.2389	16.6557	17.0724	17.4892	17.9060	18.3227	18.7395	19.1563	19.5731
3	22.4662	23.0914	23.7165	24.3418	24.9670	25.5822	26.2175	26.8428	27.4681	28.0935	28.7188	29.3442
4	29.5823	30.7659	31.5996	32.4333	33.2671	34.1010	34.9348	35.7688	36.6027	37.4337	38.2708	39.1048
5	37.3369	38.4290	39.4712	40.5136	41.5560	42.5985	43.6411	44.6837	45.7265	46.7692	47.8121	48.8550
6	44.8299	46.0806	47.3314	48.5824	49.8335	51.0848	52.3362	53.5876	54.8392	56.0909	57.3426	58.5944
7	52.2612	53.7205	55.1800	56.6397	58.0996	59.5597	61.0199	62.4803	63.9409	65.4015	66.8623	68.3232
8	59.6908	61.3488	63.0170	64.6855	66.3542	68.0232	69.6924	71.3618	73.0313	74.7011	76.3710	78.0410
9	67.0086	68.9652	70.8422	72.7195	74.5972	76.4751	78.3533	80.2318	82.1105	83.9894	85.8696	87.7479
10	74.4844	76.5698	78.6555	80.7417	82.8284	84.9153	87.0027	89.0903	91.1783	93.2655	95.3550	97.4438
11	81.8683	84.1623	86.4570	88.7521	91.0477	93.3438	95.6404	97.9373	100.2346	102.5322	104.8302	107.1285
12	89.2400	91.7428	94.2463	96.7505	99.2552	101.7605	104.2663	106.7726	109.2793	111.7864	114.2940	116.8019
13	96.5996	99.3112	102.0236	104.7368	107.4506	110.1652	112.8803	115.5560	118.3123	121.0290	123.7462	126.4639
14	103.9468	106.8673	109.7896	112.7109	115.6340	118.5578	121.4823	124.4076	127.3334	130.2599	133.1869	136.1143
15	111.2817	114.4110	117.5414	120.6727	123.8051	126.9383	130.0723	133.2071	136.3427	139.4789	142.6158	145.7532
16	118.6041	121.9423	125.2817	128.6222	131.9638	135.3065	138.6501	141.9946	145.3399	148.6860	152.0329	155.3803
17	125.9140	129.4611	133.0094	136.5592	140.1102	143.6623	147.2155	150.7698	154.3250	157.8811	161.4380	164.9956
18	133.2112	136.9671	140.7246	144.4886	148.2440	152.0056	155.7696	159.5326	163.2978	167.0639	170.6310	174.5990
19	140.4956	144.4605	148.4270	152.3953	156.3851	160.3364	164.3091	168.2831	172.2582	176.2345	180.2119	184.1902
20	147.7673	151.9410	156.1167	160.2942	164.4735	168.6545	172.8370	177.0209	181.2062	185.3928	189.5605	193.7693

21	155.0259	159.4096	163.7934	168.1903	172.5691	176.9598	181.3521	185.7461	190.1416	194.5385	198.9366	203.3360
22	162.2715	166.6631	171.4571	176.0533	180.8517	185.2522	189.8545	194.4585	199.0643	203.8715	208.2803	212.8903
23	169.5040	174.3045	179.1077	183.9133	188.7213	193.5315	198.3448	203.1615	207.9741	212.7919	217.6112	222.4320
24	176.7333	181.7327	186.7450	191.7600	196.7777	201.7977	206.8201	211.8445	216.8710	221.9933	226.9294	231.9611
25	183.9292	189.1475	194.3690	199.5935	204.8332	210.0517	215.2831	220.5179	225.7548	230.9938	236.2347	241.4773
26	191.1217	196.5489	201.9796	207.4135	212.8505	218.2904	223.7329	229.1825	234.6255	240.0752	245.5269	250.9906
27	198.3006	203.9368	209.5766	215.2200	220.8667	226.5165	232.1633	237.8248	243.4828	249.1433	254.6061	260.4709
28	205.4659	211.3110	217.1600	223.0129	228.8693	234.7281	240.5921	246.4580	252.3268	258.1981	264.0719	269.9479
29	212.6175	218.6714	224.7296	230.7920	236.8582	242.9280	249.0012	255.0777	261.1571	267.2394	273.3243	279.4117
30	219.7552	226.0180	232.2854	238.5572	244.8332	251.1130	257.3966	263.6836	269.9739	276.2671	282.5632	288.8620
31	226.8790	233.3506	239.8272	246.0456	252.7942	259.2842	265.7781	272.2757	278.7768	285.2811	291.7885	298.2997
32	233.9887	240.6691	247.3549	254.0456	260.7412	267.4412	274.1455	280.8638	287.5657	294.2812	300.9999	307.7217
33	241.0843	247.9735	254.8684	261.7686	268.6740	275.5841	282.4988	289.4178	296.3407	303.2673	310.1975	317.1308
34	248.1656	255.2636	262.3675	269.4773	276.5925	283.7128	290.8379	297.9675	305.1014	312.2393	319.3909	326.5260
35	255.2326	262.5398	269.8523	277.1715	284.4965	291.8269	299.1625	306.5029	313.8479	321.1971	328.5502	335.9071
36	262.2850	269.8004	277.3225	284.8612	292.3860	299.9266	307.4726	315.0239	322.5799	330.1404	337.7052	345.2739
37	269.3229	277.0469	284.7781	292.5162	300.2608	308.0116	315.7681	323.5302	331.2973	339.0692	346.8457	354.6263
38	276.3461	284.2796	292.2189	300.1864	308.1208	316.0818	324.0488	332.0217	340.0000	347.9834	355.9716	363.9641
39	283.3545	291.4966	299.6448	307.8017	315.5659	324.1371	332.3147	340.4964	348.6879	356.8828	365.0822	373.2873
40	290.3479	298.6975	307.0557	315.4220	323.7960	332.1773	340.5654	348.9601	357.3608	365.7672	374.1790	382.5957
41	297.3264	305.8644	314.4515	323.0271	331.6109	340.2024	348.8011	357.4066	366.0186	374.6366	383.2602	391.8891
42	304.2897	313.0561	321.8320	330.6619	339.4105	348.2161	357.0214	365.6379	374.4611	383.4907	392.3263	401.1674
43	311.2377	320.2124	329.1972	338.1914	347.1947	356.2065	365.2263	374.2537	383.2882	392.3296	401.3770	410.4304
44	318.1704	327.3533	336.5468	345.7503	354.9633	364.1852	373.4156	382.6540	391.8998	401.1528	410.4123	419.6780
45	325.0875	334.4787	343.8809	353.2936	362.7163	372.1483	381.5892	391.0386	400.4968	409.9604	419.4320	428.9100
46	331.9891	341.5684	351.1992	360.8211	370.4534	380.0965	389.7470	399.4073	409.0759	418.4359	428.4359	438.1264
47	338.8750	348.6623	358.5017	368.3327	378.1746	388.0268	397.8888	407.7601	417.6400	427.5281	437.4239	447.3268
48	345.7450	355.7603	365.7882	375.8282	385.8797	395.9420	406.0145	416.0967	426.1880	436.3958	446.3958	456.5513
49	352.5991	362.8222	373.0586	383.3076	393.5686	403.8409	414.1239	424.4171	434.7198	445.0314	455.3515	465.6795
50	359.4371	369.8680	380.3128	390.7707	401.2412	411.7235	422.2170	432.7211	443.2351	453.7586	464.2809	474.6314

Table 7.7-1. (continued) 20-YEAR TERM Interest Rate

j	12.00	12.25	12.50	12.75	13.00	13.25	13.50	13.75	14.00	14.25	14.50	14.75
1	10.0000	10.2083	10.4167	10.6250	10.8333	11.0417	11.2500	11.4583	11.6667	11.8750	12.0833	12.2917
2	19.9899	20.4067	20.8235	21.2403	21.6571	22.0739	22.4907	22.9075	23.3244	23.7412	24.1590	24.5748
3	29.9696	30.5960	31.2204	31.8458	32.4712	33.0967	33.7221	34.3475	34.9730	35.5985	36.2239	36.8494
4	39.9389	40.7731	41.6072	42.4414	43.2756	44.1098	44.9440	45.7782	46.6124	47.4467	48.2810	49.1152
5	49.8979	50.9409	51.9839	53.0269	54.0700	55.1131	56.1563	57.1994	58.2426	59.2858	60.3290	61.3722
6	59.8463	61.0983	62.3503	63.6024	64.8545	66.1067	67.3589	68.6111	69.8634	71.1157	72.3680	73.6203
7	69.7641	71.2452	72.7064	74.1676	75.6289	77.0903	78.5517	80.0132	81.4747	82.9362	84.3978	85.8594
8	79.7712	81.3815	83.0520	84.7225	86.3931	88.0638	89.7346	91.4054	93.0763	94.7473	96.4182	98.0893
9	89.6275	91.5071	93.3870	95.2669	97.1470	99.0272	100.9075	102.7878	104.6683	106.5488	108.4293	110.3099
10	99.5828	101.6219	103.7113	105.6008	107.8905	109.9603	112.0702	114.1602	116.2504	118.3406	120.4308	122.5211
11	109.4270	111.7258	114.0248	116.3240	118.6234	120.9230	123.2227	125.5225	127.8225	130.1226	132.4227	134.7229
12	119.3101	121.8186	124.3274	126.8364	129.3457	131.8552	134.3648	136.8746	139.3846	141.8946	144.4048	146.9151
13	129.1819	131.9003	134.6190	137.3380	140.0572	142.7768	145.4965	148.2164	150.9365	153.6567	156.3770	159.0975
14	139.0423	141.9706	144.8994	147.8285	150.7579	153.6876	156.6175	159.5477	162.4781	165.4086	168.3393	171.2701
15	148.8912	152.0296	155.1685	158.3079	161.4475	164.5876	167.7279	170.8684	174.0092	177.1502	180.2914	183.4327
16	158.7285	162.0771	165.4263	168.7760	172.1261	175.4765	178.8274	182.1785	185.5298	188.8814	192.2332	195.5852
17	168.5540	172.1130	175.6726	179.2327	182.7934	186.3544	189.9159	193.4777	197.0398	200.6021	204.1647	207.7275
18	178.3677	182.1372	185.9073	189.6780	193.4493	197.2211	200.9933	204.7660	208.5389	212.3122	216.0857	219.8594
19	188.1694	192.1495	196.1302	200.1117	204.0938	208.0766	212.0596	216.0432	220.0271	224.0115	227.9961	231.9809
20	197.9580	202.1498	206.3413	210.5336	214.7266	218.9203	223.1145	227.3092	231.5043	235.6998	239.8957	244.0918

21	207.7365	212.1380	216.5404	220.9437	225.3478	229.7525	234.1579	238.5639	242.9703	247.3772	251.7844	256.1920
22	217.5016	222.1140	226.7274	231.3418	235.9670	240.5737	245.1898	249.8071	254.4250	259.0434	263.6622	268.2813
23	227.2542	232.0776	236.9022	241.7277	246.5543	251.3817	256.2099	261.0398	265.9683	270.6963	275.5288	280.3536
24	236.9942	242.0288	247.0645	252.1015	257.1396	262.1784	267.2182	272.2597	277.2999	282.3417	287.3841	292.4268
25	246.7216	251.9673	257.2144	262.4628	267.7124	272.9630	278.2145	283.4668	288.7199	293.9737	299.2290	304.4828
26	256.4361	261.8931	267.3517	272.8817	278.2729	283.7353	289.1997	294.6629	300.1280	305.5539	311.0603	316.5273
27	266.1376	271.8061	277.4763	283.1479	288.8209	294.4962	300.1706	305.8469	311.5242	317.2022	322.8810	328.5603
28	275.8260	281.7061	287.5879	293.4713	299.3563	305.2426	311.1301	317.0187	322.9082	328.7996	334.6896	340.5818
29	285.5013	291.5929	297.6965	303.7819	309.8789	315.9773	322.0771	328.1790	334.2900	340.3829	346.4866	352.5910
30	295.1631	301.4665	307.7720	314.0794	320.3885	326.6992	333.0114	339.3248	345.6393	351.9548	358.2713	364.5886
31	304.8115	311.3267	317.8442	324.3637	330.8851	337.4082	343.9329	350.4589	356.9961	363.5145	370.0438	376.5739
32	314.4462	321.1734	327.9030	334.6347	341.3686	348.1041	354.4841	361.5801	368.8302	375.0615	381.9038	388.5471
33	324.0672	331.0064	337.9481	344.8922	351.8385	358.7368	365.7368	372.6884	379.6415	386.5968	393.5513	400.5078
34	333.6743	340.8256	347.9796	355.1362	362.2961	369.4561	376.6190	383.7836	390.9498	398.1173	405.2860	412.4559
35	343.2674	350.6308	357.9972	365.3663	372.7380	380.1118	387.4877	394.8655	402.2449	409.8258	417.0079	424.3913
36	352.8462	360.4220	368.0004	375.5826	383.1671	390.7533	398.3429	405.9339	413.5267	421.1210	428.7168	436.3138
37	362.4108	370.1989	377.9904	385.7849	393.5822	401.3821	409.1844	416.9888	424.7950	432.6030	440.4124	448.2232
38	371.9609	379.9614	387.9655	396.9729	403.9833	411.9964	420.0120	428.0299	436.0498	444.0715	452.0948	460.1195
39	381.4563	389.7095	397.9263	406.1466	414.3701	422.5966	430.8256	439.0571	447.2908	455.5263	463.7636	472.0024
40	391.0171	399.4428	407.6725	416.3058	424.7428	433.1824	441.6251	450.0703	458.5178	466.9674	475.4187	483.8718
41	400.5229	409.1613	417.8039	426.4503	435.1005	443.7538	452.4102	461.0692	469.7307	478.3944	487.0601	495.7275
42	410.0137	418.8648	427.7204	436.5801	445.4436	454.3106	463.1808	472.0538	480.9294	489.8074	498.6874	507.5693
43	419.4893	428.5532	437.6219	446.6749	455.7719	464.8526	473.9367	483.0238	492.1137	501.2060	510.3005	519.3971
44	428.9496	438.2263	447.5081	456.7945	466.0852	475.3797	484.6778	493.9791	503.2833	512.5902	521.8993	531.2106
45	438.3942	447.8840	457.3790	466.8789	476.3833	485.8917	495.4039	504.9196	514.4382	523.9597	533.4836	543.0098
46	447.8232	457.5261	467.2344	476.9478	486.6660	496.3885	506.1149	515.8449	525.5782	535.3144	545.0532	554.7944
47	457.2365	467.1524	477.0387	487.0001	496.9332	506.8698	516.8105	526.7551	536.7031	546.6541	556.6080	566.5643
48	466.6337	476.7628	487.0101	497.0387	507.1847	517.3355	527.4906	537.6498	547.8126	557.9787	568.1477	578.3193
49	476.0149	486.8979	496.9857	507.0603	517.4203	527.7854	538.1551	548.5290	558.9071	569.2879	579.6721	590.0592
50	485.3797	495.8352	506.4974	517.0657	527.6400	538.2194	548.8037	559.3924	569.9852	580.5815	591.1812	601.7888

Table 7.7-1. (continued) 25-YEAR TERM Interest Rate

J	8.00	9.25	9.50	9.75	10.00	10.25	10.50	10.75	11.00	11.25	11.50	11.75
1	7.5000	7.7083	7.9167	8.1250	8.3333	8.5417	8.7500	8.9583	9.1667	9.3750	9.5833	9.7917
2	14.9933	15.4101	15.8268	16.2438	16.6604	17.0072	17.4389	17.9107	18.3275	18.7443	19.1611	19.5779
3	22.4799	23.1052	23.7305	24.3558	24.9811	25.6064	26.2318	26.8571	27.4825	28.1079	28.7332	29.3566
4	29.9657	30.7988	31.6275	32.4615	33.2964	34.1294	34.9835	35.7975	36.6316	37.4656	38.2987	39.1338
5	37.4328	38.4752	39.5178	40.5606	41.6033	42.6461	43.6889	44.7318	45.7746	46.8175	47.8604	48.9033
6	44.8966	46.1501	47.4016	48.6531	49.9047	51.1564	52.4081	53.6599	54.9117	56.1635	57.4154	58.6672
7	52.3577	53.8181	55.2785	56.7390	58.1996	59.6603	61.1210	62.5818	64.0426	65.5035	66.9644	68.4254
8	59.8098	61.4791	63.1486	64.8182	66.4878	68.1576	69.8275	71.4975	73.1675	74.8375	76.5076	78.1778
9	67.2549	69.1333	71.0118	72.8906	74.7694	76.6484	78.5276	80.4068	82.2961	84.1654	86.0449	87.9243
10	74.6928	76.7804	78.8862	80.8562	83.0448	85.1327	87.2211	89.3097	91.3964	93.4672	95.5761	97.6650
11	82.1237	84.4205	86.7175	89.0148	91.3124	93.6102	95.9092	98.2063	100.5045	102.6028	105.1013	107.3998
12	89.5472	92.0534	94.5599	97.0667	99.5737	102.0811	104.5886	107.0963	109.6042	112.1122	114.6203	117.1285
13	96.9636	99.6791	102.3951	105.1115	107.8282	110.5451	113.2623	115.9798	118.6974	121.4152	124.1331	126.8511
14	104.3726	107.2977	110.2232	113.1492	116.0756	119.0024	121.9294	124.8567	127.7842	130.7119	133.6397	136.5677
15	111.7742	114.9088	118.0442	121.1799	124.3161	127.4527	130.5896	133.7269	136.8644	140.0021	143.1400	146.2780
16	119.1684	122.5128	125.8678	129.2034	132.5496	135.8961	139.2431	142.5904	145.9390	149.2858	152.6339	155.9821
17	126.5552	130.1093	133.6642	137.2197	140.7758	144.3325	147.8896	151.4471	155.0049	158.5630	162.1214	165.6900
18	133.9343	137.6983	141.4632	145.2287	148.9950	152.7618	156.5291	160.2969	164.0651	167.8336	171.6024	175.3714
19	141.3059	145.2798	149.2547	153.2304	157.2069	161.1840	165.1617	169.1399	173.1185	177.0975	181.0768	185.0564
20	148.6699	152.8538	157.0388	161.1247	165.4415	169.5590	173.7871	177.9759	182.1651	186.3547	190.5447	194.7349

21	156.0261	160.4202	164.8154	169.2116	173.6088	178.0067	182.4055	186.8048	191.2047	195.6051	200.0058	204.4069
22	163.3746	167.9788	172.5843	177.1909	181.7996	186.4072	191.0166	195.6287	200.2374	204.8486	209.4602	214.0722
23	170.7152	175.5297	180.3456	185.1627	189.9810	194.8004	199.6204	204.4414	209.2830	214.0852	218.9079	223.7309
24	178.0490	183.0728	188.0991	193.1268	198.1558	203.1859	208.2169	213.2489	218.2815	223.3148	228.3496	233.3828
25	185.3728	190.6090	195.8449	201.0833	206.3230	211.5640	216.8060	222.0490	227.2928	232.5373	237.7824	243.0279
26	192.6896	198.1353	203.5828	209.0318	214.4826	219.9346	225.3877	230.8419	236.2969	241.7527	247.2092	252.6661
27	199.9983	205.6546	211.3128	216.9728	222.6344	228.2975	233.9618	239.6273	245.2937	250.9609	256.6289	262.2974
28	207.2989	213.1658	219.0348	224.9058	230.7785	236.6527	242.5284	248.4052	254.2831	260.1619	266.0415	271.9016
29	214.5913	220.6688	226.7488	232.8308	238.9147	245.0002	251.0872	257.1756	263.2651	269.3555	275.4468	281.5388
30	221.8755	228.1639	234.4547	240.7478	247.0429	253.3399	259.6384	265.9384	272.2395	278.5418	284.8449	291.1488
31	229.1514	235.6506	242.1524	248.6567	255.1632	261.6716	268.1818	274.6934	281.2064	287.7206	294.2357	300.7516
32	236.4189	243.1290	249.8420	256.5575	263.2754	269.9954	276.7173	283.4408	290.1657	296.8918	303.6130	310.3471
33	243.6780	250.5990	257.5232	264.4501	271.3795	278.3112	285.2448	292.1902	299.1172	306.0555	312.9948	319.9352
34	250.9896	258.0607	265.1360	272.3344	279.4754	286.6188	293.7644	300.9118	308.0609	315.2114	322.3631	329.5158
35	258.1706	265.5138	272.8605	280.2103	287.5631	294.9163	302.2759	309.6355	316.9968	324.3596	331.7238	339.0890
36	265.4040	272.9683	280.5164	288.0779	295.6424	303.2096	310.7792	318.3511	325.9247	333.5000	341.0767	348.6546
37	272.6287	280.3943	288.1763	295.9369	303.7133	311.4925	319.2744	327.0585	334.8447	342.6325	350.7219	358.7827
38	279.8446	287.8015	295.8026	303.7874	311.7757	319.7671	327.7612	335.7578	343.7565	351.7571	359.7592	367.7627
39	287.0517	295.2400	303.4326	311.6233	319.8287	328.0332	336.2398	344.4489	352.6602	360.8736	369.0866	377.3050
40	294.2500	302.6496	311.0539	319.4625	327.8750	336.2908	344.7098	353.1316	361.5557	369.9819	378.4100	386.8495
41	301.4392	310.0503	318.6664	327.2869	335.9116	344.5399	353.1714	361.8059	370.4429	379.0821	387.7233	396.3660
42	308.6196	317.4421	326.2700	335.1025	343.9394	352.7802	361.6244	370.4741	379.3217	388.1740	397.0284	405.8045
43	315.7907	324.8249	333.8646	342.9096	351.9585	361.0118	370.0687	379.1290	388.1920	397.2576	406.3253	415.3948
44	322.9527	332.1985	341.4501	350.7070	359.9685	369.2346	378.5044	387.7704	397.0539	406.3327	415.6139	424.8870
45	330.1055	339.5630	349.0265	358.4966	367.9698	377.4485	386.9312	396.4175	405.9071	415.3994	424.8941	434.3908
46	337.2490	346.9182	356.5938	366.2752	375.9619	385.6534	395.3491	405.0487	414.7516	424.4574	434.1658	443.8763
47	344.3832	354.2641	364.1518	374.0456	383.9449	393.8493	403.7581	413.6709	423.5873	433.5068	443.4290	453.3534
48	351.5079	361.6006	371.7004	381.8066	391.9187	402.0360	412.1580	422.2843	432.4142	442.5474	452.6835	462.8219
49	358.6231	368.9277	379.2397	389.5584	399.8832	410.2136	420.5488	430.8886	441.2322	451.5792	461.9293	472.2818
50	365.7287	376.2452	386.7695	397.3007	407.8394	418.3818	428.9305	439.4858	450.0411	460.6021	471.1663	481.7330

Table 7.7-1. (continued) 25-YEAR TERM Interest Rate

J	12.00	12.25	12.50	12.75	13.00	13.25	13.50	13.75	14.00	14.25	14.50	14.75
1	10.0000	10.2083	10.4167	10.6250	10.8333	11.0417	11.2500	11.4583	11.6667	11.8750	12.0833	12.2917
2	19.9947	20.4115	20.8283	21.2451	21.6618	22.0786	22.4954	22.9122	23.3290	23.7458	24.1626	24.5794
3	29.9840	30.6094	31.2347	31.8601	32.4855	33.1109	33.7362	34.3616	34.9870	35.6123	36.2377	36.8630
4	39.9678	40.8019	41.6360	42.4701	43.3042	44.1383	44.9724	45.8064	46.6405	47.4746	48.3086	49.1426
5	49.9462	50.9892	52.0321	53.0750	54.1179	55.1608	56.2038	57.2467	58.2896	59.3324	60.3753	61.4181
6	59.9191	61.1710	62.4229	63.6747	64.9266	66.1785	67.4304	68.6822	69.9341	71.1859	72.4377	73.6895
7	69.8863	71.3473	72.8083	74.2698	75.7302	77.1912	78.6522	80.1131	81.5740	83.0349	84.4957	85.9566
8	79.8479	81.5181	83.1883	84.8595	86.5287	88.1989	89.8690	91.5392	93.2093	94.8794	96.5494	98.2194
9	89.8038	91.6834	93.5629	95.4424	97.3220	99.2015	101.0810	102.9604	104.8399	106.7193	108.5986	110.4779
10	99.7540	101.8430	103.9320	106.0210	108.1100	110.1990	112.2879	114.3769	116.4657	118.5545	120.6433	122.7320
11	109.6983	111.9969	114.2965	116.5541	118.8927	121.1913	123.4898	125.7883	128.0968	130.3852	132.6835	134.9917
12	119.6367	122.1450	124.6563	127.1617	129.8700	132.1783	134.6866	137.1948	139.7030	142.2110	144.7190	147.2269
13	129.5692	132.2874	135.0056	137.7237	140.4419	143.1601	145.8782	148.5962	151.3142	154.0321	156.7499	159.4676
14	139.4957	142.4239	145.3520	148.2602	151.2084	154.1365	157.0646	159.9926	162.9205	165.8483	168.7761	171.7037
15	149.4162	152.5544	155.6927	158.8309	161.9692	165.1075	168.2457	171.3838	174.5218	177.6597	180.7975	183.9351
16	159.3305	162.6790	166.0275	169.3760	172.7245	176.0730	179.4214	182.7697	186.1179	189.4660	192.8140	196.1618
17	169.2386	172.7975	176.3563	179.9152	183.4741	187.0329	190.5917	194.1504	197.7090	201.2674	204.8257	208.3838
18	179.1405	182.9099	186.6792	190.4498	194.2180	197.9873	201.7566	205.5257	209.2948	213.0637	216.8324	220.6009
19	189.0362	193.0160	196.9960	200.9760	204.9561	208.9360	212.9159	216.8957	220.8753	224.8548	228.8340	232.8131
20	198.9254	203.1160	207.3067	211.4975	215.6883	219.8790	224.0696	228.2602	232.4505	236.6407	240.8306	245.0204

21	208.8082	213.2087	217.6113	222.0129	226.4146	230.8162	235.2177	239.6191	244.0203	248.4214	252.8221	257.2226
22	218.6845	223.2077	227.9096	232.5222	237.1349	241.7476	246.3801	250.9725	255.5847	260.1967	264.9084	269.4199
23	228.5543	233.3778	238.2016	243.0254	247.8492	252.6730	257.4367	262.3202	267.1435	271.9666	276.7894	281.6119
24	238.4174	243.4522	248.4872	253.5223	258.5574	263.5924	268.6274	273.6622	278.6936	283.7311	288.7651	293.7998
25	248.2738	253.5200	258.7864	264.0128	269.2594	274.5059	279.7522	284.9984	290.2444	295.4901	300.7354	305.9904
26	258.1235	263.5812	269.0391	274.4971	279.9551	285.4132	290.8711	296.3288	301.7863	307.2434	312.7003	318.1567
27	267.9663	273.6357	279.3052	284.9748	290.6446	296.3143	301.9838	307.8532	313.3224	318.9912	324.6596	330.3276
28	277.8023	283.6834	289.5647	295.4461	301.1277	307.2091	313.0905	318.9717	324.8526	330.7332	336.6133	342.4331
29	287.6313	293.7242	299.8174	305.9108	312.0043	318.0977	324.1910	330.2841	336.3769	342.4694	348.5614	354.6530
30	297.4533	303.7582	310.0634	316.3688	322.6744	328.9799	335.2852	341.5904	347.8953	354.1998	360.5038	366.6074
31	307.2691	313.7862	320.3025	326.8201	333.3379	339.8556	346.3731	352.8905	359.4075	365.9242	372.4404	378.9561
32	317.0750	323.6901	330.5348	337.2647	343.9947	350.7247	357.4547	364.1848	370.9137	377.6426	384.3711	391.0990
33	326.8762	333.8179	340.7800	347.7023	354.6448	361.5873	368.5297	375.4718	382.4136	389.3550	396.2959	403.2362
34	336.6694	343.8235	350.9781	358.1330	365.2881	372.4432	379.5982	386.7529	393.9073	401.0613	408.2147	415.3675
35	346.4551	353.8219	361.1892	368.5567	375.9246	383.2924	390.6601	398.0275	405.3947	412.7613	420.1274	427.4928
36	356.2334	363.8129	371.3930	378.9734	386.5540	394.1347	401.7153	409.2956	416.8756	424.4551	432.0339	439.6122
37	366.0041	373.7965	381.5895	389.3828	397.1765	404.9702	412.7637	420.5570	428.3500	436.1424	443.9343	451.7254
38	375.7672	383.7726	391.7786	399.7851	407.7918	415.7986	423.8053	431.8118	439.8178	447.8234	455.8283	463.8325
39	385.5226	393.7411	401.9603	410.1800	418.4000	426.6200	434.8400	443.0597	451.2790	459.4978	467.7160	475.9334
40	395.2703	403.7020	412.1345	420.5675	429.0009	437.4343	445.8677	454.3008	462.7335	471.1657	479.5972	488.0279
41	405.0101	413.6552	422.3011	430.9476	439.5944	448.2414	456.8883	465.5349	474.1812	482.8269	491.4719	500.1161
42	414.7420	423.6006	432.4600	441.3201	450.1906	459.0412	467.9017	476.7621	485.6220	494.4813	503.3399	512.1977
43	424.4658	433.5391	442.8112	451.6850	460.7592	469.8336	478.9080	487.9821	497.0558	506.1289	515.2013	524.2728
44	434.1816	443.4676	452.7545	462.0421	471.3303	480.6186	489.9069	499.1949	508.4826	517.7696	527.0559	536.3413
45	443.8893	453.3891	462.8899	472.3915	481.8937	491.3360	500.8984	510.4005	519.9022	529.4033	538.9037	548.4031
46	453.5886	463.3024	473.0173	482.7330	492.4493	502.1658	511.8824	521.5968	531.3147	541.0300	550.7445	560.4581
47	463.2797	473.2076	483.1366	493.0665	502.9971	512.9280	522.8586	532.7896	542.7198	552.6495	562.5783	572.5062
48	472.9623	483.1044	493.2478	503.3920	513.5370	523.6823	533.8277	543.9729	554.1176	564.2617	574.4050	584.5473
49	482.6365	492.9929	503.3507	513.7094	524.0690	534.4288	544.7888	555.1485	565.5079	575.8667	586.2245	596.5814
50	492.3021	502.8729	513.4452	524.0186	534.5928	545.1673	555.7420	566.3166	576.8907	587.4642	598.0368	608.6083

Table 7.7-1. (continued) 30-YEAR TERM Interest Rate

J	8.00	8.25	8.50	8.75	10.00	10.25	10.50	10.75	11.00	11.25	11.50	11.75
1	7.5000	7.7083	7.9167	8.1250	8.3333	8.5417	8.7500	8.9583	9.1667	9.3750	9.5833	9.7917
2	14.9969	15.4127	15.8294	16.2462	16.6630	17.0799	17.4965	17.9133	18.3301	18.7468	19.1636	19.5904
3	22.4877	23.1130	23.7383	24.3636	24.9888	25.6142	26.2395	26.8648	27.4902	28.1155	28.7408	29.3661
4	29.8763	30.8092	31.6432	32.4771	33.3111	34.1450	34.9790	35.8130	36.6469	37.4609	38.3148	39.1488
5	37.4587	38.5014	39.5441	40.5868	41.6296	42.6722	43.7149	44.7576	45.8003	46.8430	47.8857	48.9284
6	44.9379	46.1894	47.4410	48.6925	49.9441	51.1957	52.4472	53.6988	54.9504	56.2019	57.4535	58.7050
7	52.4129	53.8733	55.3338	56.7943	58.2548	59.7154	61.1759	62.6364	64.0970	65.5575	67.0190	68.4784
8	59.8836	61.5530	63.2226	64.8921	66.5617	68.2313	69.9009	71.5705	73.2401	74.9097	76.5792	78.2488
9	67.3499	69.2285	71.1072	72.9859	74.8647	76.7434	78.6222	80.5010	82.3798	84.2585	86.1372	88.0159
10	74.8119	76.8898	78.9877	81.0757	83.1637	85.2517	87.3398	89.4279	91.5159	93.6034	95.6919	97.7799
11	82.2696	84.5667	86.6640	89.1613	91.4587	93.7562	96.0536	98.3511	100.6485	102.9459	105.2433	107.5406
12	89.7227	92.2294	94.7361	97.2429	99.7498	102.2567	104.7637	107.2706	109.7775	112.2944	114.7913	117.2980
13	97.1715	99.8876	102.6039	105.3203	108.0368	110.7533	113.4699	116.1864	118.9029	121.6194	124.3358	127.0522
14	104.6158	107.5416	110.4675	113.3936	116.3197	119.2460	122.1722	125.0985	128.0247	130.9509	133.8770	136.8030
15	112.0555	115.1910	118.3268	121.4628	124.5966	127.7346	130.8707	134.0067	137.1428	140.2788	143.4147	146.5505
16	119.4908	122.8361	126.1817	129.5274	132.8733	136.2192	139.5652	142.9112	146.2571	149.6030	152.9488	156.2945
17	126.9214	130.4767	134.0322	137.5879	141.1438	144.6997	148.2557	151.8118	155.3678	158.5237	162.4796	166.0352
18	134.3474	138.1127	141.8783	145.6441	149.4101	153.1762	156.9423	160.7085	164.4746	168.2406	172.0066	175.7724
19	141.7688	145.7442	149.7199	153.6969	157.6721	161.6485	165.6248	169.6012	173.5776	177.5539	181.5300	185.5060
20	149.1855	153.3711	157.5571	161.7434	165.9299	170.1166	174.3033	178.4901	182.6768	186.8634	191.0499	195.2362

21	156.5974	160.9934	165.3897	169.7664	174.1834	178.5605	182.9777	187.3749	191.7720	196.1691	200.5661	204.9628
22	164.0046	168.6110	173.2178	177.8250	182.4325	187.0401	191.6479	196.2557	200.8634	205.4710	210.0785	214.6858
23	171.4070	176.2239	181.0413	185.8659	190.6772	195.4565	200.3139	205.1324	209.9608	214.7691	219.5672	224.4051
24	178.8046	183.8321	188.8602	193.8887	198.9175	203.9466	208.9758	214.0050	219.0342	224.0633	229.0922	234.1208
25	186.1973	191.4355	196.6743	201.9137	207.1534	212.3383	217.6333	222.8735	228.1136	233.3535	238.5303	243.8328
26	193.5851	199.0341	204.4838	209.9341	215.3847	220.8356	226.2866	231.7378	237.1889	242.6398	248.0906	253.5411
27	200.9680	206.6279	212.2886	217.9498	223.6115	229.2735	234.9356	240.5979	246.2601	251.9221	257.5640	263.2455
28	208.3459	214.2168	220.0885	225.9609	231.8337	237.7069	243.5802	249.4537	255.3271	261.2004	267.0735	272.9462
29	215.7188	221.9008	227.8837	233.9672	240.0513	246.1358	252.2205	258.3052	264.3900	270.4746	276.5590	282.6430
30	223.0866	229.3798	235.6739	241.9688	248.2643	254.5601	260.8562	267.1524	273.4486	279.7447	286.0405	292.3359
31	230.4494	236.9538	243.4593	249.9656	256.4726	262.9799	269.4875	275.9953	282.5030	289.0106	295.5179	302.0249
32	237.8070	244.5228	251.2398	257.9576	264.6761	271.3961	278.1143	284.8337	291.5531	298.2723	304.9913	311.7099
33	245.1594	252.0868	259.0153	265.9447	272.8749	279.8056	286.7365	293.6677	300.5989	307.5299	314.4606	321.3909
34	252.5067	259.6456	266.7868	273.9269	281.0689	288.2113	295.3542	302.4972	309.6402	316.7831	323.9257	331.0679
35	259.8487	267.1993	274.5512	281.9041	289.2580	296.6124	303.9672	311.3222	318.6772	326.0321	333.3866	340.7407
36	267.1064	274.7470	282.3115	289.8764	297.4422	305.0086	312.5755	320.1426	327.7097	335.2767	342.8433	350.4095
37	274.5168	282.2950	290.0667	297.8436	305.6215	313.4001	321.1791	328.9584	336.7377	344.5169	352.2957	360.0741
38	281.8429	289.8430	297.8167	305.8058	313.7968	321.7866	329.7780	337.7695	345.7612	353.7526	361.7438	369.7345
39	289.1635	297.3910	305.5615	313.7628	321.9652	330.1683	338.3720	346.5760	354.7801	362.9840	371.1875	379.3906
40	296.4787	304.8880	313.3011	321.7147	330.1294	338.5450	346.9612	355.3777	363.7943	372.2108	380.6289	389.0425
41	303.7885	312.2409	321.0354	329.8613	338.2886	346.9168	355.5455	364.1747	372.8039	381.4330	390.0618	398.6900
42	311.0927	319.9274	328.7643	337.6028	346.4426	355.2834	364.1249	372.9668	381.8088	390.6506	399.4922	408.3331
43	318.3913	327.4365	336.4478	345.5389	354.5915	363.6451	372.6994	381.7541	390.8089	399.8637	408.9181	417.9719
44	325.6843	334.4940	344.2059	353.4698	362.7351	372.0016	381.2688	390.5385	399.8043	409.0720	418.3394	427.6061
45	332.9717	342.4439	351.9106	361.3962	370.8735	380.3529	389.8331	399.3139	408.7948	418.2756	427.7560	437.2359
46	340.2534	349.9383	359.6257	369.3153	379.0065	388.6990	398.3924	408.0063	417.7804	427.4744	437.1681	446.8611
47	347.5283	357.4270	367.3273	377.2299	387.1342	397.0399	406.9465	416.8537	426.7611	436.6684	446.5754	456.4817
48	354.7995	364.4900	375.0233	385.1130	395.2565	405.3756	415.4954	425.6160	435.7368	445.8576	455.9790	466.0977
49	362.0639	372.3873	382.7137	393.0425	403.3734	413.7057	424.0418	434.3732	444.7075	455.0418	465.3758	475.7091
50	369.3224	378.8588	390.3984	400.9405	411.4847	422.0305	432.5775	443.1251	453.8731	464.2211	474.7687	485.3156

Table 7.7-1. (continued) 30-YEAR TERM Interest Rate

J	12.00	12.25	12.50	12.75	13.00	13.25	13.50	13.75	14.00	14.25	14.50	14.75
1	10.0000	10.2083	10.4167	10.6250	10.8333	11.0417	11.2500	11.4583	11.6667	11.8750	12.0833	12.2917
2	19.9971	20.4139	20.8307	21.2474	21.6642	22.0809	22.4977	22.9145	23.3312	23.7480	24.1647	24.5815
3	29.9914	30.6167	31.2420	31.8673	32.4925	33.1178	33.7431	34.3683	34.9938	35.6198	36.2441	36.8693
4	39.9827	40.8166	41.6506	42.4845	43.3184	44.1522	44.9861	45.8200	46.6538	47.4877	48.3215	49.1553
5	49.9711	51.0138	52.0564	53.0990	54.1416	55.1416	56.2268	57.2699	58.3118	59.3543	60.3968	61.4398
6	59.9565	61.2080	62.4595	63.7109	64.9823	66.2137	67.4650	68.7163	69.9676	71.2189	72.4701	73.7213
7	69.9389	71.3993	72.8597	74.3200	75.7604	77.2406	78.7009	80.1610	81.6212	83.0813	84.5413	86.0013
8	79.9186	81.5877	83.2571	84.9265	86.5958	88.2650	89.9342	91.6034	93.2724	94.9415	96.6104	98.2799
9	89.8945	91.7731	93.6517	95.5301	97.4085	99.2869	101.1651	103.0433	104.9214	106.7994	108.6774	110.5553
10	99.8677	101.9556	104.0433	106.1310	108.2186	110.3061	112.3335	114.4808	116.5680	118.6552	120.7422	122.8291
11	109.8378	112.1350	114.4320	116.7290	119.0259	121.3227	123.6190	125.9159	128.2123	130.5096	132.8048	135.1009
12	119.8047	122.3113	124.8178	127.3242	129.8305	132.2366	134.8428	137.3485	139.8542	142.3598	144.8653	147.3706
13	129.7684	132.4846	135.2006	137.9165	140.6322	143.3478	146.0633	148.7766	151.4537	154.2086	156.9234	159.6381
14	139.7289	142.6547	145.5803	148.5058	151.4312	154.3563	157.2813	160.2061	163.1307	166.0551	168.9798	171.9034
15	149.6861	152.8217	155.9570	159.0922	162.2273	165.3821	168.4567	171.6311	174.7653	177.8992	181.0330	184.1665
16	159.6401	162.9855	166.3307	169.6757	173.0205	176.3651	179.7094	183.0535	186.3974	189.7410	193.0843	196.4274
17	169.5907	173.1461	176.7012	180.2561	183.8108	187.3652	190.9194	194.4733	198.0269	201.5802	205.1332	208.6860
18	179.5380	183.3034	187.0686	190.8335	194.5982	198.3626	202.1266	205.6904	209.6539	213.4170	217.1798	220.9423
19	189.4818	193.4574	197.4327	201.4078	205.3826	209.3570	213.3311	217.3049	221.2763	225.2513	229.2240	233.1963
20	199.4223	203.6082	207.7937	211.9790	216.1639	220.3485	224.5328	228.7166	232.9001	237.0831	241.2857	245.4480

21	209.3593	213.7555	218.1915	222.5470	226.9423	231.3377	235.7318	240.1256	244.5198	248.9123	253.3050	257.8973
22	219.2928	223.8995	228.5059	233.1119	237.7178	242.3228	246.9275	251.5318	256.1356	260.7390	265.3418	269.9442
23	229.2228	234.0401	238.8570	243.6736	248.4897	253.3054	258.1206	262.9352	267.7494	272.5630	277.3761	282.1886
24	239.1432	244.1772	249.2048	254.2320	259.2567	264.2850	269.3107	274.3358	279.3604	284.3844	289.4078	294.4306
25	249.0720	254.3108	259.5492	264.7871	270.0248	275.2615	280.4978	285.7335	290.9696	296.2031	301.4369	306.6701
26	258.9912	264.4409	269.8902	275.3390	280.7872	286.2349	291.6819	297.1283	302.5740	308.0191	313.4635	318.9071
27	268.9067	274.5675	280.2278	285.8875	291.5466	297.2052	302.8630	308.5202	314.1766	319.8324	325.4873	331.1416
28	278.8186	284.6904	290.5618	296.4326	302.3028	308.1722	314.0410	319.9091	325.7763	331.6428	337.5086	343.3734
29	288.7266	294.8097	300.8923	306.9743	313.0556	319.1361	325.2159	331.2950	337.3732	343.4505	349.5270	355.6026
30	298.6309	304.9254	311.2193	317.5125	323.8050	330.0968	336.3877	342.6778	348.9670	355.2553	361.5427	367.8292
31	308.5314	315.0373	321.5426	328.0472	334.5611	341.0541	347.5563	354.0576	360.5579	367.0573	373.5557	380.0531
32	318.4280	325.1455	331.8623	338.5784	345.2938	352.0082	358.7271	365.4342	372.1458	378.8563	385.5658	392.2743
33	328.3207	335.2499	342.1794	349.1061	356.0329	362.9589	369.8838	376.8078	383.7307	390.6525	397.5731	404.4927
34	338.2095	345.3055	352.4907	359.6301	366.7686	373.9060	381.0420	388.1781	395.3124	402.4456	409.5776	416.7084
35	348.0943	355.4472	362.7993	370.1505	377.5008	384.8500	392.1982	399.5452	406.8911	414.2357	421.5791	428.9212
36	357.9751	365.5400	373.1041	380.6672	388.2294	395.7964	403.3504	410.9091	418.4666	426.0228	433.5778	441.1312
37	367.8618	375.6289	383.4050	391.1802	398.9544	406.7274	414.4991	422.2697	430.0389	437.8067	445.5732	453.3383
38	377.7440	385.7137	393.7021	401.6894	409.6757	417.6080	425.6080	433.6269	441.6080	449.5876	457.5658	465.5425
39	387.5930	395.7946	403.9953	412.1948	420.3933	428.5905	436.7863	444.9808	453.1738	461.3653	469.5553	477.7437
40	397.4573	405.8714	414.2845	422.6964	431.1072	439.5166	447.9247	456.3313	464.7363	473.1396	481.5417	489.9419
41	407.3175	415.9441	424.5687	433.1941	441.8173	450.4399	459.0595	467.6783	476.2955	484.9111	493.5249	502.1371
42	417.1733	426.0128	434.8509	443.6879	452.5237	461.3579	470.1937	479.0219	487.8513	496.6791	505.5050	514.3298
43	427.0249	436.0770	445.1280	454.1777	463.2261	472.2730	481.3183	490.3619	499.4037	508.4438	517.4818	526.5183
44	436.8721	446.1371	455.4010	464.6635	473.9247	483.1843	492.4422	501.6983	510.9527	520.2051	529.4556	538.7041
45	446.7149	456.1930	465.6698	475.1453	484.6199	494.0917	503.5624	513.0312	522.4981	531.9631	541.4260	550.8868
46	456.5633	466.2445	475.9344	485.6229	495.3100	504.9953	514.6798	524.3604	534.0400	543.7176	553.3930	563.0663
47	466.3872	476.2917	486.1948	496.0965	505.9986	515.8949	525.7914	535.6859	545.5783	555.4686	565.3567	575.2425
48	476.2166	486.3344	496.4509	506.5658	516.6792	526.7907	536.9002	547.0077	557.1130	567.2161	577.3169	587.4155
49	486.0415	496.3727	506.7026	517.0309	527.3578	537.6824	548.0051	558.3257	568.6441	578.9601	589.2738	599.5850
50	495.8617	506.4065	516.9600	527.4918	538.0319	548.5700	559.1061	569.6399	580.1714	590.7005	601.2271	611.7512

Table 7.7-1. (continued) 35-YEAR TERM Interest Rate

j	8.00	8.25	8.50	8.75	10.00	10.25	10.50	10.75	11.00	11.25	11.50	11.75
1	7.5000	7.7083	7.9167	8.1250	8.3333	8.5417	8.7500	8.9583	9.1667	9.3750	9.5833	9.7917
2	14.9974	15.4142	15.8310	16.2477	16.6645	17.0812	17.4980	17.9147	18.3315	18.7482	19.1650	19.5817
3	22.4923	23.1176	23.7429	24.3681	24.9934	25.6187	26.2439	26.8692	27.4944	28.1196	28.7449	29.3701
4	29.9846	30.8185	31.6524	32.4862	33.3201	34.1539	34.9878	35.8016	36.6554	37.4892	38.3230	39.1568
5	37.4743	38.5169	39.5594	40.6020	41.6445	42.6871	43.7296	44.7721	45.8146	46.8570	47.8895	48.9419
6	44.9614	46.2127	47.4641	48.7154	49.9667	51.2180	52.4639	53.7205	54.9718	56.2229	57.4741	58.7253
7	52.4458	53.9060	55.3662	56.8264	58.2866	59.7467	61.2069	62.6670	64.1270	65.5870	67.0470	68.5069
8	59.9275	61.5967	63.2659	64.9350	66.6042	68.2733	69.9423	71.6113	73.2803	74.9492	76.6180	78.2868
9	67.4066	69.2848	71.1631	73.0413	74.9194	76.7975	78.6756	80.5536	82.4316	84.3095	86.1873	88.0650
10	74.8829	76.9703	79.0577	81.1450	83.2323	85.3196	87.4067	89.4939	91.5809	93.6678	95.7547	97.8415
11	82.3566	84.6532	86.9498	89.2464	91.5429	93.8393	96.1357	98.4320	100.7282	103.0242	105.3202	107.6161
12	89.8275	92.3334	94.8393	97.3452	99.8510	102.3568	104.8624	107.3680	109.8734	112.3787	114.8839	117.3890
13	97.2956	100.0109	102.7263	105.4416	108.1568	110.8719	113.5869	116.3018	119.0166	121.7312	124.4457	127.1600
14	104.7609	107.6858	110.6106	113.5354	116.4601	119.3847	122.3092	125.2335	128.1577	131.0317	134.0056	136.9292
15	112.2234	115.3579	118.4924	121.6267	124.7610	127.8952	131.0298	134.1630	137.2367	140.4302	143.5635	146.6966
16	119.6834	123.0273	126.3714	129.7154	133.0594	136.4032	139.7469	143.0903	146.4336	149.7767	153.1195	156.4621
17	127.1409	130.6939	134.2476	137.8016	141.3553	144.9089	148.4623	152.0154	155.5684	159.1211	162.6735	166.2257
18	134.5939	138.3577	142.1216	145.8852	149.6488	153.4122	157.1753	160.9383	164.7010	168.4634	172.2256	175.9874
19	142.0439	146.0170	149.9925	153.9661	157.9397	161.9130	165.8861	169.8589	173.8314	177.8037	181.7756	185.7472
20	149.4931	153.6770	157.8608	162.0445	166.2260	170.4113	174.5944	178.7772	182.9597	187.1418	191.3236	195.5050

21	156.9383	161.3323	165.7263	170.1201	174.5138	178.9072	183.3004	187.6932	192.0857	196.4779	200.8696	205.2609
22	164.3805	168.9848	173.5690	178.1931	182.7970	187.4006	192.0039	196.6069	201.2096	205.8118	210.4135	215.0148
23	171.8198	176.4448	181.4440	186.2633	191.0776	195.8915	200.7051	205.5183	210.3311	215.1435	219.9554	224.7667
24	179.2561	184.2811	189.3061	194.3309	199.3555	204.3798	209.4037	214.4273	219.4504	224.4730	229.4951	234.5166
25	186.6883	191.9249	197.1603	202.3957	207.6308	212.8659	218.0999	223.3339	228.5674	233.8003	239.0327	244.2645
26	194.1195	199.5657	205.0018	210.4577	215.9034	221.3487	226.7936	232.2381	237.6820	243.1254	248.5682	254.0103
27	201.5466	207.2035	212.8603	218.5169	224.1733	229.8293	235.4848	241.1399	246.7944	252.4483	258.1015	263.7540
28	208.9706	214.8283	220.7059	226.5733	232.4405	238.3072	244.1735	250.0392	255.9044	261.7688	267.6328	273.4957
29	216.3915	222.4370	228.5486	234.6269	240.7049	246.7825	252.8596	258.9361	265.0120	271.0871	277.1615	283.2352
30	223.8092	230.0888	236.3883	242.6778	248.9666	255.2551	261.5431	267.8305	274.1172	280.4031	286.6882	292.9725
31	231.1238	237.7245	244.2951	250.7254	257.2254	263.7250	270.2240	276.7223	283.2199	289.7167	296.2127	302.7077
32	238.6352	245.3470	252.0588	258.7703	265.4815	272.1922	278.9022	285.6117	292.3203	299.0280	305.7349	312.4408
33	246.0434	252.9665	259.8885	266.8123	273.7347	280.6566	287.5779	294.4984	301.4181	308.3369	315.2548	322.1716
34	253.4484	260.5828	267.7172	274.8513	281.9851	289.1183	296.2508	303.3826	310.5135	317.6434	324.7724	331.9002
35	260.8500	268.1969	275.5418	282.8874	290.2325	297.5771	304.9211	312.2642	319.6063	326.9475	334.2876	341.6266
36	268.2464	275.8059	283.3633	290.9204	298.4771	306.0032	313.5886	321.1431	328.6597	336.2491	343.6005	351.3507
37	275.6435	283.4916	291.1816	298.9504	306.7187	314.4864	322.2534	330.0194	337.7844	345.5483	353.3110	361.0725
38	283.0353	291.0161	298.9968	306.9773	314.9674	322.9368	330.9154	338.9800	346.8698	354.8450	362.8192	370.7919
39	290.4236	298.6163	306.8089	315.0012	323.1931	331.3842	339.5746	347.7639	355.9522	364.1392	372.3248	380.5091
40	297.8086	306.2132	314.6177	323.0220	331.4257	339.8288	348.2310	356.6321	365.0321	373.4308	381.8881	390.2239
41	305.1902	313.8068	322.4233	331.0396	339.6554	348.2704	356.8845	365.4976	374.1094	382.7196	391.3289	399.9363
42	312.5684	321.3970	330.2257	339.0541	347.8820	356.7091	365.5352	374.3602	383.1840	392.0063	400.8271	409.6463
43	319.9431	328.9839	338.0248	347.0654	356.1055	365.1447	374.1830	383.2201	392.2559	401.2902	410.3229	419.3539
44	327.3142	336.5674	345.8206	355.0735	364.3259	373.5774	382.8279	392.0770	401.3251	410.5714	419.8161	429.0590
45	334.6819	344.1475	353.6131	363.0764	372.5431	382.0070	391.4698	400.9314	410.3915	419.8500	429.3068	438.7617
46	342.0461	351.7241	361.4022	371.0800	380.7572	390.4335	400.1148	409.7887	419.4500	429.1259	438.7748	448.4619
47	349.4066	359.2972	369.1879	379.0783	388.9681	398.8570	408.7447	418.6311	428.5159	438.3990	448.2803	458.1595
48	356.7696	366.8669	376.9702	387.0733	397.1758	407.2773	417.3777	427.4766	437.5739	447.6695	457.7631	467.6546
49	364.1170	374.4330	384.7491	395.0650	405.3602	415.6945	426.0075	436.3192	446.6291	456.9372	467.2432	477.5471
50	371.4687	381.9956	392.5246	403.0533	413.5814	424.1085	434.6344	445.1587	455.6814	466.2020	476.7207	487.2370

Table 7.7-1. (continued) 35-YEAR TERM Interest Rate

J	12.00	12.25	12.50	12.75	13.00	13.25	13.50	13.75	14.00	14.25	14.50	14.75
1	10.0000	10.2083	10.4167	10.6250	10.8333	11.0417	11.2500	11.4583	11.6667	11.8750	12.0833	12.2917
2	19.9984	20.4152	20.8319	21.2486	21.6654	22.0821	22.4988	22.9156	23.3323	23.7490	24.1657	24.5824
3	29.9953	30.6205	31.2457	31.8709	32.4961	33.1213	33.7465	34.3717	34.9968	35.6220	36.2471	36.8723
4	39.9906	40.8244	41.6581	42.4918	43.3256	44.1598	44.9930	45.8266	46.6603	47.4940	48.3276	49.1612
5	49.9843	51.0267	52.0690	53.1114	54.1537	55.1960	56.2382	57.2805	58.3227	59.3649	60.4071	61.4492
6	59.9764	61.2274	62.4795	63.7295	64.9804	66.2314	67.4823	68.7331	69.9840	71.2348	72.4856	73.7363
7	69.9668	71.4266	72.8864	74.3462	75.8059	77.2655	78.7251	80.1847	81.6442	83.1036	84.5630	86.0224
8	79.9556	81.6243	83.2929	84.9614	86.6299	88.2983	89.9667	91.6350	93.3032	94.9714	96.6395	98.3075
9	89.9427	91.8203	93.6978	95.5752	97.4526	99.3298	101.2070	103.0841	104.9611	106.8381	108.7149	110.5917
10	99.9281	102.0147	104.1012	106.1875	108.2738	110.3600	112.4460	114.5320	116.6179	118.7036	120.7883	122.8749
11	109.9118	112.2075	114.5030	116.7984	119.0937	121.3888	123.6838	125.9787	128.2735	130.5681	132.8628	135.1571
12	119.8939	122.3986	124.9033	127.4077	129.9121	132.4162	134.9203	137.4241	139.9279	142.4315	144.9349	147.4382
13	129.8741	132.5881	135.3019	138.0156	140.7290	143.4423	146.1554	148.8683	151.5811	154.2937	157.0061	159.7183
14	139.8527	142.7759	145.6990	148.6219	151.5445	154.4670	157.3892	160.3113	163.2331	166.1547	169.0762	171.9974
15	149.8294	152.9621	156.0945	159.2266	162.3585	165.4902	168.6217	171.7529	174.8839	178.0146	181.1451	184.2755
16	159.8044	163.1465	166.4883	169.8298	173.1711	176.5121	179.8528	183.1932	186.5334	189.8733	193.2130	196.5524
17	169.7776	173.3291	176.8804	180.4314	183.9821	187.5325	191.0825	194.6323	198.1817	201.7309	205.2797	208.8283
18	179.7489	183.5101	187.2709	191.0314	194.7916	198.5514	202.3109	206.0700	209.8288	213.5872	217.3453	221.1031
19	189.7184	193.6893	197.6597	201.6298	205.5995	209.5689	213.5378	217.5063	221.4745	225.4423	229.4097	233.3768
20	199.6860	203.8666	208.0468	212.2266	216.4059	220.5848	224.7633	228.9413	233.1190	237.2962	241.4730	245.6494

21	209.6518	214.0422	218.4322	222.8217	227.2107	231.5993	235.9874	240.3750	244.7621	249.1488	253.5350	257.9208
22	219.6157	224.2160	228.8158	233.4151	238.0140	242.6122	247.2100	251.8072	256.4039	261.0002	265.5959	270.191
23	229.5776	234.3879	239.1977	244.0069	248.8156	253.6226	258.4311	263.2381	268.0444	272.8502	277.6555	282.4602
24	239.5376	244.5580	249.5778	254.5970	259.6155	264.6335	269.6508	274.6675	279.6836	284.6990	289.7139	294.7282
25	249.4967	254.7262	259.9561	265.1853	270.4139	275.6417	280.8689	286.0955	291.3213	296.5465	301.7710	306.9950
26	259.4518	264.8925	270.3326	275.7719	281.2105	286.6484	292.0856	297.5220	302.9577	308.3927	313.8269	319.2605
27	269.4058	275.0569	280.7072	286.3567	292.0055	297.6535	303.3007	308.9470	314.5926	320.2375	325.8815	331.5249
28	279.3579	285.2194	291.0800	296.9398	302.7988	308.6569	314.5142	320.3706	326.2262	332.0809	337.9348	343.7880
29	289.3079	295.3799	301.4509	307.5211	313.5904	319.6587	325.7262	331.7827	337.8583	343.9230	349.9868	356.0498
30	299.2559	305.5384	311.8200	318.1006	324.3802	330.6589	336.9365	343.2132	349.4889	355.7637	362.0375	368.3104
31	309.2018	315.6950	322.1871	328.6782	335.1683	341.6573	348.1453	354.6322	361.1181	367.6030	374.0868	380.5697
32	319.1457	325.8496	332.5523	339.2540	345.9546	352.6541	359.3524	366.0497	372.7458	379.4409	386.1348	392.8278
33	329.0874	336.0020	342.9155	349.8279	356.7391	363.6499	370.5579	377.4655	384.3720	391.2773	398.1814	405.0845
34	339.0269	346.1525	353.2768	360.3999	367.5218	374.6424	381.7617	388.8798	395.9967	403.1123	410.2266	417.3398
35	348.9643	356.3008	363.6361	370.9700	378.3026	385.6339	392.9639	400.2925	407.6198	414.9458	422.2704	429.5939
36	358.8995	366.4471	373.9933	381.5381	389.0816	396.6237	404.1643	411.7035	419.2413	426.7778	434.3128	441.8466
37	368.8325	376.5913	384.3486	392.1044	399.8588	407.6116	415.3630	423.1129	430.8613	438.6093	446.3538	454.0978
38	378.7633	386.7333	394.7017	402.6686	410.6340	418.5978	426.5600	434.5207	442.4797	450.4372	458.3932	466.3478
39	388.6919	396.8732	405.0528	413.2309	421.4073	429.5821	437.7552	445.9267	454.0965	462.2647	470.4301	478.5962
40	398.6182	407.0108	415.4018	423.7911	432.1787	440.5646	448.9487	457.3310	465.7717	474.0905	482.4677	490.8433
41	408.5421	417.1463	425.7487	434.3493	442.9482	451.5451	460.1403	468.7336	477.3251	486.9148	494.5027	503.0889
42	418.4638	427.2796	436.0934	444.9054	453.7156	462.5238	471.3301	480.1345	488.9370	497.7375	506.5362	515.3331
43	428.3831	437.4105	446.4369	455.4595	464.4811	473.5006	482.5181	491.5336	500.5471	509.5586	518.5681	527.5757
44	438.3001	447.5392	456.7764	466.0114	475.2445	484.4754	493.7042	502.9309	512.1555	521.3780	530.5985	539.8169
45	448.2147	457.6657	467.1145	476.5613	486.0059	495.4483	504.8885	514.3264	523.7662	533.1956	542.6272	552.0565
46	458.1269	467.7898	477.4505	487.1089	496.7652	506.4192	516.0708	525.7201	535.3671	545.0119	554.6544	564.2947
47	468.0366	477.9115	487.7842	497.6545	507.5225	517.3880	527.2512	537.1120	546.9703	556.6803	566.6799	576.5312
48	477.9439	488.0309	498.1156	508.1978	518.2778	528.3549	538.4297	548.5019	558.5717	568.6330	578.7038	588.7662
49	487.8487	498.1479	508.4447	518.7389	529.0306	539.3197	549.6062	559.8900	570.1713	580.4499	590.7260	600.9996
50	497.7510	508.2625	518.7714	529.2277	539.7815	550.2824	560.7807	571.2762	581.7690	592.2591	602.7465	613.2313

Table 7.7-1. (continued) 40-YEAR TERM Interest Rate

J	9.00	9.25	9.50	9.75	10.00	10.25	10.50	10.75	11.00	11.25	11.50	11.75
1	7.5000	7.7083	7.9167	8.1250	8.3333	8.5417	8.7500	8.9583	9.1667	9.3750	9.5833	9.7917
2	14.9984	15.4151	15.8319	16.2486	16.6653	17.0821	17.4988	17.9155	18.3323	18.7490	19.1657	19.5824
3	22.4952	23.1204	23.7456	24.3708	24.9960	25.6212	26.2464	26.8716	27.4968	28.1220	28.7471	29.3723
4	29.9903	30.8241	31.6579	32.4916	33.3254	34.1591	34.9928	35.8265	36.6602	37.4939	38.3276	39.1612
5	37.4889	38.5283	39.5687	40.6110	41.6534	42.6957	43.7380	44.7803	45.8226	46.8648	47.9070	48.9492
6	44.9757	46.2268	47.4779	48.7290	49.9800	51.2310	52.4820	53.7329	54.9838	56.2347	57.4855	58.7363
7	52.4659	53.9258	55.3857	56.8455	58.3053	59.7650	61.2247	62.6843	64.1439	65.6035	67.0630	68.5224
8	59.9545	61.6232	63.2919	64.9605	66.6291	68.2977	69.9662	71.6346	73.3029	74.9712	76.6395	78.3076
9	67.4413	69.3190	71.1966	73.0741	74.9516	76.8290	78.7064	80.5836	82.4608	84.3379	86.2149	88.0918
10	74.9264	77.0131	79.0997	81.1862	83.2727	85.3590	87.4453	89.5315	91.6175	93.7035	95.7893	97.8751
11	82.4099	84.7056	87.0013	89.2969	91.5923	93.8877	96.1829	98.4781	100.7731	103.0679	105.3627	107.6573
12	89.8916	92.3365	94.8013	97.4060	99.9106	102.4150	104.9193	107.4234	109.9274	112.4313	114.5930	117.4386
13	97.3715	100.0857	102.7997	105.5136	108.2273	110.9409	113.6543	116.3676	119.0607	121.7783	124.5063	127.2188
14	104.8497	107.7732	110.6965	113.6197	116.5427	119.4655	122.3881	125.3105	128.2327	131.1547	134.0765	136.9981
15	112.3262	115.4590	118.5917	121.7242	124.8565	127.9886	131.1205	134.2521	137.3835	140.5147	143.6456	146.7763
16	119.8008	123.1432	126.4853	129.8272	133.1689	136.5103	139.8515	143.1924	146.5331	149.8735	153.2136	156.5535
17	127.2737	130.8256	134.3772	137.9286	141.4798	145.0306	148.5812	152.1315	155.6815	159.2312	162.7806	166.3236
18	134.7448	138.5063	142.2675	146.0284	149.7891	153.5496	157.3096	161.0693	164.8287	168.5877	172.3464	176.1047
19	142.2140	146.1852	150.1561	154.1267	158.0970	162.0669	166.0365	170.0057	173.9746	177.9430	181.9111	185.8788
20	149.6814	153.8624	158.0430	162.2233	166.4033	170.5829	174.7621	178.9409	183.1192	187.2971	191.4747	195.6517

21	157.1470	161.5378	165.9283	170.3194	174.7081	179.0974	183.4862	187.8747	192.2626	196.6501	201.0371	205.4236
22	164.6107	169.2114	173.8118	178.4118	183.0113	187.6104	192.2090	196.8071	201.4047	206.0018	210.5984	215.1944
23	172.0726	176.8833	181.6936	186.5035	191.3130	196.1219	200.9303	205.7382	210.5455	215.3523	220.1585	224.9641
24	179.5325	184.5533	189.5737	194.5936	199.6131	204.6319	209.6502	214.6679	219.6850	224.7015	229.7174	234.7326
25	186.9905	192.2215	197.4521	202.6821	207.9116	213.1404	218.3687	223.5563	228.8232	234.0496	239.2751	244.5001
26	194.4467	199.8879	205.3286	210.7688	216.2084	221.6474	227.0856	232.5232	237.9601	243.3963	248.8317	254.2664
27	201.9009	207.5524	213.2034	218.8539	224.5037	230.1528	235.8011	241.4488	247.0956	252.7417	258.3870	264.0315
28	209.3531	215.2151	221.0765	226.9372	232.7973	238.6566	244.5152	250.3729	256.2298	262.0859	267.9411	273.7955
29	216.8034	222.8759	228.9477	235.0198	241.0893	247.1589	253.2277	259.2956	265.3626	271.4288	277.4940	283.5583
30	224.2517	230.5347	236.8171	243.0987	249.3736	255.6536	261.9307	268.2169	274.4941	280.7703	287.0456	293.3199
31	231.6980	238.1917	244.6847	251.1768	257.6682	264.1596	270.6481	277.1366	283.6241	290.1106	296.5960	303.0804
32	239.1424	245.8467	252.5504	259.2532	265.9551	272.6561	279.3561	286.0550	292.7528	299.4495	306.1451	312.8396
33	246.5847	253.4998	260.4143	267.3278	274.2404	281.1519	288.0624	294.9718	301.8800	308.7871	315.6929	322.5976
34	254.0249	261.1510	268.2762	275.4006	282.5239	289.6461	296.7672	303.8871	311.0059	318.1233	325.2395	332.3544
35	261.4631	268.8002	276.1364	283.4715	290.8057	298.1387	305.4704	312.8010	320.1302	327.4591	334.7847	342.1099
36	268.8993	276.4474	283.9946	291.5407	299.0857	306.6295	314.1721	321.7133	329.2531	336.7916	344.3296	351.8642
37	276.3334	284.0926	291.8508	299.6080	307.3640	315.1187	322.8721	330.6240	338.3745	346.1236	353.8712	361.6173
38	283.7653	291.7358	299.7052	307.6735	315.6405	323.6062	331.5704	339.5333	347.4945	355.4542	363.4124	371.3690
39	291.1952	299.3769	307.5576	315.7370	323.9152	332.0919	340.2872	348.4409	356.6130	364.7835	372.9523	381.1194
40	298.6209	307.0160	315.4060	323.7967	332.1881	340.5760	348.9623	357.3470	365.7300	374.1112	382.4908	390.8686
41	306.0485	314.6531	323.2565	331.8595	340.4592	349.0583	357.6557	366.2515	374.8454	383.4376	392.0279	400.6164
42	313.4719	322.2880	331.1029	339.9164	348.7284	357.5388	366.3474	375.1543	383.9593	392.7624	401.5637	410.3629
43	320.8932	329.9209	338.9474	347.9724	356.9958	366.0176	375.0375	384.0556	393.0717	402.0858	411.0990	420.1081
44	328.3102	337.5517	346.7898	356.0264	365.2614	374.4945	383.7258	392.9552	402.1825	411.4077	420.6309	429.8519
45	335.7291	345.1803	354.6301	364.0784	373.5250	382.9697	392.4124	401.8531	411.2917	420.7281	430.1623	439.5943
46	343.1437	352.8068	362.4685	372.1285	381.7867	391.4430	401.0973	410.7494	420.3993	430.0470	439.6923	449.3354
47	350.5561	360.4311	370.3047	380.1766	390.0466	399.9146	409.7804	419.6440	429.5053	439.3643	449.2209	459.0750
48	357.9662	368.0533	378.1338	388.2226	398.3045	408.3842	418.4617	428.5369	438.6097	448.6901	458.7429	468.8133
49	365.3741	375.6733	385.9709	396.2666	406.5604	416.8520	427.1413	437.4282	447.7125	457.9943	468.2735	478.5501
50	372.7798	383.2910	393.8008	404.3086	414.8144	425.3179	435.8190	446.3176	456.8138	467.3069	477.7976	488.2855

Table 7.7-1. (continued) 40-YEAR TERM Interest Rate

j	12.00	12.25	12.50	12.75	13.00	13.25	13.50	13.75	14.00	14.25	14.50	14.75
1	10.0000	10.2083	10.4167	10.6250	10.8333	11.0417	11.2500	11.4583	11.6667	11.8750	12.0833	12.2917
2	19.9991	20.4159	20.8326	21.2493	21.6660	22.0827	22.4994	22.9161	23.3328	23.7495	24.1662	24.5829
3	29.9974	30.6226	31.2477	31.8729	32.4980	33.1231	33.7482	34.3733	34.9984	35.6235	36.2496	36.8737
4	39.9949	40.8285	41.6621	42.4957	43.3293	44.1629	44.9964	45.8300	46.6635	47.4970	48.3305	49.1641
5	49.9914	51.0036	52.0757	53.1178	54.1599	55.2020	56.2440	57.2860	58.3280	59.3700	60.4120	61.4540
6	59.9871	61.2378	62.4885	63.7392	64.9899	66.2404	67.4910	68.7415	69.9920	71.2425	72.4930	73.7434
7	69.9818	71.4412	72.9005	74.3598	75.8190	77.2782	78.7373	80.1964	81.6555	83.1145	84.5735	86.0324
8	79.9757	81.6438	83.3117	84.9796	86.6475	88.3153	89.9830	91.6507	93.3184	94.9859	96.6535	98.3210
9	89.9687	91.8454	93.7221	95.5987	97.4753	99.3517	101.2281	103.1044	104.9807	106.8569	108.7330	110.6091
10	99.9607	102.0463	104.1317	106.2170	108.3023	110.3875	112.4725	114.5575	116.6424	118.7272	120.8120	122.8967
11	109.9518	112.2462	114.5404	116.8346	119.1286	121.4225	123.7163	126.0100	128.3036	130.5971	132.8905	135.1838
12	119.9420	122.4452	124.9484	127.4513	129.9542	132.4569	134.9594	137.4619	139.9642	142.4664	144.9684	147.4704
13	129.9312	132.6434	135.3554	138.0673	140.7790	143.4905	146.2019	148.9131	151.6241	154.3351	157.0459	159.7565
14	139.9195	142.8406	145.7616	148.6824	151.6030	154.5234	157.4436	160.3637	163.2835	166.2032	169.1228	172.0422
15	149.9068	153.0370	156.1670	159.2967	162.4263	165.5556	168.6847	171.8136	174.9423	178.0708	181.1992	184.3273
16	159.8931	163.2324	166.5714	169.9102	173.2488	176.5871	179.9251	183.2629	186.6005	189.9378	193.2750	196.6119
17	169.8784	173.4269	176.9750	180.5229	184.0705	187.6178	191.1648	194.7115	198.2580	201.8043	205.3503	208.8961
18	179.8627	183.6204	187.3777	191.1347	194.8914	198.6477	202.4038	206.1596	209.9149	213.6701	217.4250	221.1796
19	189.8461	193.8130	197.7796	201.7457	205.7115	209.6769	213.6420	217.6068	221.5712	225.5353	229.4991	233.4627
20	199.8284	204.0046	208.1804	212.3558	216.5308	220.7054	224.8796	229.0534	233.2269	237.4000	241.5727	245.7452

21	209.8087	214.1952	218.5604	222.9650	227.3492	231.7330	236.1184	240.4933	244.8818	249.2640	253.6458	258.0272
22	219.7899	224.3849	228.9794	233.5734	238.1869	242.7599	247.3524	251.9445	256.5382	261.1274	265.7182	270.3096
23	229.7691	234.5736	239.3775	244.1908	248.9837	253.7860	258.5878	263.3890	268.1898	272.9902	277.7900	282.5895
24	239.7472	244.7612	249.7746	254.7796	259.7996	264.8113	269.8223	274.8328	279.8428	284.8523	289.8613	294.8698
25	249.7243	254.9479	260.1708	265.3391	270.6147	275.8357	281.0561	286.2759	291.4961	296.7138	301.9319	307.1495
26	259.7003	265.1335	270.5660	275.9978	281.4289	286.8594	292.2899	297.7182	303.1467	308.5746	314.0018	319.4287
27	269.6752	275.3181	280.9603	286.6016	292.2423	297.8822	303.5214	309.1598	314.7977	320.4348	326.0713	331.7073
28	279.6490	285.5017	291.3535	297.2045	303.0548	308.9042	314.7528	320.6007	326.4479	332.2943	338.1401	343.9653
29	289.6217	295.6842	301.7458	307.8065	313.8683	319.9253	325.9835	332.0408	338.0974	344.1532	350.2088	356.2627
30	299.5933	305.8656	312.1370	318.4074	324.6770	330.9456	337.2133	343.4801	349.7461	356.0118	362.2758	368.5394
31	309.5637	316.0460	322.5272	329.0075	335.4867	341.9650	348.4423	354.9187	361.3942	367.8688	374.3426	380.8156
32	319.5330	326.2253	332.9164	339.6065	346.2956	352.9835	359.6705	366.3565	373.0415	379.7256	386.4088	393.0912
33	329.5011	336.4034	343.3046	350.2045	357.1034	364.0012	370.8978	377.7935	384.6881	391.5817	398.4743	405.3661
34	339.4681	346.5805	353.6917	360.8016	367.9104	375.0179	382.1244	389.2297	396.3339	403.4370	410.5392	417.6404
35	349.4339	356.7564	364.0777	371.3976	378.7164	386.0338	393.3500	400.6650	407.9789	415.2917	422.6033	429.9140
36	359.3984	366.9313	374.4627	381.9927	389.5214	397.0487	404.5748	412.0996	419.6227	427.1456	434.6668	442.1870
37	369.3618	377.1049	384.8465	392.5867	400.3254	408.0627	415.7987	423.5333	431.2667	438.9987	446.7296	454.4598
38	379.3240	387.2774	395.2293	403.1756	411.1285	419.0758	427.0217	434.9662	442.9093	450.8511	458.7917	466.7310
39	389.2849	397.4488	405.6110	413.7715	421.9305	430.0860	438.2449	446.3983	454.5512	462.7028	470.8530	479.0020
40	399.2446	407.6189	415.9915	424.3624	432.7318	441.0981	449.4651	457.8294	466.1923	474.5537	482.9136	491.2723
41	409.2031	417.7879	426.3709	434.9521	443.5316	452.1093	460.6854	469.2598	477.8326	486.4038	494.9735	503.5419
42	419.1603	427.9557	436.7492	445.5408	454.3306	463.1186	471.9048	480.6892	489.4720	498.2531	507.0327	515.8108
43	429.1162	438.1222	447.1263	456.1284	465.1286	474.1268	483.1232	492.1178	501.1106	510.1017	519.0911	528.0730
44	439.0708	448.2876	457.5023	466.7148	475.9255	485.1341	494.3407	503.5454	512.7483	521.9494	531.1487	540.3465
45	449.0241	458.4517	467.8770	477.3002	486.7213	496.1403	505.5572	514.9722	524.3852	533.7963	543.2056	552.6132
46	458.9761	468.6145	478.2506	487.8844	497.5161	507.1455	516.7728	526.3960	536.0212	545.6424	555.2617	564.8792
47	468.9267	478.7770	488.6230	498.4675	508.3100	518.1487	527.9874	537.8229	547.6563	557.4877	567.3170	577.1445
48	478.8760	488.9364	498.9941	509.0494	519.1024	529.1528	539.2010	549.2469	559.2906	569.3321	579.3715	589.4090
49	488.8240	498.9963	509.3641	519.6302	529.8938	540.1549	550.4136	560.6699	570.9239	581.1756	591.4252	601.6728
50	498.7706	509.2530	519.7327	530.2097	540.6842	551.1559	561.6256	572.0820	582.5663	593.0194	603.4781	613.9357

CHAPTER 8

KNOW THE LEGAL ASPECTS OF MORTGAGES

8.0 HOW THE STATES VIEW MORTGAGES

Most real property is purchased with the aid of a loan. A bond or promissory note is the evidence of the debt. It gives the details of the debt and the requirements for payment.

However, since the loan amount is usually very large, the lender wants more than simply the promise to pay. Hence, it is customary that the subject property be pledged as security for the loan.[1] The mortgage is the evidence of the pledge of security. The bond and the mortgage are considered parts of a single transaction.

State law governs property rights; in most states the mortgage is viewed as creating a lien, in some of the others it is viewed as conveying title, and in a few it is viewed as a combination (Table 8.0-1). That is, in lien-theory states the mortgage creates a lien on the property that terminates when the mortgage is satisfied. The mortgagor (borrower) retains title to the property and the right to possession and to collect rents. If the mortgage is not satisfied, the mortgagee (lender) can acquire the property through foreclosure. In title-theory states the mortgage conveys title to the mortgagee with the provision that if the mortgage is satisfied the conveyance is void. The mortgagor acquires the right to take possession and

Actually any interest that can be purchased or inherited can be pledged.

collect rent. In most other states the mortgage becomes a lien when it is written, and title passes to the mortgagee only in the event of default and foreclosure. The mortgagee has no interest in real property, only intangible personal property (i.e., the mortgage).

In some states a trust deed is used in place of a mortgage (Table 8.0-1). In this case, the borrower conveys the property in trust as security for payment of the debt. The conveyance is void upon payment of the debt. The trustee has the right to advertise and sell the property at public auction if the debt is not paid (rather than through to pursue a formal court action). He then uses the proceeds to satisfy the debt.

The mortgage involves only two parties: the borrower and the lender. The trust deed involves three parties: the borrower (trustor), the lender (beneficiary), and a trustee. (The borrower conveys the land to the trustee.)

8.1 HOW TO USE BONDS AND PROMISSORY NOTES

A bond is a sealed written agreement in which the borrower promises to repay the lender under certain stated conditions. A promissory note is similar to a bond except it lacks a seal. The bond or promissory note is evidence of the debt whereas the mortgage is evidence of the pledge of security for the debt. The bond or note is delivered, together with the mortgage, to the lender at the closing of the transaction. It is usually not recorded since it represents a personal obligation and not real property. The promissory note is used much more frequently than the bond, and it is always used in those states employing the deed of trust (Table 8.0-1).

The following are minimum requirements for the bond or note to be valid and enforceable:

- It must be in writing;
- The parties must be competent;
- There must be a promise to pay;

Table 8.0-1. Mortgage Concepts of States

State	Mortgage Theory			Evidence of Pledge of Security		Usual Method of Foreclosure			
	Lien Theory	Title Theory	Intermediate Theory	Trust Deed	Mortgage	Strict Foreclosure	Judicial Sale	Power of Sale	Entry and Possession
Alabama	X	X			X		X	X	
Alaska	X				X				
Arizona		X			X		X		
Arkansas					X		X		
California	X			X			X		
Colorado	X			X			X		
Connecticut		X			X	X			
Delaware			X	X					
District of Colombia		X		X				X	
Florida	X				X		X	X	

State	1	2	3	4	5	6	7	8	9
Georgia			X		X				X
Hawaii			X		X				X
Idaho			X		X				X
Illinois			X				X		
Indiana			X		X				X
Iowa			X		X				X
Kansas			X		X				X
Kentucky			X		X				X
Louisiana					X				
Maine	X	X			X				
Maryland		X			X			X	
Massachusetts	X				X			X	
Michigan		X	X					X	X
Minnesota		X	X						X
Mississippi			X			X	X		
Missouri						X	X		
Montana			X		X				X
Nebraska			X		X				X
Nevada					X				X
New Hampshire	X							X	

Table 8.0-1. (continued) Mortgage Concepts of States

State								
New Jersey	X			X		X		
New Mexico	X			X		X		
New York				X		X	X	
North Carolina	X			X		X		
North Dakota				X			X	
Ohio	X	X		X		X		
Oklahoma	X			X		X		
Oregon				X				
Pennsylvania		X		X				
Rhode Island		X		X				
South Carolina	X			X			X	X
South Dakota	X	X		X		X	X	
Tennessee	X		X	X				
Texas	X		X	X		X		
Utah						X		
Vermont		X			X			
Virginia		X	X	X				
Washington	X		X			X		
West Virginia		X	X					
Wisconsin	X			X			X	
Wyoming	X			X		X		

- The payment terms must be specified;
- The lender's recourse in the event of default must be specified; and
- The borrower must sign.

In event of default, many states allow the lender to sue on the note instead of foreclosing (Section 8.3). Generally, he may bring legal action under both the note and the mortgage so that if the net proceeds are less than the debt, he may recover the deficiency from the suit on the note.

8.2 HOW TO ASSIGN A MORTGAGE

From the mortgagee's point of view, the mortgage represents an investment (an annuity) that can be sold (Section 7.4). If sells the mortgage, he assigns his rights in the mortgage to the buyer of the mortgage (assignee). The assignee (and new mortgagee) receives exactly the same rights as were held by the previous mortgagee; moreover, the lien priority is unaltered by the assignment.

The assignment is usually made through a written instrument.[2] This instrument names the parties, identifies the mortgage (by its recording book and page number), the consideration, the remaining indebtedness, the property description (sometimes), and states that the assignor's interest is being transferred. The assignee should record the assignment immediately to give notice that the mortgagee's rights have been terminated. Recordation protects the assignee from a previous mortgagee who could fraudulently make a subsequent assignment of the mortgage. The mortgagee should give the mortgagor official notice of the assignment (otherwise the mortgagor needn't make payments to the assignee).

Sometimes the mortgage contains a covenant intended to protect the assignee. This covenant (called the estoppel covenant) states that the mortgagor is to execute and furnish to the mortgagee a

[2] The promissory note must be assigned with the mortgage; when the mortgage is satisfied, the mortgagor must insist on receiving both instruments.

statement declaring the validity of the mortgage, the remaining indebtedness, and whether or not the mortgagor has a defense in the event of fore-closure action. Otherwise, the assignee could not necessarily determine the amount of indebtedness (i.e., this is not stated on the mortgage).

8.3 WHAT HAPPENS AFTER DEFAULT?

Mortgage default is the failure to perform an act as required by the mortgage agreement. In particular, a mortgagor is in default if he violates one of the mortgage covenants. Usually, default occurs from the failure to pay the debt as specified, failure to pay assessments such as taxes and insurance, or failure to maintain the property.

I. Action by the Mortgagee

After default, the mortgagee can take action against the mortgagor by virtue of either provisions in the mortgage or state law. He usually chooses foreclosure. On the other hand, the mortgagee might wish to sue on the note and also act to foreclose the mortgage (i.e., to recover a deficiency resulting from foreclosure sale proceeds that are less than the loan balance). However, a few states may limit him to one action, usually foreclosure (See Table 8.0-1).

II. Time to Correct

The mortgagor is granted time to correct the deficiency by law (and sometimes by contract)[3]. It is usually terminated by

A. Sale. from a foreclosure action,

B. The Statute of Limitations.

C. Mortgagor's Failure to Perform.

Even after foreclosure sale, most states grant another period of time during which the mort-

[3] As are others with lawful interest in the property such as owners, past owners, heirs, assigns, legal representa-tives, grantees, life tenants, lessees, junior mortgagees, etc.

gagor can redeem the property. It may last as long as one year.

Hence, in order to exercise his rights, a mortgagee generally must declare a default, institute foreclosure proceedings, bid on the property at a public sale, and, finally, may have to wait up to one year to acquire clear title. For these reasons, mortgagees often cooperate with the mortgagor to avoid foreclosure.

III. Foreclosure

Foreclosure is a legal action taken upon default to end all of the mortgagor's rights to the property. Foreclosure proceedings vary greatly from state to state, but there are generally four methods of foreclosure.

A. Judicial Sale. Generally, the secured property is sold, and the proceeds are used to satisfy the debt. Figure 8.3-1 is a diagram showing the flow of events resulting from judicial sale. If the sale nets an amount less than the mortgage balance, most states hold the mortgagor liable for some of the deficiency (although the extent varies greatly).

B. Strict Foreclosure. Strict foreclosure is an action brought to determine the amount due under the mortgage and to foreclose the mortgagor's rights in the property. After determining the amount due, the Court issues its order stating the amount due under the mortgage, orders the amount due paid within a specified time, and provides that in default of such payment the mortgagor's (debtor's) right and equity of redemption shall be forever barred. This is done obviously without public sale as contrasted to most other foreclosure proceedings. The flow of events for strict foreclosure is as depicted in Figure 8.3-1 until the period of equitable right of redemption ends.

C. Foreclosure by Exercise of the Power of Sale. This form of foreclosure is possible because of the mortgage provision giving the power of sale to the mortgagee[4]: Notice of default is given to the

[4] Or to the trustee in the case of a trust deed.

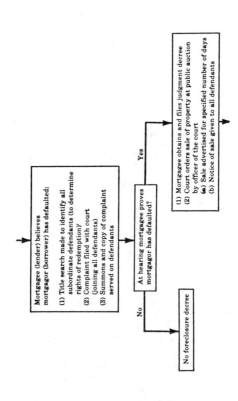

Mortgagee (lender) believes
mortgagor (borrower) has defaulted:

(1) Title search made to identify all
subordinate defendants (to determine
rights of redemption)
(2) Complaint filed with court
(joining all defendants)
(3) Summons and copy of complaint
served on defendants

At hearing mortgagee proves
mortgagor has defaulted?

No → No foreclosure decree

Yes →

(1) Mortgagee obtains and files judgment decree
(2) Court orders sale of property at public auction
by officer of the court
(a) Sale advertised for specified number of days
(b) Notice of sale given to all defendants

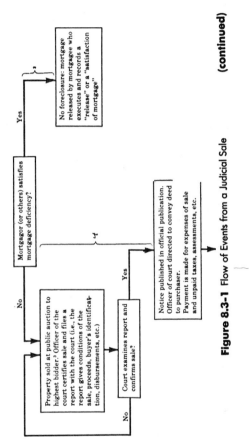

Figure 8.3-1 Flow of Events from a Judicial Sale **(continued)**

No

Yes

Remaining proceeds exceed mortgage balance*

Mortgagee obtains a deficiency judgment⁴ (mortgagor is liable)

Excess funds divided among defendants according to results of a "surplus money action"⁵

¹ If the mortgage had been assigned to the current mortgagee by a previous one, the previous mortgagee should be joined as a defendant to terminate his rights to the mortgage.

² Period during which mortgagor can retain property (period of equitable right of redemption). Time at which mortgagor must pay indebtedness when a strict foreclosure action has been brought.

³ Generally, the highest bidder is bound to buy if court provides marketable title as advertised. The mortgagee can bid if he chooses, but the mortgagor is generally not liable for a resulting deficiency (i.e., net sale proceeds less than mortgage balance). If statutory rights of redemption granted, purchaser receives only a certificate of sale and won't receive the deed until this period expires.

⁴ Period of statutory right of redemption (granted by some states). This period begins immediately after sale. Mortgagor can still redeem property during this period, which usually lasts one year.

⁵ Excess paid to junior-lien claimants in order of their priority and then to mortgagor.

⁶ Some states limit or prohibit deficiency judgments.

Figure 8.3-1 Flow of Events from a Judicial Sale

204

mortgagor, time is provided for the equitable right of redemption, the property is advertised, and a public sale is held. This procedure avoids the courts but is rarely used because of the strict statutory regulations (Table 8.0-1). This procedure is also known as statutory foreclosure or foreclosure by advertisement.

D. Foreclosure by Entry and Possession. In some states (Table 8.0-1), foreclosure can occur if the mortgagee takes possession of the property without opposition from the mortgagor. If the mortgagee gives legal notice of foreclosure and is able to possess the property without opposition from the mortgagor, he makes a witnessed written certification of the fact. Recordation of the certification then gives notice of complete foreclosure. The mortgagor is given one to three years in which to recover the property. After this period of redemption, title rests irrevocably with the mortgagee. On the other hand, if the mortgagor opposes possession, the mortgagee must use other means of foreclosure.

There is an alternative to foreclosure: The mortgagor gives a deed to the mortgagee. The mortgagee then replaces the mortgagor but is subject to junior liens that would have been removed by foreclosure. This procedure is much faster than foreclosure.

8.4 HOW MORTGAGE PRIORITY IS DETERMINED

The priority of a mortgage is the order in which it has claim to the property that is offered as security. Priority is important in the event of default by the mortgagor. If a foreclosure sale occurs and is confirmed by the court, the net proceeds are distributed according to a surplus money action as determined by lien priority.

Notice of the mortgage is necessary to establish lien priority. Actual notice comes from occupying the property, but since the mortgagee ordinarily does not occupy the property, notice must come from constructive notice—by recording the mortgage with the county recorder. Priority is determined by the time of recordation. However, a prior mortgage can voluntarily be subordinated to another.

Table 8.4-1 lists the priority of mortgages according to the time of recordation, the time of execution and delivery, and qualifications as expressed in the mortgage document.

It is not only mortgages that vie for lien priority, but also mechanics' liens, future after-acquired property, recorded judgments, and taxes (Sections 10.1–10.11). Statutes vary considerably with respect to priority of these liens. In the case of recorded construction loans, most states determine lien priority based upon whether advances for construction are optional or obligatory. Optional advances have priority over intervening liens only if the mortgagee did not receive actual notice (constructive notice is not sufficient since he is not obligated to search records). Obligatory advances have priority over all intervening liens. In any case, prospective lenders should examine the subject property for evidence of recent improvements.

8.5 WHAT ARE THE MINIMUM REQUIREMENTS AND PROVISIONS OF A MORTGAGE?

This section discusses the minimum requirements for a mortgage, provisions included in most statutory forms, and additional provisions that should be considered.

I. Minimum Requirements for a Mortgage

A mortgage is a contract, so it must contain those requirements of a valid contract. States vary somewhat in the conditions they consider minimal.

A. *Form.* It must be in writing.

B. *Execution.* It must be signed (executed) and dated.

C. *Parties.* The mortgagor and mortgagee must be competent and of legal age. The mortgagor's name should appear as it did when he acquired title, and, if married, the spouse should also sign. The addresses of all parties should be included.

Table 8.4-1. Priority Among Mortgages Depending Upon Time of Recordation, Time of Execution and Delivery, and Qualification as Expressed in the Mortgage Document. (t is any time you choose.)

Time of Recordation	Time of Execution & Delivery	Documented Qualification	Resulting Mortgage Priority
Recorded at time t	Time of exec. & del. is irrelevant	None	1
Recorded after time t	Time of exec. & del. is irrelevant	None	2
Not recorded	Exec. & del. at time t	None	3
Not recorded	Exec. & del. after time t	None	4
Recordation irrelevant	Time of exec. & del. is irrelevant	". . . subject to . . ."*	5

*This mortgage is subject to any of the above mortgages.

D. *Mortgaging Clause.* The words creating the mortgage are either "grants and conveys" or "conveys and warrants" in title-theory states and "mortgages" in lien-theory states.

E. *Interest.* The mortgagor must possess an interest that can be purchased or inherited.

F. *Debt or Performance.* The debt must exist and should be described. It can be pre-existing, created concurrently with the mortgage, or created by advances from the mortgagee in future installments (as in a construction loan). The mortgage can also secure performance (instead of debt) provided that the damage of non-performance can be expressed monetarily. The debt can be evidenced by one or more bonds or promissory notes, referred to in the mortgage.

G. *Description of Property.* The mortgaged property must be described with certainty. If not, the mortgage will probably still be valid, but other interested parties might not receive adequate notice of its existence. Since the mortgagee doesn't ordinarily possess the property (actual notice), he must rely upon recordation (constructive notice). If the description is inadequate, these parties are not bound by the notice and the priority the mortgage would receive.

In many cases the mortgage will cover not only real property but personal property as well (called a package mortgage). However, if the amount of personal property is extensive, a separate chattel mortgage (Section 8.2) might be preferable.

H. *Mortgagee's Recourse.* The mortgagee's recourse in event of default should be described.

I. *Delivery and Acceptance.* The mortgage should be voluntarily delivered to the mortgagee, his agent, or escrow. It should also be voluntarily accepted (i.e., either the mortgagee records it, or he fails to protest when the mortgagor records it). Although a mortgage can be valid without being acknowledged (i.e., the executor declares before an authorized officer that his act is voluntary), acknowledgment is necessary to gain the benefits of recordation.

II. Provisions Included in Most Statutory Forms

The statutory form of a mortgage contains this statement: "And the mortgagor covenants with the mortgagee as follows:". Then these provisions (covenants) are added. Note that all but the last are demands upon the mortgagor:

A. *Promise to Pay.* See that specific reference is made to the bond or promissory note (the evidence of the debt).

B. *Fire Insurance.* The mortgagor agrees to carry adequate fire insurance with the mortgagee as beneficiary. If the property is subject to other hazards such as wind and water, he should be responsible for extended coverage. Additionally, he should agree to assign and deliver the policies to the mortgagee and to reimburse him for any premiums that he must pay because of his failure to do so.

C. *Alteration or Destruction.* The mortgagor should agree that neither he nor others will be permitted to demolish, remove, or alter the realty without permission of the mortgagee.

D. *Taxes.* The mortgagor should agree to pay all taxes, assessments, and charges when due. Otherwise the mortgagee may do so and add that amount to the loan balance.

E. *Transfer or Default by Mortgagor (Acceleration Clause).* If the mortgagor transfers the property or defaults by violating one of the covenants (usually one of the four listed above), the mortgagee can call the loan balance due and payable at his option. Since this is a drastic measure, the default must be genuine and the provision clearly defined. In the case of transfer, the mortgagee will be interested in the acceleration clause because interest rates may have risen since the loan was made and he might be able to make a new loan at the higher rate. Although the acceleration clause is self-executing, most states give the mortgagee the option of exercising it; however, if he has knowledge of the transfer and delays too long, the equitable doctrine of estoppel would deny him the right to exercise it.

F. *Warranty of Title.* The mortgagor guarantees that he has good title.

G. *Termination of Mortgagee's Rights (Defeasance Clause).* The defeasance clause terminates the rights of the mortgagee if and when the debt is paid or performance is completed. In those states where the mortgage is considered to be a transfer of title (title theory states), the defeasance clause is essential.

III. Additional Provisions that Should Be Considered

A. *Subordination.* If the mortgage is intended to be "subject to" and subordinate to other mortgages, this should be so stated (i.e., a junior mortgage). The other mortgages should be clearly identified.

B. *Refinancing Protection (Lifting Clause).* The mortgagor may want to refinance the first mortgage. However, this could allow junior mortgages to replace the first mortgage, and refinancing would be denied on that basis. To prevent replacement, the first mortgagor should see that the junior mortgage contains a waiver: the junior mortgagee waives priority over a first mortgage subsequently executed to refinance as long as the indebtedness does not exceed the present amount. However, from the junior mortgagee's point of view, the clause should prevent the refinancing from increasing the payments.

C. *Multiple Properties (Partial Release Clause).* If the mortgage covers more than one parcel, it is desirable that each can be released separately.

D. *Life Estates.* A homestead is a life estate whereby the family home cannot be seized due to the husband's debts. If a homestead is mortgaged, the mortgage should contain a waiver of the homestead rights. Also, some states recognize the life estate that a wife has in her deceased husband's realty (dower's rights). In these states the mortgagee should require that the wife sign the note and mortgage, creating a personal liability for her.

E. *Foreclosure Costs.* The mortgagor should pay the costs of advertising and sale if a foreclosure sale is necessary. These costs can include attorney's fees, documentary evidence, and title searches.

F. *Good Repair.* To prevent the security from being impaired, the mortgagor should be required to keep the property in "reasonably good repair."

G. *Rent.* After foreclosure action, the mortgagor should be required to pay a reasonable rent while he possesses the property.

H. *Variable Interest Rate.* The interest rate can be tied to a standard rate.

I. *Prepayment.* Prepayment is a privilege, not a right. Hence, it is not permitted unless expressly granted in the mortgage. Prepayment is generally not desired by lenders if interest rates have subsequently fallen, and they may require a prepayment penalty on the loan balance. However, consider prepayment without penalty if there is a variable interest rate.

J. *Equity Participation.* When loans are difficult to obtain, some lenders also include provisions entitling them to some of the cash flow, capital gain, etc.

K. *Subordination of Purchase Money Mortgage.* Purchase money mortgages have unusual priority rights. Lenders should be very interested in having the grantor of such a mortgage subordinate it to the mortgage he will take.

8.6 HOW MORTGAGES CAN BE SATISFIED

The mortgage can be satisfied in several ways; however, most often it is satisfied by payment of debt.

I. Methods of Satisfaction

A. *Payment of Debt or Completion of Performance.* Suppose the mortgagor offers to pay the debt as specified. If the mortgagee accepts the payment, he issues a written statement to this effect. On the other hand, if the mortgagee refuses a valid offer of payment, the secured property is discharged (however, only payment will discharge the debt), accumulation of interest ceases, and the mortgagee cannot hold the mortgagor liable for court costs resulting from foreclosure action.

B. *Gratuity of Mortgagee.* A mortgagee can consider a mortgage satisfied whenever he wishes, even though the debt has not been paid.

C. *Conveyance by Mortgagor.* The mortgage lien is satisfied if the mortgagor conveys the property to the mortgagee.

D. *Statute of Limitations.* The statute of limitations requires that, after default, the mortgagee must bring action to enforce payment within a certain period of time (usually 8 to 20 years, but 6 years in New York). After this period of time, any party with an interest in the property can bring action to have the property released from the mortgage (provided the mortgagee is not in possession). Note that a statute of limitations does not discharge the debt, but bars the remedy.

II. The Satisfaction Document

Upon satisfaction, the mortgagee must give the mortgagor a receipt, commonly called a "satisfaction of mortgage." It should clearly identify both the mortgage and the mortgagee. It is signed by the mortgagee and states that the indebtedness has been satisfied.

Have the satisfaction acknowledged and recorded immediately with the county clerk (some states also stamp "discharged" or "released" in the margin of the mortgage). Recordation prevents the mortgagee from fraudulently assigning the satisfied mortgage and allows the mortgagor to refinance his property.

8.7 HOW LIABILITY IS ASSIGNED WHEN A MORTGAGE IS TRANSFERRED

When mortgaged property is transferred liability for the mortgage is assigned in one of two ways, depending upon the state (Table 8.0-1).

I. Mortgagor-Grantor Retains Liability.

In about half of the states, the grantee (e.g., buyer) recognizes the existence of the mortgage but promises nothing to the mortgagee. (It is said that he takes the property "subject to" the mortgage.) However, the mortgagor had earlier agreed to comply with the terms of the mortgage. Hence, if, after transfer, a deficiency results from a foreclosure sale, the mortgagor is liable to the mortgagee for this deficiency. The foreclosed-upon grantee, at most, loses his equity in the property.

II. Grantee Assumes Liability.

Conversely, in the other states, the grantee assumes liability for the mortgage (i.e., he "assumes" the mortgage). Hence, if, after transfer, a deficiency results from a foreclosure sale, the grantee is liable to the mortgagee for this deficiency. In this case, there is a separate agreement between the mortgagor and the grantee (for the benefit of the mortgagee), and they both sign the deed. The mortgagor is liable only for that part of the deficiency not paid by the grantee. However, because of their agreement, he can seek the unpaid portion from the grantee.

Sometimes the mortgagee insists on his approval of the grantee before transfer; however, there is a trend away from this.

Table 8.7-1 lists whether an amount is due the mortgagee from each party.

Table 8.7-1. Amount Due Mortgagee From Mortgagor and Grantee if there Is a Deficiency After Foreclosure Sale of Property in which the Mortgage Is Assumed.

	Mortgagor-Grantor	Grantee
Mortgagor-Grantor retains liability	Deficiency	0
Grantee assumes liability	Deficiency not paid by grantee	Deficiency

PART IV

PROPERTY MANAGEMENT

CHAPTER 9

LEASES: THEIR CONDITIONS AND VALUE

9.1 LEASE PROVISIONS TO CONSIDER

Every lease should contain a number of provisions in addition to those required. Since uncertainty increases with time, long-term leases, in particular, should be laden with provisions.

This section contains an extensive list of provisions that should be considered, depending upon the interests of the parties.

I. Rent

Rent is the usual consideration to the lessor in exchange for possession, use, and enjoyment of the premises.

At common law, rent is due at the *end* of each rental period. Therefore, if rent is to be paid in advance, this must be specified in the lease. The amount of rent, the payment schedule, and the recipient should all be specified.

The amount of rent stated in the lease is called the contract rent, and the rent dictated by prevailing supply and demand is called economic rent. When the lease is executed they are probably close, but they may diverge with time. Consequently, short-term leases usually call for constant rent, but long-term leases usually call for the contract rent to be periodically adjusted to approximate the economic rent. If the contract rent far exceeds the economic rent, the tenant will be tempted to default on the lease. On the other hand, if the economic rent exceeds the contract rent, the lease has value to the tenant; he can either occupy the property at the low rent, or he can sublet it at a profit. See Section 9.4.

In the case of net rent, the lease should provide that rent increase enough to cover increases in taxes and assessments so that rent is, in fact, net.

Rent can be tied to an index. The index

* can be general, such as the cost of living index;
* can be very specific, such as a percentage of the tenant's income; or it
* can tie rent to either a certain percentage of the tenant's income, or to a constant rent, whichever is higher.

If the lessor is entitled to a percentage of the tenant's income (called a percentage lease), he is not only an investor in real estate, but also an investor in business. Although tenant selection is always important, it is more important when rent is tied to his income. In selecting the tenant, the lessor should at least see that the tenant is engaged in an activity that will put the property to its "highest and best use."

A. Amount of Rent. Although the rent can be tied to the tenant's profits, it is more common to tie it to his gross income. If the rent is tied to profits, the relationship between lessor and lessee can become so close that the courts view them as partners; consequently, the lessor would be equally responsible for debts, liability, etc. Moreover, profits can be more difficult to define than gross income.

Some standard percentages of gross income are used throughout the country for different types of retail businesses. These percentages, of course, vary somewhat depending upon the size of the community, the income of the residents, the characteristics of the location, and the functional suitability of the property for the business.

The following is a partial list of percentage rents as determined by the Realtors National Marketing Institute of the National Association of Realtors.

Type of Business	Percentage of Gross Income
Automobile Accessories	3 to 4
Automobile Dealers	3
Bakeries	5 to 7
Barber Shops	8 to 10
Beauty Shops	8 to 10
Book and Stationery Stores	5 to 8
Bowling Alleys	8 to 10
Camera-Photography Stores	6 to 10
Candy Stores	6 to 10
Children's Clothing	5 to 8
Cocktail Bars-Taverns	8 to 10
Delicatessens	5 to 6
Department Stores	2 to 3
Discount Stores	1 to 2½
Drapery	4 to 5
Drug Store (Chain)	2 to 4
Drug Store (Individual)	3 to 5
Dry Cleaning & Laundry	6 to 8
Dry Cleaning & Laundry (Coin Operated)	8 to 10
Family Apparel	5 to 6
Florists	8 to 10
Florists (Garden Supply)	6 to 8
Furniture Stores	4 to 5
Furriers	6 to 8
Gift Shops	8 to 10
Hardware Stores	4 to 6
Hosiery-Lingerie	6 to 8
Household Appliances-Radios-T.V.	3 to 5
Jewelry Stores	7 to 10
Liquor Stores (Package)	4 to 6
Luggage Stores	6 to 8
Men's Apparel	4 to 6
Men's Furnishings	6 to 8
Millinery	10 to 12
Music-Musical Instruments	4 to 6
Office Supplies	5 to 6
Optical Stores	8 to 10
Paint-Wallpaper	4 to 6
Parking Lots (Attended)	40 to 50
Parking Lots (Non-Attended)	50 to 60

Type of Business	Percentage of Gross Income
Photography Shops	5 to 8
Restaurants	6 to 8
Sewing Machine Stores	4 to 5
Shoe Repair	8 to 10
Sport Goods	4 to 6
Supermarkets	$1^{1}/_{2}$ to 2
Variety Stores	$2^{1}/_{2}$ to 4
Women's Apparel	5 to 8
Women's-Children's Furnishings	6 to 8

B. Tenant's Income. In order to define the tenant's income, the following items should be specified.

• Merchandise—Consider different percentages for retail and wholesale and also for different products.

• Services—exchanged for goods and other services.

• Income of subtenants, concessionaires, licensees, etc.

• Charges, cash, and uncollected sales.

• Returned and exchanged merchandise.

• Sales tax.

• Merchandise sold through mail order and branch stores—Guard against sales that are diverted to branch stores to take advantage of their lower percentage rental.

C. Accounting and Inspection.

• The lessee should be required to keep records for this property separate from others.

• The lessor should reserve the right to enter the premises and inspect all records necessary to determine the income, whenever reasonable.

• The lessee should provide a statement on a specified date following each income period.

• The lessee should bear the expense of an audit when requested by the lessor and when an underpayment is also discovered.

D. Building Under Construction. If the building is under construction, specify the conditions under which the tenant can occupy it.

E. Tenant Operations.

• The minimum rental is to be increased if the tenant ceases or reduces operation.

• The tenant should conduct business in a competent way. If he fails to obtain a minimum gross income and there is no minimum rental, he should be dispossessed.

• The tenant should be restricted from engaging in a competitive business at other nearby locations.

• The lessor's permission should be required for subletting or assignment.

II. Improvements

If the lease is a short-term lease, only maintenance needs to be specified. Long-term leases should deal with the erection of new buildings (including the architect) and the demolition of older or improper buildings. Provide for cancellation of the lease if construction guidelines are violated This is essential in the case of a ground lease (a lease in which the tenant will build the improvements). The type of land qualifying for the construction of improvements is almost always prime commercial land; since location is not so important to industrial users, they are more likely to purchase their sites.

The owner might prefer a tenant to construct improvements because the value of the land will be increased (particularly if the tenant has a good reputation), and the property can be more readily sold or mortgaged. The tenant could prefer to lease the ground and construct improvements because he needn't have the capital to purchase the land, and the rent he will pay is a deductible business expense.

At the termination of a ground lease, the improvements might revert automatically to the owner, or one party may be required to purchase the improvements at its appraised value.

III. Maintenance

At common law, the tenant is responsible for keeping the property in the same condition as when he assumed possession. However, some states have enacted legislation requiring the landlord to maintain the property.

A. Tenant Recourse. If the landlord does not maintain the property, the tenant has some recourse:

1. He can maintain the property and recover the cost from the landlord, or (in some states) he can deduct the cost from rent.

2. If the need for maintenance is quite extensive, the landlord has breached the implied covenant of quiet enjoyment, and the tenant can claim he has been constructively evicted. He can then either abandon the property or remain without paying rent.

B. Tenant Responsibilities. Long-term leases contain detailed provisions for maintenance:

1. The tenant should keep the premises in good condition. In this case, the tenant must comply whether he caused the damage or not. The lease should call for termination if the tenant does not comply. Otherwise, the landlord may have to sue for damages for breach of contract.

2. Usually, if the tenant leases the entire premises, the landlord repairs only those deficiencies expressly stated.

IV. Term

The term of the lease should depend on the use, the type of tenant, and the needs of the parties. Long-term tenants usually pay all operating expenses including real estate tax (called a net lease).

V. Use

The lease should specify:

• the use of the property (e.g., " . . . a retail store and no other . . . ");

• that the lease will be terminated if the tenant does anything to diminish or injure the value of the owner's fee interest; and

• that the landlord has the right to make frequent inspections.

VI. Insurance

In the case of a long-term lease:

• the policies should be in the names of both parties. (The lessee should pay the premium);

• the policy should remain in the possession of the lessor; and

• the type of insurance and the amount allocated between the lessor and lessee depend upon the use of the property and the terms of the lease.

A. Fire Insurance. For short-term leases, the landlord usually insures the improvements, and the tenant usually insures his personal property.

B. Liability Insurance. Leases for residential rental property usually provide that the lessor is responsible for injury occurring only in the common areas such as stairs, walks, parking lots, etc. Leases for commercial and industrial property usually specify that the lessee is responsible for injury occurring anywhere on the property.

VII. Option to Purchase

When the tenant erects a building on the property it is common to give him the option to purchase. It can be unqualified or it can merely give the tenant the first right of refusal under the same conditions offered to others.

A. Purchase Price. The price can be specified or the parties can agree to a method to determine the price. Each appoints an appraiser and the appraisers appoint an umpire. If the umpire and at least one appraiser agree on a price, it shall be binding upon the parties. Without agreement, the lease can call for a suit for specific performance in a court of equity.

B. Time. Specify the time period during which the purchase option must be exercised.

C. Rent Credit. The lease might provide for some rent to be applied to the down payment upon purchase.

VIII. Mortgaging the Leasehold

Unless expressly prohibited, the lessee can mortgage the lease (The leasehold mortgage is discussed in Section 5.6.)

Some leases require the loan proceeds to be used for the property only and specify that the lessor's rights are not to be impaired by the mortgage.

If the lessee defaults on the lease and is evicted, the mortgagee would lose his security. Hence, the mortgagee should provide that the lessee notify him of possible default and permit him to correct it.

IX. Subleasing

Subleasing is the leasing of property by the lessee to a third party. However, he remains bound by the provisions of his lease with the original lessor. Generally, subleasing is not permitted unless expressly provided in the lease or subsequently permitted by the landlord.

X. Assignment

The assignment of a lease is the transfer of all rights of the lessee to another. Assignment is permitted unless the lease expressly forbids it.

XI. Extension

An extension is the continuation of the lease for an extra period of time and under the same conditions. The lessee can extend the lease simply by remaining in possession after the termination date. Some states that permit extensions limit the time to the length of the lease or one year, whichever is shorter. Since the extension option runs with the land, it binds assignees.

XII. Renewal

When a lease is renewed, a new agreement

must be executed (even if the provisions are to be the same). If the lessee desires to renew the lease, he usually must give proper notice.[1]

XIII. Abandonment

Unless the lessee has been constructively evicted, his abandonment of the property does not relieve him of the obligations of the lease. Since abandonment causes default, the lessor can terminate the lease.

The lease should specify that upon abandonment, the landlord can repossess, relet, and charge the tenant with lost rental and the expenses of reletting.

XIV. Security

The tenant should always be required to deposit something of value with the lessor to cover the cost of possible damage or default. Usually the security is cash, but it can be anything of value such as a bond or a deed to other property. The extent of the security should depend upon the likelihood of damage or default. This, of course, depends upon the property, the use, the integrity and solvency of the tenant, etc. Sometimes the lessor is required to deposit the security (if cash) in an interest-bearing account for the lessee and to notify him of the location of the account.

In the case of a ground lease in which the tenant constructs a building, the lessor should require some security before the building is complete. Usually the security is cash or a completion bond. After it is complete, the building becomes the security.

In any case, the lease should specify that, if the lease is assigned by the lessor, the security can be transferred to the new lessor; otherwise, the original lessor remains liable for its return.

---

[1]However, New York holds that a renewal is automatic unless the lessee provides proper notice that he will not renew. Moreover, the lessor is required to remind the lessee of this fact.

XV. Arbitration

To avoid court action over disputes, important leases should describe a method of arbitration; e.g., the method of arbitration and the number and types of arbitrators.

XVI. Taxes

Long-term leases usually require the tenant to pay property tax and assessments. Some leases even require the tenant to pay corporate franchise tax and income tax.

XVII. Municipal Ordinances

The lease should define the responsibility of each party with respect to municipal safety, sanitation, building, fire, and other codes that regulate occupancy.

XVIII. Bankruptcy

The lessor should express the right to terminate the lease if the lessee declares bankruptcy.

XIX. Condemnation and Destruction

The lease should provide for premature termination due to condemnation or destruction of the property. For example, a long-term lease should equitably allocate the condemnation award or insurance award between the lessor and lessee after mortgages and other encumbrances are satisfied. Provision should be made for partial condemnation. In most cases the tenant remains responsible for rent. See Section 9.3.

XX. Default

This provision can cause termination and is discussed in Section 9.3.

XXI. Mortgage Payments

In a long-term lease, the tenant has a great interest in the property. Consequently, he would want the right to make mortgage payments for the mortgagor-lessor to prevent default.

9.2 REQUIREMENTS FOR VALIDITY OF A LEASE

The substance of a lease is important, but its form is not. In fact, leases can be either written or oral. However, the Statute of Frauds usually requires that a lease of one year or longer be in writing to be enforceable. The following seven requirements are usually considered sufficient for the validity of a lease.

I. Parties

The parties to the lease should be identified by legal names and address. Although both parties should sign, only the lessor is required to sign. Spouses should be a party to the lease if there are dower rights in their state or if the title is held as tenancy by the entirety. Actually the lessee needn't sign the lease because his acceptance is evidenced by his possession of the property and payment of rent.

II. Property Description

The property should be described as in a deed, but it often must be more specific because only part of the property might be leased. A blueprint of the leased property is sometimes included as part of the lease. The amount of detail in the description depends upon the use of the property and the length of the term.

III. Term

The term of the lease should be specified by stating the beginning date and the length of time. If the term is not specified, a tenancy at will or a month-to-month tenancy will probably result. (It can be terminated by either party at any time.)

In some states the term is limited by statute. For example, agricultural leases are sometimes limited to 10–20 years. To discourage leases that run for centuries, some states hold that leasehold estates that run for 100 years or more become freehold estates; hence the frequent use of 99 years.[2]

[2]Leaseholds that have several extensive renewal options also risk becoming freehold estates.

IV. Statement of Intent to Lease

The lease must contain a statement that the lessor voluntarily transfers the right of possession (and sometimes the right of use and enjoyment) to the lessee.

V. Delivery and Acceptance

The lessor must deliver the signed lease to the lessee. Delivery occurs when the lease passes into the lessee's control.

VI. Acknowledgment

Acknowledgment is generally not required although some states require leases of one year or longer to be either witnessed or acknowledged.

VII. Recordation

Recordation (with the county clerk and recorder) gives constructive notice that the lease exists. This protects third parties such as claimants and purchasers of the freehold estate. Short-term leases are usually not recorded, but some states require long-term leases to be. If the lease is not recorded in those states that require it, it remains valid between the lessor and lessee (and third parties having knowledge of its existence), but it is void with regard to others.

9.3 HOW TO TERMINATE A LEASE

A lease can terminate either at maturity or prematurely due to a variety of reasons.

I. Natural Termination

If the tenant remains in possession of the property until the intended term, the extent of notice required of the parties is dictated by statute. It generally depends upon the length of the lease.

A. More than One Year. A tenancy of more than one year (called an estate for years) requires no notice.

B. *One Year or Less.* Tenancies of this type are called periodic tenancies. The lessor is usually required to give a 30-day notice for both month-to-month and year-to-year leases and a 7-day notice for week-to-week tenancies. In any case, when a tenant remains in possession after the lease expires, neither party is required to give notice.

II. Premature Termination

Leases can be terminated prematurely for a variety of reasons and costly litigation can be minimized if some of the possible reasons are included as provisions when the lease is drafted.

A. *Mutual Agreement.* Both parties might agree to premature termination with some consideration paid to, or conditions imposed on, one of the parties.

B. *Default.* Default on a lease results from the breach of one of its provisions. If the lessee defaults, the lessor can bring dispossess proceedings to have him evicted. The proceedings require certain documents to be served and statutory notice.

If the lessor defaults, the lessee can prematurely terminate the lease by abandoning the property. A common cause of default by the lessor is through either actual or constructive eviction.

1. Actual Eviction. Occurs when some party rightfully dispossesses the lessee through possession of a title superior to that of the lessor.

2. Constructive Eviction. Occurs when the lessor fails to keep the property in tenantable condition[3] (e.g., unsanitary plumbing, leaky roof, inadequate heat, vermin infestation, unrepaired damage, etc.). Before the lessee can abandon the property legally, he must give the lessor an opportunity to remedy the situation and give proper notice.

---

[3]Such condition is necessary for quiet enjoyment, a right of the lessee that is implied and needn't be expressed in the lease.

C. Condemnation (Eminent Domain). The lease is prematurely terminated when government condemns the property.

D. Destruction. The lease might include a provision calling for termination in the event of destruction of the premises. Otherwise, the lessee may still be responsible for rent. The lessee owns the leasehold estate, and, at common law, he has the responsibilities of an owner (such as the owner of a freehold estate). Hence, he is responsible for the provisions of the lease (including rent) even though the property is untenantable due to destruction. However, some states have enacted statutes to modify common law. For example, the lessor may be responsible for restoring the usefulness of the realty within a reasonable time at his expense; during this time the tenant would not be responsible for rent. The lease should provide for partial rent in the event damage renders the realty only partially untenantable.

E. Purchase by Tenant. Provide for termination of the lease if the lessee purchases the freehold estate.

9.4. HOW TO DETERMINE THE VALUE OF A LEASE

The rent from a lease constitutes an annuity to the lessor. Hence, the value of the lease is the present value of an annuity.

When the lease is executed, the contract rent is probably near the economic rent. However, as time passes, these two values will probably diverge because of market conditions or the condition of the property.

I. Leased Fee Interest

The owner's interest is called the leased fee interest. In the case of net rental, its present value is the sum of these two values:

• the rent payments, discounted at the leased fee interest rate (which is proportional to the risk of collecting rent), and

• the forecast value of the lessor's equity discounted at the property interest rate.

The formula for gross rental is more complicated than for net rental because it also accounts for operating expenses.

II. Leasehold Interest

The lessee's interest is called the leasehold interest. If the economic rent exceeds the contract rent, it has value. The value depends upon whether or not the lessee remains in possession of the property or subleases his interest (operating a sandwich lease interest).

If the lessee remains in possession of the property, the value to him is the difference between economic rent and contract rent, discounted at the leasehold interest rate. Generally, the leasehold interest rate is rather high because the difference between economic rent and contract rent is not certain to remain favorable.

III. Sandwich Lease Interest

If the property is subleased at a higher rent, the original lessee's interest (called a sandwich lease interest) has value. The value is the difference between the two contract rents, discounted at the sandwich lease interest rate. This rate is related to the risk of the sublease. It is usually less than the leasehold interest rate and greater than the leased fee interest rate.

IV. Formulas

The following formulas can be used to determine the present value of the lease. If the rent is constant, the formulas in Table A.4.2-1 for the present value are easier to use than these.

$$
v_f = \begin{cases}
\sum_{i=1}^{m} \dfrac{x_j}{c(r_f,i,q)} + \dfrac{V}{c(r_p,m,q)} & \text{(net rental)} \\[2ex]
\sum_{i=1}^{m} \dfrac{y_i}{c(r_f,i,q)} - w \sum_{i=1}^{m} \dfrac{1}{c(r'',i,q)} + \dfrac{V}{c(r_p,m,q)} & \text{(gross rental)}
\end{cases}
$$

$$
v_h = \sum_{i=1}^{m} \dfrac{(y'_i - y_i)}{c(r_h,i,q)} \approx \sum_{i=1}^{m} \dfrac{(x'_i - x_i)}{c(r_h,i,q)}
$$

$$\mathbf{v_s} = \sum_{i=1}^{m} \frac{y_{2i} - y_{1i}}{c(r_s,i,q)} = \sum_{i=1}^{m} \frac{(x_{2i} - x_{1i})}{c(r_s,i,q)}$$

where

v_f, v_h, v_s = present value of the leased fee interest, leasehold interest, and sandwich lease interest, respectively

x_i, x'_i = periodic net rental that is contract rent and economic rent, respectively

y_i, y'_i = periodic gross rental that is contract rent and economic rent, respectively

x_{1i}, x_{2i} = periodic net contract rental on original lease and sublease, respectively

y_{1i}, y_{2i} = periodic gross contract rental on original lease and sublease, respectively

w = operating expenses in first rental period

r_f, r_h, r_s, r_p = interest rate of leased fee interest, leasehold interest, sandwich lease, and property,[4] respectively

r' = annual rate of change of operating expenses (positive, zero, or negative)

$r'' = q \cdot \dfrac{r_f - r'}{q + r'}$ (r_f and r' must be expressed as decimals)

V = forecast value of reversion (lessor's equity) when the lease expires. See Section 1.1

q = number of rental periods per year

m = number of remaining rental periods

$c(r_f,i,1)$ etc. = amount of 1 at compound interest. See Table 1

EXAMPLE

So that this example will be concise, assume that rental payments are made annually and that only

[4] See Section 4.4.

five years remain on the lease. The lease specifies annual net rental of $50,000.

(a) Determine the present value of the leased fee interest if the lessor's equity value at the expiration of the lease is expected to be $600,000, the leased fee interest rate is 12%, and the property interest rate is 15%; (b) Determine the present value of the leasehold interest if the economic net rent over the next five years is expected to be $55,000, $57,000, $60,000, $64,000, and $69,000. The leasehold interest rate is 14%; and (c) Determine the present value of the sandwich lease if the sublease calls for net rent of $57,000 for each of the remaining 5 years and the sandwich lease interest rate is 13%.

SOLUTION

In this example, $q = 1$, $m = 5$, and $x_i = x_2 = x_3 = x_4 = x_5 = \$50,000$.

(a) For this part of the problem,

$$V = \$600,000, r_f = 12\%, \text{ and } r_p = 15\%.$$

From Table 1,

$$c(12,1,1) = 1.1200,$$
$$c(12,2,1) = 1.2544,$$
$$c(12,3,1) = 1.4049,$$
$$c(12,4,1) = 1.5735,$$
$$c(12,5,1) = 1.7623, \text{ and}$$
$$c(15,5,1) = 2.0114.$$

Now, the present value of the leased fee interest is

$$
\begin{aligned}
v_f &= \left(\frac{\$50,000}{1.1200} + \frac{\$50,000}{1.2544} + \frac{\$50,000}{1.4049} \right.\\
&\qquad \left. + \frac{\$50,000}{1.5735} + \frac{\$50,000}{1.7623} \right) + \frac{\$600,000}{2.0114} \\
&= (\$44,642.86 + \$39,859.69 + \$35,589.72 \\
&\qquad + \$31,776.29 + \$28,372.01) + \$298,299.69 \\
&= \$180,240.57 + \$298,299.69 \\
&= \$478,540.26.
\end{aligned}
$$

(b) In this case,

$x'_1 = \$55,000$, $x'_2 = \$57,000$, $x'_3 = \$60,000$,
$x'_4 = \$64,000$, $x'_5 = \$69,000$, and $r_h = 14\%$.

From Table 1,

$$c(14,1,1) = 1.1400,$$
$$c(14,2,1) = 1.2996,$$
$$c(14,3,1) = 1.4815,$$
$$c(14,4,1) - 1.6890, \text{ and}$$
$$c(14,5,1) = 1.9254.$$

Now, the present value of the leasehold interest is

$$
\begin{aligned}
v_h &= \frac{\$55,000 - \$50,000}{1.1410} + \frac{\$57,000 - \$50,000}{1.2996} \\
&\quad + \frac{\$60,000 - \$50,000}{1.4815} + \frac{\$64,000 - \$50,000}{1.6890} \\
&\quad\quad\quad\quad\quad + \frac{\$69,000 - \$50,000}{1.9254} \\
&= \frac{\$5,000}{1.1400} + \frac{\$7,000}{1.2996} + \frac{\$10,000}{1.4815} + \frac{\$14,000}{1.6890} \\
&\quad + \frac{\$19,000}{1.9254} \\
&= \$4,385.96 + \$5,386.27 + \$6,749.92 \\
&\quad + \$8,288.93 + \$9,868.08 \\
&= \$34,679.16.
\end{aligned}
$$

(c) In this case,

$$x_{11} = x_{12} = x_{13} = x_{14} = x_{15} = \$50,000,$$
$$x_{21} = x_{22} = x_{23} = x_{24} = x_{25} = \$57,000,$$
$$\text{and } r_s = 13\%.$$

From Table 1,

$$c(13,1,1) = 1.1300,$$
$$c(13,2,1) = 1.2769,$$
$$c(13,3,1) = 1.4429,$$
$$c(13,4,1) = 1.6305, \text{ and}$$
$$c(13,5,1) = 1.8424.$$

Now, the present value of the sandwich lease interest is

$$
v_8 = \frac{\$57,000 - \$50,000}{1.1300} + \frac{\$57,000 - \$50,000}{1.2769}
$$

$$+ \frac{\$57,000 - \$50,000}{1.4429} + \frac{\$57,000 - \$50,000}{1.6305}$$

$$+ \frac{\$57,000 - \$50,000}{1.8424}$$

$$= \frac{\$7,000}{1.1300} + \frac{\$7,000}{1.2769} + \frac{\$7,000}{1.4429} + \frac{\$7,000}{1.6305} + \frac{\$7,000}{1.8424}$$

$$= \$6,194.69 + \$5,482.03 + \$4,851.34$$

$$+ \$4,293.16 + \$3,799.39$$

$$= \$24,620.61.$$

CHAPTER 10

TYPES OF LIENS

10.0 GENERAL PROPERTIES OF LIENS

A lien is a right of certain creditors to have their debts paid from the debtor's realty, usually by sale. Depending upon the reason for the debt, the lien can affect a specific property (specific lien) or all properties of the debtor (general lien).

At common law, realty cannot be used involuntarily to satisfy a debt.[1] However, statutes have been enacted to provide this right to certain creditors. Hence, the details of liens vary greatly from state to state. These involuntary liens are called statutory liens. On the other hand, equitable liens arise when the owner voluntarily pledges his realty as security for a debt. Table 10.0-1 lists characteristics of liens.

To create a lien, the creditor first files the notice of lien with the county clerk and recorder in the county in which the realty is located. The notice of lien is then recorded. Generally, it must be filed with a certain period of time after the debt occurs, and right to the lien lasts for only a certain period of time.

During this period of time the debt can be satisfied by the debtor or the lien can be enforced by foreclosure proceedings.[2] If there is a foreclosure sale, the proceeds are applied toward the debt. If the debt is not enforced during the lien period, the lien right is lost forever. The owner can

---

[1]Common law is a body of law that has evolved through use and acceptance (English unwritten law) rather than through codified law (Roman law).

[2]The foreclosure proceedings are similar to those following default on a mortgage (detailed in Section 8.3).

sell his property to a third party, but that party takes title subject to the lien right.

The priority among liens of the same type generally follows the order in which they were recorded with the county clerk and recorder. However, the priority between liens of a different type is not so easily determined. For example, property tax liens generally have priority over all other liens regardless of the time of recording, and some mechanic's liens have priority over prior recorded mortgage liens. Again, state laws vary considerably.

Since states hold that debts are assignable, liens are assignable.

10.1 ASSESSMENT LIEN

An assessment (or special tax) is a charge against a specific real property by local government for the cost of an improvement (such as streets, sewers, etc.). Like a real property tax lien, it has priority over all other liens.

After a given period of time, the unpaid assessment becomes an assessment lien. To enforce the lien, the government can sell the property at public auction to the highest bidder. The former owner has the right to redeem the property if he pays the assessment, plus interest, within a given period of time.

10.2 ATTACHMENT LIEN

An attachment lien is a lien against the real property of a defendant *prior* to a law suit for money damages. The purpose of the attachment lien is to take a specific property into legal custody to help satisfy the money damage if the suit is successful. The plaintiff (person filing the suit) should have some reason to believe the property might not otherwise be available.[3] Since the suit may not be

---

[3] Generally, an attachment lien is allowed when the defendant (1) is a non-resident or a foreign (out-of-state) corporation, (2) has absconded or is in hiding, or (3) is about to dispose of the property. The defendant is usually given proper notice and a fair hearing.

Table 10.0-1. Characteristics of Liens

Reason for Debt	Name of Lien	Property Affected	Origin of Lien	Section
Unpaid Municipal Improvement	Assessment Lien	Specific	Statutory	10.1
Unpaid Money Damages	Attachment Lien	Specific	Statutory	10.2
Unpaid Bail	Bail Bond Lien	Specific	Equitable	10.3
Unpaid Corporate Franchise Tax	Corporate Franchise Tax Lien	General	Statutory	10.4
Unpaid Federal Tax	Federal Income and Estate Tax Lien	General	Statutory	10.5
Unpaid Money Awarded by Court Action	Judgment Lien	General	Statutory	10.6

Unpaid Labor and Materials	Mechanic's Lien	Specific	Statutory	10.7
Unpaid Loan	Mortgage Lien	Specific	Equitable	10.8
Unpaid Real Property Tax	Real Property Tax Lien	Specific	Statutory	10.9
Unpaid State Tax	State Income and Estate Tax Lien	General	Statutory	10.10
Unreturned Deposit on Defaulted Contract for Sale	Vendee's Lien	Specific	Statutory*	10.11
Full Purchase Price Not Paid by Purchaser	Vendor's Lien	Specific	Statutory*	10.12

* Sometimes equitable.

successful, the plaintiff should file a bond to compensate the defendant for any loss due to the suit.

10.3 BAIL BOND LIEN

A bail bond lien is a lien on a specific property as security for the payment of bail.

After arrest on a criminal charge, the suspect might be released provided a certain amount of value (bail) is secured to encourage him to return for trial. Bail can be satisfied in one of three ways: cash, a bond placed by a bondsman, or a lien on real property. The first two ways are liquid and have known value. But, since the third is neither liquid nor of well-known value, equity should be at least twice the amount of bail.

If real property is offered for bail, notice of the bail bond lien is filed with the county clerk and recorder in the county where the property is located. The lien is discharged when bail is discharged, and a certificate to this effect is obtained from the district attorney and recorded.

10.4 CORPORATE FRANCHISE TAX LIEN

Most states impose a franchise tax on corporations that do business in their state. If this tax is not paid, the state may file a lien against the corporate property (a general lien).

10.5 FEDERAL INCOME AND ESTATE TAX LIEN

A Federal tax lien is imposed against all property of a taxpayer for delinquent tax and lien is imposed against all property of a beneficiary or descendant for an estate tax.

The Federal tax lien is valid after notice is filed in the county clerk's office in the county where the debtor owns property. The lien lasts for 10 years. It is subordinate to existing mortgages, but superior to subsequent mortgages.

10.6 JUDGMENT LIEN

A judgment is a money award arising from a successful court action. A judgment lien is a lien on all of the defendant's non-exempt property to secure the money award.

The judgment becomes a lien when it is recorded with the county clerk and perfected (satisfies all judgments). It lasts from 1 to 10 years. The lien applies to all property within the county in which the judgment is entered and to all property acquired after the lien exists.[4]

A supplementary proceeding is served upon the debtor ordering him to submit his records so that his assets can be determined. The creditor must request the clerk of the court in which the judgment was entered to issue an order of execution. An official, often the sheriff, serves a copy of the execution on the debtor, thereby demanding payment. If the debt is not paid, the official seizes and sells all realty necessary to satisfy the judgment.[5] If the proceeds from the sale are at least equal to the money award, the judgment is satisfied. The purchaser should record the satisfaction of judgment (the seller has no reason to do it).

10.7 MECHANIC'S LIEN

A mechanic's lien is a lien on a specific improved property to secure unpaid labor or materials that improved the property. Because the mechanic's lien is due to improvement, it can be placed against the improved property only.

Since mechanics' liens do not exist at common law, but are created solely by statute, provisions vary greatly from state to state.

I. Persons Entitled to a Mechanic's Lien

Generally, those entitled to a mechanic's lien are contractors, subcontractors, materialmen

[4] The lien can be extended to any county in the state by filing an abstract of judgment in that county. It can be extended to property in another state, if the plaintiff brings suit and obtains a judgment in the appropriate county of that state.

[5] In some states, the property must be appraised before the sale, and the sale price must be at least a certain fraction (e.g., 2/3) of the appraised value before the sale can be consummated.

(those who supply materials), engineers, architects, employees of contractors, etc. However, they are entitled only if they contributed to the improvement.

A subcontractor is usually entitled to a mechanic's lien, and, if he is, so are his employees who contributed to the improvement. Materialmen who supply materials are entitled, but those who supply materialmen are not.

If the contractor does not pay the subcontractor, he may be required to show his records. If it is found that he has diverted funds paid to him by the owner, he may be held for grand larceny.

A lessee usually cannot claim a mechanic's lien against the leased property unless:

• the lease (or other contract) requires him to improve the property or,

• in those states requiring only consent of the owner, the owner realizes the lessee is making improvements but does not give him notice of nonresponsibility.

If a contract to improve property is assigned to another with the owner's consent, the assignee is entitled to a mechanic's lien.

Two systems are used to determine those entitled to a mechanic's lien. All states use one of these systems or a combination of them.

A. Pennsylvania System. The contractor's right to a lien is subordinate to that of his subcontractors, laborers, and materialmen. It is important for the owner in states using this system to re alize that the subcontractors, laborers, and materialmen are entitled to a mechanic's lien even though he has paid the contractor. Moreover, the total amount of the debt can legally exceed the cost of the improvements.

B. New York System. Usually, only the contractor has the right to a lien on the property. However, subcontractors, laborers, and materialmen can substitute their lien rights for those of the contractor if they give proper notice. That is, if the subcontractor gives the owner notice of the amount due him, the owner can withhold that amount from the contractor.

II. Persons Subject to a Mechanic's Lien

Owners of realty are generally responsible for debts due to improvements to their property, and, hence, are subject to a mechanic's lien.

Generally, for lien purposes, an owner is one who

• Owns a fee estate,

• Owns a lesser estate,

• Owns a leasehold for a term of years (but usually not less),

• Is in possession of the realty and also under contract to purchase it, or

• Has a right, interest, or title in the realty.

The following are generally not subject to a mechanic's lien:

• Publicly owned improvements.

• A tenant who orders improvements without proof of the lessor's consent.[6]

• A spouse who does not have authority to contract for improvements to the other's realty.[7]

III. Conditions Necessary for a Mechanic's Lien

One of the most important conditions necessary for a mechanic's lien is the degree of consent of the owner or his agent. Generally, an obligation cannot be imposed on a person without his knowledge or consent. In many states, if the owner or his agent consents to improvement, the contractor is entitled to a lien, but as a general rule, mere evidence of improvement is not sufficient. Some states require a contract as a necessary condition for a lien.

The improvements must be of a permanent nature and materials must be used for improvement. That is, tools, machinery, and so on, do not qualify.

---

[6] Owners of multiple-unit property should post a notice of non-responsibility for improvements contracted by lessees. Such notice should also be recorded.

[7] However, New York statute provides that either spouse will be responsible unless they give notice to the contrary within 10 days.

IV. How to File Notice of a Mechanic's Lien

Since mechanics' liens do not exist at common law, the claimant must exercise great care to file a statement of claim and a notice of lien according to state law.

The notice of lien must be served on the owner (usually by registered mail), posted on the property, or both. Usually the notice must include the name of the claimant, the name of the owner, an itemized list of the claim, the dates of improvements or materials delivered, and a description of the property. The notice is verified (sworn to be correct before a duly qualified officer) by the claimant.

The notice must be filed within a certain time after completion of the work or delivery of materials. The length of time depends on the state, the type of claimant, and the type of owner. Allow four months to file.

V. Assignment

Unless otherwise specified in a contract (such as the contract for improvement) all states hold that a debt is assignable; hence, perfected mechanics' liens are assignable.

VI. Priority Between Liens

Priority of liens is usually established by the order in which the notice of lien is recorded by the county clerk. However, one of three dates might be used for mechanics' liens, depending upon the state: the date the notice of lien was recorded, the contract for improvement was signed, or the work began.

Priority among mechanics' liens would be established by one of these dates. However, criteria for priority between a mechanic's lien and another lien such as a mortgage, varies among the states. Some states give priority to a mechanic's lien over a prior recorded mortgage. In other states, there is no priority among lien claimants, and if the proceeds from the sale are insufficient to pay them all, they are distributed ratably.

VII. Satisfaction or Enforcement

If the lien has been released or satisfied, a satisfaction of lien should be signed, acknowledged, and recorded. The lien is then effectively discharged.

On the other hand, if the lien is neither released nor satisfied it is enforced by foreclosure proceedings. In most states the procedure is similar to that of mortgage foreclosure (Section 8.3). An action is brought to foreclose the lien; if the claim is valid, the court will determine the amount of the claim, order the real estate sold, and distribute the sale proceeds according to statute. The lienor has only a certain period of time within which he can foreclose after the lien has been perfected. The period is usually 18 months, but it can range from 6 months to 6 years.

After the period of foreclosure passes, the lien terminates (unless a lis pendens has been filed to extend it). If, the recorded lien still appears on the records of the county clerk after the foreclosure period ends, it can be removed by court order. The county clerk then issues an order to discharge the lien.

10.8 MORTGAGE LIEN

A mortgage is the pledge of a specific property to secure payment of a debt (or other obligation). Since it is voluntary, it is an equitable lien.

Some states (called title theory states) view the mortgagee as having title to the property; others (called lien theory states) view the mortgagee as having a lien on the property, and others use a combination of these theories.

10.9 REAL PROPERTY TAX LIEN

Real property tax is a tax levied by local government, based on the assessed value of real property. It becomes a lien on the specific property when due (usually on the first of the year), and it has priority over all other liens. If necessary, the property is sold, and a tax certificate is delivered to the purchaser. However, the owner usually has the right to redeem the property within three years after the date of sale. Even then, the owner is usually given notice and time to redeem. To redeem, he must pay the purchaser the amount of the delinquent taxes plus interest.

If the owner does not redeem the property, the purchaser is issued a quitclaim deed. If the purchaser has only a quitclaim deed, lenders will be reluctant to lend on the property until one of the following occurs:

- The period for adverse possession passes.

- The purchaser institutes a tax foreclosure proceeding (if statute provides for this) and a marketable deed is issued.

- The title is registered with an insurance fund (called the Torrens proceeding). Then, the fund pays losses due to title defects.

10.10 STATE INCOME AND ESTATE TAX LIEN

States impose an income tax and usually an estate tax. The income tax lien is a general lien against all property of the delinquent taxpayer, and the estate tax lien is a general lien against all property received by the benficiary or descendant.

10.11 VENDEE AND VENDOR'S LIEN

A vendee's lien can arise when the purchaser of real property places a deposit on the property, but the seller defaults on the contract for sale and refuses to return the deposit.

A vendor's lien can arise when the seller of real property adheres to the contract for sale, but the purchaser does not pay the entire purchase price.

A vendor's lien also occurs when the seller retains title until the purchaser completes the contract (e.g., installment land contract). These liens generally include the amount owed the parties, and, unless specified in the contract for sale, they do not include damages, attorney fees, title fees, etc. They must be recovered through a suit for damages. Enforcement of these liens is by foreclosure.

CHAPTER 11

TIPS ON PROPERTY MANAGEMENT

11.1 HOW TO ACQUIRE AND KEEP TENANTS

This section discusses the techniques of getting the prospective tenant to the property, renting the unit, selecting tenants, and lease renewal.

I. Attracting the Prospective Tenant to the Property

In most cases, prospective tenants are brought to the property by some form of advertising, including "word of mouth." The amount of advertising required depends upon the location of the property, the number of vacancies, the fairness of rents, and the use. Advertising should be considered before vacancies occur. In fact, owners of large properties should consider continuous advertising. The three principal forms of advertising (other than "word of mouth") are signs on the property, newspapers, and direct mail.

A. Signs on the Property. Specify the type of unit that is available.

B. Newspapers. Classified advertising is the most effective form for residential rentals. Display advertising at selected locations in the paper is sometimes suitable for large or new properties. Consider daily advertising versus advertising on Sunday only.

C. Direct Mail. This is effective only if prospective tenants can be identified by address. The ability to locate the market is more important than the presentation. Many mailing lists are neither carefully prepared nor maintained.

II. Technique of Renting

To fill a vacancy in residential rental units it is believed that approximately three prospects are needed for furnished units, five for unfurnished, and six or seven for luxury units and houses.

If the prospective tenant has come to inspect a unit it is clear that he approves of the location and the building.

To create the desire to rent, the common areas and the units must be clean and well-maintained. The manager should:

• Be pleasant and introduce himself;

• Be enthusiastic, but not anxious;

• Determine the needs of the prospective tenant (space, price, equipment, aesthetics, etc.);

• On the way to show the unit, describe it, its qualities, and its unique features;

• When reaching the unit, say something like "Here is a unit I think you will like";

• Notice the features of the unit that seem to interest the prospective tenant. Then mention some qualities of those features that the prospective tenant may not realize; and

• Mention other features that may have been overlooked.

III. Selecting Tenants

The most obvious reason to reject a prospective tenant is his inability to pay the security deposit and the first month's rent. (How can he be expected to pay the second month's rent if he can't pay the first?) Check the prospective tenant's previous record, job stability, personal habits, and compatibility with the other tenants.

A. Previous Record.   Obtain the rental history in person from one or more previous managers or landlords. Obtain additional credit records from credit bureaus and finance companies.

B. Job Stability. Since most tenants can pay rent for only a month or two after losing their jobs, the property manager should be able to analyze job stability. Generally speaking, salaried employees have more stable income than commissioned employees. Jobs ranked in order of decreasing stability follow:

- Government
- Professions
- Commerce and Finance
- Services
- Industry

The length of time spent in a job is an important measure of stability. Not only does longevity indicate stability, it often creates it, due to acquired seniority.

C. Personal Habits. Notice the personal cleanliness of the prospective tenant and, perhaps, that of his car. Although it is rather easy to evict tenants for non-payment, laws extensively protect tenants from eviction due to their living habits.

D. Compatibility. Since tenants live close together and share common areas, it is important that their living habits be similar. Noise is, of course, a major consideration. Even though children can be destructive and noisy, families with children are usually more stable and desirable than some other tenants.

IV. Lease Renewal

It is far more important to renew a lease than to make a new one. Vacancies not only cause loss of income, but cause expenses for renovation, advertising, and recordkeeping.

If complaints are responded to promptly and adequately and if the lease is respected by the landlord, the tenant is likely to remain after its term.

If the landlord has some information about the needs of the tenant, he is more able to negotiate a favorable lease renewal. For example, a tenant with a grand piano is more likely to absorb a rent increase than a tenant in a furnished unit.

11.2 TIPS ON COLLECTING RENT

Collecting rent is certainly one of the most important aspects of property management, and the key word is *diligence.*

I. When to Collect

Rent is paid in advance. Almost all professional property managers agree that rent should be due on the first of the month, regardless of when tenancy began. If this is done, it is much easier to notice delinquency.

II. Collection Policy

A rigid collection policy is essential. The tenant should be informed of all management policies, especially rent collection. Specifically, he should be informed that management will take prompt legal action against delinquent payments.

Property managers seem to differ on the virtue of billing the tenant. Of course, billing is necessary when the payment also reflects services rendered.

III. Delinquency

Most tenants pay promptly, and delinquencies usually result from the delinquency of management. Tenants must be "trained" to pay promptly. It is human nature to pay bills first to those who press hardest and to those who could cause the most inconvenience.

IV. Eviction

It is better to have a vacancy than a non-paying tenant; the tenant will cause wear and tear, use utilities, let other tenants know that nonpayment is tolerated, and preclude the unit from being rented.

If the tenant is late with the rent, remind him that legal action will be taken if it is more than, say, five days late. If he does not pay after this time:

- Complete two copies of a demand for payment or possession form.[1]
- The manager then hands a copy of the form to the tenant.
- If the tenant has neither paid nor surrendered possession by the number of days specified by statute (perhaps three days), the copy of the form, a summons, and complaint are filed with the court; a court date is also arranged.
- When the tenant appears in court, he is usually given the opportunity to pay the rent.
- If he does not, the judge sets a date by which he must vacate.
- If he does not vacate, a writ of eviction is given to the bailiff who executes the orders of the court.

The entire period required for eviction often takes about 30 days. For this reason alone, it is essential to begin action promptly.

The owner might also obtain a judgment against the tenant for non-payment, but this is often impractical. The tenant who does not pay his rent probably doesn't have a job (whose wages could be garnished) or assets sufficient to satisfy the judgment.

11.3 HOW TO SET THE RENT

The proper rental depends upon supply and demand rather than a rate of return desired by the owner. However, owners frequently undertake a renovation of the property in an attempt to increase demand and increase rental. See Section 1.3.

---

[1] The legal procedure for eviction varies from state to state.

Generally, it is thought that a vacancy rate of 5% or less allows rents to increase. Such a small vacancy rate makes relocating so expensive and difficult that increases will be absorbed. If a rent increase is attempted, it should be done with a few units at a time, otherwise misjudgment can cause many vacancies. Vacancies not only cause loss of income, but expenses for renovation, advertising and recordkeeping.

An excess of rental units can result from two causes. A technical excess is caused by the construction of too many comparable units. An economic excess is caused by the tenant's loss of purchasing power and the consequent "doubling up."

The rental of each unit should depend upon its characteristics: the location within the building, condition, amenities, facilities, etc. Some owners determine a base rent (say for units on the middle floors), and then set the rent for other units as a fraction of the base rent. In any case, rental should be determined from rent data collected from comparable units in the area. The statistical methods discussed in Section 3.3 might be useful.

11.4 HOW TO IMPROVE YOUR DAILY OPERATIONS

The operations of the property include the day-to-day management duties and decisions concerning expenses.

I. Manager

The owner can either handle the management of his property or pay a professional management company to do it.

A. Owner Management. Residential rentals of, say, 10 units or more should have an on-site manager.

1. Finding the Manager

• One of the best places to obtain a manager is from the tenants in the building. By living there he has shown that he likes the property and fits socially and economically. Moreover, his unit can be checked for neatness.

• Find a building that is well-managed and offer the manager a job.

• Advertising and employment agencies can help, but are not as good as the two other methods because there is not as much information about the applicant.

2. Points to Remember

• Be skeptical of references. Verify their identity.

• Check the applicant's appearance, domestic relations, manners, health, drinking habits, capabilities and experience.

• Try to obtain a long-term manager because repeated training is time-consuming, expensive and disruptive to operations.

• Managers should never be trusted completely. Be skeptical. Discourage them from fraternizing with tenants because this could divide their loyalty.

• Always check vacant units to see that they are, in fact, vacant.

• Make regular (and irregular) visits to the property.

• Have the manager bonded.

• Require tenants to pay by check or money order.

• Do not rehire former managers or rent to them.

• Consider paying the manager a percentage of collections.

• Let the manager be familiar with the budget. He will be more sympathetic to the burdens of ownership.

B. Professional Management. If a professional management company is retained, the management contract should specify the following:

• Terms
• Degree of diligence

- Services provided
- Employees to be provided and the degree to which the agent is responsible for them
- Agent's authority to contract for utilities, cleaning, waste disposal, laundry and other services
- The creation of a special bank account in the owner's name
- Agents and employees to be bonded
- Expenditures by agent to be limited except for emergencies and recurring operating expenses
- On or before the 10th day of each month the owner should be provided a remittance and a statement of the previous month's operations.
- The agent should cooperate with other brokers so that two commissions will not be charged when a tenant is located.
- Responsibility for advertising.

II. Expenses

Bills should be paid only after inspection. Resist paying for poor workmanship and goods not delivered. Establish a work order and purchase order system; no charges are paid unless the orders have been recorded. Avoid double payment. The following discusses some major categories of expenses. Table 11.4-1 is a checklist of possible expenses.

A. Utilities. Utilities usually include fuel, electricity, water and telephone.

1. *Fuel.* Watch closely. Compare costs with costs in similar buildings. Consult the fuel company's experts on conservation.

2. *Electricity.* It is desirable to have tenants pay their own electricity.

3. *Water.* Sudden cost increases might be evidence of a leak or break.

B. Taxes. Little can be done to minimize taxes. Contract labor to save FICA and minimize personal property.

Table 11.4-1. Possible Expenses to Include in the Budget

air conditioning repair	licenses
advertising and promotion	locks and keys
	management
appliance repair	office supplies
carpeting	painting
cleaning	plumbing repair
concrete and asphalt repair	rain gutter repair
	renovation
door repair	secretary costs
electrical repair	snow removal
electricity	supplies
elevator repair	taxes (payroll)
employee benefits	taxes (personal property)
equipment rental	
extermination	taxes (real property)
fixture repair	telephone
floor repair	trash removal
ground care	travel
heat	water and sewer
heating system repair	window screen repair
insurance	window repair
legal	

C. Insurance. The insurance coverage should fit the characteristics of the property. The coverage should protect the rents that are collected and should include bonding the employees.

D. Contracted Services. Obtain competitive bids for services such as trash removal, pest control, security, gardening, laundry, elevator maintenance, and air conditioning maintenance.

E. Supplies. Store supplies in a secure place and take inventory frequently.

F. Maintenance. Maintenance is frequently deferred because the budget does not provide for the rare large expenses (e.g., roof repair). The amount of maintenance can be estimated from Section 1.1.

APPENDIX   A

MATHEMATICAL NOTES

APPENDIX A.1

INTERPOLATION (ESTIMATING A VALUE BETWEEN TWO KNOWN VALUES)

Often it is necessary to know a value that is not listed in a table. If the formula from which the table is derived is known, the unknown value can theoretically be determined. However, often either the formula is not known or it is quite complicated. In either event the unknown value can be estimated by using the two nearest tabulated values. If the unknown value lies beyond the table it can sometimes be estimated by *extrapolation*. On the other hand, if the unknown value lies between two listed values, it can be estimated by *interpolation*.

Interpolation assumes that the formula is a straight line.[1] This assumption is of course usually not true, but it generally provides a good estimate of the true value.

As an example, Figure A.1-1 shows a portion of a curve, some of whose values might be listed in a table. Consider the listed values y_1 and y_2 corresponding to x_1 and x_2. Also consider a straight line through the points $P_1 = (x_1, y_1)$ and $P_2 = (x_2, y_2)$. The straight line, although not identical to the curve, can be used to approximate values on the curve between x_1 and x_2.

For instance, the value on the curve corre-

[1] The word interpolation usually refers to linear interpolation although it needn't be so restrictive.

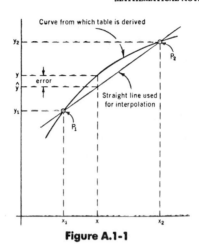

Figure A.1-1

sponding to x is y and the value on the straight line corresponding to x is $\hat{y}$. Therefore, $\hat{y}$ is the estimate of y obtained by using linear interpolation.

The following formula determines the estimate of y.

FORMULA

$$\hat{y} = \left(\frac{x_2 - x}{x_2 - x_1}\right) \cdot y_1 + \left(\frac{x - x_1}{x_2 - x_1}\right) \cdot y_2$$

where

$\hat{y}$ = estimate of y using linear interpolation

y = nonlisted value to be estimated by $\hat{y}$

x_1, x_2 = first and second listed parameter values that straddle x

x = nonlisted parameter value (between x_1 and x_2)

y_1, y_2 = first and second listed value corresponding to x_1 and x_2, respectively

EXAMPLE

Find the present value of an annuity of 1 corresponding to q = 1, r = 10%, and m = 20.25. (See Table 1.)

SOLUTION

Since m = 20.25 is the non-listed parameter value
(i.e. x = 20.25)., we will interpolate. Let

$$x_1 = 20 \text{ and } x_2 = 21$$

be the nearest listed values that straddle **x**.

The present values of an annuity of 1 corresponding to x_1 and x_2 (obtained from Table 1) are

$$y_1 = a(10,20,1) = 8.51356, \text{ and}$$
$$y_2 = a(10,21,1) = 8.64869.$$

Now, using the formula, the estimate of y is

$$\hat{y} = \left(\frac{21 - 20.25}{21 - 20}\right) \times 8.51356$$
$$+ \left(\frac{20.25 - 20}{21 - 20}\right) \times 8.64869$$
$$= .75 \times 8.51356 + .25 \times 8.64869$$
$$= 6.38517 + 2.16217$$
$$= 8.54734$$

(Note: The actual value using the formula in Appendix A.4.2 is y = 8.54856. These two values differ by only 0.01427%.)

APPENDIX A.2

PRODUCTS OF VALUES

When n numbers (say $a_1, a_2, \ldots, a_n$) are to be multiplied, we can write

$$a_1 \cdot a_2 \cdot \ldots \cdot a_n.$$

However, it is usually more convenient to write

$$\prod_{i=1}^{n} a_i.$$

The symbol "Π" is the Greek equivalent of "p" and is used in mathematics to indicate the taking of products. Hence $\prod_{i=1}^{n} a_i$ means: multiply all of the numbers a_i, starting with $i = 1$ and ending with $i = n$.

EXAMPLE 1

If the numbers being multiplied are the same, the product can also be expressed as an exponent. For example, if a $50,000 property is expected to increase at the rate of 12% annually for 4 years, the value will be

$$\$50,000 \times \prod_{i=1}^{4} (1.12) = \$50,000 \times (1.12)^4$$
$$= \$50,000 \times 1.5735$$
$$= \$78,675.$$

EXAMPLE 2

If the numbers being multiplied are different, the product notation is needed. For example, if a $50,000 property is expected to increase by 10, 11,

13, and 15% for four consecutive years (e.g., $r_1 = .10$, $r_2 = .11$, $r_3 = .13$, and $r_4 = .15$), the value will be

$$\$50,000 \times \prod_{i=1}^{4} (1 + r_i) = \$50,000$$

$$\times [(1.10)(1.11)(1.13)(1.15)]$$

APPENDIX A.3

SUMMATION OF VALUES

When n numbers (say $a_1, a_2, \ldots, a_n$) are to be added, we can write

$$a_1 + a_2 + \ldots + a_n.$$

However, it is more convenient to write

$$\sum_{i=1}^{n} a_i.$$

The symbol "Σ" is the Greek equivalent of "s" and is used in mathematics to indicate summation. Hence, $\sum_{i=1}^{n} a_i$ means: add all of the numbers a_i, starting with i = 1 and ending with i = n. Sometimes when a summation is known or understood only Σa_i is used.

EXAMPLE 1

If we are asked to find the sum of the first 100 integers, we could write

$$1 + 2 + 3 + \ldots + 100,$$

or we can write,

$$\sum_{i=1}^{100} i^*.$$

*The sum of the first n integers is $\dfrac{n(n + 1)}{2}$.

EXAMPLE 2

If $a_i = (1 + r)^i$, (for $i = 1,2,3 \ldots$) the sum of the first 4 values can be written

$$\sum_{i=1}^{4} (1 + r)^i$$

to represent

$$(1 + r)^1 + (1 + r)^2 + (1 + r)^3 + (1 + r)^4.$$

APPENDIX A.4

ANNUITIES: PRESENT AND FUTURE VALUE

A.4.0 INTRODUCTION

An annuity is a series of payments to be received over a period of time.

The mortgage lender receives an annuity in the traditional sense when he receives equal monthly payments. However, cash flow received by the equity investor constitutes an annuity, usually with variable payments. Even capital gain and balloon payments are annuities consisting of a single payment to be received in the future. In fact, the methods used to evaluate an annuity can (and should) be used to evaluate any payment to be received in the future.

Three methods are commonly used to evaluate an annuity. The most elementary method is to simply sum the payments. But since the payments are made over a period of time, and time has value,[1] most investors prefer to evaluate an annuity in ways that account for time, such as by the present value of an annuity and the future value of an annuity.

For example, suppose payments of the amounts $x_1, x_2, \ldots, x_n$ are received annually over n years. The following describes the three methods to evaluate an annuity.

A. The Sum of an Annuity. The sum of the annuity is simply the sum of the payments (as if time has no value):

[1] Actually time has no inherent value, but can have it if used beneficially. Of course, all investors believe they will use it beneficially. Hence, the saying, "Time has value."

$$\sum_{i=1}^{n} x_1 = x_1 + x_2 + \ldots + x_n.^2$$

B. The Present Value of an Annuity. If you normally invest money at the annual rate of interest, r, the first payment is not worth x_1 to you, but only $x_1/(1 + r)$ because you had to wait a year to receive it. In other words, its present value is $x_1/(1 + r)$. In the same way, the present value of the second payment is $x_2/(1 + r)^2$, the present value of the third payment is $x_3/(1 + r)^3$, etc. Now the present value, A, of the annuity is the sum of the present values of all n payments:

$$A = \sum_{i=1}^{n} \frac{x_1}{(1 + r)^i}$$
$$= \frac{x_1}{(1 + r)^1} + \frac{x_2}{(1 + r)^2} + \ldots + \frac{x_n}{(1 + r)^n}.$$

C. The Future Value of an Annuity. The concept of the future value of an annuity is derived from the assumption that each payment can be invested at the rate of interest, r, from the time it is received until the annuity terminates.

That is, the first payment is invested at the rate r for the remaining $n - 1$ years of the annuity (i.e., interest is compounded for $n - 1$ years). Hence, its future value is $x_1(1 + r)^{n-1}$. The second payment is invested for $n - 2$ years, and its future value is $x_2(1 + r)^{n-2}$. Finally, the last payment cannot be invested at all, so its future value is simply x_n. Then the future value, S, of the annuity is the sum of the future values of all n payments:

$$S = \sum_{i=1}^{n} x_1(1 + r)^{n-i} = x_1(1 + r)^{n-1}$$
$$+ x_2(1 + r)^{n-2} + \ldots + x_n(1 + r)^{n-n}.^3$$

Figure A.4.0-1 shows the relationship among the sum, the present value, and the future value of

[2] The mathematical notation $\sum_{i=1}^{n}$ means: sum all the values, x_i, for $i = 1$ through $i = n$. See Appendix A.3.
[3] Recall that $(1 + r)^{n-n} = (1 + r)^0 = 1$.

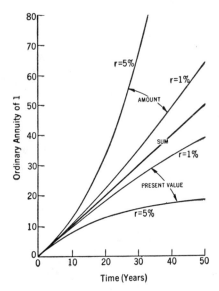

Figure A.4.0-1

an annuity for equal payments and for two inter-est rates (1% and 5%). Notice that the sum is a straight line because equal payments are being re-ceived at equal intervals of time. The future value of the annuity is greater than the sum because the payments are being invested at interest as they are received. Conversely, the present value is less than the sum because you must wait to receive payments that you otherwise could have invested. Of course, all three formulas are equal if time has no value, i.e., if $r = 0$.

Annuities are separated into three types, de-pending upon when they begin.

1. *Ordinary Annuity.* Begins now, and payments are made at the end of each period.

2. *Annuity Due.* Begins now, and payments are made at the beginning of each period (as in rent).

3. *Deferred Annuity.* Begins at some future date

(then it can be called a deferred ordinary annuity or a deferred annuity due, depending upon when the payments are considered to have been made within the period).

A.4.1 FUTURE VALUE OF AN ANNUITY

The future value of an annuity is the amount accumulated at its term if each payment is promptly invested when it is received.

Table A.4.1-1 lists many formulas for the future value of an annuity for different conditions of income and interest rates. The simplest and most frequently used formulas are those of constant income and constant interest rate. The other formulas are more general and can be used in unusual situations. For instance, those labeled variable can be used for almost any annuity, but those labeled linear and exponential have specific applications:

• *Linear Annuity.* A linear annuity is one in which income either decreases or increases by a *fixed amount* relative to the previous period.

• *Exponential Annuity.* An exponential annuity is one in which income either decreases or increases by a *fixed percentage* of its previous value. Any payment that is changing in proportion to its value is changing exponentially (like an amount at compound interest).

where

S = future value of an annuity

x = constant periodic payment of initial payment in linear and exponential annuities

x_1 = payment in the ith period

x' = fixed amount of change of payment (positive or negative)

r = constant annual interest rate

r_j = interest rate in the jth year

r' = fixed rate of change of payment (positive or negative), expressed as a decimal

q = number of periods per year

n = number of years of the annuity

$m = nq$ = total number of periods

Table A.4.1-1. Future Value of an Annuity for Different Conditions of Income and Interest Rates.
(Note: The amount of a deferred ordinary annuity is not included here because it is equal to the amount of an ordinary annuity.)

Income			Interest Rate	
			Constant	Variable
Constant		Ordinary Annuity	$x \cdot \sum_{i=1}^{m} (1 + r/q)^{m-i} = x \cdot s(r,m,q)$	$x + x \cdot \sum_{i=1}^{m-1} \left[\prod_{j=m+1-i}^{m} (1 + r_j/q) \right]$
		Annuity Due	$x \cdot \sum_{i=1}^{m} (1 + r/q)^{m+1-i} = x \cdot s(r,m,q) \cdot c(r,1,q)$	$x \cdot \sum_{i=1}^{m} \left[\prod_{j=m+1-i}^{m} (1 + r_j/q) \right]$
Variable		Ordinary Annuity	$\sum_{i=1}^{m} x_i (1 + r/q)^{m-i} = \sum_{i=1}^{m} x_i \cdot c(r, m - i, q)$	$x_m + \sum_{i=1}^{m-1} \left[x_{m-i} \cdot \prod_{j=m+1-i}^{m} (1 + r_j/q) \right]$
		Annuity Due	$\sum_{i=1}^{m} x_i (1 + r/q)^{m+1-i} = \sum_{i=1}^{m} x_i \cdot c(r, m + 1 - i, q)$	$\sum_{i=1}^{m} \left[x_{m+1-i} \cdot \prod_{j=m+1-i}^{m} (1 + r_j/q) \right]$

Income		Formula 1	Formula 2
Linear	*Ordinary Annuity*	$\left[x + x'\left(1+\dfrac{q}{r}\right)\right]\cdot s(r,m,q) - \dfrac{x'mq}{r}$	$(x+mx') + \displaystyle\sum_{i=1}^{m-1}\left\{[x+(m-i)x']\cdot \prod_{j=m+1-i}^{m}(1+r_j/q)\right\}$
	Annuity Due	$\left[\left(x+x'\dfrac{q}{r}\right)\cdot s(r,m,q) - \dfrac{x'mq}{r}\right]\cdot c(r,1,q)$	$\displaystyle\sum_{i=1}^{m}\left\{[x+(m+1-i)x']\cdot \prod_{j=m+1-i}^{m}(1+r_j/q)\right\}$
Exponential	*Ordinary Annuity*	$x\cdot s(w,m,q)\cdot c(r',m,q)$ if $r \geq r'$ $x\cdot a(w,m,q)\cdot c(r,m,q)$ if $r' \geq r$	$x\cdot c(r',m,q) + x\cdot \displaystyle\sum_{i=1}^{m-1}\left[c(r',m-i,q)\cdot \prod_{j=m+1-i}^{m}(1+r_j/q)\right]$
	Annuity Due	$x\cdot s(w,m,q)\cdot c(r',m,q)\cdot c(w,1,q)$ if $r \geq r'$ $x\cdot a(w,m,q)\cdot c(r,m,q)\cdot c(w,1,q)$ if $r' \geq r$	$x\cdot \displaystyle\sum_{i=1}^{m}\left[c(r',m+1-i,q)\cdot \prod_{j=m+1-i}^{m}(1+r_j/q)\right]$

$$w = \begin{cases} q(r - r')/(q + r') \text{ if } r > r' \\ q(r' - r)/(q + r) \text{ if } r' \geq r \end{cases}$$

$s(r,m,q)$, $s(w,m,q)$ = future value of an annuity of 1

$c(r,1,q)$, $c(r,m - 1,q)$, etc. = amount of 1 at compound interest

EXAMPLE 1

(constant income and constant interest rate). Robert Johnson has been depositing $1,000 at the end of each month in a fund that pays 8% compounded monthly. How much will the fund (an ordinary annuity) be worth after 13 years?

SOLUTION

In this example,

$x = \$1,000$, $q = 12$, $r = 8\%$, $n = 13$,

and $m = nq = 156$,

From Table 1, $s(r,m,q) = s(8,156,12) = 272.92039$, Now, from Table A.4.1-1,

$$S = x \cdot s(r,m,q),$$

Specifically, the fund will be worth

$$S = \$1,000 \times 272.92039 = \$272,920.39.$$

EXAMPLE 2

(constant income and variable interest rate). Suppose $5,000 is to be invested at the beginning of each year for three years. If these funds earn 10, 15, and 20% each year, what is the future value of this annuity due?

SOLUTION

In this example,

$x = \$5,000$, $q = 1$, $n = 3$, $m = nq = 3$,

$r_1 = 10\%$, $r_2 = 15\%$, and $r_3 = 20\%$.

Since the funds are deposited at the beginning of each period, this is an annuity due. From Table A.4.1-1,

$$S = x \cdot \sum_{i=1}^{m} \left[\prod_{j=m+1-i}^{m} (1 + r_j/q) \right].$$

Specifically, the future value of the annuity will be

$$
\begin{aligned}
S &= \$5,000 \times \sum_{i=1}^{3} \left[\prod_{j=4-i}^{3} (1 + r_j) \right] \\
&= \$5,000 \times [(1 + r_3) + (1 + r_2)(1 + r_3) \\
&\qquad\qquad\qquad + (1 + r_1)(1 + r_2)(1 + r_3)] \\
&= \$5,000 \times [(1.20) + (1.15)(1.20) \\
&\qquad\qquad\qquad\qquad + (1.10)(1.15)(1.20)] \\
&= \$5,000 \times 4.098 \\
&= \$20,490.
\end{aligned}
$$

EXAMPLE 3

(variable income and constant interest rate). Suppose you will receive \$5,000, \$4,000, and \$7,000 at the end of the each of the next three years. If these funds earn 12% annually, what is the future value of this ordinary annuity?

SOLUTION

In this example,

$$x_1 = \$5,000, \ x_2 = \$4,000, \ x_3 = \$7,000, \ q = 1,$$
$$n = 3, \ m = nq = 3, \text{ and } r = 12\%.$$

From Table A.4.1-1,

$$S = \sum_{i=1}^{m} x_i \cdot c(r, m - i, q).$$

Specifically,

$$S = \sum_{i=1}^{3} x_i \cdot c(12, 3 - i, 1).$$

From Table 1,

$$c(12, 3 - i, 1) = \begin{cases} c(12,2,1) = 1.254400 & \text{for } i = 1 \\ c(12,1,1) = 1.120000 & \text{for } i = 2 \\ c(12,0,1) = 1.000000 & \text{for } i = 3. \end{cases}$$

Now, the future value of this ordinary annuity is

$$
\begin{aligned}
S &= \$5,000 \times 1.254400 + \$4,000 \times 1.120000 \\
&\qquad\qquad + \$7,000 \times 1.000000 = \$17,752.
\end{aligned}
$$

A.4.2 PRESENT VALUE OF AN ANNUITY

The present value of an annuity measures the penalty for having to wait to receive the payments. Since the payments are received over a period of time, and time has value,[4] the value of each payment is less than its face value. How much less depends on the rate of return (interest rate) you could achieve if you had the payment to invest. It is subjective. Figure A.4.2-1 shows the present value of an ordinary annuity for various interest rates. It can be used for a quick estimate of the present value of 1.

Table A.4.2-1 lists many formulas for the present value of an annuity. The most frequently used formulas are relatively simple because they provide for constant payments and constant interest rate. However, the other formulas are more general and can be used in unusual situations. For instance, those labeled variable can be used for most any annuity, but those labeled linear and exponential have specific applications nad are explained in Section A.4.1.

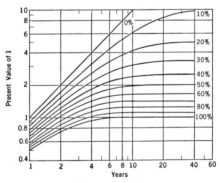

Figure A.4.2-1

[4] Actually time has no inherent value but can have it if used beneficially. Of course all investors believe they will use it beneficially. Hence, the saying, "Time has value."

where

A = present value of an annuity

x = constant periodic payment or initial payment in linear and exponential annuities

x_i = payment in the ith period

x' = fixed amount of change of payment (positive or negative)

r = constant annual interest rate

r_j = interest rate in the jth year

r' = fixed rate of change of payment (positive or negative), expressed as a decimal

q = number of periods per year

n = number of years of annuity

$m = nq$ = total number of periods

$w = q(r - r')/(q + r')$, an interest rate if $r > r'$

v = number of periods the annuity is deferred

$a(r,m,q)$, $a(w,m,q)$ = present value of an annuity of 1

$c(r,1,q)$, $c(r,v,q)$, etc. = amount of 1 at compound interest

EXAMPLE 1

(constant income and constant interest rate). Suppose you expect to receive a \$5,000 cash flow at the beginning of each month for 10 years. If you normally expect a 10% return on your investments, what is the present value of this annuity due?

SOLUTION

In this example,

$x = \$5,000$, $q = 12$, $n = 10$, $m = nq = 120$, and $r = 10\%$.

From Table A.4.2-1,

$$A = x \cdot a(r,m,q) \cdot c(r,1,q)$$

From Table 1,

$a(r,m,q) = a(10,120,12) = 75.6711633$, and
$c(r,1,q) = c(10,1,12) = 1.0083333$.

Table A.4.2-1. Present Value of an Annuity for Different Conditions of Income and Interest Rates.

Income		Interest Rate	
Constant		**Constant**	**Variable**
	Ordinary Annuity	$x \cdot \sum_{i=1}^{m} \dfrac{1}{(1+r/q)^i} = x \cdot a(r,m,q)$	$x \cdot \sum_{i=1}^{m} \left[\dfrac{1}{\prod_{j=1}^{i}(1+r_j/q)} \right]$
	Annuity Due	$x \cdot \sum_{i=1}^{m} \dfrac{1}{(1+r/q)^{i-1}} = x \cdot a(r,m,q) \cdot c(r,1,q)$	$x \cdot \left\{ 1 + \sum_{i=1}^{m-1} \left[\dfrac{1}{\prod_{j=1}^{i}(1+r_j/q)} \right] \right\}$
	Deferred Ordinary Annuity	$x \cdot \sum_{i=1}^{m} \dfrac{1}{(1+r/q)^{i+v}} = x \cdot a(r,m,q)/c(r,v,q)$	$x \cdot \sum_{i=1}^{m} \left[\dfrac{1}{\prod_{j=1}^{i+v}(1+r_j/q)} \right]$

276

Income			
Variable			
Ordinary Annuity	$\displaystyle\sum_{i=1}^{m} \frac{x_i}{(1+r/q)^{i-1}} = \sum_{i=1}^{m} \frac{x_i}{c(r,i,q)}$		$\displaystyle\sum_{i=1}^{m}\left[\frac{x_i}{\prod_{i=1}^{i-1}(1+r_j/q)}\right]$
Annuity Due	$\displaystyle\sum_{i=1}^{m} \frac{x_i}{(1+r/q)^{i-1}} = \sum_{i=1}^{m} \frac{x_i}{c(r,i-1,q)}$		$\displaystyle x_1 + \sum_{i=1}^{m-1}\left[\frac{x_{i+1}}{\prod_{i=1}^{i}(1+r_j/q)}\right]$
Deferred Ordinary Annuity	$\displaystyle\sum_{i=1}^{m} \frac{x_i}{(1+r/q)^{i+v}} = \sum_{i=1}^{m} \frac{x_i}{c(r,i+v,q)}$		$\displaystyle\sum_{i=1}^{m}\left[\frac{x_i}{\prod_{i=1}^{i+v}(1+r_j/q)}\right]$

† In mathematics, the Greek symbol Σ (sigma) means to sum, and the Greek symbol Π (pi) means to take the product (see the examples in this section).

Table A.4.2-1. (Continued)

Income	Linear		Interest Rate	
			Constant	Variable
		Ordinary Annuity	$\left[x + x'\left(m+1+\dfrac{q}{r}\right)\right]\cdot a(r,m,q) - \dfrac{x'mq}{r}$	$\displaystyle\sum_{i=1}^{m}\left[\dfrac{x+ix'}{\prod_{j=1}^{i}(1+r_j/q)}\right]$
		Annuity Due	$\left\{\left[x + x'\left(m+\dfrac{q}{r}\right)\right]\cdot a(r,m,q) - \dfrac{x'mq}{r}\right\}c(r,1,q)$	$x+\displaystyle\sum_{i=1}^{m-1}\left[\dfrac{x+ix'}{\prod_{j=1}^{i}(1+r_j/q)}\right]$
		Deferred Ordinary Annuity	$\left\{\left[x + x'\left(m+1+\dfrac{q}{r}\right)\right]\cdot a(r,m,q) - \dfrac{x'mq}{r}\right\}\dfrac{1}{c(r,v,q)}$	$\displaystyle\sum_{i=1}^{m}\left[\dfrac{x+ix'}{\prod_{j=1}^{i+v}(1+r_j/q)}\right]$

Income			
Exponential			
Ordinary Annuity	$x \cdot a(w,m,q)$		$x \cdot \sum_{i=1}^{m}\left[\dfrac{c(r_i',i,q)}{\prod_{j=1}^{i}(1+r_j/q)}\right]$
Annuity Due	$x \cdot a(w,m,q) \cdot c(w,1,q)$		$x \cdot \left\{1 + \sum_{i=1}^{m-1}\left[\dfrac{c(r_i',i,q)}{\prod_{j=1}^{i}(1+r_j/q)}\right]\right\}$
Deferred Ordinary Annuity	$x \cdot a(w,m,q)/c(w,v,q)$		$x \cdot \sum_{i=1+v}^{m}\left[\dfrac{c(r_i',i,q)}{\prod_{j=1}^{i}(1+r_j/q)}\right]$

Now, the present value of this annuity due is

$$A = \$5,000 \times 75.6711633 \times 1.0083333$$
$$= \$381,508.77$$

EXAMPLE 2

(constant income and variable interest rate). Suppose you expect to receive \$5,000 at the end of each year for three years. If you could have made a 10%, 15%, and 20% return over each of the next three years, what is the present value of this ordinary annuity?

SOLUTION

In this example,

$$x = \$5,000, q = 1, n = 3, m = nq = 3, r_1 = 0.10,$$
$$r_2 = 0.15, \text{ and } r_3 = 0.20.$$

Now from Table A.4.2-1, the present value of this ordinary annuity is

$$A = x \cdot \sum_{i=1}^{m} \frac{1}{\left[\prod_{j=1}^{i} (1 + r_j/q)\right]}$$

$$= \$5,000 \left[\frac{1}{\prod_{j=1}^{1} (1 + r_j/1)} + \frac{1}{\prod_{j=1}^{2} (1 + r_j/1)} \right.$$

$$\left. + \frac{1}{\prod_{j=1}^{3} (1 + r_j/1)} \right]$$

$$= \$5000 \left(\frac{1}{1.10} + \frac{1}{(1.10) \times (1.15)} \right.$$

$$\left. + \frac{1}{(1.10) \times (1.15) \times (1.20)} \right)$$

$$= \$5,000(0.909091 + 0.790514 + 0.658762)$$
$$= \$5,000 \times 2.358367$$
$$= \$11,791.84.$$

EXAMPLE 3: (variable income and constant interest rate).

Suppose you will receive $5,000, $4,000, and $7,000 at the end of three consecutive years, but this income will not begin for four years. If you could make 10% annually on your investments, what is the present value of this deferred ordinary annuity?

SOLUTION

In this example,

$x_1 = \$5,000$, $x_2 = \$4,000$, $x_3 = \$7,000$, $n = 3$,
$$q = 1, m = nq = 3, \text{ and } v = 4.$$

From Table A.4.2-1,

$$A = \sum_{i=1}^{3} \frac{x_i}{c(r, i + v, q)}.$$

From Table 1,

$c(r, i + v, q) =$
$$c(10, i + 4, 1) = \begin{cases} c(10,5,1) = 1.610510 & \text{for } i = 1 \\ c(10,6,1) = 1.771561 & \text{for } i = 2 \\ c(10,7,1) = 1.948717 & \text{for } i = 3 \end{cases}$$

Now, the present value of this deferred ordinary annuity is

$$A = \frac{\$5,000}{1.610510} + \frac{\$4,000}{1.771561} + \frac{\$7,000}{1.948717}$$
$$= \$3,104.61 + \$2,257.90 + \$3,592.11$$
$$= \$8,954.62.$$

TABLE 1

ANNUITIES

This table lists values of the three functions needed to solve interest and value problems when interest and income are constant. The functions are:

compound interest of 1 (the amount of $1 drawing interest, compounded at regular periods)

$$c(r,m,q) = (1 + r/q)^m,$$

the present value of an annuity of 1 (the present value of $1 received at regular periods)

$$a(r,m,q) = \frac{(1 + r/q)^m - 1}{(r/q)(1 + r/q)^m},$$

and the future value of an annuity of 1 (the future value of $1 deposited at regular periods)

$$s(r,m,q) = \frac{(1 + r/q)^m - 1}{(r/q)}.^{[1]}$$

where

r = annual interest rate, expressed as a decimal

q = number of interest periods per year

$m = nq$ = total number of interest periods, where n is the number of years

EXAMPLE

What is the amount of $1 that is drawing interest at $r = 9\%$ compounded $q = 4$ times/year over $m = 12$ months?

---

[1] Notice the relationship among the three functions:

$$s(r,m,q) = a(r,m,q) \cdot c(r,m,q).$$

SOLUTION

Generally, this annuity is labeled c(r,m,q). For the values in this example, it is labeled c(9,12,4). The value is listed in Table 1 on page 284. It is found in the column labeled c(9,m,4) at row m = 12. That is,

$$c(9,12,4) = 1.30605.$$

The \$1 will be worth \$1.31.

For further discussions of compound interest, amount of an annuity, and present value of an annuity see Section A.4.

This table lists the values for annual compounding (q = 1) and monthly compounding (q = 12).

For annual compounding the interest rates are listed for every $\frac{1}{4}$% from 5% through 7.75%, for every 1% from 8% through 19%, and for every 5% from 20% through 45%, for every 10% from 50% through 100%.

For monthly compounding the interest rates are every $\frac{1}{4}$% from 5% through 14%.

Table 1 begins on p. 284.

Table 1. Annuities

m	C(8.00.M.1)	A(8.00.M.1)	S(8.00.M.1)	C(9.00.M.1)	A(9.00.M.1)	S(9.00.M.1)	C(10.00.M.1)	A(10.00.M.1)	S(10.00.M.1)
1/12	1.0064340	.0799136	.0804250	1.0072073	.0795081	.0800811	1.0079741	.0790101	.0797410
1/4	1.0194265	.2381978	.2428313	1.0217782	.2367554	.2419800	1.0241137	.2354713	.2411370
1/2	1.0392305	.4718694	.4903813	1.0440307	.4686581	.4892300	1.0488088	.4653741	.4880880
1	1.0800000	.9259259	1.0000000	1.0900000	.9174312	1.0000000	1.1000000	.9090909	1.0000000
2	1.1664000	1.7832647	2.0800000	1.1881000	1.7591112	2.0900000	1.2100000	1.7355372	2.1000000
3	1.2597120	2.5770970	3.2464000	1.2950290	2.5312947	3.2781000	1.3310000	2.4868520	3.3100000
4	1.3604890	3.3121269	4.5061120	1.4115816	3.2397199	4.5731290	1.4641000	3.1698654	4.6410000
5	1.4693281	3.9927100	5.8666010	1.5386240	3.8896513	5.9847111	1.6105100	3.7907868	6.1051000
6	1.5868743	4.6228797	7.3359290	1.6771001	4.4859186	7.5233344	1.7715610	4.3552607	7.7156100
7	1.7138243	5.2063701	8.9228034	1.8280391	5.0329528	9.2004344	1.9487171	4.8684188	9.4871710
8	1.8509302	5.7466390	10.6366276	1.9925626	5.5348191	11.0284733	2.1435888	5.3349262	11.4358881
9	1.9990046	6.2468879	12.4875578	2.1718933	5.9952469	13.0210367	2.3579477	5.7590238	13.5794770
10	2.1589250	6.7100814	14.4865625	2.3673637	6.4176577	15.1929300	2.5937425	6.1445671	15.9374246
11	2.3316390	7.1389643	16.6454875	2.5804264	6.8051906	17.5602933	2.8531167	6.4950610	18.5311671
12	2.5181701	7.5360780	18.9771265	2.8126648	7.1607253	20.1407200	3.1384284	6.8136918	21.3842838
13	2.7196237	7.9037759	21.4952966	3.0658046	7.4869040	22.9533844	3.4522712	7.1033562	24.5227122
14	2.9371936	8.2442370	24.2149203	3.3417270	7.7861505	26.0191889	3.7974983	7.3666874	27.9749834
15	3.1721691	8.5594787	27.1521139	3.6424825	8.0606885	29.3609167	4.1772482	7.6060794	31.7724817
16	3.4259426	8.8513692	30.3242830	3.9703059	8.3125583	33.0033989	4.5949730	7.8237096	35.9497299
17	3.7000181	9.1216381	33.7502257	4.3276334	8.5436314	36.9737044	5.0544703	8.0215367	40.5447029
18	3.9960195	9.3718871	37.4502437	4.7171204	8.7556251	41.3013378	5.5599173	8.2014212	45.5991732
19	4.3157011	9.6035992	41.4462632	5.1416612	8.9501148	46.0184578	6.1159090	8.3649265	51.1590905
20	4.6609571	9.8181474	45.7619643	5.6044108	9.1285457	51.1601200	6.7274999	8.5135696	57.2749996
21	5.0338337	10.0168031	50.4229215	6.1088078	9.2922437	56.7645311	7.4002499	8.6486996	64.0024996
22	5.4365404	10.2007436	55.4567552	6.6586005	9.4424254	62.8733389	8.1402749	8.7715451	71.4027495
23	5.8714636	10.3710589	60.8932956	7.2578745	9.5801976	69.5319389	8.9543024	8.8832229	79.5430245
24	6.3411807	10.5287583	66.7647593	7.9110832	9.7066033	76.7898133	9.8497327	8.9847428	89.4973269
25	6.8484752	10.6747762	73.1059400	8.6230807	9.8225720	84.7008967	10.8347059	9.0770416	98.3470596

n								
26	7.3963532	79.9544153	9.3991579	9.9289721	93.3239770	11.9181766	9.1609455	109.1817655
27	7.9880615	87.3507685	10.2450822	10.0265799	102.7231350	13.1099942	9.2372231	121.1099421
28	8.9177749	95.1804300	12.1721821	10.1982829	113.1612824	15.2600936	9.3696059	148.6309360
29	9.0626569	103.9859364	13.2876785	10.2736540	124.1353567	15.6200930	9.4269145	164.4940230
30	10.0626569	113.2832113	14.4617696	10.3428019	136.3075388	17.4494023	9.4790131	181.9434253
31	10.8676695	123.3458682	15.7633288	10.4002402	149.5752173	19.1943425	9.5283756	201.1377679
32	11.7370830	134.2135377	16.9203284	10.4644400	164.0369969	21.1137768	9.5849335	221.1377679
33	12.6766497	145.9502207	18.7284110	10.5173354	181.0303157	23.1133545	9.6085749	245.4765992
34	13.6901336	158.6266704	20.4139680	10.5688215	198.9823441	25.5476899	9.6441590	271.1023691
35	14.7853443	172.3168041	22.2512251	10.6117628	215.7107551	28.1024369	9.6765081	299.1268060
36	15.9681719	187.1021464	24.3568306	10.6593994	236.1247231	30.9126806	9.7059185	330.2348967
37	17.2456756	203.0763203	26.4358404	10.6938199	255.3754042	34.0039487	9.7329165	344.4433438
38	18.7866690	221.8766890	28.8159818	10.7255226	285.6299784	37.4433438	9.7569558	401.1477789
39	20.1152978	238.9412218	31.4094202	10.7573602	309.0664641	41.1447779	9.7790507	442.2595569
40	21.7245216	259.0555194	34.2362680	10.7573602	337.8824459	45.2592557	9.7991370	487.8518126
41	23.4624833	280.7810410	37.3658481	10.7855690	369.2918661	49.7851813	9.8139997	532.4006933
42	25.4280605	304.7818159	40.6817921	10.8378905	405.7605994	54.7505994	9.8490887	592.4006933
43	27.0770736	337.8370505	44.3389599	10.8605050	440.8456662	60.2605662	9.8628073	652.6407628
44	29.5559718	356.9496468	48.3272863	10.8811973	481.5217762	66.2640763	9.8752799	718.9046391
45	31.9204495	386.5056186	52.6767421	10.9001810	525.8567361	72.8904840	9.8871928	791.7953231
46	34.4740855	418.4260681	57.3735666	10.9001810	574.1860224	80.1795324	9.8986935	791.7953231
47	37.2496733	452.5859566	62.5852377	10.9235752	624.2804134	87.0172348	9.8996281	960.1723411
48	40.2106723	490.1801365	68.2179085	10.9482344	684.8655508	96.7169576	9.9052959	1057.1895753
49	43.4274192	530.3427392	74.3575204	10.9616829	746.8655508	106.7199534	9.9062959	1057.1895753
50	46.9016127	573.7701584	74.3575204	10.9616829	815.0835593	117.3908534	9.9148145	1183.9085530

Table 1. (continued) Annuities

M	C(11.00,M,1)	A(11.00,M,1)	S(11.00,M,1)	C(12.00,M,1)	A(12.00,M,1)	S(12.00,M,1)	C(13.00,M,1)	A(13.00,M,1)	S(13.00,M,1)
1/12	1.0087346	.0787172	.0794055	1.0094888	.0783300	.0790733	1.0102368	.0779470	.0787446
1/4	1.0264335	.2341145	.2403045	1.0287373	.2327882	.2394779	1.0310260	.2314795	.2386615
1/2	1.0535654	.4622000	.4869582	1.0583005	.4590738	.4858377	1.0630146	.4559933	.4847277
1	1.1100000	.9009009	1.0000000	1.1200000	.8928571	1.0000000	1.1300000	.8849558	1.0000000
2	1.2321000	1.7125236	2.1100000	1.2544000	1.6900510	2.1200000	1.2769000	1.6681025	2.1300000
3	1.3676310	2.4437145	3.3421000	1.4049280	2.4018313	3.3744000	1.4428970	2.3611527	3.4069000
4	1.5180704	3.1024455	4.7097310	1.5735194	3.0373493	4.7793280	1.6304736	2.9744714	4.8497969
5	1.6850582	3.6958968	6.2278014	1.7623417	3.6047762	6.3528474	1.8424352	3.5172313	6.4802708
6	1.8704146	4.2305377	7.9128596	1.9738227	4.1114073	8.1151890	2.0819518	3.9975454	8.3227062
7	2.0761602	4.7121961	9.7832741	2.2106814	4.5637565	10.0890117	2.3526055	4.4226065	10.4046577
8	2.3045378	5.1461226	11.8594343	2.4759632	4.9676398	12.2996931	2.6584442	4.7987677	12.7572631
9	2.5580369	5.5370474	14.1639721	2.7730788	5.3282498	14.7756564	3.0040419	5.1316528	15.4157069
10	2.8394210	5.8892364	16.7220090	3.1058482	5.6502230	17.5487351	3.3945674	5.4262414	18.4197492
11	3.1517573	6.2065182	19.5614300	3.4785500	5.9376991	20.6545833	3.8358612	5.6869393	21.8143169
12	3.4984506	6.4923545	22.7131873	3.8959760	6.1943742	24.1331333	4.3345231	5.9176454	25.6501777
13	3.8832802	6.7498727	26.2116379	4.3634931	6.4235417	28.0291092	4.8980111	6.1218101	29.9847008
14	4.3104410	6.9818727	30.0949180	4.8871123	6.6281667	32.3926024	5.5347525	6.3024868	34.8827115
15	4.7845895	7.1908818	34.4053590	5.4735658	6.8108667	37.2797147	6.2542703	6.4623769	40.4174638
16	5.3108943	7.3791545	39.1899485	6.1303937	6.9739833	42.7532805	7.0673255	6.6038769	46.6717346
17	5.8950927	7.5487909	44.5008428	6.8660410	7.1196333	48.8836748	7.9860778	6.7290923	53.7390600
18	6.5435529	7.7016182	50.3959355	7.6899659	7.2496750	55.7497158	9.0242679	6.8399077	61.7251377
19	7.2633437	7.8392909	56.9394884	8.6127618	7.3657750	63.4396817	10.1974227	6.9379692	70.7494054
20	8.0623116	7.9633273	64.2028321	9.6462932	7.4694417	72.0524435	11.5230877	7.0247516	80.9468285
21	8.9491658	8.0750636	72.2651437	10.8038484	7.5620000	81.6987367	13.0210891	7.1015501	92.4699162
22	9.9335740	8.1757364	81.2143093	12.1003102	7.6446417	92.5025851	14.7138307	7.1695131	105.4910054
23	11.0262672	8.2664182	91.1478834	13.5523474	7.7184250	104.6028953	16.6266287	7.2296569	120.2048362
24	12.2391566	8.3481364	102.1741506	15.1786291	7.7843167	118.1552427	18.7880904	7.2828838	136.8314646
25	13.5854638	8.4217455	114.4133073	17.0000646	7.8431392	133.3338717	21.2305421	7.3299831	155.6195546

287

n					n			n			
26	15.0798640	8.4880583	127.9987713	19.0400722	26	7.8956599	180.339347	26	23.9905128	7.3716681	178.0500985
27	16.5799015	8.5170002	143.0786362	21.0766808	27	7.9445535	190.3740069	27	27.1092785	7.4085559	200.8406113
28	18.5799015	8.5618218	159.8172862	23.1836655	28	7.9844228	190.6988877	28	30.6334858	7.4411999	227.9498908
29	20.6235907	8.6501097	178.3971876	26.7499305	29	8.0218060	214.5827543	29	34.6158390	7.4700884	258.5833766
30	22.8922966	8.6937926	199.0208763	29.9599222	30	8.0551840	241.3326848	30	39.1158981	7.4955534	293.1992156
31	25.4104493	8.7184465	221.9311749	33.5857264	31	8.0858817	241.0998817	31	44.2099648	7.5121774	332.1531537
32	28.2655987	8.7786006	247.3336242	37.3336242	32	8.1135944	304.6477199	32	49.9070902	7.5382986	376.5160785
33	31.3082145	8.8005409	275.5292229	42.0915336	33	8.1353521	342.494463	33	56.4402120	7.5560184	426.4631687
34	34.7521181	8.8293161	306.0374374	47.1425176	34	8.1565644	384.5209799	34	63.7774395	7.5716980	482.9033807
35	38.5748511	8.8552398	341.5895556	52.7996197	35	8.1755039	431.663497	35	72.0685067	7.5855716	546.6908203
36	42.6180848	8.8895944	380.1440067	59.3355741	36	8.1924172	484.631173	36	81.4314726	7.5978510	618.4637370
37	47.5500741	8.9100741	423.9240615	66.2330440	37	8.2089761	544.586913	37	91.0242762	7.6059517	700.1867395
38	52.7561623	8.9185897	470.5105656	74.1796642	38	8.2209935	609.8305344	38	103.9874321	7.6183343	792.3110157
39	58.5593401	8.9356664	523.2667729	83.0812239	39	8.2330299	684.0101986	39	117.5057993	7.6268445	896.1984479
40	73.0008675	8.9510508	581.8260680	93.0509708	40	8.2437787	767.091425	40	132.7815521	7.6343758	1013.7042463
41	81.1509630	8.9649106	718.2103873	104.2101749	41	8.2519768	860.354805	41	149.5487639	7.6453539	1296.5289522
42	88.8972015	8.9866362	744.3213673	116.2137078	42	8.2599887	1081.0826183	42	191.5901032	7.6521579	1466.0777161
43	96.6758937	8.9804459	799.0654674	130.7299143	43	8.2694188	1211.8125326	43	216.4966167	7.6567769	1857.6678193
44	109.5302420	8.9987801	887.9626689	146.4175040	44	8.2825185	1358.2300366	44	244.6414029	7.6860645	1874.1066360
45	121.5325586	9.0079100	986.6385628	163.9876045	45	8.2842518	1584.8818823	45	283.8826074	7.6683123	2118.8065241
46	149.7069544	9.0136451	1219.7413733	203.7660512	46	8.2929224	1705.8837582	46	312.3826074	7.6676831	2395.2508241
47	164.5640276	9.0181331	1302.3907773	230.3907773	47	8.2971629	1911.5898094	47	352.5923464	7.6705180	2707.6334315
48	149.7069544	9.0302209	1352.6995844	258.0376708	48	8.3010383	2141.9805867	48	398.8813514	7.6730230	3080.6257779
49	164.5640276	9.0382350	1660.7711982	289.0021911	49	8.3044985	2400.0183573	49	450.7359272	7.6752416	3459.5071293

Table 1. (continued) Annuities

M	C(14.00,M,1)	A(14.00,M,1)	S(14.00,M,1)	C(15.00,M,1)	A(15.00,M,1)	S(15.00,M,1)	C(16.00,M,1)	A(16.00,M,1)	S(16.00,M,1)
1/12	1.0109789	.0775688	.0784204	1.0117149	.0771951	.0780994	1.0124451	.0768263	.0777821
1/4	1.0332995	.2301883	.2378535	1.0355581	.2288941	.2370538	1.0378020	.2277063	.2362625
1/2	1.0677078	.4529585	.4836273	1.0723805	.4499679	.4825369	1.0770330	.4470207	.4814563
1	1.1400000	.8771930	1.0000000	1.1500000	.8695652	1.0000000	1.1600000	.8620690	1.0000000
2	1.2996000	1.6466605	2.1400000	1.3225000	1.6257089	2.1500000	1.3456000	1.6052319	2.1600000
3	1.4815440	2.3216320	3.4396000	1.5208750	2.2832251	3.4725000	1.5608960	2.2458896	3.5056000
4	1.6889602	2.9137120	4.9211440	1.7490063	2.8549784	4.9933750	1.8106394	2.7981808	5.0664960
5	1.9254146	3.4330811	6.6101042	2.0113572	3.3521551	6.7423813	2.1003417	3.2742937	6.8771354
6	2.1949726	3.8886675	8.5355187	2.3130608	3.7844827	8.7537384	2.4363963	3.6847419	8.9774770
7	2.5022688	4.2883051	10.7304914	2.6600199	4.1604197	11.0667992	2.8262197	4.0385661	11.4138731
8	2.8525864	4.6388631	13.2327600	3.0590229	4.4873213	13.7268191	3.2784149	4.3435875	14.2400931
9	3.2519485	4.9463102	16.0853464	3.5178763	4.7715831	16.7858419	3.8029613	4.6065496	17.5185081
10	3.7072213	5.2161102	19.3372950	4.0455577	5.0187686	20.3037182	4.4114351	4.8332125	21.3214694
11	4.2262323	5.4527086	23.0445164	4.6523914	5.2337118	24.3492760	5.1172647	5.0286494	25.7329044
12	4.8179048	5.6602123	27.2707486	5.3502501	5.4206190	29.0016674	5.9360270	5.1971063	30.8501688
13	5.4924115	5.8423389	32.0886536	6.1527876	5.5831468	34.3519175	6.8857913	5.3423375	36.7861956
14	6.2613491	6.0020392	37.5810651	7.0757058	5.7244758	40.5047051	7.9875179	5.4675319	43.6719869
15	7.1379380	6.1421577	43.8424142	8.1370616	5.8473701	47.5804109	9.2655208	5.5754500	51.6595050
16	8.1372493	6.2650584	50.9803522	9.3576209	5.9542349	55.7174725	10.7480041	5.6684938	60.9250256
17	9.2764642	6.3728319	59.1176015	10.7612640	6.0471610	65.0750934	12.4676848	5.7487044	71.6730300
18	10.5751692	6.4674087	68.3940657	12.3754536	6.1279659	75.8363574	14.4625144	5.8178500	84.1407150
19	12.0556929	6.5504076	78.9692350	14.2317716	6.1982372	88.2118110	16.7765167	5.8774563	98.6032294
20	13.7434899	6.6231237	91.0249278	16.3665374	6.2593315	102.4435827	19.4607594	5.9288375	115.3797463
21	15.6675785	6.6869838	104.7684177	18.8215180	6.3124621	118.8101202	22.5744810	5.9731375	134.8405062
22	17.8610395	6.7429390	120.4359964	21.6447457	6.3586627	137.6316381	26.1863980	6.0113250	157.4149875
23	20.3615850	6.7920316	138.2970356	24.8914575	6.3988572	159.2763839	30.3762217	6.0442438	183.6013856
24	23.2122069	6.8351374	158.6586207	28.6251761	6.4337714	184.1678415	35.2364172	6.0726250	213.9776075
25	26.4619159	6.8729274	181.8708275	32.9189526	6.4641491	212.7930178	40.8742439	6.0970938	249.2140239

n			
26	30.1865841	6.9060767	208.3327434
27	34.3899550	6.9351550	238.4993376
28	42.6931217	6.9266523	312.0937260
29	49.9630377	6.9630377	356.7868477
30	50.9501587	7.0026641	407.7370064
31	58.0831809	7.0198808	485.0201817
32	56.2148263	7.0349832	565.6320187
33	72.8446920	7.0423308	685.0201817
34	86.0527882	7.0598518	807.5199156
35	98.1001786	7.0700453	693.5727039
36	111.8342036	7.0898971	791.6728825
37	127.4909321	7.0863308	903.9907993
38	146.3339331	7.0933723	1003.9907993
39	165.6872934	7.0997467	1176.3378093
40	188.8835145	7.1050409	1342.0251028
41	215.3272066	7.1096850	1530.9086173
42	245.8390375	7.1119388	1941.7088304
43	281.1173388	7.1173388	2271.5480771
44	319.0167310	7.1204669	2954.2436815
45	363.6790734	7.1232168	3941.4753491
46	414.5941437	7.1256288	919.5826818
47	472.5324730	7.1276003	4360.2818063
48	538.8065493	7.1296003	4994.8213045
49	614.2394082	7.1312204	
50	700.2339915	7.1326508	

n			
26	37.8567958	6.4905644	245.7119705
27	43.5353149	6.5135081	283.1400761
28	50.6586122	6.5586122	327.1040861
29	57.5754540	6.5508796	377.1696932
30	66.2117721	6.5659996	434.7451472
31	76.1435360	6.5791127	500.9869194
32	87.6950687	6.5995328	577.1107553
33	107.6930290	6.6004833	664.6655269
34	115.8046033	6.6090985	765.3653549
35	133.1755238	6.6166074	881.1701583
36	153.1518524	6.6231369	1014.3456821
37	176.1246348	6.6287147	1165.3425345
38	205.5433248	6.6337519	1343.6221648
39	232.9248238	6.6380451	1546.1654897
40	287.8635472	6.6417784	1779.0903133
41	308.0430793	6.6450247	2046.9938604
42	385.3857354	6.6503022	2709.2464809
43	468.4950183	6.6524367	3116.6334533
44	538.7692711	6.6542928	3585.1284716
45	619.5986618	6.6559053	4123.8624045
46	919.5845610	6.6573068	4723.9022047
47	942.3108228	6.6585304	5455.0047656
48	1083.6574463	6.6593919	6275.4054810
49		6.6605147	7217.7163038
50			

n			
26	0.1181847	47.4441220	390.0832078
27	0.1583647	63.0004380	337.5023907
28	0.1920383	83.0004438	392.5027713
29	0.1855503	74.0085148	456.3032170
30	0.1771985	85.8498771	530.3173317
31	0.1854901	99.5958575	718.7476093
32	0.1858592	115.5999547	831.2670610
33	0.2033592	134.0027390	985.2697909
34	0.2097924	155.4431666	1120.7129575
35	0.2153383	180.3140733	1310.1913559
36	0.2201172	209.0423751	1510.1913559
37	0.2241407	242.6365475	1752.8219730
38	0.2277937	281.4515159	2034.2734968
39	0.2308566	326.4837584	2380.7872477
40	0.2334971	378.7211598	3178.7949525
41	0.2357386	439.0075927	3689.4021452
42	0.2377356	509.1443438	4278.5464888
43	0.2394273	665.7274386	4965.7739243
44	0.2408856	795.4382769	5683.7799243
45	0.2421427	1070.3492163	6683.4325979
46	0.2432140	1241.6050910	7753.7816142
47	0.2441608	1440.2619057	8935.3869053
48	0.2449662	1670.7036108	10435.6488110
49	0.2456605		
50	0.2462591		

Table 1. (continued) Annuities

M	C(17.00,M,1)	A(17.00,M,1)	S(17.00,M,1)	C(18.00,M,1)	A(18.00,M,1)	S(18.00,M,1)	C(19.00,M,1)	A(19.00,M,1)	S(19.00,M,1)
1/12	1.0131698	.0764613	.0774683	1.0138884	.0761010	.0771579	1.0146017	.0757450	.0768510
1/4	1.0400314	.2264153	.2354790	1.0422466	.2251900	.2347035	1.0444478	.2239804	.2339358
1/2	1.0816654	.4441157	.4803846	1.0862780	.4412521	.4793225	1.0908712	.4384290	.4782695
1	1.1700000	.8547009	1.0000000	1.1800000	.8474578	1.0000000	1.1900000	.8403361	1.0000000
2	1.3689000	1.5851144	2.1700000	1.3924000	1.5656421	2.1800000	1.4161000	1.5464000	2.1900000
3	1.6016130	2.2372800	3.5389000	1.6430320	2.1742729	3.5724000	1.6851590	2.1398319	3.6061000
4	1.8738972	2.7432350	5.1405130	1.9387778	2.6900618	5.2154320	2.0053392	2.6385855	5.2912590
5	2.1924480	3.1993462	7.0144002	2.2877578	3.1271710	7.1542098	2.3863537	3.0576349	7.2965992
6	2.5651642	3.5891848	9.2068482	2.6995542	3.4976026	9.4419675	2.8397609	3.4097772	9.6829519
7	3.0012421	3.9223801	11.7720125	3.1854739	3.8115276	12.1415217	3.3793154	3.7055850	12.5227127
8	3.5114533	4.2055692	14.7834658	3.7588592	4.0775658	15.3269956	4.0213953	3.9610857	15.9020281
9	4.1084003	4.4586036	18.2847078	4.4354539	4.3030018	19.0858548	4.7854486	4.1633225	19.9234135
10	4.8068294	4.6356036	22.3931062	5.2338356	4.4940863	23.5213086	5.6946838	4.4864999	24.7088621
11	5.6239892	4.8356134	27.1999366	6.1759260	4.6560053	28.7551442	6.7766737	4.6105041	30.4035449
12	6.5800674	4.9883875	32.8239258	7.2875926	4.7932349	34.9310702	8.0642417	4.7110504	37.1802196
13	7.6986788	5.1192991	39.4039932	8.5993593	4.9095126	42.2186628	9.5984417	4.7714717	45.2444613
14	9.0074543	5.2192991	47.1026232	10.1472440	5.0080615	50.8180221	11.4197727	4.8022767	54.8409090
15	10.5387215	5.3241872	56.1101263	11.9737419	5.0915776	60.9652661	13.5895295	4.8756628	66.2606817
16	12.3302041	5.4052882	66.6488478	14.1290225	5.1623539	72.9330140	16.1715401	4.9376998	79.8502112
17	14.4263558	5.4564279	79.0459479	16.6722660	5.2223142	87.0620365	19.2440828	4.9833039	96.0216513
18	16.8788463	5.5344279	93.4722516	19.6732510	5.2731831	103.7602801	22.9005180	5.0333039	115.2658841
19	19.7483754	5.5844878	110.2845610	23.2144361	5.3162409	123.4135341	27.2516164	5.0700259	138.1664021
20	23.1055992	5.6277673	130.0329364	27.3930347	5.3527465	146.6279702	32.4294235	5.1008621	165.4180185
21	27.0335511	5.6647584	153.1385356	32.3237809	5.3836835	174.0210049	38.5910140	5.1267749	197.8474420
22	31.6292548	5.6924088	180.2081314	38.1420615	5.4099014	206.3447858	45.9233067	5.1485453	236.4384560
23	37.0062281	5.7213972	210.8013414	45.0076325	5.4321197	244.4858472	54.6487349	5.1668490	282.3617626
24	43.2972868	5.7464933	248.8075695	53.1090064	5.4509489	289.4944797	65.0319946	5.1822261	337.0104976
25	50.6578256	5.7662336	292.1048563	62.6686275	5.4669058	342.6034861	77.3880735	5.1951480	402.0424921

n				
26	59.2696560	5.7831058	342.7626820	73.9489805
27	69.3454975	5.7925262	402.0323379	87.2597970
28	81.1342321	5.8009956	471.7128854	102.5665505
29	94.2707515	5.8093858	551.3726851	120.3170855
30	111.0646503	5.8233896	647.4391190	143.3706388
31	129.9456409	5.8370851	758.5037693	169.1773538
32	152.0363998	5.8436625	888.4940102	199.6292475
33	178.8025678	5.8540894	1040.3689100	235.5625475
34	207.8825877	5.8540894	1218.3683978	277.9630060
35	243.5034745	5.8581958	1426.4910255	327.9972912
36	284.8990652	5.8617058	1669.9945000	387.0368036
37	333.3319063	5.8670586	1954.8935554	456.7033283
38	389.8990464	5.8699464	2287.8999000	538.7044283
39	456.2980466	5.8694615	2678.2238018	635.9138537
40	533.8687145	5.8713348	3134.5218484	750.3783474
41	624.6263961	5.8729355	3668.3905629	885.4464500
42	730.8128835	5.8743039	4293.0198590	1044.2956372
43	853.8773039	5.8774273	5023.0189844	1454.8168520
44	1000.4097563	5.8767430	5878.8809161	1454.8168520
45	1170.4794150	5.8773273	6879.2905725	1716.6838855
46	1369.4609157	5.8780578	8049.7700875	2025.6869850
47	1602.2692715	5.8786817	9419.9009231	2920.5665584
48	1876.0518478	5.8790710	11026.0003190	3328.2685392
49	2193.3454081	5.8796710	12906.1553224	3927.3568766
50	2568.2153995	5.8800607	15099.5017285	

n				
26	479.4305057	5.2060087	92.0918075	405.2721136
27	531.5218242	5.2127907	109.5892087	479.2210941
28	611.5228329	5.2192435	132.8120871	566.2408911
29	966.7121712	5.2346584	155.1893383	669.4479516
30	1151.3874838	5.2392087	184.6753126	790.9479929
31	1337.1051058	5.2430325	219.7636220	934.3186317
32	1632.6598161	5.2462458	261.2072552	1103.4359850
33	1943.8770813	5.2489461	311.2072552	1303.1202630
34	2314.2137269	5.2512152	370.3366456	1538.6878105
35	2754.9143533	5.2531220	440.7006083	1816.6516165
36	3278.4840593	5.2551224	524.4337240	2144.6489077
37	3903.4241908	5.2560709	724.6555967	2531.9857396
38	4648.0747875	5.2572024	883.7542101	2981.0851850
39	5529.8289976	5.2581533	1051.6675101	3527.2991850
40	6581.4965077	5.2589524	1251.4843371	4163.2130386
41	9322.2472061	5.2598701	1779.2263701	4913.5913860
42	1094.4741762	5.2601681	2108.9500946	5843.8608471
43	13203.4242708	5.2606623	2509.6506128	8076.7602842
44	15713.0748835	5.2610607	2986.4842294	9531.5771361
45	18713.3106693	5.2611956	3223.1603180	11248.2860216
46	22253.4753463	5.2619134	5032.7027789	15664.2586491
47	26482.6356643	5.2621121		18484.8252075
48	31515.3364432	5.2622781	5968.9139274	21813.0937468

M	C(20.00,M,1)	A(20.00,M,1)	S(20.00,M,1)	M	C(25.00,M,1)	A(25.00,M,1)	S(25.00,M,1)	M	C(30.00,M,1)	A(30.00,M,1)	S(30.00,M,1)
1/12	1.0153095	.0753931	.0765474	1/12	1.0187693	.0736939	.0750771	1/12	1.0221045	.0720880	.0736815
1/4	1.0468351	.2227770	.2331757	1/4	1.0573713	.2170336	.2294851	1/4	1.0677900	.2116208	.2259666
1/2	1.0954451	.4356455	.4772256	1/2	1.1180340	.4222913	.4721360	1/2	1.1401754	.4098066	.4672514
1	1.2000000	.8333333	1.0000000	1	1.2500000	.8000000	1.0000000	1	1.3000000	.7692308	1.0000000
2	1.4400000	1.5277778	2.2000000	2	1.5625000	1.4400000	2.2500000	2	1.6900000	1.3609467	2.3000000
3	1.7280000	2.1064815	3.6400000	3	1.9531250	1.9520000	3.8125000	3	2.1970000	1.8161129	3.9900000
4	2.0736000	2.5887346	5.3680000	4	2.4414063	2.3616000	5.7656250	4	2.8561000	2.1662407	6.1870000
5	2.4883200	2.9906121	7.4416000	5	3.0517578	2.6892800	8.2070313	5	3.7129300	2.4355698	9.0431000
6	2.9859840	3.3255101	9.9299200	6	3.8146973	2.9514240	11.2587891	6	4.8268090	2.6427460	12.7560300
7	3.5831808	3.6045918	12.9159040	7	4.7683716	3.1611392	15.0734863	7	6.2748517	2.8021123	17.5828390
8	4.2998170	3.8371598	16.4990848	8	5.9604645	3.3289114	19.8418579	8	8.1573072	2.9247018	23.8576907
9	5.1597804	4.0309665	20.7989018	9	7.4505806	3.4631291	25.8023224	9	10.6044994	3.0190014	32.0149979
10	6.1917365	4.1924721	25.9586821	10	9.3132257	3.5705033	33.2529030	10	13.7858492	3.0915395	42.6194973
11	7.4300838	4.3270601	32.1504186	11	11.6415322	3.6564026	42.5661288	11	17.9216040	3.1473381	56.4053465
12	8.9161005	4.4392167	39.5805023	12	14.5519152	3.7251221	54.2076610	12	23.2980851	3.1902601	74.3269505
13	10.6993206	4.5326806	48.4966027	13	18.1898940	3.7800976	68.7595762	13	30.2875107	3.2232770	97.6250356
14	12.8391847	4.6105672	59.1959233	14	22.7373675	3.8240781	86.9494703	14	39.3737639	3.2486746	127.9125463
15	15.4070217	4.6754727	72.0359079	15	28.4217094	3.8592625	109.6868378	15	51.1858930	3.2682112	167.2863102
16	18.4884260	4.7295606	87.4421300	16	35.5271368	3.8874100	138.1085473	16	66.5416610	3.2832394	218.4722033
17	22.1861112	4.7746338	105.9305560	17	44.4089210	3.9099280	173.6356841	17	86.5041593	3.2947995	285.0138643
18	26.6233334	4.8121948	128.1166670	18	55.5111512	3.9279424	218.0446051	18	112.4554071	3.3036920	371.5180236
19	31.9480001	4.8434957	154.7400005	19	69.3889390	3.9423539	273.5557564	19	146.1920292	3.3105323	483.9734307
20	38.3376001	4.8695797	186.6880005	20	86.7361738	3.9538831	342.9446955	20	190.0496380	3.3157941	630.1654599
21	46.0051202	4.8913164	225.0256010	21	108.4202172	3.9631065	429.6808693	21	247.0645294	3.3198416	820.2150979
22	55.2061442	4.9094304	271.0307210	22	135.5252716	3.9704852	538.1010867	22	321.1838882	3.3229551	1067.2796273
23	66.2473730	4.9245253	326.2368650	23	169.4065895	3.9763882	673.6263584	23	417.5390546	3.3253500	1388.4635155
24	79.4968476	4.9371044	392.4842380	24	211.7582368	3.9811105	842.0329480	24	542.8007710	3.3271923	1806.0025701
25	95.3962171	4.9475870	471.9810855	25	264.6977960	3.9848884	1054.7911850	25	705.6410023	3.3286095	2348.8033412
26	114.4754606	4.9563225	567.3773030	26	330.8722451	3.9879108	1319.4889813	26	917.3333030	3.3296996	3054.4443436
27	137.3705527	4.9636021	681.8527635	27	413.5903063	3.9903286	1650.3612266	27	1192.5332939	3.3305382	3971.7776466
28	164.8446632	4.9696684	819.2233160	28	516.9878829	3.9922629	2063.9515333	28	1550.2932821	3.3311832	5164.3109406
29	197.8135959	4.9747237	984.0679795	29	646.2348536	3.9938103	2580.9394166	29	2015.3812667	3.3316794	6714.6042228
30	237.3763150	4.9789364	1181.8815750	30	807.7935670	3.9950483	3227.1742708	30	2619.9956467	3.3320611	8729.9854896
31	284.8515781	4.9824470	1419.2578905	31	1009.7419587	3.9960386	4034.9678385	31	3405.9943407	3.3323547	11349.9811365
32	341.8218937	4.9853725	1704.1094685	32	1262.1774484	3.9968309	5044.7097981	32	4427.7926429	3.3325805	14755.9754774
33	410.1862724	4.9878104	2045.9313620	33	1577.7218105	3.9974647	6306.8872476	33	5756.1304358	3.3327542	19183.7681206
34	492.2235269	4.9898420	2456.1176345	34	1972.1522631	3.9979718	7884.6090595	34	7482.9695665	3.3328879	24939.8985568
35	590.6682323	4.9915350	2948.3411615	35	2465.1903289	3.9983774	9856.7613244	35	9727.8604365	3.3329907	32422.8681238

Table 1. (continued) Annuities

M	C(35.00,M,1)	A(35.00,M,1)	S(35.00,M,1)	M	C(40.00,M,1)	A(40.00,M,1)	S(40.00,M,1)	M	C(45.00,M,1)	A(45.00,M,1)	S(45.00,M,1)
1/12	1.0253241	.0705674	.0723544	1/12	1.0284362	.0691247	.0710904	1/12	1.0314480	.0877537	.0898844
1/4	1.0779123	.2065165	.2226067	1/4	1.0877573	.2016932	.2193933	1/4	1.0973420	.1971268	.2163155
1/2	1.1618950	.3981058	.4625572	1/2	1.1832160	.3871144	.4680399	1/2	1.2041465	.3895551	.4356807
1	1.3200000	.7894376	1.0000000	1	1.4000000	.7142857	1.0000000	1	1.4500000	.8952981	1.0000000
2	1.7424376	1.2894376	2.3200000	2	1.9600000	1.2144898	2.4000000	2	2.1025000	1.4932982	2.4500000
3	2.4603750	1.6958797	4.1725000	3	2.7440000	1.5889213	4.3600000	3	3.0486250	1.7195146	4.5525000
4	3.3215062	1.9969479	6.5328750	4	3.8416000	2.0351639	7.1040000	4	4.4205062	2.0435223	7.6011250
5	4.4840334	2.2199614	9.9436812	5	5.3782400	2.0351639	10.9456000	5	6.4097341	2.0573257	10.8216086
6	6.0591451	2.3845656	14.4336448	6	7.5295360	2.2828387	16.3238400	6	9.2941344	2.1085005	14.4319456
7	8.1731509	2.5075234	20.4918598	7	10.5413504	2.3305991	24.3533760	7	13.4764659	2.1437934	18.9252133
8	11.0324038	2.5981655	28.6640108	8	14.7578906	2.3789994	35.8947264	8	19.5408755	2.1691334	24.5248205
9	14.8937451	2.6653078	39.6964145	9	20.6610468	2.4135650	52.8526170	9	28.3342695	2.1849196	31.7254797
10	20.1065559	2.7115428	54.5901596	10	28.9254655	2.4559036	76.9936637	10	41.0846900	2.1964963	41.2019456
11	27.1438504	2.7419335	74.7935755	11	40.4956517	2.4685025	111.8933633	11	59.5728016	2.2044802	53.0742001
12	36.6441991	2.7791730	101.8405655	12	56.6939124	2.4751518	159.3347809	12	86.3805523	2.2099863	67.0779906
13	49.4696674	2.7993874	138.4847640	13	79.3714773	2.4798299	195.9206933	13	125.2518153	2.2138786	89.0779906
14	66.7840510	2.8143610	187.9544314	14	111.1200683	2.4818610	275.3011706	14	181.6151322	2.2164025	130.1617813
15	90.1584688	2.8236686	254.0884824	15	155.5680956	2.4893385	440.4212369	15	263.3419416	2.2182086	189.7345829
16	121.7139036	2.8337545	344.6108841	16	217.7953338	2.4914355	616.9893345	16	381.8458158	2.2194542	276.1151452
17	164.3138094	2.8442628	466.5108841	17	304.9134673	2.4941435	759.7836682	17	553.6764326	2.2203053	501.1809906
18	221.8236427	2.8476019	630.9246935	18	426.8788542	2.4958166	1064.6971355	18	802.8308272	2.2213143	846.3240346
19	299.4619177	2.8519078	852.7483363	19	597.6303959	2.4968366	1491.5759947	19	1164.3052466	2.2215981	1228.1698501
20	404.2635880	2.8532650	1155.4324329	20	836.6825760	2.4976655	2925.8868366	20	1687.9518144	2.2217904	1781.8462827
21	545.7886158	2.8542704	1556.4322429	21	1171.3555760	2.4984755	4097.2459536	21	2447.5301306	2.2217904	3748.7810039
22	736.7886158	2.8552650	2102.2531877	22	1639.8978063	2.4989111	5737.1423222	22	3548.9186893	2.2215981	5436.7336235
23	994.6646313	2.8550161	2839.0418037	23	2295.8559289	2.4992222	8032.9925310	23	5145.9320995	2.2217904	7884.2637541
24	1342.7972552	2.8550161	3833.7064350	24	3214.1997004	2.4992510		24	7461.6015543	2.2219244	11433.1824434
											16579.1145429

Table 1. (continued) Annuities

M	C(50.00,M,1)	A(50.00,M,1)	S(50.00,M,1)	M	C(60.00,M,1)	A(60.00,M,1)	S(60.00,M,1)	M	C(70.00,M,1)	A(70.00,M,1)	S(70.00,M,1)
1/12	1.0343661	.0664480	.0687322	1/12	1.0399441	.0640164	.0665735	1/12	1.0452113	.0617937	.0645875
1/4	1.1066819	.1927960	.2133638	1/4	1.1246827	.1847672	.2078044	1/4	1.1418583	.1774780	.2026547
1/2	1.2247449	.3670068	.4494897	1/2	1.2649110	.3490510	.4415184	1/2	1.3038405	.3329051	.4340579
1	1.5000000	.6666667	1.0000000	1	1.6000000	.6250000	1.0000000	1	1.7000000	.5882353	1.0000000
2	2.2500000	1.1111111	2.5000000	2	2.5600000	1.0156250	2.6000000	2	2.8900000	.9342561	2.7000000
3	3.3750000	1.4074074	4.7500000	3	4.0960000	1.2597656	5.1600000	3	4.9130000	1.1377977	5.5900000
4	5.0625000	1.6049383	8.1250000	4	6.5536000	1.4123535	9.2560000	4	8.3521000	1.2575280	10.5030000
5	7.5937500	1.7366255	13.1875000	5	10.4857600	1.5077210	15.8096000	5	14.1985700	1.3279577	18.8551000
6	11.3906250	1.8244170	20.7812500	6	16.7772160	1.5673256	26.2953600	6	24.1375690	1.3693869	33.0536700
7	17.0859375	1.8829447	32.1718750	7	26.8435456	1.6045785	43.0725760	7	41.0338673	1.3937570	57.1912390
8	25.6289063	1.9219631	49.2578125	8	42.9496730	1.6278616	69.9161216	8	69.7575744	1.4080923	98.2251063
9	38.4433594	1.9479754	74.8867188	9	68.7194767	1.6424135	112.8657946	9	118.5878765	1.4165249	167.9826807
10	57.6650391	1.9653169	113.3300781	10	109.9511628	1.6515084	181.5852713	10	201.5993900	1.4214856	286.5705572
11	86.4975586	1.9768780	170.9951172	11	175.9218605	1.6571928	291.5364341	11	342.7189631	1.4244031	488.1699473
12	129.7463379	1.9845853	257.4926758	12	281.4749767	1.6607455	467.4582945	12	582.6222372	1.4261195	830.8889103
13	194.6195068	1.9897236	387.2390137	13	450.3599627	1.6629659	748.9332712	13	990.4578033	1.4271291	1413.5111476
14	291.9292603	1.9931490	581.8585205	14	720.5759404	1.6643537	1199.2932340	14	1683.7782656	1.4277230	2403.9689508
15	437.8938904	1.9954327	873.7877808	15	1152.9215046	1.6652211	1919.8691743	15	2862.4230515	1.4280724	4087.7472164
16	656.8408356	1.9969551	1311.6816712	16	1844.6744074	1.6657632	3072.7906790	16	4866.1191876	1.4282779	6950.1702680
17	985.2612534	1.9979701	1968.5225067	17	2951.4790518	1.6661020	4917.4650863	17	8272.4026189	1.4283987	11816.2894555

M	C(80.00,M,1)	A(80.00,M,1)	S(80.00,M,1)
1/12	1.0502017	.0597524	.0627521
1/4	1.1582922	.1708240	.1978653
1/2	1.3416408	.3183050	.4270510
1	1.8000000	.5555556	1.0000000
2	3.2400000	.8641975	2.8000000
3	5.8320000	1.0356653	6.0400000
4	10.4976000	1.1309252	11.8720000
5	18.8956800	1.1838471	22.3696000
6	34.0122240	1.2132485	41.2652800
7	61.2220032	1.2295824	75.2775040
8	110.1996058	1.2386568	136.4995072
9	198.3592904	1.2436983	246.6991130
10	357.0467227	1.2464991	445.0584033
11	642.6841008	1.2480550	802.1051260
12	1156.8318184	1.2489195	1444.7897730
13	2082.2964866	1.2493997	2601.6206082

M	C(90.00,M,1)	A(90.00,M,1)	S(90.00,M,1)
1/12	1.0549441	.0578691	.0610490
1/4	1.1740540	.1647222	.1933943
1/2	1.3784048	.3050284	.4204494
1	1.9000000	.5263158	1.0000000
2	3.6100000	.8033242	2.9000000
3	6.8590000	.9491179	6.5100000
4	13.0321000	1.0258516	13.3690000
5	24.7609900	1.0662377	26.4011000
6	47.0458810	1.0874935	51.1620900
7	89.3871739	1.0986808	98.2079710
8	169.8356304	1.1045688	187.5951449
9	322.6876978	1.1076678	357.4307753
10	613.1066258	1.1092988	680.1184731
11	1164.9025890	1.1101573	1293.2250989
12	2213.3149191	1.1106091	2458.1276877
13	4205.2983462	1.1108469	4671.4426069

M	C(100.00,M,1)	A(100.00,M,1)	S(100.00,M,1)
1/12	1.0594631	.0561287	.0594631
1/4	1.1892071	.1591038	.1892071
1/2	1.4142136	.2928932	.4142136
1	2.0000000	.5000000	1.0000000
2	4.0000000	.7500000	3.0000000
3	8.0000000	.8750000	7.0000000
4	16.0000000	.9375000	15.0000000
5	32.0000000	.9687500	31.0000000
6	64.0000000	.9843750	63.0000000
7	128.0000000	.9921875	127.0000000
8	256.0000000	.9960937	255.0000000
9	512.0000000	.9980469	511.0000000
10	1024.0000000	.9990234	1023.0000000
11	2048.0000000	.9995117	2047.0000000
12	4096.0000000	.9997559	4095.0000000
13	8192.0000000	.9998779	8191.0000000

Table 1. (continued) Annuities

M	C(5.00,M,12)	A(5.00,M,12)	S(5.00,M,12)	M	C(5.25,M,12)	A(5.25,M,12)	S(5.25,M,12)	M	C(5.50,M,12)	A(5.50,M,12)	S(5.50,M,12)
1	1.00417	0.99585	1.00000	1	1.00437	0.99564	1.00000	1	1.00458	0.99544	1.00000
2	1.00835	1.98757	2.00417	2	1.00877	1.98695	2.00437	2	1.00918	1.98633	2.00458
3	1.01255	2.97571	3.01252	3	1.01318	2.97394	3.01314	3	1.01381	2.97271	3.01377
4	1.01677	3.95868	4.02507	4	1.01762	3.95663	4.02633	4	1.01846	3.95458	4.02758
5	1.02101	4.93810	5.04184	5	1.02207	4.93504	5.04394	5	1.02313	4.93198	5.04604
6	1.02526	5.91346	6.06285	6	1.02654	5.90919	6.06601	6	1.02782	5.90491	6.06917
7	1.02953	6.88478	7.08811	7	1.03103	6.87909	7.09255	7	1.03253	6.87341	7.09699
8	1.03382	7.85206	8.11764	8	1.03554	7.84477	8.12358	8	1.03726	7.83749	8.12952
9	1.03813	8.81533	9.15147	9	1.04007	8.80624	9.15912	9	1.04201	8.79717	9.16678
10	1.04246	9.77460	10.18960	10	1.04462	9.76353	10.19919	10	1.04679	9.75247	10.20879
11	1.04680	10.72989	11.23205	11	1.04919	10.71664	11.24381	11	1.05159	10.70341	11.25558
12	1.05116	11.68122	12.27886	12	1.05378	11.66560	12.29300	12	1.05641	11.65002	12.30717
13	1.05554	12.62860	13.33002	13	1.05839	12.61043	13.34678	13	1.06125	12.59230	13.36358
14	1.05994	13.57205	14.38556	14	1.06302	13.55115	14.40518	14	1.06611	13.53029	14.42463
15	1.06436	14.51159	15.44550	15	1.06767	14.48776	15.46820	15	1.07100	14.46399	15.49094
16	1.06879	15.44722	16.50985	16	1.07234	15.42030	16.53587	16	1.07591	15.39344	16.56194
17	1.07324	16.37898	17.57865	17	1.07704	16.34877	17.60822	17	1.08084	16.31865	17.63786
18	1.07772	17.30687	18.65189	18	1.08175	17.27320	18.68525	18	1.08579	17.23963	18.71869
19	1.08221	18.23090	19.72961	19	1.08648	18.19361	19.76700	19	1.09077	18.15642	19.80448
20	1.08672	19.15111	20.81181	20	1.09123	19.11000	20.85348	20	1.09577	19.06902	20.89525
21	1.09124	20.06749	21.89853	21	1.09601	20.02240	21.94472	21	1.10079	19.97745	21.99102
22	1.09579	20.98007	22.98977	22	1.10080	20.93083	23.04072	22	1.10584	20.88174	23.09182
23	1.10036	21.88887	24.08556	23	1.10562	21.83530	24.14153	23	1.11091	21.78191	24.19765
24	1.10494	22.78390	25.18592	24	1.11046	22.73583	25.24714	24	1.11600	22.67797	25.30856
25	1.10955	23.69517	26.29086	25	1.11531	23.63244	26.35760	25	1.12111	23.56994	26.42456

n				n				n			
26	1.11417	24.59270	27.40041	26	1.12019	24.52514	27.47292	26	1.12625	24.45784	27.54567
27	1.11881	25.40650	28.51457	27	1.12509	25.41396	28.59311	27	1.13141	25.34169	28.87192
28	1.12347	26.37660	29.63338	28	1.13002	26.29890	29.71820	28	1.13660	26.22151	29.80333
29	1.12815	27.26301	30.75686	29	1.13496	27.17999	30.84822	29	1.14181	27.09731	30.93993
30	1.13285	28.14573	31.88501	30	1.13993	28.05723	31.96318	30	1.14704	27.96912	32.08174
31	1.13757	29.02480	33.01786	31	1.14491	28.93066	33.12311	31	1.15230	28.83695	33.22878
32	1.14231	29.90021	34.15544	32	1.14992	29.80029	34.28802	32	1.15758	29.70082	34.38108
33	1.14707	30.77199	35.29775	33	1.15496	30.66612	35.41795	33	1.16289	30.56075	35.53866
34	1.15186	31.64016	36.44483	34	1.16001	31.52819	36.57290	34	1.16822	31.41676	36.70155
35	1.15665	32.50472	37.59668	35	1.16508	32.38649	37.73291	35	1.17357	32.26898	37.86976
36	1.16147	33.36570	38.75333	36	1.17018	33.24107	38.89799	36	1.17895	33.11707	39.04333
37	1.16631	34.22310	39.91481	37	1.17530	34.09191	40.06816	37	1.18435	33.96142	40.22228
38	1.17117	35.07695	41.08112	38	1.18044	34.93905	41.24346	38	1.18978	34.80191	41.40663
39	1.17605	35.92725	42.25229	39	1.18560	35.78251	42.42390	39	1.19523	35.63857	42.59641
40	1.18095	36.77403	43.42834	40	1.19079	36.62228	43.60961	40	1.20071	36.47141	43.79165
41	1.18587	37.61729	44.60929	41	1.19600	37.45840	44.80030	41	1.20621	37.30045	44.99236
42	1.19081	38.45705	45.79616	42	1.20123	38.29088	45.99630	42	1.21174	38.12570	46.19857
43	1.19577	39.29333	46.98598	43	1.20649	39.11973	47.19754	43	1.21730	38.94719	47.41031
44	1.20076	40.12614	48.18175	44	1.21177	39.94497	48.40402	44	1.22288	39.76494	48.62761
45	1.20576	40.95549	49.38251	45	1.21707	40.76662	49.61579	45	1.22848	40.57895	49.85049
46	1.21078	41.78140	50.58827	46	1.22239	41.58469	50.83206	46	1.23411	41.38825	51.07897
47	1.21583	42.60388	51.79905	47	1.22774	42.39919	52.05526	47	1.23977	42.19685	52.31308
48	1.22090	43.42295	53.01488	48	1.23311	43.21014	53.28300	48	1.24545	42.99878	53.55285
49	1.22598	44.23862	54.23578	49	1.23851	44.01757	54.51611	49	1.25116	43.79803	54.79803
50	1.23109	45.05091	55.46176	50	1.24393	44.82147	55.75462	50	1.25689	44.53865	56.04948

Table 1. (continued) Annuities

M	CI 5.00,M,12	AI 5.00,M,12	SI 5.00,M,12	M	CI 5.25,M,12	AI 5.25,M,12	SI 5.25,M,12	M	CI 5.50,M,12	AI 5.50,M,12	SI 5.50,M,12
51	1.23822	45.86983	56.69285	51	1.24907	45.62188	56.99854	51	1.26255	45.38563	57.30635
52	1.24137	46.66533	57.92307	52	1.25483	46.41890	58.24797	52	1.26844	46.17400	58.56901
53	1.24454	47.26761	59.16944	53	1.26032	47.21224	59.50275	53	1.27425	46.96877	59.83746
54	1.24770	48.06208	60.41999	54	1.26584	48.00223	60.76307	54	1.28010	47.73996	61.11170
55	1.25185	48.85435	61.66872	55	1.27138	48.78878	62.02891	55	1.28596	48.51759	62.39180
56	1.26219	49.85435	62.92568	56	1.27694	49.57190	63.30028	56	1.29186	49.29167	63.67778
57	1.26745	50.64333	64.18787	57	1.28253	50.35162	64.57722	57	1.29778	50.06222	64.96961
58	1.27273	51.42905	65.45531	58	1.28814	51.12793	65.85975	58	1.30373	50.82925	66.26740
59	1.27803	52.21150	66.72804	59	1.29377	51.90086	67.14789	59	1.30970	51.59278	67.57112
60	1.28336	52.99070	68.00608	60	1.29943	52.67043	68.44166	60	1.31570	52.35283	68.88082
61	1.28871	53.76668	69.28944	61	1.30512	53.43665	69.74109	61	1.32173	53.10942	70.19653
62	1.29408	54.53943	70.57814	62	1.31083	54.19952	71.04620	62	1.32778	53.86255	71.51826
63	1.29947	55.30898	71.87222	63	1.31656	54.95908	72.35703	63	1.33388	54.61224	72.84605
64	1.30488	56.07533	73.17168	64	1.32232	55.71532	73.67360	64	1.33999	55.35851	74.17992
65	1.31032	56.83850	74.47657	65	1.32811	56.46827	74.99592	65	1.34613	56.10138	75.51992
66	1.31578	57.59851	75.78689	66	1.33392	57.21795	76.32403	66	1.35230	56.84086	76.86605
67	1.32126	58.35536	77.10267	67	1.33975	57.96435	77.65794	67	1.35850	57.57697	78.21835
68	1.32677	59.10907	78.42393	68	1.34561	58.70751	78.99770	68	1.36473	58.30972	79.57686
69	1.33229	59.85966	79.75069	69	1.35150	59.44742	80.34331	69	1.37098	59.03912	80.94158
70	1.33785	60.60713	81.08299	70	1.35741	60.18412	81.69482	70	1.37727	59.76519	82.31256
71	1.34342	61.35149	82.42084	71	1.36335	60.91760	83.05223	71	1.38358	60.48796	83.68983
72	1.34902	62.09278	83.76425	72	1.36932	61.64790	84.41558	72	1.38992	61.20742	85.07341
73	1.35464	62.83096	85.11327	73	1.37531	62.37500	85.78490	73	1.39629	61.92361	86.46333
74	1.36028	63.56612	86.46791	74	1.38133	63.09895	87.16021	74	1.40268	62.63652	87.85962
75	1.36595	64.29821	87.82819	75	1.38737	63.81973	88.54153	75	1.40912	63.34619	89.28231

n				n				n			
76	1.37164	65.02726	89.19415	76	1.39344	64.53738	89.98890	76	1.41558	64.05261	90.87142
77	1.37736	65.75329	90.56579	77	1.39954	65.25191	91.32234	77	1.42207	64.75581	92.08701
78	1.38310	66.47630	91.94315	78	1.40566	65.96332	92.72188	78	1.42858	65.45580	93.50907
79	1.38886	67.19632	93.32624	79	1.41181	66.67162	94.12753	79	1.43513	66.15260	94.93765
80	1.39465	67.91335	94.71510	80	1.41798	67.37695	95.53934	80	1.44171	66.84623	96.37279
81	1.40046	68.62740	96.10975	81	1.42419	68.07901	96.95733	81	1.44832	67.53668	97.81449
82	1.40629	69.33849	97.51020	82	1.43042	68.77810	98.38152	82	1.45496	68.22399	99.26281
83	1.41215	70.04663	98.91650	83	1.43668	69.47415	99.81194	83	1.46162	68.90816	100.71777
84	1.41804	70.75183	100.32865	84	1.44296	70.16718	101.24961	84	1.46832	69.58921	102.17939
85	1.42394	71.45411	101.74668	85	1.44928	70.85717	102.69157	85	1.47505	70.26715	103.64771
86	1.42988	72.15347	103.17063	86	1.45562	71.54417	104.14085	86	1.48181	70.94200	105.12276
87	1.43584	72.84992	104.60051	87	1.46198	72.22816	105.59647	87	1.48860	71.61378	106.60458
88	1.44182	73.54350	106.03634	88	1.46838	72.90919	107.05845	88	1.49543	72.28248	108.03318
89	1.44783	74.23418	107.47816	89	1.47480	73.58724	108.52683	89	1.50228	72.94814	109.50861
90	1.45386	74.92201	108.92599	90	1.48126	74.26234	110.00164	90	1.50917	73.61075	111.09089
91	1.45992	75.60698	110.37984	91	1.48774	74.93451	111.48289	91	1.51608	74.27035	112.60005
92	1.46600	76.28911	111.83976	92	1.49425	75.60374	112.97063	92	1.52303	74.92653	114.11613
93	1.47211	76.96841	113.30576	93	1.50078	76.27007	114.46488	93	1.53001	75.58508	115.63917
94	1.47824	77.64489	114.77787	94	1.50735	76.93348	115.96566	94	1.53703	76.23112	117.16918
95	1.48440	78.31856	116.25611	95	1.51394	77.59400	117.47301	95	1.54407	76.87877	118.70621
96	1.49059	78.98943	117.74051	96	1.52057	78.25166	118.96696	96	1.55115	77.52345	120.25027
97	1.49680	79.65753	119.23109	97	1.52722	78.90644	120.50752	97	1.55826	78.16519	121.80142
98	1.50303	80.32285	120.72769	98	1.53390	79.55837	122.03474	98	1.56540	78.80401	123.35968
99	1.50930	80.98541	122.23033	99	1.54061	80.20746	123.56865	99	1.57257	79.43991	124.92508
100	1.51558	81.64523	123.74022	100	1.54735	80.85373	125.10926	100	1.57978	80.07291	126.49765

Table 1. (continued) Annuities

M	C(5.00,M,12)	A(5.00,M,12)	S(5.00,M,12)	M	C(5.25,M,12)	A(5.25,M,12)	S(5.25,M,12)	M	C(5.50,M,12)	A(5.50,M,12)	S(5.50,M,12)
101	1.52190	82.30230	125.25581	101	1.55412	81.49718	126.65662	101	1.58702	80.70302	128.07742
102	1.52824	82.95664	126.77770	102	1.56092	82.13783	128.21074	102	1.59430	81.33025	129.66446
103	1.53461	83.60828	128.30594	103	1.56775	82.77568	129.77165	103	1.60160	81.95463	131.25874
104	1.54100	84.25720	129.84055	104	1.57461	83.41076	131.33940	104	1.60894	82.57616	132.86035
105	1.54742	84.90344	131.38155	105	1.58150	84.04307	132.91402	105	1.61632	83.19485	134.46930
106	1.55387	85.54700	132.92897	106	1.58842	84.67262	134.49551	106	1.62373	83.81071	136.08562
107	1.56035	86.18788	134.48285	107	1.59537	85.29944	136.08394	107	1.63117	84.42377	137.70584
108	1.56685	86.82610	136.04318	108	1.60235	85.92352	137.67931	108	1.63864	85.03403	139.34050
109	1.57338	87.46166	137.61003	109	1.60936	86.54489	139.28165	109	1.64615	85.64151	140.97914
110	1.57993	88.09462	139.18341	110	1.61640	87.16355	140.89101	110	1.65370	86.24622	142.62531
111	1.58651	88.72493	140.76334	111	1.62347	87.77952	142.50740	111	1.66128	86.84816	144.27901
112	1.59312	89.35263	142.34985	112	1.63057	88.39290	144.13087	112	1.66889	87.44736	145.94028
113	1.59976	89.97772	143.94298	113	1.63771	89.00341	145.76144	113	1.67654	88.04392	147.60918
114	1.60643	90.60022	145.54274	114	1.64487	89.61136	147.39915	114	1.68423	88.63757	149.28572
115	1.61312	91.22014	147.14917	115	1.65207	90.21666	149.04402	115	1.69195	89.22861	150.96994
116	1.61984	91.83748	148.76230	116	1.65930	90.81933	150.69609	116	1.69970	89.81694	152.66188
117	1.62659	92.45226	150.38214	117	1.66655	91.41936	152.35539	117	1.70749	90.40260	154.36159
118	1.63337	93.06449	152.00873	118	1.67385	92.01679	154.02194	118	1.71532	90.98558	156.06908
119	1.64018	93.67419	153.64209	119	1.68117	92.61162	155.69579	119	1.72318	91.56590	157.78439
120	1.64701	94.28135	155.28227	120	1.68852	93.20385	157.37695	120	1.73108	92.14358	159.50757
121	1.65387	94.88599	156.92928	121	1.69591	93.79350	159.06548	121	1.73901	92.71862	161.23865
122	1.66076	95.48812	158.58316	122	1.70333	94.38058	160.76140	122	1.74698	93.29103	162.97766
123	1.66768	96.08775	160.24391	123	1.71078	94.96512	162.46472	123	1.75499	93.86084	164.72464
124	1.67463	96.68490	161.91161	124	1.71827	95.54710	164.17551	124	1.76303	94.42804	166.47963
125	1.68161	97.27957	163.55623	125	1.72579	96.12654	165.89377	125	1.77111	94.99266	168.24266

n				n				n			
126	1.68962	97.87177	165.26784	126	1.73334	96.70347	167.61955	126	1.77923	95.55470	170.01378
127	1.69565	98.46152	166.99645	127	1.74092	97.27788	169.35289	127	1.78738	96.11418	171.79300
128	1.70272	99.04881	168.65211	128	1.74854	97.84978	171.03381	128	1.79558	96.67110	173.58038
129	1.70981	99.63367	170.35483	129	1.75619	98.41920	172.84235	129	1.80381	97.22549	175.37596
130	1.71694	100.21610	172.06464	130	1.76387	98.98614	174.59854	130	1.81207	97.77734	177.17978
131	1.72409	100.73612	173.78157	131	1.77159	99.55060	176.36240	131	1.82038	98.32668	178.99185
132	1.73127	101.37373	175.50566	132	1.77934	100.11261	178.13399	132	1.82872	98.87350	180.81223
133	1.73849	101.94894	177.23694	133	1.78712	100.67216	179.91333	133	1.83710	99.41784	182.64095
134	1.74573	102.52177	178.97542	134	1.79494	101.22929	181.70044	134	1.84552	99.95969	184.47806
135	1.75300	103.09222	180.72116	135	1.80279	101.76398	183.49539	135	1.85398	100.49907	186.32358
136	1.76031	103.66030	182.47417	136	1.81068	102.33627	185.28917	136	1.86248	101.03599	188.17757
137	1.76764	104.22602	184.23447	137	1.81860	102.88614	187.10886	137	1.87102	101.57046	190.04004
138	1.77501	104.78940	186.00211	138	1.82656	103.43362	188.92746	138	1.87959	102.10249	191.91106
139	1.78240	105.35044	187.77871	139	1.83455	103.97871	190.75401	139	1.88821	102.63209	193.79065
140	1.78983	105.90916	189.55962	140	1.84257	104.52142	192.58856	140	1.89686	103.15928	195.67886
141	1.79729	106.46555	191.34337	141	1.85064	105.06178	194.43114	141	1.90556	103.68406	197.57571
142	1.80478	107.01963	193.14665	142	1.85873	105.59978	196.28177	142	1.91429	104.20644	199.48128
143	1.81230	107.57142	194.96143	143	1.86686	106.13544	198.14050	143	1.92306	104.72645	201.39557
144	1.81985	108.12091	196.76372	144	1.87503	106.66876	200.00737	144	1.93188	105.24408	203.31862
145	1.82743	108.66813	198.58357	145	1.88324	107.19976	201.88240	145	1.94073	105.75935	205.25050
146	1.83505	109.21307	200.41100	146	1.89147	107.72845	203.76564	146	1.94973	106.27227	207.19124
147	1.84269	109.75578	202.24805	147	1.89975	108.25483	205.65712	147	1.95856	106.78284	209.14085
148	1.85037	110.29619	204.09875	148	1.90806	108.77893	207.55687	148	1.96754	107.29110	211.09943
149	1.85808	110.83438	205.95912	149	1.91641	109.30074	209.46492	149	1.97656	107.79703	213.06696
150	1.86582	111.37034	207.79720	150	1.92479	109.82027	211.38133	150	1.98562	108.30065	215.04352

Table 1. (continued) Annuities

M	CI 5.00,M,12	AI 5.00,M,12	SI 5.00,M,12	M	CI 5.25,M,12	AI 5.25,M,12	SI 5.25,M,12	M	CI 5.50,M,12	AI 5.50,M,12	SI 5.50,M,12
151	1.87360	111.90408	209.66301	151	1.93321	110.33755	213.30614	151	1.99472	108.80197	217.02913
152	1.88140	112.43659	211.53661	152	1.94167	110.85257	215.23985	152	2.00386	109.30101	219.02386
153	1.88924	112.96450	213.41801	153	1.95017	111.36534	217.18102	153	2.01304	109.79777	221.02371
154	1.89711	113.49202	215.30725	154	1.95870	111.87589	219.13118	154	2.02227	110.29827	223.04076
155	1.90502	114.01696	217.20436	155	1.96727	112.38421	221.08989	155	2.03154	110.78450	225.06302
156	1.91296	114.53970	219.10939	156	1.97588	112.89031	223.05714	156	2.04085	111.27449	227.09456
157	1.92093	115.06028	221.02234	157	1.98452	113.39421	225.03302	157	2.05020	111.76225	229.13542
158	1.92893	115.57870	222.94327	158	1.99320	113.89592	227.01755	158	2.05960	112.24778	231.18562
159	1.93697	116.09498	224.87219	159	2.00192	114.39544	229.01074	159	2.06904	112.73109	233.24522
160	1.94504	116.60911	226.80916	160	2.01068	114.89278	231.01266	160	2.07852	113.21220	235.31425
161	1.95314	117.12110	228.75420	161	2.01948	115.38795	233.02335	161	2.08805	113.69112	237.39278
162	1.96128	117.63097	230.70735	162	2.02831	115.88098	235.04283	162	2.09762	114.16785	239.48083
163	1.96945	118.13873	232.66862	163	2.03719	116.37185	237.07114	163	2.10723	114.64241	241.57846
164	1.97766	118.64437	234.63808	164	2.04610	116.86059	239.10832	164	2.11689	115.11480	243.68568
165	1.98590	119.14793	236.61574	165	2.05505	117.34719	241.15442	165	2.12660	115.58504	245.80258
166	1.99417	119.64938	238.60164	166	2.06404	117.83168	243.20947	166	2.13634	116.05312	247.92918
167	2.00248	120.14877	240.59581	167	2.07307	118.31406	245.27351	167	2.14613	116.51908	250.06552
168	2.01083	120.64607	242.59830	168	2.08214	118.79433	247.34659	168	2.15597	116.98291	252.21165
169	2.01920	121.14132	244.60912	169	2.09125	119.27251	249.42873	169	2.16585	117.44462	254.36763
170	2.02762	121.63451	246.62833	170	2.10040	119.74861	251.51997	170	2.17578	117.90423	256.53348
171	2.03607	122.12565	248.65594	171	2.10959	120.22264	253.62038	171	2.18575	118.36173	258.70926
172	2.04455	122.61475	250.69200	172	2.11882	120.69460	255.72997	172	2.19577	118.81715	260.89499
173	2.05307	123.10183	252.73656	173	2.12809	121.16451	257.84879	173	2.20583	119.27050	263.09076
174	2.06162	123.58688	254.78963	174	2.13740	121.63236	259.97687	174	2.21594	119.72177	265.29660
175	2.07021	124.06993	256.85123	175	2.14675	122.09818	262.11426	175	2.22610	120.17099	267.51254

n									
176	2.07884	258.92145	124.55096	2.15614	122.56197	264.26102	2.23630	120.61816	269.73865
177	2.08750	261.00031	125.03001	2.16558	123.02374	266.41714	2.24655	121.06329	271.97495
178	2.09620	263.08780	125.50706	2.17505	123.48351	268.58273	2.25685	121.50618	274.22150
179	2.10493	265.18399	125.98213	2.18457	123.94126	270.75378	2.26719	121.94746	276.47633
180	2.11370	267.28894	126.45524	2.19412	124.39703	272.94235	2.27758	122.38651	278.74554
181	2.12251	269.40262	126.92638	2.20372	124.85081	275.13647	2.28802	122.82358	281.02313
182	2.13135	271.52515	127.39556	2.21336	125.30260	277.34018	2.29851	123.25864	283.31113
183	2.14024	273.65649	127.86280	2.22305	125.75244	279.53356	2.30904	123.69172	285.60965
184	2.14915	275.79672	128.32809	2.23277	126.20031	281.77681	2.31963	124.12283	287.91870
185	2.15811	277.94589	128.79147	2.24254	126.64623	284.00537	2.33026	124.55196	290.23831
186	2.16710	280.10400	129.25291	2.25235	127.09022	286.25192	2.34094	124.97914	292.56857
187	2.17613	282.27109	129.71245	2.26221	127.53226	288.50427	2.35167	125.40437	294.90952
188	2.18520	284.44724	130.17007	2.27210	127.97238	290.76648	2.36245	125.82766	297.26120
189	2.19430	286.63242	130.62579	2.28204	128.41058	293.03857	2.37328	126.24902	299.62363
190	2.20344	288.82672	131.07964	2.29203	128.84688	295.32062	2.38415	126.66845	301.99692
191	2.21263	291.03018	131.53159	2.30206	129.28127	297.61264	2.39508	127.08598	304.38107
192	2.22184	293.24280	131.99166	2.31213	129.71378	299.91470	2.40606	127.50159	306.77615
193	2.23110	295.46463	132.42987	2.32224	130.14439	302.22684	2.41708	127.91531	309.18219
194	2.24040	297.69574	132.87622	2.33240	130.57314	304.54907	2.42816	128.32715	311.59927
195	2.24973	299.93615	133.32071	2.34261	131.00002	306.88147	2.43929	128.73711	314.02747
196	2.25911	302.18588	133.76337	2.35286	131.42502	309.22409	2.45047	129.14519	316.46674
197	2.26852	304.44498	134.20418	2.36315	131.84819	311.57693	2.46170	129.55141	318.91721
198	2.27797	306.71350	134.64317	2.37349	132.26952	313.94009	2.47299	129.95578	321.37891
199	2.28746	308.99149	135.08034	2.38387	132.68600	316.31357	2.48432	130.35831	323.85190
200	2.29700	311.27893	135.51569	2.39430	133.10666	318.69745	2.49571	130.75899	326.33624

Table 1. (continued) Annuities

M	C(5.00,M,12)	A(5.00,M,12)	S(5.00,M,12)	M	C(5.25,M,12)	A(5.25,M,12)	S(5.25,M,12)	M	C(5.50,M,12)	A(5.50,M,12)	S(5.50,M,12)
201	2.30657	135.94923	313.57593	201	2.40478	133.52249	321.09177	201	2.50715	131.15795	328.88194
202	2.31618	136.36098	315.88251	202	2.41530	133.93652	323.49652	202	2.51964	131.55489	331.33908
203	2.32583	136.81093	318.19867	203	2.42586	134.34877	325.91183	203	2.53218	131.95012	333.86373
204	2.33552	137.26550	320.52451	204	2.43648	134.75924	328.33768	204	2.54178	132.34354	336.38791
205	2.34525	137.66550	322.86012	205	2.44714	135.16792	330.77417	205	2.55343	132.73517	338.90368
206	2.35502	138.05012	325.20529	206	2.45784	135.57468	333.22131	206	2.56513	133.12502	341.48309
207	2.36483	138.51299	327.56030	207	2.46960	135.97977	335.67914	207	2.57689	133.51308	344.04825
208	2.37469	138.93408	329.92514	208	2.47940	136.38309	338.14774	208	2.58870	133.89837	346.62512
209	2.38458	139.35345	332.29984	209	2.49024	136.78465	340.62714	209	2.60056	134.28391	349.21384
210	2.39452	139.77107	334.68442	210	2.50114	137.18448	343.11737	210	2.61248	134.66669	351.81439
211	2.40450	140.18695	337.07892	211	2.51208	137.58255	345.61853	211	2.62446	135.04771	354.42658
212	2.41451	140.60112	339.48343	212	2.52307	137.97890	348.13062	212	2.63649	135.42700	357.05133
213	2.42457	141.01357	341.89792	213	2.53411	138.37350	350.65369	213	2.64857	135.80457	359.68781
214	2.43468	141.42430	344.32251	214	2.54520	138.76640	353.18777	214	2.66071	136.18040	362.33640
215	2.44482	141.83333	346.75717	215	2.55633	139.15759	355.73297	215	2.67290	136.55453	364.99710
216	2.45501	142.24065	349.20200	216	2.56752	139.54707	358.28931	216	2.68515	136.92686	367.66998
217	2.46524	142.64630	351.65701	217	2.57875	139.93496	360.85684	217	2.69746	137.29767	370.35513
218	2.47551	143.05025	354.12225	218	2.59003	140.32095	363.43558	218	2.70982	137.66670	373.05261
219	2.48582	143.45253	356.59775	219	2.60136	140.70537	366.02560	219	2.72224	138.03404	375.76242
220	2.49618	143.85315	359.08359	220	2.61274	141.08810	368.62698	220	2.73472	138.39972	378.48468
221	2.50658	144.25209	361.57977	221	2.62417	141.46918	371.23972	221	2.74726	138.76372	381.21939
222	2.51703	144.64938	364.08636	222	2.63565	141.84859	373.86389	222	2.75985	139.12605	383.96664
223	2.52751	145.04503	366.60336	223	2.64719	142.22635	376.49954	223	2.77250	139.48674	386.72650
224	2.53805	145.43904	369.13080	224	2.65877	142.60246	379.14673	224	2.78520	139.84578	389.49099
225	2.54862	145.83141	371.66895	225	2.67040	142.97694	381.80548	225	2.79797	140.20319	392.28421

n				n				n			
226	2.55924	146.22215	374.21756	226	2.88208	143.34978	384.47589	226	2.81079	140.55894	395.08218
227	2.58930	146.28127	376.77679	227	2.69392	143.72101	387.15799	227	2.82368	140.91310	397.89297
228	2.59861	146.99878	373.34671	228	2.70560	144.09061	389.85181	228	2.83662	141.26563	400.71664
229	2.59136	147.39467	381.92731	229	2.71744	144.45860	392.55740	229	2.84962	141.61656	403.55325
230	2.60216	147.76897	384.51968	230	2.72933	144.82500	395.27484	230	2.86268	141.96588	406.40289
231	2.61300	148.15167	387.12085	231	2.74127	145.18979	398.00415	231	2.87580	142.31361	409.26556
232	2.62389	148.53278	389.73383	232	2.75326	145.55299	400.74542	232	2.88898	142.65974	412.14136
233	2.63482	148.91231	392.35773	233	2.76531	145.91461	403.49969	233	2.90222	143.00432	415.03033
234	2.64580	149.29027	394.99255	234	2.77741	146.27466	406.26401	234	2.91552	143.34731	417.93256
235	2.65683	149.66666	397.63837	235	2.78956	146.63315	409.04141	235	2.92889	143.68874	420.84808
236	2.66790	150.04149	400.29620	236	2.80176	146.99007	411.83096	236	2.94231	144.02859	423.77698
237	2.67901	150.41476	402.96307	237	2.81402	147.34543	414.63272	237	2.95590	144.36691	426.71930
238	2.69018	150.78648	405.64209	238	2.82633	147.69925	417.44675	238	2.96934	144.70369	429.67508
239	2.70138	151.15666	408.33228	239	2.83869	148.05151	420.27307	239	2.98295	145.03893	432.64444
240	2.71264	151.52530	411.03366	240	2.85111	148.40225	423.11176	240	2.99663	145.37263	435.62738
241	2.72394	151.89243	413.74631	241	2.86359	148.75146	425.96296	241	3.01036	145.70483	438.62399
242	2.73529	152.25801	418.47025	242	2.87612	149.09917	428.82648	242	3.02416	146.03549	441.63437
243	2.74669	152.62209	419.20554	243	2.88870	149.44534	431.70258	243	3.03802	146.36465	444.65851
244	2.75813	152.98465	421.96221	244	2.90134	149.79001	434.59128	244	3.05194	146.69232	447.69658
245	2.76963	153.34570	424.71036	245	2.91403	150.13318	437.43061	245	3.06593	147.01948	450.74847
246	2.78117	153.70528	427.47998	246	2.92678	150.47484	440.28665	246	3.07998	147.34315	453.81442
247	2.79275	154.06334	430.26114	247	2.93958	150.81503	443.33344	247	3.09410	147.66635	456.89441
248	2.80439	154.41992	433.05389	248	2.95244	151.15373	446.27301	248	3.10828	147.98908	458.98849
249	2.81608	154.77502	435.85831	249	2.96536	151.49095	449.22546	249	3.12253	148.30833	463.09677
250	2.82781	155.12866	438.67438	250	2.97833	151.82672	452.19083	250	3.13684	148.62712	466.21890

Table 1. (continued) Annuities

M	C(5.00,M,12)	A(5.00,M,12)	S(5.00,M,12)	M	C(5.25,M,12)	A(5.25,M,12)	S(5.25,M,12)	M	C(5.50,M,12)	A(5.50,M,12)	S(5.50,M,12)
251	2.83959	155.48082	441.50217	251	2.99136	152.16101	455.16916	251	3.15122	148.94446	469.35614
252	2.85142	155.83153	444.34177	252	3.00445	152.43385	458.16052	252	3.16566	149.26036	472.50735
253	2.86330	156.18077	447.19321	253	3.01760	152.82524	461.16498	253	3.18017	149.57480	475.67300
254	2.87524	156.52856	450.05649	254	3.03080	153.15447	464.18256	254	3.19474	149.88782	478.85318
255	2.88722	156.87492	452.93173	255	3.04406	153.48370	467.21335	255	3.20939	150.19940	482.04794
256	2.89925	157.21983	455.81894	256	3.05738	153.81078	470.25742	256	3.22410	150.50957	485.25732
257	2.91133	157.56332	458.71920	257	3.07075	154.13643	473.31479	257	3.23887	150.81831	488.48141
258	2.92346	157.90538	461.62966	258	3.08419	154.44855	476.38556	258	3.25372	151.12566	491.72028
259	2.93564	158.24603	464.55298	259	3.09768	154.76066	479.46973	259	3.26863	151.43159	494.97400
260	2.94787	158.58525	467.48862	260	3.11123	155.10490	482.56741	260	3.28361	151.73615	498.24265
261	2.96015	158.92308	470.43649	261	3.12484	155.42491	485.67965	261	3.29866	152.03929	501.52625
262	2.97249	159.25949	473.39664	262	3.13852	155.74353	488.80350	262	3.31378	152.34106	504.82492
263	2.98487	159.59451	476.36911	263	3.15225	156.06078	491.94202	263	3.32897	152.64145	508.13870
264	2.99731	159.92815	479.35400	264	3.16604	156.37662	495.09424	264	3.34423	152.94048	511.46765
265	3.00980	160.26041	482.35132	265	3.17989	156.69042	498.28028	265	3.35955	153.23813	514.81189
266	3.02234	160.59126	485.36111	266	3.19380	157.00421	501.44019	266	3.37495	153.53444	518.17145
267	3.03493	160.92076	488.38345	267	3.20777	157.31598	504.63397	267	3.39042	153.82939	521.54639
268	3.04758	161.24890	491.41837	268	3.22181	157.62633	507.84177	268	3.40596	154.12299	524.92677
269	3.06027	161.57567	494.46594	269	3.23590	157.93536	511.06357	269	3.42157	154.41525	528.34277
270	3.07303	161.90108	497.52621	270	3.25006	158.24306	514.29944	270	3.43725	154.70618	531.76434
271	3.08583	162.22514	500.59924	271	3.26428	158.54939	517.54950	271	3.45301	154.99579	535.20160
272	3.09869	162.54785	503.68509	272	3.27856	158.85442	520.81378	272	3.46883	155.28406	538.65460
273	3.11160	162.86923	506.78375	273	3.29290	159.15810	524.09235	273	3.48473	155.57103	542.12341
274	3.12456	163.18929	509.89536	274	3.30731	159.46045	527.38525	274	3.50070	155.85669	545.60815
275	3.13758	163.50800	513.01990	275	3.32178	159.76151	530.69857	275	3.51675	156.14104	549.10889

276	3.15066	163.82539	516.15747	276	3.33631	160.06123	534.01434	276	3.53287	156.42410	552.82561
277	3.16378	164.14146	519.30817	277	3.35091	160.35966	537.35065	277	3.54906	156.70596	556.15845
278	3.17697	164.45624	522.47192	278	3.36557	160.65678	540.70154	278	3.56533	156.98634	559.70752
279	3.19020	164.76968	525.64893	279	3.38029	160.95262	544.06714	279	3.58167	157.26555	563.27289
280	3.20350	165.08185	528.83911	280	3.39508	161.24716	547.44745	280	3.59808	157.54347	566.85455
281	3.21684	165.39272	532.04260	281	3.40994	161.54042	550.84253	281	3.61457	157.82013	570.45264
282	3.23025	165.70229	535.25946	282	3.42485	161.83240	554.25244	282	3.63114	158.09552	574.06720
283	3.24371	166.01057	538.48969	283	3.43984	162.12311	557.67731	283	3.64778	158.36966	577.69830
284	3.25722	166.31758	541.73340	284	3.45489	162.41257	561.11713	284	3.66450	158.64255	581.34613
285	3.27079	166.62332	544.99060	285	3.47000	162.70074	564.57202	285	3.68130	158.91418	585.01062
286	3.28442	166.92780	548.26141	286	3.48518	162.98767	568.04205	286	3.69817	159.18460	588.69189
287	3.29811	167.23099	551.54584	287	3.50043	163.27335	571.52722	287	3.71512	159.45377	592.39008
288	3.31186	167.53294	554.84393	288	3.51575	163.55779	575.02765	288	3.73215	159.72171	596.10522
289	3.32565	167.83363	558.15582	289	3.53113	163.84099	578.54342	289	3.74925	159.98843	599.83734
290	3.33951	168.13307	561.48145	290	3.54658	164.12294	582.07452	290	3.76644	160.25394	603.58661
291	3.35342	168.43128	564.82098	291	3.56209	164.40369	585.62109	291	3.78370	160.51822	607.35303
292	3.36739	168.72824	568.17438	292	3.57768	164.68320	589.18317	292	3.80104	160.78131	611.13678
293	3.38142	169.02399	571.54175	293	3.59333	164.96149	592.76086	293	3.81846	161.04320	614.93781
294	3.39551	169.31848	574.92322	294	3.60905	165.23857	596.35419	294	3.83597	161.30398	618.75629
295	3.40966	169.61177	578.31873	295	3.62484	165.51443	599.96326	295	3.85355	161.56339	622.59222
296	3.42387	169.90384	581.72839	296	3.64070	165.78911	603.58907	296	3.87121	161.82170	626.44580
297	3.43813	170.19469	585.15222	297	3.65663	166.06259	607.22876	297	3.88895	162.07884	630.31702
298	3.45246	170.48434	588.59039	298	3.67262	166.33487	610.88644	298	3.90678	162.33481	634.20593
299	3.46685	170.77280	592.04285	299	3.68869	166.60597	614.55804	299	3.92468	162.58960	638.11273
300	3.48129	171.06004	595.50970	300	3.70483	166.87589	618.24670	300	3.94267	162.84323	642.03741

Table 1. (continued) Annuities

M	C(5.00,M,12)	A(5.00,M,12)	S(5.00,M,12)	M	C(5.25,M,12)	A(5.25,M,12)	S(5.25,M,12)	M	C(5.50,M,12)	A(5.50,M,12)	S(5.50,M,12)
301	3.49580	171.34610	598.99097	301	3.72104	167.14464	621.96154	301	3.96074	163.08672	645.99004
302	3.51036	171.63097	602.48676	302	3.73732	167.41220	625.67261	302	3.97890	163.34705	649.94080
303	3.52499	171.91466	605.99713	303	3.75367	167.67860	629.40991	303	3.99713	163.59721	653.91974
304	3.53968	172.19717	609.52209	304	3.77009	167.94385	633.16357	304	4.01546	163.84825	657.91697
305	3.55442	172.47852	613.06177	305	3.78658	168.20795	636.93365	305	4.03386	164.09416	661.93231
306	3.56923	172.75868	616.61621	306	3.80315	168.47089	640.72028	306	4.05235	164.34088	665.96313
307	3.58411	173.03769	620.18542	307	3.81979	168.73268	644.52338	307	4.07092	164.58658	670.01649
308	3.59904	173.31554	623.76963	308	3.83650	168.99333	648.34320	308	4.08958	164.83110	674.08942
309	3.61404	173.59224	627.36859	309	3.85329	169.25285	652.17969	309	4.10832	165.07451	678.17902
310	3.62909	173.86780	630.98260	310	3.87014	169.51125	656.03286	310	4.12715	165.31680	682.28729
311	3.64422	174.14220	634.61169	311	3.88708	169.76851	659.90314	311	4.14607	165.55800	686.41449
312	3.65940	174.41547	638.25592	312	3.90408	170.02464	663.79022	312	4.16507	165.79910	690.56055
313	3.67465	174.68761	641.91534	313	3.92116	170.27968	667.69427	313	4.18416	166.03709	694.72569
314	3.68996	174.95960	645.58997	314	3.93832	170.53358	671.61548	314	4.20334	166.27499	698.90373
315	3.70533	175.22849	649.27997	315	3.95555	170.78639	675.55377	315	4.22260	166.51181	703.11310
316	3.72077	175.49725	652.98529	316	3.97285	171.03810	679.50934	316	4.24196	166.74756	707.33569
317	3.73628	175.76489	656.70605	317	3.99023	171.28871	683.48218	317	4.26140	166.98222	711.57764
318	3.75184	176.03143	660.44232	318	4.00769	171.53824	687.47241	318	4.28093	167.21582	715.83905
319	3.76748	176.29686	664.19415	319	4.02523	171.78667	691.48010	319	4.30055	167.44835	720.12000
320	3.78317	176.56119	667.96167	320	4.04284	172.03403	695.50531	320	4.32026	167.67981	724.42053
321	3.79894	176.82442	671.74481	321	4.06052	172.28029	699.54816	321	4.34006	167.91022	728.74078
322	3.81477	177.08656	675.54376	322	4.07829	172.52550	703.60870	322	4.35995	168.13959	733.08087
323	3.83066	177.34761	679.35852	323	4.09613	172.76962	707.68696	323	4.37994	168.36789	737.44080
324	3.84662	177.60759	683.18921	324	4.11405	173.01270	711.78308	324	4.40001	168.59617	741.82074
325	3.86265	177.86647	687.03583	325	4.13205	173.25471	715.89716	325	4.42018	168.82140	746.22076

n				n				n			
326	3.87874	178.12428	690.89644	326	4.15013	173.49567	720.02917	326	169.04660	4.44044	**750.84093**
327	3.89491	178.38103	694.77722	327	4.16828	173.73557	724.17932	327	169.27078	4.46079	**755.08136**
328	3.91113	178.63672	698.67212	328	4.18652	173.97444	728.34760	328	169.49393	4.48124	**759.54218**
329	3.92743	178.89133	702.56325	329	4.20484	174.21225	732.53412	329	169.71606	4.50177	**764.02338**
330	3.94379	179.14490	706.51068	330	4.22323	174.44904	736.73896	330	169.93719	4.52241	**768.52515**
331	3.96023	179.39740	710.45447	331	4.24171	174.68480	740.96222	331	170.15730	4.54313	**773.04755**
332	3.97673	179.64886	714.41467	332	4.26027	174.91963	745.20392	332	170.37640	4.56396	**777.59070**
333	3.99330	179.89929	718.39142	333	4.27891	175.15323	749.46417	333	170.59451	4.58488	**782.15466**
334	4.00994	180.14867	722.38470	334	4.29763	175.38591	753.74310	334	170.81163	4.60589	**786.73956**
335	4.02664	180.39702	726.39465	335	4.31643	175.61758	758.04071	335	171.02776	4.62700	**791.34546**
336	4.04342	180.64433	730.42128	336	4.33531	175.84825	762.35712	336	171.24289	4.64821	**795.97241**
337	4.06027	180.89063	734.46472	337	4.35428	176.07791	766.69244	337	171.45705	4.66951	**800.62067**
338	4.07718	181.13588	738.52496	338	4.37333	176.30656	771.04675	338	171.67023	4.69091	**805.29016**
339	4.09418	181.38014	742.60217	339	4.39246	176.53423	775.42004	339	171.88243	4.71241	**809.98108**
340	4.11123	181.62037	746.69635	340	4.41168	176.76089	779.81250	340	172.03367	4.73401	**814.69348**
341	4.12837	181.86560	750.80756	341	4.43098	176.99659	784.22418	341	172.30394	4.75571	**819.42749**
342	4.14557	182.10683	754.93597	342	4.45037	177.23131	788.65521	342	172.51328	4.77751	**824.18323**
343	4.16284	182.34705	759.08154	343	4.46984	177.43501	793.10553	343	172.72162	4.79940	**828.96069**
344	4.18018	182.58626	763.24438	344	4.48939	177.65776	797.57538	344	172.92902	4.82140	**833.76013**
345	4.19760	182.82449	767.42456	345	4.50903	177.87953	802.06476	345	173.13548	4.84350	**838.58148**
346	4.21509	183.06174	771.62213	346	4.52876	178.10034	806.57379	346	173.34100	4.86570	**843.42499**
347	4.23266	183.29900	775.83722	347	4.54857	178.32019	811.10260	347	173.54559	4.88800	**848.29071**
348	4.25029	183.53328	780.06999	348	4.56847	178.53908	815.65112	348	173.74924	4.91040	**853.17871**
349	4.26800	183.76758	784.32019	349	4.58846	178.75702	820.21960	349	173.96197	4.93291	**858.08911**
350	4.28578	184.00090	788.58820	350	4.60854	178.97401	824.90811	350	174.15375	4.95552	**863.02203**

Table 1. (continued) Annuities

M	C(5.00,M,12)	AI 5.00,M,12)	SI 5.00,M,12)	M	C(5.25,M,12)	AI 5.25,M,12)	SI 5.25,M,12)	M	C(5.50,M,12)	AI 5.50,M,12)	SI 5.50,M,12)
351	4.30364	184.23326	792.87398	351	4.62870	179.19005	829.41683	351	4.97823	174.35463	867.97754
352	4.32157	184.46466	797.17781	352	4.64895	179.40515	834.04529	352	5.00116	174.55458	872.95575
353	4.33968	184.63610	801.49921	353	4.66929	179.61932	838.69427	353	5.02397	174.75363	877.95679
354	4.35788	184.92458	805.83875	354	4.68972	179.83255	843.36353	354	5.04700	174.95177	882.98076
355	4.37382	185.16311	810.19641	355	4.71023	180.04486	848.05328	355	5.07013	175.14900	888.02776
356	4.39405	185.38069	814.57227	356	4.73084	180.25624	852.76349	356	5.09337	175.34534	893.09730
357	4.41236	185.60733	818.96631	357	4.75154	180.46669	857.49432	357	5.11671	175.54077	898.19128
358	4.43074	185.83032	823.37866	358	4.77233	180.67624	862.24591	358	5.14016	175.73532	903.30798
359	4.44921	186.05779	827.80939	359	4.79322	180.88487	867.01819	359	5.16372	175.92899	908.44812
360	4.46774	186.28162	832.25841	360	4.81417	181.09259	871.81140	360	5.18739	176.12175	913.61188
361	4.48636	186.50450	836.72618	361	4.83524	181.29939	876.62561	361	5.21116	176.31364	918.79826
362	4.50505	186.72649	841.21271	362	4.85639	181.50531	881.46082	362	5.23505	176.50467	924.01044
363	4.52382	186.94753	845.71777	363	4.87764	181.71033	886.31720	363	5.25904	176.69482	929.24548
364	4.54267	187.16766	850.24158	364	4.89898	181.91446	891.19482	364	5.28315	176.88409	934.50452
365	4.56160	187.38689	854.78424	365	4.92041	182.11769	896.09381	365	5.30736	177.07253	939.78766
366	4.58061	187.60519	859.34589	366	4.94194	182.32004	901.01422	366	5.33169	177.26007	945.09503
367	4.59969	187.82260	863.92645	367	4.96356	182.52151	905.95618	367	5.35612	177.44678	950.42670
368	4.61886	188.03911	868.52618	368	4.98527	182.72211	910.91974	368	5.38067	177.63263	955.78284
369	4.63810	188.25471	873.14502	369	5.00708	182.92181	915.90503	369	5.40533	177.81763	961.16351
370	4.65743	188.46942	877.76314	370	5.02899	183.12067	920.91211	370	5.43011	178.00179	966.56885
371	4.67684	188.68324	882.44055	371	5.05099	183.31865	925.94110	371	5.45500	178.18510	971.99896
372	4.69632	188.89618	887.11737	372	5.07309	183.51576	930.99207	372	5.48000	178.36758	977.45392
373	4.71589	189.10823	891.89372	373	5.09528	183.71202	936.06519	373	5.50511	178.54924	982.93390
374	4.73554	189.31940	896.52960	374	5.11758	183.90742	941.16046	374	5.53035	178.73006	988.43903
375	4.75527	189.52969	901.26514	375	5.13997	184.10197	946.27602	375	5.55569	178.91005	993.96936

n				n			n				
376	4.77508	189.7391	906.02045	376	5.16245	184.29868	376	5.58116	951.41797	179.08923	999.52509
377	4.79498	189.94766	910.79853	377	5.18504	184.48856	377	5.60674	956.58044	179.26759	1005.10620
378	4.81496	190.15535	915.55045	378	5.20772	184.68057	378	5.63243	961.76550	179.44513	1010.71296
379	4.83502	190.36217	920.40546	379	5.23051	184.87177	379	5.65825	966.97321	179.62186	1016.34540
380	4.85517	190.56813	925.24048	380	5.25339	185.06212	380	5.68418	972.20374	179.7979	1022.00366
381	4.87540	190.77325	930.09564	381	5.27637	185.25226	381	5.71024	977.45709	179.97292	1027.68774
382	4.89571	190.97751	934.97101	382	5.29946	185.44034	382	5.73641	982.73352	180.14723	1033.39807
383	4.91611	191.18092	939.86676	383	5.32264	185.62820	383	5.76270	988.03296	180.32077	1039.13440
384	4.93659	191.38348	944.78284	384	5.34593	185.81528	384	5.78911	993.35559	180.49350	1044.89709
385	4.95716	191.58522	949.71948	385	5.36932	186.00151	385	5.81565	998.70154	180.66545	1050.68628
386	4.97782	191.78610	954.67664	386	5.39281	186.18695	386	5.84230	1004.07086	180.83662	1056.50196
387	4.99856	191.98616	959.65442	387	5.41640	186.37157	387	5.86908	1009.46368	181.00700	1062.34424
388	5.01939	192.18539	964.65302	388	5.44010	186.55539	388	5.89598	1014.88007	181.17662	1068.21326
389	5.04030	192.38379	969.67236	389	5.46390	186.73840	389	5.92300	1020.32013	181.34544	1074.10925
390	5.06130	192.58138	974.71271	390	5.48781	186.92062	390	5.95015	1025.78406	181.51350	1080.03223
391	5.08239	192.77814	979.77399	391	5.51181	187.10207	391	5.97742	1031.27185	181.68080	1085.98242
392	5.10357	192.97408	984.85638	392	5.53593	187.28270	392	6.00482	1036.76369	181.84734	1091.95984
393	5.12483	193.16920	989.95996	393	5.56015	187.46255	393	6.03234	1042.31968	182.01311	1097.96460
394	5.14619	193.36353	995.08478	394	5.58447	187.64162	394	6.05999	1047.87978	182.17813	1103.93695
395	5.16763	193.55704	1000.23036	395	5.60891	187.81990	395	6.08776	1053.46423	182.34239	1110.05701
396	5.18916	193.74976	1005.39962	396	5.63344	187.99742	396	6.11566	1059.07312	182.50591	1116.14478
397	5.21078	193.94165	1010.58777	397	5.65809	188.17415	397	6.14369	1064.70654	182.66867	1122.26038
398	5.23249	194.13277	1015.79852	398	5.68285	188.35013	398	6.17185	1070.36462	182.83070	1128.40405
399	5.25430	194.32309	1021.03107	399	5.70771	188.52533	399	6.20014	1076.04749	182.99199	1134.57598
400	5.27619	194.51262	1026.28528	400	5.73268	188.69977	400	6.22856	1081.75825	183.15254	1140.77612

Table 1. (continued) Annuities

M	C(5.00,M,12)	A(5.00,M,12)	SI 5.00,M,12)	M	C(5.25,M,12)	A(5.25,M,12)	SI 5.25,M,12)	M	C(5.50,M,12)	A(5.50,M,12)	SI 5.50,M,12)
401	5.29817	194.70135	1031.56152	401	5.75776	188.87344	1087.48792	401	8.25710	183.31236	1147.00464
402	5.32025	194.88533	1036.85962	402	5.78295	189.04636	1093.24561	402	8.28578	183.47145	1153.26172
403	5.34242	195.07651	1042.17993	403	5.80825	189.21854	1099.02856	403	8.31459	183.62981	1159.54749
404	5.36468	195.26291	1047.52234	404	5.83366	189.38995	1104.83679	404	8.34353	183.78745	1165.86218
405	5.38703	195.44953	1052.88698	405	5.85918	189.56061	1110.67053	405	8.37261	183.94437	1172.20569
406	5.40948	195.63339	1058.27405	406	5.88482	189.73055	1116.52966	406	8.40182	184.10059	1178.57825
407	5.43201	195.81749	1063.68347	407	5.91056	189.89973	1122.41455	407	8.43116	184.25607	1184.98010
408	5.45465	196.00082	1069.11548	408	5.93642	190.06819	1128.32507	408	8.46063	184.41086	1191.41125
409	5.47738	196.18340	1074.57019	409	5.96239	190.23592	1134.26147	409	8.49025	184.56493	1197.87183
410	5.50020	196.36520	1080.04761	410	5.98848	190.40289	1140.22388	410	8.51999	184.71831	1204.36218
411	5.52312	196.54626	1085.54773	411	6.01468	190.56915	1146.21240	411	8.54988	184.87099	1210.88208
412	5.54613	196.72656	1091.07092	412	6.04099	190.73470	1152.22705	412	8.57990	185.02298	1217.43201
413	5.56924	196.90613	1096.61694	413	6.06742	190.89951	1158.26907	413	8.61005	185.17424	1224.01194
414	5.59244	197.08498	1102.18628	414	6.09397	191.06360	1164.33545	414	8.64035	185.32484	1230.62195
415	5.61574	197.26300	1107.77869	415	6.12063	191.22699	1170.42944	415	8.67079	185.47475	1237.26233
416	5.63914	197.44034	1113.39441	416	6.14741	191.38966	1176.55005	416	8.70136	185.62396	1243.93311
417	5.66264	197.61693	1119.03357	417	6.17430	191.55162	1182.69751	417	8.73207	185.77251	1250.63440
418	5.68623	197.79280	1124.69617	418	6.20131	191.71288	1188.87061	418	8.76293	185.92038	1257.36658
419	5.70993	197.96798	1130.38245	419	6.22844	191.87343	1195.07312	419	8.79393	186.06757	1264.12893
420	5.73372	198.14233	1136.09241	420	6.25569	192.03328	1201.30151	420	8.82507	186.21408	1270.92334
421	5.75761	198.31602	1141.82605	421	6.28306	192.19244	1207.55725	421	8.85635	186.35994	1277.74841
422	5.78160	198.48898	1147.58374	422	6.31055	192.35091	1213.84033	422	8.88777	186.50513	1284.60474
423	5.80569	198.66122	1153.36523	423	6.33816	192.50868	1220.15088	423	8.91934	186.64964	1291.49255
424	5.82988	198.83276	1159.17102	424	6.36589	192.66577	1226.48901	424	8.95105	186.79350	1298.41187
425	5.85417	199.00357	1165.00085	425	6.39374	192.82217	1232.85486	425	8.98291	186.93671	1305.36292

n				n				n			
426	5.87856	199.17369	1170.85498	426	6.42171	192.97789	1239.24966	426	7.01492	187.07927	1312.34563
427	5.90306	199.34309	1176.73384	427	6.44981	193.13293	1245.67029	427	7.04707	187.22118	1319.36084
428	5.92765	199.51180	1182.63660	428	6.47803	193.28731	1252.12012	428	7.07937	187.36243	1326.40784
429	5.95235	199.67918	1188.56433	429	6.50637	193.44039	1258.59914	429	7.11182	187.50304	1333.48718
430	5.97715	199.84709	1194.51660	430	6.53483	193.59402	1265.10449	430	7.14441	187.64301	1340.59900
431	6.00206	200.01370	1200.43877	431	6.56342	193.74638	1271.63940	431	7.17716	187.78233	1347.74341
432	6.02707	200.17563	1206.49585	432	6.59214	193.89609	1278.20276	432	7.21005	187.92104	1354.92065
433	6.05218	200.34485	1212.52295	433	6.62098	194.04912	1284.79492	433	7.24310	188.05910	1362.13062
434	6.07740	200.50940	1218.57507	434	6.64994	194.19949	1291.41589	434	7.27630	188.19653	1369.37378
435	6.10272	200.67326	1224.65247	435	6.67904	194.34921	1298.06580	435	7.30965	188.33333	1376.65002
436	6.12815	200.83644	1230.75525	436	6.70826	194.49829	1304.74487	436	7.34315	188.46951	1383.95972
437	6.15368	200.99895	1236.88342	437	6.73761	194.64670	1311.45313	437	7.37680	188.60507	1391.30286
438	6.17932	201.16078	1243.03711	438	6.76708	194.73448	1318.19080	438	7.41061	188.74002	1398.67969
439	6.20507	201.32198	1249.21643	439	6.79669	194.94160	1324.95782	439	7.44458	188.87434	1406.09033
440	6.23092	201.48242	1255.42139	440	6.82643	195.08810	1331.75452	440	7.47870	189.00806	1413.53491
441	6.25689	201.64224	1261.65234	441	6.85629	195.23395	1338.58093	441	7.51298	189.14116	1421.01355
442	6.28296	201.80141	1267.90930	442	6.88629	195.37917	1345.43726	442	7.54741	189.27365	1428.52649
443	6.30913	201.95990	1274.19026	443	6.91642	195.52376	1352.32349	443	7.58201	189.40555	1436.07397
444	6.33542	202.11775	1280.50134	444	6.94667	195.66771	1359.23999	444	7.61676	189.53686	1443.65601
445	6.36182	202.27439	1286.83679	445	6.97707	195.81104	1366.19665	445	7.65167	189.66753	1451.27271
446	6.38833	202.43147	1293.19661	446	7.00761	195.96374	1373.16370	446	7.68674	189.79762	1458.92444
447	6.41495	202.58736	1299.59691	447	7.03825	196.09581	1380.17126	447	7.72197	189.92712	1466.81108
448	6.44167	202.74260	1306.00183	448	7.06904	196.23727	1387.20947	448	7.75736	190.05603	1474.33313
449	6.46851	202.89720	1312.44348	449	7.09997	196.37813	1394.27856	449	7.79291	190.18436	1482.09045
450	6.49547	203.05115	1318.91199	450	7.13103	196.51836	1401.37854	450	7.82863	190.31209	1489.88342

Table 1. (continued) Annuities

M	CI(5.00,M,12)	AI(5.00,M,12)	SI(5.00,M,12)	M	CI(5.25,M,12)	AI(5.25,M,12)	SI(5.25,M,12)	M	CI(5.50,M,12)	AI(5.50,M,12)	SI(5.50,M,12)
451	6.52253	203.20447	1325.40747	451	7.16223	196.65797	1408.50962	451	7.86451	190.43924	1497.71204
452	6.54971	203.35715	1331.93005	452	7.19356	196.79714	1415.67175	452	7.90056	190.56581	1505.57654
453	6.57700	203.50919	1338.47974	453	7.22504	196.93540	1422.86536	453	7.93723	190.69180	1513.47705
454	6.60440	203.66060	1345.05676	454	7.25665	197.07320	1430.03045	454	7.97315	190.81723	1521.41382
455	6.63192	203.81139	1351.66113	455	7.28839	197.21040	1437.34705	455	8.00968	190.94208	1529.38698
456	6.65956	203.96155	1358.29440	456	7.32028	197.34702	1444.63550	456	8.04640	191.06636	1537.39673
457	6.68730	204.11108	1364.96264	457	7.35231	197.48302	1451.96569	457	8.08328	191.19006	1545.44312
458	6.71517	204.25999	1371.63989	458	7.38447	197.61844	1459.30798	458	8.12033	191.31322	1553.52637
459	6.74315	204.40829	1378.35510	459	7.41678	197.75327	1466.69050	459	8.15755	191.43581	1561.64673
460	6.77124	204.55599	1385.09027	460	7.44923	197.88751	1474.10925	460	8.19494	191.55783	1569.80420
461	6.79946	204.70305	1391.86961	461	7.48182	198.02118	1481.55847	461	8.23250	191.67931	1577.99915
462	6.82779	204.84952	1398.66895	462	7.51455	198.15425	1489.04028	462	8.27023	191.80022	1586.23169
463	6.85624	204.99536	1405.49670	463	7.54743	198.26674	1496.55433	463	8.30813	191.92058	1594.50196
464	6.88480	205.14061	1412.35503	464	7.58045	198.41866	1504.10229	464	8.34621	192.04039	1602.81006
465	6.91349	205.28526	1419.23779	465	7.61361	198.55000	1511.68274	465	8.38447	192.15967	1611.15625
466	6.94230	205.42931	1426.15125	466	7.64692	198.69077	1519.29039	466	8.42289	192.27838	1619.54077
467	6.97122	205.57275	1433.09051	467	7.68038	198.81177	1526.94324	467	8.46150	192.39653	1627.96362
468	7.00027	205.71561	1440.06482	468	7.71398	198.94061	1534.62366	468	8.50028	192.51421	1636.42517
469	7.02944	205.85786	1447.06506	469	7.74773	199.06969	1542.33765	469	8.53924	192.63132	1644.92542
470	7.05873	205.99953	1454.09448	470	7.78162	199.19820	1550.08533	470	8.57838	192.74789	1653.46460
471	7.08814	206.14061	1461.15320	471	7.81567	199.32946	1557.86394	471	8.61770	192.86394	1662.04297
472	7.11767	206.28111	1468.24133	472	7.84986	199.45354	1565.68262	472	8.65720	192.97945	1670.66077
473	7.14733	206.42102	1475.35920	473	7.88420	199.59037	1573.53247	473	8.69687	193.09442	1679.31787
474	7.17711	206.56035	1482.50640	474	7.91870	199.70665	1581.41675	474	8.73673	193.20889	1688.01477
475	7.20701	206.69910	1489.68240	475	7.95334	199.83238	1589.33545	475	8.77678	193.32283	1696.75146

n				n				n			
476	7.23704	206.83728	1496.89050	476	7.99814	199.95757	1597.28882	476	8.81700	193.43623	1705.52832
477	7.26720	206.97488	1504.12756	477	8.02309	200.08221	1605.27686	477	8.85742	193.54913	1714.34534
478	7.29748	207.11192	1511.39478	478	8.05819	200.20630	1613.30005	478	8.89801	193.66153	1723.20276
479	7.32788	207.24838	1518.69226	479	8.09344	200.32986	1621.35815	479	8.93801	193.77339	1732.10071
480	7.35842	207.38428	1526.02014	480	8.12685	200.45288	1629.45166	480	8.97976	193.88475	1741.03955
481	7.38908	207.51962	1533.37854	481	8.16441	200.57536	1637.59044	481	9.02092	193.99561	1750.01929
482	7.41987	207.65439	1540.76758	482	8.20013	200.69731	1645.74487	482	9.06227	194.10596	1759.04016
483	7.45078	207.78860	1548.18750	483	8.23601	200.81873	1653.94507	483	9.10380	194.21581	1768.10243
484	7.48163	207.92226	1555.63818	484	8.27204	200.93962	1662.18103	484	9.14553	194.32515	1777.20630
485	7.51300	208.05536	1563.12012	485	8.30823	201.05998	1670.45313	485	9.18745	194.43399	1786.35181
486	7.54430	208.18791	1570.63306	486	8.34458	201.17982	1678.76135	486	9.22956	194.54234	1795.53931
487	7.57574	208.31992	1578.17737	487	8.38109	201.29913	1687.10596	487	9.27186	194.65019	1804.76880
488	7.60730	208.45137	1585.75305	488	8.41778	201.41794	1696.49694	488	9.31435	194.75755	1814.04065
489	7.63900	208.58228	1593.36035	489	8.45458	201.53621	1703.90479	489	9.35704	194.86443	1823.35498
490	7.67083	208.71265	1600.99939	490	8.49157	201.65398	1712.35938	490	9.39993	194.97081	1832.71204
491	7.70279	208.84247	1608.67029	491	8.52872	201.77122	1720.85096	491	9.44301	195.07671	1842.11194
492	7.73489	208.97174	1616.37305	492	8.56604	201.88797	1729.37964	492	9.48629	195.18211	1851.55505
493	7.76712	209.10049	1624.10791	493	8.60351	202.00420	1737.94568	493	9.52977	195.28705	1861.04128
494	7.79948	209.22871	1631.87500	494	8.64115	202.11992	1746.54919	494	9.57345	195.39151	1870.57104
495	7.83198	209.35638	1639.67456	495	8.67896	202.23514	1755.19031	495	9.61733	195.49548	1880.14453
496	7.86461	209.48354	1647.50647	496	8.71693	202.34987	1763.86826	496	9.66141	195.59900	1889.76184
497	7.89738	209.61017	1655.37109	497	8.75506	202.46408	1772.58618	497	9.70569	195.70203	1899.42322
498	7.93029	209.73627	1663.26843	498	8.79337	202.57780	1781.34131	498	9.75017	195.80460	1909.12891
499	7.96333	209.86185	1671.19873	499	8.83184	202.69104	1790.13464	499	9.79486	195.90668	1918.87915
500	7.99651	209.98689	1679.16211	500	8.87048	202.80377	1798.96643	500	9.83976	196.00832	1928.67395

Table 1. (continued) Annuities

M	C(5.75,M,12)	A(5.75,M,12)	S(5.75,M,12)	M	C(6.00,M,12)	A(6.00,M,12)	S(6.00,M,12)	M	C(6.25,M,12)	A(6.25,M,12)	S(6.25,M,12)
1	1.00479	0.99523	1.00000	1	1.00500	0.99502	1.00000	1	1.00521	0.99482	1.00000
2	1.00961	1.98572	2.00479	2	1.01002	1.98510	2.00500	2	1.01044	1.98448	2.00521
3	1.01444	2.97148	3.01440	3	1.01506	2.97025	3.01502	3	1.01571	2.96902	3.01565
4	1.01930	3.95254	4.02884	4	1.02015	3.95050	4.03010	4	1.02100	3.94845	4.03136
5	1.02419	4.92892	5.04815	5	1.02525	4.92587	5.05025	5	1.02631	4.92281	5.05236
6	1.02910	5.90065	6.07234	6	1.03038	5.89638	6.07550	6	1.03166	5.89213	6.07867
7	1.03403	6.86774	7.10143	7	1.03553	6.86207	7.10588	7	1.03703	6.85642	7.11033
8	1.03898	7.83022	8.13546	8	1.04071	7.82296	8.14141	8	1.04243	7.81571	8.14736
9	1.04396	8.78811	9.17444	9	1.04591	8.77906	9.18212	9	1.04786	8.77003	9.18980
10	1.04896	9.74143	10.21840	10	1.05114	9.73041	10.22803	10	1.05332	9.71941	10.23766
11	1.05399	10.69021	11.26737	11	1.05640	10.67703	11.27917	11	1.05881	10.66387	11.29098
12	1.05904	11.63446	12.32136	12	1.06168	11.61893	12.33556	12	1.06432	11.60343	12.34979
13	1.06411	12.57421	13.38040	13	1.06699	12.55615	13.39724	13	1.06987	12.53813	13.41411
14	1.06921	13.50947	14.44451	14	1.07232	13.48871	14.46423	14	1.07544	13.46799	14.48397
15	1.07434	14.44028	15.51372	15	1.07768	14.41662	15.53655	15	1.08105	14.39302	15.55941
16	1.07948	15.36665	16.58806	16	1.08307	15.33993	16.61423	16	1.08667	15.31326	16.64045
17	1.08466	16.28860	17.66754	17	1.08849	16.25862	17.69730	17	1.09233	16.22874	17.72712
18	1.08985	17.20615	18.75220	18	1.09393	17.17277	18.78579	18	1.09802	17.13947	18.81945
19	1.09508	18.11933	19.84205	19	1.09940	18.08236	19.87971	19	1.10374	18.04548	19.91747
20	1.10032	19.02815	20.93713	20	1.10490	18.98742	20.97911	20	1.10949	18.94680	21.02120
21	1.10560	19.93264	22.03745	21	1.11042	19.88798	22.08401	21	1.11528	19.84345	22.13069
22	1.11089	20.83282	23.14305	22	1.11597	20.78406	23.19443	22	1.12107	20.73545	23.24596
23	1.11622	21.72870	24.25394	23	1.12155	21.67568	24.31040	23	1.12691	21.62284	24.36703
24	1.12157	22.62032	25.37016	24	1.12716	22.56287	25.43195	24	1.13278	22.50562	25.49394
25	1.12694	23.50767	26.49173	25	1.13280	23.44564	26.55911	25	1.13868	23.38383	26.62672

n				n				n			
26	1.13234	24.39480	27.61967	26	1.13846	24.32402	27.69191	26	1.14461	24.25749	27.76540
27	1.13777	25.26972	28.75101	27	1.14415	25.19803	28.83037	27	1.15057	25.12662	28.91001
28	1.14322	26.14444	29.88877	28	1.14987	26.06769	29.97452	28	1.15657	25.99125	30.06058
29	1.14869	27.01500	31.03199	29	1.15562	26.93302	31.12439	29	1.16259	26.85140	31.21715
30	1.15420	27.88140	32.19068	30	1.16140	27.79405	32.28001	30	1.16864	27.70709	32.37974
31	1.15973	28.74367	33.33488	31	1.16721	28.65080	33.44141	31	1.17473	28.55835	33.54838
32	1.16529	29.60182	34.49461	32	1.17304	29.50328	34.60862	32	1.18085	29.40520	34.72311
33	1.17087	30.45589	35.65990	33	1.17891	30.35152	35.78167	33	1.18700	30.24766	35.90396
34	1.17648	31.30588	36.83077	34	1.18480	31.19555	36.96058	34	1.19318	31.08575	37.09096
35	1.18212	32.15182	38.00725	35	1.19073	32.03537	38.14537	35	1.19940	31.91950	38.28415
36	1.18778	32.99372	39.18937	36	1.19668	32.87101	39.33610	36	1.20564	32.74694	39.48354
37	1.19347	33.83162	40.37715	37	1.20266	33.70250	40.53278	37	1.21192	33.57407	40.68918
38	1.19919	34.66551	41.57063	38	1.20868	34.52985	41.73545	38	1.21823	34.39453	41.90111
39	1.20494	35.49543	42.76982	39	1.21472	35.35309	42.94413	39	1.22458	35.21154	43.11934
40	1.21071	36.32139	43.97475	40	1.22079	36.17223	44.15884	40	1.23096	36.02391	44.34392
41	1.21651	37.14341	45.18547	41	1.22690	36.98729	45.37964	41	1.23737	36.83208	45.57498
42	1.22234	37.96151	46.40196	42	1.23303	37.79830	46.60654	42	1.24381	37.63606	46.81225
43	1.22820	38.77571	47.62432	43	1.23920	38.60527	47.83877	43	1.25029	38.43587	48.05606
44	1.23408	39.58603	48.85252	44	1.24539	39.40823	49.07677	44	1.25680	39.23154	49.30635
45	1.24000	40.39248	50.08652	45	1.25162	40.20720	50.32416	45	1.26335	40.02309	50.56316
46	1.24594	41.19509	51.32661	46	1.25788	41.00218	51.57578	46	1.26993	40.81053	51.82651
47	1.25191	41.99386	52.57245	47	1.26417	41.79417	52.83366	47	1.27654	41.59389	53.09644
48	1.25791	42.78884	53.82446	48	1.27049	42.58031	54.09783	48	1.28319	42.37320	54.37298
49	1.26394	43.58004	55.08237	49	1.27684	43.36350	55.36832	49	1.28988	43.14847	55.65617
50	1.26999	44.36742	56.34630	50	1.28323	44.14278	56.64516	50	1.29659	43.91972	56.94605

Table 1. (continued) Annuities

M	C(5.75,M,12)	A(5.75,M,12)	S(5.75,M,12)	M	C(6.00,M,12)	A(6.00,M,12)	S(6.00,M,12)	M	C(6.25,M,12)	A(6.25,M,12)	S(6.25,M,12)
51	1.27608	45.15107	57.61629	51	1.28964	44.91819	57.92839	51	1.30335	44.68698	58.24265
52	1.28219	45.83099	58.89237	52	1.28609	45.68974	59.21803	52	1.31014	45.45028	59.54599
53	1.28834	46.70718	60.17456	53	1.30257	46.45746	60.51412	53	1.31696	46.20968	60.85613
54	1.29451	47.47868	61.46290	54	1.30908	47.21735	61.81669	54	1.32382	46.96497	62.17308
55	1.30071	48.24849	62.75741	55	1.31563	47.97145	63.12577	55	1.33071	47.71645	63.49690
56	1.30695	49.01363	64.05812	56	1.32221	48.79775	64.44140	56	1.33764	48.46404	64.82761
57	1.31321	49.77512	65.36507	57	1.32882	49.49330	65.76361	57	1.34461	49.20774	66.16526
58	1.31950	50.53299	66.67828	58	1.33546	50.23391	67.09242	58	1.35161	49.94760	67.50987
59	1.32582	51.28723	67.99777	59	1.34214	50.98419	68.42789	59	1.35865	50.68362	68.86148
60	1.33218	52.03788	69.32360	60	1.34885	51.72556	69.77003	60	1.36573	51.41583	70.22014
61	1.33856	52.78496	70.65578	61	1.35559	52.46324	71.11887	61	1.37284	52.14425	71.58587
62	1.34497	53.52847	71.99433	62	1.36237	53.19726	72.47447	62	1.37999	52.86889	72.95871
63	1.35142	54.26843	73.33930	63	1.36918	53.92762	73.83686	63	1.38718	53.58978	74.33871
64	1.35789	55.00496	74.69072	64	1.37603	54.65435	75.20602	64	1.39441	54.30693	75.72588
65	1.36440	55.73779	76.04861	65	1.38291	55.37746	76.58206	65	1.40167	55.02036	77.12029
66	1.37094	56.46722	77.41302	66	1.38982	56.09697	77.96497	66	1.40897	55.73010	78.52196
67	1.37751	57.13916	78.78396	67	1.39677	56.81291	79.35479	67	1.41631	56.43616	79.93092
68	1.38411	57.91565	80.16148	68	1.40376	57.52528	80.75156	68	1.42368	57.13857	81.34724
69	1.39074	58.63469	81.54557	69	1.41078	58.23411	82.15533	69	1.43110	57.83733	82.77092
70	1.39740	59.35031	82.93630	70	1.41783	58.93941	83.56610	70	1.43855	58.53247	84.20202
71	1.40410	60.06251	84.33371	71	1.42492	59.64121	84.98333	71	1.44604	59.22401	85.64057
72	1.41083	60.77131	85.73781	72	1.43204	60.33951	86.40885	72	1.45358	59.91197	87.06662
73	1.41759	61.47674	87.14864	73	1.43920	61.03434	87.84090	73	1.46115	60.59637	88.50419
74	1.42438	62.17879	88.56622	74	1.44640	61.72571	89.28010	74	1.46876	61.27721	90.00134
75	1.43120	62.87751	89.99060	75	1.45363	62.41364	90.72650	75	1.47641	61.95454	91.47009

76	1.43906	63.57289	91.42181	1.46090	63.09815	92.19013	76	1.49410	62.62835	92.94650
77	1.44495	64.26495	92.85987	1.46821	63.77925	93.64104	77	1.49183	63.29966	94.43060
78	1.45188	64.95371	94.30482	1.47555	64.45697	95.10924	78	1.49960	63.96551	95.92242
79	1.45883	65.63919	95.75670	1.48292	65.13131	96.58479	79	1.50741	64.62890	97.42202
80	1.46582	66.32140	97.21554	1.49034	65.80230	98.06771	80	1.51526	65.28896	98.92342
81	1.47285	67.00036	98.68136	1.49779	66.46996	99.55405	81	1.52315	65.94539	100.44468
82	1.47991	67.67608	100.15421	1.50528	67.13428	101.05584	82	1.53108	66.59852	101.96783
83	1.48700	68.34857	101.63412	1.51281	67.79630	102.56112	83	1.53906	67.24827	103.49892
84	1.49412	69.01786	103.12111	1.52037	68.45304	104.07392	84	1.54707	67.89465	105.03797
85	1.50128	69.68396	104.61523	1.52797	69.10750	105.59429	85	1.55513	68.53768	106.58504
86	1.50847	70.34689	106.11652	1.53561	69.75871	107.12226	86	1.56323	69.17738	108.14017
87	1.51570	71.00665	107.62498	1.54329	70.40668	108.65788	87	1.57137	69.81377	109.70341
88	1.52297	71.66325	109.14069	1.55101	71.05141	110.20116	88	1.57956	70.44686	111.27477
89	1.53026	72.31673	110.66366	1.55876	71.69296	111.75217	89	1.58778	71.07667	112.85433
90	1.53760	72.96710	112.19392	1.56655	72.33130	113.31093	90	1.59605	71.70322	114.44212
91	1.54496	73.61436	113.73151	1.57439	72.96646	114.87749	91	1.60437	72.32652	116.03817
92	1.55237	74.25854	115.27648	1.58226	73.59847	116.45187	92	1.61272	72.94659	117.64253
93	1.55980	74.89965	116.82885	1.59017	74.22733	118.03413	93	1.62112	73.56345	119.25526
94	1.56728	75.53770	118.38865	1.59812	74.85307	119.62431	94	1.62956	74.17710	120.87637
95	1.57479	76.17271	119.95593	1.60611	75.47569	121.22243	95	1.63805	74.78758	122.50594
96	1.58233	76.80468	121.53072	1.61414	76.09521	122.82854	96	1.64658	75.39491	124.14399
97	1.58992	77.43365	123.11305	1.62221	76.71165	124.44268	97	1.65516	75.99908	125.79057
98	1.59754	78.05961	124.70297	1.63032	77.32503	126.06490	98	1.66378	76.60011	127.44573
99	1.60519	78.68259	126.30051	1.63848	77.93588	127.69522	99	1.67245	77.19804	129.10651
100	1.61288	79.30260	127.90569	1.64667	78.54264	129.33369	100	1.68116	77.79287	130.76195

Table 1. (continued) Annuities

M	C(5.75,M,12)	A(5.75,M,12)	S(5.75,M,12)	M	C(6.00,M,12)	A(6.00,M,12)	S(6.00,M,12)	M	C(6.25,M,12)	A(6.25,M,12)	S(6.25,M,12)
101	1.62061	79.91965	129.51857	101	1.65490	79.14690	130.96036	101	1.68991	78.38462	132.46312
102	1.62838	80.53376	131.13919	102	1.66318	79.74817	132.63525	102	1.69871	78.97330	134.15303
103	1.63618	81.14494	132.76756	103	1.67149	80.34644	134.31843	103	1.70756	79.55893	135.85173
104	1.64402	81.75320	134.40373	104	1.67985	80.94173	135.97060	104	1.71645	80.14153	137.55930
105	1.65190	82.35857	136.04776	105	1.68825	81.53406	137.64978	105	1.72539	80.72110	139.27576
106	1.65981	82.96105	137.69965	106	1.69669	82.12344	139.33803	106	1.73438	81.29768	141.00114
107	1.66776	83.56065	139.35947	107	1.70517	82.70988	141.03471	107	1.74341	81.87128	142.73549
108	1.67578	84.15740	141.02722	108	1.71370	83.29342	142.73990	108	1.75249	82.44188	144.47894
109	1.68379	84.75130	142.70299	109	1.72227	83.87405	144.45360	109	1.76162	83.00954	146.23145
110	1.69185	85.34237	144.38676	110	1.73088	84.45179	146.17586	110	1.77080	83.57426	147.99306
111	1.69996	85.93062	146.07861	111	1.73953	85.02666	147.90674	111	1.78002	84.13605	149.76385
112	1.70811	86.51606	147.77858	112	1.74823	85.59866	149.64627	112	1.78929	84.69433	151.54388
113	1.71629	87.09872	149.48668	113	1.75697	86.16782	151.39450	113	1.79861	85.25092	153.33318
114	1.72451	87.67859	151.20297	114	1.76576	86.73415	153.15147	114	1.80798	85.80402	155.13177
115	1.73278	88.25569	152.92749	115	1.77459	87.29767	154.91724	115	1.81739	86.35426	156.93976
116	1.74108	88.83005	154.66026	116	1.78346	87.85838	156.69182	116	1.82686	86.90164	158.75716
117	1.74942	89.40166	156.40135	117	1.79238	88.41629	158.47528	117	1.83637	87.44619	160.59401
118	1.75781	89.97056	158.15077	118	1.80134	88.97144	160.26765	118	1.84594	87.98792	162.42038
119	1.76623	90.53674	159.90857	119	1.81034	89.52382	162.06900	119	1.85555	88.52685	164.26633
120	1.77469	91.10021	161.67480	120	1.81940	90.07345	163.87933	120	1.86522	89.06297	166.12189
121	1.78320	91.66100	163.44949	121	1.82849	90.62035	165.69873	121	1.87493	89.59633	167.98709
122	1.79174	92.21912	165.23270	122	1.83764	91.16453	167.52724	122	1.88470	90.12691	169.86203
123	1.80033	92.77458	167.02443	123	1.84682	91.70599	169.36487	123	1.89451	90.65475	171.74673
124	1.80895	93.32738	168.82475	124	1.85606	92.24047	171.21169	124	1.90438	91.17986	173.64125
125	1.81762	93.87756	170.63371	125	1.86534	92.78087	173.06775	125	1.91430	91.70225	175.54562

n			
126	1.82633	94.42510	172.45132
127	1.83508	94.97004	174.27766
128	1.84387	95.51237	176.11275
129	1.85271	96.05212	177.95662
130	1.86159	96.58930	179.80933
131	1.87051	97.12392	181.67091
132	1.87947	97.65598	183.54141
133	1.88848	98.18551	185.42088
134	1.89752	98.71251	187.30936
135	1.90662	99.23700	189.20688
136	1.91575	99.75899	191.11349
137	1.92493	100.27849	193.02925
138	1.93416	100.79651	194.95418
139	1.94342	101.31007	196.88834
140	1.95274	101.82217	198.83176
141	1.96209	102.33183	200.78450
142	1.97149	102.83906	202.74660
143	1.98094	103.34386	204.71808
144	1.99043	103.84627	206.69902
145	1.99997	104.34628	208.68945
146	2.00965	104.84389	210.68942
147	2.01918	105.33915	212.69899
148	2.02886	105.83204	214.71817
149	2.03858	106.32257	216.74702
150	2.04835	106.81078	218.78560

n			
126	1.87467	93.31429	174.93309
127	1.88404	93.84507	176.80775
128	1.89346	94.37321	178.69179
129	1.90293	94.89871	180.58525
130	1.91244	95.42160	182.48817
131	1.92200	95.94189	184.40062
132	1.93161	96.45959	186.32262
133	1.94127	96.97472	188.25423
134	1.95098	97.48728	190.19551
135	1.96073	97.99730	192.14648
136	1.97054	98.50478	194.10721
137	1.98039	99.00973	196.07776
138	1.99029	99.51216	198.05814
139	2.00024	100.01211	200.04843
140	2.01024	100.50596	202.04868
141	2.02029	101.00453	204.05891
142	2.03040	101.49705	206.07921
143	2.04055	101.98711	208.10960
144	2.05075	102.47474	210.15016
145	2.06100	102.95994	212.20091
146	2.07131	103.44273	214.26192
147	2.08167	103.92311	216.33322
148	2.09207	104.40111	218.41489
149	2.10253	104.87672	220.50696
150	2.11305	105.34987	222.60950

n			
126	1.92427	92.22192	177.45593
127	1.93429	92.73891	179.38420
128	1.94437	93.25321	181.31848
129	1.95449	93.76485	183.26286
130	1.96467	94.27385	185.21735
131	1.97491	94.78020	187.18202
132	1.98519	95.28333	189.15694
133	1.99553	95.78505	191.14212
134	2.00593	96.28357	193.13765
135	2.01637	96.77951	195.14359
136	2.02687	97.27288	197.15596
137	2.03743	97.76369	199.18663
138	2.04804	98.25197	201.22426
139	2.05871	98.73771	203.27231
140	2.06943	99.22033	205.33101
141	2.08021	99.70165	207.40044
142	2.09104	100.17989	209.48065
143	2.10194	100.65563	211.57170
144	2.11288	101.12892	213.67363
145	2.12389	101.59975	215.78651
146	2.13495	102.06815	217.91040
147	2.14607	102.53412	220.04536
148	2.15725	102.99787	222.19142
149	2.16848	103.45882	224.34668
150	2.17978	103.91759	226.51715

Table 1. (continued) Annuities

M	C(5.75,M,12)	A(5.75,M,12)	S(5.75,M,12)	M	C(6.00,M,12)	A(6.00,M,12)	S(6.00,M,12)	M	C(6.25,M,12)	A(6.25,M,12)	S(6.25,M,12)
151	2.05816	107.29565	220.83395	151	2.12361	105.82087	224.72255	151	2.19113	104.37397	228.69693
152	2.06802	107.78020	222.89212	152	2.13423	106.28942	226.84616	152	2.20254	104.82800	230.88806
153	2.07789	108.26144	224.96014	153	2.14490	106.75564	228.98019	153	2.21401	105.27966	233.09061
154	2.08789	108.74039	227.03807	154	2.15563	107.21954	231.12529	154	2.22554	105.72898	235.30463
155	2.09790	109.21706	229.12598	155	2.16640	107.68114	233.28091	155	2.23714	106.17599	237.53017
156	2.10795	109.69146	231.22386	156	2.17724	108.14043	235.44733	156	2.24879	106.62067	239.76730
157	2.11805	110.16359	233.33180	157	2.18812	108.59745	237.62456	157	2.26050	107.06306	242.01608
158	2.12820	110.63348	235.44986	158	2.19906	109.05219	239.81268	158	2.27227	107.50314	244.27660
159	2.13839	111.10111	237.57805	159	2.21006	109.50466	242.01175	159	2.28411	107.94095	246.54986
160	2.14864	111.56652	239.71645	160	2.22111	109.95489	244.22180	160	2.29601	108.37649	248.83298
161	2.15894	112.02972	241.86508	161	2.23221	110.40288	246.44292	161	2.30795	108.80977	251.12698
162	2.16928	112.49070	244.02402	162	2.24338	110.84863	248.67513	162	2.31998	109.24081	253.43694
163	2.17968	112.94948	246.19331	163	2.25459	111.29218	250.91850	163	2.33207	109.66961	255.76699
164	2.19012	113.40607	248.37299	164	2.26587	111.73351	253.17310	164	2.34421	110.09619	258.08899
165	2.20061	113.86050	250.56311	165	2.27719	112.17264	255.43896	165	2.35642	110.52057	260.43320
166	2.21116	114.31274	252.76372	166	2.28858	112.60960	257.71616	166	2.36870	110.94274	262.78961
167	2.22175	114.76284	254.97487	167	2.30002	113.04437	260.00473	167	2.38103	111.36272	265.15833
168	2.23240	115.21079	257.19662	168	2.31152	113.47699	262.30475	168	2.39343	111.78053	267.53934
169	2.24310	115.65660	259.42902	169	2.32308	113.90745	264.61627	169	2.40590	112.19618	269.93277
170	2.25386	116.10029	261.67212	170	2.33470	114.33577	266.93936	170	2.41843	112.60967	272.33968
171	2.26465	116.54185	263.92596	171	2.34637	114.76196	269.27405	171	2.43103	113.02102	274.75711
172	2.27550	116.98132	266.19061	172	2.35810	115.18603	271.62042	172	2.44369	113.43024	277.18814
173	2.28640	117.41869	268.46609	173	2.36989	115.60799	273.97852	173	2.45642	113.83733	279.63184
174	2.29736	117.85397	270.75250	174	2.38174	116.02785	276.34842	174	2.46921	114.24232	282.08826
175	2.30836	118.28718	273.04987	175	2.39365	116.44563	278.73016	175	2.48207	114.64521	284.55746

n				n				n			
176	2.31942	118.71832	275.35822	176	2.40562	116.86131	281.12381	176	2.49500	115.0601	287.03952
177	2.33054	119.14741	277.67764	177	2.41765	117.27494	283.52942	177	2.50799	115.44474	289.53452
178	2.34171	119.57445	280.00821	178	2.42974	117.68651	285.94708	178	2.52105	115.94140	294.04251
179	2.35293	119.99945	282.34991	179	2.44188	118.09603	288.37690	179	2.53419	116.28600	296.56357
180	2.36420	120.42242	284.70282	180	2.45409	118.50351	290.81870	180	2.54738	116.62656	297.09775
181	2.37553	120.84338	287.06702	181	2.46636	118.90897	293.27280	181	2.56065	117.01909	299.64514
182	2.38691	121.26234	289.44257	182	2.47870	119.31240	295.73917	182	2.57399	117.40759	302.20578
183	2.39835	121.67929	291.82947	183	2.49109	119.71384	298.21786	183	2.58739	117.79408	304.77979
184	2.40984	122.09425	294.22781	184	2.50354	120.11327	300.70895	184	2.60087	118.17857	307.36719
185	2.42139	122.50724	296.63766	185	2.51606	120.51071	303.21249	185	2.61442	118.56106	309.96805
186	2.43299	122.91826	299.05905	186	2.52864	120.90618	305.72855	186	2.62803	118.94157	312.58246
187	2.44465	123.32732	301.49203	187	2.54129	121.29968	308.25720	187	2.64172	119.32011	315.21051
188	2.45636	123.73442	303.93668	188	2.55399	121.69123	310.79846	188	2.65548	119.69669	317.85220
189	2.46813	124.13959	306.33307	189	2.56676	122.08083	313.35248	189	2.66931	120.07132	320.50769
190	2.47996	124.54282	308.86116	190	2.57960	122.46848	315.91922	190	2.68321	120.44401	323.17700
191	2.49184	124.94412	311.34116	191	2.59249	122.85421	318.49884	191	2.69719	120.81477	325.86023
192	2.50378	125.34352	313.83298	192	2.60546	123.23802	321.10931	192	2.71124	121.18360	328.55740
193	2.51578	125.74101	316.33676	193	2.61848	123.61992	323.68678	193	2.72536	121.55053	331.26865
194	2.52784	126.13660	318.85254	194	2.63158	123.99992	326.31528	194	2.73955	121.91555	333.99402
195	2.53996	126.53032	321.38040	195	2.64473	124.37803	328.96684	195	2.75382	122.27868	336.73355
196	2.55212	126.92215	323.92035	196	2.65796	124.75426	331.59158	196	2.76816	122.63993	339.48737
197	2.56435	127.31211	326.47244	197	2.67125	125.12862	334.24964	197	2.78258	122.99931	342.25555
198	2.57663	127.70021	329.03680	198	2.68460	125.50111	336.92078	198	2.79707	123.35683	345.03812
199	2.58898	128.08646	331.61343	199	2.69803	125.87175	339.60538	199	2.81164	123.71249	347.83521
200	2.60139	128.47087	334.20242	200	2.71152	126.24055	342.30341	200	2.82629	124.06631	350.64686

Table 1. (continued) Annuities

M	C(5.75,M,12)	A(5.75,M,12)	S(5.75,M,12)	M	C(6.00,M,12)	A(6.00,M,12)	S(6.00,M,12)	M	C(6.25,M,12)	A(6.25,M,12)	S(6.25,M,12)
201	2.81385	128.85345	336.80380	201	2.72507	126.60751	345.01492	201	2.84101	124.41830	353.47311
202	2.82638	129.23421	339.41766	202	2.73870	126.99387	347.73999	202	2.85580	124.76846	356.31412
203	2.83896	129.61314	342.04404	203	2.75016	127.36597	350.47870	203	2.87068	125.11681	359.16992
204	2.85161	129.99026	344.68298	204	2.76916	127.70748	353.23111	204	2.88563	125.46336	362.04062
205	2.86431	130.36560	347.33459	205	2.77999	128.05719	355.99725	205	2.90066	125.80811	364.90624
206	2.87708	130.73914	349.99850	206	2.79369	128.41512	358.77722	206	2.91577	126.15107	367.82690
207	2.88991	131.11090	352.67599	207	2.80786	128.77126	361.57114	207	2.93095	126.49226	370.74268
208	2.90279	131.48090	355.36591	208	2.82189	129.12563	364.37897	208	2.94622	126.83167	373.67361
209	2.91575	131.84911	358.06870	209	2.83600	129.47824	367.20087	209	2.96156	127.16933	376.61984
210	2.92876	132.21558	360.78442	210	2.85018	129.82910	370.03687	210	2.97699	127.50525	379.58139
211	2.94183	132.58029	363.51318	211	2.86444	130.17821	372.88705	211	2.99249	127.83942	382.55838
212	2.95497	132.94328	366.25504	212	2.87876	130.52557	375.75150	212	3.00808	128.17184	385.55097
213	2.96817	133.30453	369.01001	213	2.89315	130.87122	378.63025	213	3.02374	128.50256	388.55896
214	2.98144	133.66405	371.77817	214	2.90762	131.21515	381.52341	214	3.03949	128.83157	391.58270
215	2.99476	134.02187	374.55960	215	2.92216	131.55736	384.43103	215	3.05532	129.15886	394.62219
216	3.00816	134.37798	377.35437	216	2.93677	131.89758	387.35318	216	3.07124	129.48447	397.67752
217	3.02161	134.73238	380.16254	217	2.95145	132.23668	390.28995	217	3.08723	129.80838	400.74875
218	3.03513	135.08510	382.98413	218	2.96621	132.57382	393.24139	218	3.10331	130.13062	403.83597
219	3.04872	135.43613	385.81927	219	2.98104	132.90927	396.20761	219	3.11948	130.45119	406.93930
220	3.06237	135.78549	388.66600	220	2.99594	133.24306	399.18863	220	3.13572	130.77010	410.05878
221	3.07608	136.13319	391.53036	221	3.01092	133.57518	402.18457	221	3.15205	131.08734	413.19449
222	3.08986	136.47922	394.40643	222	3.02598	133.90565	405.19650	222	3.16847	131.40295	416.34656
223	3.10371	136.82361	397.29633	223	3.04111	134.23448	408.22150	223	3.18497	131.71693	419.51501
224	3.11762	137.16635	400.20001	224	3.05631	134.56168	411.26260	224	3.20156	132.02928	422.69998
225	3.13161	137.50746	403.11765	225	3.07159	134.88724	414.31891	225	3.21824	132.34001	425.90155

n			n					n			n		
226	2.94565	137.84695	226	3.06695	135.21118	406.04926		226	3.23500	132.64912	226	417.39050	429.11978
227	2.96977	138.18481	227	3.10289	135.53351	408.99490		227	3.25185	132.95663	227	420.47745	432.35480
228	2.97396	138.52107	228	3.11750	135.85423	411.95468		228	3.26878	133.26256	228	423.57963	435.60663
229	2.98620	138.85571	229	3.13349	136.17337	414.92862		229	3.28581	133.56691	229	426.69772	438.87543
230	3.00252	139.18877	230	3.14916	136.49092	417.91681		230	3.30292	133.86986	230	429.83124	442.16122
231	3.01639	139.52023	231	3.16490	136.80688	420.91934		231	3.32013	134.17085	231	432.98038	445.46414
232	3.03136	139.85013	232	3.18073	137.12128	423.93825		232	3.33742	134.47049	232	436.14529	448.78427
233	3.04589	140.17844	233	3.19663	137.43411	426.96762		233	3.35480	134.76857	233	439.32602	452.12170
234	3.06048	140.50517	234	3.21261	137.74538	430.01349		234	3.37227	135.06511	234	442.52264	455.47650
235	3.07515	140.83037	235	3.22868	138.05510	433.07397		235	3.38984	135.36011	235	445.73526	458.84879
236	3.08989	141.15401	236	3.24482	138.36328	436.14911		236	3.40749	135.65358	236	448.96399	462.23862
237	3.10469	141.47610	237	3.26104	138.66994	439.23901		237	3.42524	135.94553	237	452.20874	465.64609
238	3.11956	141.79666	238	3.27735	138.97507	442.34369		238	3.44308	136.23596	238	455.46979	469.07135
239	3.13451	142.11560	239	3.29374	139.27867	445.46326		239	3.46101	136.52490	239	458.74713	472.51443
240	3.14953	142.43320	240	3.31020	139.59076	448.59778		240	3.47904	136.81233	240	462.04089	475.97543
241	3.16462	142.74919	241	3.32676	139.88136	451.74728		241	3.49716	137.09828	241	465.35107	479.45447
242	3.17979	143.06367	242	3.34339	140.19045	454.91193		242	3.51537	137.38275	242	468.67783	482.96163
243	3.19502	143.37666	243	3.36011	140.47906	458.09171		243	3.53368	137.66574	243	472.02124	486.46701
244	3.21033	143.68816	244	3.37691	140.77420	461.28671		244	3.55209	137.94727	244	475.38135	490.00070
245	3.22571	143.99815	245	3.39379	141.06885	464.49707		245	3.57059	138.22733	245	478.75824	493.55276
246	3.24117	144.30669	246	3.41076	141.36205	467.72278		246	3.58918	138.50594	246	482.15204	497.12335
247	3.25670	144.61375	247	3.42781	141.65376	470.96396		247	3.60788	138.78311	247	485.56281	500.71255
248	3.27231	144.91934	248	3.44495	141.94405	474.22064		248	3.62667	139.05885	248	488.99060	504.32043
249	3.28799	145.22348	249	3.46218	142.23288	477.49295		249	3.64556	139.33316	249	492.43555	507.94708
250	3.30374	145.52617	250	3.47949	142.52028	480.78094		250	3.66455	139.60605	250	495.89774	511.55265

Table 1. (continued) Annuities

M	C(5.75,M,12)	A(5.75,M,12)	S(5.75,M,12)	M	C(6.00,M,12)	A(6.00,M,12)	S(6.00,M,12)	M	C(6.25,11,12)	A(6.25,M,12)	S(6.25,M,12)
251	3.31967	145.82741	484.08469	251	3.43689	142.80626	499.37723	251	3.68363	139.87752	515.25720
252	3.33548	146.12723	487.40427	252	3.51437	143.09081	502.87411	252	3.70282	140.14758	518.94080
253	3.35148	146.42560	490.73975	253	3.53194	143.37393	506.38849	253	3.72210	140.41624	522.64362
254	3.36752	146.72255	494.09119	254	3.54960	143.65565	509.92044	254	3.74149	140.68352	526.36572
255	3.38356	147.01810	497.45871	255	3.56735	143.93597	513.47003	255	3.76098	140.94940	530.10724
256	3.39987	147.01023	500.84238	256	3.58519	144.21489	517.03735	256	3.78056	141.21391	533.86823
257	3.41616	147.60495	504.24225	257	3.60311	144.49243	520.62256	257	3.80025	141.47705	537.64874
258	3.43253	147.89627	507.65842	258	3.62113	144.76859	524.22565	258	3.82005	141.73883	541.44504
259	3.44898	148.18622	511.09094	259	3.63923	145.04338	527.84680	259	3.83994	141.99925	545.26904
260	3.46550	148.47478	514.53992	260	3.65743	145.31679	531.48602	260	3.85994	142.25833	549.10901
261	3.48211	148.76196	518.00537	261	3.67572	145.58885	535.14343	261	3.88005	142.51605	552.96893
262	3.49879	149.04778	521.48749	262	3.69410	145.85964	538.81915	262	3.90026	142.77245	556.84900
263	3.51556	149.33221	524.98633	263	3.71257	146.12891	542.51324	263	3.92057	143.02751	560.74927
264	3.53240	149.61531	528.50189	264	3.73113	146.39691	546.22583	264	3.94099	143.28125	564.66980
265	3.54933	149.89706	532.03424	265	3.74978	146.66360	549.95697	265	3.96151	143.53368	568.61078
266	3.56634	150.17746	535.58362	266	3.76853	146.92896	553.70673	266	3.98215	143.78491	572.57233
267	3.58343	150.45651	539.14996	267	3.78738	147.19299	557.47528	267	4.00289	144.03462	576.55444
268	3.60060	150.73425	542.73334	268	3.80631	147.45572	561.26263	268	4.02374	144.28314	580.55737
269	3.61786	151.01065	546.33398	269	3.82534	147.71713	565.06897	269	4.04469	144.53038	584.58112
270	3.63519	151.28575	549.96184	270	3.84447	147.97723	568.89435	270	4.06576	144.77634	588.62579
271	3.65260	151.55952	553.58698	271	3.86369	148.23605	572.73877	271	4.08694	145.02103	592.69153
272	3.67011	151.83200	557.23962	272	3.88301	148.43359	576.60248	272	4.10822	145.26443	596.77850
273	3.68769	152.10316	560.90973	273	3.90243	148.74985	580.48547	273	4.12962	145.50659	600.88672
274	3.70536	152.37305	564.59741	274	3.92194	149.00482	584.38794	274	4.15113	145.74750	605.01630
275	3.72312	152.64163	568.30280	275	3.94155	149.25853	588.30988	275	4.17275	145.98714	609.16742

276	3.74096	152.90895	276	572.02598	3.96126	149.51097	276	592.25140	4.19448	146.22556	813.34021
277	3.75888	153.17499	277	575.76685	3.98106	149.76216	277	596.21265	4.21633	146.46272	817.53467
278	3.77889	153.43976	278	579.31570	4.00097	150.01210	278	600.19373	4.23829	146.69967	821.75098
279	3.79499	153.70526	279	583.26261	4.02057	150.26080	279	604.19470	4.26036	146.93340	825.98932
280	3.81318	153.96552	280	587.09760	4.04108	150.50826	280	608.21570	4.28255	147.16690	830.24963
281	3.83145	154.22850	281	590.91077	4.06128	150.75449	281	612.25677	4.30486	147.39919	834.53223
282	3.84981	154.48827	282	594.74225	4.08159	150.99948	282	616.31805	4.32728	147.63028	838.83704
283	3.86825	154.74478	283	598.59204	4.10200	151.24327	283	620.39966	4.34981	147.86018	843.16431
284	3.88679	155.00206	284	602.46027	4.12251	151.48584	284	624.50165	4.37247	148.08888	847.51416
285	3.90541	155.25812	285	606.34711	4.14312	151.72720	285	628.62415	4.39524	148.31641	851.88660
286	3.92413	155.51294	286	610.25250	4.16384	151.96736	286	632.76727	4.41813	148.54274	856.28196
287	3.94296	155.76556	287	614.17664	4.18466	152.20633	287	636.93109	4.44115	148.76791	860.70001
288	3.96192	156.01897	288	618.11957	4.20558	152.44411	288	641.11572	4.46428	148.99191	865.14111
289	3.98081	156.27017	289	622.08136	4.22661	152.68071	289	645.32135	4.48753	149.21475	869.60541
290	3.99988	156.52019	290	626.06219	4.24774	152.91612	290	649.54791	4.51090	149.43643	874.09296
291	4.01905	156.76900	291	630.06207	4.26898	153.15038	291	653.79565	4.53439	149.65697	878.60382
292	4.03831	157.01663	292	634.08110	4.29032	153.38345	292	658.06464	4.55801	149.87636	883.13824
293	4.05766	157.26308	293	638.11945	4.31177	153.61539	293	662.35498	4.58175	150.09462	887.69623
294	4.07710	157.50835	294	642.17706	4.33333	153.84615	294	666.66675	4.60561	150.31175	892.27802
295	4.09663	157.75245	295	646.25415	4.35500	154.07578	295	671.00006	4.62960	150.52774	896.88361
296	4.11626	157.99539	296	650.35083	4.37678	154.30424	296	675.35510	4.65371	150.74263	701.51324
297	4.13599	158.23717	297	654.46704	4.39866	154.53160	297	679.73187	4.67795	150.95641	706.11603
298	4.15560	158.47780	298	658.60309	4.42065	154.75781	298	684.13049	4.70232	151.16307	710.84491
299	4.17572	158.71727	299	662.75885	4.44276	154.98288	299	688.55115	4.72681	151.36862	715.54718
300	4.19573	158.95561	300	666.93457	4.46497	155.20688	300	692.99336	4.75143	151.59108	720.27399

Table 1. (continued) Annuities

M	C(5.75,M,12)	A(5.75,M,12)	B(5.75,M,12)	M	C(6.00,M,12)	A(6.00,M,12)	B(6.00,M,12)	M	C(6.25,M,12)	A(6.25,M,12)	B(6.25,M,12)
301	4.21583	159.19981	671.13031	301	4.48729	155.42970	697.45892	301	4.77617	151.80046	725.02545
302	4.23603	159.42888	675.34613	302	4.50973	155.65144	701.94617	302	4.80105	152.00874	729.00164
303	4.25633	159.58215	679.58215	303	4.53228	155.87209	706.45593	303	4.82606	152.21156	734.60266
304	4.27673	159.87660	683.83650	304	4.55494	156.09163	710.96822	304	4.85119	152.42209	739.42871
305	4.29722	160.13036	688.11523	305	4.57772	156.31007	715.54315	305	4.87646	152.62715	744.27991
306	4.31781	160.36197	692.41248	306	4.60060	156.52745	720.12085	306	4.90186	152.83116	749.15637
307	4.33860	160.59945	696.73029	307	4.62361	156.74373	724.72150	307	4.92739	153.03410	754.05823
308	4.35929	160.82185	701.06879	308	4.64673	156.95892	729.34509	308	4.95305	153.23601	758.98560
309	4.38018	161.05016	705.42804	309	4.66996	157.17507	734.01505	309	4.97885	153.43684	763.93866
310	4.40116	161.27736	709.80823	310	4.69331	157.38614	738.68174	310	5.00478	153.63666	768.91754
311	4.42225	161.50349	714.20941	311	4.71678	157.59814	743.35504	311	5.03085	153.83543	773.92230
312	4.44344	161.72855	718.63165	312	4.74036	157.80910	748.07184	312	5.05705	154.03317	778.95313
313	4.46473	161.95251	723.07507	313	4.76406	158.01900	752.81219	313	5.08319	154.22989	784.01019
314	4.48613	162.17543	727.53996	314	4.78788	158.22786	757.57629	314	5.10966	154.42560	789.03357
315	4.50762	162.39728	732.02594	315	4.81182	158.43568	762.36414	315	5.13648	154.62029	794.20343
316	4.52922	162.61807	736.53357	316	4.83588	158.64247	767.17596	316	5.16323	154.81396	799.33990
317	4.55093	162.83780	741.06281	317	4.86006	158.84824	772.01184	317	5.19012	155.00664	804.50311
318	4.57273	163.05649	745.61371	318	4.88436	159.05296	776.87189	318	5.21715	155.19830	809.69324
319	4.59464	163.27414	750.18646	319	4.90878	159.25668	781.75629	319	5.24433	155.38899	814.91040
320	4.61666	163.49074	754.78113	320	4.93333	159.45938	786.66504	320	5.27164	155.57869	820.15472
321	4.63878	163.70631	759.39777	321	4.95799	159.66109	791.59839	321	5.29910	155.76740	825.42639
322	4.66101	163.92087	764.03656	322	4.98278	159.86177	796.55640	322	5.32669	155.95512	830.72546
323	4.68334	164.13438	768.69757	323	5.00770	160.06146	801.53912	323	5.35444	156.14189	836.05219
324	4.70578	164.34689	773.38092	324	5.03273	160.26016	806.54691	324	5.38233	156.32768	841.40662
325	4.72833	164.55838	778.08667	325	5.05790	160.45787	811.57969	325	5.41036	156.51251	846.78894

n			n			n			n			
326	4.75099	164.76886	326	782.81500	5.08319	326	160.65460	816.63745	326	5.43854	156.89638	852.19928
327	4.77375	164.97835	327	787.56598	5.10860	327	160.85036	821.72064	327	5.46636	156.80780	857.67500
328	4.79665	165.18655	328	792.33576	5.13415	328	161.04512	826.82928	328	5.49534	157.06128	863.10468
329	4.81961	165.39430	329	797.13641	5.15982	329	161.23892	831.96344	329	5.52398	157.24231	868.60004
330	4.84271	165.60080	330	801.95599	5.18562	330	161.43178	837.12323	330	5.55273	157.42241	874.12396
331	4.86591	165.80632	331	806.79871	5.21154	331	161.62366	842.30884	331	5.58165	157.60156	879.67670
332	4.88923	166.01085	332	811.66461	5.23760	332	161.81458	847.52039	332	5.61072	157.77979	885.25836
333	4.91265	166.21440	333	816.55383	5.26379	333	162.00456	852.75800	333	5.63714	157.95706	890.86908
334	4.93619	166.41699	334	821.46649	5.29011	334	162.19359	858.02179	334	5.66932	158.13348	896.50903
335	4.95985	166.61861	335	826.40271	5.31656	335	162.38168	863.31189	335	5.69985	158.30896	902.17834
336	4.98361	166.81926	336	831.36255	5.34314	336	162.56883	868.62848	336	5.72853	158.48352	907.87720
337	5.00749	167.01897	337	836.34613	5.36996	337	162.75507	873.97162	337	5.75836	158.65718	913.60571
338	5.03149	167.21771	338	841.35384	5.39671	338	162.94035	879.34143	338	5.78835	158.82994	919.36407
339	5.05560	167.41551	339	846.38513	5.42369	339	163.12474	884.73816	339	5.81850	159.00182	925.15247
340	5.07982	167.61237	340	851.44073	5.45081	340	163.30820	890.16187	340	5.84881	159.17279	930.97035
341	5.10416	167.80829	341	856.52057	5.47806	341	163.49074	895.61267	341	5.87927	159.34288	936.81976
342	5.12862	168.00327	342	861.62469	5.50545	342	163.67238	901.09070	342	5.90989	159.51208	942.69904
343	5.15319	168.19733	343	866.75330	5.53298	343	163.85312	906.59619	343	5.94066	159.68042	948.60889
344	5.17789	168.39048	344	871.90649	5.56065	344	164.03294	912.12915	344	5.97161	159.84787	954.54856
345	5.20270	168.58266	345	877.08441	5.58845	345	164.21188	917.68982	345	6.00271	160.01447	960.52118
346	5.22763	168.77396	346	882.28711	5.61637	346	164.38994	923.28028	346	6.03398	160.18019	966.52538
347	5.25267	168.96434	347	887.51475	5.64443	347	164.56711	928.90465	347	6.06541	160.34506	972.55792
348	5.27784	169.15381	348	892.76740	5.67270	348	164.74339	934.55912	348	6.09700	160.50908	978.63329
349	5.30313	169.34238	349	898.04533	5.70106	349	164.91879	940.21179	349	6.12875	160.67224	984.72028
350	5.32854	169.53004	350	903.34889	5.72956	350	165.09332	945.91290	350	6.16067	160.83456	990.84306

Table 1. (continued) Annuities

M	C(5.75,M,12)	A(5.75,M,12)	S(5.75,M,12)		M	C(6.00,M,12)	A(6.00,M,12)	S(6.00,M,12)		M	C(6.25,M,12)	A(6.25,M,12)	S(6.25,M,12)
351	5.35408	169.71681	908.87694		351	5.75821	165.26698	961.64246		351	6.19276	160.99605	997.00970
352	5.37973	169.90269	914.03101		352	5.78700	165.43979	967.40063		352	6.22501	161.15668	1003.20245
353	5.40561	170.08769	919.41071		353	5.81594	165.61178	973.18768		353	6.25743	161.31650	1009.42749
354	5.43141	170.27180	924.81622		354	5.84502	165.78282	969.00360		354	6.28003	161.47548	1015.68494
355	5.45744	170.45505	930.24782		355	5.87424	165.96305	974.84963		355	6.32279	161.63364	1021.97498
356	5.48359	170.63741	935.70508		356	5.90361	166.12244	980.72284		356	6.35572	161.79097	1028.29773
357	5.50986	170.81889	941.18866		357	5.93313	166.29099	996.62646		357	6.38882	161.94749	1034.65344
358	5.53626	170.99953	946.89855		358	5.96280	166.45869	992.55963		358	6.42210	162.10321	1041.04224
359	5.56279	171.17929	952.23490		359	5.99261	166.62556	998.52240		359	6.45554	162.25812	1047.46436
360	5.58945	171.35820	957.79781		360	6.02257	166.79161	1004.51501		360	6.48917	162.41222	1053.91992
361	5.61623	171.53625	963.38702		361	6.05269	166.95682	1010.53760		361	6.52296	162.56552	1060.40906
362	5.64314	171.71347	969.00323		362	6.08295	167.12122	1016.59027		362	6.55694	162.71803	1066.93201
363	5.67018	171.88983	974.64642		363	6.11337	167.28479	1022.87322		363	6.59109	162.86975	1073.48889
364	5.69735	172.06534	980.31659		364	6.14393	167.44756	1028.78662		364	6.62542	163.02069	1080.08008
365	5.72465	172.24004	986.01392		365	6.17465	167.60951	1034.93054		365	6.65992	163.17034	1086.70544
366	5.75208	172.41388	991.73859		366	6.20553	167.77066	1041.10510		366	6.69461	163.32021	1093.36536
367	5.77964	172.58690	997.49066		367	6.23655	167.93100	1047.31067		367	6.72948	163.46881	1100.05994
368	5.80734	172.75909	1003.27032		368	6.26774	168.09055	1053.54724		368	6.76453	163.61664	1106.78943
369	5.83516	172.93047	1009.07764		369	6.29908	168.24930	1059.81494		369	6.79976	163.76370	1113.55396
370	5.86312	173.10103	1014.91284		370	6.33057	168.40728	1066.11401		370	6.83518	163.91000	1120.35378
371	5.89122	173.27077	1020.77554		371	6.36222	168.56444	1072.44458		371	6.87078	164.05556	1127.18896
372	5.91945	173.43971	1026.66711		372	6.39403	168.72084	1078.80688		372	6.90656	164.20035	1134.05969
373	5.94781	173.60783	1032.58655		373	6.42600	168.87645	1085.20033		373	6.94253	164.34438	1140.96631
374	5.97631	173.77516	1038.53442		374	6.45813	169.03130	1091.62663		374	6.97869	164.48767	1147.90881
375	6.00495	173.94170	1044.51074		375	6.49043	169.18538	1098.08496		375	7.01504	164.63022	1154.88745

376	8.03372	174.10742	1050.51563	376	6.52288	169.33868	1104.57564	376	7.05156	164.77203	1161.90259
377	8.06263	174.27237	1056.54432	377	6.55549	169.49123	1111.09827	377	7.08830	164.91312	1168.95410
378	8.09168	174.43652	1062.61194	378	6.58827	169.64301	1117.65381	378	7.12522	165.05347	1176.04248
379	8.12087	174.59990	1068.70374	379	6.62121	169.79404	1124.24207	379	7.16233	165.19308	1183.16760
380	8.15020	174.76250	1074.82458	380	6.65432	169.94432	1130.96328	380	7.19964	165.33197	1190.32996
381	8.17967	174.92432	1080.97473	381	6.68759	170.03384	1137.51758	381	7.23713	165.47015	1197.52866
382	8.20928	175.08537	1087.15442	382	6.72103	170.24263	1144.20520	382	7.27483	165.60760	1204.76672
383	8.23903	175.24565	1093.36385	383	6.75463	170.39069	1150.92627	383	7.31272	165.74435	1212.04163
384	8.26893	175.40517	1099.60278	384	6.78840	170.53799	1157.68079	384	7.35080	165.88040	1219.35425
385	8.29897	175.56393	1105.87170	385	6.82235	170.68457	1164.46924	385	7.38909	166.01573	1226.70508
386	8.32915	175.72192	1112.17065	386	6.85646	170.83041	1171.29163	386	7.42757	166.15038	1234.09424
387	8.35948	175.87917	1118.49976	387	6.89074	170.97554	1178.14807	387	7.46626	166.28430	1241.52173
388	8.38995	176.03568	1124.85925	388	6.92519	171.11993	1185.03882	388	7.50615	166.41754	1248.98804
389	8.42057	176.19142	1131.24917	389	6.95962	171.26361	1191.96369	389	7.54424	166.55008	1256.49316
390	8.45133	176.34642	1137.66900	390	6.99462	171.40659	1198.92383	390	7.58353	166.68196	1264.03735
391	8.48225	176.50069	1144.12109	391	7.02959	171.54884	1205.91846	391	7.62303	166.81314	1271.62097
392	8.51331	176.65422	1150.60309	392	7.06474	171.69038	1212.94900	392	7.66273	166.94365	1279.24390
393	8.54452	176.80702	1157.11670	393	7.10006	171.83124	1220.01282	393	7.70264	167.07347	1286.90674
394	8.57588	176.95909	1163.66125	394	7.13556	171.97137	1227.11279	394	7.74276	167.20262	1294.60938
395	8.60739	177.11044	1170.23706	395	7.17124	172.11082	1234.24841	395	7.78308	167.33110	1302.35205
396	8.63905	177.26106	1176.84448	396	7.20710	172.24957	1241.41968	396	7.82362	167.45892	1310.13513
397	8.67086	177.41036	1183.48272	397	7.24313	172.38763	1248.62671	397	7.86437	167.58607	1317.95874
398	8.70282	177.56017	1190.15442	398	7.27935	172.52501	1255.86987	398	7.90533	167.71259	1325.82312
399	8.73434	177.70805	1196.85716	399	7.31575	172.66170	1263.14917	399	7.94650	167.83842	1333.72852
400	8.76721	177.85641	1203.59216	400	7.35232	172.79771	1270.46497	400	7.98789	167.96361	1341.67438

Table 1. (continued) Annuities

M	C(5.75,M,12)	A(5.75,M,12)	S(5.75,M,12)	M	C(6.00,M,12)	A(6.00,M,12)	S(6.00,M,12)	M	C(6.25,M,12)	A(6.25,M,12)	S(6.25,M,12)
401	6.79964	178.00348	1210.35338	401	7.38909	172.93304	1277.81726	401	8.02949	188.08815	1349.66284
402	6.83222	178.14984	1217.15894	402	7.42603	173.06770	1285.20642	402	8.07131	188.21205	1357.69238
403	6.86496	178.29552	1223.99121	403	7.46316	173.20171	1292.63245	403	8.11335	188.33530	1365.76367
404	6.89785	178.44048	1230.85620	404	7.50048	173.33502	1300.09558	404	8.15561	188.45792	1373.87708
405	6.93090	178.58476	1237.75403	405	7.53798	173.46768	1307.59607	405	8.19809	188.57990	1382.03259
406	6.96412	178.72836	1244.68494	406	7.57567	173.59969	1315.13403	406	8.24078	188.70125	1390.23071
407	6.99749	178.87126	1251.64905	407	7.61355	173.73103	1322.70972	407	8.28371	188.82198	1398.47156
408	7.03101	179.01349	1258.64648	408	7.65162	173.86172	1330.32324	408	8.32685	188.94205	1406.75525
409	7.06470	179.15504	1265.67749	409	7.68987	173.99176	1337.97485	409	8.37022	189.06152	1415.08203
410	7.09856	179.29591	1272.74219	410	7.72832	174.12115	1345.66479	410	8.41381	189.18037	1423.45227
411	7.13257	179.43611	1279.84088	411	7.76697	174.24991	1353.39307	411	8.45764	189.29861	1431.86609
412	7.16675	179.57565	1286.97339	412	7.80580	174.37801	1361.16003	412	8.50169	189.41624	1440.32373
413	7.20109	179.71452	1294.14014	413	7.84483	174.50549	1368.96582	413	8.54597	189.53325	1448.82544
414	7.23559	179.85272	1301.34243	414	7.88405	174.63232	1376.81067	414	8.59048	189.64966	1457.37134
415	7.27026	179.99026	1308.57878	415	7.92347	174.75854	1384.69470	415	8.63522	189.76547	1465.96191
416	7.30510	180.12717	1315.84705	416	7.96309	174.88412	1392.61816	416	8.68019	189.88068	1474.59705
417	7.34010	180.26340	1323.15210	417	8.00291	175.00908	1400.58130	417	8.72540	189.99529	1483.27734
418	7.37528	180.39899	1330.49231	418	8.04292	175.13341	1408.58423	418	8.77085	190.10930	1492.00269
419	7.41062	180.53394	1337.86755	419	8.08314	175.25713	1416.62708	419	8.81653	190.22272	1500.77356
420	7.44612	180.66823	1345.27820	420	8.12355	175.39022	1424.71021	420	8.86245	190.33556	1509.59009
421	7.48190	180.80188	1352.72424	421	8.16417	175.50270	1432.83374	421	8.90861	190.44780	1518.45251
422	7.51765	180.93491	1360.20605	422	8.20499	175.62466	1440.99792	422	8.95501	190.55946	1527.36108
423	7.55368	181.06729	1367.72375	423	8.24601	175.74585	1449.20300	423	9.00165	190.67056	1536.31616
424	7.58987	181.19905	1375.27747	424	8.28724	175.86612	1457.44897	424	9.04853	190.78108	1545.31775
425	7.62624	181.33017	1382.66731	425	8.32868	175.98659	1465.73621	425	9.09566	190.89102	1554.36633

426	7.66278	181.46068	1390.43353	426	8.37032	176.10606	1474.06494	426	9.14303	171.00040	1563.46191
427	7.69950	181.59055	1398.15625	427	8.41218	176.22433	1482.43518	427	9.19065	171.10919	1572.60498
428	7.73639	181.71980	1405.85583	428	8.45424	176.34322	1490.84741	428	9.23852	171.21744	1581.79565
429	7.77346	181.84845	1413.59216	429	8.49651	176.46091	1499.30164	429	9.28664	171.32512	1591.03418
430	7.81071	181.97649	1421.36560	430	8.53899	176.57802	1507.79810	430	9.33500	171.43225	1600.32090
431	7.84814	182.10390	1429.17639	431	8.58169	176.69455	1516.33716	431	9.38362	171.53882	1609.65576
432	7.88574	182.23071	1437.02454	432	8.62459	176.81050	1524.91882	432	9.43250	171.64484	1619.03943
433	7.92353	182.35692	1444.91028	433	8.66772	176.92587	1533.54346	433	9.48162	171.75031	1628.47192
434	7.96150	182.48253	1452.83374	434	8.71106	177.04066	1542.21118	434	9.53101	171.85522	1637.95349
435	7.99964	182.60753	1460.79529	435	8.75461	177.15489	1550.92224	435	9.58065	171.95959	1647.48462
436	8.03798	182.73193	1468.79492	436	8.79838	177.26854	1559.67676	436	9.63055	172.06343	1657.06519
437	8.07649	182.85576	1476.83289	437	8.84238	177.38164	1568.47522	437	9.68071	172.16673	1666.69580
438	8.11519	182.97897	1484.90942	438	8.88659	177.49417	1577.31750	438	9.73113	172.26950	1676.37646
439	8.15408	183.10162	1493.02454	439	8.93102	177.60614	1586.20410	439	9.78181	172.37172	1686.10754
440	8.19315	183.22366	1501.17871	440	8.97568	177.71754	1595.13513	440	9.83276	172.47342	1695.88940
441	8.23241	183.34514	1509.37183	441	9.02055	177.82840	1604.11084	441	9.88397	172.57460	1705.72217
442	8.27185	183.46603	1517.60425	442	9.06566	177.93871	1613.13135	442	9.93545	172.67525	1715.60608
443	8.31149	183.58635	1525.87610	443	9.11098	178.04848	1622.19702	443	9.98720	172.77538	1725.54163
444	8.35132	183.70609	1534.18750	444	9.15654	178.15768	1631.30798	444	10.03921	172.87498	1735.52881
445	8.39133	183.82526	1542.53882	445	9.20232	178.26638	1640.46460	445	10.09150	172.97408	1745.56799
446	8.43154	183.94396	1550.93036	446	9.24833	178.37448	1649.66687	446	10.14406	173.07266	1755.65955
447	8.47194	184.06190	1559.38169	447	9.29458	178.48207	1658.91528	447	10.19689	173.17073	1765.80359
448	8.51254	184.17937	1567.87634	448	9.34105	178.58913	1668.20984	448	10.25000	173.26830	1776.00049
449	8.55333	184.29630	1576.34619	449	9.38775	178.69565	1677.55090	449	10.30339	173.36534	1786.25049
450	8.59431	184.41264	1584.89954	450	9.43469	178.80164	1686.93860	450	10.35705	173.46190	1796.55383

Table 1. (continued) Annuities

M	C(5.75,M,12)	A(5.75,M,12)	S(5.75,M,12)	M	C(6.00,M,12)	A(6.00,M,12)	S(6.00,M,12)	M	C(6.25,M,12)	A(6.25,M,12)	S(6.25,M,12)
451	8.63549	184.52844	1593.49390	451	9.48187	178.90710	1696.37329	451	10.41099	173.55795	1806.91089
452	8.67687	184.64369	1602.12939	452	9.52928	179.01204	1705.85522	452	10.46522	173.65360	1817.32190
453	8.71845	184.75639	1610.80627	453	9.57652	179.11646	1715.38440	453	10.51972	173.74857	1827.78711
454	8.76022	184.87254	1619.52466	454	9.62481	179.22035	1724.96143	454	10.57451	173.84312	1838.30676
455	8.80220	184.98616	1628.28491	455	9.67293	179.32373	1734.58618	455	10.62959	173.93721	1848.88135
456	8.84438	185.09921	1637.08704	456	9.72130	179.42661	1744.25916	456	10.68495	174.03079	1859.51099
457	8.88675	185.21175	1645.93152	457	9.76990	179.52898	1753.98047	457	10.74060	174.12390	1870.19592
458	8.92934	185.32373	1654.81824	458	9.81875	179.63080	1763.75037	458	10.79654	174.21652	1880.93652
459	8.97212	185.43520	1663.74756	459	9.86785	179.73215	1773.56909	459	10.85278	174.30867	1891.73303
460	9.01511	185.54611	1672.71973	460	9.91718	179.83298	1783.43689	460	10.90930	174.40033	1902.58582
461	9.05831	185.65651	1681.73474	461	9.96677	179.93332	1793.35413	461	10.96612	174.49152	1913.49512
462	9.10172	185.76639	1690.79309	462	10.01660	180.03314	1803.32092	462	11.02324	174.58224	1924.46118
463	9.14533	185.87573	1699.89478	463	10.06669	180.13248	1813.33752	463	11.08065	174.67249	1935.48450
464	9.18915	185.98456	1709.04016	464	10.11702	180.23132	1823.40417	464	11.13836	174.76227	1946.56506
465	9.23318	186.09288	1718.23925	465	10.16761	180.32968	1833.52112	465	11.19637	174.85158	1957.70349
466	9.27742	186.20065	1727.46252	466	10.21844	180.42754	1843.68884	466	11.25469	174.94043	1968.89990
467	9.32188	186.30792	1736.73987	467	10.26954	180.52491	1853.90723	467	11.31330	175.02882	1980.15454
468	9.36655	186.41469	1746.06177	468	10.32088	180.62181	1864.17676	468	11.37223	175.11676	1991.46790
469	9.41143	186.52094	1755.42834	469	10.37249	180.71822	1874.49768	469	11.43146	175.20424	2002.84009
470	9.45652	186.62668	1764.83972	470	10.42435	180.81415	1884.87012	470	11.49100	175.29126	2014.27148
471	9.50184	186.73193	1774.29626	471	10.47647	180.90959	1895.29443	471	11.55085	175.37784	2025.76257
472	9.54737	186.83667	1783.79810	472	10.52885	181.00458	1905.77100	472	11.61101	175.46396	2037.31335
473	9.59311	186.94090	1793.34546	473	10.58150	181.09908	1916.29990	473	11.67148	175.54964	2048.92432
474	9.63908	187.04465	1802.93860	474	10.63441	181.19312	1926.88135	474	11.73227	175.63487	2060.59570
475	9.68527	187.14790	1812.57764	475	10.68758	181.28668	1937.51575	475	11.79338	175.71967	2072.32813

n				n				n			
476	9.73168	187.25066	1822.28294	476	10.74102	181.37978	1948.20325	476	11.85480	175.80402	2094.12134
477	9.77831	187.35294	1831.99463	477	10.79472	181.47241	1968.94434	477	11.91654	175.88794	2095.97632
478	9.82516	187.45471	1841.77295	478	10.84869	181.56459	1969.73901	478	11.97861	175.97142	2107.89282
479	9.87224	187.55600	1851.59814	479	10.90294	181.65631	1990.58777	479	12.04100	176.05447	2119.87134
480	9.91955	187.65681	1861.47034	480	10.95745	181.74757	1991.49072	480	12.10371	176.13708	2131.91235
481	9.96708	187.75714	1871.38989	481	11.01224	181.83838	2002.44812	481	12.16675	176.21928	2144.01611
482	10.01484	187.86999	1881.35693	482	11.06730	181.92874	2013.46033	482	12.23012	176.30104	2156.18286
483	10.08282	187.96638	1891.37183	483	11.12264	182.01865	2024.52771	483	12.29382	176.38239	2168.41309
484	10.11104	188.05527	1901.43457	484	11.17825	182.10811	2035.65027	484	12.35786	176.46330	2180.70679
485	10.15949	188.15376	1911.54565	485	11.23414	182.19713	2046.82861	485	12.42221	176.54381	2193.06470
486	10.20817	188.25166	1921.70520	486	11.29031	182.28569	2058.06274	486	12.48691	176.62389	2205.49692
487	10.25708	188.34915	1931.91333	487	11.34676	182.37383	2069.35303	487	12.55195	176.70357	2217.97388
488	10.30623	188.44618	1942.17041	488	11.40350	182.46152	2080.69971	488	12.61732	176.78282	2230.52563
489	10.35562	188.54278	1952.47668	489	11.46052	182.54877	2092.10327	489	12.68304	176.86166	2243.14307
490	10.40524	188.63885	1962.83228	490	11.51782	182.63559	2103.56372	490	12.74909	176.94009	2255.82617
491	10.45510	188.73450	1973.23755	491	11.57541	182.72198	2115.08154	491	12.81550	177.01813	2268.57520
492	10.50519	188.82970	1983.69263	492	11.63328	182.80794	2126.65698	492	12.88224	177.09575	2281.39063
493	10.55553	188.92444	1994.19775	493	11.69145	182.89348	2138.29028	493	12.94934	177.17297	2294.27295
494	10.60611	189.01872	2004.75330	494	11.74991	182.97858	2149.98169	494	13.01678	177.24980	2307.22217
495	10.65693	189.11255	2015.35938	495	11.80866	183.06326	2161.73169	495	13.08458	177.32623	2320.23901
496	10.70799	189.20595	2026.01636	496	11.86770	183.14754	2173.54028	496	13.15273	177.40227	2333.32349
497	10.75930	189.29889	2036.72437	497	11.92704	183.23137	2185.40796	497	13.22123	177.47789	2346.47632
498	10.81086	189.39139	2047.48364	498	11.98668	183.31480	2197.33496	498	13.29009	177.55315	2359.69751
499	10.86266	189.48344	2058.29443	499	12.04661	183.39781	2209.32178	499	13.35831	177.62799	2372.96755
500	10.91471	189.57506	2069.15723	500	12.10684	183.48041	2221.36841	500	13.42889	177.70245	2386.34692

Table 1. (continued) Annuities

N	C(6.50,M,12)	A(6.50,M,12)	S(6.50,M,12)	M	C(6.75,M,12)	A(6.75,M,12)	S(6.75,M,12)	M	C(7.00,M,12)	A(7.00,M,12)	S(7.00,M,12)
1	1.00542	0.99461	1.00000	1	1.00562	0.99441	1.00000	1	1.00583	0.99420	1.00000
2	1.01086	1.98387	2.00542	2	1.01128	1.98325	2.00562	2	1.01170	1.98264	2.00583
3	1.01634	2.96779	3.01628	3	1.01697	2.96656	3.01691	3	1.01760	2.96534	3.01753
4	1.02184	3.94641	4.03262	4	1.02269	3.94438	4.03388	4	1.02354	3.94234	4.03514
5	1.02738	4.91977	5.05446	5	1.02844	4.91672	5.06657	5	1.02951	4.91368	5.05867
6	1.03294	5.88787	6.08184	6	1.03423	5.88362	6.09501	6	1.03551	5.87938	6.08818
7	1.03854	6.85076	7.11478	7	1.04005	6.84512	7.11924	7	1.04155	6.83948	7.12370
8	1.04416	7.80847	8.15332	8	1.04590	7.80124	8.15928	8	1.04763	7.79402	8.16525
9	1.04982	8.76101	9.19748	9	1.05178	8.75201	9.20518	9	1.05374	8.74302	9.21288
10	1.05551	9.70843	10.24730	10	1.05770	9.69748	10.25696	10	1.05989	9.68651	10.26662
11	1.06122	10.65073	11.30281	11	1.06364	10.63762	11.31465	11	1.06607	10.62454	11.32651
12	1.06697	11.58797	12.36403	12	1.06963	11.57253	12.37830	12	1.07229	11.55712	12.39258
13	1.07275	12.52015	13.43101	13	1.07564	12.50220	13.44793	13	1.07855	12.48429	13.46488
14	1.07856	13.44731	14.50376	14	1.08170	13.42666	14.52257	14	1.08484	13.40609	14.54342
15	1.08440	14.36947	15.58232	15	1.08778	14.34598	15.60527	15	1.09116	14.32254	15.62826
16	1.09028	15.28667	16.66672	16	1.09390	15.26014	16.63305	16	1.09753	15.23368	16.71942
17	1.09618	16.19893	17.75700	17	1.10005	16.16919	17.78695	17	1.10393	16.13863	17.81896
18	1.10212	17.10627	18.85318	18	1.10624	17.07315	18.88700	18	1.11037	17.04013	18.92088
19	1.10809	18.00872	19.95531	19	1.11246	17.97206	19.99823	19	1.11685	17.93551	20.03126
20	1.11409	18.90631	21.06340	20	1.11872	18.86594	21.10570	20	1.12336	18.82569	21.14910
21	1.12013	19.79907	22.17745	21	1.12501	19.75482	22.22442	21	1.12992	19.71071	22.27147
22	1.12620	20.68701	23.29762	22	1.13134	20.63673	23.34943	22	1.13651	20.59060	23.40138
23	1.13230	21.57017	24.42381	23	1.13770	21.51769	24.48077	23	1.14314	21.46539	24.53789
24	1.13843	22.44858	25.55611	24	1.14410	22.39174	25.61847	24	1.14981	22.33510	25.68103
25	1.14460	23.32225	26.69454	25	1.15054	23.26089	26.76258	25	1.15651	23.19977	26.88084

n						
26	1.15080	24.19121	27.89913	1.15701	24.12519	27.91312
27	1.15703	25.05549	28.96998	1.16352	24.99465	29.07013
28	1.16330	25.91512	30.14636	1.17006	25.83391	30.23365
29	1.16960	26.77012	31.41026	1.17665	26.68918	31.40371
30	1.17593	27.62051	32.47966	1.18326	27.53430	32.59036
31	1.18230	28.46631	33.85578	1.18992	28.37469	33.76362
32	1.18871	29.30756	34.83809	1.19661	29.21038	34.95054
33	1.19515	30.14428	36.02679	1.20334	30.04140	36.15016
34	1.20162	30.97649	37.22194	1.21011	30.86777	37.35350
35	1.20813	31.80422	30.40356	1.21692	31.68650	38.56361
36	1.21467	32.62749	38.63168	1.22377	32.50666	39.79053
37	1.22125	33.44632	40.84636	1.23065	33.31924	41.00430
38	1.22787	34.26074	42.06760	1.23757	34.12728	42.23496
39	1.23452	35.07077	43.29547	1.24453	34.93079	43.47252
40	1.24120	35.87644	44.52999	1.25153	35.72981	44.71705
41	1.24793	36.67777	45.77119	1.25857	36.52436	45.95859
42	1.25469	37.47478	47.01912	1.26565	37.31447	47.22716
43	1.26148	38.28750	48.27381	1.27277	38.10015	48.49281
44	1.26832	39.05596	49.53529	1.27993	38.88145	49.76559
45	1.27519	39.84015	50.80361	1.28713	39.85837	51.04552
46	1.28209	40.62012	52.07879	1.29437	40.43094	52.33265
47	1.28904	41.39569	53.36089	1.30165	41.19920	53.62702
48	1.29602	42.16749	54.64933	1.30897	41.96315	54.92667
49	1.30304	42.93492	55.94596	1.31634	42.72284	56.23764
50	1.31010	43.69822	57.24899	1.32374	43.47828	57.55398

n			
26	1.16326	24.05942	27.99735
27	1.17005	24.91409	29.15061
28	1.17687	25.76380	30.32065
29	1.18374	26.60858	31.49752
30	1.19064	27.44847	32.68126
31	1.19759	28.28348	33.87190
32	1.20457	29.11365	35.06948
33	1.21160	29.93900	36.27406
34	1.21867	30.75957	37.48566
35	1.22578	31.57538	38.70432
36	1.23293	32.38646	39.89010
37	1.24012	33.19284	41.18302
38	1.24735	33.99454	42.40314
39	1.25463	34.79158	43.65049
40	1.26195	35.58401	44.90512
41	1.26931	36.37194	46.18707
42	1.27671	37.15511	47.43637
43	1.28416	37.93392	48.71309
44	1.29165	38.70803	49.99725
45	1.29919	39.47774	51.28890
46	1.30676	40.24299	52.58809
47	1.31439	41.00380	53.89485
48	1.32205	41.76020	55.20924
49	1.32977	42.51221	56.53129
50	1.33752	43.25986	57.86105

Table 1. (continued) Annuities

M	C(6.50,M,12)	A(6.50,M,12)	S(6.50,M,12)	M	C(6.75,M,12)	A(6.75,M,12)	S(6.75,M,12)	M	C(7.00,M,12)	A(7.00,M,12)	S(7.00,M,12)
51	1.31719	44.45741	58.55909	51	1.33119	44.20948	58.87772	51	1.34532	44.00318	59.19858
52	1.32433	45.21251	59.87628	52	1.33868	44.97649	60.20981	52	1.35317	44.74210	60.54930
53	1.33150	45.96354	61.20061	53	1.34621	45.74192	61.54758	53	1.36107	45.47650	61.89708
54	1.33872	46.71053	62.53211	54	1.35378	46.50132	62.89379	54	1.36901	46.20736	63.25814
55	1.34597	47.45349	63.87063	55	1.36139	47.25799	64.24757	55	1.37699	46.93358	64.62714
56	1.35326	48.19249	65.21600	56	1.36905	48.01234	65.60896	56	1.38502	47.65559	66.00414
57	1.36059	48.92742	66.57005	57	1.37675	48.69297	66.97801	57	1.39310	48.37341	67.38916
58	1.36796	49.65844	67.93064	58	1.38450	49.37160	68.35476	58	1.40123	49.08707	68.78226
59	1.37537	50.38552	69.29860	59	1.39228	50.00884	69.73926	59	1.40940	49.78659	70.18349
60	1.38282	51.10868	70.67397	60	1.40011	50.80407	71.13154	60	1.41763	50.50199	71.59230
61	1.39031	51.82794	72.05678	61	1.40799	51.51431	72.53165	61	1.42589	51.20330	73.01052
62	1.39784	52.54333	73.44709	62	1.41591	52.22056	73.93164	62	1.43421	51.90055	74.43642
63	1.40541	53.25487	74.84492	63	1.42387	52.92287	75.35555	63	1.44258	52.59375	75.87063
64	1.41302	53.96257	76.25034	64	1.43188	53.62125	76.77543	64	1.45099	53.28294	77.31321
65	1.42068	54.66646	77.66336	65	1.43994	54.31573	78.21131	65	1.45946	53.96812	78.76421
66	1.42837	55.36656	79.08404	66	1.44804	55.00632	79.65125	66	1.46797	54.64934	80.22366
67	1.43611	56.06289	80.51241	67	1.45618	55.69004	81.09929	67	1.47653	55.32660	81.69964
68	1.44389	56.75546	81.94852	68	1.46437	56.37599	82.55547	68	1.48515	55.99993	83.16817
69	1.45171	57.44431	83.39240	69	1.47261	57.05499	84.01695	69	1.49381	56.66936	84.65331
70	1.45957	58.12944	84.84412	70	1.48090	57.73026	85.49246	70	1.50252	57.33491	86.14713
71	1.46748	58.81088	86.30369	71	1.48923	58.40125	86.97336	71	1.51129	57.99659	87.64965
72	1.47543	59.48865	87.77116	72	1.49760	59.06948	88.46259	72	1.52011	58.65444	89.16094
73	1.48342	60.16277	89.24659	73	1.50603	59.73349	89.96018	73	1.52897	59.30848	90.68105
74	1.49145	60.83325	90.73001	74	1.51450	60.39377	91.46621	74	1.53789	59.95872	92.21001
75	1.49953	61.50013	92.22147	75	1.52302	61.05036	92.99071	75	1.54686	60.60519	93.74791

n		
76	1.50786	82.18341
77	1.51582	82.82312
78	1.52403	83.47927
79	1.53229	84.13189
80	1.54059	84.78099
81	1.54893	85.42660
82	1.55732	86.06873
83	1.56576	86.70739
84	1.57424	87.34262
85	1.58277	87.97443
86	1.59134	88.60283
87	1.59996	89.22784
88	1.60863	89.84949
89	1.61734	90.46779
90	1.62610	91.08276
91	1.63491	91.69441
92	1.64376	92.30277
93	1.65267	92.90756
94	1.66162	93.50968
95	1.67063	94.10826
96	1.67967	94.70361
97	1.68877	95.25976
98	1.69791	95.88472
99	1.70711	96.47050
100	1.71636	97.05313

n		
76	93.72100	1.53158
77	95.22865	1.54020
78	96.74448	1.54886
79	98.26851	1.55757
80	99.80090	1.56634
81	101.34138	1.57515
82	102.89031	1.58401
83	104.44764	1.59292
84	106.01340	1.60188
85	107.58764	1.61089
86	109.17040	1.61995
87	110.76174	1.62906
88	112.36170	1.63922
89	113.97033	1.64744
90	115.58767	1.65671
91	117.21377	1.66603
92	118.84967	1.67540
93	120.49756	1.68482
94	122.14510	1.69430
95	123.80672	1.70383
96	125.47734	1.71341
97	127.15701	1.72305
98	128.84578	1.73274
99	130.54369	1.74249
100	132.25081	1.75229

n		
76	81.70328	94.50372
77	82.35255	96.03531
78	82.99818	97.57551
79	83.64021	99.12437
80	84.27864	100.68196
81	84.91350	102.24828
82	85.54481	103.82343
83	86.17259	105.40743
84	86.79686	107.00035
85	87.41763	108.60223
86	88.03493	110.21311
87	88.64879	111.83306
88	89.25920	113.46212
89	89.86620	115.10035
90	90.46981	116.74779
91	91.07005	118.40450
92	91.66692	120.07052
93	92.26045	121.74592
94	92.85067	123.43073
95	93.43756	125.12503
96	94.02121	126.82897
97	94.60158	128.54227
98	95.17870	130.26532
99	95.75259	131.99906
100	96.32327	133.74655

n			
76	1.55589	81.24791	96.29477
77	1.56496	81.86630	96.85066
78	1.57409	82.52219	98.41562
79	1.58327	83.15379	99.98972
80	1.59251	83.78173	101.57298
81	1.60180	84.40603	103.16550
82	1.61114	85.02670	104.76730
83	1.62054	85.64378	106.37843
84	1.62999	86.25728	107.99898
85	1.63950	86.86723	109.62897
86	1.64907	87.47363	111.26947
87	1.65969	88.07652	112.95754
88	1.66936	88.67590	114.57623
89	1.67909	89.27192	116.24458
90	1.68798	89.86427	117.90268
91	1.69773	90.45330	119.61057
92	1.70763	91.03890	121.30829
93	1.71759	91.62112	123.01592
94	1.72761	92.19995	124.73351
95	1.73769	92.77543	126.46113
96	1.74783	93.34756	128.19601
97	1.75802	93.91639	129.94664
98	1.76828	94.48191	131.70467
99	1.77859	95.04415	133.47295
100	1.78897	95.60313	135.25153

Table 1. (continued) Annuities

M	C(6.50,M,12)	A(6.50,M,12)	S(6.50,M,12)	M	C(6.75,M,12)	A(6.75,M,12)	S(6.75,M,12)	M	C(7.00,M,12)	A(7.00,M,12)	S(7.00,M,12)
101	1.72566	77.63262	133.96716	101	1.76215	76.89076	135.49284	101	1.79940	76.15887	137.04050
102	1.73500	78.20390	135.69281	102	1.77206	77.45508	137.25499	102	1.80990	76.71139	138.83990
103	1.74440	78.78226	137.42783	103	1.78203	78.01624	139.02705	103	1.82046	77.26070	140.64990
104	1.75386	79.35242	139.17223	104	1.79205	78.57426	140.80908	104	1.83108	77.80683	142.47026
105	1.76335	79.91953	140.92607	105	1.80213	79.12915	142.60114	105	1.84176	78.34978	144.30133
106	1.77290	80.46357	142.68942	106	1.81227	79.68095	144.40326	106	1.85250	78.88960	146.14310
107	1.78250	81.04459	144.46233	107	1.82246	80.22965	146.21553	107	1.86331	79.42628	147.99559
108	1.79216	81.60257	146.24483	108	1.83271	80.77529	148.03799	108	1.87418	79.95985	149.85690
109	1.80187	82.15755	148.05699	109	1.84302	81.31788	149.87070	109	1.88511	80.49032	151.73308
110	1.81163	82.70954	149.83885	110	1.85339	81.85743	151.71373	110	1.89611	81.01772	153.61819
111	1.82144	83.25856	151.65048	111	1.86382	82.39397	153.56712	111	1.90717	81.54205	155.51430
112	1.83131	83.80462	153.47192	112	1.87430	82.92750	155.43094	112	1.91829	82.06335	157.42146
113	1.84123	84.34773	155.30322	113	1.88484	83.45805	157.30524	113	1.92948	82.58163	159.33975
114	1.85120	84.86792	157.14445	114	1.89544	83.98563	159.19008	114	1.94074	83.09689	161.26924
115	1.86123	85.42520	158.99565	115	1.90611	84.51026	161.08551	115	1.95206	83.60917	163.20996
116	1.87131	85.95959	160.85687	116	1.91683	85.03195	162.99162	116	1.96345	84.11848	165.16203
117	1.88144	86.49010	162.72818	117	1.92761	85.55073	164.90045	117	1.97490	84.62484	167.12547
118	1.89164	87.01974	164.60963	118	1.93845	86.06660	166.83606	118	1.98642	85.12826	169.10037
119	1.90188	87.54553	166.50127	119	1.94936	86.57960	168.77452	119	1.99801	85.62875	171.08679
120	1.91218	88.06850	168.40315	120	1.96032	87.08971	170.72388	120	2.00966	86.12635	173.08478
121	1.92254	88.58864	170.31532	121	1.97135	87.59698	172.68419	121	2.02138	86.62106	175.09447
122	1.93296	89.10598	172.23787	122	1.98244	88.10141	174.65555	122	2.03318	87.11290	177.11584
123	1.94343	89.62054	174.17082	123	1.99359	88.60302	176.63799	123	2.04504	87.60189	179.14902
124	1.95396	90.13232	176.11426	124	2.00480	89.10182	178.63156	124	2.05697	88.08904	181.14906
125	1.96454	90.64135	178.06821	125	2.01608	89.59783	180.63637	125	2.06896	88.57138	183.25102

n			n				n		n			
126	1.97518	91.14763	126	180.03275	90.09407	2.02744	126	182.85245	126	2.08103	89.05191	185.31999
127	1.96588	91.65118	127	182.00792	90.58155	2.03882	127	184.67997	127	2.09317	89.59966	187.40102
128	1.98663	92.15203	128	183.95379	91.06969	2.05029	128	186.71969	128	2.10538	90.00462	189.49419
129	2.00745	92.65018	129	185.99043	91.55429	2.06183	129	188.76898	129	2.11766	90.47694	191.59958
130	2.01832	93.14564	130	187.99788		2.07342	130	190.83081	130	2.13002	90.94632	193.71724
131	2.02925	93.63843	131	190.01620	92.51618	2.08505	131	192.92424	131	2.14244	91.41308	195.84726
132	2.04025	94.12856	132	192.04546	92.93310	2.09681	132	194.96932	132	2.15494	91.87713	197.96970
133	2.05130	94.61606	133	194.08669	93.46735	2.10861	133	197.06614	133	2.16751	92.33849	200.14464
134	2.06241	95.10033	134	196.13699	93.93893	2.12047	134	199.19475	134	2.18015	92.79717	202.31215
135	2.07358	95.58319	135	198.19940	94.40789	2.13240	135	201.31522	135	2.19287	93.25320	204.45231
136	2.08481	96.06285	136	200.27298	94.87423	2.14439	136	203.44762	136	2.20566	93.70657	206.68518
137	2.09610	96.53992	137	202.35780	95.33796	2.15646	137	205.59201	137	2.21853	94.15733	208.89084
138	2.10746	97.01443	138	204.45290	95.79908	2.16859	138	207.74846	138	2.23147	94.60545	211.10338
139	2.11887	97.48638	139	206.56136	96.25763	2.18078	139	209.97705	139	2.24449	95.05099	213.34084
140	2.13035	97.95579	140	208.68024	96.71362	2.19305	140	212.09784	140	2.25758	95.43994	215.56533
141	2.14189	98.42266	141	210.80973	97.16705	2.20539	141	214.29088	141	2.27075	95.93433	217.84291
142	2.15349	98.88702	142	212.95247	97.61796	2.21779	142	216.43628	142	2.28400	96.37215	220.11366
143	2.16516	99.34888	143	215.10557	98.06633	2.23027	143	218.71407	143	2.29732	96.80745	222.39766
144	2.17689	99.80826	144	217.27113	98.52140	2.24281	144	220.94432	144	2.31072	97.24021	224.69498
145	2.18868	100.26515	145	219.44901	98.95527	2.25543	145	223.18713	145	2.32420	97.67047	227.00569
146	2.20053	100.71959	146	221.63659	99.39647	2.26811	146	225.44237	146	2.33776	98.09823	229.32990
147	2.21245	101.17158	147	223.83722	99.83489	2.28087	147	227.71068	147	2.35139	98.52351	231.66765
148	2.22444	101.62112	148	226.04967	100.27087	2.29370	148	229.99155	148	2.36511	98.94632	234.01904
149	2.23648	102.06826	149	228.27411	100.70441	2.30660	149	232.28526	149	2.37891	99.36668	236.38416
150	2.24860	102.51298	150	230.51059	101.13552	2.31968	150	234.59186	150	2.39278	99.76461	238.76308

Table 1. (continued) Annuities

M	C(6.50,M,12)	A(6.50,M,12)	S(6.50,M,12)	M	C(6.75,M,12)	A(6.75,M,12)	S(6.75,M,12)	M	C(7.00,M,12)	A(7.00,M,12)	S(7.00,M,12)
151	2.26078	102.95531	232.75919	151	2.33263	101.56422	236.91144	151	2.40674	100.20010	241.15585
152	2.27302	103.39625	235.01897	152	2.34575	101.99052	239.24406	152	2.42078	100.61320	243.56259
153	2.28524	103.83282	237.29199	153	2.35894	102.41444	241.58961	153	2.43490	101.02389	245.98338
154	2.29772	104.26804	239.57834	154	2.37221	102.83599	243.94876	154	2.44911	101.43220	248.41827
155	2.31016	104.70090	241.87605	155	2.38556	103.25510	246.32097	155	2.46339	101.83814	250.86739
156	2.32268	105.13144	244.11622	156	2.39897	103.67203	248.70653	156	2.47776	102.24174	253.33078
157	2.33526	105.55066	246.50888	157	2.41247	104.08654	251.10550	157	2.49222	102.64298	255.80855
158	2.34791	105.98557	248.84415	158	2.42604	104.49873	253.51796	158	2.50675	103.04191	258.30075
159	2.36062	106.40919	251.19205	159	2.43968	104.90862	255.94400	159	2.52138	103.43851	260.80750
160	2.37341	106.83052	253.55267	160	2.45341	105.31622	258.38370	160	2.53609	103.83282	263.32889
161	2.38627	107.24959	255.96609	161	2.46721	105.72153	260.83710	161	2.55088	104.22485	265.86496
162	2.39919	107.66640	258.31235	162	2.48109	106.12459	263.30429	162	2.56576	104.61459	268.41586
163	2.41219	108.08096	260.71155	163	2.49504	106.52538	265.78540	163	2.58073	105.00208	270.98160
164	2.42525	108.43329	263.12372	164	2.50908	106.92393	268.28043	164	2.59578	105.38732	273.56235
165	2.43839	108.90339	265.54898	165	2.52319	107.32026	270.78952	165	2.61092	105.77032	276.15811
166	2.45160	109.31125	267.98737	166	2.53738	107.71436	273.31271	166	2.62615	106.15112	278.76904
167	2.46488	109.71691	270.43896	167	2.55166	108.10628	275.85010	167	2.64147	106.52969	281.39520
168	2.47823	110.12050	272.90384	168	2.56601	108.49598	278.40173	168	2.65688	106.90607	284.03665
169	2.49165	110.52192	275.38208	169	2.58044	108.88351	280.96774	169	2.67238	107.28027	286.69354
170	2.50515	110.92102	277.87372	170	2.59496	109.26887	283.54819	170	2.68797	107.65230	289.36594
171	2.51872	111.31805	280.37888	171	2.60956	109.65208	286.14316	171	2.70365	108.02217	292.05389
172	2.53236	111.71294	282.89758	172	2.62423	110.03314	288.75272	172	2.71942	108.38989	294.75754
173	2.54608	112.10570	285.42996	173	2.63900	110.41207	291.37695	173	2.73528	108.75549	297.47696
174	2.55987	112.49634	287.97604	174	2.65384	110.78889	294.01553	174	2.75124	109.11896	300.21225
175	2.57374	112.88488	290.53589	175	2.66877	111.16359	296.66977	175	2.76729	109.48032	302.96347

176	2.58768	113.27133	176	2.68379	111.53619	259.33853	176	2.78343	109.83969	305.73077
177	2.60169	113.65569	177	2.69888	111.90872	302.02231	177	2.79967	110.19678	308.51419
178	2.61579	114.03799	178	2.71406	112.27518	304.72119	178	2.81600	110.55190	311.31387
179	2.62996	114.41822	179	2.72932	112.64156	307.43524	179	2.83242	110.90496	314.12985
180	2.64420	114.73641	180	2.74468	113.00591	310.16458	180	2.84895	111.25596	316.96228
181	2.65852	115.17255	181	2.76011	113.36821	312.90924	181	2.86557	111.60459	319.81122
182	2.67292	115.54668	182	2.77564	113.72849	315.66937	182	2.88228	111.96187	322.67679
183	2.68740	115.91879	183	2.79125	114.08675	318.44501	183	2.89909	112.29681	325.55908
184	2.70196	116.28889	184	2.80696	114.44301	321.23627	184	2.91601	112.63974	328.45816
185	2.71659	116.65700	185	2.82274	114.79727	324.04321	185	2.93302	112.96069	331.37418
186	2.73131	117.02312	186	2.83962	115.14956	326.86597	186	2.95013	113.31966	334.30719
187	2.74610	117.38728	187	2.85459	115.49987	329.70459	187	2.96733	113.65666	337.25732
188	2.76099	117.74547	188	2.87065	115.84822	332.55917	188	2.98464	113.99171	340.22464
189	2.77552	118.10970	189	2.88679	116.19463	335.42981	189	3.00205	114.32481	343.20929
190	2.79097	118.46800	190	2.90303	116.53910	336.31662	190	3.01957	114.65599	346.21136
191	2.80609	118.82437	191	2.91936	116.88164	341.21964	191	3.03718	114.98524	349.23033
192	2.82129	119.17882	192	2.93578	117.22226	344.13901	192	3.05490	115.31258	352.26810
193	2.83657	119.53136	193	2.95230	117.56098	347.07477	193	3.07272	115.63803	355.32300
194	2.85193	119.88200	194	2.96890	117.89780	350.02707	194	3.09064	115.96159	358.39572
195	2.86738	120.23074	195	2.98560	118.23275	352.99597	195	3.10867	116.28326	361.48636
196	2.88291	120.57761	196	3.00240	118.56581	355.98157	196	3.12680	116.60308	364.59503
197	2.89853	120.92262	197	3.01928	118.89702	358.98398	197	3.14504	116.92104	367.72183
198	2.91423	121.26576	198	3.03627	119.22637	362.00327	198	3.16339	117.23716	370.86688
199	2.93002	121.60706	199	3.05335	119.55388	365.03952	199	3.18184	117.55145	374.03027
200	2.94589	121.94651	200	3.07052	119.87955	368.09286	200	3.20040	117.86390	377.21210

Table 1. (continued) Annuities

M	C(6.50,M,12)	A(6.50,M,12)	S(6.50,M,12)	M	C(6.75,M,12)	A(6.75,M,12)	S(6.75,M,12)	M	C(7.00,M,12)	A(7.00,M,12)	S(7.00,M,12)
201	2.96184	122.28414	362.19649	201	3.08779	120.20341	371.16339	201	3.21907	118.17455	380.41251
202	2.97789	122.61996	365.14835	202	3.10516	120.52546	374.25119	202	3.23786	118.48340	383.63159
203	2.99402	122.95396	368.13622	203	3.12263	120.84570	377.35635	203	3.25674	118.77045	386.86945
204	3.01023	123.28615	371.12024	204	3.14019	121.16415	380.47900	204	3.27574	119.09673	390.12616
205	3.02654	123.61656	374.13046	205	3.15796	121.48082	383.61917	205	3.29484	119.39923	393.40192
206	3.04293	123.94519	377.15701	206	3.17562	121.79572	386.77704	206	3.31406	119.70097	396.69675
207	3.05942	124.27205	380.19995	207	3.19348	122.10886	389.95267	207	3.33340	120.00097	400.01090
208	3.07599	124.59718	383.25937	208	3.21145	122.42024	393.14615	208	3.35284	120.28922	403.34421
209	3.09265	124.92049	386.33536	209	3.22951	122.72989	396.35760	209	3.37240	120.58675	406.69705
210	3.10940	125.24210	389.42801	210	3.24761	123.03780	399.58710	210	3.39207	120.89056	410.06946
211	3.12624	125.56197	392.53741	211	3.26595	123.34339	402.83478	211	3.41186	121.18365	413.46152
212	3.14318	125.88012	395.66364	212	3.28432	123.64847	406.10074	212	3.43176	121.47504	416.87338
213	3.16020	126.19656	398.80682	213	3.30279	123.96124	409.38504	213	3.45178	121.76476	420.30515
214	3.17732	126.51128	401.96704	214	3.32137	124.25233	412.68784	214	3.47192	122.05278	423.75698
215	3.19453	126.82433	405.14435	215	3.34005	124.55172	416.00922	215	3.49217	122.33913	427.22885
216	3.21184	127.13567	408.33890	216	3.35884	124.84944	419.34924	216	3.51254	122.62383	430.72101
217	3.22923	127.44534	411.55072	217	3.37773	125.14550	422.70810	217	3.53303	122.90687	434.23355
218	3.24672	127.75334	414.77997	218	3.39673	125.43990	426.08592	218	3.55364	123.18827	437.76657
219	3.26431	128.05968	418.02667	219	3.41584	125.73265	429.48257	219	3.57437	123.46804	441.32022
220	3.28199	128.36438	421.29099	220	3.43505	126.02377	432.89841	220	3.59522	123.74619	444.89459
221	3.29977	128.66743	424.57300	221	3.45438	126.31326	436.33347	221	3.61619	124.02272	448.48981
222	3.31764	128.96884	427.87274	222	3.47381	126.60113	439.76784	222	3.63728	124.29765	452.10599
223	3.33561	129.26865	431.19040	223	3.49335	126.88738	443.26163	223	3.65850	124.57099	455.74326
224	3.35368	129.56682	434.52600	224	3.51300	127.17204	446.75497	224	3.67984	124.84274	459.40179
225	3.37185	129.86339	437.87970	225	3.53276	127.46511	450.26797	225	3.70131	125.11292	463.08163

n										
226	3.39011	130.15837	441.25156	3.55263	127.79859	3.72290	125.38152	453.80075	468.78283
227	3.40848	130.45175	444.64166	3.57261	128.01649	3.74462	125.64857	457.35336	470.50583
228	3.42694	130.74356	448.05014	3.59271	128.29483	3.76646	125.91407	460.92599	474.25046
229	3.44550	131.03380	451.45708	3.61292	128.57162	3.78843	126.17803	464.51868	478.01691
230	3.46416	131.32246	454.52258	3.63324	128.84685	3.81053	126.44047	468.13162	481.80536
231	3.48288	131.60957	458.39675	3.65368	129.12054	3.83276	126.70137	471.76496	485.61588
232	3.50179	131.89514	461.86966	3.67423	129.39272	3.85512	126.96077	475.41852	489.44864
233	3.52076	132.17918	465.37146	3.69490	129.66336	3.87761	127.21866	479.09274	493.30374
234	3.53983	132.46167	468.89221	3.71568	129.93250	3.90022	127.47506	482.78766	497.18137
235	3.55901	132.74266	472.43204	3.73658	130.20012	3.92298	127.72997	486.50333	501.08157
236	3.57828	133.02213	475.99106	3.75760	130.46625	3.94586	127.98340	490.23990	505.00455
237	3.59767	133.30008	479.56934	3.77874	130.73068	3.96888	128.23535	493.99750	508.96041
238	3.61715	133.57654	483.16702	3.79999	130.99403	3.99203	128.48586	497.77625	512.91931
239	3.63675	133.85150	486.78418	3.82137	131.25572	4.01532	128.73489	501.57623	516.91132
240	3.65645	134.12500	490.42093	3.84286	131.51595	4.03874	128.98250	505.39761	520.90664
241	3.67625	134.39702	494.07736	3.86448	131.77472	4.06230	129.22867	509.24048	524.98539
242	3.69617	134.66756	497.75360	3.88622	132.03203	4.08599	129.47340	513.10492	529.02765
243	3.71619	134.93666	501.44977	3.90808	132.28792	4.10983	129.71672	516.99115	533.11365
244	3.73632	135.20430	505.16595	3.93006	132.54236	4.13380	129.95863	520.89923	537.22351
245	3.75655	135.47050	508.90228	3.95216	132.79539	4.15792	130.19914	524.82928	541.35730
246	3.77690	135.73528	512.65891	3.97440	133.04700	4.18217	130.43825	528.78143	545.51620
247	3.79736	135.99861	516.43573	3.99675	133.29721	4.20657	130.67596	532.75586	549.67939
248	3.81793	136.26053	520.23309	4.01923	133.54601	4.23111	130.91231	536.75256	553.90393
249	3.83861	136.52104	524.05103	4.04184	133.79343	4.25579	131.14729	540.77185	558.13507
250	3.85940	136.78015	527.88965	4.06458	134.03944	4.28061	131.38091	544.81368	562.39037

Table 1. (continued) Annuities

M	CI(6.50,M,12)	AI(6.50,M,12)	SI(6.50,M,12)	M	CI(6.75,M,12)	AI(6.75,M,12)	SI(6.75,M,12)	M	CI(7.00,M,12)	AI(7.00,M,12)	SI(7.00,M,12)
251	3.88031	137.03786	531.74302	251	4.08744	134.28410	548.87823	251	4.30558	131.61316	566.67145
252	3.90133	137.29419	535.62833	252	4.11043	134.52739	552.96570	252	4.33070	131.84407	570.97705
253	3.92246	137.54913	539.53064	253	4.13355	134.76930	557.07611	253	4.35596	132.07364	575.30774
254	3.94370	137.80269	543.45313	254	4.15680	135.00987	561.20966	254	4.38137	132.30188	579.66370
255	3.96507	138.05490	547.39679	255	4.18019	135.24910	565.36646	255	4.40693	132.52879	584.04510
256	3.98654	138.30574	551.36188	256	4.20370	135.48698	569.54669	256	4.43264	132.75439	588.45203
257	4.00814	138.55524	555.34845	257	4.22735	135.72354	573.75037	257	4.45849	132.97868	592.88464
258	4.02985	138.80338	559.35657	258	4.25112	135.95877	577.97772	258	4.48450	133.20168	597.34314
259	4.05168	139.05020	563.39641	259	4.27504	136.19269	582.22882	259	4.51066	133.42337	601.82764
260	4.07362	139.29567	567.43811	260	4.29908	136.42529	586.50385	260	4.53697	133.64378	606.33832
261	4.09568	139.53984	571.51172	261	4.32327	136.65660	590.80298	261	4.56344	133.86292	610.87531
262	4.11787	139.78268	575.60742	262	4.34758	136.88661	595.12622	262	4.59006	134.08078	615.43872
263	4.14018	140.02422	579.72528	263	4.37204	137.11534	599.47382	263	4.61683	134.29738	620.02875
264	4.16260	140.26445	583.86548	264	4.39663	137.34279	603.84563	264	4.64377	134.51271	624.64563
265	4.18515	140.50339	588.02808	265	4.42136	137.56897	608.24249	265	4.67085	134.72681	629.28837
266	4.20782	140.74104	592.21320	266	4.44623	137.79387	612.66382	266	4.69810	134.93967	633.96021
267	4.23061	140.97742	596.42102	267	4.47124	138.01752	617.11011	267	4.72551	135.15128	638.65833
268	4.25353	141.21251	600.65167	268	4.49639	138.23993	621.58130	268	4.75307	135.36166	643.38386
269	4.27657	141.44635	604.90515	269	4.52169	138.46107	626.07770	269	4.78080	135.57083	648.13690
270	4.29973	141.67891	609.18176	270	4.54712	138.68100	630.59943	270	4.80869	135.77879	652.91772
271	4.32302	141.91023	613.48151	271	4.57270	138.89969	635.14655	271	4.83674	135.98555	657.72638
272	4.34644	142.14030	617.80450	272	4.59842	139.11716	639.71924	272	4.86496	136.19110	662.56311
273	4.36998	142.36914	622.15094	273	4.62429	139.33340	644.31763	273	4.89333	136.39546	667.42810
274	4.39365	142.59674	626.52094	274	4.65030	139.54845	648.94196	274	4.92188	136.59863	672.32141
275	4.41745	142.82312	630.91461	275	4.67646	139.76228	653.59222	275	4.95059	136.80063	677.24329

n				n				n			
276	4.44138	143.04828	635.33203	276	4.70276	139.97493	658.26868	276	4.97946	137.00145	682.19391
277	4.46544	143.27222	639.77344	277	4.72921	140.18637	662.97144	277	5.00851	137.20111	687.17334
278	4.48963	143.49495	644.25944	278	4.75582	140.39664	667.70068	278	5.03773	137.39981	692.18182
279	4.51395	143.71649	648.72852	279	4.78257	140.60573	672.45648	279	5.06711	137.59697	697.21960
280	4.53840	143.93683	653.24243	280	4.80947	140.81366	677.23907	280	5.09667	137.73917	702.28668
281	4.56298	144.15599	657.78082	281	4.83652	141.02042	682.04852	281	5.12640	137.98824	707.38336
282	4.58770	144.37396	662.34381	282	4.86373	141.22603	686.88507	282	5.15631	138.18217	712.50377
283	4.61255	144.59076	666.93152	283	4.89109	141.43048	691.74878	283	5.18639	138.37498	717.66608
284	4.63753	144.80640	671.54407	284	4.91860	141.63379	696.63983	284	5.21664	138.56668	722.85248
285	4.66265	145.02086	676.18158	285	4.94627	141.83595	701.55847	285	5.24707	138.75726	728.06909
286	4.68791	145.23418	680.84424	286	4.97409	142.03700	706.50470	286	5.27768	138.94675	733.31616
287	4.71330	145.44633	685.53217	287	5.00207	142.23692	711.47882	287	5.30846	139.13513	738.53997
288	4.73883	145.65736	690.24542	288	5.03020	142.43571	716.48090	288	5.33943	139.32240	743.90234
289	4.76450	145.86725	694.98425	289	5.05850	142.63341	721.51111	289	5.37058	139.50861	749.24476
290	4.79031	146.07600	699.74878	290	5.08695	142.82999	726.56968	290	5.40191	139.69373	754.61230
291	4.81625	146.28363	704.53908	291	5.11557	143.02547	731.65656	291	5.43342	139.87778	760.01422
292	4.84234	146.49014	709.35535	292	5.14434	143.21985	736.77209	292	5.46511	140.06076	765.44763
293	4.86857	146.69554	714.19769	293	5.17328	143.41316	741.91644	293	5.49699	140.24268	770.91279
294	4.89494	146.89984	719.06622	294	5.20238	143.60538	747.08972	294	5.52906	140.42354	776.40973
295	4.92146	147.10303	723.96118	295	5.23164	143.79652	752.29211	295	5.56131	140.60335	781.93078
296	4.94811	147.30513	728.88263	296	5.26107	143.98660	757.52374	296	5.59375	140.78212	787.50012
297	4.97492	147.50613	733.83075	297	5.29066	144.17561	762.78485	297	5.62638	140.95986	793.03387
298	5.00186	147.70605	738.80566	298	5.32042	144.36356	768.07550	298	5.65920	141.13655	798.72028
299	5.02896	147.90491	743.80726	299	5.35035	144.55046	773.39594	299	5.69221	141.31224	804.37946
300	5.05620	148.10269	748.83649	300	5.38045	144.73633	778.74628	300	5.72542	141.49689	810.07166

Table 1. (continued) Annuities

M	C(6.50,M,12)	A(6.50,M,12)	S(6.50,M,12)	M	C(6.75,M,12)	A(6.75,M,12)	S(6.75,M,12)	M	C(7.00,M,12)	A(7.00,M,12)	S(7.00,M,12)
301	5.08359	148.29939	753.89270	301	5.41071	144.92114	784.12871	301	5.75882	141.66054	815.79706
302	5.11112	148.49506	758.97628	302	5.44115	145.10493	789.53941	302	5.79241	141.83318	821.55591
303	5.13881	148.68985	764.08740	303	5.47175	145.28769	794.97858	303	5.82620	142.00492	827.34833
304	5.16664	148.88319	769.22620	304	5.50253	145.46542	800.45032	304	5.86018	142.17546	833.17450
305	5.19463	149.07570	774.39282	305	5.53348	145.65013	805.96288	305	5.89437	142.34512	839.03467
306	5.22277	149.26717	779.58746	306	5.56461	145.82985	811.49633	306	5.92875	142.51379	844.92908
307	5.25106	149.45761	784.81024	307	5.59591	146.00854	817.05096	307	5.96334	142.68147	850.85779
308	5.27950	149.64702	790.06128	308	5.62739	146.16625	822.64685	308	5.99812	142.84819	856.82117
309	5.30810	149.83542	795.34082	309	5.65904	146.36236	828.27429	309	6.03311	143.01395	862.81927
310	5.33685	150.02280	800.64896	310	5.69087	146.53868	833.92421	310	6.06831	143.17874	868.85236
311	5.36576	150.20915	805.98572	311	5.72289	146.71341	839.82421	311	6.10370	143.34258	874.92072
312	5.39482	150.39452	811.35150	312	5.75508	146.88718	845.54705	312	6.13931	143.50548	881.02441
313	5.42404	150.57889	816.74634	313	5.78745	147.05997	851.10217	313	6.17512	143.66740	887.16370
314	5.45342	150.76225	822.17035	314	5.82000	147.23178	856.88959	314	6.21114	143.82840	893.33881
315	5.48296	150.94464	827.62378	315	5.85274	147.40265	862.70959	315	6.24737	143.98846	899.54999
316	5.51266	151.12604	833.10675	316	5.88566	147.57254	868.56232	316	6.28382	144.14761	905.79736
317	5.54252	151.30646	838.61938	317	5.91877	147.74150	874.44800	317	6.32047	144.30582	912.08118
318	5.57254	151.48592	844.16193	318	5.95206	147.90952	880.36678	318	6.35734	144.46312	918.40161
319	5.60273	151.66440	849.73450	319	5.98554	148.07658	886.31885	319	6.39443	144.61951	924.75897
320	5.63308	151.84190	855.33722	320	6.01921	148.24271	892.30438	320	6.43173	144.77498	931.15338
321	5.66359	152.01849	860.97028	321	6.05307	148.40791	898.32361	321	6.46925	144.92957	937.58514
322	5.69427	152.19411	866.63385	322	6.08712	148.57220	904.37665	322	6.50698	145.08325	944.05438
323	5.72511	152.36877	872.32813	323	6.12136	148.73557	910.46381	323	6.54494	145.23604	950.56134
324	5.75612	152.54250	878.05322	324	6.15579	148.89801	916.58514	324	6.58312	145.38794	957.10632
325	5.78730	152.71529	883.80339	325	6.19042	149.05956	922.74091	325	6.62152	145.53896	963.68945

n				n				n			
326	5.81865	152.88716	889.59668	326	6.22524	149.22018	928.59134	326	6.66015	145.68910	970.31097
327	5.85017	153.05809	896.41534	327	6.26026	149.37993	935.15662	327	6.69400	145.83838	976.97107
328	5.88185	153.22810	901.26550	328	6.29547	149.53877	941.41687	328	6.73808	145.98680	983.67010
329	5.9137	153.39720	907.14734	329	6.33088	149.69673	947.71234	329	6.77738	146.13434	990.40814
330	5.94575	153.56538	913.06104	330	6.36649	149.85381	954.04321	330	6.81692	146.28104	997.18555
331	5.97796	153.73267	919.00677	331	6.40230	150.00999	960.40967	331	6.85668	146.42688	1004.00244
332	6.01033	153.89905	924.98474	332	6.43832	150.16531	966.81201	332	6.89668	146.57188	1010.85913
333	6.04289	154.06453	930.99512	333	6.47453	150.31976	973.25031	333	6.93691	146.71603	1017.75560
334	6.07562	154.22913	937.03796	334	6.51095	150.47334	979.72485	334	6.97737	146.85936	1024.69275
335	6.10853	154.39284	943.11359	335	6.54758	150.62608	986.23578	335	7.01808	147.00186	1031.67004
336	6.14162	154.55565	949.22211	336	6.58441	150.77795	992.78339	336	7.05901	147.14351	1038.68811
337	6.17489	154.71761	955.36377	337	6.62144	150.92897	999.36760	337	7.10019	147.28435	1045.74719
338	6.20833	154.87868	961.53864	338	6.65969	151.07916	1005.98920	338	7.14161	147.42438	1052.84741
339	6.24196	155.03888	967.74695	339	6.69614	151.22850	1012.64789	339	7.18327	147.56358	1059.98901
340	6.27577	155.19823	973.98895	340	6.73381	151.37700	1019.34406	340	7.22517	147.70200	1067.17224
341	6.30977	155.35672	980.26471	341	6.77169	151.52467	1026.07788	341	7.26732	147.83960	1074.39746
342	6.34396	155.51434	986.57446	342	6.80978	151.67152	1032.84949	342	7.30971	147.97639	1081.66479
343	6.37831	155.67113	992.91840	343	6.84808	151.81755	1039.65380	343	7.35235	148.11241	1088.97449
344	6.41286	155.82708	999.29675	344	6.88660	151.96275	1046.50745	344	7.39524	148.24763	1096.32678
345	6.44759	155.98218	1005.70969	345	6.92534	152.10716	1053.39404	345	7.43838	148.38206	1103.72205
346	6.48252	156.13641	1012.15717	346	6.96430	152.25076	1060.31384	346	7.48177	148.51573	1111.16040
347	6.51763	156.28984	1018.63971	347	7.00437	152.39356	1067.28369	347	7.52541	148.64861	1118.64221
348	6.55294	156.44244	1025.15705	348	7.04287	152.53552	1074.28711	348	7.56931	148.78072	1126.16760
349	6.58843	156.59422	1031.71021	349	7.08248	152.67671	1081.32996	349	7.61347	148.91206	1133.73694
350	6.62412	156.74519	1038.26671	350	7.12232	152.81711	1088.41248	350	7.65788	149.04265	1141.35034

Table 1. (continued) Annuities

M	C(6.50,M,12)	A(6.50,M,12)	S(6.50,M,12)	M	C(6.75,M,12)	A(6.75,M,12)	S(6.75,M,12)	M	C(7.00,M,12)	A(7.00,M,12)	S(7.00,M,12)
351	6.66000	156.89534	1044.92273	351	7.16238	152.95674	1095.53479	351	7.70255	149.17249	1149.00830
352	6.63607	157.04469	1051.58276	352	7.20267	153.09557	1102.69714	352	7.74748	149.30156	1156.71082
353	6.73234	157.13222	1056.27881	353	7.24319	153.23363	1109.89978	353	7.79267	149.42989	1164.45825
354	6.76881	157.34036	1065.01123	354	7.28393	153.37093	1117.14307	354	7.83813	149.55746	1172.25098
355	6.80548	157.43405	1071.78003	355	7.32490	153.50745	1124.42700	355	7.88385	149.68430	1180.08911
356	6.84234	157.49405	1078.58545	356	7.36610	153.64320	1131.75193	356	7.92984	149.81041	1188.97290
357	6.87940	157.77940	1085.42746	357	7.40754	153.77820	1139.11792	357	7.97610	149.93578	1196.00283
358	6.91666	157.92398	1092.30725	358	7.44921	153.91246	1146.52551	358	8.02263	150.06042	1203.87891
359	6.95413	158.06779	1099.22388	359	7.49111	154.04598	1153.97473	359	8.06943	150.18436	1211.90149
360	6.99180	158.21082	1106.17798	360	7.53325	154.17868	1161.46582	360	8.11650	150.30756	1219.97095
361	7.02967	158.35307	1113.16990	361	7.57562	154.31068	1168.99902	361	8.16384	150.43005	1228.08740
362	7.06775	158.49455	1120.19946	362	7.61823	154.44194	1176.57471	362	8.21147	150.55183	1236.25122
363	7.10603	158.63528	1127.26721	363	7.66109	154.57246	1184.19287	363	8.25937	150.67291	1244.46277
364	7.14452	158.77525	1134.37329	364	7.70418	154.70227	1191.85400	364	8.30755	150.79327	1252.72217
365	7.18322	158.91446	1141.45746	365	7.74751	154.83134	1199.55811	365	8.35601	150.91295	1261.02986
366	7.22213	159.05292	1148.70105	366	7.79109	154.95970	1207.30566	366	8.40475	151.03194	1269.38562
367	7.26125	159.19064	1155.92310	367	7.83492	155.08733	1215.09680	367	8.45378	151.15022	1277.79041
368	7.30058	159.32762	1163.18445	368	7.87899	155.21425	1222.93164	368	8.50309	151.26782	1286.24414
369	7.34013	159.46385	1170.48499	369	7.92331	155.34045	1230.81067	369	8.55269	151.38475	1294.74731
370	7.37989	159.59935	1177.82507	370	7.96788	155.46596	1238.73401	370	8.60258	151.50099	1303.29993
371	7.41986	159.73413	1185.20496	371	8.01270	155.59076	1246.70190	371	8.65276	151.61656	1311.90259
372	7.46005	159.86818	1192.62488	372	8.05777	155.71487	1254.71460	372	8.70324	151.73146	1320.55530
373	7.50046	160.00150	1200.08496	373	8.10309	155.83827	1262.77234	373	8.75401	151.84570	1329.25854
374	7.54109	160.13411	1207.58533	374	8.14867	155.96100	1270.87549	374	8.80507	151.95927	1338.01257
375	7.58193	160.26601	1215.12646	375	8.19451	156.08304	1279.02417	375	8.85644	152.07217	1346.81763

n							n			
376	7.62300	160.39719	1222.70837	8.24060	156.20438	1287.21963	376	8.90810	152.18443	1355.67407
377	7.66430	160.52766	1230.33142	8.28636	156.32506	1296.45683	377	8.96006	152.28605	1364.58215
378	7.70581	160.65742	1237.99573	8.33357	156.44505	1303.74622	378	9.01233	152.40700	1373.54224
379	7.74755	160.76650	1245.70154	8.38045	156.56438	1312.07971	379	9.06490	152.51732	1382.55457
380	7.78952	160.91489	1253.44910	8.42759	156.68303	1320.46021	380	9.11778	152.62700	1391.61951
381	7.83171	161.04257	1261.23853	8.47499	156.80103	1328.88782	381	9.17097	152.73604	1400.73730
382	7.87413	161.16957	1269.07031	8.52267	156.91837	1337.36279	382	9.22446	152.84444	1409.90820
383	7.91678	161.29588	1276.94446	8.57061	157.03503	1345.88550	383	9.27827	152.95222	1419.13269
384	7.95966	161.42151	1284.86121	8.61882	157.15106	1354.45605	384	9.33240	153.05937	1428.41101
385	8.00278	161.54646	1292.82060	8.66730	157.26643	1363.07483	385	9.38684	153.16591	1437.74341
386	8.04613	161.67076	1300.82361	8.71605	157.38116	1371.74219	386	9.44159	153.27192	1447.13025
387	8.08971	161.79437	1308.96975	8.76508	157.49525	1380.45825	387	9.49667	153.37712	1456.57178
388	8.13353	161.91731	1316.95947	8.81438	157.60872	1389.22327	388	9.55207	153.48181	1466.06848
389	8.17759	162.03960	1325.09302	8.86396	157.72153	1398.03772	389	9.60779	153.58589	1475.62048
390	8.22188	162.16122	1333.27063	8.91382	157.83371	1406.90161	390	9.66383	153.68938	1485.22827
391	8.26642	162.28220	1341.49243	8.96396	157.94527	1415.81543	391	9.72020	153.79225	1494.89209
392	8.31119	162.40251	1349.75891	9.01438	158.05620	1424.77542	392	9.77651	153.89453	1504.61230
393	8.35621	162.52219	1358.07007	9.06509	158.16652	1433.73382	393	9.83394	153.99622	1514.38928
394	8.40146	162.64122	1366.42627	9.11608	158.27621	1442.85589	394	9.89930	154.05732	1524.22314
395	8.44698	162.75960	1374.82760	9.16736	158.38530	1451.97498	395	9.94900	154.19783	1534.11450
396	8.49274	162.87735	1383.27478	9.21893	158.49377	1461.14233	396	10.00704	154.29776	1544.06348
397	8.53874	162.99446	1391.76746	9.27078	158.60164	1470.36133	397	10.06541	154.39711	1554.07056
398	8.58499	163.11096	1400.30627	9.32293	158.70889	1479.63208	398	10.12413	154.45888	1564.13599
399	8.63149	163.22681	1408.89124	9.37537	158.81557	1488.95496	399	10.18318	154.59409	1574.26013
400	8.67825	163.34203	1417.52271	9.42811	158.92163	1498.33032	400	10.24259	154.69973	1584.44324

Table 1. (continued) Annuities

M	C(6.50,M,12)	A(6.50,M,12)	S(6.50,M,12)	M	C(6.75,M,12)	A(6.75,M,12)	S(6.75,M,12)	M	C(7.00,M,12)	A(7.00,M,12)	S(7.00,M,12)
401	8.72526	163.45663	1426.20038	401	9.48114	159.02710	1507.75842	401	10.30233	154.78879	1594.88579
402	8.77292	163.57063	1434.92627	402	9.53447	159.12117	1517.23960	402	10.36243	154.88528	1604.98016
403	8.82003	163.68473	1443.68810	403	9.58810	159.29628	1526.77405	403	10.42288	154.98123	1615.35059
404	8.86701	163.79878	1452.51890	404	9.64204	159.34000	1536.36218	404	10.48368	155.07661	1625.77344
405	8.91414	163.90894	1461.38660	405	9.69627	159.44312	1546.00427	405	10.54483	155.17145	1636.25920
406	8.96114	164.02049	1470.30249	406	9.75082	159.54767	1555.70044	406	10.60635	155.26573	1646.80260
407	9.01269	164.13145	1479.26640	407	9.80566	159.64766	1565.45129	407	10.66821	155.35947	1657.40833
408	9.06151	164.24151	1488.27980	408	9.86082	159.74907	1575.25696	408	10.73045	155.45267	1668.07854
409	9.11060	164.35156	1497.34082	409	9.91629	159.84997	1585.11780	409	10.79304	155.54532	1678.80701
410	9.15994	164.46074	1506.45142	410	9.97207	159.94991	1595.03406	410	10.85600	155.63744	1689.60010
411	9.20956	164.56932	1515.61133	411	10.02616	160.04991	1605.00610	411	10.91933	155.72902	1700.45605
412	9.25945	164.67732	1524.82092	412	10.08457	160.14508	1615.03430	412	10.98302	155.82005	1711.37537
413	9.30960	164.78473	1534.08032	413	10.14129	160.24768	1625.11890	413	11.04709	155.91058	1722.35840
414	9.36003	164.89157	1543.38988	414	10.19834	160.34573	1635.26013	414	11.11153	156.00058	1733.40552
415	9.41073	164.99783	1552.75000	415	10.25570	160.44324	1645.45860	415	11.17635	156.09006	1744.51697
416	9.46170	165.10353	1562.16064	416	10.31339	160.54021	1655.71423	416	11.24154	156.17900	1755.69336
417	9.51296	165.20865	1571.62244	417	10.37141	160.63663	1666.02759	417	11.30712	156.26744	1766.93494
418	9.56448	165.31320	1581.13536	418	10.42974	160.73250	1676.39905	418	11.37308	156.35538	1778.24207
419	9.61629	165.41719	1590.69983	419	10.48841	160.82783	1686.82874	419	11.43942	156.44279	1789.61511
420	9.66838	165.52061	1600.31616	420	10.54741	160.92265	1697.31714	420	11.50615	156.52971	1801.05457
421	9.72075	165.62349	1609.98450	421	10.60674	161.01694	1707.86462	421	11.57327	156.61610	1812.56067
422	9.77340	165.72581	1619.70520	422	10.66640	161.11069	1718.47131	422	11.64078	156.70201	1824.13391
423	9.82634	165.82758	1629.47864	423	10.72640	161.20392	1729.13770	423	11.70869	156.78741	1835.77478
424	9.87957	165.92879	1639.30505	424	10.78674	161.29663	1739.86414	424	11.77699	156.87233	1847.48340
425	9.93308	166.02946	1649.18457	425	10.84741	161.38881	1750.65088	425	11.84569	156.95676	1859.26038

426	8.99689	10.90843	1658.11768	166.12959
427	10.04098	10.96979	1668.10449	166.22919
428	10.09637	11.03149	1679.14551	166.32825
429	10.15005	11.09354	1689.24084	166.42677
430	10.20503	11.15595	1659.39099	166.52477
431	10.26031	11.21870	1709.15985	166.62222
432	10.31589	11.28180	1719.85632	166.71916
433	10.37177	11.34526	1730.17224	166.81556
434	10.42795	11.40906	1740.54395	166.91147
435	10.48443	11.47326	1750.97192	167.00685
436	10.54122	11.53779	1761.45630	167.10172
437	10.59832	11.60269	1771.99756	167.19608
438	10.65573	11.66796	1782.59683	167.28992
439	10.71345	11.73359	1793.25159	167.38326
440	10.77148	11.79958	1803.96609	167.47609
441	10.82982	11.86597	1814.73657	167.56844
442	10.88848	11.93271	1825.56641	167.66028
443	10.94746	11.99983	1836.45483	167.75162
444	11.00676	12.06733	1847.40234	167.84247
445	11.06638	12.13521	1858.40906	167.93283
446	11.12633	12.20347	1869.47646	168.02272
447	11.18659	12.27212	1880.60181	168.11211
448	11.24719	12.34115	1891.78833	168.20102
449	11.30811	12.41057	1903.03552	168.28944
450	11.36856	12.48038	1914.34363	168.37741

426	11.91479	1761.49826	161.49048	157.04068	1871.10608
427	11.98429	1772.40674	161.57164	157.12411	1883.02087
428	12.05420	1783.37646	161.66229	157.20708	1895.00513
429	12.12451	1794.40798	161.75244	157.28955	1907.05803
430	12.19524	1805.50159	161.84207	157.37155	1919.18384
431	12.26638	1816.65747	161.93121	157.45308	1931.37915
432	12.33788	1827.87622	162.01985	157.53413	1943.64551
433	12.40990	1839.15736	162.10799	157.61472	1955.98340
434	12.48229	1850.50330	162.19565	157.69482	1968.33031
435	12.55511	1861.91235	162.28281	157.77448	1980.87561
436	12.62835	1873.38562	162.36948	157.85367	1993.43079
437	12.70201	1884.92334	162.45566	157.93239	2006.05908
438	12.77611	1896.52612	162.54137	158.01067	2018.76111
439	12.85063	1908.19197	162.62659	158.08847	2031.53723
440	12.92560	1919.92781	162.71133	158.16585	2044.38780
441	13.00099	1931.72717	162.79561	158.24277	2057.31348
442	13.07683	1943.58314	162.87941	158.31923	2070.31445
443	13.15312	1955.52588	162.96275	158.39526	2083.39111
444	13.22994	1967.52576	163.04562	158.47084	2096.54443
445	13.30702	1979.59302	163.12802	158.54599	2109.77417
446	13.38464	1991.72827	163.20996	158.62071	2123.08130
447	13.46272	2003.93176	163.29146	158.69499	2136.46582
448	13.54125	2016.20386	163.37248	158.76893	2149.92847
449	13.62024	2028.54504	163.45306	158.84225	2163.46973
450	13.68969	2040.96557	163.53319	158.91525	2177.09009

Table 1. (continued) Annuities

M	C(6.50,M,12)	A(6.50,M,12)	S(6.50,M,12)	M	C(6.75,M,12)	A(6.75,M,12)	S(6.75,M,12)	M	C(7.00,M,12)	A(7.00,M,12)	S(7.00,M,12)
451	11.43095	168.46489	1905.71301	451	12.55058	163.61287	2053.43579	451	13.77961	158.98782	2190.78879
452	11.49286	168.55190	1937.14392	452	12.62117	163.69209	2065.98657	452	13.85999	159.05997	2204.56934
453	11.55512	166.63844	1948.63684	453	12.69217	163.77089	2078.60767	453	13.94084	159.13170	2218.42944
454	11.61771	168.72452	1960.19189	454	12.76356	163.84923	2091.29990	454	14.02216	159.20302	2232.37012
455	11.68064	168.81012	1971.80969	455	12.83536	163.92714	2104.06348	455	14.10396	159.27398	2246.39233
456	11.74391	168.89528	1983.49203	456	12.90756	164.00461	2116.89968	456	14.18623	159.34449	2260.49634
457	11.80752	168.97997	1995.23425	457	12.98016	164.08165	2129.60640	457	14.26898	159.41449	2274.68262
458	11.87148	169.06421	2007.04170	458	13.05317	164.15826	2142.78638	458	14.35222	159.48416	2288.95142
459	11.93578	169.14798	2018.91321	459	13.12660	164.23446	2155.03980	459	14.43594	159.55344	2303.30371
460	12.00043	169.23132	2030.84900	460	13.20043	164.31020	2168.96631	460	14.52015	159.62231	2317.73975
461	12.06543	169.31419	2042.85397	461	13.27469	164.38553	2182.16675	461	14.60485	159.69078	2332.25977
462	12.13079	169.39664	2054.91479	462	13.34936	164.46044	2195.44141	462	14.69004	159.75885	2346.86475
463	12.19650	169.47862	2067.04565	463	13.42445	164.53493	2208.79077	463	14.77574	159.82654	2361.55469
464	12.26256	169.56017	2079.24215	464	13.49996	164.60901	2222.21509	464	14.86193	159.89381	2376.33032
465	12.32898	169.64128	2091.50464	465	13.57590	164.68266	2235.71509	465	14.94862	159.96071	2391.19818
466	12.39577	169.72195	2103.83350	466	13.65226	164.75592	2249.29102	466	15.03582	160.02722	2406.14097
467	12.46291	169.80219	2116.22949	467	13.72906	164.82875	2262.94336	467	15.12353	160.09334	2421.17676
468	12.53042	169.88200	2128.69638	468	13.80628	164.90118	2276.67236	468	15.21175	160.15909	2436.30029
469	12.59829	169.96138	2141.22966	469	13.88394	164.97321	2290.47652	469	15.30049	160.22444	2451.51221
470	12.66653	170.04033	2153.82104	470	13.96204	165.04483	2304.36255	470	15.38974	160.28941	2466.81250
471	12.73514	170.11885	2166.48755	471	14.04058	165.11606	2318.32471	471	15.47951	160.35402	2482.20239
472	12.80412	170.19695	2179.22266	472	14.11965	165.18687	2332.36523	472	15.56981	160.41824	2497.68198
473	12.87348	170.27463	2192.02686	473	14.19898	165.25731	2346.48462	473	15.66063	160.48210	2513.25171
474	12.94321	170.35188	2204.90039	474	14.27885	165.32735	2360.68359	474	15.75199	160.54558	2528.91235
475	13.01332	170.42873	2217.84351	475	14.35916	165.39699	2374.96265	475	15.84387	160.60870	2544.66431

476	13.08081	170.50516	2230.85660	476	14.43933	2389.32171	165.46623	476	15.93830	160.67145	2560.50906
477	13.15468	170.58110	2243.94067	477	14.52116	2403.76172	165.53510	477	16.02926	160.73394	2575.44434
478	13.22593	170.65678	2257.05821	478	14.60284	2418.28271	165.60358	478	16.12276	160.79685	2592.47363
479	13.29757	170.73199	2270.32129	479	14.68490	2432.88574	165.67168	479	16.21681	160.85753	2608.59644
480	13.36960	170.80678	2283.61890	480	14.76758	2447.57056	165.73940	480	16.31141	160.91884	2624.81323
481	13.44202	170.88118	2296.98828	481	14.85065	2462.33813	165.80673	481	16.40656	160.97978	2641.12476
482	13.51483	170.95517	2310.43042	482	14.93419	2477.18896	165.87369	482	16.50227	161.04037	2657.53125
483	13.58904	171.02876	2323.94531	483	15.01819	2492.12305	165.94028	483	16.59853	161.10063	2674.03345
484	13.66164	171.10196	2337.53320	484	15.10267	2507.14136	166.00648	484	16.69534	161.16052	2690.63208
485	13.73564	171.17477	2351.19482	485	15.18762	2522.24340	166.07233	485	16.79274	161.22008	2707.32739
486	13.81004	171.24718	2364.93066	486	15.27305	2537.43164	166.13780	486	16.89070	161.27928	2724.12012
487	13.88484	171.31920	2378.74072	487	15.35896	2552.70459	166.20291	487	16.98923	161.33813	2741.01074
488	13.96005	171.39084	2392.62543	488	15.44536	2568.06348	166.26765	488	17.08833	161.39665	2758.00000
489	14.03567	171.46208	2406.58545	489	15.53224	2583.50903	166.33205	489	17.18801	161.45483	2775.08838
490	14.11170	171.53294	2420.62109	490	15.61961	2599.04126	166.39606	490	17.28828	161.51268	2792.27637
491	14.18814	171.60342	2434.73291	491	15.70747	2614.66064	166.45973	491	17.38913	161.57019	2809.56470
492	14.26499	171.67352	2448.92114	492	15.79582	2630.36916	166.52304	492	17.49056	161.62737	2826.95386
493	14.34226	171.74326	2463.18604	493	15.88467	2646.16406	166.58598	493	17.59259	161.68420	2844.44434
494	14.41994	171.81259	2477.52832	494	15.97402	2662.04883	166.64859	494	17.69522	161.74072	2862.03711
495	14.49805	171.88158	2491.94824	495	16.06398	2678.02271	166.71085	495	17.79944	161.79657	2879.73218
496	14.57658	171.95018	2506.44629	496	16.15424	2694.06667	166.77275	496	17.90226	161.85275	2897.53076
497	14.65554	172.02295	2521.02295	497	16.24510	2710.24097	166.83430	497	18.00669	161.90829	2915.43286
498	14.73493	172.09627	2535.67847	498	16.33648	2726.49608	166.89552	498	18.11173	161.96350	2933.43970
499	14.81474	172.15378	2550.41333	499	16.42838	2742.82251	166.95619	499	18.21738	162.01840	2951.55127
500	14.89499	172.22092	2565.22903	500	16.52079	2759.25073	167.01692	500	18.32265	162.07297	2969.76880

Table 1. (continued) Annuities

M	C(7.25,M,12)	A(7.25,M,12)	S(7.25,M,12)	M	C(7.50,M,12)	A(7.50,M,12)	S(7.50,M,12)	M	C(7.75,M,12)	A(7.75,M,12)	S(7.75,M,12)
1	1.00604	0.99399	1.00000	1	1.00625	0.99379	1.00000	1	1.00646	0.99358	1.00000
2	1.01212	1.98202	2.00604	2	1.01254	1.98141	2.00625	2	1.01298	1.99079	2.00646
3	1.01823	2.96411	3.01816	3	1.01887	2.96269	3.01879	3	1.01950	2.96166	3.01942
4	1.02439	3.94031	4.03640	4	1.02524	3.93829	4.03766	4	1.02608	3.93624	4.03892
5	1.03058	4.91064	5.06078	5	1.03164	4.90760	5.06289	5	1.03271	4.90457	5.06500
6	1.03680	5.87514	6.09136	6	1.03809	5.87094	6.09453	6	1.03938	5.86668	6.09771
7	1.04307	6.83385	7.12816	7	1.04458	6.82823	7.13263	7	1.04609	6.82261	7.13709
8	1.04937	7.78681	8.17123	8	1.05111	7.77951	8.17720	8	1.05285	7.77242	8.18319
9	1.05571	8.73404	9.22059	9	1.05768	8.72508	9.22831	9	1.05965	8.71613	9.23604
10	1.06209	9.67558	10.27630	10	1.06429	9.66467	10.28599	10	1.06649	9.65378	10.29569
11	1.06850	10.61147	11.33839	11	1.07094	10.59843	11.35028	11	1.07338	10.58541	11.36218
12	1.07496	11.54174	12.40689	12	1.07763	11.52639	12.42122	12	1.08031	11.51107	12.43556
13	1.08145	12.46642	13.48185	13	1.08437	12.44859	13.49885	13	1.08729	12.43079	13.51587
14	1.08798	13.38555	14.56330	14	1.09115	13.36506	14.58322	14	1.09431	13.34461	14.60316
15	1.09456	14.29916	15.65129	15	1.09796	14.27583	15.67436	15	1.10138	14.25256	15.69748
16	1.10117	15.20729	16.74585	16	1.10483	15.18095	16.77233	16	1.10849	15.15468	16.79885
17	1.10783	16.10995	17.84702	17	1.11173	16.08045	17.87715	17	1.11565	16.05102	17.90735
18	1.11452	17.00720	18.95486	18	1.11868	16.97436	18.98888	18	1.12286	16.94161	19.02300
19	1.12125	17.89906	20.06936	19	1.12567	17.86272	20.10756	19	1.13011	17.82648	20.14585
20	1.12803	18.78556	21.19062	20	1.13271	18.74556	21.23324	20	1.13741	18.70567	21.27596
21	1.13484	19.66674	22.31864	21	1.13979	19.62291	22.36595	21	1.14475	19.57922	22.41337
22	1.14170	20.54263	23.45349	22	1.14691	20.49482	23.50573	22	1.15215	20.44716	23.55812
23	1.14860	21.41326	24.59518	23	1.15408	21.36131	24.65264	23	1.15959	21.30954	24.71027
24	1.15554	22.27866	25.74378	24	1.16129	22.22242	25.80672	24	1.16708	22.16638	25.86986
25	1.16252	23.13886	26.89931	25	1.16855	23.07818	26.96801	25	1.17461	23.01773	27.03698

n							n			
26	1.16954	23.93990	28.06183	1.17585	23.92963	28.13656	26	1.18220	23.96361	28.21155
27	1.17661	24.84390	29.23137	1.18320	24.77379	29.31242	27	1.18983	24.70406	29.39375
28	1.18371	25.68860	30.40798	1.19060	25.61371	30.40562	28	1.19752	25.53912	30.58358
29	1.19087	26.50832	31.59169	1.19904	26.44841	31.68602	29	1.20525	26.36882	31.78110
30	1.19806	27.36301	32.78256	1.20553	27.27792	32.88425	30	1.21304	27.19320	32.96635
31	1.20530	28.19068	33.98062	1.21306	28.10228	34.08978	31	1.22087	28.01229	34.19939
32	1.21258	29.01736	35.18592	1.22064	28.92152	35.30285	32	1.22876	28.82612	35.42026
33	1.21991	29.83710	36.39850	1.22827	29.73567	36.52349	33	1.23669	29.63473	36.64902
34	1.22728	30.65191	37.61841	1.23595	30.54477	37.75176	34	1.24468	30.43815	37.88571
35	1.23469	31.46183	38.84569	1.24367	31.34884	38.98771	35	1.25272	31.23641	39.13039
36	1.24215	32.26688	40.08038	1.25145	32.14791	40.23138	36	1.26081	32.02965	40.38310
37	1.24966	33.06710	41.32253	1.25927	32.94202	41.48283	37	1.26895	32.81761	41.64391
38	1.25721	33.86251	42.57219	1.26714	33.73120	42.74209	38	1.27715	33.60060	42.91286
39	1.26490	34.65315	43.82940	1.27506	34.51548	44.00923	39	1.28539	34.37857	44.19001
40	1.27244	35.43904	45.09400	1.28303	35.29489	45.28429	40	1.29370	35.15155	45.47540
41	1.28013	36.22021	46.36664	1.29105	36.06945	46.56732	41	1.30205	35.91967	46.76910
42	1.28787	36.99669	47.64677	1.29911	36.83921	47.85836	42	1.31046	36.68266	48.07115
43	1.29565	37.76850	48.93464	1.30723	37.60418	49.15748	43	1.31892	37.44086	49.38161
44	1.30347	38.53568	50.23029	1.31540	38.36441	50.46471	44	1.32744	38.19419	50.70053
45	1.31135	39.29826	51.53376	1.32363	39.11991	51.76012	45	1.33601	38.94268	52.02797
46	1.31927	40.05625	52.84166	1.33190	39.87072	53.10374	46	1.34464	39.68637	53.36398
47	1.32724	40.80969	54.16438	1.34022	40.61686	54.43564	47	1.35333	40.42530	54.70863
48	1.33526	41.55861	55.49163	1.34860	41.35837	55.77586	48	1.36207	41.15947	56.06195
49	1.34333	42.30303	56.82689	1.35703	42.09527	57.12446	49	1.37086	41.88894	57.42402
50	1.35145	43.04298	58.17022	1.38551	42.82760	58.48149	50	1.37972	42.61373	58.79488

Table 1. (continued) Annuities

M	C(7.25,M,12)	A(7.25,M,12)	S(7.25,M,12)	M	C(7.50,M,12)	A(7.50,M,12)	S(7.50,M,12)	M	C(7.75,M,12)	A(7.75,M,12)	S(7.75,M,12)
51	1.35961	43.77848	59.52166	51	1.37404	43.55538	59.84700	51	1.38863	43.33396	60.17460
52	1.36782	44.50572	60.88127	52	1.38263	44.27064	61.22104	52	1.39760	44.04308	61.56323
53	1.37609	45.23627	62.24910	53	1.39127	44.99741	62.60368	53	1.40662	44.76030	62.93082
54	1.38440	45.95660	63.62519	54	1.39997	45.71171	63.99496	54	1.41571	45.46668	64.36745
55	1.39277	46.67659	65.00968	55	1.40872	46.42157	65.39491	55	1.42485	46.16849	65.78315
56	1.40118	47.39028	66.40285	56	1.41752	47.12703	66.80363	56	1.43405	46.86561	67.20800
57	1.40965	48.09968	67.80354	57	1.42638	47.82810	68.22115	57	1.44331	47.55667	68.64205
58	1.41816	48.80481	69.21318	58	1.43530	48.52482	69.64754	58	1.45263	48.24707	70.08537
59	1.42673	49.50572	70.63134	59	1.44427	49.21721	71.08293	59	1.46202	48.93106	71.53900
60	1.43535	50.20241	72.05807	60	1.45329	49.90531	72.52710	60	1.47146	49.61065	73.00032
61	1.44402	50.89492	73.49345	61	1.46238	50.58912	73.98039	61	1.48096	50.28589	74.47147
62	1.45275	51.59327	74.93745	62	1.47152	51.26870	75.44277	62	1.49053	50.95679	75.95244
63	1.46152	52.26749	76.39020	63	1.48071	51.94405	76.91429	63	1.50015	51.62339	77.44296
64	1.47035	52.94760	77.85172	64	1.48997	52.61520	78.39500	64	1.50984	52.28572	78.94312
65	1.47924	53.62362	79.32207	65	1.49928	53.28218	79.88497	65	1.51959	52.94379	80.45296
66	1.48817	54.29559	80.80131	66	1.50865	53.94503	81.39425	66	1.52941	53.59764	81.97255
67	1.49717	54.96351	82.28948	67	1.51808	54.60376	82.89291	67	1.53928	54.24729	83.50195
68	1.50621	55.62743	83.78665	68	1.52757	55.25939	84.41099	68	1.54922	54.89277	85.04124
69	1.51531	56.28736	85.29286	69	1.53712	55.90896	85.93855	69	1.55923	55.53411	86.59046
70	1.52447	56.94333	86.80817	70	1.54672	56.55549	87.47567	70	1.56930	56.17134	88.14969
71	1.53368	57.59536	88.33264	71	1.55639	57.19900	89.02239	71	1.57944	56.80448	89.71899
72	1.54294	58.24347	89.86632	72	1.56612	57.83652	90.57879	72	1.58964	57.43356	91.29842
73	1.55226	58.88769	91.40926	73	1.57591	58.47108	92.14491	73	1.59990	58.05659	92.88806
74	1.56164	59.52804	92.96152	74	1.58575	59.10169	93.72081	74	1.61023	58.67962	94.48797
75	1.57108	60.16455	94.52316	75	1.59567	59.72839	95.30656	75	1.62063	59.23666	96.09820

n				n				n			
76	1.59057	60.79723	96.09424	76	1.60564	60.35120	96.90223	76	1.63110	59.90974	97.71883
77	1.59012	61.42611	97.67481	77	1.61567	60.97013	98.50787	77	1.64163	60.51889	99.34994
78	1.59973	62.05122	99.26433	78	1.62577	61.58522	100.12354	78	1.65224	61.12413	100.99957
79	1.60939	62.67258	100.86465	79	1.63593	62.19650	101.74931	79	1.66291	61.72549	102.64391
80	1.61911	63.29020	102.47404	80	1.64816	62.80397	103.38525	80	1.67365	62.32299	104.30672
81	1.62890	63.90411	104.03318	81	1.65645	63.40767	105.03140	81	1.68446	62.91665	105.98036
82	1.63874	64.51434	105.72205	82	1.66690	64.00762	106.68785	82	1.69534	63.50650	107.66482
83	1.64964	65.12010	107.36079	83	1.67722	64.60385	108.35465	83	1.70628	64.09258	109.36015
84	1.65960	65.72382	108.00943	84	1.68770	65.19637	110.03187	84	1.71730	64.67488	111.06644
85	1.66862	66.32311	110.66803	85	1.69825	65.78522	111.71967	85	1.72839	65.25345	112.78374
86	1.67870	66.91881	112.33665	86	1.70886	66.37040	113.41782	86	1.73956	65.82831	114.51214
87	1.68884	67.51093	114.01535	87	1.71954	66.95196	115.12668	87	1.75079	66.39948	116.25169
88	1.69905	68.09949	115.70419	88	1.73029	67.52988	116.84621	88	1.76210	66.96699	118.00249
89	1.70931	68.68452	117.40324	89	1.74110	68.10423	118.57651	89	1.77348	67.53085	119.76459
90	1.71964	69.26604	119.11255	90	1.75199	68.67502	120.31761	90	1.78493	68.09109	121.53807
91	1.73003	69.84407	120.83219	91	1.76283	69.24226	122.06960	91	1.79646	68.64774	123.32300
92	1.74048	70.41862	122.56222	92	1.77396	69.80597	123.82253	92	1.80806	69.20082	125.11946
93	1.75100	70.98973	124.30270	93	1.78504	70.36618	125.60648	93	1.81974	69.75035	126.92753
94	1.76157	71.55740	126.05370	94	1.79620	70.92291	127.39153	94	1.83149	70.29636	128.74727
95	1.77222	72.12167	127.81522	95	1.80742	71.47618	129.18771	95	1.84332	70.83885	130.57875
96	1.78292	72.68254	129.59748	96	1.81872	72.02602	130.99613	96	1.85523	71.37797	132.42207
97	1.79370	73.24005	131.37041	97	1.83009	72.57247	132.81396	97	1.86721	71.91343	134.27730
98	1.80453	73.79421	133.16547	98	1.84152	73.11547	134.64396	98	1.87927	72.44555	136.14452
99	1.81544	74.34505	134.96963	99	1.85303	73.65513	136.48547	99	1.89140	72.97426	138.02377
100	1.82640	74.89257	136.76407	100	1.86462	74.19143	138.33550	100	1.90362	73.49957	139.91518

Table 1. (continued) Annuities

M	CI 7.25,M,12	AI 7.25,M,12	SI 7.25,M,12	M	CI 7.50,M,12	AI 7.50,M,12	SI 7.50,M,12	M	CI 7.75,M,12	AI 7.75,M,12	SI 7.75,M,12
101	1.83744	75.43681	138.81047	101	1.87627	74.72440	140.20313	101	1.91591	74.02151	141.81950
102	1.84864	75.97777	140.44791	102	1.88800	75.25407	142.07939	102	1.92829	74.54012	143.73471
103	1.85971	76.51549	142.29645	103	1.89960	75.76043	143.96739	103	1.94074	75.05538	145.66299
104	1.87094	77.04998	144.15616	104	1.91167	76.30354	145.86719	104	1.95327	75.56734	147.60374
105	1.88225	77.58126	146.02710	105	1.92362	76.82339	147.77885	105	1.96589	76.07602	149.55701
106	1.89362	78.10935	147.90935	106	1.93564	77.34002	149.70247	106	1.97859	76.58143	151.52290
107	1.90506	78.63427	149.80298	107	1.94774	77.85343	151.63811	107	1.99138	77.08360	153.50148
108	1.91657	79.15604	151.70802	108	1.95991	78.36366	153.58585	108	2.00422	77.58254	155.49284
109	1.92815	79.67467	153.62460	109	1.97216	78.87072	155.54578	109	2.01717	78.07829	157.49707
110	1.93980	80.19019	155.55275	110	1.98449	79.37463	157.51738	110	2.03020	78.57085	159.51424
111	1.95152	80.70261	157.49254	111	1.99689	79.87540	159.50241	111	2.04331	79.06026	161.54443
112	1.96331	81.21195	159.44406	112	2.00937	80.37308	161.49930	112	2.05650	79.54652	163.58775
113	1.97517	81.71823	161.40736	113	2.02198	80.86765	163.50867	113	2.06979	80.02966	165.64426
114	1.98710	82.22148	163.38254	114	2.03457	81.35915	165.53059	114	2.08315	80.50970	167.71404
115	1.99911	82.72170	165.36964	115	2.04729	81.84760	167.56517	115	2.09661	80.98666	169.79720
116	2.01119	83.21892	167.36874	116	2.06008	82.33303	169.61244	116	2.11015	81.46056	171.89380
117	2.02334	83.71316	169.37994	117	2.07296	82.81543	171.67253	117	2.12378	81.93142	174.00395
118	2.03556	84.20442	171.40327	118	2.08591	83.29484	173.74548	118	2.13749	82.39926	176.12772
119	2.04786	84.69273	173.43884	119	2.09895	83.77127	175.83139	119	2.15130	82.86410	178.26521
120	2.06023	85.17812	175.48669	120	2.11206	84.24474	177.93033	120	2.16519	83.32595	180.41650
121	2.07268	85.66058	177.54692	121	2.12526	84.71527	180.04240	121	2.17917	83.78484	182.58170
122	2.08520	86.14015	179.61961	122	2.13855	85.18288	182.16766	122	2.19325	84.24078	184.76088
123	2.09780	86.61684	181.70490	123	2.15191	85.64758	184.30621	123	2.20741	84.69360	186.95412
124	2.11047	87.09067	183.80261	124	2.16536	86.10940	186.45813	124	2.22167	85.14391	189.16153
125	2.12322	87.56165	185.91309	125	2.17890	86.56834	188.62349	125	2.23602	85.59114	191.38319

n				n				n			
126	2.13605	88.02981	189.03630	126	2.19251	87.02444	190.80238	126	2.25046	86.03549	193.61922
127	2.14886	88.49515	190.17236	127	2.20622	87.47771	192.99490	127	2.26499	86.47700	195.86987
128	2.16194	88.95770	192.32132	128	2.22001	87.92815	195.20113	128	2.27982	86.91566	198.13466
129	2.17500	89.41747	194.48326	129	2.23388	88.37590	197.42113	129	2.29434	87.35152	200.41429
130	2.18814	89.87447	196.65826	130	2.24784	88.82067	199.65501	130	2.30916	87.78458	202.70863
131	2.20136	90.32874	198.84641	131	2.26189	89.26278	201.90286	131	2.32407	88.21486	205.01779
132	2.21466	90.78027	201.04778	132	2.27603	89.70214	204.16475	132	2.33908	88.64237	207.34186
133	2.22804	91.22910	203.26244	133	2.29025	90.13878	206.44078	133	2.35419	89.06715	209.68094
134	2.24150	91.67522	205.49048	134	2.30457	90.57270	208.73103	134	2.36939	89.48920	212.03514
135	2.25505	92.11868	207.73198	135	2.31897	91.00392	211.03560	135	2.38470	89.90854	214.40453
136	2.26867	92.55946	209.98703	136	2.33347	91.43247	213.35457	136	2.40010	90.32519	216.78923
137	2.28238	92.99760	212.25571	137	2.34805	91.85835	215.68803	137	2.41560	90.73917	219.18932
138	2.29617	93.43311	214.53803	138	2.36273	92.28159	218.03609	138	2.43120	91.15048	221.60492
139	2.31004	93.86600	216.83424	139	2.37749	92.70221	220.33882	139	2.44690	91.55917	224.03612
140	2.32400	94.29630	219.14429	140	2.39235	93.12020	222.77831	140	2.46270	91.96523	226.48302
141	2.33804	94.72401	221.46829	141	2.40730	93.53561	225.16666	141	2.47861	92.36868	228.94572
142	2.35216	95.14915	223.80632	142	2.42235	93.94843	227.57596	142	2.49462	92.76954	231.42433
143	2.36637	95.57173	226.15849	143	2.43749	94.35869	229.99031	143	2.51073	93.18783	233.91896
144	2.38067	95.99178	228.52486	144	2.45272	94.76640	232.43581	144	2.52694	93.56356	236.42967
145	2.39505	96.40931	230.90553	145	2.46805	95.17158	234.88852	145	2.54326	93.95678	238.95660
146	2.40952	96.82433	233.30058	146	2.48348	95.57423	237.35658	146	2.55969	94.34743	241.49988
147	2.42408	97.23686	235.71011	147	2.49900	95.97440	239.84006	147	2.57622	94.73560	244.05056
148	2.43873	97.64690	238.13419	148	2.51462	96.37207	242.33905	148	2.59286	95.12128	246.63577
149	2.45346	98.05450	240.57292	149	2.53034	96.76727	244.85358	149	2.60960	95.50447	249.22864
150	2.46828	98.45563	243.02638	150	2.54615	97.16003	247.38402	150	2.62646	95.88522	251.63824

Table 1. (continued) Annuities

M	C(7.25,M,12)	A(7.25,M,12)	S(7.25,M,12)	M	C(7.50,M,12)	A(7.50,M,12)	S(7.50,M,12)	M	C(7.75,M,12)	A(7.75,M,12)	S(7.75,M,12)
151	2.48320	96.86334	245.49466	151	2.56206	97.55034	249.93016	151	2.64342	96.26351	254.46469
152	2.49820	98.26263	247.97786	152	2.57808	97.93822	252.49223	152	2.66049	96.63338	257.10809
153	2.51329	99.66051	250.47606	153	2.59419	98.32370	255.07030	153	2.67767	97.01284	259.76859
154	2.52848	100.05601	252.98935	154	2.61040	98.70678	257.66448	154	2.69497	97.38390	262.44628
155	2.54375	100.44913	255.51784	155	2.62672	99.08749	260.27490	155	2.71237	97.75259	265.14124
156	2.55912	100.83989	258.06158	156	2.64314	99.46582	262.90181	156	2.72989	98.11890	267.85361
157	2.57458	101.22830	260.62070	157	2.65965	99.84181	265.54474	157	2.74752	98.48286	270.58350
158	2.59014	101.61438	263.19528	158	2.67628	100.21546	268.20441	158	2.76526	98.84450	273.33099
159	2.60579	101.99814	265.78543	159	2.69300	100.58680	270.88068	159	2.78312	99.20380	276.09628
160	2.62153	102.37959	268.39120	160	2.70984	100.95583	273.57367	160	2.80110	99.56081	278.87939
161	2.63737	102.75876	271.01273	161	2.72677	101.32256	276.28351	161	2.81919	99.91552	281.68048
162	2.65330	103.13565	273.65012	162	2.74381	101.68701	279.01028	162	2.83739	100.28736	284.49966
163	2.66933	103.51028	276.30341	163	2.76096	102.04921	281.75409	163	2.85572	100.61813	287.33707
164	2.68546	103.88265	278.97275	164	2.77822	102.40915	284.51508	164	2.87416	100.96606	290.19278
165	2.70168	104.25279	281.65821	165	2.79558	102.76685	287.29327	165	2.89272	101.31175	293.06696
166	2.71801	104.62070	284.35989	166	2.81306	103.12234	290.08887	166	2.91141	101.65523	295.95966
167	2.73443	104.98641	287.07791	167	2.83064	103.47562	292.90193	167	2.93021	101.99650	298.87106
168	2.75095	105.34992	289.81232	168	2.84833	103.82670	295.73254	168	2.94913	102.33559	301.80130
169	2.76757	105.71126	292.56326	169	2.86613	104.17560	298.58087	169	2.96818	102.67249	304.75043
170	2.78429	106.07041	295.33084	170	2.88404	104.52234	301.44702	170	2.98735	103.00723	307.71960
171	2.80111	106.42741	298.11514	171	2.90207	104.86692	304.33105	171	3.00664	103.33964	310.70598
172	2.81804	106.78227	300.91626	172	2.92021	105.20937	307.23312	172	3.02606	103.67030	313.71259
173	2.83506	107.13499	303.73428	173	2.93846	105.54967	310.15335	173	3.04560	103.99863	316.73865
174	2.85219	107.48560	306.56934	174	2.95682	105.88788	313.09190	174	3.06527	104.32487	319.78427
175	2.86942	107.83411	309.42154	175	2.97530	106.22398	316.04861	175	3.08507	104.64302	322.84952

n			
176	2.88676	108.18051	312.29095
177	2.90420	108.52484	315.17770
178	2.92174	108.86710	318.08191
179	2.93940	109.20731	321.00366
180	2.95716	109.54547	323.94305
181	2.97502	109.88161	326.90021
182	2.99300	110.21572	329.87524
183	3.01108	110.54783	332.86823
184	3.02927	110.87794	335.87930
185	3.04757	111.20607	338.90857
186	3.06598	111.53223	341.95615
187	3.08451	111.85643	345.02213
188	3.10314	112.17868	348.10666
189	3.12189	112.49900	351.20978
190	3.14075	112.81740	354.33170
191	3.15973	113.13398	357.47244
192	3.17882	113.44846	360.63217
193	3.19802	113.76115	363.81057
194	3.21735	114.07197	367.00900
195	3.23678	114.39092	370.22635
196	3.25634	114.68801	373.46313
197	3.27601	114.98326	376.71948
198	3.29581	115.29668	379.99548
199	3.31572	115.59827	383.29129
200	3.33575	115.88805	386.60703

n			
176	2.99390	106.55799	319.02393
177	3.01261	106.88993	322.01782
178	3.03144	107.21980	325.03043
179	3.05039	107.54763	328.06196
180	3.06945	107.87342	331.11227
181	3.08864	108.19719	334.18170
182	3.10794	108.51894	337.27036
183	3.12736	108.83871	340.37830
184	3.14691	109.15648	343.50566
185	3.16658	109.47227	346.65256
186	3.18637	109.78611	349.81915
187	3.20628	110.10600	353.00552
188	3.22632	110.40795	356.21179
189	3.24649	110.71597	359.43811
190	3.26678	111.02209	362.68460
191	3.28720	111.32629	365.96139
192	3.30774	111.62862	369.23859
193	3.32841	111.92906	372.54633
194	3.34922	112.22764	375.87473
195	3.37015	112.52436	379.22397
196	3.39121	112.81924	382.55412
197	3.41241	113.11229	385.98532
198	3.43374	113.40352	389.37974
199	3.45520	113.69294	392.83145
200	3.47679	113.96056	396.28665

n			
176	3.10499	104.97108	325.83460
177	3.12505	105.29107	329.03958
178	3.14523	105.60902	332.16464
179	3.16554	105.92491	335.30988
180	3.18599	106.23879	338.47540
181	3.20656	106.55065	341.66141
182	3.22727	106.86051	344.86795
183	3.24812	107.16838	348.09525
184	3.26909	107.47427	351.34335
185	3.29021	107.77821	354.61246
186	3.31145	108.08019	357.90265
187	3.33284	108.38023	361.21411
188	3.35437	108.67835	364.54694
189	3.37603	108.97456	367.90131
190	3.39783	109.26887	371.27734
191	3.41978	109.56128	374.67517
192	3.44186	109.85182	378.09494
193	3.46409	110.14050	381.53680
194	3.48646	110.42732	385.00092
195	3.50898	110.71230	388.48737
196	3.53164	110.99546	391.99534
197	3.55445	111.27679	395.52798
198	3.57741	111.55633	399.08246
199	3.60051	111.83407	402.65995
200	3.62376	112.11002	406.26038

Table 1. (continued) Annuities

M	C(7.25,M,12)	A(7.25,M,12)	S(7.25,M,12)	M	C(7.50,M,12)	A(7.50,M,12)	S(7.50,M,12)	M	C(7.75,M,12)	A(7.75,M,12)	S(7.75,M,12)
201	3.35590	116.19604	365.94278	201	3.49852	114.26640	399.76346	201	3.64717	112.38421	409.88412
202	3.37618	116.49223	383.28968	202	3.52039	114.55045	403.26196	202	3.67072	112.65663	413.53131
203	3.39658	116.76664	396.67487	203	3.54239	114.83275	406.78235	203	3.69443	112.92731	417.20203
204	3.41710	117.07928	400.07144	204	3.56453	115.11329	410.32474	204	3.71829	113.19625	420.89545
205	3.43774	117.37018	403.48853	205	3.58681	115.39209	413.88928	205	3.74230	113.46346	424.61475
206	3.45851	117.65532	406.92627	206	3.60923	115.66916	417.47607	206	3.76647	113.72897	428.35706
207	3.47941	117.94672	410.38490	207	3.63178	115.94450	421.08533	207	3.79080	113.99278	432.12350
208	3.50043	118.23240	413.86420	208	3.65448	116.21814	424.71710	208	3.81528	114.25487	435.91431
209	3.52158	118.51637	417.36462	209	3.67732	116.49007	428.37158	209	3.83992	114.51529	439.72958
210	3.54285	118.79662	420.88620	210	3.70031	116.76032	432.04889	210	3.86472	114.77404	443.56562
211	3.56426	119.07919	424.42905	211	3.72343	117.02889	435.74921	211	3.88968	115.03113	447.43423
212	3.58579	119.35906	427.99332	212	3.74670	117.29580	439.47263	212	3.91480	115.28658	451.32391
213	3.60746	119.63427	431.57910	213	3.77012	117.56104	443.21833	213	3.94008	115.54037	455.23871
214	3.62925	119.90680	435.18655	214	3.79368	117.82464	446.98947	214	3.96553	115.79255	459.17880
215	3.65118	120.18469	438.81583	215	3.81739	118.08659	450.78314	215	3.99114	116.04310	463.14432
216	3.67324	120.45653	442.46701	216	3.84125	118.34692	454.60056	216	4.01692	116.29205	467.13547
217	3.69543	120.72753	446.14023	217	3.86526	118.60564	458.44190	217	4.04286	116.53940	471.15237
218	3.71776	120.99511	449.83566	218	3.88942	118.86275	462.30707	218	4.06897	116.78516	475.19525
219	3.74022	121.26388	453.55344	219	3.91373	119.11826	466.19647	219	4.09525	117.02934	479.26422
220	3.76282	121.52964	457.29364	220	3.93819	119.37218	470.11020	220	4.12170	117.27197	483.35947
221	3.78555	121.79380	461.05646	221	3.96280	119.62453	474.04940	221	4.14832	117.51302	487.48117
222	3.80842	122.05637	464.84201	222	3.98757	119.87531	478.01120	222	4.17511	117.75254	491.62949
223	3.83143	122.31738	468.65042	223	4.01249	120.12453	481.99978	223	4.20207	117.99052	495.80460
224	3.85458	122.57681	472.48187	224	4.03757	120.37221	486.01126	224	4.22921	118.22697	500.00665
225	3.87787	122.83468	476.33643	225	4.06281	120.61634	490.04883	225	4.25652	118.46191	504.23587

n				n				n			
226	3.90129	123.09100	480.21429	226	4.08820	120.86295	494.11163	226	4.28401	118.69533	508.43240
227	3.92487	123.34579	484.11560	227	4.11375	121.10603	498.19983	227	4.31168	118.92726	512.77637
228	3.94858	123.59904	488.04047	228	4.13966	121.34761	502.51360	228	4.33953	119.15770	517.08807
229	3.97243	123.85078	491.98904	229	4.16533	121.58768	506.45303	229	4.36755	119.38666	521.42761
230	3.99643	124.10101	495.96149	230	4.19136	121.82627	510.61838	230	4.39676	119.61415	525.75617
231	4.02058	124.34972	499.95792	231	4.21756	122.06338	514.80975	231	4.42415	119.84018	530.19032
232	4.04487	124.59695	503.97849	232	4.24392	122.29901	519.02728	232	4.45272	120.06477	534.61505
233	4.06931	124.84270	508.02335	233	4.27044	122.53318	523.27118	233	4.48148	120.28790	539.06781
234	4.09389	125.08696	512.09265	234	4.29714	122.76589	527.54163	234	4.51042	120.50961	543.54928
235	4.11863	125.32976	516.18652	235	4.32399	122.99715	531.83881	235	4.53955	120.72990	548.05969
236	4.14351	125.57110	520.30518	236	4.35102	123.22699	536.16278	236	4.56887	120.94877	552.59924
237	4.16854	125.81099	524.44867	237	4.37821	123.45539	540.51379	237	4.59838	121.16624	557.16809
238	4.19373	126.04945	528.61725	238	4.40557	123.68238	544.89203	238	4.62808	121.38232	561.76648
239	4.21507	126.28646	532.81099	239	4.43311	123.90795	549.29761	239	4.65796	121.59700	566.39453
240	4.24456	126.52206	537.03003	240	4.46082	124.13213	553.73071	240	4.68805	121.81031	571.05255
241	4.27020	126.75624	541.27460	241	4.48870	124.35491	558.19153	241	4.71832	122.02225	575.74060
242	4.29600	126.98901	545.54490	242	4.51675	124.57631	562.68024	242	4.74880	122.23283	580.45892
243	4.32195	127.22039	549.84076	243	4.54498	124.78633	567.19636	243	4.77947	122.44205	585.20770
244	4.34607	127.45038	554.16272	244	4.57339	125.01498	571.74194	244	4.81033	122.64994	589.98718
245	4.37434	127.67899	558.51090	245	4.60197	125.23228	576.31531	245	4.84140	122.85649	594.79749
246	4.40076	127.90622	562.88513	246	4.63073	125.44823	580.91730	246	4.87267	123.06172	599.63892
247	4.42735	128.13208	567.28589	247	4.65968	125.66284	585.54903	247	4.90414	123.26563	604.51154
248	4.45410	128.35660	571.71326	248	4.68880	125.87611	590.20770	248	4.93581	123.46823	609.41571
249	4.48101	128.57976	576.16736	249	4.71810	126.08807	594.89648	249	4.96769	123.66953	614.35150
250	4.50808	128.80159	580.64838	250	4.74759	126.29870	599.61462	250	4.99977	123.86954	619.31921

Table 1. (continued) Annuities

M	C(7.25,M,12)	A(7.25,M,12)	S(7.25,M,12)	M	C(7.50,M,12)	A(7.50,M,12)	S(7.50,M,12)	M	C(7.75,M,12)	A(7.75,M,12)	S(7.75,M,12)
251	4.53532	129.02208	585.15643	251	4.77726	126.50802	604.36218	251	5.03206	124.06827	624.31897
252	4.56272	129.24124	589.69177	252	4.80712	126.71605	609.13947	252	5.06456	124.26572	629.35101
253	4.59029	129.45909	594.25452	253	4.83717	126.90278	613.94659	253	5.09727	124.46190	634.41559
254	4.61802	129.67563	598.84479	254	4.86740	127.12823	618.78375	254	5.13019	124.65682	639.51288
255	4.64592	129.89008	603.46283	255	4.89782	127.33240	623.65112	255	5.16332	124.85049	644.64307
256	4.67399	130.10483	608.10870	256	4.92843	127.53530	628.54895	256	5.19667	125.04293	649.80634
257	4.70223	130.31749	612.78271	257	4.95923	127.73695	633.47742	257	5.23023	125.23412	655.00305
258	4.73064	130.52888	617.48492	258	4.99023	127.93734	638.43665	258	5.26401	125.42410	660.23328
259	4.75922	130.73900	622.21558	259	5.02142	128.13649	643.42688	259	5.29800	125.61285	665.49725
260	4.78797	130.94786	626.97479	260	5.05280	128.33440	648.44830	260	5.33222	125.80038	670.79629
261	4.81690	131.15548	631.76276	261	5.08438	128.53107	653.50110	261	5.36666	125.98672	676.12750
262	4.84600	131.36182	636.57965	262	5.11616	128.72653	658.58545	262	5.40132	126.17186	681.49414
263	4.87528	131.56693	641.42566	263	5.14814	128.92078	663.70160	263	5.43620	126.35581	686.89545
264	4.90474	131.77091	646.30096	264	5.18031	129.11382	668.84979	264	5.47131	126.53858	692.33167
265	4.93437	131.97348	651.20569	265	5.21263	129.30566	674.03009	265	5.50664	126.72018	697.80298
266	4.96418	132.17493	656.14008	266	5.24527	129.49631	679.24274	266	5.54221	126.90062	703.30963
267	4.99417	132.37515	661.10423	267	5.27805	129.68578	684.48804	267	5.57800	127.07990	708.85181
268	5.02434	132.57419	666.09839	268	5.31104	129.87405	689.76605	268	5.61403	127.25802	714.42981
269	5.05470	132.77202	671.12274	269	5.34423	130.06117	695.07715	269	5.65028	127.43500	720.04382
270	5.08524	132.96867	676.17743	270	5.37763	130.24713	700.42133	270	5.69677	127.61085	725.69415
271	5.11596	133.16414	681.26270	271	5.41124	130.43193	705.79901	271	5.72350	127.78556	731.38092
272	5.14687	133.35843	686.37866	272	5.44506	130.61559	711.21021	272	5.76047	127.95916	737.10443
273	5.17797	133.55156	691.52551	273	5.47910	130.79810	716.65527	273	5.79767	128.13164	742.86487
274	5.20925	133.74352	696.70349	274	5.51334	130.97948	722.13440	274	5.83511	128.30301	748.66254
275	5.24072	133.93433	701.91272	275	5.54780	131.15973	727.64771	275	5.87280	128.47330	754.49768

n				n				n			
276	5.27239	134.12399	707.15344	276	5.58247	131.33885	733.19656	276	5.91073	128.64247	760.37048
277	5.30424	134.31253	712.42564	277	5.61736	131.51688	738.77802	277	5.94490	128.81058	766.28119
278	5.33629	134.49992	717.73010	278	5.65247	131.69379	744.39539	278	5.98732	128.97760	772.23010
279	5.36853	134.68619	723.06641	279	5.68760	131.86960	750.04785	279	6.02599	129.14354	778.21741
280	5.40096	134.87135	728.43488	280	5.72335	132.04433	755.73566	280	6.06491	129.30843	784.24341
281	5.43359	135.05539	733.83588	281	5.75912	132.21797	761.45898	281	6.10407	129.47224	790.30829
282	5.46642	135.23833	739.26947	282	5.79511	132.39052	767.21808	282	6.14350	129.63503	796.41235
283	5.49945	135.42017	744.73590	283	5.83133	132.56201	773.01318	283	6.18317	129.79675	802.55585
284	5.53267	135.60091	750.23535	284	5.86778	132.73244	778.84454	284	6.22311	129.95744	808.73901
285	5.56610	135.78056	755.76901	285	5.90445	132.90179	784.71234	285	6.26330	130.11711	814.96216
286	5.59973	135.95914	761.33411	286	5.94135	133.07011	790.61676	286	6.30375	130.27574	821.22546
287	5.63356	136.13666	766.93364	287	5.97849	133.23738	796.55811	287	6.34446	130.43336	827.52917
288	5.66759	136.31310	772.56738	288	6.01585	133.40359	802.53662	288	6.38543	130.58937	833.87366
289	5.70184	136.48848	778.23499	289	6.05345	133.56880	808.55249	289	6.42667	130.74556	840.25909
290	5.73628	136.66280	783.93683	290	6.09129	133.73297	814.60596	290	6.46818	130.90018	846.68573
291	5.77094	136.83609	789.67310	291	6.12936	133.89612	820.69720	291	6.50995	131.05379	853.15393
292	5.80581	137.00833	796.44403	292	6.16767	134.05826	826.82660	292	6.55200	131.20641	859.66398
293	5.84088	137.17953	801.24982	293	6.20621	134.21938	832.99426	293	6.59431	131.35805	866.21588
294	5.87617	137.34972	807.09076	294	6.24500	134.37950	839.20044	294	6.63690	131.50873	872.81018
295	5.91167	137.51888	812.96692	295	6.28403	134.53864	845.44543	295	6.67976	131.65843	879.44708
296	5.94739	137.68701	818.87860	296	6.32331	134.69679	851.72949	296	6.72290	131.80717	886.12663
297	5.98332	137.85414	824.82599	297	6.36283	134.85280	858.05280	297	6.76632	131.95497	892.84973
298	6.01947	138.02026	830.80927	298	6.40260	135.01013	864.41565	298	6.81002	132.10181	899.61609
299	6.05584	138.18539	836.82880	299	6.44261	135.16536	870.81824	299	6.85400	132.24771	906.42609
300	6.09243	138.34953	842.88458	300	6.48288	135.31961	877.26096	300	6.89827	132.39267	913.28009

Table 1. (continued) Annuities

M	C(7.25,M,12)	A(7.25,M,12)	S(7.25,M,12)	M	C(7.50,M,12)	A(7.50,M,12)	S(7.50,M,12)	M	C(7.75,M,12)	A(7.75,M,12)	S(7.75,M,12)
301	6.12924	138.51270	848.97705	301	6.52340	135.47290	883.74371	301	6.94282	132.53871	920.17834
302	6.16627	138.67487	855.10626	302	6.56417	135.62524	890.26709	302	6.98766	132.67981	927.12122
303	6.20352	138.83606	861.27252	303	6.60520	135.77664	896.83130	303	7.03279	132.82001	934.10883
304	6.24100	138.99629	867.47607	304	6.64648	135.92709	903.43646	304	7.07821	132.96329	941.14166
305	6.27871	139.15556	873.71704	305	6.68802	136.07661	910.08295	305	7.12392	133.10365	948.21985
306	6.31664	139.31367	879.99579	306	6.72982	136.22520	916.77100	306	7.16993	133.24313	955.34375
307	6.35480	139.47124	886.31244	307	6.77188	136.37288	923.50079	307	7.21623	133.38171	962.51367
308	6.39320	139.62766	892.66724	308	6.81420	136.51962	930.27271	308	7.26284	133.51939	969.72992
309	6.43182	139.78313	899.06042	309	6.85679	136.66547	937.06691	309	7.30974	133.65620	976.99274
310	6.47068	139.93767	905.49225	310	6.89965	136.81041	943.94366	310	7.35695	133.79213	984.30249
311	6.50978	140.09128	911.96289	311	6.94277	136.95444	950.84332	311	7.40447	133.92717	991.65948
312	6.54911	140.24317	918.47272	312	6.98616	137.09758	957.78607	312	7.45229	134.06137	999.06390
313	6.58867	140.39590	925.02149	313	7.02983	137.23982	964.77228	313	7.50042	134.19469	1006.51624
314	6.62848	140.54862	931.60866	314	7.07376	137.38120	971.80206	314	7.54886	134.32716	1014.01666
315	6.66853	140.69658	938.23895	315	7.11797	137.52168	978.87585	315	7.59761	134.45879	1021.56549
316	6.70882	140.84563	944.90747	316	7.16246	137.66105	985.99384	316	7.64668	134.58955	1029.16309
317	6.74935	140.99379	951.61627	317	7.20723	137.79899	993.15631	317	7.69606	134.71950	1036.80969
318	6.79013	141.14107	958.36566	318	7.25227	137.93693	1000.36353	318	7.74577	134.84860	1044.50596
319	6.83115	141.28746	965.15576	319	7.29760	138.07487	1007.61578	319	7.79579	134.97687	1052.25159
320	6.87242	141.43297	971.99694	320	7.34321	138.21115	1014.91339	320	7.84614	135.10432	1060.04736
321	6.91394	141.57761	978.85938	321	7.38910	138.34648	1022.25659	321	7.89681	135.23096	1067.89355
322	6.95571	141.72136	985.77332	322	7.43529	138.48099	1029.64563	322	7.94781	135.35678	1075.79028
323	6.99774	141.86427	992.72900	323	7.48176	138.61464	1037.09693	323	7.99914	135.48178	1083.73816
324	7.04002	142.00632	999.72675	324	7.52852	138.74743	1044.56274	324	8.05080	135.60600	1091.73730
325	7.08255	142.14751	1006.76878	325	7.57557	138.87947	1052.09119	325	8.10280	135.72942	1098.78809

	n			n				n			
7.12634	326	1019.84830	142.28796	326	7.62292	139.01065	1059.66675	326	8.15513	135.85804	1107.89087
7.16639	327	1020.97467	142.42735	327	7.67756	139.14102	1067.28967	327	8.20780	135.97388	1116.04602
7.21170	328	1028.14294	142.56601	328	7.71850	139.27056	1074.96033	328	8.26081	136.09492	1124.25378
7.25527	329	1035.35474	142.70384	329	7.76574	139.37924	1082.67883	329	8.31416	136.21519	1132.51465
7.29910	330	1042.60999	142.84085	330	7.81528	139.52728	1090.44556	330	8.36785	136.33470	1140.82874
7.34320	331	1049.90906	142.97704	331	7.86413	139.65445	1098.26086	331	8.42190	136.45345	1149.19666
7.38757	332	1057.25232	143.11240	332	7.91328	139.79062	1106.12488	332	8.47628	136.57143	1157.61853
7.43220	333	1064.63989	143.24695	333	7.96274	139.90640	1114.03821	333	8.53103	136.68864	1166.09495
7.47710	334	1072.07202	143.38069	334	8.01251	140.03120	1122.00098	334	8.58613	136.80511	1174.62595
7.52228	335	1079.54919	143.51363	335	8.06258	140.15524	1130.01343	335	8.64158	136.92082	1183.21191
7.56772	336	1087.07141	143.64577	336	8.11298	140.27850	1138.07605	336	8.69739	137.03580	1191.85352
7.61344	337	1094.63916	143.77711	337	8.16368	140.40099	1146.18896	337	8.75356	137.15004	1200.55090
7.65944	338	1102.25256	143.90767	338	8.21470	140.52272	1154.35266	338	8.81009	137.26355	1208.30444
7.70572	339	1109.91199	144.03745	339	8.26605	140.64371	1162.56738	339	8.86699	137.37633	1218.11462
7.75227	340	1117.61780	144.16644	340	8.31771	140.76393	1170.83350	340	8.92426	137.48839	1226.98157
7.79911	341	1125.37000	144.29466	341	8.36969	140.86341	1179.15112	341	8.98189	137.59972	1235.90598
7.84623	342	1133.16919	144.42210	342	8.42201	141.00214	1187.52087	342	9.03990	137.71034	1244.88770
7.89363	343	1141.01538	144.54878	343	8.47464	141.12015	1196.94287	343	9.09828	137.82025	1253.92761
7.94133	344	1148.90906	144.67471	344	8.52761	141.23741	1204.41748	344	9.15704	137.92946	1263.02588
7.98930	345	1156.85034	144.77998	345	8.56091	141.35394	1212.94507	345	9.21618	138.03796	1272.18298
8.03757	346	1164.83980	144.92430	346	8.63454	141.46976	1221.52600	346	9.27570	138.14577	1281.39917
8.08613	347	1172.87720	145.04795	347	8.68850	141.58485	1230.16052	347	9.33561	138.25288	1290.67480
8.13499	348	1180.93338	145.17088	348	8.74281	141.65923	1238.84912	348	9.39590	138.35931	1300.01050
8.18414	349	1189.09827	145.25308	349	8.79745	141.81290	1247.59192	349	9.45658	138.46506	1309.40637
8.23358	350	1197.28247	145.41454	350	8.85243	141.92587	1256.38928	350	9.51766	138.57013	1318.66292

Table 1. (continued) Annuities

M	C(7.25,M,12)	A(7.25,M,12)	S(7.25,M,12)	M	C(7.50,M,12)	A(7.50,M,12)	S(7.50,M,12)	M	C(7.75,M,12)	A(7.75,M,12)	S(7.75,M,12)
351	8.28833	145.53526	1205.51599	351	8.90776	142.03813	1265.24182	351	9.57912	138.67451	1328.38062
352	8.33337	145.65526	1213.79832	352	8.96343	142.14964	1274.14964	352	9.64099	138.77824	1337.95972
353	8.38372	145.77454	1222.13269	353	9.01946	142.26056	1283.11292	353	9.70325	138.88130	1347.60071
354	8.43437	145.89310	1230.51648	354	9.07583	142.37074	1292.13245	354	9.76592	138.98370	1357.30356
355	8.48533	146.01094	1238.96081	355	9.13255	142.48024	1301.20825	355	9.82899	139.08543	1367.06982
356	8.53659	146.12810	1247.43816	356	9.18963	142.58907	1310.34082	356	9.89247	139.18652	1376.89880
357	8.58817	146.24452	1255.97278	357	9.24706	142.69720	1319.53040	357	9.95636	139.28697	1386.79138
358	8.64006	146.36028	1264.56091	358	9.30486	142.80468	1328.77747	358	10.02066	139.38678	1396.74768
359	8.69226	146.47531	1273.20093	359	9.36301	142.91148	1338.08240	359	10.08538	139.48592	1406.76831
360	8.74477	146.58968	1281.83319	360	9.42153	143.01762	1347.44531	360	10.15051	139.58443	1416.85376
361	8.79760	146.70334	1290.63806	361	9.48042	143.12309	1356.86694	361	10.21607	139.68231	1427.00427
362	8.85076	146.81631	1299.43555	362	9.53967	143.22792	1366.34729	362	10.28205	139.77957	1437.22034
363	8.90423	146.92862	1308.28568	363	9.59929	143.33211	1375.88698	363	10.34845	139.87621	1447.50232
364	8.95803	147.04025	1317.19055	364	9.65929	143.43562	1385.46633	364	10.41529	139.97221	1457.85083
365	9.01215	147.15121	1326.14568	365	9.71966	143.53651	1395.14563	365	10.48255	140.06761	1468.26611
366	9.06660	147.26152	1335.16077	366	9.78041	143.64076	1404.86523	366	10.55025	140.16240	1478.74866
367	9.12137	147.37115	1344.22472	367	9.84154	143.74237	1414.64563	367	10.61839	140.25658	1489.29895
368	9.17648	147.48012	1353.34875	368	9.90304	143.84335	1424.48718	368	10.68697	140.35014	1499.91736
369	9.23192	147.58844	1362.52527	369	9.96494	143.94370	1434.39026	369	10.75599	140.44312	1510.60425
370	9.28770	147.69611	1371.75720	370	10.02722	144.04343	1444.35510	370	10.82545	140.53549	1521.36023
371	9.34381	147.80262	1381.04460	371	10.08989	144.14253	1454.38232	371	10.89537	140.62727	1532.18567
372	9.40026	147.90962	1390.38667	372	10.15295	144.24103	1464.47229	372	10.96573	140.71848	1543.08105
373	9.45706	148.01526	1399.78694	373	10.21641	144.33891	1474.62524	373	11.03655	140.80908	1554.04675
374	9.51419	148.12036	1409.24597	374	10.28026	144.43619	1484.84167	374	11.10783	140.89911	1565.08337
375	9.57168	148.22484	1418.76013	375	10.34451	144.53285	1495.12195	375	11.17957	140.98856	1576.19116

n				n				n			
376	9.62951	148.32969	1426.33191	376	10.40917	144.62890	1505.46643	376	11.25177	141.07742	1587.37073
377	9.68768	148.43190	1437.96130	377	10.47422	144.72440	1515.87561	377	11.32444	141.16573	1598.62256
378	9.74621	148.53452	1447.64905	378	10.53969	144.81927	1526.34973	378	11.39757	141.25346	1609.94702
379	9.60510	148.63851	1457.39526	379	10.60556	144.91356	1536.88953	379	11.47118	141.34064	1621.34448
380	9.86434	148.73787	1467.20032	380	10.67184	145.00726	1547.49500	380	11.54527	141.42726	1632.81567
381	9.92393	148.83864	1477.06470	381	10.73854	145.10039	1558.16687	381	11.61983	141.51332	1644.36096
382	9.98389	148.93600	1486.98960	382	10.80566	145.19293	1568.90540	382	11.69488	141.59883	1655.98083
383	10.04421	149.03606	1496.97253	383	10.87319	145.28491	1579.71106	383	11.77041	141.68379	1667.67566
384	10.10488	149.13733	1507.01672	384	10.94115	145.37630	1590.58423	384	11.84642	141.76820	1679.44617
385	10.16594	149.23569	1517.12158	385	11.00953	145.46713	1601.52832	385	11.92293	141.85207	1691.29248
386	10.22736	149.33347	1527.28760	386	11.07834	145.55740	1612.53491	386	11.99993	141.93541	1703.21545
387	10.28915	149.40666	1537.51465	387	11.14758	145.64711	1623.61328	387	12.07743	142.01820	1715.21545
388	10.35132	149.50408	1547.80408	388	11.21726	145.73625	1634.76096	388	12.15543	142.10048	1727.29286
389	10.41386	149.63229	1558.15540	389	11.28736	145.82484	1645.97815	389	12.23394	142.18221	1739.44824
390	10.47677	149.71873	1568.56921	390	11.35791	145.91289	1657.26550	390	12.31296	142.26343	1751.68225
391	10.54007	149.81961	1579.04602	391	11.42890	146.00040	1668.62841	391	12.39247	142.34412	1763.99512
392	10.60375	149.90793	1589.59606	392	11.50033	146.08734	1680.05237	392	12.47250	142.42430	1776.38757
393	10.66781	150.00166	1600.20166	393	11.57220	146.17375	1691.55261	393	12.55305	142.50396	1788.86011
394	10.73226	150.09483	1610.85767	394	11.64453	146.25964	1703.12488	394	12.63413	142.58311	1801.41321
395	10.79711	150.18745	1621.58997	395	11.71731	146.34499	1714.76941	395	12.71572	142.66176	1814.04736
396	10.86234	150.27961	1632.39696	396	11.79054	146.42979	1726.48669	396	12.79784	142.73988	1826.76306
397	10.92797	150.37103	1643.24939	397	11.86423	146.51408	1738.27722	397	12.88050	142.81752	1839.56091
398	10.99399	150.46199	1654.17737	398	11.93838	146.59784	1750.14148	398	12.96368	142.89467	1852.44141
399	11.06041	150.55240	1665.17126	399	12.01300	146.68109	1762.07983	399	13.04741	142.97131	1865.40503
400	11.12723	150.64227	1676.23169	400	12.08808	146.76381	1774.09290	400	13.13167	143.04745	1878.45251

Table 1. (continued) Annuities

M	C(7.25,M,12)	A(7.25,M,12)	S(7.25,M,12)	M	C(7.50,M,12)	A(7.50,M,12)	S(7.50,M,12)	M	C(7.75,M,12)	A(7.75,M,12)	S(7.75,M,12)
401	11.19446	150.73160	1687.35501	401	12.16363	146.84602	1796.16091	401	13.21648	143.12312	1891.58411
402	11.26209	150.82039	1696.55347	402	12.23965	146.92773	1798.34460	402	13.30184	143.19830	1904.80066
403	11.33014	150.90965	1709.81555	403	12.31615	147.00883	1810.58423	403	13.38774	143.27299	1918.10242
404	11.39859	150.99938	1721.14563	404	12.39313	147.08961	1822.90039	404	13.47421	143.34721	1931.49023
405	11.46745	151.08359	1732.54419	405	12.47058	147.16960	1835.23046	405	13.56123	143.42096	1944.96436
406	11.53674	151.17026	1744.01172	406	12.54853	147.24960	1847.76404	406	13.64881	143.49422	1958.52563
407	11.60644	151.25642	1755.54846	407	12.62695	147.32869	1860.31262	407	13.73699	143.56702	1972.17444
408	11.67656	151.34206	1767.15491	408	12.70587	147.40739	1872.93968	408	13.82568	143.63934	1985.91138
409	11.74711	151.42719	1778.83142	409	12.78528	147.48561	1885.64539	409	13.91497	143.71121	1999.73706
410	11.81808	151.51181	1790.57849	410	12.86519	147.56334	1898.43066	410	14.00484	143.78261	2013.65210
411	11.88948	151.59592	1802.39661	411	12.94560	147.64058	1911.29590	411	14.09528	143.85356	2027.65686
412	11.96131	151.67952	1814.28613	412	13.02651	147.71735	1924.24146	412	14.18632	143.92406	2041.75220
413	12.03358	151.76262	1826.24744	413	13.10793	147.79364	1937.26907	413	14.27794	143.99409	2055.93848
414	12.10628	151.84521	1838.28101	414	13.18985	147.86945	1950.37598	414	14.37015	144.06367	2070.21631
415	12.17942	151.92732	1850.38733	415	13.27229	147.94479	1963.56580	415	14.46295	144.13281	2084.58643
416	12.25301	152.00894	1862.56665	416	13.35524	148.01967	1976.83813	416	14.55636	144.20150	2099.04956
417	12.32704	152.09006	1874.81970	417	13.43671	148.09409	1990.13836	417	14.65037	144.26978	2113.60571
418	12.40154	152.17070	1887.14673	418	13.52270	148.16803	2003.63208	418	14.74499	144.33760	2128.26610
419	12.47644	152.25085	1899.54862	419	13.60722	148.24153	2017.15479	419	14.84022	144.40498	2143.00122
420	12.55182	152.33052	1912.02466	420	13.69228	148.31456	2030.76198	420	14.93606	144.47192	2157.84131
421	12.62765	152.40971	1924.57654	421	13.77784	148.38715	2044.45422	421	15.03252	144.53845	2172.77759
422	12.70394	152.48842	1937.20410	422	13.86396	148.45927	2058.23193	422	15.12961	144.60455	2187.81006
423	12.78069	152.56667	1949.90908	423	13.95060	148.53094	2072.09565	423	15.22733	144.67023	2202.93970
424	12.85791	152.64444	1962.68884	424	14.03779	148.60219	2086.04663	424	15.32566	144.73547	2218.16699
425	12.93559	152.72174	1975.54675	425	14.12553	148.67299	2100.08423	425	15.42464	144.80031	2233.49268

426	13.01375	152.79858	1988.48230
427	13.09237	152.87487	2001.49609
428	13.17747	152.96090	2014.58838
429	13.25105	153.02635	2027.75989
430	13.33111	153.10136	2041.01099
431	13.41165	153.17593	2054.34204
432	13.49268	153.25005	2067.75366
433	13.57420	153.32372	2081.24634
434	13.65621	153.39694	2094.82056
435	13.73871	153.46973	2108.47681
436	13.82172	153.54208	2122.21533
437	13.90522	153.61400	2136.03711
438	13.98924	153.68547	2149.94238
439	14.07375	153.75653	2163.93164
440	14.15878	153.82716	2178.00537
441	14.24433	153.89737	2192.16406
442	14.33039	153.96715	2206.40845
443	14.41696	154.03650	2220.73877
444	14.50407	154.10545	2235.15576
445	14.59170	154.17398	2249.65991
446	14.67985	154.24211	2264.25171
447	14.76854	154.30981	2278.93140
448	14.85777	154.37712	2293.69995
449	14.94754	154.44402	2308.55786
450	15.03784	154.51053	2323.50537

426	14.21381	148.74333	2114.20996
427	14.30265	148.81325	2128.42358
428	14.39204	148.88274	2142.72632
429	14.48199	148.96178	2157.11841
430	14.57250	149.02042	2171.60034
431	14.66358	149.08861	2186.17285
432	14.75523	149.15637	2200.63643
433	14.84745	149.22372	2215.59155
434	14.94024	149.29066	2230.43921
435	15.03362	149.35718	2245.37939
436	15.12758	149.42328	2260.41309
437	15.22213	149.48898	2275.54053
438	15.31727	149.55426	2290.76270
439	15.41300	149.61914	2306.07983
440	15.50933	149.68362	2321.49292
441	15.60626	149.74770	2337.00220
442	15.70380	149.81137	2352.60864
443	15.80195	149.87466	2368.31226
444	15.90071	149.93755	2384.11426
445	16.00009	150.00005	2400.01514
446	16.10009	150.06216	2416.01514
447	16.20072	150.12389	2432.11523
448	16.30198	150.18523	2448.31592
449	16.40386	150.24619	2464.61792
450	16.50639	150.30678	2481.02173

426	15.52428	144.86472	2248.47724
427	15.62452	144.92873	2264.44141
428	15.72543	144.99231	2280.06592
429	15.82699	145.05550	2296.79150
430	15.92920	145.11827	2311.61841
431	16.03208	145.18065	2327.54761
432	16.13562	145.24261	2343.57959
433	16.23983	145.30420	2359.71533
434	16.34471	145.36539	2375.95508
435	16.45027	145.42618	2392.28990
436	16.55651	145.48657	2408.75024
437	16.66344	145.54659	2425.30664
438	16.77106	145.60620	2441.96997
439	16.87937	145.66545	2458.74121
440	16.98838	145.72432	2475.62061
441	17.09810	145.78281	2492.60889
442	17.20852	145.84091	2509.70703
443	17.31966	145.89865	2526.91553
444	17.43152	145.95601	2544.23511
445	17.54410	146.01302	2561.86675
446	17.65740	146.06966	2579.21069
447	17.77144	146.12592	2596.86816
448	17.88621	146.18182	2614.63985
449	18.00173	146.23738	2632.52598
450	18.11798	146.29257	2650.52759

Table 1. (continued) Annuities

M	C(7.25,M,12)	A(7.25,M,12)	S(7.25,M,12)	M	C(7.50,M,12)	A(7.50,M,12)	S(7.50,M,12)	M	C(7.75,M,12)	A(7.75,M,12)	S(7.75,M,12)
451	15.12870	154.57661	2338.54321	451	16.60955	150.36697	2497.52908	451	18.23500	146.34741	2868.64551
452	15.22010	154.64232	2353.67188	452	16.71336	150.42682	2514.13770	452	18.35277	146.40190	2886.88062
453	15.31206	154.70763	2368.89185	453	16.81782	150.48627	2530.85107	453	18.47130	146.45604	2905.23340
454	15.40457	154.77255	2384.20410	454	16.92293	150.54536	2547.66895	454	18.59059	146.50983	2923.70459
455	15.49763	154.83707	2399.60864	455	17.02870	150.60410	2564.55180	455	18.71066	146.56328	2942.28517
456	15.59127	154.90121	2415.10620	456	17.13513	150.66245	2581.62061	456	18.83150	146.61638	2961.00506
457	15.68546	154.96497	2430.69751	457	17.24222	150.72044	2598.75562	457	18.95312	146.66914	2979.83740
458	15.78023	155.02834	2446.38281	458	17.34999	150.77808	2615.99780	458	19.07552	146.72156	2998.79053
459	15.87557	155.09132	2462.16309	459	17.45842	150.83536	2633.34790	459	19.19872	146.77365	3017.98597
460	15.97148	155.15393	2478.03882	460	17.56754	150.89229	2650.80640	460	19.32271	146.82539	3037.06470
461	16.06798	155.21617	2494.01025	461	17.67734	150.94885	2668.37378	461	19.44750	146.87682	3056.38745
462	16.16506	155.27803	2510.07813	462	17.78782	151.00508	2686.05127	462	19.57310	146.92792	3075.83496
463	16.26272	155.33952	2526.24316	463	17.89899	151.06094	2703.83887	463	19.69951	146.97867	3095.40798
464	16.36097	155.40065	2542.50586	464	18.01086	151.11647	2721.73804	464	19.82674	147.02911	3115.10767
465	16.45982	155.46140	2558.86694	465	18.12343	151.17165	2739.74878	465	19.95478	147.07922	3134.93433
466	16.55927	155.52179	2575.32666	466	18.23670	151.22647	2757.87231	466	20.08366	147.12901	3154.88916
467	16.65931	155.58182	2591.88599	467	18.35068	151.28098	2776.10889	467	20.21337	147.17848	3174.97266
468	16.75996	155.64148	2608.54541	468	18.46537	151.33513	2794.45972	468	20.34391	147.22765	3195.19604
469	16.86122	155.70078	2625.30542	469	18.58078	151.38895	2812.92505	469	20.47530	147.27649	3215.53003
470	16.96308	155.75974	2642.16650	470	18.69691	151.44243	2831.50586	470	20.60753	147.32501	3236.00537
471	17.06557	155.81834	2659.12964	471	18.81377	151.49557	2850.20264	471	20.74063	147.37323	3256.61279
472	17.16868	155.87659	2676.19531	472	18.93135	151.54840	2869.01660	472	20.87457	147.42113	3277.35352
473	17.27241	155.93448	2693.36377	473	19.04967	151.60091	2887.94775	473	21.00939	147.46872	3298.22803
474	17.37678	155.99203	2710.63623	474	19.16873	151.65306	2906.99756	474	21.14507	147.51602	3319.23755
475	17.48174	156.04922	2728.01204	475	19.28854	151.70491	2926.16626	475	21.28164	147.56300	3340.38257

476	17.58736	156.10609	2745.49487	476	19.40909	151.75644	2945.45583	476	21.41908	147.60970	3161.66406
477	17.63062	156.16261	2763.08228	477	19.53040	151.80763	2964.06401	477	21.55741	147.65608	3183.08325
478	17.80052	156.21878	2780.77588	478	19.65246	151.85852	2984.39429	478	21.69664	147.70218	3204.64063
479	17.90807	156.27463	2798.57642	479	19.77529	151.90909	3004.04688	479	21.83676	147.74797	3226.33740
480	18.01626	156.33012	2816.48438	480	19.89889	151.95934	3023.82202	480	21.97779	147.79347	3248.17407
481	18.12511	156.38530	2834.50073	481	20.02326	152.00928	3043.72095	481	22.11973	147.83867	3270.15186
482	18.23461	156.44014	2852.62573	482	20.14840	152.05891	3063.74414	482	22.26259	147.88359	3292.27148
483	18.34478	156.49466	2870.86035	483	20.27433	152.10825	3083.89258	483	22.40637	147.92822	3314.53418
484	18.45561	156.54884	2889.20508	484	20.40104	152.15726	3104.16699	484	22.55107	147.97256	3336.94067
485	18.56712	156.60269	2907.66064	485	20.52855	152.20596	3124.56787	485	22.69672	148.01663	3359.49970
486	18.67929	156.65623	2926.22778	486	20.65685	152.25438	3145.09644	486	22.84330	148.06041	3382.18823
487	18.79215	156.70944	2944.90723	487	20.78596	152.30249	3165.75342	487	22.99083	148.10390	3405.03174
488	18.90568	156.76234	2963.69922	488	20.91587	152.35030	3186.53931	488	23.13931	148.14711	3428.02246
489	19.01991	156.81491	2982.60459	489	21.04659	152.39781	3207.45532	489	23.28875	148.19005	3451.16187
490	19.13482	156.86717	3001.62500	490	21.17814	152.44504	3228.50171	490	23.43916	148.23271	3474.45044
491	19.25042	156.91913	3020.75977	491	21.31050	152.49196	3249.67993	491	23.59054	148.27512	3497.88965
492	19.36673	156.97076	3040.01025	492	21.44369	152.53859	3270.99048	492	23.74289	148.31723	3521.48022
493	10.48373	157.02208	3055.37655	493	21.57771	152.58493	3292.43408	493	23.89623	148.35907	3545.22314
494	19.60145	157.07310	3078.86060	494	21.71257	152.63100	3314.01196	494	24.05056	148.40065	3569.11938
495	19.71988	157.12381	3098.46216	495	21.84828	152.67676	3335.72437	495	24.20589	148.44197	3593.16992
496	19.83902	157.17422	3118.18188	496	21.98483	152.72224	3357.57275	496	24.36222	148.48302	3617.37573
497	19.95888	157.22432	3138.02100	497	22.12223	152.76746	3379.55762	497	24.51956	148.52379	3641.73804
498	20.07946	157.27412	3157.97974	498	22.26050	152.81238	3401.67969	498	24.67791	148.56432	3666.25977
499	20.20078	157.32362	3178.05933	499	22.39963	152.85701	3423.94019	499	24.83729	148.60458	3690.93555
500	20.32282	157.37283	3198.26001	500	22.53962	152.90138	3446.33984	500	24.99770	148.64458	3715.77271

Table 1. (continued) Annuities

M	C(8.00,M,12)	A(8.00,M,12)	S(8.00,M,12)	M	C(8.25,M,12)	A(8.25,M,12)	S(8.25,M,12)	M	C(8.50,M,12)	A(8.50,M,12)	S(8.50,M,12)
1	1.00667	0.99338	1.00000	1	1.00687	0.99317	1.00000	1	1.00708	0.99297	1.00000
2	1.01338	1.99018	2.00667	2	1.01380	1.97956	2.00687	2	1.01422	1.97895	2.00708
3	1.02013	2.96044	3.02004	3	1.02077	2.95962	3.02067	3	1.02140	2.95800	3.02130
4	1.02693	3.93421	4.04018	4	1.02779	3.93218	4.04144	4	1.02864	3.93016	4.04270
5	1.03378	4.90154	5.06711	5	1.03485	4.89851	5.06922	5	1.03592	4.89648	5.07134
6	1.04067	5.86245	6.10089	6	1.04197	5.85823	6.10407	6	1.04326	5.85402	6.10726
7	1.04761	6.81701	7.14157	7	1.04913	6.81140	7.14604	7	1.05065	6.80581	7.15052
8	1.05459	7.76524	8.18918	8	1.05634	7.75807	8.19517	8	1.05809	7.75091	8.20117
9	1.06163	8.70719	9.24377	9	1.06360	8.69827	9.25151	9	1.06559	8.68936	9.25926
10	1.06870	9.64290	10.30540	10	1.07092	9.63204	10.31511	10	1.07313	9.62121	10.32485
11	1.07583	10.57242	11.37410	11	1.07828	10.55945	11.38603	11	1.08074	10.54650	11.39798
12	1.08300	11.49578	12.44993	12	1.08569	11.48052	12.46431	12	1.08839	11.46529	12.47872
13	1.09022	12.41303	13.53292	13	1.09316	12.39530	13.55000	13	1.09610	12.37781	13.56711
14	1.09749	13.32420	14.62314	14	1.10067	13.30384	14.64316	14	1.10386	13.28352	14.66321
15	1.10480	14.22934	15.72063	15	1.10824	14.20617	15.74383	15	1.11168	14.18306	15.76707
16	1.11217	15.12848	16.82544	16	1.11596	15.10234	16.85207	16	1.11956	15.07627	16.87875
17	1.11958	16.02167	17.93760	17	1.12353	15.99239	17.96793	17	1.12749	15.96320	17.99831
18	1.12705	16.90894	19.05719	18	1.13125	16.87637	19.09146	18	1.13547	16.84388	19.12580
19	1.13456	17.79034	20.18424	19	1.13903	17.75431	20.22271	19	1.14352	17.71838	20.26127
20	1.14213	18.66590	21.31880	20	1.14686	18.62625	21.36174	20	1.15162	18.58672	21.40479
21	1.14974	19.53566	22.46092	21	1.15475	19.49224	22.50860	21	1.15977	19.44896	22.55641
22	1.15740	20.39967	23.61066	22	1.16269	20.35232	23.66335	22	1.16799	20.30513	23.71618
23	1.16512	21.25795	24.76807	23	1.17068	21.20653	24.82604	23	1.17626	21.15528	24.88447
24	1.17289	22.11054	25.93319	24	1.17873	22.05490	25.99672	24	1.18459	21.99945	26.06044
25	1.18071	22.95749	27.10608	25	1.18683	22.89748	27.17544	25	1.19298	22.83768	27.24508

n			n				n			
26	1.18858	23.79683	26	1.19499	23.73431	28.36227	26	1.20144	23.67002	28.43802
27	1.19650	24.63460	27	1.20321	24.56542	29.55726	27	1.20996	24.49651	29.63945
28	1.20448	25.46484	28	1.21148	25.39086	30.76047	28	1.21852	25.31718	30.84940
29	1.21251	26.28957	29	1.21981	26.21066	31.97195	29	1.22715	26.13207	32.06791
30	1.22059	27.10885	30	1.22819	27.02496	33.19175	30	1.23584	26.94124	33.29506
31	1.22873	27.92270	31	1.23664	27.83351	34.41995	31	1.24459	27.74471	34.53090
32	1.23692	28.73116	32	1.24514	28.63663	35.65659	32	1.25341	28.54254	35.77550
33	1.24517	29.53426	33	1.25370	29.43427	36.90173	33	1.26229	29.33475	37.02891
34	1.25347	30.33205	34	1.26232	30.22646	38.15542	34	1.27123	30.12139	38.29119
35	1.26182	31.12455	35	1.27100	31.01325	39.41774	35	1.28023	30.90250	39.56242
36	1.27024	31.91190	36	1.27974	31.79466	40.68874	36	1.28930	31.67811	40.84266
37	1.27871	32.69384	37	1.28853	32.57073	41.96848	37	1.29943	32.44827	42.13196
38	1.28723	33.47071	38	1.29739	33.34151	43.25701	38	1.30763	33.21301	43.43039
39	1.29581	34.24242	39	1.30631	34.10703	44.55440	39	1.31689	33.97237	44.73803
40	1.30445	35.00903	40	1.31529	34.86731	45.86071	40	1.32622	34.72639	46.05432
41	1.31315	35.77056	41	1.32433	35.62241	47.17600	41	1.33560	35.47511	47.38114
42	1.32190	36.52705	42	1.33344	36.37235	48.50034	42	1.34508	36.21856	48.71676
43	1.33071	37.27852	43	1.34261	37.11717	49.83378	43	1.35460	36.95679	50.06184
44	1.33958	38.02502	44	1.35184	37.85690	51.17638	44	1.36420	37.68982	51.41644
45	1.34852	38.76658	45	1.36113	38.59158	52.52822	45	1.37386	38.41769	52.78064
46	1.35751	39.50322	46	1.37049	39.32125	53.88935	46	1.38359	39.14045	54.15450
47	1.36656	40.23499	47	1.37991	40.04593	55.25984	47	1.39039	39.85812	55.53810
48	1.37567	40.96191	48	1.38940	40.76567	56.63976	48	1.40326	40.57074	56.93148
49	1.38484	41.68402	49	1.39895	41.48049	58.02915	49	1.41320	41.27835	58.33476
50	1.39407	42.40134	50	1.40857	42.18043	59.42810	50	1.42321	41.96099	59.74796

Table 1. (continued) Annuities

M	C(8.00,M,12)	A(8.00,M,12)	S(8.00,M,12)	M	C(8.25,M,12)	A(8.25,M,12)	S(8.25,M,12)	M	C(8.50,M,12)	A(8.50,M,12)	S(8.50,M,12)
51	1.40336	43.11391	60.50449	51	1.41825	42.89553	60.83667	51	1.43330	42.87068	61.17118
52	1.41272	43.82177	61.90785	52	1.42960	43.59681	62.26492	52	1.44345	43.37147	62.60447
53	1.42214	44.52494	63.32057	53	1.43782	44.29330	63.68293	53	1.45367	44.05938	64.04792
54	1.43162	45.23345	64.74271	54	1.44771	44.98205	65.12074	54	1.46397	44.74245	65.50159
55	1.44116	45.91733	66.17432	55	1.45766	45.66908	66.56845	55	1.47434	45.42072	66.96556
56	1.45077	46.60662	67.61549	56	1.46768	46.34943	68.02611	56	1.48478	46.09422	68.43990
57	1.46044	47.29135	69.06625	57	1.47777	47.02613	69.49379	57	1.49530	46.76299	69.92468
58	1.47018	47.97153	70.52670	58	1.48793	47.69820	70.97156	58	1.50589	47.42704	71.41998
59	1.47998	48.64722	71.99687	59	1.49816	48.36568	72.45949	59	1.51656	48.08643	72.90587
60	1.48985	49.31843	73.47685	60	1.50848	49.02861	73.96765	60	1.52730	48.74118	74.44244
61	1.49978	49.98520	74.96687	61	1.51883	49.68702	75.46610	61	1.53812	49.39133	75.96973
62	1.50978	50.64754	76.46648	62	1.52927	50.34092	76.98433	62	1.54901	50.03690	77.50786
63	1.51984	51.30551	77.97625	63	1.53979	50.99036	78.51421	63	1.55999	50.67793	79.05687
64	1.52997	51.95991	79.49609	64	1.55037	51.63537	80.05399	64	1.57104	51.31445	80.61886
65	1.54017	52.60839	81.02607	65	1.56103	52.27597	81.60436	65	1.58216	51.94650	82.18789
66	1.55044	53.25337	82.56624	66	1.57176	52.91220	83.16539	66	1.59337	52.57410	83.77005
67	1.56078	53.89408	84.11668	67	1.58257	53.54409	84.73715	67	1.60466	53.19728	85.36343
68	1.57118	54.53054	85.67746	68	1.59345	54.17166	86.31973	68	1.61602	53.81609	86.96809
69	1.58166	55.16279	87.24864	69	1.60440	54.79494	87.91317	69	1.62747	54.43053	88.58411
70	1.59220	55.79085	88.83030	70	1.61543	55.41397	89.51757	70	1.63900	55.04066	90.21158
71	1.60282	56.41475	90.42251	71	1.62654	56.02854	91.13301	71	1.65061	55.64650	91.85058
72	1.61350	57.03452	92.02532	72	1.63772	56.63338	92.75964	72	1.66230	56.24808	93.50118
73	1.62426	57.65018	93.63882	73	1.64898	57.24581	94.39727	73	1.67407	56.84542	95.16348
74	1.63509	58.26177	95.26308	74	1.66032	57.84811	96.04625	74	1.68593	57.43857	96.83756
75	1.64599	58.86931	96.89817	75	1.67173	58.44629	97.70657	75	1.69787	58.02754	98.52349

76	100.22137	58.61237	1.70990	99.37830	59.04039	1.68323	98.54416	59.47283	1.65696
77	101.38127	59.13008	1.72201	101.06152	59.63042	1.69460	100.20112	60.07235	1.66801
78	103.53328	59.76971	1.73421	102.75632	60.21644	1.70645	101.86913	60.66789	1.67913
79	105.38749	60.34228	1.74649	104.46278	60.79845	1.71818	103.54826	61.26949	1.69032
80	107.13399	60.91084	1.75887	106.18095	61.37648	1.72999	105.23858	61.84718	1.70159
81	108.89285	61.47539	1.77132	107.91095	61.95057	1.74189	106.94016	62.43097	1.71233
82	110.66418	82.03596	1.78387	109.65284	62.52074	1.75396	108.65310	63.01090	1.72435
83	112.44805	82.59260	1.79651	111.40670	63.08702	1.76592	110.37746	63.50699	1.73585
84	114.24455	63.14532	1.80923	113.17262	63.64943	1.77806	112.11330	64.15926	1.74742
85	116.05379	63.69416	1.82205	114.95068	64.20900	1.79029	113.86073	64.72774	1.75907
86	117.87583	64.23913	1.83495	116.74097	64.76276	1.80259	115.61980	65.29246	1.77080
87	119.71079	64.79027	1.84795	118.54356	65.31372	1.81499	117.39059	65.85343	1.78260
88	121.55874	65.31760	1.86104	120.35855	65.86093	1.82747	119.17320	66.41070	1.79449
89	123.41978	65.85115	1.87422	122.18601	66.40440	1.84003	120.96769	66.96426	1.80645
90	125.29401	66.38096	1.88750	124.02605	66.94416	1.85268	122.77414	67.51418	1.81849
91	127.18150	66.90703	1.90087	125.87872	67.48023	1.86542	124.59264	68.06043	1.83062
92	129.08237	87.42941	1.91433	127.74414	68.01264	1.87824	126.42325	68.60308	1.84282
93	130.99670	87.94810	1.92789	129.62238	68.54142	1.89115	128.26607	69.14214	1.85511
94	132.92459	88.46316	1.94155	131.51353	69.06659	1.90416	130.12117	69.67762	1.86747
95	134.86615	88.97459	1.95530	133.41769	69.58817	1.91725	131.98965	70.20956	1.87992
96	136.82144	89.48242	1.96915	135.33493	70.10619	1.93043	133.86858	70.73797	1.89246
97	138.79060	89.98668	1.98310	137.26537	70.62067	1.94370	135.76103	71.26288	1.90507
98	140.77370	70.48740	1.99715	139.20906	71.13165	1.95706	137.66611	71.78432	1.91777
99	142.77094	70.98459	2.01129	141.16612	71.63912	1.97032	139.58388	72.30230	1.93056
100	144.78214	71.47829	2.02554	143.13664	72.14314	1.98406	141.51443	72.81686	1.94343

Table 1. (continued) Annuities

M	C(8.00,M,12)	A(8.00,M,12)	S(8.00,M,12)	C(8.25,M,12)	A(8.25,M,12)	S(8.25,M,12)	C(8.50,M,12)	A(8.50,M,12)	S(8.50,M,12)
101	1.95639	73.32800	143.45787	1.99770	72.64371	145.12070	2.03989	71.96851	146.80768
102	1.96943	73.63576	145.41426	2.01144	73.14087	147.11841	2.05434	72.45528	148.84756
103	1.98256	74.34016	147.38368	2.02527	73.63464	149.12985	2.06889	72.93864	150.90190
104	1.99577	74.84122	149.36624	2.03919	74.12502	151.15512	2.08354	73.41859	152.97079
105	2.00908	75.33897	151.36201	2.05321	74.61207	153.19431	2.09830	73.89516	155.05434
106	2.02247	75.83340	153.37109	2.06733	75.09578	155.24751	2.11316	74.36839	157.15263
107	2.03596	76.32458	155.39357	2.08154	75.57619	157.31485	2.12813	74.83828	159.26581
108	2.04953	76.81249	157.42953	2.09585	76.05333	159.39638	2.14321	75.30487	161.39394
109	2.06319	77.29718	159.47306	2.11026	76.52721	161.49223	2.15839	75.76818	163.53714
110	2.07695	77.77866	161.54225	2.12477	76.99784	163.60249	2.17368	76.22823	165.69653
111	2.09079	78.25694	163.61820	2.13937	77.46527	165.72726	2.18907	76.68504	167.86920
112	2.10473	78.73206	165.70999	2.15408	77.92960	167.86664	2.20458	77.13865	170.05829
113	2.11876	79.20403	167.81473	2.16889	78.39057	170.02072	2.22020	77.58906	172.26286
114	2.13289	79.67288	169.93349	2.18380	78.84849	172.18961	2.23592	78.03630	174.48306
115	2.14711	80.13863	172.06638	2.19882	79.30328	174.37341	2.25176	78.48040	176.71898
116	2.16142	80.60128	174.21349	2.21393	79.75496	176.57224	2.26771	78.92137	178.97073
117	2.17583	81.06087	176.37491	2.22915	80.20356	178.78616	2.28377	79.35925	181.23845
118	2.19034	81.51743	178.55075	2.24448	80.64910	181.01532	2.29995	79.79404	183.52222
119	2.20494	81.97095	180.74109	2.25991	81.09159	183.25980	2.31624	80.22577	185.82217
120	2.21964	82.42148	182.94603	2.27545	81.53107	185.51971	2.33265	80.65448	188.13841
121	2.23444	82.86902	185.16566	2.29109	81.96754	187.79517	2.34917	81.08015	190.47105
122	2.24933	83.31359	187.40010	2.30684	82.40103	190.09626	2.36581	81.50284	192.82022
123	2.26433	83.75523	189.64944	2.32270	82.83157	192.39310	2.38257	81.92255	195.18604
124	2.27943	84.18393	191.91377	2.33867	83.25916	194.71581	2.39944	82.33932	197.56860
125	2.29462	84.62973	194.13919	2.35475	83.68383	197.05447	2.41644	82.75314	199.96805

No.				No.				No.		
126	2.30992	85.06265	196.48782	126	2.37094	84.10561	199.40923	126	2.43356	83.16407	202.38449
127	2.32532	85.48270	198.79973	127	2.38724	84.52451	201.78015	127	2.45079	83.57210	204.81804
128	2.34082	85.91990	201.12305	128	2.40365	84.94054	204.16740	128	2.46815	83.97728	207.26884
129	2.35643	86.34427	203.46387	129	2.42018	85.35373	206.57104	129	2.48564	84.37957	209.73700
130	2.37214	86.76583	205.82030	130	2.43681	85.76410	208.99123	130	2.50324	84.77305	212.22263
131	2.38795	87.18460	208.19243	131	2.45357	86.17167	211.42804	131	2.52097	85.17573	214.72588
132	2.40387	87.60059	210.58038	132	2.47044	86.57645	213.88161	132	2.53883	85.56960	217.24686
133	2.41989	88.01384	212.98425	133	2.48742	86.97848	216.35204	133	2.55682	85.96072	219.78568
134	2.43603	88.42434	215.40414	134	2.50452	87.37775	218.83946	134	2.57433	86.34908	222.34250
135	2.45227	88.83213	217.84018	135	2.52174	87.77431	221.34398	135	2.59316	86.73471	224.91742
136	2.46862	89.23721	220.29245	136	2.53908	88.16815	223.86572	136	2.61153	87.11762	227.51059
137	2.48507	89.63962	222.76106	137	2.55653	88.55931	226.40490	137	2.63003	87.49785	230.12212
138	2.50164	90.03935	225.24614	138	2.57411	88.94779	228.96133	138	2.64966	87.87540	232.75215
139	2.51832	90.43645	227.74677	139	2.59181	89.33363	231.53545	139	2.66742	88.25029	235.40082
140	2.53511	90.83090	230.26610	140	2.60962	89.71682	234.12724	140	2.68632	88.62255	238.06824
141	2.55201	91.22276	232.80121	141	2.62757	90.09740	236.73688	141	2.70534	88.99219	240.75455
142	2.56902	91.61201	235.35321	142	2.64563	90.47538	239.36444	142	2.72451	89.35922	243.45990
143	2.58615	91.99868	237.92223	143	2.66382	90.85078	242.01007	143	2.74381	89.72369	246.18440
144	2.60339	92.38280	240.50838	144	2.68213	91.22362	244.67389	144	2.76324	90.08558	248.92821
145	2.62074	92.76437	243.11177	145	2.70057	91.53391	247.35602	145	2.78281	90.44492	251.67405
146	2.63822	93.14341	245.73251	146	2.71914	91.96018	250.05099	146	2.80253	90.80174	254.47427
147	2.65580	93.51994	248.37073	147	2.73783	92.32693	252.77574	147	2.82238	91.15606	257.27679
148	2.67351	93.89398	251.02654	148	2.75666	92.68069	255.51357	148	2.84237	91.50787	260.09915
149	2.69133	94.26555	253.70004	149	2.77561	93.04996	258.27020	149	2.86250	91.85722	262.94153
150	2.70928	94.63465	256.39136	150	2.79469	93.40779	261.04584	150	2.88278	92.20411	265.80405

Table 1. (continued) Annuities

M	CI 8.00,M,12)	AI 8.00,M,12)	SI 8.00,M,12)	M	CI 8.25,M,12)	AI 8.25,M,12)	SI 8.25,M,12)	M	CI 8.50,M,12)	AI 8.50,M,12)	SI 8.50,M,12)
151	2.72734	95.00130	259.10065	151	2.81390	93.76317	263.84082	151	2.90320	92.54855	268.68683
152	2.74552	95.36554	261.82797	152	2.83325	94.11612	266.65442	152	2.92378	92.89058	271.59003
153	2.76382	95.72798	264.57352	153	2.85273	94.46666	269.48767	153	2.94447	93.23020	274.51376
154	2.78225	96.08678	267.33734	154	2.87234	94.81481	272.34039	154	2.96533	93.56743	277.45825
155	2.80080	96.44382	270.11957	155	2.89209	95.16058	275.21274	155	2.98633	93.90229	280.42358
156	2.81947	96.79849	272.92038	156	2.91197	95.50399	278.10483	156	3.00749	94.23479	283.40991
157	2.83827	97.15003	275.73984	157	2.93199	95.84505	281.01678	157	3.02879	94.56496	286.41739
158	2.85719	97.50082	278.57813	158	2.95215	96.18379	283.94879	158	3.05024	94.89290	289.44620
159	2.87624	97.84850	281.43530	159	2.97244	96.52022	286.90094	159	3.07185	95.21834	292.49643
160	2.89541	98.19387	284.31152	160	2.99288	96.85434	289.87338	160	3.09361	95.54159	295.56827
161	2.91471	98.53696	287.20694	161	3.01346	97.18619	292.86627	161	3.11552	95.86256	298.66190
162	2.93414	98.87777	290.12164	162	3.03417	97.51576	295.87970	162	3.13759	96.18127	301.77740
163	2.95371	99.21632	293.05579	163	3.05503	97.84309	298.91388	163	3.15981	96.49775	304.91501
164	2.97340	99.55264	296.00949	164	3.07604	98.16819	301.96893	164	3.18220	96.81200	308.07483
165	2.99322	99.88673	298.98291	165	3.09718	98.49106	305.04496	165	3.20474	97.12404	311.25702
166	3.01317	100.21861	301.97614	166	3.11848	98.81173	308.14215	166	3.22744	97.43388	314.46176
167	3.03326	100.54829	304.98929	167	3.13992	99.13021	311.26062	167	3.25030	97.74154	317.68918
168	3.05348	100.87578	308.02255	168	3.16150	99.44652	314.40054	168	3.27332	98.04704	320.93948
169	3.07384	101.20110	311.07605	169	3.18324	99.76066	317.56204	169	3.29651	98.35040	324.21200
170	3.09433	101.52428	314.14987	170	3.20512	100.07266	320.74527	170	3.31986	98.65161	327.50831
171	3.11496	101.84531	317.24420	171	3.22716	100.38253	323.95041	171	3.34337	98.95071	330.82916
172	3.13573	102.16422	320.35919	172	3.24935	100.69028	327.17755	172	3.36706	99.24770	334.17255
173	3.15663	102.48101	323.49490	173	3.27168	100.99594	330.42691	173	3.39091	99.54261	337.53961
174	3.17768	102.79570	326.65155	174	3.29418	101.29951	333.69858	174	3.41492	99.83544	340.93051
175	3.19886	103.10831	329.82922	175	3.31683	101.60100	336.99277	175	3.43911	100.12622	344.34543

n			
176	3.22019	103.41895	333.02908
177	3.24186	103.72734	336.48936
178	3.26327	104.03378	339.48993
179	3.28502	104.33820	342.75317
180	3.30692	104.64059	346.03821
181	3.32897	104.94098	349.34512
182	3.35116	105.23939	352.67410
183	3.37350	105.53581	356.02527
184	3.39599	105.83028	359.39877
185	3.41863	106.12290	362.79474
186	3.44142	106.41337	366.21338
187	3.46437	106.70203	369.65482
188	3.48746	106.98876	373.11917
189	3.51071	107.27361	376.60663
190	3.53412	107.55656	380.11734
191	3.55768	107.83765	383.65146
192	3.58139	108.11687	387.20914
193	3.60527	108.39424	390.73580
194	3.62931	108.66978	394.39581
195	3.65350	108.94348	398.02512
196	3.67786	109.21538	401.67862
197	3.70238	109.48548	405.35648
198	3.72706	109.75378	409.05884
199	3.75191	110.02032	412.75589
200	3.77692	110.28508	416.53781

n			
176	3.33963	101.90044	340.30960
177	3.36259	102.19782	343.64923
178	3.38571	102.49318	347.01181
179	3.40898	102.78652	350.39752
180	3.43242	103.07787	353.80649
181	3.45602	103.36722	357.23892
182	3.47978	103.65459	360.69495
183	3.50370	103.94000	364.17471
184	3.52779	104.22346	367.67841
185	3.55204	104.50500	371.20621
186	3.57646	104.78460	374.75824
187	3.60105	105.06229	378.33472
188	3.62581	105.33810	381.93576
189	3.65074	105.61201	385.56158
190	3.67583	105.88406	389.21231
191	3.70111	106.15425	392.88815
192	3.72655	106.42259	396.58923
193	3.75217	106.68911	400.31580
194	3.77797	106.95360	404.06796
195	3.80394	107.21668	407.84595
196	3.83019	107.47778	411.64987
197	3.85642	107.74098	415.47998
198	3.88294	107.99462	419.33640
199	3.90963	108.24040	423.21303
200	3.93651	108.50443	427.12897

n			
176	3.46347	100.41495	347.78455
177	3.48801	100.70164	351.24802
178	3.51271	100.98632	354.73602
179	3.53760	101.26900	358.24875
180	3.56265	101.54969	361.78635
181	3.58789	101.82841	365.34900
182	3.61130	102.10516	368.93689
183	3.63890	102.37997	372.55017
184	3.66467	102.65285	376.18909
185	3.69063	102.92380	379.85376
186	3.71677	103.19285	383.54437
187	3.74310	103.46001	387.26117
188	3.76961	103.72529	391.00424
189	3.79631	103.98870	394.77386
190	3.82321	104.25026	398.57019
191	3.85029	104.50999	402.33340
192	3.87756	104.76788	406.24368
193	3.90503	105.02396	410.12125
194	3.93269	105.27824	414.02628
195	3.96054	105.53073	417.95895
196	3.98860	105.78144	421.91949
197	4.01685	106.03040	425.90808
198	4.04530	106.27760	429.92493
199	4.07396	106.52306	433.97025
200	4.10281	106.76679	438.04419

Table 1. (continued) Annuities

M	C(8.00,M,12)	A(8.00,M,12)	S(8.00,M,12)	M	C(8.25,M,12)	A(8.25,M,12)	S(8.25,M,12)	M	C(8.50,M,12)	A(8.50,M,12)	S(8.50,M,12)
201	3.80210	110.54810	420.31473	201	3.96358	108.75673	431.06549	201	4.13187	107.00881	442.14700
202	3.82745	110.80936	424.11692	202	3.99082	109.00730	435.02905	202	4.16114	107.24913	446.27887
203	3.85296	111.06873	427.94427	203	4.01826	109.25616	439.01987	203	4.19062	107.48776	450.44003
204	3.87865	111.32623	431.79727	204	4.04589	109.50333	443.03815	204	4.22030	107.72471	454.63065
205	3.90451	111.58265	435.67587	205	4.07370	109.74881	447.08401	205	4.25019	107.95999	458.85095
206	3.93054	111.83727	439.59038	206	4.10171	109.99261	451.15775	206	4.28030	108.19362	463.10114
207	3.95674	112.09000	443.51093	207	4.12991	110.23475	455.25943	207	4.31062	108.42561	467.38144
208	3.98312	112.34106	447.46765	208	4.15830	110.47523	459.38934	208	4.34115	108.65596	471.69205
209	4.00967	112.59045	451.45078	209	4.18689	110.71407	463.54764	209	4.37190	108.88469	476.03320
210	4.03640	112.83820	455.46045	210	4.21567	110.95128	467.73453	210	4.40287	109.11182	480.40512
211	4.06331	113.08430	459.49686	211	4.24466	111.18687	471.95023	211	4.43406	109.33734	484.80798
212	4.09040	113.32877	463.56015	212	4.27384	111.42085	476.19489	212	4.46546	109.56129	489.24203
213	4.11767	113.57163	467.65057	213	4.30322	111.65324	480.46872	213	4.49709	109.78365	493.70749
214	4.14512	113.81288	471.76825	214	4.33281	111.88403	484.77194	214	4.52895	110.00446	498.20459
215	4.17276	114.05253	475.91336	215	4.36260	112.11325	489.10474	215	4.56103	110.22370	502.73355
216	4.20057	114.29060	480.08612	216	4.39259	112.34091	493.46735	216	4.59334	110.44141	507.29359
217	4.22858	114.52708	484.28668	217	4.42279	112.56701	497.85992	217	4.62587	110.65759	511.88791
218	4.25677	114.76200	488.51526	218	4.45319	112.79157	502.28271	218	4.65864	110.87224	516.51379
219	4.28515	114.99536	492.77203	219	4.48381	113.01460	506.73550	219	4.69164	111.08538	521.17242
220	4.31371	115.22718	497.05719	220	4.51464	113.23610	511.21973	220	4.72487	111.29703	525.86407
221	4.34247	115.45747	501.37088	221	4.54567	113.45609	515.73431	221	4.75834	111.50719	530.58893
222	4.37142	115.68623	505.71338	222	4.57693	113.67458	520.28003	222	4.79204	111.71587	535.34723
223	4.40057	115.91347	510.08478	223	4.60839	113.89157	524.85693	223	4.82599	111.92308	540.13928
224	4.42990	116.13921	514.48535	224	4.64007	114.10708	529.46533	224	4.86017	112.12888	544.96527
225	4.45943	116.36345	518.91522	225	4.67197	114.32112	534.10541	225	4.89460	112.33314	549.82544

226	4.48916	116.59620	523.37469
227	4.51909	116.80749	527.86388
228	4.54922	117.02731	532.38238
229	4.57955	117.24567	536.93213
230	4.61008	117.46259	541.51172
231	4.64081	117.67607	546.12177
232	4.67175	117.89212	550.76257
233	4.70290	118.10475	555.43433
234	4.73425	118.31598	560.13727
235	4.76581	118.52581	564.87146
236	4.79758	118.73425	569.63733
237	4.82957	118.94131	574.43488
238	4.86176	119.14700	579.26447
239	4.89417	119.35132	584.12622
240	4.92680	119.55429	589.02039
241	4.95965	119.75591	593.94720
242	4.99271	119.96621	598.90696
243	5.02600	120.15517	603.89954
244	5.05950	120.35282	608.92554
245	5.09323	120.54916	613.98505
246	5.12719	120.74420	619.07831
247	5.16137	120.93794	624.20544
248	5.19578	121.13041	629.36682
249	5.23042	121.32160	634.56262
250	5.26529	121.51152	639.79303

226	4.70409	114.53371	538.77740
227	4.73643	114.74483	543.48745
228	4.76900	114.95452	548.24790
229	4.80178	115.16278	552.96698
230	4.83490	115.36961	557.78870
231	4.86804	115.57504	562.62347
232	4.90150	115.77905	567.49152
233	4.93520	115.98167	572.33301
234	4.96913	116.18292	577.32825
235	5.00329	116.38279	582.29736
236	5.03769	116.58129	587.30066
237	5.07233	116.77844	592.33838
238	5.10720	116.97424	597.41071
239	5.14231	117.16871	602.51788
240	5.17766	117.36195	607.66016
241	5.21326	117.55367	612.83783
242	5.24910	117.74417	618.05109
243	5.28519	117.93338	623.30023
244	5.32152	118.12130	628.58539
245	5.35811	118.30739	633.90692
246	5.39495	118.49329	639.26501
247	5.43204	118.67738	644.65997
248	5.46938	118.86021	650.09204
249	5.50698	119.04190	655.56140
250	5.54485	119.22215	661.06836

226	4.99927	112.53601	554.72003
227	4.96418	112.73745	559.64929
228	4.99335	112.93748	564.61353
229	5.03476	113.13610	569.81295
230	5.07042	113.33332	574.64758
231	5.10634	113.52915	579.71902
232	5.14251	113.72361	584.82434
233	5.17893	113.91670	589.96696
234	5.21562	114.10844	595.14581
235	5.25256	114.29882	600.36139
236	5.28977	114.48786	605.81395
237	5.32723	114.67558	610.90375
238	5.36497	114.86197	616.23056
239	5.40297	115.04706	621.59595
240	5.44124	115.23083	626.99890
241	5.47978	115.41332	632.44019
242	5.51860	115.59453	637.91992
243	5.55769	115.77446	643.43854
244	5.59706	115.95313	648.99622
245	5.63670	116.13054	654.58032
246	5.67663	116.30669	660.22998
247	5.71684	116.48162	665.90662
248	5.75733	116.65531	671.62347
249	5.79811	116.82278	677.38080
250	5.83918	116.99904	683.17989

Table 1. (continued) Annuities

M	C[8.00,M,12]	A[8.00,M,12]	S[8.00,M,12]	M	C[8.25,M,12]	A[8.25,M,12]	S[8.25,M,12]	M	C[8.50,M,12]	A[8.50,M,12]	S[8.50,M,12]
251	5.30039	121.70019	645.05835	251	5.58297	119.40127	666.61322	251	5.88054	117.16909	689.01907
252	5.33572	121.88760	650.35870	252	5.62135	119.57916	672.19623	252	5.92220	117.33794	694.89862
253	5.37130	122.07378	655.69446	253	5.66000	119.75584	677.81757	253	5.96415	117.50562	700.82096
254	5.40710	122.25872	661.06573	254	5.69891	119.93131	683.47754	254	6.00639	117.67210	706.78497
255	5.44315	122.44244	666.47284	255	5.73809	120.10558	689.17645	255	6.04894	117.83742	712.79938
256	5.47944	122.62494	671.91602	256	5.77754	120.27867	694.91455	256	6.09179	118.00158	718.84033
257	5.51597	122.80623	677.39645	257	5.81726	120.45057	700.69208	257	6.13494	118.16457	724.93213
258	5.55274	122.98632	682.91138	258	5.85725	120.62130	706.50384	258	6.17839	118.32643	731.06702
259	5.58976	123.16521	688.46417	259	5.89752	120.79086	712.36658	259	6.22216	118.48714	737.24542
260	5.62703	123.34290	694.05389	260	5.93807	120.95927	718.26410	260	6.26623	118.64674	743.46759
261	5.66454	123.51941	699.68091	261	5.97889	121.12653	724.20215	261	6.31061	118.80520	749.73388
262	5.70230	123.69484	705.34546	262	6.01999	121.29264	730.18109	262	6.35531	118.96255	756.04443
263	5.74032	123.86904	711.04779	263	6.06138	121.45762	736.20105	263	6.40033	119.11879	762.39972
264	5.77859	124.04210	716.78909	264	6.10305	121.62147	742.26245	264	6.44567	119.27393	768.80011
265	5.81711	124.21400	722.56671	265	6.14501	121.78420	748.36548	265	6.49132	119.42798	775.24573
266	5.85589	124.38477	728.38379	266	6.18726	121.94582	754.51050	266	6.53730	119.58095	781.73706
267	5.89493	124.55441	734.23969	267	6.22990	122.10635	760.69075	267	6.58361	119.73284	788.27435
268	5.93423	124.72292	740.13464	268	6.27263	122.26576	766.92755	268	6.63024	119.88367	794.85797
269	5.97379	124.89032	746.06885	269	6.31575	122.42410	773.20020	269	6.67721	120.03343	801.48822
270	6.01362	125.05661	752.04266	270	6.35917	122.58135	779.51598	270	6.72450	120.18214	808.16547
271	6.05371	125.22179	758.05627	271	6.40289	122.73752	785.87512	271	6.77214	120.32980	814.88996
272	6.09407	125.38589	764.10999	272	6.44691	122.89265	792.27802	272	6.82011	120.47643	821.66211
273	6.13469	125.54890	770.20404	273	6.49123	123.04670	798.72491	273	6.86842	120.62202	828.48218
274	6.17559	125.71082	776.33875	274	6.53586	123.19970	805.21619	274	6.91707	120.76659	835.35059
275	6.21676	125.87168	782.51434	275	6.58080	123.35166	811.75201	275	6.96606	120.91015	842.26770

n				n				n			
276	8.25821	126.03147	788.73108	276	8.62604	123.50258	818.33282	276	7.01541	121.05269	849.23376
277	8.29993	126.19020	794.98932	277	8.67159	123.65247	824.96866	277	7.06510	121.19423	856.24915
278	8.34198	126.34789	801.34789	278	8.71746	123.80133	831.63043	278	7.11514	121.33478	863.31427
279	8.38421	126.50452	807.63116	279	8.76364	123.94918	838.34790	279	7.16554	121.47433	870.42838
280	8.42677	126.66012	814.01538	280	8.81014	124.09602	845.11157	280	7.21630	121.61291	877.59491
281	8.46961	126.81469	820.44214	281	8.85696	124.24186	851.92169	281	7.26741	121.75051	884.81122
282	8.51274	126.96823	826.91174	282	8.90410	124.38670	858.77863	282	7.31889	121.88714	892.07861
283	8.55616	127.12076	833.42450	283	8.95157	124.53056	865.68274	283	7.37073	122.02281	899.39752
284	8.59987	127.27228	839.96065	284	8.99936	124.67342	872.63434	284	7.42294	122.15753	906.76825
285	8.64387	127.42280	846.58051	285	9.04748	124.81532	879.63367	285	7.47552	122.29130	914.19122
286	8.68816	127.57231	853.22437	286	9.09593	124.95625	886.68115	286	7.52847	122.42413	921.66675
287	8.73275	127.72084	859.84254	287	9.14472	125.09621	893.77710	287	7.58190	122.55602	929.19519
288	8.77764	127.86839	866.64254	288	9.19384	125.23521	900.92191	288	7.63550	122.68699	936.77698
289	8.82282	128.01496	873.42291	289	9.24330	125.37328	908.11566	289	7.68959	122.81704	944.41248
290	8.86831	128.16054	880.24579	290	9.29309	125.51039	915.35895	290	7.74406	122.94617	952.10211
291	8.91409	128.30518	887.11407	291	9.34323	125.64657	922.65204	291	7.79691	123.07439	959.84613
292	8.96019	128.44885	894.02814	292	9.39373	125.78182	929.99530	292	7.85415	123.20171	967.64508
293	9.00659	128.59157	900.98834	293	9.44455	125.91613	937.38898	293	7.90979	123.32814	975.49821
294	9.05330	128.73335	907.99493	294	9.49573	126.04955	944.83356	294	7.96581	123.45367	983.40900
295	9.10032	128.87419	915.04822	295	9.54726	126.18205	952.32928	295	8.02224	123.57833	991.37482
296	9.14766	129.01410	922.14856	296	9.59915	126.31365	959.87653	296	8.07906	123.70210	999.39703
297	9.19531	129.15308	929.29208	297	9.65140	126.44434	967.47571	297	8.13629	123.82501	1007.47614
298	9.24328	129.29114	936.49152	298	9.70400	126.57415	975.12708	298	8.19392	123.94705	1015.61243
299	9.29157	129.42828	943.73480	299	9.75696	126.70306	982.83105	299	8.25196	124.06824	1023.80634
300	9.34018	129.56451	951.02837	300	9.81029	126.83110	990.58807	300	8.31041	124.18857	1032.05823

Table 1. (continued) Annuities

M	C(8.00,M,12)	A(8.00,M,12)	S(8.00,M,12)	C(8.25,M,12)	A(8.25,M,12)	S(8.25,M,12)	C(8.50,M,12)	A(8.50,M,12)	S(8.50,M,12)
301	7.38811	129.69984	956.36652	7.86399	126.95826	998.39832	8.36928	124.30905	1040.36965
302	7.43837	129.83429	965.75568	7.91905	127.08456	1006.26233	8.42856	124.42670	1048.73792
303	7.48796	129.96763	973.19403	7.97249	127.20398	1014.18039	8.48838	124.54450	1057.16650
304	7.53788	130.10049	980.68201	8.02730	127.33456	1022.15289	8.54838	124.66148	1065.65478
305	7.58813	130.23228	988.21965	8.08249	127.45828	1030.18018	8.60894	124.77764	1074.20313
306	7.63872	130.36319	995.80798	8.13806	127.58116	1038.26257	8.66992	124.89298	1082.81213
307	7.68964	130.49324	1003.44672	8.19401	127.70320	1046.40063	8.73133	125.00751	1091.48206
308	7.74091	130.62242	1011.13635	8.25034	127.82441	1054.59473	8.79318	125.12124	1100.21338
309	7.79252	130.75075	1018.87726	8.30706	127.94479	1062.84509	8.85546	125.23416	1109.00647
310	7.84447	130.87823	1026.66980	8.36417	128.06435	1071.15210	8.91819	125.34630	1117.86194
311	7.89676	131.00487	1034.51416	8.42167	128.18309	1079.51624	8.98136	125.45763	1126.78015
312	7.94941	131.13066	1042.41092	8.47957	128.30101	1087.93799	9.04498	125.56820	1135.76147
313	8.00240	131.25562	1050.36035	8.53787	128.41814	1096.41748	9.10905	125.67798	1144.80652
314	8.05575	131.37976	1058.36279	8.59657	128.53447	1104.95544	9.17357	125.78699	1153.91553
315	8.10946	131.50307	1066.41858	8.65567	128.64999	1113.55200	9.23855	125.89523	1163.08911
316	8.16352	131.62556	1074.52796	8.71518	128.76474	1122.20764	9.30399	126.00271	1172.32764
317	8.21794	131.74725	1082.69153	8.77509	128.87869	1130.92285	9.36989	126.10944	1181.63771
318	8.27273	131.86813	1090.90942	8.83542	128.99188	1139.69788	9.43626	126.21541	1191.00159
319	8.32788	131.98820	1099.18225	8.89617	129.10429	1148.53333	9.50310	126.32063	1200.43787
320	8.38340	132.10750	1107.51013	8.95733	129.21593	1157.42944	9.57041	126.42513	1209.94092
321	8.43929	132.22598	1115.88343	9.01891	129.32681	1166.38684	9.63821	126.52888	1219.51135
322	8.49555	132.34363	1124.33276	9.08091	129.43694	1175.40576	9.70648	126.63190	1229.14964
323	8.55219	132.46062	1132.82837	9.14335	129.54630	1184.48669	9.77523	126.73420	1238.85598
324	8.60920	132.57678	1141.38049	9.20621	129.65492	1193.63000	9.84447	126.83578	1248.63123
325	8.66660	132.69217	1149.98975	9.26960	129.76280	1202.83618	9.91420	126.93665	1258.47571

326	8.72438	132.90678	1158.65637	326	9.33323	129.86995	1212.10571	326	9.99443	127.03680	1268.38988
327	8.78254	132.96965	1167.30074	327	9.39739	129.97636	1221.43896	327	10.05515	127.13625	1278.37439
328	8.84109	133.03375	1176.16321	328	9.46200	130.08205	1230.83630	328	10.12638	127.23501	1288.42944
329	8.90003	133.14612	1185.00427	329	9.52705	130.18701	1240.29834	329	10.19910	127.33306	1298.55591
330	8.95936	133.25774	1193.90430	330	9.59255	130.29126	1249.82532	330	10.27034	127.43044	1308.75403
331	9.01909	133.36961	1202.86365	331	9.65850	130.39479	1259.41797	331	10.34309	127.52711	1319.02429
332	9.07922	133.47874	1211.88281	332	9.72490	130.49762	1269.07642	332	10.41635	127.62312	1329.36743
333	9.13975	133.58817	1220.86204	333	9.79178	130.59975	1278.80127	333	10.49014	127.71844	1339.78381
334	9.20068	133.69695	1230.10181	334	9.85908	130.70117	1288.59302	334	10.56444	127.81310	1350.27393
335	9.26202	133.80481	1239.30249	335	9.92686	130.80191	1298.45215	335	10.63927	127.90710	1360.83838
336	9.32376	133.91206	1248.56445	336	9.99511	130.90196	1308.37903	336	10.71463	128.00043	1371.47766
337	9.38592	134.01962	1257.88818	337	10.06382	131.00133	1318.37415	337	10.79053	128.09309	1382.19026
338	9.44849	134.12445	1267.27417	338	10.13301	131.10002	1328.43799	338	10.86696	128.18512	1392.98279
339	9.51148	134.22958	1276.72266	339	10.20267	131.19803	1338.57092	339	10.94394	128.27649	1403.84973
340	9.57489	134.33403	1286.23413	340	10.27282	131.29538	1348.77368	340	11.02145	128.36722	1414.78370
341	9.63873	134.43777	1295.90886	341	10.34344	131.39206	1359.04639	341	11.09952	128.45732	1425.81519
342	9.70298	134.54083	1305.44775	342	10.41456	131.48807	1369.38989	342	11.17815	128.54678	1436.91467
343	9.76767	134.64320	1315.15076	343	10.49616	131.58344	1379.80444	343	11.25732	128.63560	1448.09277
344	9.83279	134.74492	1324.91046	344	10.55825	131.67815	1390.29065	344	11.33706	128.72382	1459.35010
345	9.89834	134.84533	1334.75122	345	10.63084	131.77222	1400.84888	345	11.41737	128.81140	1470.68713
346	9.96433	134.94630	1344.64954	346	10.70392	131.86563	1411.47974	346	11.49824	128.89838	1482.10461
347	10.03076	135.04599	1354.60189	347	10.77751	131.95842	1422.18359	347	11.57969	128.98473	1493.60278
348	10.09763	135.14502	1364.64465	348	10.85161	132.05058	1432.96106	348	11.66171	129.07048	1505.18250
349	10.16495	135.24339	1374.74231	349	10.92621	132.14211	1443.81274	349	11.74431	129.15562	1516.84424
350	10.23271	135.34113	1384.90723	350	11.00133	132.23300	1454.73989	350	11.82750	129.24017	1528.58850

Table 1. (continued) Annuities

M	CI 8.00,M,12	AI 8.00,M,12	SI 8.00,M,12	M	CI 8.25,M,12	AI 8.25,M,12	SI 8.25,M,12	M	CI 8.50,M,12	AI 8.50,M,12	SI 8.50,M,12
351	10.30093	135.43820	1396.13969	351	11.07696	132.32327	1465.74023	351	11.91128	129.32413	1540.41602
352	10.36961	135.53464	1405.44000	352	11.15312	132.41293	1476.81726	352	11.99665	129.40749	1552.32727
353	10.43874	135.63043	1415.81042	353	11.22980	132.50198	1487.97034	353	12.08062	129.49026	1564.32300
354	10.50833	135.72660	1426.24915	354	11.30700	132.59042	1499.20020	354	12.16619	129.57246	1576.40356
355	10.57838	135.82013	1436.75757	355	11.38474	132.67827	1510.50720	355	12.25237	129.65408	1588.56970
356	10.64891	135.91403	1447.33594	356	11.46301	132.76550	1521.89185	356	12.33916	129.73512	1600.82214
357	10.71990	136.00732	1457.98406	357	11.54181	132.85214	1533.35498	357	12.42656	129.81560	1613.16125
358	10.79136	136.09999	1468.70471	358	11.62117	132.93819	1544.89673	358	12.51458	129.89551	1625.58789
359	10.86331	136.19205	1479.49609	359	11.70106	133.02365	1556.51782	359	12.60323	129.97485	1638.10242
360	10.93573	136.28349	1490.35938	360	11.78151	133.10854	1568.21899	360	12.69250	130.05363	1650.70569
361	11.00863	136.37433	1501.29517	361	11.86250	133.19284	1580.00049	361	12.78240	130.13187	1663.39819
362	11.08202	136.46455	1512.30371	362	11.94406	133.27655	1591.86292	362	12.87295	130.20955	1676.19054
363	11.15550	136.55420	1523.38574	363	12.02617	133.35971	1603.80701	363	12.96413	130.28668	1689.05347
364	11.23028	136.64325	1534.54163	364	12.10885	133.44229	1615.83313	364	13.05596	130.36328	1702.01758
365	11.30515	136.73170	1545.77197	365	12.19210	133.52431	1627.94202	365	13.14844	130.43933	1715.07361
366	11.39051	136.81956	1557.07715	366	12.27592	133.60577	1640.13416	366	13.24157	130.51485	1728.22205
367	11.45638	136.90686	1568.45764	367	12.36032	133.68668	1652.41003	367	13.33537	130.58984	1741.46362
368	11.53276	136.99356	1579.91406	368	12.44530	133.76703	1664.77039	368	13.42983	130.66431	1754.79695
369	11.60964	137.07970	1591.44678	369	12.53096	133.84683	1677.21570	369	13.52496	130.73824	1768.22876
370	11.68704	137.16527	1603.05640	370	12.61701	133.92609	1689.74658	370	13.62076	130.81166	1781.75378
371	11.76496	137.25026	1614.74341	371	12.70375	134.00481	1702.36353	371	13.71724	130.88457	1795.37451
372	11.84339	137.33470	1626.50842	372	12.79109	134.08298	1715.06726	372	13.81440	130.95696	1809.09180
373	11.92235	137.41858	1638.35376	373	12.87903	134.16063	1727.85840	373	13.91225	131.02882	1822.90613
374	12.00183	137.50189	1650.27417	374	12.96757	134.23775	1740.73743	374	14.01060	131.10020	1836.81836
375	12.08184	137.58467	1662.27600	375	13.05672	134.31433	1753.70496	375	14.11004	131.17107	1850.82922

n				n				n			
376	12.16238	137.66689	1674.35779	376	13.14649	134.33040	1766.76172	376	14.20999	131.24144	1864.93921
377	12.24347	137.74857	1686.52014	377	13.23687	134.46594	1779.90820	377	14.31064	131.31133	1879.14917
378	12.32509	137.82970	1698.76367	378	13.32787	134.54097	1793.14502	378	14.41201	131.38071	1893.45984
379	12.40726	137.91029	1711.08875	379	13.41960	134.61549	1806.47290	379	14.51409	131.44962	1907.87183
380	12.48997	137.99036	1723.49597	380	13.51176	134.68950	1819.89246	380	14.61690	131.51802	1922.38599
381	12.57324	138.06990	1735.98596	381	13.60645	134.76302	1833.40417	381	14.72044	131.58596	1937.00281
382	12.65706	138.14890	1748.55920	382	13.69819	134.83601	1847.00879	382	14.82471	131.65341	1951.72327
383	12.74144	138.22739	1761.21631	383	13.79236	134.90851	1860.70703	383	14.92972	131.72040	1966.54797
384	12.82638	138.30534	1773.96776	384	13.88718	134.99053	1874.49939	384	15.03547	131.78690	1981.47766
385	12.91189	138.38280	1786.78418	385	13.98266	135.05205	1888.39660	385	15.14197	131.85294	1996.51318
386	12.99797	138.45973	1799.69604	386	14.07879	135.12308	1902.36926	386	15.24922	131.91852	2011.65515
387	13.08463	138.53616	1812.69397	387	14.17558	135.18362	1916.44900	387	15.35724	131.98363	2026.90442
388	13.17186	138.61208	1825.77856	388	14.27304	135.26367	1930.62366	388	15.46602	132.04829	2042.28160
389	13.25967	138.68750	1838.96044	389	14.37116	135.33327	1944.89681	389	15.57557	132.11250	2057.72754
390	13.34807	138.76241	1852.21021	390	14.46997	135.40237	1969.26782	390	15.68590	132.17625	2073.30322
391	13.43705	138.83684	1865.55833	391	14.56945	135.47101	1973.73779	391	15.79701	132.23965	2088.98901
392	13.52664	138.91077	1878.99524	392	14.66961	135.53917	1988.30725	392	15.90890	132.30241	2104.78613
393	13.61681	138.98419	1892.52185	393	14.77047	135.60687	2002.97681	393	16.02159	132.36482	2120.63607
394	13.70759	139.05714	1906.13867	394	14.87201	135.67412	2017.74731	394	16.13507	132.42680	2136.71655
395	13.79897	139.12962	1919.84631	395	14.97428	135.74091	2032.61928	395	16.24936	132.48834	2152.85156
396	13.89037	139.20161	1933.64528	396	15.07721	135.80722	2047.53063	396	16.36447	132.54945	2169.43107
397	13.98357	139.27312	1947.53825	397	15.18086	135.87039	2062.87065	397	16.48038	132.61012	2186.46558
398	14.07680	139.34416	1961.51978	398	15.28523	135.93852	2077.85156	398	16.59712	132.67038	2201.94580
399	14.17064	139.41473	1975.59608	399	15.39032	136.00349	2093.13672	399	16.71468	132.73021	2218.54297
400	14.26511	139.48483	1969.76733	400	15.43612	136.06802	2108.52710	400	16.83307	132.78961	2235.25757

Table 1. (continued) Annuities

N	C(8.00,M,12)	A(8.00,M,12)	S(8.00,M,12)	N	C(8.25,M,12)	A(8.25,M,12)	S(8.25,M,12)	N	C(8.50,M,12)	A(8.50,M,12)	S(8.50,M,12)
401	14.36022	139.55447	2004.03235	401	15.60266	136.13213	2124.02319	401	16.95231	132.84960	2252.09082
402	14.45595	139.62364	2018.39258	402	15.70993	136.19577	2139.62598	402	17.07239	132.90718	2269.04297
403	14.55232	139.69237	2032.84851	403	15.81793	136.25899	2155.33594	403	17.19332	132.96533	2286.11548
404	14.64934	139.76062	2047.40088	404	15.92668	136.32178	2171.15381	404	17.31510	133.02309	2303.30884
405	14.74700	139.82843	2062.05005	405	16.03618	136.38414	2187.06057	405	17.43775	133.08044	2320.62378
406	14.84531	139.89680	2076.79712	406	16.14643	136.44608	2203.11670	406	17.56127	133.13737	2338.06152
407	14.94428	139.96271	2091.64258	407	16.25743	136.50758	2219.26294	407	17.68566	133.19392	2355.62280
408	15.04391	140.02917	2106.56667	408	16.36920	136.56868	2235.52051	408	17.81094	133.25008	2373.30859
409	15.14421	140.09521	2121.63062	409	16.48174	136.62935	2251.88965	409	17.93710	133.30582	2391.11938
410	15.24517	140.16081	2136.77490	410	16.59505	136.68961	2268.37134	410	18.06415	133.36118	2409.05664
411	15.34680	140.22597	2152.02002	411	16.70914	136.74945	2284.96655	411	18.19210	133.41615	2427.12061
412	15.44911	140.29070	2167.36694	412	16.82402	136.80888	2301.67554	412	18.32096	133.47073	2445.31274
413	15.55211	140.35500	2182.81592	413	16.93969	136.86792	2318.49976	413	18.45074	133.52493	2463.63379
414	15.65579	140.41887	2198.36816	414	17.05614	136.92656	2335.43945	414	18.58143	133.57875	2482.08447
415	15.76016	140.48232	2214.02393	415	17.17341	136.98479	2352.49661	415	18.71305	133.63219	2500.66602
416	15.86523	140.54535	2229.78394	416	17.29147	137.04262	2369.66895	416	18.84560	133.68524	2519.37891
417	15.97099	140.60797	2245.64917	417	17.41035	137.10005	2386.96045	417	18.97909	133.73793	2538.22461
418	16.07747	140.67017	2261.62036	418	17.53005	137.15710	2404.37085	418	19.11353	133.79025	2557.20435
419	16.18465	140.73195	2277.69775	419	17.65057	137.21375	2421.90088	419	19.24891	133.84221	2576.31714
420	16.29255	140.79333	2293.88232	420	17.77192	137.27002	2439.55127	420	19.38526	133.89380	2595.56616
421	16.40117	140.85431	2310.17480	421	17.89410	137.32591	2457.32324	421	19.52257	133.94502	2614.95142
422	16.51051	140.91487	2326.57617	422	18.01712	137.38141	2475.21729	422	19.66096	133.99588	2634.47388
423	16.62058	140.97504	2343.08667	423	18.14098	137.43654	2493.23438	423	19.80012	134.04639	2654.13477
424	16.73138	141.03481	2359.70728	424	18.26571	137.49127	2511.37549	424	19.94037	134.09653	2673.93506
425	16.84292	141.09418	2376.43848	425	18.39128	137.54565	2529.64111	425	20.08162	134.14633	2699.87524

426	16.95521	141.15315	2398.28149
427	17.06824	141.21175	2410.23657
428	17.18203	141.26994	2427.30493
429	17.29658	141.32776	2444.48706
430	17.41189	141.38519	2461.78345
431	17.52797	141.44225	2479.19631
432	17.64482	141.49892	2496.72339
433	17.76245	141.55522	2514.36816
434	17.88087	141.61115	2532.13062
435	18.00008	141.66670	2550.01147
436	18.12008	141.72188	2568.00172
437	18.24088	141.77670	2586.13159
438	18.36248	141.83116	2604.37256
439	18.48490	141.88525	2622.73511
440	18.60813	141.93900	2641.21997
441	18.73219	141.99239	2659.82813
442	18.85707	142.04541	2678.56030
443	18.98278	142.09810	2697.41748
444	19.10933	142.15042	2716.40015
445	19.23673	142.20241	2735.50952
446	19.36497	142.25404	2754.74634
447	19.49407	142.30534	2774.11108
448	19.62403	142.35631	2793.60522
449	19.75486	142.40692	2813.22925
450	19.88656	142.45721	2832.98413

426	18.51772	137.59966	2548.03247
427	18.64503	137.65329	2566.55029
428	18.77322	137.70656	2585.19631
429	18.90228	137.75946	2603.96861
430	19.03224	137.81200	2622.87061
431	19.16308	137.86418	2641.90308
432	19.29483	137.91602	2661.06616
433	19.42748	137.96748	2680.36084
434	19.56104	138.01662	2699.78833
435	19.69553	138.06338	2719.34337
436	19.83093	138.11981	2739.04492
437	19.96727	138.16989	2758.87598
438	20.10455	138.21964	2778.84302
439	20.24277	138.26903	2798.94775
440	20.38194	138.31810	2819.13043
441	20.52206	138.36682	2839.57227
442	20.66315	138.41522	2860.09448
443	20.80521	138.46329	2880.75757
444	20.94824	138.51102	2901.56274
445	21.09226	138.55843	2922.51099
446	21.23727	138.60551	2943.60327
447	21.38328	138.65228	2964.84058
448	21.53029	138.69873	2986.22388
449	21.67831	138.74486	3007.75415
450	21.82735	138.79066	3029.43237

426	20.22396	134.19577	2713.96703
427	20.36711	134.24487	2734.19091
428	20.51138	134.29362	2754.54785
429	20.65667	134.34204	2775.05033
430	20.80299	134.39011	2795.71606
431	20.95034	134.43784	2816.51904
432	21.09974	134.48523	2837.46924
433	21.24819	134.53230	2858.56812
434	21.39870	134.57903	2879.81616
435	21.55027	134.62543	2901.21484
436	21.70292	134.67151	2922.76514
437	21.85665	134.71727	2944.46802
438	22.01147	134.76270	2966.32471
439	22.16738	134.80780	2988.33618
440	22.32440	134.85260	3010.50366
441	22.48253	134.89708	3032.82813
442	22.64178	134.94124	3055.31055
443	22.80216	134.98511	3077.96239
444	22.96368	135.02864	3100.75439
445	23.12634	135.07188	3123.71826
446	23.29015	135.11482	3146.84448
447	23.45512	135.15746	3170.13477
448	23.62126	135.19980	3193.58984
449	23.78858	135.24184	3217.21118
450	23.95708	135.28357	3240.99976

Table 1. (continued) Annuities

M	CI(8.00,M,12)	AI(8.00,M,12)	SI(8.00,M,12)	M	CI(8.25,M,12)	AI(8.25,M,12)	SI(8.25,M,12)	M	CI(8.50,M,12)	AI(8.50,M,12)	SI(8.50,M,12)
451	20.01914	142.50716	2852.87085	451	21.97741	138.83817	3051.25977	451	24.12678	135.32501	3264.95679
452	20.15260	142.55678	2872.88999	452	22.12851	138.88136	3073.23730	452	24.29767	135.36618	3289.08350
453	20.28695	142.60608	2890.04248	453	22.28064	138.92424	3096.36572	453	24.46978	135.40704	3313.38110
454	20.42220	142.65504	2913.32935	454	22.43382	138.97083	3117.84648	454	24.64311	135.44762	3337.85107
455	20.55834	142.70369	2933.75171	455	22.58805	139.01509	3140.08008	455	24.81767	135.48792	3362.49414
456	20.69540	142.75200	2954.31006	456	22.74334	139.05907	3162.66821	456	24.99346	135.52792	3387.31177
457	20.83337	142.80000	2975.00537	457	22.89970	139.10272	3185.41162	457	25.17050	135.56766	3412.30518
458	20.97226	142.84769	2996.83862	458	23.05714	139.14610	3208.31128	458	25.34879	135.60710	3437.47559
459	21.11207	142.89505	3016.81104	459	23.21566	139.18918	3231.36841	459	25.52834	135.64627	3462.82446
460	21.25282	142.94211	3037.92310	460	23.37527	139.23195	3254.58398	460	25.70917	135.68518	3488.35278
461	21.39451	142.98885	3059.17578	461	23.53597	139.27444	3277.95947	461	25.89127	135.72380	3514.06201
462	21.53714	143.03528	3080.57031	462	23.69778	139.31664	3301.49536	462	26.07467	135.76215	3539.95337
463	21.68072	143.08141	3102.10742	463	23.86070	139.35855	3325.19312	463	26.25937	135.80023	3566.02783
464	21.82525	143.12723	3123.78833	464	24.02474	139.40018	3349.05371	464	26.44537	135.83904	3592.28735
465	21.97074	143.17273	3145.61353	465	24.18991	139.44151	3373.07661	465	26.63269	135.87560	3618.73267
466	22.11720	143.21793	3167.58423	466	24.35622	139.48257	3397.26855	466	26.82134	135.91287	3645.36548
467	22.26463	143.26286	3189.70142	467	24.52367	139.52335	3421.62476	467	27.01132	135.94989	3672.10677
468	22.41311	143.30748	3211.96606	468	24.69227	139.56384	3446.14844	468	27.20265	135.98666	3699.19800
469	22.56253	143.35181	3234.37939	469	24.86203	139.60406	3470.84058	469	27.39534	136.02316	3726.40063
470	22.71296	143.39583	3256.94189	470	25.03296	139.64401	3495.70264	470	27.58939	136.05940	3753.79690
471	22.86436	143.43966	3279.65479	471	25.20506	139.68369	3520.73560	471	27.76481	136.09540	3781.38550
472	23.01679	143.48302	3302.51904	472	25.37834	139.72310	3545.94067	472	27.98162	136.13113	3809.17017
473	23.17024	143.52617	3325.53589	473	25.55282	139.76222	3571.31909	473	28.17982	136.16663	3837.15106
474	23.32471	143.56905	3348.70605	474	25.72849	139.80110	3596.87183	474	28.37943	136.20186	3865.33179
475	23.48021	143.61163	3372.03076	475	25.90538	139.83969	3622.60034	475	28.59045	136.23685	3893.71118

n				n				n			n	
476	23.63674	143.65395	3395.51099	476	26.08348	139.87904	3648.50562	476	136.27159	28.76290	476	3922.29150
477	23.79432	143.69597	3419.14771	477	26.26290	139.91611	3674.58911	477	136.30609	28.96678	477	3951.07446
478	23.96295	143.73772	3442.94214	478	26.44336	139.95393	3700.85205	478	136.34035	29.19210	478	3980.06128
479	24.11263	143.77919	3466.89502	479	26.62516	139.99149	3727.29541	479	136.37436	29.39818	479	4009.25342
480	24.27338	143.82039	3491.00781	480	26.80820	140.02879	3753.92041	480	136.40814	29.60712	480	4038.65210
481	24.43521	143.86131	3515.28101	481	26.99251	140.06584	3780.72876	481	136.44167	29.81884	481	4068.25928
482	24.59811	143.90196	3539.71631	482	27.17808	140.10263	3807.72119	482	136.47498	30.02804	482	4098.07617
483	24.76210	143.94235	3564.31445	483	27.36493	140.13918	3834.89941	483	136.50804	30.24074	483	4128.10400
484	24.92718	143.98247	3589.07642	484	27.55307	140.17548	3862.26416	484	136.54088	30.45494	484	4158.34473
485	25.09336	144.02231	3614.00366	485	27.74249	140.21152	3889.81738	485	136.57349	30.67067	485	4188.79980
486	25.26065	144.06190	3639.09692	486	27.93322	140.24731	3917.55991	486	136.60587	30.88792	486	4219.47021
487	25.42905	144.10123	3664.35767	487	28.12527	140.28287	3945.49292	487	136.63800	31.10671	487	4250.35840
488	25.59858	144.14029	3689.78687	488	28.31863	140.31818	3973.61841	488	136.66992	31.32705	488	4281.46484
489	25.76924	144.17909	3715.38525	489	28.51332	140.35326	4001.93701	489	136.70163	31.54894	489	4312.79199
490	25.94103	144.21765	3741.15454	490	28.70934	140.38809	4030.45020	490	136.73309	31.77242	490	4344.34082
491	26.11397	144.25594	3767.09570	491	28.90672	140.42268	4059.15967	491	136.76434	31.99747	491	4376.11328
492	26.28806	144.29398	3793.20947	492	29.10546	140.45703	4088.06641	492	136.79538	32.22412	492	4408.11084
493	26.46332	144.33177	3819.49756	493	29.30556	140.49117	4117.17188	493	136.82620	32.45237	493	4440.33456
494	26.63974	144.36931	3845.96094	494	29.50703	140.52505	4146.47705	494	136.85680	32.68224	494	4472.78760
495	26.81734	144.40660	3872.60059	495	29.70989	140.55872	4175.98438	495	136.88718	32.91374	495	4505.46973
496	26.99612	144.44363	3899.41797	496	29.91415	140.59213	4205.69434	496	136.91734	33.14688	496	4538.38330
497	27.17609	144.48044	3926.41418	497	30.11981	140.62840	4235.60840	497	136.94730	33.38167	497	4571.53027
498	27.35727	144.51698	3953.59033	498	30.32688	140.65831	4265.72803	498	136.97705	33.61813	498	4604.91211
499	27.53965	144.55330	3980.94751	499	30.53538	140.69106	4295.05518	499	137.00659	33.85625	499	4638.53027
500	27.72325	144.58937	4008.48706	500	30.74531	140.72359	4326.59033	500	137.03592	34.09607	500	4672.38623

Table 1. (continued) Annuities

M	C(8.75,M,12)	A(8.75,M,12)	S(8.75,M,12)	M	C(9.00,M,12)	A(9.00,M,12)	S(9.00,M,12)	M	C(9.25,M,12)	A(9.25,M,12)	S(9.25,M,12)
1	1.00729	0.99276	1.00000	1	1.00750	0.99256	1.00000	1	1.00771	0.99235	1.00000
2	1.01464	1.97834	2.00729	2	1.01506	1.97772	2.00750	2	1.01548	1.97711	2.00771
3	1.02203	2.95678	3.02193	3	1.02267	2.95556	3.02256	3	1.02330	2.95434	3.02318
4	1.02949	3.92813	4.04396	4	1.03034	3.92611	4.04523	4	1.03119	3.92409	4.04649
5	1.03699	4.89246	5.07345	5	1.03807	4.88944	5.07556	5	1.03914	4.88642	5.07768
6	1.04456	5.84980	6.11044	6	1.04585	5.84560	6.11363	6	1.04715	5.84140	6.11682
7	1.05217	6.80022	7.15500	7	1.05370	6.79464	7.15948	7	1.05522	6.79106	7.16397
8	1.05984	7.74375	8.20717	8	1.06160	7.73661	8.21318	8	1.06336	7.72948	8.21919
9	1.06757	8.68046	9.26701	9	1.06956	8.67158	9.27478	9	1.07155	8.66271	9.28255
10	1.07536	9.61038	10.33459	10	1.07758	9.59958	10.34434	10	1.07981	9.58879	10.35410
11	1.08320	10.53358	11.40994	11	1.08566	10.52067	11.42192	11	1.08814	10.50790	11.43392
12	1.09110	11.45009	12.49314	12	1.09381	11.43491	12.50759	12	1.09652	11.41977	12.52205
13	1.09905	12.35996	13.58424	13	1.10201	12.34234	13.60139	13	1.10498	12.32476	13.61858
14	1.10707	13.26325	14.68329	14	1.11028	13.24302	14.70340	14	1.11349	13.22284	14.72355
15	1.11514	14.16000	15.79035	15	1.11860	14.13699	15.81368	15	1.12208	14.11404	15.83705
16	1.12327	15.05026	16.90549	16	1.12699	15.02431	16.93228	16	1.13073	14.99843	16.95912
17	1.13146	15.93407	18.02876	17	1.13544	15.90502	18.05927	17	1.13944	15.87605	18.08985
18	1.13971	16.81149	19.16022	18	1.14396	16.77918	19.19472	18	1.14823	16.74696	19.22929
19	1.14802	17.68255	20.29993	19	1.15254	17.64683	20.33868	19	1.15708	17.61121	20.37752
20	1.15639	18.54731	21.44795	20	1.16118	18.50802	21.49122	20	1.16600	18.46884	21.53459
21	1.16482	19.40581	22.60434	21	1.16989	19.36280	22.65240	21	1.17498	19.31992	22.70059
22	1.17332	20.25810	23.76917	22	1.17867	20.21531	23.82229	22	1.18404	20.16448	23.87557
23	1.18187	21.10421	24.94248	23	1.18751	21.05331	25.00096	23	1.19317	21.00259	25.05961
24	1.19049	21.94420	26.12436	24	1.19641	21.88914	26.18847	24	1.20237	21.83428	26.25278
25	1.19917	22.77811	27.31484	25	1.20539	22.71875	27.38488	25	1.21163	22.65561	27.45515

n									
26	1.20791	23.60598	28.51402	1.21443	23.54219	28.50027	1.22097	23.47863	28.66678
27	1.21672	24.42786	29.72193	1.22354	24.35949	29.60470	1.23038	24.29139	29.88775
28	1.22559	25.24380	30.93965	1.23271	25.17071	31.02823	1.23987	25.09793	31.11814
29	1.23453	26.05382	32.16425	1.24196	25.97589	32.26094	1.24943	25.89929	32.35801
30	1.24353	26.85798	33.39878	1.25127	26.77508	33.50290	1.25906	26.69254	33.60743
31	1.25260	27.65632	34.64231	1.26066	27.56832	34.75417	1.26876	27.48071	34.86649
32	1.26173	28.44888	35.89491	1.27011	28.35565	36.01483	1.27854	28.26285	36.13525
33	1.27093	29.23570	37.15664	1.27964	29.13712	37.28494	1.28840	29.03901	37.41360
34	1.28020	30.01683	38.42758	1.28923	29.91278	38.56458	1.29833	29.80923	38.70219
35	1.28954	30.79230	39.70778	1.29890	30.68266	39.85381	1.30834	30.57355	40.00052
36	1.29894	31.56216	40.99731	1.30865	31.44680	41.15271	1.31842	31.33204	41.30886
37	1.30841	32.32645	42.29625	1.31846	32.20527	42.46136	1.32859	32.08472	42.62729
38	1.31795	33.08520	43.60466	1.32835	32.95808	43.77982	1.33883	32.83164	43.95587
39	1.32756	33.84946	44.92262	1.33835	33.70529	45.10817	1.34915	33.57285	45.29470
40	1.33724	34.58627	46.25018	1.34835	34.44694	46.44648	1.35955	34.30839	46.64384
41	1.34699	35.32867	47.58741	1.35846	35.18306	47.79483	1.37003	35.03830	48.00339
42	1.35681	36.06569	48.93441	1.36865	35.91371	49.15329	1.39059	35.76263	49.37341
43	1.36671	36.79737	50.29122	1.37891	36.63992	50.52194	1.39123	36.48142	50.75400
44	1.37667	37.52376	51.65738	1.38926	37.35873	51.90085	1.40195	37.19471	52.14523
45	1.38671	38.24489	53.03460	1.39968	38.07318	53.29011	1.41276	37.90255	53.54718
46	1.39682	38.96090	54.42131	1.41017	38.78231	54.68979	1.42365	38.60497	54.95994
47	1.40701	39.67153	55.81813	1.42075	39.49616	56.09596	1.43462	39.30201	56.38359
48	1.41727	40.37711	57.22514	1.43141	40.18478	57.52071	1.44568	39.99372	57.81821
49	1.42760	41.07759	58.64241	1.44214	40.87819	58.95211	1.45683	40.68015	59.26390
50	1.43801	41.77299	60.07001	1.45296	41.56644	60.39426	1.46806	41.36132	60.72072

Table 1. (continued) Annuities

M	CI 8.75,M,12	AI 8.75,M,12	SI 8.75,M,12	M	CI 9.00,M,12	AI 9.00,M,12	SI 9.00,M,12	M	CI 9.25,M,12	AI 9.25,M,12	SI 9.25,M,12
51	1.44850	42.46337	61.50802	51	1.46385	42.24957	61.84721	51	1.47337	42.03728	62.18878
52	1.45906	43.14874	62.99651	52	1.47483	42.90762	63.31120	52	1.48078	42.70808	63.66815
53	1.46970	43.83615	64.54557	53	1.48599	43.60061	64.78590	53	1.50227	43.37374	65.15892
54	1.48041	44.50464	65.98557	54	1.49704	44.26160	66.27179	54	1.51365	44.03431	66.66119
55	1.49121	45.17504	67.36568	55	1.50827	44.93161	67.76883	55	1.51852	44.68982	68.17504
56	1.50208	45.84098	68.85689	56	1.51958	45.58969	69.27710	56	1.52728	45.34032	69.70055
57	1.51303	46.50190	70.35897	57	1.53097	46.24287	70.75668	57	1.54912	45.98585	71.23783
58	1.52407	47.15804	71.87200	58	1.54246	46.89118	72.32765	58	1.56107	46.62644	72.78596
59	1.53518	47.80943	73.39607	59	1.55403	47.53467	73.87011	59	1.57310	47.26213	74.34902
60	1.54637	48.45611	74.93125	60	1.56568	48.17337	75.42413	60	1.58523	47.89295	75.92112
61	1.55765	49.09810	76.47762	61	1.57742	48.80732	76.98981	61	1.59744	48.51895	77.50635
62	1.56901	49.73545	78.03527	62	1.58925	49.43654	78.56724	62	1.60976	49.14016	79.10379
63	1.58045	50.36818	79.60428	63	1.60117	50.06108	80.15649	63	1.62217	49.75662	80.71355
64	1.59197	50.99633	81.18473	64	1.61318	50.68098	81.75767	64	1.63467	50.36837	82.33572
65	1.60358	51.61993	82.77670	65	1.62528	51.29626	83.37085	65	1.64727	50.97543	83.97038
66	1.61527	52.23903	84.38028	66	1.63747	51.90695	84.99613	66	1.65997	51.57785	85.61766
67	1.62705	52.85363	85.99555	67	1.64975	52.51310	86.63360	67	1.67277	52.17566	87.27763
68	1.63891	53.46379	87.62260	68	1.66213	53.11474	88.28336	68	1.68566	52.76890	88.95039
69	1.65087	54.06954	89.26152	69	1.67459	53.71191	89.94548	69	1.69965	53.35760	90.63605
70	1.66290	54.67089	90.91238	70	1.68715	54.30462	91.62007	70	1.71175	53.94180	92.33470
71	1.67503	55.26790	92.57529	71	1.69980	54.89290	93.30722	71	1.72494	54.52153	94.04645
72	1.68724	55.86058	94.25031	72	1.71255	55.47685	95.00703	72	1.73824	55.09683	95.77139
73	1.69954	56.44897	95.93756	73	1.72540	56.05642	96.71967	73	1.75164	55.66772	97.50963
74	1.71194	57.03311	97.63710	74	1.73834	56.63169	98.44498	74	1.76514	56.23425	99.26127
75	1.72442	57.61301	99.34904	75	1.75137	57.20267	100.18331	75	1.77875	56.79644	101.02641

n				n				n			
76	1.73899	58.18872	101.07346	76	1.76451	57.76639	101.93468	76	1.79246	57.35434	102.80515
77	1.74966	58.76026	102.81046	77	1.77774	58.33191	103.69920	77	1.80627	57.90796	104.59761
78	1.76242	59.32766	104.56011	78	1.79108	58.89023	105.47694	78	1.82020	58.45736	106.40388
79	1.77527	59.89096	106.32253	79	1.80451	59.44440	107.26801	79	1.83423	59.00254	108.22408
80	1.78821	60.45018	108.09790	80	1.81804	59.99444	109.07253	80	1.84837	59.54356	110.05830
81	1.80125	61.00534	109.88601	81	1.83168	60.54039	110.89057	81	1.86261	60.08044	111.90667
82	1.81439	61.55650	111.68726	82	1.84542	61.08227	112.72225	82	1.87697	60.61322	113.76929
83	1.82762	62.10366	113.50165	83	1.85926	61.62012	114.56767	83	1.89144	61.14191	115.64626
84	1.84094	62.64686	115.32927	84	1.87320	62.15396	116.42693	84	1.90602	61.66657	117.53770
85	1.85437	63.18612	117.17021	85	1.88725	62.68383	118.30013	85	1.92071	62.18721	119.44372
86	1.86789	63.72149	119.02457	86	1.90141	63.20976	120.18738	86	1.93552	62.70387	121.36443
87	1.88151	64.25298	120.89246	87	1.91567	63.73177	122.08878	87	1.95044	63.21657	123.29994
88	1.89523	64.78062	122.77397	88	1.93003	64.24999	124.00445	88	1.96547	63.72535	125.25038
89	1.90905	65.30444	124.66920	89	1.94451	64.76417	125.93448	89	1.98062	64.23025	127.21585
90	1.92297	65.82447	126.57825	90	1.95909	65.27460	127.87899	90	1.99589	64.73128	129.19647
91	1.93699	66.34074	128.50121	91	1.97379	65.78124	129.83907	91	2.01127	65.22847	131.19237
92	1.95111	66.85326	130.43820	92	1.98859	66.28412	131.81186	92	2.02678	65.72186	133.20364
93	1.96534	67.36208	132.38931	93	2.00350	66.78249	133.80046	93	2.04240	66.21149	135.23041
94	1.97967	67.86722	134.35464	94	2.01853	67.27965	135.80396	94	2.05814	66.69736	137.27281
95	1.99410	68.36869	136.33432	95	2.03367	67.77037	137.82249	95	2.07401	67.17952	139.33096
96	2.00864	68.86654	138.32841	96	2.04892	68.25844	139.85616	96	2.09000	67.65799	141.40497
97	2.02329	69.36079	140.33707	97	2.06429	68.74287	141.90508	97	2.10611	68.13280	143.49458
98	2.03804	69.85146	142.36035	98	2.07977	69.22369	143.96386	98	2.12234	68.60397	145.60107
99	2.05290	70.33857	144.39841	99	2.09537	69.70093	146.04913	99	2.13870	89.07155	147.72342
100	2.06787	70.82216	146.45131	100	2.11108	70.17462	148.14450	100	2.15519	89.53555	149.86212

Table 1. (continued) Annuities

M	C(8.75,M,12)	A(8.75,M,12)	S(8.75,M,12)	M	C(9.00,M,12)	A(9.00,M,12)	S(9.00,M,12)	M	C(9.25,M,12)	A(9.25,M,12)	S(9.25,M,12)
101	2.08296	71.30225	148.51918	101	2.12692	70.64478	150.25558	101	2.17190	69.99599	152.01730
102	2.09814	71.77885	150.60213	102	2.14287	71.11145	152.38251	102	2.18854	70.45236	154.18910
103	2.11344	72.25201	152.70027	103	2.15894	71.57444	154.52538	103	2.20524	70.90635	156.37764
104	2.12885	72.72176	154.81371	104	2.17513	72.03438	156.68431	104	2.22241	71.36631	158.58305
105	2.14437	73.18810	156.94257	105	2.19145	72.49070	158.85945	105	2.23968	71.80283	160.80547
106	2.16001	73.65105	159.08693	106	2.20788	72.94352	161.05089	106	2.25681	72.24593	163.04501
107	2.17576	74.11063	161.24695	107	2.22444	73.39281	163.25877	107	2.27420	72.68565	165.30182
108	2.19162	74.56686	163.42270	108	2.24112	73.83838	165.48322	108	2.29173	73.12200	167.57602
109	2.20760	75.01993	165.61432	109	2.25793	74.28226	167.72433	109	2.30940	73.55502	169.86775
110	2.22370	75.46963	167.82193	110	2.27487	74.72185	169.98027	110	2.32720	73.98471	172.17714
111	2.23992	75.91607	170.04564	111	2.29193	75.15816	172.25714	111	2.34514	74.41113	174.50435
112	2.25625	76.35928	172.28555	112	2.30912	75.59122	174.54907	112	2.36321	74.83428	176.84949
113	2.27270	76.79929	174.54179	113	2.32644	76.02106	176.85818	113	2.38143	75.25420	179.21269
114	2.28927	77.23611	176.81450	114	2.34388	76.44769	179.18462	114	2.39979	75.67090	181.59413
115	2.30596	77.66977	179.10378	115	2.36146	76.87118	181.52850	115	2.41829	76.08442	183.99391
116	2.32278	78.10029	181.40973	116	2.37917	77.29149	183.88997	116	2.43693	76.49477	186.41220
117	2.33972	78.52769	183.73251	117	2.39702	77.70868	186.26915	117	2.45571	76.90199	188.84914
118	2.35678	78.95200	186.07224	118	2.41500	78.12276	188.66617	118	2.47464	77.30608	191.30484
119	2.37396	79.37323	188.42900	119	2.43311	78.53375	191.08116	119	2.49372	77.70709	193.77948
120	2.39127	79.79142	190.80296	120	2.45136	78.94169	193.51427	120	2.51294	78.10503	196.27321
121	2.40871	80.20658	193.19424	121	2.46974	79.34659	195.96562	121	2.53231	78.49992	198.78615
122	2.42627	80.61874	195.60205	122	2.48827	79.74847	198.43536	122	2.55183	78.89180	201.31845
123	2.44396	81.02791	198.02822	123	2.50693	80.14737	200.92363	123	2.57150	79.28068	203.87029
124	2.46178	81.43412	200.47319	124	2.52573	80.54330	203.43056	124	2.59132	79.66658	206.44179
125	2.47973	81.83739	202.93497	125	2.54467	80.93627	205.96628	125	2.61130	80.04954	209.03310

126	2.49782	82.23774	205.41470	126	2.56376	81.32632	208.50096	126	2.63143	80.42956	211.54439
127	2.51603	82.63519	207.92252	127	2.58299	81.71348	211.06473	127	2.65171	80.80667	214.27582
128	2.53437	83.02976	210.42854	128	2.60236	82.10774	213.64771	128	2.67215	81.19090	216.92754
129	2.55285	83.42148	212.92292	129	2.62188	82.47915	216.25006	129	2.69275	81.55227	219.59969
130	2.57147	83.81036	215.51578	130	2.64154	82.85771	218.87193	130	2.71350	81.92080	222.29243
131	2.59022	84.19643	218.00725	131	2.66131	83.23347	221.51347	131	2.73442	82.29651	225.00594
132	2.60911	84.57970	220.67746	132	2.68131	83.60641	224.17484	132	2.75550	82.64941	227.74036
133	2.62813	84.96021	223.28659	133	2.70142	83.97659	226.85614	133	2.77674	83.00955	230.49685
134	2.64729	85.33794	225.91470	134	2.72168	84.34401	229.55756	134	2.79814	83.36693	233.27260
135	2.66660	85.71296	228.56200	135	2.74209	84.70869	232.27925	135	2.81971	83.72158	236.07074
136	2.68604	86.08525	231.22859	136	2.76266	85.07066	235.02133	136	2.84145	84.07351	238.89046
137	2.70563	86.45485	233.91464	137	2.78338	85.42994	237.78400	137	2.86335	84.42275	241.73190
138	2.72536	86.82178	236.62027	138	2.80426	85.78654	240.56738	138	2.88542	84.76932	244.59625
139	2.74523	87.18604	239.34563	139	2.82529	86.14049	243.37163	139	2.90766	85.11324	247.49067
140	2.76525	87.54768	242.09085	140	2.84648	86.49180	246.19691	140	2.93008	85.45453	250.38834
141	2.78541	87.90669	244.85609	141	2.86783	86.84050	249.04340	141	2.95266	85.79321	253.31841
142	2.80572	88.26311	247.64151	142	2.88933	87.18660	251.91122	142	2.97542	86.12930	256.27106
143	2.82618	88.61694	250.44722	143	2.91100	87.53012	254.80055	143	2.99836	86.46281	259.24649
144	2.84679	88.96822	253.27341	144	2.93284	87.87109	257.71155	144	3.02147	86.79377	262.24484
145	2.86754	89.31694	256.12018	145	2.95483	88.20952	260.64438	145	3.04476	87.12221	265.26633
146	2.88845	89.66315	258.98773	146	2.97699	88.54543	263.59921	146	3.06823	87.44813	268.31107
147	2.90951	90.00685	261.87616	147	2.99932	88.87884	266.57623	147	3.09188	87.77155	271.37300
148	2.93073	90.34806	264.78568	148	3.02182	89.21039	269.57553	148	3.11572	88.09251	274.47119
149	2.95210	90.66681	267.71643	149	3.04448	89.53822	272.59735	149	3.13973	88.41100	277.56691
150	2.97362	91.02309	270.66852	150	3.06731	89.86424	275.64185	150	3.16393	88.72707	280.72865

Table 1. (continued) Annuities

M	C(8.75,M,12)	A(8.75,M,12)	S(8.75,M,12)	M	C(9.00,M,12)	A(9.00,M,12)	S(9.00,M,12)	M	C(9.25,M,12)	A(9.25,M,12)	S(9.25,M,12)
151	2.99531	91.35696	273.64215	151	3.09032	90.18784	278.70914	151	3.18832	89.04071	283.89056
152	3.01715	91.68839	276.63745	152	3.11350	90.50902	281.79947	152	3.21290	89.35196	287.07889
153	3.03915	92.01743	279.65460	153	3.13685	90.82780	284.91236	153	3.23767	89.66082	290.29181
154	3.06131	92.34409	282.69375	154	3.16037	91.14423	288.04980	154	3.26262	89.96732	293.52945
155	3.08363	92.66838	285.75505	155	3.18408	91.45829	291.21017	155	3.28777	90.27148	296.79208
156	3.10612	92.99033	288.83868	156	3.20796	91.77001	294.39426	156	3.31312	90.57331	300.07986
157	3.12876	93.30994	291.94480	157	3.23202	92.07941	297.60223	157	3.33865	90.87283	303.39297
158	3.15158	93.62724	295.07356	158	3.25626	92.38652	300.83423	158	3.36439	91.17007	306.73163
159	3.17456	93.94225	298.22514	159	3.28068	92.69134	304.09048	159	3.39032	91.46502	310.09601
160	3.19771	94.25497	301.39970	160	3.30528	92.99388	307.37119	160	3.41646	91.75772	313.48633
161	3.22102	94.56543	304.59741	161	3.33007	93.29417	310.67645	161	3.44279	92.04819	316.90260
162	3.24451	94.87364	307.81843	162	3.35505	93.59223	314.00653	162	3.46933	92.33643	320.34558
163	3.26817	95.17963	311.06294	163	3.38021	93.88807	317.36157	163	3.49607	92.62246	323.81491
164	3.29200	95.48339	314.33111	164	3.40556	94.18171	320.74179	164	3.52302	92.90630	327.31100
165	3.31600	95.78496	317.62311	165	3.43111	94.47316	324.14737	165	3.55018	93.18798	330.83401
166	3.34018	96.08434	320.93911	166	3.45684	94.76244	327.57846	166	3.57754	93.46751	334.38419
167	3.36454	96.38156	324.27929	167	3.48276	95.04957	331.03531	167	3.60512	93.74489	337.98173
168	3.38907	96.67663	327.64383	168	3.50889	95.33456	334.51907	168	3.63291	94.02015	341.56686
169	3.41378	96.96956	331.03290	169	3.53520	95.61743	338.02695	169	3.66091	94.29330	345.19877
170	3.43867	97.26037	334.44669	170	3.56172	95.89819	341.56216	170	3.68913	94.56437	348.86069
171	3.46375	97.54907	337.88535	171	3.58843	96.17686	345.12387	171	3.71757	94.83337	352.54984
172	3.48900	97.83569	341.34909	172	3.61534	96.45347	348.71231	172	3.74623	95.10030	356.26740
173	3.51444	98.12022	344.83810	173	3.64246	96.72800	352.32764	173	3.77510	95.36519	360.01361
174	3.54007	98.40271	348.35254	174	3.66978	97.00050	355.97009	174	3.80420	95.62806	363.78873
175	3.56588	98.68314	351.89261	175	3.69730	97.27097	359.63986	175	3.83353	95.88892	367.59293

n									
176	3.59188	98.96155	355.45850	3.72503	97.53942	363.33716	3.86308	96.14777	371.42645
177	3.61908	99.23794	359.05038	3.75297	97.80588	367.06219	3.89296	96.40466	375.28955
178	3.64446	99.51233	362.66846	3.78111	98.07035	370.81516	3.92298	96.65957	379.18240
179	3.67103	99.78473	366.31293	3.80947	98.33286	374.59628	3.95310	96.91254	383.10526
180	3.69790	100.05516	369.98395	3.83804	98.59341	378.40576	3.98357	97.16357	387.05838
181	3.72475	100.32363	373.68176	3.86683	98.85201	382.24360	4.01428	97.41268	391.04198
182	3.75192	100.59016	377.40652	3.89583	99.10870	386.11063	4.04523	97.65988	395.05621
183	3.77928	100.85477	381.15845	3.92505	99.36347	390.00647	4.07641	97.90520	399.10144
184	3.80694	101.11745	384.93771	3.95449	99.61635	393.93152	4.10783	98.14864	403.17796
185	3.83460	101.37823	388.74454	3.98414	99.86735	397.88599	4.13949	98.39021	407.28568
186	3.86256	101.63713	392.57916	4.01403	100.11647	401.87016	4.17140	98.62994	411.42517
187	3.89072	101.89415	396.44171	4.04413	100.36375	405.88416	4.20356	98.86784	415.59659
188	3.91909	102.14931	400.33243	4.07446	100.60918	409.92828	4.23596	99.10390	419.90014
189	3.94767	102.40263	404.25133	4.10502	100.85278	414.00275	4.26861	99.33817	424.03610
190	3.97645	102.65411	408.19919	4.13581	101.09457	418.10779	4.30152	99.57065	428.30472
191	4.00545	102.90377	412.17563	4.16683	101.33456	422.24359	4.33467	99.80135	432.60623
192	4.03465	103.15162	416.18109	4.19808	101.57276	426.41040	4.36809	100.03028	436.94089
193	4.06407	103.39768	420.21573	4.22956	101.80920	430.60849	4.40176	100.25746	441.30899
194	4.09371	103.64196	424.27982	4.26129	102.04387	434.83904	4.43569	100.48291	445.71075
195	4.12356	103.88447	428.37350	4.29324	102.27679	439.09933	4.46988	100.70663	450.14642
196	4.15362	104.12522	432.49707	4.32544	102.50798	443.39258	4.50433	100.92983	454.61630
197	4.18391	104.36423	436.65070	4.35788	102.73745	447.71902	4.53905	101.14895	459.12064
198	4.21442	104.60151	440.83463	4.39057	102.96521	452.07553	4.57404	101.36757	463.65970
199	4.24515	104.83707	445.04904	4.42350	103.19128	456.46649	4.60930	101.58453	468.23373
200	4.27610	105.07093	449.29419	4.45667	103.41566	460.88998	4.64483	101.79982	472.84305

Table 1. (continued) Annuities

M	C(8.75,M,12)	A(8.75,M,12)	S(8.75,M,12)	M	C(9.00,M,12)	A(9.00,M,12)	S(9.00,M,12)	M	C(9.25,M,12)	A(9.25,M,12)	S(9.25,M,12)
201	4.30728	105.30309	453.57028	201	4.49010	103.63837	465.34665	201	4.69064	102.01347	477.48798
202	4.33869	105.53358	457.87756	202	4.52378	103.85943	469.83676	202	4.71672	102.22548	482.16652
203	4.37033	105.76240	462.21625	203	4.55770	104.07888	474.36053	203	4.73971	102.43587	486.88522
204	4.40219	105.98956	466.58658	204	4.59189	104.29661	478.91824	204	4.76971	102.64465	491.62831
205	4.43428	106.21507	470.98877	205	4.62633	104.51276	483.51013	205	4.83847	102.85183	496.43801
206	4.46663	106.43896	475.43307	206	4.66102	104.72731	488.13644	206	4.90133	103.05743	501.25464
207	4.49920	106.66122	479.88971	207	4.69598	104.94025	492.79749	207	4.93911	103.26146	506.11847
208	4.53200	106.88187	484.38889	208	4.73120	105.15162	497.49347	208	4.97718	103.46392	511.01901
209	4.56505	107.10092	488.92090	209	4.76669	105.36141	502.22467	209	5.01555	103.66484	515.95892
210	4.59833	107.31840	493.48593	210	4.80243	105.56963	506.99133	210	5.05421	103.86422	520.93610
211	4.63186	107.53429	498.08429	211	4.83845	105.77631	511.79376	211	5.09317	104.06207	525.95166
212	4.66564	107.74863	502.71616	212	4.87474	105.98145	516.63220	212	5.13243	104.25942	531.00596
213	4.69966	107.96140	507.38177	213	4.91130	106.18507	521.50698	213	5.17199	104.45325	536.09000
214	4.73393	108.17265	512.08143	214	4.94814	106.38716	526.41827	214	5.21186	104.64661	541.23145
215	4.76845	108.38235	516.81537	215	4.98525	106.58775	531.36639	215	5.25203	104.83847	546.40344
216	4.80322	108.59055	521.58380	216	5.02264	106.78685	536.35162	216	5.29252	105.02888	551.61530
217	4.83824	108.79724	526.38702	217	5.06031	106.98447	541.37427	217	5.33332	105.21782	556.86737
218	4.87352	109.00243	531.22526	218	5.09826	107.18061	546.43457	218	5.37443	105.40532	562.15985
219	4.90905	109.20613	536.09875	219	5.13650	107.37530	551.53284	219	5.41585	105.59138	567.49316
220	4.94485	109.40836	541.00781	220	5.17502	107.56853	556.66937	220	5.45760	105.77603	572.86761
221	4.98091	109.60913	545.95270	221	5.21383	107.76033	561.84436	221	5.49467	105.95926	578.28345
222	5.01722	109.80844	550.93359	222	5.25294	107.95070	567.05823	222	5.54206	106.14109	583.74109
223	5.05381	110.00632	555.95081	223	5.29233	108.13966	572.31116	223	5.58478	106.32153	589.24072
224	5.09066	110.20275	561.00464	224	5.33203	108.32720	577.60345	224	5.58478	106.50059	594.78278
225	5.12778	110.39777	566.09528	225	5.37202	108.51335	582.93549	225	5.62783	106.67828	600.36755

226	5.16517	110.59138	226	571.22302	226	5.41231	108.69811	226	588.30750	5.87121	226	106.85461	605.99542
227	5.20283	110.76358	227	576.38024	227	5.45230	108.88150	227	593.71979	5.71493	227	107.02959	611.66663
228	5.24077	110.97419	228	581.59106	228	5.49360	109.08353	228	599.17273	5.75898	228	107.20322	617.38153
229	5.27898	111.16382	229	586.83179	229	5.53500	109.24419	229	604.66650	5.80338	229	107.37554	623.14056
230	5.31747	111.35188	230	592.11078	230	5.57651	109.43352	230	610.20154	5.84811	230	107.54653	628.94391
231	5.35625	111.53857	231	597.42828	231	5.61834	109.60151	231	615.77802	5.83319	231	107.71622	634.79205
232	5.39530	111.72392	232	602.78455	232	5.66047	109.77818	232	621.39636	5.93862	232	107.88461	640.68524
233	5.43464	111.90733	233	608.17981	233	5.70293	109.96352	233	627.05682	5.99439	233	108.05171	646.62384
234	5.47427	112.09060	234	613.61444	234	5.74570	110.12756	234	632.75977	6.03052	234	108.21754	652.60822
235	5.51419	112.27195	235	619.08875	235	5.78879	110.30031	235	638.50543	6.07701	235	108.38209	658.63873
236	5.55440	112.45199	236	624.60291	236	5.83221	110.47177	236	644.29425	6.12385	236	108.54539	664.71576
237	5.59490	112.63072	237	630.15735	237	5.87595	110.64196	237	650.12646	6.17106	237	108.70744	670.83960
238	5.63569	112.80817	238	635.75220	238	5.92002	110.81087	238	656.00238	6.21862	238	108.86824	677.01068
239	5.67679	112.98432	239	641.38794	239	5.96442	110.97854	239	661.92242	6.26656	239	109.02782	683.22831
240	5.71818	113.15920	240	647.06470	240	6.00915	111.14495	240	667.86684	6.31486	240	109.18617	689.49585
241	5.75988	113.33282	241	652.78230	241	6.05422	111.31013	241	673.89600	6.36354	241	109.34332	695.81073
242	5.80187	113.50517	242	658.54279	242	6.09963	111.47407	242	679.95020	6.41259	242	109.49926	702.17426
243	5.84418	113.67628	243	664.34467	243	6.14537	111.63680	243	686.04987	6.46202	243	109.65401	708.58685
244	5.88679	113.84615	244	670.79830	244	6.19146	111.79818	244	692.19519	6.51184	244	109.80758	715.04889
245	5.92972	114.01479	245	676.07562	245	6.23790	111.95662	245	698.38666	6.56203	245	109.95997	721.56073
246	5.97296	114.18222	246	682.00531	246	6.28468	112.11773	246	704.62457	6.61261	246	110.11120	728.12274
247	6.01651	114.34843	247	687.97827	247	6.33182	112.27567	247	710.90924	6.66358	247	110.26127	734.73535
248	6.06038	114.51344	248	693.99481	248	6.37931	112.43242	248	717.24109	6.71495	248	110.41019	741.39693
249	6.10457	114.67725	249	700.05518	249	6.42715	112.58801	249	723.62036	6.76671	249	110.55797	748.11389
250	6.14908	114.83987	250	706.15973	250	6.47536	112.74245	250	730.04755	6.81887	250	110.70462	754.88062

Table 1. (continued) Annuities

M	CI 8.75,M,12)	AI 8.75,M,12)	SI 8.75,M,12)	M	CI 9.00,M,12)	AI 9.00,M,12)	SI 9.00,M,12)	M	CI 9.25,M,12)	AI 9.25,M,12)	SI 9.25,M,12)
251	6.19392	115.00132	712.30884	251	6.52392	112.89573	736.52289	251	6.87143	110.85015	761.89946
252	6.23908	115.16160	718.50275	252	6.57285	113.04787	743.04691	252	6.92140	110.99457	768.57092
253	6.28458	115.32072	724.74182	253	6.62215	113.19808	749.61969	253	6.97778	111.13788	775.49530
254	6.33040	115.47969	731.02643	254	6.67181	113.34878	756.24182	254	7.03196	111.28010	782.47308
255	6.37656	115.63551	737.35681	255	6.72185	113.49753	762.91364	255	7.08576	111.42123	789.50464
256	6.42306	115.79320	743.73334	256	6.77227	113.64519	769.63550	256	7.14038	111.56127	796.59039
257	6.46989	115.94576	750.15643	257	6.82306	113.79175	776.40778	257	7.19543	111.70025	803.73077
258	6.51707	116.09921	756.62628	258	6.87423	113.93722	783.23083	258	7.25089	111.83817	810.92621
259	6.56459	116.25154	763.14337	259	6.92579	114.08161	790.10504	259	7.30678	111.97502	818.17712
260	6.61245	116.40277	769.70795	260	6.97773	114.22492	797.03082	260	7.36310	112.11084	825.48389
261	6.66067	116.55290	776.32043	261	7.03006	114.36717	804.00854	261	7.41986	112.24561	832.84698
262	6.70924	116.70195	782.98108	262	7.08279	114.50835	811.03864	262	7.47706	112.37936	840.26685
263	6.75816	116.84992	789.69031	263	7.13591	114.64849	818.12140	263	7.53469	112.51207	847.74390
264	6.80744	116.99682	796.44849	264	7.18943	114.78758	825.25732	264	7.59277	112.64378	855.27863
265	6.85707	117.14265	803.25592	265	7.24335	114.92564	832.44678	265	7.65130	112.77448	862.87140
266	6.90707	117.28743	810.11298	266	7.29768	115.06268	839.69012	266	7.71028	112.90417	870.52264
267	6.95744	117.43117	817.02008	267	7.35241	115.19868	846.98779	267	7.76971	113.03288	878.23297
268	7.00817	117.57385	823.97748	268	7.40755	115.33368	854.34021	268	7.82960	113.16060	886.00269
269	7.05927	117.71552	830.98566	269	7.46311	115.46767	861.74774	269	7.88996	113.28734	893.83228
270	7.11074	117.85615	838.04492	270	7.51908	115.60067	869.21088	270	7.95078	113.41312	901.72223
271	7.16259	117.99576	845.15570	271	7.57547	115.73267	876.72992	271	8.01206	113.53793	909.67297
272	7.21482	118.13436	852.31830	272	7.63229	115.86369	884.30542	272	8.07382	113.66178	917.68506
273	7.26743	118.27197	859.53308	273	7.68953	115.99374	891.93768	273	8.13606	113.78469	925.75891
274	7.32042	118.40857	866.80054	274	7.74720	116.12282	899.62726	274	8.19877	113.90666	933.89496
275	7.37380	118.54418	874.12097	275	7.80531	116.25094	907.37445	275	8.26197	114.02769	942.08875

276	7.42757	118.67882	881.49475
277	7.48173	118.81248	888.92230
278	7.53628	118.94517	896.40405
279	7.59123	119.07690	903.94031
280	7.64658	119.20767	911.53156
281	7.70234	119.33751	919.17816
282	7.75850	119.46640	926.88049
283	7.81508	119.59435	934.63898
284	7.87206	119.72138	942.45404
285	7.92946	119.84750	950.32611
286	7.98728	119.97269	958.25562
287	8.04552	120.09699	966.24296
288	8.10419	120.22038	974.28839
289	8.16328	120.34288	982.39258
290	8.22280	120.46449	990.55585
291	8.28276	120.58523	998.77869
292	8.34316	120.70509	1007.06140
293	8.40399	120.82408	1015.40460
294	8.46527	120.94221	1023.80859
295	8.52700	121.05948	1032.27360
296	8.58917	121.17591	1040.80078
297	8.65180	121.29149	1049.39001
298	8.71489	121.40623	1058.04475
299	8.77843	121.52015	1066.76213
300	8.84244	121.63324	1075.53516

276	7.86395	116.37811	915.17975
277	7.92883	116.50432	923.04358
278	7.98225	116.62960	930.96643
279	8.04212	116.75394	938.94867
280	8.10243	116.87737	946.99078
281	8.16320	116.99986	955.09320
282	8.22442	117.12145	963.25641
283	8.28611	117.24213	971.48083
284	8.34825	117.36192	979.76697
285	8.41086	117.48082	988.11517
286	8.47395	117.59882	996.52606
287	8.53750	117.71596	1005.00000
288	8.60153	117.83221	1013.53754
289	8.66604	117.94761	1022.13904
290	8.73104	118.06214	1030.80505
291	8.79652	118.17582	1039.53613
292	8.86249	118.28866	1048.33264
293	8.92896	118.40065	1057.19507
294	8.99533	118.51181	1066.12402
295	9.06340	118.62215	1075.12020
296	9.13138	118.73166	1084.18335
297	9.19986	118.84035	1093.31482
298	9.26884	118.94823	1102.51465
299	9.33838	119.05533	1111.78345
300	9.40841	119.16162	1121.12183

276	8.32566	114.14781	950.35571
277	8.38994	114.26700	958.68134
278	8.45451	114.38528	967.07117
279	8.51968	114.50266	975.52570
280	8.58535	114.61913	984.04535
281	8.65153	114.73472	992.63074
282	8.71822	114.84942	1001.28823
283	8.78542	114.96325	1010.00049
284	8.85314	115.07620	1018.78689
285	8.92138	115.18829	1027.63904
286	8.99015	115.29952	1036.56042
287	9.05945	115.40990	1045.55054
288	9.12928	115.51944	1054.60999
289	9.19966	115.62814	1063.73326
290	9.27057	115.73601	1072.93896
291	9.34203	115.84306	1082.20947
292	9.41404	115.94928	1091.55151
293	9.48661	116.05469	1100.96558
294	9.55974	116.15929	1110.45215
295	9.63343	116.26310	1120.01196
296	9.70768	116.36611	1129.64539
297	9.78251	116.46834	1139.35303
298	9.85792	116.56978	1149.13550
299	9.93391	116.67044	1158.99353
300	10.01048	116.77034	1168.92737

Table 1. (continued) Annuities

M	C(8.75,M,12)	A(8.75,M,12)	S(8.75,M,12)	M	C(9.00,M,12)	A(9.00,M,12)	S(9.00,M,12)	M	C(9.25,M,12)	A(9.25,M,12)	S(9.25,M,12)
301	8.90692	121.74551	1084.37756	301	9.47899	119.26711	1130.53027	301	10.08765	116.86947	1178.93787
302	8.97187	121.85697	1093.28442	302	9.55007	119.37183	1140.00928	302	10.16541	116.98784	1189.02551
303	9.03729	121.96763	1102.25635	303	9.62169	119.47576	1149.55933	303	10.24376	117.06546	1199.19092
304	9.10318	122.07748	1111.29358	304	9.69386	119.57892	1159.18103	304	10.32273	117.16234	1209.43469
305	9.16956	122.18654	1120.39685	305	9.76656	119.68131	1168.87488	305	10.40230	117.25847	1219.75745
306	9.23642	122.29480	1129.56641	306	9.83981	119.78294	1178.64148	306	10.48248	117.35387	1230.15967
307	9.30377	122.40228	1138.80273	307	9.91361	119.88380	1188.48132	307	10.56328	117.44853	1240.64221
308	9.37161	122.50900	1148.10657	308	9.98796	119.98392	1198.39490	308	10.64471	117.54247	1251.20544
309	9.43995	122.61492	1157.47815	309	10.06287	120.08330	1208.38281	309	10.72676	117.63570	1261.85022
310	9.50878	122.72009	1166.91809	310	10.13834	120.18194	1218.44568	310	10.80945	117.72821	1272.57690
311	9.57811	122.82449	1176.42688	311	10.21438	120.27984	1228.58411	311	10.89277	117.82001	1283.38635
312	9.64795	122.92815	1186.00500	312	10.29099	120.37701	1238.79846	312	10.97674	117.91112	1294.27917
313	9.71830	123.03104	1195.65296	313	10.36817	120.47346	1249.08948	313	11.06135	118.00153	1305.25596
314	9.78917	123.13319	1205.37122	314	10.44593	120.56919	1259.45764	314	11.14661	118.09124	1316.31726
315	9.86055	123.23461	1215.16040	315	10.52428	120.66421	1269.90356	315	11.23253	118.18027	1327.46397
316	9.93244	123.33529	1225.02100	316	10.60321	120.75852	1280.42786	316	11.31912	118.26861	1338.69641
317	10.00487	123.43524	1234.95337	317	10.68273	120.85213	1291.03101	317	11.40639	118.35628	1350.01550
318	10.07782	123.53447	1244.95825	318	10.76285	120.94504	1301.71375	318	11.49429	118.44328	1361.42188
319	10.15131	123.63298	1255.03613	319	10.84357	121.03726	1312.47656	319	11.58280	118.52962	1372.91614
320	10.22532	123.73077	1265.18738	320	10.92490	121.12880	1323.32019	320	11.67218	118.61529	1384.49902
321	10.29988	123.82787	1275.41272	321	11.00684	121.21965	1334.24512	321	11.76215	118.70031	1396.17126
322	10.37498	123.92425	1285.71265	322	11.08939	121.30982	1345.25195	322	11.85282	118.78468	1407.93335
323	10.45064	124.01994	1296.08765	323	11.17256	121.39933	1356.34131	323	11.94419	118.86840	1419.78625
324	10.52684	124.11493	1306.53821	324	11.25635	121.48817	1367.51392	324	12.03625	118.95148	1431.73035
325	10.60360	124.20924	1317.06506	325	11.34078	121.57635	1378.77026	325	12.12903	119.03398	1443.76660

n									
326	10.68092	124.30286	1327.68870	11.42583	121.66386	1390.11096	12.22253	119.11575	1455.89575
327	10.75880	124.39581	1338.34861	11.51153	121.75073	1401.53687	12.31674	119.19593	1468.11816
328	10.83725	124.48909	1349.10840	11.59796	121.83696	1413.04834	12.41169	119.27750	1490.43494
329	10.91627	124.57970	1359.94568	11.68485	121.92254	1424.64624	12.50736	119.35745	1492.84668
330	10.99587	124.67064	1370.86194	11.77248	122.00748	1436.33105	12.60377	119.43690	1505.35400
331	11.07605	124.76093	1381.85779	11.86078	122.09180	1448.10352	12.70092	119.51553	1517.96776
332	11.15681	124.85056	1392.93384	11.94973	122.17548	1459.96436	12.79883	119.59367	1530.85969
333	11.23816	124.93954	1404.09070	12.03936	122.25854	1471.91406	12.89748	119.67120	1543.45752
334	11.32011	125.02787	1415.32886	12.12965	122.34098	1483.95337	12.99690	119.74814	1556.35498
335	11.40265	125.11557	1426.64893	12.22062	122.42281	1496.08301	13.09709	119.82449	1569.35198
336	11.48579	125.20264	1438.05151	12.31228	122.50403	1508.30371	13.19804	119.90026	1582.44897
337	11.56954	125.28907	1449.53735	12.40462	122.58465	1520.61597	13.29978	119.97545	1595.64709
338	11.65390	125.37488	1461.10693	12.49765	122.66466	1533.02063	13.40230	120.05006	1608.94690
339	11.73880	125.46007	1472.76086	12.59139	122.74408	1545.51919	13.50561	120.12411	1622.34912
340	11.82448	125.54464	1484.49963	12.68582	122.82291	1558.10962	13.60971	120.19759	1635.86474
341	11.91070	125.62859	1496.32422	12.78097	122.90115	1570.79541	13.71462	120.27050	1649.46448
342	11.99755	125.71194	1508.23486	12.87682	122.97881	1583.57642	13.82034	120.34286	1663.17908
343	12.08503	125.79469	1520.23242	12.97340	123.05589	1596.45325	13.92687	120.41466	1676.99939
344	12.17315	125.87684	1532.31738	13.07070	123.13240	1609.42564	14.03422	120.48592	1690.92627
345	12.26191	125.95839	1544.49060	13.16873	123.20834	1622.49731	14.14240	120.55663	1704.96057
346	12.35132	126.03935	1556.75236	13.26750	123.28371	1635.66602	14.25142	120.62679	1718.10291
347	12.44138	126.11974	1569.10598	13.36700	123.35852	1648.93359	14.36127	120.69643	1733.35437
348	12.53210	126.19953	1581.54917	13.46725	123.43277	1662.30054	14.47197	120.76553	1747.71558
349	12.62348	126.27875	1594.07727	13.56826	123.50647	1675.76782	14.58353	120.83409	1762.18762
350	12.71553	126.35739	1606.70081	13.67002	123.57963	1689.33606	14.69594	120.90214	1776.77112

Table 1. (continued) Annuities

M	C(8.75,M,12)	A(8.75,M,12)	S(8.75,M,12)	M	C(9.00,M,12)	A(9.00,M,12)	S(9.00,M,12)	M	C(8.25,M,12)	A(8.25,M,12)	S(9.25,M,12)
351	12.80824	126.43546	1619.41626	351	13.72255	123.65224	1703.00610	351	14.80923	120.96987	1791.46704
352	12.90164	126.51297	1632.22461	352	13.87584	123.72430	1716.77868	352	14.92338	121.03667	1806.27625
353	12.9571	126.58992	1645.12622	353	13.97391	123.79583	1730.65454	353	15.03841	121.10317	1821.19971
354	13.09047	126.66631	1658.12196	354	14.08476	123.86683	1744.63440	354	15.15434	121.16916	1836.23804
355	13.18692	126.74215	1671.21240	355	14.19039	123.93730	1758.71912	355	15.27115	121.23464	1851.39248
356	13.28207	126.81744	1684.39832	356	14.29682	124.00725	1772.90955	356	15.38887	121.29962	1866.66357
357	13.37892	126.89219	1697.68042	357	14.40405	124.07668	1787.20642	357	15.50749	121.36411	1882.05249
358	13.47647	126.96639	1711.05933	358	14.51208	124.14558	1801.61047	358	15.62702	121.42810	1897.55994
359	13.57474	127.04005	1724.53577	359	14.62092	124.21397	1816.12256	359	15.74748	121.49160	1913.18701
360	13.67372	127.11319	1738.11047	360	14.73058	124.28196	1830.74341	360	15.86887	121.55462	1928.93445
361	13.77343	127.18579	1751.78418	361	14.84105	124.34924	1845.47400	361	15.99119	121.61715	1944.80334
362	13.87386	127.25787	1765.55762	362	14.95236	124.41612	1860.31506	362	16.11446	121.67921	1960.79456
363	13.97501	127.32943	1779.43152	363	15.06451	124.48251	1875.26746	363	16.23867	121.74079	1976.90894
364	14.07692	127.40047	1793.40649	364	15.17749	124.54839	1890.33191	364	16.36385	121.80190	1993.14758
365	14.17957	127.47099	1807.48352	365	15.29132	124.61378	1905.50940	365	16.48998	121.86254	2009.51147
366	14.28296	127.54100	1821.66309	366	15.40601	124.67870	1920.80078	366	16.61709	121.92272	2026.00146
367	14.38711	127.61051	1835.94604	367	15.52155	124.74313	1936.20679	367	16.74518	121.98244	2042.61853
368	14.49201	127.67951	1850.33313	368	15.63796	124.80707	1951.72827	368	16.87426	122.04170	2059.36377
369	14.59768	127.74802	1864.82507	369	15.75525	124.87054	1967.36821	369	17.00433	122.10051	2076.23804
370	14.70412	127.81602	1879.42285	370	15.87341	124.93354	1983.12146	370	17.13541	122.15887	2090.24219
371	14.81134	127.88354	1894.12696	371	15.99246	124.99607	1996.99487	371	17.26749	122.21677	2110.47769
372	14.91934	127.95057	1909.93823	372	16.11240	125.05814	2014.98743	372	17.40060	122.27425	2127.64526
373	15.02813	128.01711	1923.85577	373	16.23325	125.11974	2031.09973	373	17.53473	122.33128	2145.04590
374	15.13771	128.08316	1938.85574	374	16.35500	125.18088	2047.33301	374	17.66989	122.38787	2162.58057
375	15.24809	128.14874	1954.02344	375	16.47766	125.24157	2063.68799	375	17.80610	122.44404	2180.25049

n									
376	15.35927	128.21385	1969.27148	16.60124	125.30190	2080.16553	17.94335	122.49976	2198.05640
377	15.47127	128.27849	1984.63086	16.72575	125.36159	2096.76685	18.08167	122.55507	2215.99976
378	15.58408	128.34265	2000.10205	16.85119	125.41984	2113.43268	18.22104	122.60995	2234.08154
379	15.69771	128.40636	2015.68616	16.97758	125.47984	2130.34375	18.36150	122.66441	2252.30249
380	15.81217	128.46960	2031.38391	17.10491	125.53830	2147.32129	18.50303	122.71846	2270.66406
381	15.92747	128.53239	2047.19604	17.23320	125.59633	2164.42627	18.64566	122.77209	2289.16699
382	16.04361	128.59473	2063.12354	17.36245	125.65392	2181.65942	18.78939	122.82531	2307.81274
383	16.16059	128.65660	2079.16699	17.49266	125.71109	2199.02197	18.93423	122.87813	2326.60205
384	16.27843	128.71803	2095.32764	17.62386	125.76783	2216.51465	19.09018	122.93053	2345.53638
385	16.39713	128.77902	2111.60620	17.75604	125.82415	2234.13843	19.22725	122.98254	2364.61646
386	16.51669	128.83955	2128.00317	17.88921	125.88005	2251.89453	19.37546	123.03416	2383.84375
387	16.63713	128.89967	2144.52002	18.02338	125.93553	2269.78369	19.52481	123.08537	2403.21924
388	16.75844	128.95934	2161.15698	18.15855	125.99060	2287.90713	19.67532	123.13620	2422.74414
389	16.88063	129.01859	2177.91553	18.29474	126.04527	2305.96558	19.82698	123.18664	2442.41943
390	17.00372	129.07739	2194.79614	18.43195	126.09952	2324.26050	19.97982	123.23669	2462.24634
391	17.12771	129.13577	2211.79980	18.57019	126.15337	2342.69038	20.13383	123.28635	2482.22632
392	17.25260	129.19374	2228.92749	18.70947	126.20681	2361.26245	20.28903	123.33564	2502.36011
393	17.37840	129.25128	2246.18018	18.84979	126.25986	2379.97192	20.44542	123.38455	2522.64997
394	17.50511	129.30841	2263.55859	18.99116	126.31252	2398.82178	20.60302	123.43309	2543.09448
395	17.63276	129.36511	2281.06372	19.13360	126.36478	2417.81299	20.76184	123.48125	2563.69751
396	17.76133	129.42142	2298.69629	19.27710	126.41666	2436.94653	20.92188	123.52905	2584.45923
397	17.89084	129.47731	2316.45776	19.42168	126.46815	2456.22363	21.08315	123.57648	2605.38110
398	18.02129	129.53281	2334.34063	19.56734	126.51926	2475.64528	21.24566	123.62355	2626.46436
399	18.15270	129.58789	2352.36987	19.71410	126.56998	2495.21265	21.40943	123.67026	2647.70996
400	18.28506	129.64258	2370.52246	19.86195	126.62032	2514.92676	21.57446	123.71661	2669.11938

Table 1. (continued) Annuities

M	C(8.75,M,12)	A(8.75,M,12)	S(8.75,M,12)	M	C(9.00,M,12)	A(9.00,M,12)	S(9.00,M,12)	M	C(9.25,M,12)	A(9.25,M,12)	S(9.25,M,12)
401	18.41839	129.69687	2388.60762	401	20.01092	126.67030	2534.78882	401	21.74077	123.76260	2690.63195
402	18.55269	129.75078	2407.22607	402	20.16100	126.71990	2554.79956	402	21.90835	123.80825	2712.43481
403	18.68797	129.80429	2425.77881	403	20.31220	126.76913	2574.96069	403	22.07723	123.85355	2734.34302
404	18.82424	129.85741	2444.46655	404	20.46455	126.81799	2595.27295	404	22.24741	123.89850	2756.42017
405	18.96150	129.91014	2463.28102	405	20.61803	126.86650	2615.73730	405	22.41890	123.94310	2778.66772
406	19.09976	129.96251	2482.25244	406	20.77267	126.91463	2636.35547	406	22.59171	123.98737	2801.08667
407	19.23903	130.01448	2501.35205	407	20.92846	126.96242	2657.12817	407	22.76585	124.03129	2823.67822
408	19.37931	130.06609	2520.59106	408	21.08542	127.00985	2678.05664	408	22.94134	124.07488	2846.44409
409	19.52062	130.11731	2539.97046	409	21.24356	127.05692	2699.14209	409	23.11818	124.11813	2869.38550
410	19.66296	130.16817	2559.49121	410	21.40289	127.10365	2720.38550	410	23.29638	124.16106	2892.50366
411	19.80633	130.21866	2579.15405	411	21.56341	127.15002	2741.78857	411	23.47596	124.20366	2915.80005
412	19.95075	130.26878	2598.96045	412	21.72514	127.19604	2763.35181	412	23.65692	124.24593	2939.27612
413	20.09623	130.31854	2618.00713	413	21.88808	127.24173	2785.07690	413	23.83928	124.28788	2962.93286
414	20.24276	130.36794	2638.00732	414	22.05204	127.28708	2806.96509	414	24.02304	124.32951	2986.77222
415	20.39037	130.41698	2659.25244	415	22.21763	127.33208	2829.01733	415	24.20821	124.37081	3010.79617
416	20.53905	130.46567	2679.64063	416	22.38426	127.37676	2851.23496	416	24.39482	124.41180	3035.00342
417	20.68881	130.51401	2700.17944	417	22.55215	127.42110	2873.61914	417	24.58286	124.45248	3059.39819
418	20.83966	130.56200	2720.96841	418	22.72128	127.46512	2896.17139	418	24.77235	124.49285	3083.98120
419	20.99162	130.60963	2741.70801	419	22.89170	127.50880	2918.89258	419	24.96331	124.53291	3108.75342
420	21.14469	130.65692	2762.69971	420	23.06338	127.55216	2941.78442	420	25.15573	124.57266	3133.71690
421	21.29888	130.70387	2783.84424	421	23.23636	127.59520	2964.84766	421	25.34964	124.61211	3158.87256
422	21.45417	130.75049	2805.14331	422	23.41063	127.63791	2988.08398	422	25.54505	124.65126	3184.22217
423	21.61061	130.79675	2826.59741	423	23.58621	127.68031	3011.49463	423	25.74196	124.69010	3209.76733
424	21.76818	130.84270	2848.20901	424	23.76311	127.72239	3035.08105	424	25.94038	124.72865	3235.50928
425	21.92691	130.88831	2869.97607	425	23.94133	127.76416	3058.84399	425	26.14034	124.76691	3261.44946

idx			idx			idx		idx		
426	22.08679	130.53358	426	2891.90308	24.12089	127.60562	426	3082.78540	426	26.34184	124.80487	3287.58984
427	22.24784	130.97853	427	2913.98999	24.30190	127.84676	427	3106.90625	427	26.54489	124.84254	3313.93164
428	22.41007	131.02315	428	2936.23779	24.48406	127.88761	428	3131.20801	428	26.74951	124.87993	3340.47656
429	22.57347	131.06744	429	2958.64771	24.66769	127.96838	429	3155.69214	429	26.95570	124.91702	3367.22607
430	22.73807	131.11143	430	2981.22119	24.85270	127.96838	430	3190.35986	430	27.16348	124.95384	3394.18188
431	22.90387	131.15509	431	3003.95923	25.03909	128.00832	431	3205.21240	431	27.37287	124.99037	3421.34546
432	23.07088	131.19844	432	3026.86328	25.22689	128.04796	432	3230.25171	432	27.58387	125.02663	3448.71826
433	23.23910	131.24018	433	3049.93408	25.41609	128.08731	433	3255.07852	433	27.79650	125.06260	3476.30200
434	23.40855	131.28418	434	3073.17310	25.60671	128.12636	434	3280.89453	434	28.01076	125.09830	3504.09863
435	23.57924	131.32660	435	3096.58179	25.79876	128.16512	435	3306.50122	435	28.22668	125.13373	3532.10938
436	23.75117	131.36870	436	3120.16089	25.99225	128.20360	436	3332.30005	436	28.44426	125.16888	3560.33594
437	23.92436	131.41049	437	3143.91211	26.18719	128.24178	437	3358.29224	437	28.66352	125.20377	3588.79027
438	24.09881	131.45200	438	3167.83643	26.38360	128.27968	438	3384.47949	438	28.88446	125.23840	3617.44385
439	24.27453	131.43319	439	3191.93530	26.58147	128.31731	439	3410.86304	439	29.10711	125.27275	3646.32837
440	24.45153	131.53409	440	3216.20996	26.78083	128.35464	440	3437.44458	440	29.33148	125.30684	3675.43530
441	24.62982	131.57469	441	3240.66138	26.98169	128.39171	441	3464.22534	441	29.55758	125.34068	3704.76685
442	24.80942	131.61439	442	3265.29126	27.18405	128.42848	442	3491.20703	442	29.78542	125.37424	3734.32446
443	24.99032	131.61501	443	3289.10059	27.38793	128.46500	443	3518.39111	443	30.01501	125.40756	3764.10986
444	25.17254	131.69473	444	3315.03106	27.59334	128.50124	444	3545.77905	444	30.24638	125.44063	3794.12476
445	25.35609	131.73418	445	3340.26343	27.80029	128.53722	445	3573.37256	445	30.47953	125.47343	3824.37134
446	25.54098	131.77333	446	3365.61963	28.00879	128.57292	446	3601.17285	446	30.71448	125.50600	3854.85083
447	25.72721	131.81219	447	3391.16064	28.21896	128.60835	447	3629.18164	447	30.95123	125.53830	3885.56519
448	25.91481	131.85078	448	3416.88770	28.43050	128.64352	448	3657.40039	448	31.18981	125.57037	3916.51660
449	26.10377	131.88910	449	3442.90249	28.64373	128.67844	449	3685.88081	449	31.43024	125.60218	3947.70630
450	26.29411	131.92712	450	3468.90625	28.85856	128.71309	450	3714.47461	450	31.67251	125.63375	3979.13647

Table 1. (continued) Annuities

M	CI 8.75,M,12)	AI 8.75,M,12)	SI 8.75,M,12)	M	CI 9.00,M,12)	AI 9.00,M,12)	SI 9.00,M,12)	M	CI 9.25,M,12)	AI 9.25,M,12)	SI 9.25,M,12)
451	26.48584	131.96487	3496.20044	451	29.07500	128.74748	3743.33325	451	31.91665	125.66508	4010.90908
452	26.67898	132.00237	3521.68628	452	29.23306	128.78162	3772.40820	452	32.16268	125.69617	4042.72559
453	26.87350	132.03988	3548.36523	453	29.51276	128.81551	3801.70117	453	32.41060	125.72703	4074.88843
454	27.06945	132.07652	3575.23877	454	29.73410	128.84914	3831.21411	454	32.66043	125.75765	4107.39668
455	27.26683	132.11319	3602.30981	455	29.95711	128.88252	3860.94900	455	32.91219	125.78803	4139.95947
456	27.46563	132.14990	3629.57495	456	30.18179	128.91565	3890.90527	456	33.16589	125.81818	4172.87158
457	27.66592	132.18675	3657.04077	457	30.40815	128.94853	3921.08691	457	33.42154	125.84811	4206.03760
458	27.86765	132.22363	3684.70654	458	30.63621	128.98117	3951.49612	458	33.67916	125.87780	4239.45698
459	28.07085	132.25725	3712.57422	459	30.86599	129.01358	3982.13135	459	33.93877	125.90726	4273.13818
460	28.27554	132.29062	3740.64502	460	31.09748	129.04573	4012.99731	460	34.20038	125.93650	4307.07666
461	28.48171	132.32773	3768.92065	461	31.33071	129.07765	4044.09497	461	34.46401	125.96552	4341.27734
462	28.68939	132.36258	3797.40234	462	31.56569	129.10933	4075.42554	462	34.72967	125.99431	4375.74121
463	28.89859	132.3979	3826.09180	463	31.80243	129.14078	4106.99121	463	34.99738	126.02289	4410.47070
464	29.10930	132.43155	3854.99023	464	32.04095	129.17198	4138.73946	464	35.26715	126.05124	4445.46826
465	29.32156	132.46565	3884.05981	465	32.28126	129.20296	4170.83447	465	35.53900	126.07938	4480.73535
466	29.53536	132.49951	3913.42114	466	32.52337	129.23370	4203.11572	466	35.81295	126.10730	4516.27441
467	29.75072	132.53311	3942.95654	467	32.76729	129.26422	4235.63916	467	36.08901	126.13501	4552.08740
468	29.96766	132.56648	3972.70728	468	33.01305	129.29453	4268.40625	468	36.36719	126.16251	4588.17627
469	30.18617	132.59961	4002.67505	469	33.26065	129.32458	4301.41943	469	36.64752	126.18980	4624.54346
470	30.40628	132.63251	4032.86108	470	33.51010	129.35443	4334.68018	470	36.93002	126.21687	4661.19092
471	30.62799	132.66515	4063.26733	471	33.76143	129.38408	4368.19043	471	37.21468	126.24374	4698.12109
472	30.85132	132.69757	4093.89551	472	34.01464	129.41345	4401.95166	472	37.50155	126.27041	4735.33594
473	31.07628	132.72975	4124.74658	473	34.26975	129.44258	4435.96631	473	37.79062	126.29687	4772.83740
474	31.30288	132.76169	4155.82275	474	34.52677	129.47159	4470.23584	474	38.08192	126.32313	4810.62793
475	31.53113	132.79341	4187.12598	475	34.78572	129.50034	4504.76270	475	38.37547	126.34919	4848.70996

n			n					n			
476	31.76104	132.82489	476	4218.65674	35.04662	129.52887	4539.54834	476	38.67128	126.37505	4897.08545
477	31.99263	132.85616	477	4250.41797	35.30946	129.55719	4574.59621	477	38.96938	126.40071	4925.75684
478	32.22591	132.88718	478	4282.41064	35.57428	129.58530	4609.90479	478	39.26976	126.42617	4954.72607
479	32.46089	132.91798	479	4314.63872	35.84109	129.61320	4645.47900	479	39.57247	126.45145	5003.98961
480	32.69759	132.94856	480	4347.09717	36.10990	129.64090	4681.31982	480	39.87751	126.47652	5043.56836
481	32.93600	132.97893	481	4379.79492	36.38073	129.66838	4717.42969	481	40.18489	126.50140	5083.44580
482	33.17616	133.00908	482	4412.73096	36.65358	129.69566	4753.81055	482	40.49465	126.52610	5123.63096
483	33.41807	133.03900	483	4445.90723	36.92848	129.72273	4790.46436	483	40.80690	126.55061	5164.12549
484	33.66175	133.06871	484	4479.32520	37.20544	129.74962	4827.39258	484	41.12135	126.57492	5204.93213
485	33.90720	133.09819	485	4512.99682	37.48449	129.77631	4864.59914	485	41.43833	126.59905	5246.05371
486	34.15444	133.12747	486	4546.89404	37.76562	129.80278	4902.08252	486	41.75775	126.62300	5287.49170
487	34.40348	133.15654	487	4581.02783	38.04886	129.82906	4939.84814	487	42.07963	126.64677	5329.24951
488	34.65434	133.18539	488	4615.45215	38.33423	129.85515	4977.89697	488	42.40400	126.67035	5371.32910
489	34.90702	133.21405	489	4650.10645	38.62173	129.88104	5016.23145	489	42.73086	126.69376	5413.73340
490	35.16156	133.24249	490	4685.01367	38.91140	129.90674	5054.85303	490	43.06025	126.71698	5456.46387
491	35.41794	133.27072	491	4720.17490	39.20324	129.93225	5093.76465	491	43.39217	126.74002	5499.52441
492	35.67620	133.29875	492	4755.59277	39.49726	129.95757	5132.96777	492	43.72665	126.76289	5542.91650
493	35.93634	133.32658	493	4791.26904	39.79349	129.98270	5172.46484	493	44.06371	126.78558	5596.64307
494	36.19837	133.35420	494	4827.20557	40.09194	130.00763	5212.25830	494	44.40337	126.80811	5630.70703
495	36.46232	133.38162	495	4863.40381	40.39263	130.03239	5252.35059	495	44.74564	126.83045	5675.11035
496	36.72819	133.40886	496	4899.86621	40.69557	130.05696	5292.74316	496	45.09056	126.85263	5719.85596
497	36.99600	133.43588	497	4936.59424	41.00079	130.08136	5333.43848	497	45.43813	126.87464	5764.94629
498	37.26576	133.46272	498	4973.59033	41.30830	130.10556	5374.43945	498	45.78838	126.89648	5810.38477
499	37.53749	133.48936	499	5010.86963	41.61811	130.12969	5415.24756	499	46.14133	126.91815	5856.17285
500	37.81120	133.51581	500	5048.33355	41.93024	130.15344	5457.36572	500	46.49701	126.93966	5902.31445

Table 1. (continued) Annuities

M	C(9.50,M,12)	A(9.50,M,12)	S(9.50,M,12)	M	C(9.75,M,12)	A(9.75,M,12)	S(9.75,M,12)	M	C(10.00,M,12)	A(10.00,M,12)	S(10.00,M,12)
1	1.00792	0.99215	1.00000	1	1.00812	0.99194	1.00000	1	1.00833	0.99174	1.00000
2	1.01590	1.97650	2.00792	2	1.01632	1.97589	2.00812	2	1.01674	1.97527	2.00833
3	1.02394	2.95312	3.02381	3	1.02457	2.95005	3.02444	3	1.02521	2.96069	3.02507
4	1.03204	3.92207	4.04775	4	1.03290	3.92005	4.04901	4	1.03375	3.91904	4.05028
5	1.04022	4.88341	5.07980	5	1.04129	4.88040	5.08191	5	1.04237	4.87739	5.08403
6	1.04845	5.83720	6.12001	6	1.04975	5.83300	6.12320	6	1.05105	5.82882	6.12640
7	1.05675	6.78350	7.16846	7	1.05828	6.77793	7.17295	7	1.05981	6.77238	7.17745
8	1.06512	7.72236	8.22521	8	1.06688	7.71525	8.23123	8	1.06864	7.70815	8.23726
9	1.07355	8.65385	9.29033	9	1.07555	8.64501	9.29811	9	1.07755	8.63618	9.30591
10	1.08205	9.57802	10.36388	10	1.08429	9.56727	10.37366	10	1.08653	9.55654	10.38346
11	1.09061	10.49494	11.44592	11	1.09310	10.48211	11.45795	11	1.09558	10.46930	11.46998
12	1.09925	11.40465	12.53654	12	1.10198	11.38957	12.55104	12	1.10471	11.37451	12.56557
13	1.10795	12.30721	13.63578	13	1.11093	12.28971	13.65302	13	1.11392	12.27224	13.67028
14	1.11672	13.20270	14.74373	14	1.11996	13.18260	14.76396	14	1.12320	13.16255	14.78420
15	1.12556	14.09114	15.86046	15	1.12906	14.06830	15.88391	15	1.13256	14.04551	15.90740
16	1.13447	14.97261	16.98602	16	1.13823	14.94685	17.01296	16	1.14200	14.92116	17.03996
17	1.14345	15.84715	18.12049	17	1.14749	15.81833	18.15119	17	1.15152	15.78958	18.18196
18	1.15251	16.71483	19.26394	18	1.15680	16.68278	19.29867	18	1.16111	16.65083	19.33348
19	1.16163	17.57569	20.41645	19	1.16620	17.54027	20.45547	19	1.17079	17.50495	20.49459
20	1.17083	18.42978	21.57908	20	1.17568	18.39084	21.62168	20	1.18054	18.35202	21.66538
21	1.18010	19.27717	22.74891	21	1.18523	19.23456	22.79735	21	1.19038	19.19208	22.84592
22	1.18944	20.11791	23.92900	22	1.19486	20.07148	23.98258	22	1.20030	20.02521	24.03631
23	1.19885	20.95204	25.11844	23	1.20457	20.90166	25.17744	23	1.21030	20.85144	25.23661
24	1.20835	21.77962	26.31729	24	1.21435	21.72514	26.38200	24	1.22039	21.67085	26.44691
25	1.21791	22.60069	27.52564	25	1.22422	22.54198	27.59636	25	1.23056	22.48349	27.66730

n				n				n			
26	1.22755	23.41532	28.74355	26	1.23417	23.35225	28.88058	26	1.24082	23.28941	28.89787
27	1.23727	24.22355	29.97110	27	1.24419	24.15598	30.05475	27	1.25118	24.08967	30.13868
28	1.24707	25.02543	31.20837	28	1.25430	24.95324	31.29894	28	1.26158	24.88133	31.38984
29	1.25694	25.82102	32.45544	29	1.26450	25.74406	32.55324	29	1.27210	25.66743	32.65142
30	1.26689	26.61035	33.71238	30	1.27477	26.52852	33.81774	30	1.28270	26.44704	33.93352
31	1.27692	27.33349	34.97927	31	1.28513	27.30665	35.09251	31	1.29339	27.22021	35.20621
32	1.28703	28.17047	36.25619	32	1.29557	28.07852	36.37764	32	1.30416	27.99698	36.49960
33	1.29722	28.94135	37.54322	33	1.30609	28.84416	37.67320	33	1.31503	28.74742	37.90376
34	1.30749	29.70618	38.84044	34	1.31671	29.60363	38.97930	34	1.32599	29.50157	39.11879
35	1.31784	30.46500	40.14792	35	1.32740	30.35698	40.29601	35	1.33704	30.24949	40.44478
36	1.32827	31.21796	41.46576	36	1.33819	31.10426	41.62341	36	1.34818	30.99123	41.78192
37	1.33879	31.96490	42.79403	37	1.34906	31.84551	42.96160	37	1.35942	31.72684	43.13000
38	1.34938	32.70588	44.13282	38	1.36002	32.58079	44.31066	38	1.37075	32.45638	44.48942
39	1.36007	33.44114	45.48220	39	1.37107	33.31015	45.67068	39	1.38217	33.17987	45.86016
40	1.37083	34.17062	46.84227	40	1.38221	34.03362	47.04176	40	1.39369	33.89740	47.24233
41	1.38169	34.89437	48.21310	41	1.39344	34.75127	48.42398	41	1.40530	34.60899	48.63602
42	1.39263	35.61244	49.59479	42	1.40477	35.46313	49.81742	42	1.41701	35.31470	50.04132
43	1.40365	36.32487	50.98742	43	1.41618	36.16925	51.22219	43	1.42882	36.01458	51.45833
44	1.41476	37.03170	52.39106	44	1.42769	36.86969	52.63837	44	1.44073	36.70867	52.88715
45	1.42596	37.73298	53.80583	45	1.43929	37.56448	54.06606	45	1.45273	37.39703	54.32787
46	1.43725	38.42875	55.23179	46	1.45098	38.25367	55.50534	46	1.46484	38.07970	55.79061
47	1.44863	39.11906	56.66304	47	1.46277	38.93730	56.95632	47	1.47705	38.75673	57.24545
48	1.46010	39.80394	58.11767	48	1.47466	39.61543	58.41909	48	1.48935	39.42816	58.72249
49	1.47166	40.48345	59.57777	49	1.48664	40.28909	59.83375	49	1.50177	40.09404	60.21185
50	1.48331	41.15762	61.04943	50	1.49672	40.95532	61.36038	50	1.51428	40.75442	61.71361

Table 1. (continued) Annuities

M	CI 8.50,M,12)	AI 9.50,M,12)	SI 9.50,M,12)	M	CI 9.75,M,12)	AI 9.75,M,12)	SI 9.75,M,12)	M	C(10.00,M,12)	A(10.00,M,12)	S(10.00,M,12)
51	1.49505	41.82649	62.53273	51	1.51089	41.61718	62.87910	51	1.52610	41.40934	63.22788
52	1.50689	42.49011	64.02779	52	1.52317	42.27371	64.38999	52	1.53962	42.05885	64.75478
53	1.51882	43.14852	65.53487	53	1.53554	42.92495	65.91316	53	1.55245	42.70300	66.29441
54	1.53084	43.80176	67.05349	54	1.54802	43.57093	67.44870	54	1.56539	43.34181	67.84686
55	1.54296	44.44986	68.58433	55	1.56060	44.21171	68.99673	55	1.57844	43.97535	69.41225
56	1.55517	45.09288	70.12729	56	1.57328	44.84732	70.55792	56	1.59159	44.60385	70.99069
57	1.56749	45.73084	71.68246	57	1.58606	45.47782	72.13060	57	1.60485	45.22676	72.58228
58	1.57990	46.36390	73.24995	58	1.59895	46.10323	73.71666	58	1.61823	45.84473	74.18713
59	1.59240	46.99178	74.82984	59	1.61194	46.72360	75.31561	59	1.63171	46.45758	75.80536
60	1.60501	47.61488	76.42224	60	1.62504	47.33897	76.92755	60	1.64531	47.06537	77.43707
61	1.61772	48.23298	78.02725	61	1.63824	47.94938	78.55258	61	1.65902	47.66813	79.08237
62	1.63052	48.84628	79.64497	62	1.65155	48.55487	80.19083	62	1.67285	48.26591	80.74139
63	1.64343	49.45477	81.27549	63	1.66497	49.15549	81.84238	63	1.68679	48.85876	82.41425
64	1.65644	50.05847	82.91892	64	1.67850	49.75126	83.50735	64	1.70084	49.44670	84.10103
65	1.66955	50.65743	84.57536	65	1.69213	50.34223	85.18584	65	1.71502	50.02979	86.00187
66	1.68277	51.25169	86.24492	66	1.70588	50.92843	86.87798	66	1.72931	50.60806	87.51688
67	1.69609	51.84128	87.92770	67	1.71974	51.50991	88.58386	67	1.74372	51.18154	89.24619
68	1.70952	52.42624	89.62379	68	1.73372	52.08671	90.30360	68	1.75825	51.75029	90.98991
69	1.72306	53.00660	91.33331	69	1.74780	52.65886	92.03732	69	1.77290	52.31434	92.74816
70	1.73670	53.58241	93.05637	70	1.76200	53.22639	93.78513	70	1.78768	52.87372	94.52106
71	1.75045	54.15369	94.78306	71	1.77632	53.78935	95.54719	71	1.80257	53.42849	96.30874
72	1.76430	54.72049	96.54350	72	1.79075	54.34778	97.32345	72	1.81759	53.97866	98.11131
73	1.77827	55.28283	98.30170	73	1.80530	54.90170	99.11420	73	1.83274	54.52430	99.92890
74	1.79235	55.84076	100.08607	74	1.81997	55.45116	100.91950	74	1.84801	55.06541	101.76164
75	1.80654	56.39430	101.87843	75	1.83476	55.99619	102.73948	75	1.86341	55.60207	103.60966

n				n				n			
76	1.82084	56.94350	103.68497	76	1.84967	56.53683	104.57423	76	1.87894	56.13428	105.47308
77	1.83525	57.48838	105.50581	77	1.86469	57.07311	106.42390	77	1.89460	56.66209	107.35201
78	1.84978	58.02899	107.34106	78	1.87964	57.60507	108.28960	78	1.91039	57.18555	109.24661
79	1.86443	58.56535	109.19084	79	1.89512	58.13274	110.16844	79	1.92631	57.70468	111.15701
80	1.87919	59.09749	111.05527	80	1.91052	58.65616	112.06356	80	1.94236	58.21951	113.08331
81	1.89406	59.62545	112.93446	81	1.32604	59.17536	113.97408	81	1.95855	58.73010	115.02567
82	1.90906	60.14927	114.82852	82	1.34169	59.69038	115.90012	82	1.97487	59.23646	116.98422
83	1.92417	60.66898	116.73758	83	1.95746	60.20124	117.84190	83	1.99133	59.73864	118.95909
84	1.93941	61.18460	118.66175	84	1.97337	60.70799	119.79926	84	2.00792	60.23666	120.95042
85	1.95476	61.69617	120.60116	85	1.99940	61.21065	121.77264	85	2.02465	60.73058	122.95834
86	1.97023	62.20372	122.55598	86	2.00557	61.70926	123.76264	86	2.04152	61.22041	124.98299
87	1.98583	62.70729	124.52615	87	2.02196	62.20396	125.76761	87	2.05854	61.70619	127.02451
88	2.00155	63.20691	126.51199	88	2.03829	62.69447	127.78947	88	2.07569	62.18796	129.08305
89	2.01740	63.70259	128.51353	89	2.03485	63.18112	129.82776	89	2.09299	62.66574	131.15874
90	2.03337	64.19438	130.53093	90	2.07155	63.66385	131.88260	90	2.11043	63.13958	133.25172
91	2.04947	64.68232	132.56430	91	2.08838	64.14268	133.95415	91	2.12902	63.60950	135.36215
92	2.06569	65.16641	134.61377	92	2.10535	64.61767	136.04253	92	2.14575	64.07553	137.49017
93	2.08205	65.64671	136.67946	93	2.12245	65.08882	138.14787	93	2.16363	64.53772	139.63599
94	2.09853	66.12324	138.76151	94	2.13970	65.55618	140.27032	94	2.18166	64.99609	141.79956
95	2.11514	66.59602	140.86003	95	2.15708	66.01977	142.41002	95	2.19984	65.45066	143.98123
96	2.13189	67.06509	142.97517	96	2.17461	66.47962	144.56711	96	2.21818	65.90148	146.18106
97	2.14876	67.53047	145.10707	97	2.19228	66.93577	146.74171	97	2.23666	66.34858	148.39925
98	2.16578	67.99220	147.25583	98	2.21009	67.38824	148.93399	98	2.25530	66.79198	150.63591
99	2.18292	68.45030	149.42160	99	2.22805	67.83706	151.14407	99	2.27409	67.23171	152.89120
100	2.20020	68.90480	151.60452	100	2.24615	68.28227	153.37212	100	2.29304	67.66782	155.16530

Table 1. (continued) Annuities

M	C(8.50,M,12)	A(8.50,M,12)	S(8.50,M,12)	M	C(8.75,M,12)	A(9.75,M,12)	S(9.75,M,12)	M	C(10.00,M,12)	A(10.00,M,12)	S(10.00,M,12)
101	2.21762	69.35574	153.80473	101	2.26440	68.72388	155.61827	101	2.31215	68.10031	157.45834
102	2.23518	69.80233	156.02235	102	2.28280	69.16195	157.88266	102	2.33142	68.52924	159.77049
103	2.25287	70.24701	158.25752	103	2.30134	69.59647	160.16547	103	2.35085	68.95461	162.10191
104	2.27071	70.68740	160.51039	104	2.32004	70.02750	162.46681	104	2.37044	69.37648	164.45276
105	2.28868	71.12433	162.78111	105	2.33889	70.45506	164.78685	105	2.39019	69.79485	166.82320
106	2.30680	71.55783	165.06979	106	2.35790	70.87948	167.12575	106	2.41011	70.20977	169.21339
107	2.32506	71.98793	167.37659	107	2.37705	71.29985	169.48364	107	2.43020	70.62126	171.62350
108	2.34347	72.41464	169.70166	108	2.39637	71.71715	171.86070	108	2.45045	71.02935	174.05371
109	2.36202	72.83801	172.04514	109	2.41584	72.13108	174.25706	109	2.47087	71.43407	176.50415
110	2.38072	73.25805	174.40715	110	2.43547	72.54168	176.67290	110	2.49146	71.83544	178.97502
111	2.39957	73.67479	176.78787	111	2.45526	72.94897	179.10837	111	2.51222	72.23349	181.46648
112	2.41857	74.08826	179.18744	112	2.47520	73.35298	181.56363	112	2.53316	72.62826	183.97870
113	2.43771	74.49848	181.60602	113	2.49632	73.75373	184.03883	113	2.55427	73.01976	186.51196
114	2.45701	74.90548	184.04373	114	2.51559	74.15125	186.53415	114	2.57555	73.40803	189.06612
115	2.47646	75.30928	186.50075	115	2.53603	74.54557	189.04974	115	2.59701	73.79308	191.64168
116	2.49607	75.70991	188.97720	116	2.55663	74.93671	191.58577	116	2.61866	74.17496	194.23869
117	2.51583	76.10739	191.47328	117	2.57741	75.32469	194.14240	117	2.64048	74.55368	196.85735
118	2.53575	76.50175	193.98911	118	2.59835	75.70956	196.71980	118	2.66248	74.92927	199.49782
119	2.55582	76.89302	196.52486	119	2.61946	76.09131	199.31816	119	2.68467	75.30175	202.16031
120	2.57606	77.28120	199.08067	120	2.64074	76.46999	201.93762	120	2.70704	75.67118	204.84497
121	2.59645	77.66635	201.65672	121	2.66220	76.84562	204.57835	121	2.72960	76.03751	207.55202
122	2.61700	78.04846	204.25317	122	2.68383	77.21822	207.24055	122	2.75235	76.40084	210.28162
123	2.63772	78.42758	206.87018	123	2.70564	77.58782	209.92439	123	2.77528	76.76116	213.03397
124	2.65860	78.80372	209.50750	124	2.72762	77.95444	212.63002	124	2.79841	77.11851	215.80925
125	2.67965	79.17690	212.16550	125	2.74978	78.31811	215.35764	125	2.82173	77.47290	218.60765

126	2.70087	79.54715	214.84616	126	2.77212	78.67884	218.10742	126	2.84524	77.82438	221.42838
127	2.72225	79.91450	217.54703	127	2.79465	79.03667	220.87955	127	2.86896	78.17293	224.27463
128	2.74380	80.27896	220.26927	128	2.81735	79.43868	223.67419	128	2.89286	78.51860	227.14359
129	2.76552	80.64055	223.01308	129	2.84024	79.74370	226.49155	129	2.91697	78.86143	230.03645
130	2.78741	80.99931	225.77859	130	2.86332	80.08294	229.33179	130	2.94128	79.20141	232.95341
131	2.80948	81.35524	228.56601	131	2.88659	80.43937	232.19511	131	2.96579	79.53859	235.89470
132	2.83172	81.70838	231.37549	132	2.91004	80.78300	235.08170	132	2.99050	79.87299	238.86049
133	2.85414	82.05875	234.20721	133	2.93368	81.12388	237.99173	133	3.01542	80.20461	241.85098
134	2.87674	82.40637	237.06136	134	2.95752	81.46200	240.92542	134	3.04055	80.53350	244.86641
135	2.89951	82.75125	239.93608	135	2.98155	81.79739	243.88293	135	3.06589	80.85966	247.90697
136	2.92246	83.09343	242.83760	136	3.00577	82.13009	246.86449	136	3.09144	81.18314	250.97285
137	2.94560	83.43292	245.76006	137	3.03020	82.46010	249.87025	137	3.11720	81.50394	254.06430
138	2.96892	83.76974	248.70566	138	3.05482	82.76745	252.90045	138	3.14318	81.82209	257.18149
139	2.99242	84.10392	251.67458	139	3.07964	83.11217	255.95528	139	3.16937	82.13761	260.32468
140	3.01611	84.43547	254.66701	140	3.10466	83.43426	259.03491	140	3.19578	82.45052	263.49405
141	3.03999	84.76442	257.68311	141	3.12988	83.75376	262.13966	141	3.22242	82.76085	266.68982
142	3.06406	85.09079	260.72311	142	3.15531	84.07069	265.26944	142	3.24927	83.06861	269.91223
143	3.08832	85.41459	263.78717	143	3.18095	84.38506	268.42474	143	3.27635	83.37383	273.16158
144	3.11276	85.73585	266.87549	144	3.20680	84.61630	271.60571	144	3.30365	83.67652	276.43787
145	3.13741	86.05458	269.98825	145	3.23285	85.00622	274.81250	145	3.33118	83.97672	279.74152
146	3.16224	86.37081	273.12864	146	3.25912	85.31305	278.04535	146	3.35894	84.27443	283.07269
147	3.18728	86.68456	276.28730	147	3.28560	85.61741	281.30447	147	3.38633	84.56369	286.43164
148	3.21251	86.99584	279.47516	148	3.31228	85.91972	284.59009	148	3.41515	84.86350	289.81857
149	3.23794	87.30468	282.68758	149	3.33921	86.21979	287.90237	149	3.44361	85.15289	293.23370
150	3.26358	87.61109	285.92563	150	3.36634	86.51585	291.24158	150	3.47231	85.44088	296.67734

Table 1. (continued) Annuities

M	C(9.50,M,12)	A(9.50,M,12)	SI 9.50,M,12)	S(9.50,M,12)	M	C(9.75,M,12)	A(9.75,M,12)	SI 9.75,M,12)	S(9.75,M,12)	M	C(10.00,M,12)	A(10.00,M,12)	S(10.00,M,12)
151	3.28941	87.91510	288.18921	3.33969	151	66.81051	294.60791	3.39369	151	3.50125	85.72649	300.14963
152	3.31546	88.21671	292.47861	3.42126	152	87.10280	298.00162	3.42128	152	3.53042	86.00974	303.65088
153	3.34170	88.51536	295.79407	3.44306	153	87.39274	301.42285	3.44306	153	3.55984	86.29066	307.18130
154	3.36816	88.81206	299.13577	3.47708	154	87.68034	304.87192	3.47708	154	3.58951	86.56924	310.74115
155	3.39482	89.10743	302.50394	3.50534	155	87.96561	308.34300	3.50534	155	3.61942	86.84554	314.33046
156	3.42170	89.39868	305.89877	3.53382	156	88.24859	311.85434	3.53382	156	3.64958	87.11958	317.95007
157	3.44879	89.69064	309.32047	3.56253	157	88.52929	315.38815	3.56253	157	3.68000	87.39128	321.59967
158	3.47609	89.97732	312.76926	3.59147	158	88.80773	318.95068	3.59147	158	3.71066	87.66077	325.27966
159	3.50361	90.26273	316.24533	3.62066	159	89.08392	322.54218	3.62066	159	3.74159	87.92804	328.99033
160	3.53135	90.54591	319.74893	3.65007	160	89.35789	326.16281	3.65007	160	3.77277	88.19309	332.73193
161	3.55930	90.82687	323.28030	3.67973	161	89.62965	329.81290	3.67973	161	3.80421	88.45596	336.50470
162	3.58748	91.10561	326.83960	3.70963	162	89.89922	333.49261	3.70963	162	3.83591	88.71666	340.30890
163	3.61588	91.38217	330.42706	3.73977	163	90.16661	337.20224	3.73977	163	3.86787	88.97520	344.14481
164	3.64451	91.65656	334.04297	3.77015	164	90.43185	340.94202	3.77015	164	3.90011	89.23160	348.01266
165	3.67336	91.92879	337.68747	3.80079	165	90.69496	344.71219	3.80079	165	3.93261	89.48589	351.91278
166	3.70244	92.19888	341.36081	3.83167	166	90.96594	348.51297	3.83167	166	3.96538	89.73807	355.84540
167	3.73175	92.46685	345.06326	3.86280	167	91.21482	352.34464	3.86280	167	3.99842	89.98817	359.81076
168	3.76129	92.73272	348.79501	3.89419	168	91.47161	356.20743	3.89419	168	4.03174	90.23620	363.80917
169	3.79107	92.99650	352.55630	3.92583	169	91.72633	360.10162	3.92583	169	4.06534	90.48218	367.84094
170	3.82108	93.25820	356.34738	3.95772	170	91.97900	364.02744	3.95772	170	4.09922	90.72613	371.90628
171	3.85133	93.51785	360.16846	3.98988	171	92.22964	367.98517	3.98988	171	4.13338	90.96806	376.00549
172	3.88182	93.77546	364.01981	4.02230	172	92.47826	371.97504	4.02230	172	4.16782	91.20799	380.13885
173	3.91255	94.03105	367.90161	4.05498	173	92.72487	375.99734	4.05498	173	4.20256	91.44595	384.30670
174	3.94353	94.28463	371.81418	4.08792	174	92.96949	380.05231	4.08792	174	4.23758	91.68193	388.50925
175	3.97475	94.53622	375.75769	4.12114	175	93.21214	384.14026	4.12114	175	4.27289	91.91596	392.74683

n				n				n			
176	4.00622	94.78583	379.73245	176	4.15462	93.45284	389.26138	176	4.30850	92.14906	397.01971
177	4.03798	95.03349	383.73968	177	4.18838	93.69159	392.41602	177	4.34440	92.37824	401.32822
178	4.06990	95.27919	387.77661	178	4.22241	93.90842	396.60440	178	4.39061	92.60652	405.67261
179	4.10212	95.52296	391.84650	179	4.25672	94.16335	400.82681	179	4.41711	92.83292	410.05322
180	4.13459	95.76482	395.94961	180	4.29130	94.39638	405.08353	180	4.45392	93.05743	414.47034
181	4.16733	96.00479	400.08319	181	4.32617	94.62753	409.37482	181	4.49104	93.28010	418.92426
182	4.20032	96.24287	404.25052	182	4.36132	94.85681	413.70099	182	4.52846	93.50092	423.41528
183	4.23357	96.47907	408.45084	183	4.39676	95.08426	418.06232	183	4.56620	93.71992	427.94376
184	4.26709	96.71342	412.68442	184	4.43248	95.30986	422.45908	184	4.60425	93.93712	432.50995
185	4.30087	96.94594	416.96151	185	4.46849	95.53365	426.89154	185	4.64262	94.15251	437.11420
186	4.33491	97.17662	421.25238	186	4.50480	95.75564	431.36005	186	4.68131	94.36613	441.75681
187	4.36923	97.40549	425.58728	187	4.54140	95.97583	435.86484	187	4.72032	94.57798	446.43811
188	4.40382	97.63257	429.95651	188	4.57830	96.19425	440.40625	188	4.75965	94.78808	451.15845
189	4.43869	97.85796	434.36035	189	4.61550	96.41092	444.99456	189	4.79932	94.99644	455.91809
190	4.47383	98.08138	438.79901	190	4.65300	96.62583	449.60004	190	4.83931	95.20308	460.71741
191	4.50924	98.30315	443.27286	191	4.69081	96.83901	454.25305	191	4.87964	95.40901	465.55673
192	4.54494	98.52318	447.78210	192	4.72892	97.05048	458.94385	192	4.92030	95.61125	470.43637
193	4.58092	98.74147	452.32703	193	4.76734	97.26024	463.67276	193	4.96131	95.81281	475.35666
194	4.61719	98.96605	456.90796	194	4.80608	97.46831	468.44012	194	5.00265	96.01271	480.31796
195	4.65374	99.17294	461.52515	195	4.84513	97.67471	473.24619	195	5.04434	96.21095	485.32062
196	4.69058	99.36613	466.17889	196	4.88449	97.87943	478.09131	196	5.08637	96.40755	490.36496
197	4.72772	99.59765	470.86948	197	4.92418	98.08251	482.97580	197	5.12876	96.60283	495.45132
198	4.76514	99.80750	475.59720	198	4.96419	98.28396	487.89999	198	5.17150	96.79590	500.58011
199	4.80287	100.01572	480.36234	199	5.00452	98.48377	492.36417	199	5.21460	96.98767	505.75159
200	4.84089	100.22229	485.16519	200	5.04518	98.68198	497.06668	200	5.25805	97.17786	510.96619

Table 1. (continued) Annuities

M	C(9.50,M,12)	A(9.50,M,12)	S(9.50,M,12)	M	C(9.75,M,12)	A(9.75,M,12)	S(9.75,M,12)	M	C(10.00,M,12)	A(10.00,M,12)	S(10.00,M,12)
201	4.87921	100.42724	490.00610	201	5.08617	98.87859	502.91388	201	5.30187	97.36647	516.22424
202	4.91784	100.63058	494.88531	202	5.12750	99.07362	508.00006	202	5.34605	97.55352	521.52612
203	4.95677	100.83232	499.80316	203	5.16916	99.26707	513.12756	203	5.39060	97.73903	526.87213
204	4.99602	101.03249	504.75992	204	5.21116	99.45897	518.29669	204	5.43552	97.92300	532.26276
205	5.03557	101.23107	509.75595	205	5.25350	99.64932	523.50787	205	5.48082	98.10546	537.69824
206	5.07543	101.42810	514.79150	206	5.29619	99.83813	528.76135	206	5.52649	98.28641	543.17908
207	5.11561	101.62358	519.86694	207	5.33922	100.02543	534.05756	207	5.57255	98.46586	548.70557
208	5.15611	101.81752	524.98254	208	5.38260	100.21121	539.39679	208	5.61898	98.64382	554.27814
209	5.19699	102.00994	530.13867	209	5.42633	100.39550	544.77936	209	5.66581	98.82032	559.89709
210	5.23807	102.20085	535.33557	210	5.47042	100.57830	550.20569	210	5.71302	98.99536	565.56293
211	5.27964	102.39027	540.57367	211	5.51487	100.75963	555.67615	211	5.76063	99.16895	571.27594
212	5.32134	102.57819	545.85321	212	5.55968	100.93950	561.19098	212	5.80864	99.34111	577.03656
213	5.36347	102.76463	551.17456	213	5.60485	101.11791	566.75067	213	5.85704	99.51185	582.84521
214	5.40593	102.94962	556.53802	214	5.65039	101.29489	572.35553	214	5.90585	99.68117	588.70227
215	5.44872	103.13315	561.94391	215	5.69630	101.47044	578.00592	215	5.95507	99.84909	594.60809
216	5.49186	103.31523	567.39264	216	5.74258	101.64458	583.70221	216	6.00469	100.01563	600.56317
217	5.53534	103.49589	572.88452	217	5.78924	101.81731	589.44476	217	6.05473	100.18079	606.56787
218	5.57916	103.67513	578.41996	218	5.83628	101.98866	595.23401	218	6.10519	100.34458	612.62262
219	5.62333	103.85296	583.99902	219	5.88370	102.15862	601.07031	219	6.15606	100.50703	618.72778
220	5.66784	104.02940	589.62235	220	5.93150	102.32721	606.95398	220	6.20737	100.66812	624.88396
221	5.71271	104.20444	595.29016	221	5.97969	102.49445	612.88550	221	6.25909	100.82789	631.09125
222	5.75794	104.37811	605.00287	222	6.02828	102.66033	618.86517	222	6.31125	100.98634	637.35034
223	5.80352	104.55042	606.76080	223	6.07726	102.82487	624.89349	223	6.36385	101.14348	643.66156
224	5.84947	104.72138	612.56433	224	6.12664	102.98810	630.97070	224	6.41688	101.29932	650.02545
225	5.89578	104.89098	618.41382	225	6.17642	103.15000	637.09735	225	6.47035	101.45387	656.44232

n								
226	5.94245	105.05927	6.22660	624.30957	103.31061	643.27390	6.52427	101.60714	662.91266
227	5.98950	105.22623	6.27719	630.25201	103.46991	649.50037	6.57964	101.75915	669.43695
228	6.03691	105.39188	6.32819	636.24152	103.62794	655.77759	6.63346	101.90990	676.01556
229	6.08470	105.55623	6.37961	642.27844	103.78468	662.10577	6.68874	102.05940	682.64905
230	6.13287	105.71928	6.43144	648.36316	103.94017	668.48535	6.74448	102.20767	689.33777
231	6.18143	105.88106	6.48370	654.49603	104.09441	674.91681	6.80069	102.35471	696.08228
232	6.23036	106.04156	6.53638	660.67743	104.24739	681.40051	6.85736	102.50055	702.88283
233	6.27969	106.20081	6.58949	666.90784	104.39915	687.93689	6.91450	102.64517	709.74030
234	6.32940	106.35880	6.64303	673.18750	104.54968	694.52637	6.97212	102.78860	716.65479
235	6.37951	106.51555	6.69700	679.51691	104.69901	701.16943	7.03022	102.93084	723.62695
236	6.43001	106.67107	6.75141	685.89642	104.84712	707.86639	7.08881	103.07191	730.65717
237	6.48092	106.82537	6.80627	692.32642	104.99405	714.61786	7.14788	103.21181	737.74597
238	6.53222	106.97845	6.86157	698.80737	105.13979	721.42407	7.20745	103.35056	744.83386
239	6.58394	107.13034	6.91732	705.33960	105.28435	728.28564	7.26751	103.48815	752.10132
240	6.63606	107.28104	6.97352	711.92352	105.42775	735.20300	7.32607	103.62462	759.36884
241	6.68860	107.43054	7.03018	718.55967	105.56999	742.17651	7.38914	103.75995	766.69690
242	6.74155	107.57887	7.08730	725.24817	105.71109	749.20673	7.45072	103.89417	774.06600
243	6.79492	107.72604	7.14489	731.98975	105.85105	756.29401	7.51281	104.02727	781.48674
244	6.84871	107.87206	7.20294	738.78467	105.98988	763.43490	7.57541	104.15928	789.04856
245	6.90293	108.01692	7.26147	745.63316	106.12759	770.64185	7.63854	104.29019	795.82494
246	6.95759	108.16065	7.32046	752.53335	106.26420	777.90332	7.70220	104.42002	804.26349
247	7.01266	108.30325	7.37994	759.49384	106.39970	785.22375	7.76638	104.54878	811.96570
248	7.06818	108.44473	7.43991	766.50653	106.53411	792.60370	7.83110	104.67648	819.73206
249	7.12413	108.58510	7.50035	773.57471	106.66744	800.04364	7.89636	104.80312	827.56317
250	7.18053	108.72437	7.56129	780.69865	106.79969	807.54395	7.96216	104.92872	835.45953

Table 1. (continued) Annuities

M	CI 8.50,M,12	AI 8.50,M,12	SI 8.50,M,12	M	CI 9.75,M,12	AI 9.75,M,12	SI 9.75,M,12	M	CI 10.00,M,12	AI 10.00,M,12	SI 10.00,M,12
251	7.23738	108.86253	787.87339	251	7.62273	106.88088	815.10529	251	8.02851	105.05327	843.42168
252	7.29467	108.99962	796.11676	252	7.68467	107.06100	822.72903	252	8.09542	105.17680	851.45020
253	7.35242	109.13563	802.41144	253	7.74710	107.19009	830.41266	253	8.16288	105.29930	859.54565
254	7.41063	109.27057	809.76385	254	7.81005	107.31813	838.15979	254	8.23090	105.42090	867.70850
255	7.46930	109.40445	817.17450	255	7.87350	107.44514	845.96979	255	8.29949	105.54128	875.93939
256	7.52843	109.53728	824.64380	256	7.93748	107.57112	853.84332	256	8.36866	105.66078	884.23889
257	7.58803	109.66907	832.17218	257	8.00197	107.69609	861.78082	257	8.43840	105.77928	892.60754
258	7.64810	109.79982	839.76025	258	8.06699	107.82005	869.78278	258	8.50872	105.89681	901.04596
259	7.70865	109.92954	847.40833	259	8.13253	107.94302	877.84973	259	8.57962	106.01337	909.55469
260	7.76968	110.05825	855.11700	260	8.19861	108.06499	885.99230	260	8.65112	106.12896	918.13428
261	7.83119	110.18594	862.88666	261	8.26522	108.18597	894.19091	261	8.72321	106.24360	926.78540
262	7.89318	110.31264	870.74783	262	8.33237	108.30599	902.44611	262	8.79591	106.35728	935.50967
263	7.95567	110.43833	878.61102	263	8.40007	108.42503	910.77850	263	8.86920	106.47003	944.30457
264	8.01865	110.56304	886.56871	264	8.46833	108.54312	919.17853	264	8.94311	106.58186	953.17377
265	8.08213	110.68678	894.58533	265	8.53713	108.66026	927.64691	265	9.01764	106.69275	962.11688
266	8.14612	110.80953	902.66748	266	8.60649	108.77645	936.18402	266	9.09279	106.80273	971.13452
267	8.21061	110.93132	910.81360	267	8.67642	108.89171	944.79053	267	9.16856	106.91179	980.22729
268	8.27561	111.05216	919.02423	268	8.74692	109.00603	953.46692	268	9.24497	107.01996	989.39587
269	8.34112	111.17205	927.29990	269	8.81799	109.11944	962.21367	269	9.32201	107.12724	998.64081
270	8.40716	111.29099	935.64083	270	8.88963	109.23133	971.03186	270	9.39969	107.23362	1007.96283
271	8.47371	111.40900	944.04810	271	8.96186	109.34351	979.92145	271	9.47802	107.33913	1017.36249
272	8.54060	111.52609	952.52179	272	9.03468	109.45419	988.88336	272	9.55700	107.44376	1026.84045
273	8.60841	111.64226	961.06262	273	9.10808	109.56399	997.91603	273	9.63665	107.54753	1036.39746
274	8.67656	111.75751	969.67102	274	9.18209	109.67290	1007.02612	274	9.71695	107.65044	1046.03418
275	8.74525	111.87186	978.34760	275	9.25669	109.78092	1016.20819	275	9.79793	107.75251	1055.75110

n									
276	8.81448	111.98531	987.09283	9.33190	109.88808	1025.46484	9.87968	107.85373	1065.54907
277	8.88427	112.09766	995.90735	9.40772	109.99438	1034.73675	9.96191	107.96410	1075.42859
278	8.96460	112.20954	1004.79156	9.48416	110.09982	1044.20447	10.04492	108.05366	1085.39050
279	9.02549	112.32034	1013.74622	9.56122	110.20441	1053.68860	10.12863	108.15239	1095.43542
280	9.09694	112.43027	1022.43027	9.63891	110.30815	1063.24968	10.21303	108.25031	1105.56409
281	9.16896	112.53933	1031.06865	9.71722	110.41106	1072.88879	10.29814	108.34741	1115.77710
282	9.24155	112.64754	1041.03760	9.79617	110.51315	1082.60596	10.38396	108.44371	1126.07520
283	9.31471	112.75489	1050.27905	9.87577	110.61440	1092.40210	10.47049	108.53922	1136.45923
284	9.38845	112.86140	1059.55387	9.95601	110.71484	1102.27796	10.55775	108.63393	1146.92969
285	9.46278	112.96709	1068.98230	10.03690	110.81448	1112.23389	10.64573	108.72787	1157.48743
286	9.53769	113.07193	1078.44507	10.11845	110.91331	1122.27087	10.73444	108.82103	1168.13318
287	9.61320	113.17536	1087.98279	10.20066	111.01134	1132.38928	10.82390	108.93410	1178.86768
288	9.68930	113.27916	1097.59595	10.28354	111.10858	1142.58997	10.91410	109.00504	1189.69153
289	9.76601	113.38155	1107.28528	10.36710	111.20504	1152.87354	11.00505	109.09591	1200.60559
290	9.84332	113.48315	1117.05127	10.45133	111.30072	1163.24060	11.09676	109.16603	1211.61072
291	9.92125	113.58394	1126.89453	10.53625	111.39563	1173.69189	11.18923	109.27540	1222.70740
292	9.99979	113.68394	1136.81560	10.62185	111.48978	1184.22815	11.28247	109.36403	1233.89661
293	10.07896	113.78315	1146.81555	10.70816	111.58317	1194.84998	11.37649	109.45193	1245.17908
294	10.15875	113.88160	1156.89453	10.79516	111.67580	1205.55823	11.47130	109.53910	1256.55566
295	10.23917	113.97926	1167.05334	10.88287	111.76768	1216.35339	11.56689	109.62556	1268.02686
296	10.32023	114.07616	1177.29248	10.97129	111.85883	1227.23621	11.66328	109.71130	1279.59375
297	10.40193	114.17229	1187.61267	11.06044	111.94925	1238.20752	11.76048	109.79633	1291.25708
298	10.48428	114.26768	1198.01465	11.15030	112.03893	1249.26794	11.85848	109.88065	1303.01758
299	10.56728	114.36230	1208.49890	11.24090	112.12789	1260.41821	11.95730	109.96429	1314.87610
300	10.65094	114.45620	1219.06616	11.33223	112.21613	1271.65918	12.05694	110.04723	1325.83337

Table 1. (continued) Annuities

M	C(9.50,M,12)	A(9.50,M,12)	S(9.50,M,12)	M	C(9.75,M,12)	A(9.75,M,12)	S(9.75,M,12)	M	C(10.00,M,12)	A(10.00,M,12)	S(10.00,M,12)
301	10.73526	114.54835	1229.71716	301	11.42430	112.30367	1282.99133	301	12.15742	110.12948	1338.89026
302	10.82025	114.64177	1240.45239	302	11.51713	112.39550	1294.41565	302	12.25873	110.21105	1351.04773
303	10.90591	114.73346	1251.27271	303	11.61070	112.47662	1305.93286	303	12.36089	110.29195	1363.30640
304	10.99225	114.82443	1262.17859	304	11.70504	112.56206	1317.54346	304	12.46389	110.37218	1375.66736
305	11.07927	114.91470	1273.17078	305	11.80014	112.64660	1329.24854	305	12.56776	110.45176	1388.13123
306	11.16698	115.00424	1284.25012	306	11.89602	112.73096	1341.04871	306	12.67249	110.53067	1400.69897
307	11.25539	115.03609	1295.41711	307	11.99268	112.81425	1352.94470	307	12.77810	110.60892	1413.37146
308	11.34449	115.18124	1306.67249	308	12.09012	112.89698	1364.93738	308	12.88458	110.68654	1426.14964
309	11.43430	115.26669	1318.01697	309	12.18835	112.97900	1377.02747	309	12.99195	110.76351	1439.03418
310	11.52482	115.35546	1329.45129	310	12.28738	113.06039	1389.21582	310	13.10022	110.83984	1452.02612
311	11.61606	115.44155	1340.97607	311	12.38721	113.14111	1401.50330	311	13.20939	110.91555	1465.12634
312	11.70802	115.52596	1352.59213	312	12.48786	113.22119	1413.89050	312	13.31946	110.99062	1478.33569
313	11.80071	115.61170	1364.30017	313	12.58932	113.30063	1426.37830	313	13.43046	111.06509	1491.65515
314	11.89413	115.69578	1376.10083	314	12.69161	113.37942	1438.96765	314	13.54238	111.13892	1505.08557
315	11.98829	115.77919	1387.99500	315	12.79473	113.45757	1451.65303	315	13.65523	111.21216	1518.62805
316	12.08320	115.86195	1399.98329	316	12.89869	113.53510	1464.45396	316	13.76903	111.28478	1532.28320
317	12.17886	115.94406	1412.06653	317	13.00349	113.61201	1477.35266	317	13.88377	111.35681	1546.05225
318	12.27528	116.02553	1424.24536	318	13.10914	113.68829	1490.35620	318	13.99947	111.42824	1559.99604
319	12.37245	116.10635	1436.52063	319	13.21566	113.76395	1503.46533	319	14.11613	111.49908	1573.59555
320	12.47040	116.18654	1448.89307	320	13.32303	113.83901	1516.68091	320	14.23376	111.56934	1588.05164
321	12.56913	116.26610	1461.36353	321	13.43128	113.91347	1530.00403	321	14.35238	111.63902	1602.28540
322	12.66863	116.34503	1473.93262	322	13.54041	113.98732	1543.43530	322	14.47198	111.70811	1616.63782
323	12.76893	116.42335	1486.60132	323	13.65043	114.06058	1556.97571	323	14.59258	111.77664	1631.10974
324	12.87001	116.50105	1499.37024	324	13.76134	114.13325	1570.62610	324	14.71419	111.84460	1645.70239
325	12.97190	116.57814	1512.24023	325	13.87315	114.20533	1584.38745	325	14.83680	111.91200	1660.41650

n								
326	13.07460	116.65482	1525.21216	13.98587	114.27682	1598.26062	14.96044	111.97884	1675.25330
327	13.17810	116.73051	1538.20674	14.09950	114.34776	1612.24646	15.08511	112.04514	1690.21375
328	13.28243	116.80579	1551.46484	14.21406	114.41811	1626.34595	15.21082	112.11088	1705.29895
329	13.38758	116.88049	1564.74719	14.32955	114.48789	1640.56006	15.33758	112.17608	1720.50977
330	13.43357	116.95460	1578.13477	14.44598	114.55711	1654.88965	15.46539	112.24074	1735.84729
331	13.60039	117.02813	1591.62842	14.56335	114.62578	1669.33557	15.59427	112.30486	1751.31274
332	13.70806	117.10107	1605.22876	14.68168	114.69389	1683.89883	15.72423	112.36846	1766.90698
333	13.81658	117.17345	1618.93689	14.80097	114.76145	1696.58057	15.85526	112.43153	1782.63123
334	13.92556	117.24526	1632.75342	14.92123	114.82848	1713.38159	15.98739	112.49408	1798.48645
335	14.03621	117.31651	1646.67944	15.04246	114.89495	1728.30273	16.12062	112.55611	1814.47388
336	14.14733	117.38719	1660.71558	15.16468	114.96089	1743.34521	16.25495	112.61763	1830.59448
337	14.25933	117.45732	1674.86292	15.28789	115.02631	1758.50989	16.39041	112.67864	1846.84587
338	14.37222	117.52690	1689.12231	15.41211	115.09119	1773.79785	16.52700	112.73915	1863.23987
339	14.48600	117.59593	1703.49451	15.53733	115.15555	1789.20996	16.66472	112.79916	1879.76685
340	14.60068	117.66442	1717.98047	15.66357	115.21939	1804.74731	16.80360	112.85967	1896.43152
341	14.71627	117.73238	1732.58118	15.79084	115.28272	1820.41089	16.94363	112.91769	1913.23511
342	14.83277	117.79979	1747.29749	15.91914	115.34554	1836.20166	17.08482	112.97622	1930.17883
343	14.95020	117.86668	1762.13025	16.04848	115.40785	1852.12085	17.22720	113.03426	1947.26355
344	15.06855	117.93304	1777.08044	16.17887	115.46966	1868.16931	17.37076	113.09184	1964.49084
345	15.18785	117.99891	1792.14893	16.31033	115.53097	1884.34814	17.51551	113.14893	1981.86157
346	15.30808	118.06421	1807.33679	16.44285	115.59179	1900.65845	17.66147	113.20554	1999.37708
347	15.42927	118.12902	1822.64490	16.57645	115.65211	1917.10132	17.80965	113.26170	2017.03857
348	15.55142	118.19333	1838.07410	16.71113	115.71195	1933.67706	17.95706	113.31739	2034.84717
349	15.67454	118.25713	1853.62561	16.84691	115.77131	1950.38892	18.10670	113.37262	2052.80420
350	15.79863	118.32042	1869.30005	16.98379	115.83019	1967.23584	18.25759	113.42739	2070.91089

Table 1. (continued) Annuities

M	CI 9.50,M,12)	AI 9.50,M,12)	SI 9.50,M,12)	M	CI 9.75,M,12)	AI 9.75,M,12)	SI 9.75,M,12)	M	C(10.00,M,12)	A(10.00,M,12)	S(10.00,M,12)
351	15.92370	118.38322	1865.09875	351	17.12178	115.88860	1964.21960	351	18.40974	113.48170	2089.16846
352	16.04976	118.44553	1901.02246	352	17.26030	115.94653	2001.34143	352	18.56315	113.53558	2107.57813
353	16.17682	118.50734	1917.07214	353	17.40114	116.00400	2018.60229	353	18.71784	113.58900	2126.14136
354	16.30489	118.56867	1933.24902	354	17.54253	116.06100	2036.00342	354	18.87383	113.64196	2144.85913
355	16.43397	118.62952	1949.55396	355	17.68506	116.11755	2053.54590	355	19.03111	113.69453	2163.73315
356	16.56407	118.68990	1965.98792	356	17.82875	116.17364	2071.23096	356	19.18970	113.74664	2182.76416
357	16.69520	118.74979	1982.55200	357	17.97361	116.22927	2089.05981	357	19.34962	113.79832	2201.95396
358	16.82737	118.80922	1999.24719	358	18.11965	116.28446	2107.03345	358	19.51096	113.84958	2221.30347
359	16.96059	118.86818	2016.07446	359	18.26687	116.33920	2125.15308	359	19.67345	113.90041	2240.81445
360	17.09486	118.92667	2033.03516	360	18.41529	116.39351	2143.41992	360	19.83740	113.95081	2260.48779
361	17.23020	118.98472	2050.12988	361	18.56491	116.44737	2161.83521	361	20.00271	114.00081	2280.32520
362	17.36660	119.04230	2067.36011	362	18.71575	116.50081	2180.40015	362	20.16940	114.05039	2300.32788
363	17.50409	119.09943	2084.72691	363	18.86782	116.55380	2199.11572	363	20.33748	114.09956	2320.49731
364	17.64266	119.15611	2102.23071	364	19.02112	116.60638	2217.98364	364	20.50696	114.14832	2340.83472
365	17.78233	119.21234	2119.87354	365	19.17566	116.65853	2237.00488	365	20.67785	114.19669	2361.34180
366	17.92311	119.26814	2137.65576	366	19.33147	116.71026	2256.16042	366	20.85016	114.24464	2382.01953
367	18.06500	119.32349	2155.57886	367	19.48853	116.76157	2275.49196	367	21.02391	114.29221	2402.86987
368	18.20801	119.37841	2173.64380	368	19.64688	116.81247	2295.00049	368	21.19911	114.33939	2423.89390
369	18.35216	119.43290	2191.85191	369	19.80651	116.86295	2314.64722	369	21.37577	114.38616	2445.09277
370	18.49745	119.48696	2210.20410	370	19.96744	116.91304	2334.45396	370	21.55391	114.43256	2466.46851
371	18.64389	119.54060	2228.70142	371	20.12967	116.96272	2354.42114	371	21.73352	114.47857	2488.02246
372	18.79148	119.59382	2247.34546	372	20.29323	117.01199	2374.55103	372	21.91463	114.52420	2509.75610
373	18.94025	119.64661	2266.13696	373	20.45811	117.06087	2394.84424	373	22.09726	114.56946	2531.67065
374	19.09019	119.69900	2285.07715	374	20.62433	117.10936	2415.30225	374	22.28140	114.61434	2553.76782
375	19.24133	119.75097	2304.16724	375	20.79190	117.15746	2435.92651	375	22.46708	114.65884	2576.04832

n				n				n			
376	19.33365	119.80253	2323.40069	376	20.96084	117.20518	2456.71851	376	22.65430	114.70299	2598.51636
377	19.54719	119.85369	2342.80225	377	21.13115	117.25249	2477.67944	377	22.84309	114.74677	2621.17065
378	19.70193	119.90445	2362.34961	378	21.30284	117.29943	2498.81055	378	23.03345	114.79018	2644.01367
379	19.8579	119.95480	2382.05151	379	21.47592	117.34599	2520.11328	379	23.22539	114.83324	2667.04712
380	20.01512	120.00477	2401.90942	380	21.65041	117.39218	2541.58836	380	23.41894	114.87594	2690.27271
381	20.17357	120.05434	2421.92456	381	21.82632	117.43800	2563.23975	381	23.61410	114.91829	2713.69165
382	20.33328	120.10352	2442.05814	382	22.00366	117.48344	2585.06592	382	23.81088	114.96028	2737.30566
383	20.49425	120.15231	2462.43140	383	22.18244	117.52853	2607.06958	383	24.00930	115.00193	2761.11646
384	20.65649	120.20072	2482.02554	384	22.36267	117.57324	2629.25220	384	24.20938	115.04324	2785.12573
385	20.82002	120.24875	2503.58203	385	22.54437	117.61760	2651.61475	385	24.41113	115.08421	2809.33521
386	20.98485	120.29640	2524.40210	386	22.72754	117.66160	2674.15918	386	24.61455	115.12483	2833.74634
387	21.15098	120.34368	2545.39696	387	22.91220	117.70525	2696.88672	387	24.81967	115.16512	2858.36084
388	21.31843	120.39059	2566.53784	388	23.09837	117.74854	2719.79983	388	25.02650	115.20508	2883.18066
389	21.48720	120.43713	2587.85645	389	23.28604	117.79148	2742.89722	389	25.23506	115.24471	2908.20703
390	21.65730	120.48331	2609.34351	390	23.47524	117.83408	2766.18235	390	25.44535	115.28400	2933.44214
391	21.82876	120.52911	2631.00073	391	23.66598	117.87634	2789.65845	391	25.65740	115.32298	2958.88745
392	22.00157	120.57457	2652.82959	392	23.85826	117.91825	2813.32446	392	25.87121	115.36163	2984.54492
393	22.17575	120.61966	2674.85130	393	24.05211	117.95982	2837.18286	393	26.08680	115.39997	3010.41602
394	22.35131	120.66441	2697.00684	394	24.24753	118.00107	2861.23486	394	26.30419	115.43799	3036.50293
395	22.52825	120.70879	2719.35815	395	24.44454	118.04198	2885.48242	395	26.52339	115.47569	3062.80713
396	22.70660	120.75283	2741.88647	396	24.64316	118.08256	2909.92700	396	26.74442	115.51308	3089.33057
397	22.88636	120.79652	2764.53302	397	24.84338	118.12280	2934.57007	397	26.96729	115.55016	3116.07495
398	23.06754	120.83987	2787.47949	398	25.04523	118.16273	2959.41357	398	27.19202	115.58694	3143.04224
399	23.25016	120.88289	2810.56480	399	25.24873	118.20234	2984.45874	399	27.41862	115.62341	3170.23413
400	23.43423	120.92556	2833.73712	400	25.45367	118.24163	3009.70752	400	27.64711	115.65958	3197.65283

Table 1. (continued) Annuities

M	C(9.50,M,12)	A(9.50,M,12)	S(9.50,M,12)	M	C(9.75,M,12)	A(9.75,M,12)	SI 9.75,M,12)	M	C(10.00,M,12)	A(10.00,M,12)	S(10.00,M,12)
401	23.61975	120.96790	2857.23145	401	25.66069	110.30069	5035.16138	401	27.87750	115.69645	3225.30005
402	23.80674	121.00990	2880.85107	402	25.86918	118.31125	3060.82202	402	28.10981	115.73103	3253.17749
403	23.99521	121.05157	2904.65798	403	26.07337	118.35760	3086.69916	403	28.34406	115.76630	3281.28735
404	24.18517	121.09293	2928.65308	404	26.29126	118.39963	3112.77051	404	28.58026	115.80129	3309.63135
405	24.37664	121.13395	2952.83608	405	26.50488	118.43336	3139.06177	405	28.81843	115.83599	3338.21167
406	24.56962	121.17464	2977.21484	406	26.72023	118.47079	3165.56865	406	29.05858	115.87041	3367.03003
407	24.76413	121.21503	3001.78442	407	26.93733	118.50791	3192.28887	407	29.30074	115.90453	3396.08862
408	24.96018	121.25510	3026.54858	408	27.15620	118.54473	3219.22437	408	29.54491	115.93839	3425.38940
409	25.15778	121.29485	3051.50879	409	27.37684	118.58126	3246.38037	409	29.79112	115.97195	3454.93433
410	25.35694	121.33428	3076.66693	410	27.59928	118.61749	3273.75732	410	30.03938	116.00524	3484.72534
411	25.55769	121.37341	3102.02844	411	27.82352	118.65343	3301.35669	411	30.28971	116.03825	3514.76445
412	25.76002	121.41222	3127.58130	412	28.04959	118.68909	3329.19018	412	30.54212	116.07100	3545.05444
413	25.96395	121.45074	3153.34131	413	28.27749	118.72445	3357.22974	413	30.79664	116.10347	3575.59668
414	26.16950	121.48895	3179.30518	414	28.50725	118.75953	3385.50732	414	31.05328	116.13567	3606.39331
415	26.37667	121.52686	3205.47461	415	28.73887	118.79433	3414.01440	415	31.31205	116.16761	3637.44653
416	26.58548	121.56448	3231.85132	416	28.97237	118.82884	3442.75342	416	31.57299	116.19928	3668.75854
417	26.79595	121.60180	3258.43677	417	29.20777	118.86308	3471.72559	417	31.83610	116.23069	3700.33154
418	27.00809	121.63882	3285.23291	418	29.44508	118.89704	3500.93335	418	32.10139	116.26184	3732.16772
419	27.22191	121.67556	3312.24097	419	29.68433	118.93073	3530.37066	419	32.36891	116.29273	3764.26904
420	27.43741	121.71201	3339.46289	420	29.92551	118.96414	3560.06299	420	32.63865	116.32337	3796.63794
421	27.65463	121.74817	3366.90015	421	30.16866	118.99729	3589.98828	421	32.91064	116.35376	3829.27661
422	27.87356	121.78404	3394.55493	422	30.41378	119.03017	3620.15698	422	33.18489	116.38390	3862.18726
423	28.09422	121.81964	3422.42847	423	30.66089	119.06278	3650.57080	423	33.46143	116.41378	3895.37207
424	28.31664	121.85495	3450.52271	424	30.91001	119.09514	3681.23169	424	33.74028	116.44341	3928.83350
425	28.54081	121.88999	3478.83386	425	31.16115	119.12723	3712.14160	425	34.02145	116.47281	3962.57373

N									
426	28.76676	121.92475	8507.39013	31.41434	119.15306	3743.30298	34.30496	116.50196	3996.59521
427	28.99450	121.95924	8536.14697	31.66958	119.19064	3774.71729	34.59084	116.53087	4030.90015
428	29.22404	121.99346	8565.14136	31.92689	119.22196	3806.38672	34.87909	116.55964	4065.49097
429	29.45539	122.02741	8594.36548	32.16830	119.25303	3838.31372	35.16975	116.58797	4100.37012
430	29.68858	122.06110	8623.82080	32.44781	119.28384	3870.50000	35.46283	116.61617	4135.54004
431	29.92362	122.09451	8653.50928	32.71145	119.31441	3902.94775	35.75835	116.64413	4171.00244
432	30.16051	122.12767	8683.43311	32.97723	119.34474	3935.65918	36.05634	116.67188	4206.76123
433	30.39928	122.16056	8713.59351	33.24517	119.37482	3968.63647	36.35681	116.69938	4242.81738
434	30.63994	122.19320	8743.99268	33.51529	119.40466	4001.88159	36.65979	116.72665	4279.17432
435	30.88251	122.22558	8774.63281	33.78760	119.43426	4035.39697	36.96528	116.75371	4315.83398
436	31.12700	122.25771	8805.51514	34.06212	119.46362	4069.18457	37.27333	116.78053	4352.79932
437	31.37342	122.28959	8836.64233	34.33888	119.49274	4103.24658	37.58394	116.80714	4390.07275
438	31.62179	122.32121	8868.01563	34.61788	119.52162	4137.58545	37.89714	116.83353	4427.65625
439	31.87213	122.35258	8899.63745	34.89915	119.55028	4172.20313	38.21295	116.85970	4465.55371
440	32.12445	122.38371	8931.50952	35.18271	119.57870	4207.10254	38.53139	116.88565	4503.76660
441	32.37877	122.41460	8963.63403	35.46857	119.60689	4242.28516	38.85248	116.91139	4542.29785
442	32.63510	122.44524	8996.01270	35.75675	119.63486	4277.75391	39.17625	116.93691	4581.15039
443	32.89346	122.47564	9028.64795	36.04727	119.66260	4313.51025	39.50272	116.96223	4620.32666
444	33.15387	122.50580	9061.54126	36.34016	119.69012	4349.55762	39.83191	116.98734	4659.82959
445	33.41634	122.53573	9094.69531	36.63542	119.71741	4385.89795	40.16385	117.01224	4699.66113
446	33.68088	122.56541	9128.11133	36.93308	119.74449	4422.53320	40.49654	117.03633	4739.82580
447	33.94752	122.59487	9161.79248	37.23317	119.77135	4459.46631	40.83603	117.06142	4780.32373
448	34.21627	122.62410	9195.73975	37.53568	119.79799	4496.69971	41.17633	117.08570	4821.15967
449	34.48715	122.65309	9229.95605	37.84066	119.82442	4534.23535	41.51947	117.10979	4862.33594
450	34.76018	122.68186	9264.44336	38.14812	119.85063	4572.07617	41.86546	117.13367	4903.85547

Table 1. (continued) Annuities

M	CI 9.50,M,12	AI 9.50,M,12	SI 9.50,M,12	M	CI 9.75,M,12	AI 9.75,M,12	SI 9.75,M,12	M	C(10.00,M,12)	A(10.00,M,12)	S(10.00,M,12)
451	35.03536	122.71040	4298.20361	451	38.45807	119.87663	4610.22412	451	42.21434	117.15736	4945.72119
452	35.31273	122.73872	4334.23877	452	38.77054	119.90242	4648.68213	452	42.56813	117.18085	4987.93555
453	35.59229	122.76682	4369.55176	453	39.08555	119.92901	4687.45264	453	42.92085	117.20415	5030.50146
454	35.87405	122.79469	4405.14404	454	39.40312	119.95338	4726.53909	454	43.27852	117.22726	5073.42236
455	36.15806	122.82235	4441.01807	455	39.72327	119.97866	4765.94141	455	43.63918	117.25018	5116.70068
456	36.44431	122.84979	4477.17578	456	40.04602	120.00353	4805.66455	456	44.00283	117.27290	5160.33984
457	36.73283	122.87701	4513.62012	457	40.37140	120.02831	4845.71045	457	44.36953	117.29544	5204.34277
458	37.02363	122.90402	4550.35303	458	40.69942	120.05287	4886.08203	458	44.73927	117.31779	5248.71240
459	37.31673	122.93080	4587.37695	459	41.03010	120.07725	4926.78125	459	45.11210	117.33996	5293.45166
460	37.61216	122.95738	4624.69336	460	41.36347	120.10142	4967.81152	460	45.48803	117.36194	5338.56396
461	37.90992	122.98374	4662.30566	461	41.69955	120.12540	5009.17529	461	45.86710	117.38374	5384.05176
462	38.21004	123.00996	4700.21533	462	42.03836	120.14919	5050.87451	462	46.24932	117.40536	5429.91895
463	38.51254	123.03598	4738.42578	463	42.37992	120.17278	5092.91309	463	46.63474	117.42680	5476.16846
464	38.81743	123.06168	4776.93799	464	42.72425	120.19619	5135.29297	464	47.02336	117.44807	5522.80322
465	39.12473	123.08724	4815.75537	465	43.07139	120.21941	5178.01709	465	47.41522	117.46916	5569.82617
466	39.43447	123.11260	4854.88037	466	43.42134	120.24244	5221.08838	466	47.81034	117.49008	5617.24170
467	39.74666	123.13776	4894.31494	467	43.77414	120.26528	5264.51977	467	48.20877	117.51083	5665.05176
468	40.06132	123.16273	4934.06152	468	44.12981	120.28794	5308.28418	468	48.61050	117.53139	5713.26074
469	40.37847	123.18749	4974.12256	469	44.48836	120.31042	5352.41406	469	49.01559	117.55190	5761.87109
470	40.69814	123.21206	5014.50146	470	44.84983	120.33272	5396.90234	470	49.42406	117.57203	5810.88672
471	41.02033	123.23644	5055.19922	471	45.21424	120.35484	5441.75195	471	49.83592	117.59209	5860.31104
472	41.34507	123.26063	5096.21973	472	45.58160	120.37678	5486.96631	472	50.25122	117.61199	5910.14697
473	41.67239	123.28462	5137.56494	473	45.95195	120.39854	5532.54785	473	50.66998	117.63173	5960.39795
474	42.00229	123.30843	5179.23730	474	46.32531	120.42012	5578.50000	474	51.09203	117.65131	6011.06787
475	42.33481	123.33205	5221.23926	475	46.70171	120.44154	5624.82520	475	51.51800	117.67072	6062.16016

n					
476	42.66996	123.35549	5283.57422	120.46278	47.08115
477	43.00777	123.37874	5306.24414	120.48384	47.46389
478	43.34824	123.40181	5349.25195	120.50475	47.84811
479	43.69142	123.42470	5398.60010	120.52547	48.23811
480	44.03731	123.44740	5426.29150	120.54604	48.63004
481	44.38594	123.46993	5456.32910	120.56644	49.02516
482	44.73733	123.49229	5524.71484	120.58667	49.42349
483	45.09150	123.51447	5569.45215	120.60674	49.82506
484	45.48047	123.53647	5614.54395	120.62665	50.22969
485	45.80827	123.55830	5659.99219	120.64639	50.63000
486	46.17092	123.57996	5705.80029	120.66599	51.04944
487	46.53644	123.60145	5751.97119	120.68542	51.46421
488	46.90485	123.62276	5798.50781	120.70469	51.88236
489	47.27618	123.64391	5845.41260	120.72381	52.30391
490	47.65046	123.66490	5892.68896	120.74277	52.72887
491	48.02769	123.68572	5940.33336	120.76158	53.15730
492	48.40791	123.70638	5988.36719	120.78024	53.58920
493	48.79113	123.72688	6036.77490	120.79875	54.02461
494	49.17740	123.74722	6085.56592	120.81712	54.46356
495	49.56672	123.76739	6134.31006	120.83533	54.90608
496	49.95912	123.78740	6184.31006	120.85339	55.35219
497	50.35463	123.80726	6234.26953	120.87132	55.80193
498	50.75327	123.82697	6284.62402	120.88909	56.25532
499	51.15507	123.84651	6335.33744	120.90672	56.71239
500	51.56005	123.86591	6396.53223	120.92422	57.17318

n				
476	51.94732	117.68996	5671.52686	6113.87822
477	52.39021	117.70905	5718.60791	6165.62549
478	52.81672	117.72799	5766.07178	6218.00586
479	53.25686	117.74677	5813.92010	6270.82227
480	53.70066	117.76539	5862.15918	6324.07910
481	54.14817	117.78385	5910.78906	6377.77979
482	54.59940	117.80217	5959.81445	6431.92822
483	55.05440	117.82034	6009.29779	6486.52734
484	55.51318	117.83835	6059.06299	6541.58203
485	55.97579	117.85621	6109.29297	6597.09521
486	56.44226	117.87393	6159.93066	6653.07090
487	56.91261	117.89150	6210.99047	6709.51318
488	57.38688	117.90898	6262.44434	6766.42578
489	57.86510	117.92621	6314.32666	6823.81250
490	58.34732	117.94334	6366.63086	6881.67773
491	58.83354	117.96034	6419.35938	6940.02490
492	59.32382	117.97720	6472.51709	6996.85889
493	59.81819	117.99392	6526.10596	7058.18262
494	60.31667	118.01050	6580.13096	7118.00049
495	60.81331	118.02694	6634.59424	7178.31738
496	61.32614	118.04324	6689.50049	7239.13672
497	61.83719	118.05942	6744.85254	7300.46289
498	62.35250	118.07545	6800.65430	7362.29980
499	62.87210	118.09136	6856.90967	7424.65234
500	63.35604	118.10713	6913.62207	7487.52441

Table 1. (continued) Annuities

M	C(10.25,M,12)	A(10.25,M,12)	S(10.25,M,12)	M	C(10.50,M,12)	A(10.50,M,12)	S(10.50,M,12)	M	C(10.75,M,12)	A(10.75,M,12)	S(10.75,M,12)
1	1.00854	0.99153	1.00000	1	1.00875	0.99133	1.00000	1	1.00896	0.99112	1.00000
2	1.01716	1.97466	2.00854	2	1.01758	1.97405	2.00875	2	1.01800	1.97344	2.00896
3	1.02584	2.94947	3.02570	3	1.02648	2.94826	3.02633	3	1.02712	2.94704	3.02696
4	1.03461	3.91602	4.05154	4	1.03546	3.91401	4.05281	4	1.03632	3.91200	4.05407
5	1.04344	4.87439	5.09615	5	1.04452	4.87138	5.08827	5	1.04560	4.86838	5.09039
6	1.05236	5.82463	6.12959	6	1.05366	5.82045	6.13279	6	1.05497	5.81628	6.13599
7	1.06135	6.76683	7.18196	7	1.06288	6.76129	7.18645	7	1.06442	6.75576	7.19096
8	1.07041	7.70105	8.24330	8	1.07218	7.69397	8.24933	8	1.07395	7.68690	8.25538
9	1.07955	8.62736	9.31371	9	1.08156	8.61856	9.32152	9	1.08358	8.60977	9.32933
10	1.08878	9.54582	10.33326	10	1.09103	9.53513	10.40308	10	1.09328	9.52445	10.41291
11	1.09808	10.45651	11.48204	11	1.10057	10.44374	11.49411	11	1.10308	10.43100	11.50619
12	1.10746	11.35948	12.56011	12	1.11020	11.34448	12.59460	12	1.11296	11.32951	12.60927
13	1.11691	12.25480	13.68757	13	1.11992	12.23740	13.70488	13	1.12293	12.22004	13.72222
14	1.12645	13.14254	14.80448	14	1.12972	13.12258	14.82480	14	1.13299	13.10266	14.84515
15	1.13608	14.02277	15.93094	15	1.13960	14.00008	15.95452	15	1.14314	13.97744	15.97814
16	1.14578	14.89553	17.06701	16	1.14957	14.86997	17.09412	16	1.15338	14.84446	17.12128
17	1.15557	15.76091	18.21280	17	1.15963	15.73231	18.24369	17	1.16371	15.70378	18.27465
18	1.16544	16.61895	19.36836	18	1.16978	16.58717	19.40333	18	1.17414	16.55547	19.43837
19	1.17539	17.46973	20.53380	19	1.18001	17.43462	20.57310	19	1.18465	17.39960	20.61250
20	1.18543	18.31331	21.70919	20	1.19034	18.27471	21.75312	20	1.19627	18.23623	21.79716
21	1.19556	19.14974	22.89463	21	1.20076	19.10752	22.94346	21	1.20597	19.06544	22.99242
22	1.20577	19.97908	24.09019	22	1.21126	19.93311	24.14421	22	1.21678	19.88728	24.19839
23	1.21607	20.80140	25.29596	23	1.22186	20.75153	25.35548	23	1.22768	20.70183	25.41517
24	1.22646	21.61676	26.51202	24	1.23255	21.56286	26.57734	24	1.23868	21.50914	26.64285
25	1.23693	22.42521	27.73848	25	1.24334	22.36714	27.60989	25	1.24977	22.30929	27.88153

n				n				n			
26	1.24750	23.22682	28.97541	26	1.25422	23.16446	29.05322	26	1.26097	23.10233	29.13130
27	1.25815	24.02163	30.22231	27	1.26519	23.95485	30.30744	27	1.27226	23.88833	30.39227
28	1.26830	24.80972	31.48107	28	1.27628	24.73839	31.57263	28	1.28366	24.66735	31.66453
29	1.27374	25.59112	32.74997	29	1.28743	25.51513	32.84889	29	1.29616	25.43946	32.94819
30	1.29067	26.36592	34.02971	30	1.29989	26.28514	34.13632	30	1.30676	26.20471	34.24335
31	1.30169	27.13414	35.32038	31	1.31006	27.04846	35.43501	31	1.31847	26.96318	35.55011
32	1.31281	27.89587	36.62207	32	1.32152	27.80517	36.74507	32	1.33028	27.71488	36.86858
33	1.32403	28.65114	37.93489	33	1.33308	28.55531	38.06659	33	1.34220	28.45933	38.19086
34	1.33534	29.40001	39.25891	34	1.34475	29.29894	39.39967	34	1.35422	29.19836	39.54106
35	1.34674	30.14255	40.59425	35	1.35651	30.03613	40.74442	35	1.36635	29.93023	40.89529
36	1.35825	30.87879	41.94099	36	1.36838	30.76692	42.10093	36	1.37859	30.65561	42.26164
37	1.36985	31.60880	43.29924	37	1.38036	31.49137	43.46931	37	1.39094	31.37455	43.64023
38	1.38155	32.33262	44.66909	38	1.39243	32.20953	44.84967	38	1.40340	32.08710	45.03118
39	1.39335	33.05032	46.05063	39	1.40462	32.92147	46.24210	39	1.41598	32.73033	46.43458
40	1.40525	33.76194	47.44398	40	1.41691	33.62723	47.64672	40	1.42866	33.43328	47.85056
41	1.41725	34.46753	48.84933	41	1.42931	34.32687	49.06363	41	1.44146	34.18702	49.27922
42	1.42936	35.16714	50.26649	42	1.44181	35.02044	50.49294	42	1.45437	34.87461	50.72068
43	1.44157	35.86083	51.69585	43	1.45443	35.70800	51.93475	43	1.46740	35.55608	52.17505
44	1.45388	36.54864	53.13742	44	1.46716	36.38959	53.38918	44	1.48055	36.23151	53.64245
45	1.46630	37.23063	54.59130	45	1.47999	37.06527	54.85633	45	1.49381	36.90094	55.12300
46	1.47883	37.90684	56.05760	46	1.49294	37.73508	56.33633	46	1.50719	37.56442	56.61681
47	1.49146	38.57733	57.53642	47	1.50601	38.39909	57.82927	47	1.52069	38.22202	58.12400
48	1.50420	39.24213	59.02788	48	1.51918	39.05734	59.33528	48	1.53432	38.87377	59.64470
49	1.51704	39.90131	60.53208	49	1.53248	39.70988	60.85446	49	1.54806	39.51974	61.17901
50	1.53000	40.55490	62.04912	50	1.54589	40.35676	62.39694	50	1.56193	40.19998	62.72707

Table 1. (continued) Annuities

M	C(10.25,M,12)	A(10.25,M,12)	S(10.25,M,12)	M	C(10.50,M,12)	A(10.50,M,12)	S(10.50,M,12)	M	C(10.75,M,12)	A(10.75,M,12)	S(10.75,M,12)
51	1.54307	41.20296	63.57912	51	1.55941	40.99802	63.93282	51	1.57592	40.79453	64.28900
52	1.55625	41.84553	65.12219	52	1.57306	41.63373	65.49203	52	1.59004	41.42344	65.86492
53	1.56955	42.48266	66.67844	53	1.58682	42.26392	67.06529	53	1.60428	42.04677	67.45498
54	1.58296	43.11439	68.24799	54	1.60071	42.88865	68.65211	54	1.61866	42.66457	69.05925
55	1.59647	43.74077	69.83094	55	1.61471	43.50796	70.25282	55	1.63316	43.27688	70.67790
56	1.61011	44.36185	71.42741	56	1.62884	44.12188	71.86753	56	1.64779	43.88375	72.31106
57	1.62386	44.97766	73.03753	57	1.64309	44.73049	73.49637	57	1.66255	44.48524	73.95885
58	1.63773	45.58826	74.66138	58	1.65747	45.33382	75.13947	58	1.67744	45.08139	75.62140
59	1.65172	46.19369	76.29912	59	1.67197	45.93192	76.79694	59	1.69247	45.67224	77.26984
60	1.66583	46.79399	77.95084	60	1.68660	46.52483	78.46891	60	1.70763	46.25785	78.99131
61	1.68006	47.38921	79.61687	61	1.70136	47.11259	80.15551	61	1.72293	46.83825	80.69694
62	1.69441	47.97939	81.29673	62	1.71625	47.69526	81.85687	62	1.73836	47.41351	82.42187
63	1.70888	48.56456	82.99114	63	1.73126	48.27287	83.57312	63	1.75394	47.98365	84.16022
64	1.72348	49.14478	84.70002	64	1.74641	48.84547	85.30438	64	1.76965	48.54874	85.91416
65	1.73820	49.72009	86.42350	65	1.76169	49.41311	87.05080	65	1.78550	49.10880	87.68391
66	1.75305	50.29053	88.16171	66	1.77711	49.97582	88.81249	66	1.80150	49.66390	89.46931
67	1.76802	50.85613	89.91475	67	1.79266	50.53365	90.58960	67	1.81763	50.21407	91.27081
68	1.78312	51.41695	91.68277	68	1.80834	51.08664	92.38226	68	1.83392	50.75935	93.08844
69	1.79835	51.97301	93.46580	69	1.82417	51.63483	94.19061	69	1.85035	51.29979	94.92236
70	1.81372	52.52436	95.26425	70	1.84013	52.17828	96.01477	70	1.86692	51.83543	96.77271
71	1.82921	53.07105	97.07796	71	1.85623	52.71700	97.85490	71	1.88365	52.36631	98.63963
72	1.84483	53.61310	98.90717	72	1.87247	53.25106	99.71114	72	1.90052	52.89248	100.52328
73	1.86059	54.15057	100.75201	73	1.88886	53.78048	101.58360	73	1.91755	53.41398	102.42390
74	1.87648	54.68348	102.61259	74	1.90538	54.30531	103.47247	74	1.93472	53.93085	104.34134
75	1.89251	55.21188	104.48908	75	1.92206	54.82558	105.37785	75	1.95206	54.44313	106.27607

n				n			
76	1.90868	55.73590	106.38159	76	1.93887	55.34134	107.29990
77	1.92498	56.25529	108.23027	77	1.95584	55.85263	109.23878
78	1.94142	56.77037	110.21525	78	1.97295	56.35949	111.19462
79	1.95800	57.28110	112.15667	79	1.99022	56.86195	113.16757
80	1.97473	57.78749	114.11467	80	2.00763	57.36005	115.15778
81	1.99160	58.28960	116.08940	81	2.02520	57.85382	117.16541
82	2.00861	58.78746	118.08100	82	2.04292	58.34332	119.19061
83	2.02577	59.28110	120.08961	83	2.06079	58.82857	121.23353
84	2.04307	59.77056	122.11537	84	2.07883	59.30961	123.29433
85	2.06052	60.25587	124.15844	85	2.09701	59.78648	125.37315
86	2.07812	60.73708	126.21896	86	2.11536	60.25921	127.47016
87	2.09587	61.21421	128.29707	87	2.13387	60.72784	129.58553
88	2.11377	61.68730	130.39294	88	2.15254	61.19241	131.71941
89	2.13183	62.15638	132.50673	89	2.17138	61.65295	133.87195
90	2.15004	62.62149	134.63855	90	2.19038	62.10949	136.04332
91	2.16840	63.08265	136.78859	91	2.20954	62.56207	138.23370
92	2.18692	63.53992	138.95699	92	2.22888	63.01073	140.44325
93	2.20560	63.99331	141.14392	93	2.24838	63.45549	142.67212
94	2.22444	64.44286	143.34952	94	2.26905	63.89640	144.92050
95	2.24344	64.88660	145.57396	95	2.28730	64.33347	147.18857
96	2.26261	65.33057	147.07741	96	2.30792	64.76677	149.47646
97	2.28193	65.76679	150.CEOO2	97	2.32871	65.19610	151.78438
98	2.30142	66.20331	152.26139	98	2.34848	65.62111	154.11249
99	2.32108	66.62414	154.66338	99	2.36903	66.04422	156.46098
100	2.34091	67.06133	156.98445	100	2.38976	66.46267	158.83002

n			
76	1.96954	54.96096	108.22813
77	1.98719	55.45409	110.19767
78	2.00499	55.96284	112.18485
79	2.02295	56.4477	114.18994
80	2.04107	56.93711	116.21279
81	2.05936	57.42270	118.25387
82	2.07781	57.90397	120.31322
83	2.09642	58.38098	122.39103
84	2.11520	58.85374	124.48745
85	2.13415	59.32232	126.60265
86	2.15327	59.78673	128.73680
87	2.17256	60.24701	130.89006
88	2.19202	60.70322	133.06382
EE	2.21166	61.15536	135.25464
90	2.23147	61.60350	137.46629
91	2.25146	62.04766	139.69777
92	2.27163	62.4787	141.94922
93	2.29198	62.92418	144.22096
94	2.31251	63.35681	146.51283
95	2.33323	63.78519	148.82535
96	2.35413	64.20998	151.15857
97	2.37522	64.63099	153.51270
98	2.39650	65.04827	155.88791
99	2.41796	65.46184	158.28441
100	2.43963	65.87174	160.70238

Table 1. (continued) Annuities

M	C(10.25,M,12)	A(10.25,M,12)	S(10.25,M,12)	M	C(10.50,M,12)	A(10.50,M,12)	S(10.50,M,12)	M	C(10.75,M,12)	A(10.75,M,12)	S(10.75,M,12)
101	2.36090	67.48489	159.32536	101	2.41067	66.87749	161.21977	101	2.46148	66.27900	163.14200
102	2.38107	67.90487	161.68626	102	2.43177	67.28872	163.63045	102	2.48353	66.68065	165.60349
103	2.40141	68.32129	164.06734	103	2.45304	67.69897	166.06221	103	2.50578	67.07973	168.08701
104	2.42192	68.73418	166.46875	104	2.47451	68.10049	168.51526	104	2.52823	67.47527	170.59279
105	2.44261	69.14359	168.89067	105	2.49616	68.50111	170.98976	105	2.55088	67.86729	173.12102
106	2.46347	69.54951	171.33328	106	2.51800	68.89825	173.48593	106	2.57373	68.25583	175.67189
107	2.48451	69.95201	173.79675	107	2.54003	69.29195	176.00394	107	2.59678	68.64091	178.24562
108	2.50574	70.35110	176.28127	108	2.56226	69.68223	178.54396	108	2.62005	69.02259	180.84241
109	2.52714	70.74680	178.78700	109	2.58468	70.06912	181.10622	109	2.64352	69.40087	183.46245
110	2.54872	71.13915	181.31413	110	2.60730	70.45266	183.69090	110	2.66720	69.77580	186.10597
111	2.57050	71.52818	183.86287	111	2.63011	70.83287	186.29820	111	2.69109	70.14739	188.77318
112	2.59245	71.91392	186.43336	112	2.65312	71.20979	188.92831	112	2.71520	70.51569	191.46426
113	2.61460	72.29639	189.02580	113	2.67634	71.58344	191.58144	113	2.73952	70.88072	194.17946
114	2.63693	72.67561	191.64041	114	2.69976	71.95383	194.25777	114	2.76407	71.24251	196.91899
115	2.65945	73.05164	194.27733	115	2.72338	72.32103	196.95752	115	2.78883	71.60108	199.68306
116	2.68217	73.42447	196.93678	116	2.74721	72.68504	199.68091	116	2.81381	71.95647	202.47188
117	2.70508	73.79414	199.61896	117	2.77125	73.04588	202.42812	117	2.83902	72.30870	205.28569
118	2.72818	74.16068	202.32404	118	2.79549	73.40360	205.19936	118	2.86445	72.65781	208.12471
119	2.75149	74.52412	205.05222	119	2.81995	73.75822	207.99486	119	2.89011	73.00381	210.98917
120	2.77499	74.88448	207.80371	120	2.84463	74.10976	210.81490	120	2.91600	73.34676	213.87927
121	2.79869	75.24179	210.57869	121	2.86952	74.45824	213.65944	121	2.94212	73.68665	216.79827
122	2.82260	75.59608	213.37740	122	2.89463	74.80371	216.52896	122	2.96848	74.02351	219.73740
123	2.84671	75.94736	216.19998	123	2.91996	75.14619	219.42358	123	2.99507	74.35740	222.70589
124	2.87102	76.29567	219.04669	124	2.94551	75.48568	222.34354	124	3.02190	74.68832	225.70096
125	2.89555	76.64103	221.91772	125	2.97128	75.82224	225.28905	125	3.04898	75.01630	228.72285

126	2.98028	76.96046	224.81326	126	2.98728	76.15588	228.26033	126	3.07629	75.34136	281.77184
127	2.94522	77.32299	227.73355	127	3.02350	76.48662	231.25760	127	3.10395	75.66354	234.84813
128	2.97038	77.65565	230.67877	128	3.04996	76.81449	234.28111	128	3.13165	75.98286	237.96197
129	2.99675	77.99345	233.64915	129	3.07665	77.13962	237.33107	129	3.15971	76.29935	241.08362
130	3.02134	78.32443	236.64491	130	3.10357	77.46173	240.40771	130	3.18801	76.61302	244.24333
131	3.04715	78.65261	239.66624	131	3.13072	77.78114	243.51128	131	3.21657	76.92391	247.43135
132	3.07318	78.97800	242.71339	132	3.15812	78.09779	246.64200	132	3.24539	77.23204	250.64792
133	3.09943	79.30064	245.78658	133	3.18575	78.41169	249.80013	133	3.27446	77.53744	253.89331
134	3.12590	79.62055	248.80600	134	3.21363	78.72286	252.98587	134	3.30379	77.84012	257.18776
135	3.15260	79.93775	252.01190	135	3.24175	79.03133	256.19949	135	3.33339	78.14011	260.47156
136	3.17953	80.25227	255.16451	136	3.27011	79.33714	259.44125	136	3.36325	78.43745	263.80498
137	3.20669	80.56411	258.34402	137	3.29872	79.64028	262.71136	137	3.39338	78.73213	267.16818
138	3.23408	80.87332	261.55072	138	3.32759	79.94080	266.01007	138	3.42378	79.02421	270.56158
139	3.26170	81.17991	264.78479	139	3.35670	80.23672	269.33768	139	3.45445	79.31369	273.96535
140	3.28956	81.48390	268.04651	140	3.38608	80.53404	272.69437	140	3.48540	79.60060	277.43962
141	3.31766	81.78532	271.33606	141	3.41570	80.82681	276.08044	141	3.51662	79.88496	280.98520
142	3.34600	82.08418	274.65372	142	3.44559	81.11703	279.49615	142	3.54812	80.16690	284.44183
143	3.37458	82.38052	277.99973	143	3.47574	81.40474	282.94174	143	3.57991	80.44614	287.99958
144	3.40341	82.67434	281.37430	144	3.50615	81.68996	286.41748	144	3.61198	80.72300	291.56965
145	3.43248	82.96568	284.77771	145	3.53683	81.97269	289.92365	145	3.64434	80.99740	295.18166
146	3.46180	83.25454	288.21017	146	3.56778	82.25298	293.46045	146	3.67698	81.26936	298.92617
147	3.49936	83.54036	291.67200	147	3.59900	82.53083	297.02823	147	3.70992	81.53890	302.50317
148	3.52119	83.82496	295.16336	148	3.63049	82.80628	300.62723	148	3.74316	81.80606	306.21310
149	3.55126	84.10654	298.68454	149	3.66226	83.06628	304.25772	149	3.77668	82.07084	309.96627
150	3.58160	84.38575	302.23591	150	3.69430	83.35002	307.91998	150	3.81052	82.33327	313.73284

Table 1. (continued) Annuities

M	C(10,25,M,12)	A(10,25,M,12)	S(10,25,M,12)	M	C(10,50,M,12)	A(10,50,M,12)	S(10,50,M,12)	M	C(10,75,M,12)	A(10,75,M,12)	S(10,75,M,12)
151	3.61219	84.66259	305.81741	151	3.72662	83.81836	311.61429	151	3.84466	82.59338	317.54346
152	3.64304	84.93709	309.42960	152	3.75923	83.88438	315.34091	152	3.87910	82.65117	321.38812
153	3.67416	85.20926	313.07263	153	3.79213	84.14808	319.10013	153	3.91385	83.10667	325.26724
154	3.70555	85.47913	316.74680	154	3.82531	84.40949	322.89227	154	3.94891	83.35990	329.18109
155	3.73720	85.74670	320.45233	155	3.85878	84.66864	326.71759	155	3.98429	83.61089	333.13000
156	3.76912	86.01202	324.18954	156	3.89254	84.92554	330.57635	156	4.01998	83.86964	337.11429
157	3.80131	86.27509	327.96865	157	3.92660	85.18022	334.46890	157	4.05599	84.10619	341.13428
158	3.83378	86.53593	331.75998	158	3.96096	85.43268	338.39551	158	4.09233	84.35056	345.19028
159	3.86653	86.79456	335.55375	159	3.99562	85.68295	342.35648	159	4.12899	84.59274	349.28259
160	3.89956	87.05099	339.46030	160	4.03058	85.93106	346.35208	160	4.16598	84.83278	353.41159
161	3.93287	87.30526	343.35983	161	4.06585	86.17701	350.38266	161	4.20330	85.07069	357.57758
162	3.96646	87.55737	347.29269	162	4.10142	86.42083	354.44852	162	4.24095	85.30649	361.78085
163	4.00034	87.80735	351.25976	163	4.13731	86.66253	358.54993	163	4.27895	85.54019	366.02182
164	4.03451	88.05521	355.25949	164	4.17351	86.90214	362.68726	164	4.31728	85.77182	370.30075
165	4.06897	88.30098	359.29401	165	4.21003	87.13966	366.86075	165	4.35595	86.00139	374.61804
166	4.10373	88.54465	363.36298	166	4.24687	87.37513	371.07080	166	4.39497	86.22892	378.97400
167	4.13878	88.78628	367.46671	167	4.28403	87.60856	375.31766	167	4.43435	86.45443	383.36986
168	4.17413	89.02585	371.60550	168	4.32151	87.83996	379.60168	168	4.47407	86.67794	387.80331
169	4.20978	89.26339	375.77960	169	4.35933	88.06935	383.92322	169	4.51415	86.89947	392.27737
170	4.24574	89.49892	379.98941	170	4.39747	88.29675	388.28253	170	4.55459	87.11903	396.79153
171	4.28201	89.73245	384.23514	171	4.43595	88.52219	392.67999	171	4.59539	87.33664	401.34613
172	4.31858	89.96401	388.51716	172	4.47476	88.74566	397.11597	172	4.63656	87.55231	405.94153
173	4.35547	90.19360	392.83572	173	4.51392	88.96720	401.59073	173	4.67810	87.76608	410.57809
174	4.39267	90.42126	397.19122	174	4.55342	89.18681	406.10464	174	4.72000	87.97794	415.25616
175	4.43020	90.64698	401.58388	175	4.59326	89.40453	410.65805	175	4.76229	88.18792	419.97617

n					n				n			
176	4.46804	90.87060	4.63345	406.01407	176	4.63345	88.62035	415.25131	176	4.80495	88.39604	424.73846
177	4.50620	91.09271	4.67399	410.48212	177	4.67399	89.83430	419.88477	177	4.84799	88.60231	429.54343
178	4.54469	91.31274	4.71489	414.98831	178	4.71489	90.04639	424.55675	178	4.89142	88.00676	434.39142
179	4.58351	91.53092	4.75614	419.53302	179	4.75614	90.25665	429.27365	179	4.93524	89.00938	439.28284
180	4.62266	91.73725	4.79776	424.11652	180	4.79776	90.46507	434.02979	180	4.97945	89.21021	444.21808
181	4.66215	91.96174	4.83974	428.73920	181	4.83974	90.67170	438.82755	181	5.02406	89.40924	449.19754
182	4.70197	92.17442	4.88209	433.40134	182	4.88209	90.87653	443.66730	182	5.06907	89.60652	454.22159
183	4.74213	92.38529	4.92481	438.10330	183	4.92481	91.07968	448.54938	183	5.11448	89.80204	459.29065
184	4.78264	92.59438	4.96790	442.84543	184	4.96790	91.28088	453.47418	184	5.16030	89.99583	464.40515
185	4.82349	92.80170	5.01137	447.62808	185	5.01137	91.48042	458.44208	185	5.20652	90.18730	469.56543
186	4.86469	93.00726	5.05522	452.45157	186	5.05522	91.67824	463.45346	186	5.25317	90.37826	474.77197
187	4.90624	93.21108	5.09945	457.31625	187	5.09945	91.87434	468.50867	187	5.30022	90.56693	480.02512
188	4.94815	93.41319	5.14407	462.22250	188	5.14407	92.06873	473.60812	188	5.34771	90.75392	485.32535
189	4.99042	93.61356	5.18908	467.17065	189	5.18908	92.26144	478.75220	189	5.39561	90.93926	490.67307
190	5.03304	93.81226	5.23449	472.16107	190	5.23449	92.45248	483.94128	190	5.44395	91.12295	496.06866
191	5.07603	94.00925	5.28029	477.19409	191	5.28029	92.64187	489.17575	191	5.49272	91.30501	501.51260
192	5.11939	94.20459	5.32649	482.27014	192	5.32649	92.82961	494.45605	192	5.54192	91.48545	507.00534
193	5.16312	94.39828	5.37310	487.38953	193	5.37310	93.01572	499.78253	193	5.59157	91.66429	512.54724
194	5.20722	94.59032	5.42011	492.55264	194	5.42011	93.20022	505.15564	194	5.64166	91.84155	518.13879
195	5.25170	94.78073	5.46754	497.75996	195	5.46754	93.38312	510.57574	195	5.69220	92.01723	523.76046
196	5.29656	94.96953	5.51538	503.01157	196	5.51538	93.56443	516.04327	196	5.74319	92.19135	529.47266
197	5.34180	95.15673	5.56364	508.30814	197	5.56364	93.74417	521.55985	197	5.79464	92.36391	535.21588
198	5.38743	95.34235	5.61232	513.64990	198	5.61232	93.92235	527.12231	198	5.84655	92.53496	541.01050
199	5.43344	95.52640	5.66143	519.03735	199	5.66143	94.09898	532.73462	199	5.89893	92.70448	546.85706
200	5.47985	96.70889	5.71097	524.47076	200	5.71097	94.27409	538.39606	200	5.96177	92.87250	552.75598

Table 1. (continued) Annuities

M	C(10.25,M,12)	A(10.25,M,12)	S(10.25,M,12)	M	C(10.50,M,12)	A(10.50,M,12)	S(10.50,M,12)	M	C(10.75,M,12)	A(10.75,M,12)	S(10.75,M,12)
201	5.52866	95.88992	529.96062	201	5.76094	94.44767	544.10699	201	6.00509	93.03902	558.70776
202	5.57387	96.06924	535.47729	202	5.81134	94.61974	549.86792	202	6.05889	93.20407	564.71283
203	5.62148	96.24712	541.05115	203	5.86219	94.78033	555.67526	203	6.11316	93.36765	570.77173
204	5.66950	96.42351	546.67261	204	5.91349	94.95943	561.54144	204	6.16730	93.52979	576.88489
205	5.71792	96.59840	552.34210	205	5.96523	95.12708	567.45436	205	6.22318	93.69047	583.05280
206	5.76676	96.77192	558.06084	206	6.01743	95.28326	573.42017	206	6.27693	93.84973	589.27500
207	5.81602	96.94374	563.82784	207	6.07008	95.45600	579.43762	207	6.33518	94.00758	595.55433
208	5.86570	97.11422	569.64282	208	6.12319	95.62132	585.50769	208	6.39193	94.16403	601.89014
209	5.91580	97.28326	575.50854	209	6.17677	95.78321	591.63092	209	6.44919	94.31908	608.26204
210	5.96633	97.45087	581.42432	210	6.23082	95.94370	597.80768	210	6.50697	94.47277	614.73126
211	6.01730	97.61706	587.39069	211	6.28534	96.10280	604.03845	211	6.56526	94.62508	621.23822
212	6.06869	97.78184	593.40796	212	6.34033	96.26052	610.32379	212	6.62407	94.77605	627.80347
213	6.12053	97.94522	599.47668	213	6.39581	96.41688	616.66412	213	6.68341	94.92587	634.42755
214	6.17281	98.10722	605.59717	214	6.45177	96.57187	623.05994	214	6.74329	95.07397	641.11096
215	6.22554	98.26785	611.77002	215	6.50823	96.72552	629.51172	215	6.80369	95.22095	647.85425
216	6.27871	98.42712	617.99554	216	6.56517	96.87784	636.01996	216	6.86464	95.36662	654.65796
217	6.33234	98.58504	624.27423	217	6.62262	97.02884	642.58514	217	6.92614	95.51100	661.52258
218	6.38643	98.74162	630.60657	218	6.68057	97.17853	649.20776	218	6.98819	95.65411	668.44873
219	6.44098	98.89687	636.99304	219	6.73902	97.32692	655.88831	219	7.05079	95.79593	675.43689
220	6.49600	99.05082	643.43402	220	6.79799	97.47402	662.62730	220	7.11355	95.93650	682.48767
221	6.55149	99.20345	649.92999	221	6.85747	97.61994	669.42535	221	7.17768	96.07582	689.60162
222	6.60745	99.35480	656.48151	222	6.91747	97.76440	676.28264	222	7.24196	96.21391	696.77300
223	6.66388	99.50486	663.08893	223	6.97800	97.90771	683.20026	223	7.30686	96.35076	704.02130
224	6.72081	99.65366	669.75281	224	7.03906	98.04978	690.17828	224	7.37231	96.48640	711.32819
225	6.77821	99.80119	676.47363	225	7.10065	98.19061	697.21735	225	7.43836	96.62084	718.70050

n									
226	6.83611	99.94746	683.25183	7.16278	98.33022	704.31799	7.50499	96.75409	726.13885
227	6.89450	100.03251	690.08795	7.22546	98.46862	711.48077	7.57223	96.88615	733.64396
228	6.95339	100.23633	696.98242	7.28868	98.60582	718.70624	7.64006	97.01704	741.21606
229	7.01279	100.37892	703.93585	7.35246	98.74183	725.99493	7.70850	97.14677	748.85614
230	7.07269	100.52031	710.94861	7.41679	98.87666	733.34735	7.77756	97.27534	756.56464
231	7.13310	100.66050	718.02130	7.48169	99.01031	740.76416	7.84723	97.40277	764.34218
232	7.19403	100.79951	725.15442	7.54715	99.14281	748.24585	7.91753	97.52908	772.18939
233	7.25548	100.93733	732.34845	7.61319	99.27417	755.79803	7.98846	97.65426	780.10693
234	7.31745	101.07399	739.60394	7.67900	99.40438	763.40619	8.06002	97.77833	788.09540
235	7.37995	101.20950	746.92139	7.74700	99.53346	771.08600	8.13223	97.90129	796.15540
236	7.44299	101.34385	754.30133	7.81479	99.66142	778.83301	8.20508	98.02317	804.28766
237	7.50657	101.47707	761.74432	7.88317	99.78828	786.64777	8.27858	98.13223	812.49274
238	7.57068	101.60915	769.25085	7.95215	99.91403	794.53094	8.35274	98.26368	820.77130
239	7.63535	101.74013	776.82153	8.02173	100.03969	802.48309	8.42757	98.38234	829.12402
240	7.70057	101.86999	784.45691	8.09192	100.16227	810.50482	8.50307	98.49995	837.55164
241	7.76635	101.99875	792.15747	8.16272	100.28478	818.59674	8.57924	98.61651	846.05469
242	7.83268	102.12642	799.92383	8.23415	100.40623	826.75946	8.65610	98.73203	854.63391
243	7.89959	102.25301	807.75653	8.30619	100.52662	834.93359	8.73364	98.84653	863.29004
244	7.96706	102.37852	815.65607	8.37887	100.64597	843.29980	8.81188	98.96001	872.02366
245	8.03511	102.50298	823.62317	8.45219	100.76427	851.67871	8.90892	99.07249	880.83551
246	8.10375	102.62637	831.65806	8.52614	100.88156	860.13086	8.97046	99.18397	889.72638
247	8.17297	102.74873	839.76202	8.60075	100.98183	868.65704	9.05083	99.29446	898.69684
248	8.24278	102.87005	847.93500	8.67601	101.11309	877.25775	9.13191	99.40396	907.74762
249	8.31318	102.99034	856.17780	8.75192	101.22906	885.93378	9.21371	99.51250	916.87958
250	8.38419	103.10961	864.49037	8.82850	101.34062	894.68567	9.29625	99.62006	926.03826

Table 1. (continued) Annuities

M	C(10.25,M,12)	A(10.25,M,12)	S(10.25,M,12)	M	C(10.50,M,12)	A(10.50,M,12)	S(10.50,M,12)	M	C(10.75,M,12)	A(10.75,M,12)	S(10.75,M,12)
251	8.45581	103.22787	872.87512	251	8.90575	101.45291	903.51422	251	9.37563	99.72668	935.38953
252	8.52604	103.34513	881.33093	252	8.98367	101.56422	912.41992	252	9.46336	99.83285	944.76904
253	8.60088	103.46140	889.85901	253	9.06228	101.67457	921.40363	253	9.55233	99.93708	954.23260
254	8.67434	103.57668	898.45990	254	9.14158	101.78396	930.46558	254	9.63570	100.04008	963.78094
255	8.74844	103.69099	907.13422	255	9.22157	101.89240	939.60748	255	9.72017	100.14376	973.41479
256	8.82316	103.80433	915.88263	256	9.30225	101.99990	948.82904	256	9.80725	100.24572	983.13501
257	8.89853	103.91670	924.70581	257	9.38365	102.10647	958.13129	257	9.89511	100.34679	992.94226
258	8.97454	104.02811	933.60437	258	9.46576	102.21211	967.51495	258	9.98375	100.44695	1002.83734
259	9.05119	104.13861	942.57896	259	9.54858	102.31684	976.98071	259	10.07319	100.54622	1012.82111
260	9.12851	104.24816	951.63007	260	9.63213	102.42066	986.52930	260	10.16343	100.64462	1022.89429
261	9.20648	104.35678	960.75861	261	9.71641	102.52356	996.16144	261	10.25447	100.74213	1033.05774
262	9.28512	104.46448	969.96509	262	9.80143	102.62561	1005.87781	262	10.34634	100.83878	1043.31213
263	9.36443	104.57127	979.25018	263	9.88719	102.72675	1015.67926	263	10.43902	100.93458	1053.65845
264	9.44442	104.67715	988.61462	264	9.97371	102.82701	1025.56641	264	10.53254	101.02952	1064.09753
265	9.52509	104.78214	998.05902	265	10.06098	102.92494	1035.54016	265	10.62689	101.12362	1074.62000
266	9.60645	104.88625	1007.58411	266	10.14901	103.02494	1045.60107	266	10.72209	101.21689	1085.25696
267	9.68850	104.98945	1017.19055	267	10.23781	103.12261	1055.75012	267	10.81815	101.30933	1095.97900
268	9.77126	105.09179	1026.87903	268	10.32739	103.21944	1065.98798	268	10.91506	101.40094	1106.75724
269	9.85472	105.19326	1036.65027	269	10.41776	103.31544	1076.31531	269	11.01284	101.49474	1117.71228
270	9.93890	105.29388	1046.50500	270	10.50891	103.41059	1086.73303	270	11.11150	101.58174	1128.72510
271	10.02379	105.39364	1056.43957	271	10.60087	103.50492	1097.24154	271	11.21104	101.67094	1139.83655
272	10.10941	105.49255	1066.46765	272	10.69363	103.59843	1107.84290	272	11.31147	101.75935	1151.04761
273	10.19576	105.59064	1076.57715	273	10.78719	103.69114	1118.53650	273	11.41280	101.84696	1162.35913
274	10.28285	105.68789	1086.77283	274	10.88158	103.78304	1129.32373	274	11.51504	101.93381	1173.77185
275	10.37068	105.78431	1097.05579	275	10.97680	103.87414	1140.20532	275	11.61820	102.01988	1185.28699

n				n				n			
276	10.45927	105.87992	1107.42639	276	11.07284	103.96445	1151.16201	276	11.72227	102.10519	1196.90515
277	10.54861	105.57472	1117.88574	277	11.16973	104.05398	1162.25488	277	11.82729	102.18974	1208.62744
278	10.63871	106.06872	1128.43433	278	11.26747	104.14273	1173.42468	278	11.93324	102.27354	1220.45471
279	10.72958	106.16192	1139.07300	279	11.36606	104.23071	1184.69214	279	12.04014	102.35659	1232.38794
280	10.82123	106.25433	1149.80261	280	11.46551	104.31793	1196.05811	280	12.14800	102.43891	1244.42810
281	10.91366	106.34596	1160.62378	281	11.56583	104.40439	1207.52368	281	12.25683	102.52050	1256.57605
282	11.00688	106.43681	1171.53748	282	11.66703	104.49010	1219.08948	282	12.36663	102.60138	1268.83289
283	11.10090	106.52689	1182.54431	283	11.76912	104.57507	1230.76659	283	12.47741	102.68150	1281.19968
284	11.19572	106.61621	1193.64526	284	11.87210	104.65930	1242.52563	284	12.58919	102.76094	1293.67700
285	11.29135	106.70477	1204.84094	285	11.97598	104.74280	1254.39771	285	12.70197	102.83967	1306.26611
286	11.38780	106.79259	1216.13232	286	12.08077	104.82558	1266.37378	286	12.81576	102.91772	1318.96814
287	11.48507	106.87965	1227.52014	287	12.18648	104.90764	1278.45447	287	12.93056	102.99503	1331.78381
288	11.58317	106.96599	1239.00525	288	12.29311	104.98898	1290.64099	288	13.04640	103.07168	1344.71448
289	11.68211	107.05159	1250.58838	289	12.40067	105.06963	1302.93408	289	13.16327	103.14765	1357.76096
290	11.78189	107.13647	1262.27051	290	12.50918	105.14957	1315.33472	290	13.28119	103.22296	1370.92407
291	11.88253	107.22063	1274.05237	291	12.61863	105.22881	1327.84399	291	13.40017	103.29757	1384.20532
292	11.99403	107.30407	1285.93494	292	12.72905	105.30737	1340.46252	292	13.52022	103.37154	1397.60547
293	12.06639	107.39680	1297.91895	293	12.84043	105.38525	1353.19165	293	13.64133	103.44484	1411.12573
294	12.18963	107.46994	1310.00537	294	12.95278	105.46246	1366.03210	294	13.76354	103.51749	1424.76697
295	12.28375	107.55019	1322.14615	295	13.06612	105.53899	1378.98486	295	13.88684	103.58951	1438.53052
296	12.39876	107.63084	1334.48865	296	13.18045	105.61496	1392.05090	296	14.01124	103.66088	1452.41736
297	12.50466	107.71081	1346.88745	297	13.29577	105.69007	1405.23145	297	14.13676	103.73161	1466.42859
298	12.61147	107.79010	1359.33209	298	13.41211	105.76463	1418.52722	298	14.26340	103.80173	1480.56543
299	12.71920	107.86872	1372.00354	299	13.52947	105.83854	1431.93933	299	14.39117	103.87122	1494.82874
300	12.82784	107.94668	1384.72278	300	13.64785	105.91181	1445.46875	300	14.52010	103.94009	1509.21997

Table 1. (continued) Annuities

M	C(10.25,M,12)	A(10.25,M,12)	S(10.25,M,12)	M	C(10.50,M,12)	A(10.50,M,12)	S(10.50,M,12)	M	C(10.75,M,12)	A(10.75,M,12)	S(10.75,M,12)
301	12.93741	108.02397	1397.55066	301	13.76727	105.98845	1459.11658	301	14.65017	104.00834	1523.74011
302	13.04792	108.17062	1410.48804	302	13.88773	106.05646	1472.88391	302	14.78141	104.07600	1538.39026
303	13.17537	108.31539	1423.50601	303	14.00825	106.12784	1486.77161	303	14.91383	104.14304	1553.17163
304	13.21577	108.25165	1436.63631	304	14.13103	106.19860	1500.79088	304	15.04743	104.20950	1568.08545
305	13.30514	108.32666	1449.96716	305	14.25549	106.26975	1514.91272	305	15.18223	104.27537	1583.13298
306	13.49477	108.40074	1463.35229	306	14.38022	106.33829	1529.16821	306	15.31824	104.34065	1598.31519
307	13.61477	108.47419	1476.85168	307	14.50605	106.40723	1543.54846	307	15.45547	104.40535	1613.63342
308	13.73107	108.54702	1490.46643	308	14.63298	106.47556	1558.05444	308	15.59392	104.46948	1629.08887
309	13.84835	108.61922	1504.19751	309	14.76101	106.54331	1572.68738	309	15.73362	104.53304	1644.68274
310	13.96664	108.69083	1518.04590	310	14.89017	106.61047	1587.44849	310	15.87456	104.59603	1660.41638
311	14.08594	108.76182	1532.01257	311	15.02046	106.67705	1602.33862	311	16.01677	104.65847	1676.29089
312	14.20626	108.83221	1546.09851	312	15.15189	106.74304	1617.35913	312	16.16026	104.72034	1692.30774
313	14.32760	108.90201	1560.30481	313	15.28447	106.80847	1632.51635	313	16.31503	104.78167	1706.46802
314	14.44998	108.97121	1574.63232	314	15.41821	106.87333	1647.79641	314	16.45109	104.84246	1724.77307
315	14.57341	109.03983	1589.08240	315	15.55312	106.93762	1663.21362	315	16.59648	104.90271	1741.22412
316	14.69789	109.10786	1603.65576	316	15.68649	107.00136	1678.76672	316	16.74716	104.96243	1757.82251
317	14.82344	109.17532	1618.35364	317	15.82649	107.06454	1694.45593	317	16.89719	105.02161	1774.56970
318	14.95005	109.24222	1633.17771	318	15.96497	107.12718	1710.28247	318	17.04856	105.08026	1791.46692
319	15.07775	109.30854	1648.12720	319	16.10466	107.18928	1726.24744	319	17.20128	105.13840	1808.51550
320	15.20654	109.37430	1663.20483	320	16.24558	107.25083	1742.35217	320	17.35536	105.19601	1825.71680
321	15.33643	109.43951	1678.41138	321	16.38773	107.31185	1758.59766	321	17.51085	105.25312	1843.07214
322	15.46743	109.50416	1693.74792	322	16.53112	107.37234	1774.98647	322	17.66772	105.30972	1860.58301
323	15.59955	109.56826	1709.21533	323	16.67577	107.43231	1791.51660	323	17.82599	105.36582	1878.25073
324	15.73279	109.63182	1724.81482	324	16.82168	107.49176	1808.19238	324	17.98669	105.42142	1896.07666
325	15.86718	109.69485	1740.54761	325	16.96887	107.55069	1825.01404	325	18.14661	105.47652	1914.06238

idx				idx				idx			
326	16.00271	109.75733	1756.41479	326	17.11735	107.60911	1841.9629	326	18.30997	105.53114	1932.20923
327	16.13940	109.81930	1772.41748	327	17.26713	107.66702	1859.10022	327	18.47339	105.58627	1950.51655
328	16.27726	109.88073	1788.55688	328	17.41821	107.72443	1876.36731	328	18.63889	105.63882	1968.99194
329	16.41629	109.94164	1804.83423	329	17.57062	107.78135	1890.78552	329	18.80586	105.65210	1987.63066
330	16.55651	110.00204	1821.25049	330	17.72437	107.83777	1911.35620	330	18.97433	105.74480	2006.43677
331	16.69793	110.06194	1837.80701	331	17.87945	107.89370	1929.09057	331	19.14431	105.79704	2025.41101
332	16.84056	110.12132	1854.50488	332	18.03590	107.94914	1946.96996	332	19.31581	105.84881	2044.55542
333	16.98441	110.18019	1871.34546	333	18.19371	108.00410	1964.96597	333	19.48805	105.90012	2063.87109
334	17.12948	110.23857	1888.32996	334	18.35291	108.05859	1983.18968	334	19.66343	105.95097	2083.35996
335	17.27580	110.29646	1905.45935	335	18.51350	108.11261	2001.54248	335	19.83858	106.00138	2103.02344
336	17.42336	110.35384	1922.73523	336	18.67549	108.16615	2020.05603	336	20.01731	106.05134	2122.96304
337	17.57219	110.41076	1940.15857	337	18.83890	108.21924	2038.73157	337	20.19664	106.10085	2142.66037
338	17.72228	110.46718	1957.73071	338	19.00374	108.27186	2057.57031	338	20.37756	106.14993	2163.07690
339	17.87366	110.52313	1975.45300	339	19.17002	108.32402	2076.57422	339	20.56011	106.19856	2183.45459
340	18.02633	110.57861	1993.32666	340	19.33776	108.37573	2095.74414	340	20.74420	106.24677	2204.01465
341	18.16031	110.63361	2011.35303	341	19.50697	108.42700	2115.06179	341	20.93013	106.29455	2224.75879
342	18.33560	110.68815	2029.53333	342	19.67765	108.47782	2134.58887	342	21.11763	106.34193	2245.66866
343	18.49221	110.74223	2047.86890	343	19.84983	108.52820	2154.26660	343	21.30681	106.38883	2266.60664
344	18.65017	110.79585	2066.36108	344	20.02352	108.57814	2174.11646	344	21.49768	106.43535	2288.11353
345	18.80947	110.84901	2085.01123	345	20.19872	108.62765	2194.13969	345	21.63027	106.48145	2309.61108
346	18.97013	110.90173	2103.82090	346	20.37546	108.67673	2214.33862	346	21.80457	106.52715	2331.30151
347	19.13217	110.95399	2122.79077	347	20.55375	108.72538	2234.74411	347	22.08062	106.57243	2353.19604
348	19.29559	111.00581	2141.90310	348	20.73359	108.77361	2255.26782	348	22.27843	106.61732	2375.26660
349	19.46041	111.05721	2161.21851	349	20.91501	108.82142	2276.00146	349	22.47601	106.66181	2397.54517
350	19.62663	111.10815	2180.67988	350	21.09802	108.86882	2296.91650	350	22.67937	106.70590	2420.02319

Table 1. (continued) Annuities

M	C(10.25,M,12)	A(10.25,M,12)	S(10.25,M,12)	M	C(10.50,M,12)	A(10.50,M,12)	S(10.50,M,12)	M	C(10.75,M,12)	A(10.75,M,12)	S(10.75,M,12)
351	19.79428	111.15868	2200.30566	351	21.28863	108.91590	2318.01440	351	22.88254	106.74960	2442.70239
352	19.96335	111.20876	2220.09995	352	21.46885	108.96239	2339.29712	352	23.08753	106.79292	2465.58496
353	20.13387	111.25843	2240.06323	353	21.65670	109.00856	2360.76587	353	23.29436	106.83585	2488.67261
354	20.30585	111.30768	2260.19727	354	21.84620	109.05434	2382.42261	354	23.50304	106.87840	2511.96680
355	20.47930	111.35651	2280.50293	355	22.03735	109.09971	2404.26880	355	23.71358	106.92056	2535.46997
356	20.65422	111.40492	2300.98242	356	22.23018	109.14470	2426.30615	356	23.92602	106.96236	2559.18359
357	20.83064	111.45293	2321.63647	357	22.42469	109.18929	2448.53638	357	24.14036	107.00378	2583.10962
358	21.00857	111.50053	2342.46729	358	22.62091	109.23350	2470.96094	358	24.35661	107.04484	2607.25000
359	21.18802	111.54773	2363.47583	359	22.81884	109.27732	2493.58203	359	24.57491	107.08553	2631.60645
360	21.36900	111.59452	2384.66382	360	23.01851	109.32076	2516.40088	360	24.79496	107.12586	2656.18140
361	21.55153	111.64092	2406.03271	361	23.21992	109.36383	2539.41919	361	25.01708	107.16584	2680.97632
362	21.73562	111.68694	2427.58423	362	23.42309	109.40652	2562.63916	362	25.24119	107.20545	2705.99341
363	21.92127	111.73255	2449.31982	363	23.62804	109.44864	2586.06226	363	25.46731	107.24472	2731.23462
364	22.10852	111.77778	2471.24121	364	23.83479	109.49090	2609.69043	364	25.69545	107.28364	2756.70190
365	22.29736	111.82263	2493.34961	365	24.04334	109.53239	2633.52515	365	25.92564	107.32221	2782.39722
366	22.48782	111.86710	2515.64697	366	24.25373	109.57362	2657.56860	366	26.15789	107.36044	2808.32300
367	22.67990	111.91119	2538.13403	367	24.46594	109.61449	2681.82227	367	26.39833	107.39833	2834.44096
368	22.87363	111.95491	2560.81470	368	24.66002	109.65501	2706.28909	368	26.62965	107.43588	2860.87305
369	23.06901	111.99825	2583.68848	369	24.89597	109.69518	2730.96826	369	26.86720	107.47311	2887.50171
370	23.26605	112.04124	2606.75732	370	25.11381	109.73500	2755.86426	370	27.10789	107.50999	2914.36890
371	23.46478	112.08385	2630.02344	371	25.33356	109.77448	2780.97803	371	27.35073	107.54655	2941.47681
372	23.66521	112.12611	2653.48828	372	25.55623	109.81361	2806.31152	372	27.59575	107.58279	2968.82764
373	23.86735	112.16801	2677.15356	373	25.77163	109.85239	2831.86670	373	27.84296	107.61871	2996.42334
374	24.07122	112.20955	2701.02075	374	26.00440	109.89085	2857.64551	374	28.03938	107.65430	3024.26636
375	24.27683	112.25075	2725.09204	375	26.23194	109.92897	2883.64990	375	28.34405	107.68958	3052.35864

376	24.48419	112.29959	2749.36890	376	26.46147	109.96677	2909.88194	376	28.59736	107.72456	3090.70264
377	24.61833	112.33208	2773.85303	377	26.63300	110.00423	2936.34351	377	28.85415	107.75921	3109.30054
378	24.90425	112.37224	2798.54639	378	26.92657	110.04137	2963.03638	378	29.11264	107.79356	3138.15479
379	25.11697	112.41205	2823.45068	379	27.16218	110.07818	2989.96289	379	29.37344	107.82761	3167.26733
380	25.33151	112.45153	2848.56763	380	27.39985	110.11468	3017.12524	380	29.63657	107.86134	3196.64087
381	25.54789	112.49067	2873.89917	381	27.63959	110.15006	3044.52490	381	29.90207	107.89479	3226.27734
382	25.76611	112.52948	2899.44702	382	27.88144	110.18672	3072.16455	382	30.16994	107.92798	3256.17944
383	25.98619	112.56796	2925.21313	383	28.12540	110.22227	3100.04614	383	30.44021	107.96078	3286.34937
384	26.20816	112.60612	2961.19946	384	28.37150	110.25752	3128.17139	384	30.71291	107.99335	3316.78979
385	26.43202	112.64395	2977.40747	385	28.61975	110.29247	3156.54297	385	30.98804	108.02561	3347.50269
386	26.65779	112.68147	3003.83960	386	28.87017	110.32710	3185.16260	386	31.26564	108.05760	3378.49072
387	26.88550	112.71866	3030.49731	387	29.12279	110.36144	3214.03296	387	31.54573	108.08930	3409.75635
388	27.11514	112.75554	3057.39281	388	29.37761	110.39548	3243.15576	388	31.82833	108.12072	3441.30200
389	27.34675	112.79211	3084.49805	389	29.63467	110.42922	3272.53320	389	32.11346	108.15186	3473.30037
390	27.58034	112.82836	3111.84473	390	29.89397	110.46268	3302.16797	390	32.40114	108.18272	3505.24230
391	27.81592	112.86431	3139.42505	391	30.15554	110.49583	3332.06201	391	32.69140	108.21331	3537.64502
392	28.05352	112.89996	3167.24097	392	30.41940	110.52871	3362.21753	392	32.96426	108.24363	3570.33643
393	28.29314	112.93530	3195.29443	393	30.68557	110.56130	3392.63696	393	33.27275	108.27367	3602.32056
394	28.53481	112.97035	3223.58765	394	30.96407	110.59361	3423.32251	394	33.57798	108.30346	3636.60034
395	28.77855	113.00510	3252.12256	395	31.22498	110.62563	3454.27637	395	33.87968	108.33298	3670.17602
396	29.02436	113.03955	3280.90112	396	31.48914	110.65738	3485.50146	396	34.18217	108.36223	3704.05688
397	29.27228	113.07372	3309.92529	397	31.77375	110.68885	3516.99961	397	34.48839	108.39123	3738.23901
398	29.52231	113.10759	3339.19775	398	32.05177	110.72005	3548.77319	398	34.79735	108.41996	3772.72754
399	29.77448	113.14117	3368.71997	399	32.33222	110.75098	3580.82495	399	35.10907	108.44845	3807.52490
400	30.02881	113.17448	3398.49438	400	32.61512	110.78164	3613.15723	400	35.42360	108.47668	3842.63403

Table 1. (continued) Annuities

M	C(10.25,M,12)	A(10.25,M,12)	S(10.25,M,12)	M	C(10.50,M,12)	A(10.50,M,12)	S(10.50,M,12)	M	C(10.75,M,12)	A(10.75,M,12)	S(10.75,M,12)
401	30.26530	113.20749	3428.52319	401	32.90051	110.81203	3645.77246	401	35.74059	108.50465	3878.05762
402	30.54399	113.24023	3458.80069	402	33.18839	110.84616	3678.87295	402	36.06111	108.53239	3913.79834
403	30.80489	113.27270	3489.35254	403	33.47879	110.87204	3711.86133	403	36.38416	108.55987	3949.85562
404	31.06901	113.30488	3520.15747	404	33.77172	110.90165	3746.34009	404	36.71010	108.58711	3986.24365
405	31.33338	113.33680	3551.22559	405	34.06723	110.93100	3779.11192	405	37.03896	108.61411	4022.95366
406	31.60102	113.36844	3582.55884	406	34.36531	110.96010	3813.17896	406	37.37077	108.64087	4059.99268
407	31.87095	113.39992	3614.15991	407	34.66601	110.98895	3847.54443	407	37.70555	108.66739	4097.36328
408	32.14318	113.43093	3646.03076	408	34.96934	111.01754	3882.21045	408	38.04333	108.69367	4135.06805
409	32.41774	113.46178	3678.17407	409	35.27532	111.04589	3917.17969	409	38.38413	108.71973	4173.11230
410	32.69464	113.49236	3710.59180	410	35.58398	111.07400	3952.45508	410	38.72799	108.74554	4211.45658
411	32.97390	113.52269	3743.28638	411	35.89534	111.10185	3988.03906	411	39.07493	108.77114	4250.22461
412	33.25555	113.55255	3776.26025	412	36.20942	111.12947	4023.93433	412	39.42497	108.79650	4289.29332
413	33.53961	113.58257	3809.51587	413	36.52626	111.15685	4060.14390	413	39.77816	108.82164	4328.72412
414	33.82610	113.61214	3843.05542	414	36.84586	111.18399	4096.66992	414	40.13450	108.84656	4368.50244
415	34.11503	113.64145	3876.88159	415	37.16826	111.21089	4133.51563	415	40.49404	108.87125	4408.63721
416	34.40643	113.67052	3910.99656	416	37.43348	111.23756	4170.68408	416	40.85690	108.89573	4449.13086
417	34.70032	113.69933	3945.40308	417	37.82155	111.26400	4208.17773	417	41.22281	108.91999	4489.98779
418	34.99672	113.72791	3980.10327	418	38.15249	111.29021	4245.99902	418	41.59209	108.94403	4531.21045
419	35.29565	113.75624	4015.10010	419	38.48632	111.31620	4284.15137	419	41.96469	108.96786	4572.80273
420	35.59713	113.78433	4050.39575	420	38.82308	111.34196	4322.63770	420	42.34063	108.99148	4614.76758
421	35.90119	113.81219	4085.99292	421	39.16278	111.36749	4361.46194	421	42.71700	109.01490	4656.07611
422	36.20784	113.83981	4121.89404	422	39.50546	111.39280	4400.62402	422	43.10263	109.03809	4699.06108
423	36.51712	113.86719	4156.10156	423	39.85113	111.41789	4440.12639	423	43.48875	109.06108	4742.93066
424	36.82904	113.89434	4194.61865	424	40.19963	111.44277	4479.96047	424	43.87634	109.08367	4786.41943
425	37.14362	113.92126	4231.44775	425	40.55157	111.46743	4520.16018	425	44.27142	109.10646	4830.29785

426	37.46088	113.94796	4266.59131	40.90640	111.49187	4560.73198	426	44.66601	109.12895	4874.56934
427	37.78096	113.97443	4306.05225	41.26434	111.51611	4601.63818	427	45.06816	109.15104	4919.23730
428	38.10358	114.00067	4343.83350	41.62540	111.54014	4642.90234	428	45.47190	109.17303	4964.30518
429	38.42904	114.02670	4381.93701	41.98962	111.56335	4684.52703	429	45.67925	109.19492	5009.77734
430	38.75729	114.05249	4420.36572	42.35703	111.58756	4726.51758	430	46.29026	109.21643	5055.65625
431	39.08834	114.07808	4459.12305	42.72765	111.61096	4768.87451	431	46.70494	109.23784	5100.94673
432	39.42222	114.10345	4498.21143	43.10152	111.63416	4811.60205	432	47.12334	109.25906	5148.65196
433	39.75896	114.12859	4537.63379	43.47966	111.65777	4854.70361	433	47.54548	109.28005	5196.77490
434	40.09856	114.15353	4577.39258	43.85910	111.67996	4898.18092	434	47.97141	109.30093	5243.32031
435	40.44107	114.17826	4617.49121	44.24296	111.70257	4942.04150	435	48.40118	109.32160	5291.29199
436	40.78651	114.20278	4657.92213	44.62999	111.72498	4996.20418	436	48.63475	109.34208	5339.69287
437	41.13489	114.22709	4696.71875	45.02050	111.74718	5030.91455	437	49.27223	109.36237	5388.52783
438	41.48625	114.25119	4738.86352	45.41443	111.76920	5075.98506	438	49.71363	109.38248	5437.79960
439	41.84061	114.27509	4781.33964	45.81181	111.79103	5121.34912	439	50.15899	109.40242	5487.51367
440	42.19800	114.29879	4823.19068	46.21266	111.81268	5167.16113	440	50.60832	109.42218	5537.67205
441	42.55844	114.32229	4865.37042	46.61702	111.83412	5213.37354	441	51.06168	109.44176	5588.28078
442	42.92196	114.34559	4907.93701	47.02492	111.85539	5258.99072	442	51.51917	109.46117	5639.34277
443	43.28859	114.36869	4960.85889	47.43639	111.87647	5307.01563	443	51.98064	109.48042	5690.86192
444	43.65834	114.39159	4994.14746	47.85146	111.89737	5354.45215	444	52.44630	109.49948	5742.84229
445	44.03126	114.41431	5037.00615	48.27016	111.91608	5402.30371	445	52.91613	109.51838	5795.28857
446	44.40736	114.43682	5081.03740	48.69252	111.93862	5450.33017	446	53.3017	109.53711	5848.20459
447	44.78667	114.45915	5126.24463	49.11958	111.95898	5498.26611	447	53.86645	109.55567	5901.59521
448	45.16922	114.48129	5171.03125	49.54837	111.97916	5548.38477	448	54.35102	109.57407	5955.46339
449	45.55505	114.50324	5216.20068	49.98191	111.99917	5597.93311	449	54.83792	109.59231	6009.81445
450	45.94416	114.52501	5261.74627	50.41926	112.01900	5647.91504	450	55.32918	109.61038	6064.65234

Table 1. (continued) Annuities

M	C(10.25,M,12)	A(10.25,M,12)	S(10.25,M,12)	M	C(10.50,M,12)	A(10.50,M,12)	S(10.50,M,12)	M	C(10.75,M,12)	A(10.75,M,12)	S(10.75,M,12)
451	46.33660	114.54659	5307.89971	451	50.86042	112.03867	5696.33447	451	55.82483	109.62830	6119.98145
452	46.73239	114.56799	5354.03613	452	51.30545	112.05816	5749.19482	452	56.32438	109.64605	6175.80664
453	47.13157	114.58920	5400.76855	453	51.75438	112.07748	5800.50049	453	56.82951	109.66364	6232.13135
454	47.53415	114.61024	5447.90039	454	52.20723	112.09663	5852.25439	454	57.33861	109.68108	6288.96094
455	47.94017	114.63110	5495.43457	455	52.66404	112.11562	5904.46191	455	57.85226	109.69837	6346.29302
456	48.34966	114.65176	5542.37451	456	53.12495	112.13445	5957.12598	456	58.37053	109.71560	6404.11135
457	48.76265	114.67225	5591.72412	457	53.58969	112.15311	6010.25098	457	58.89343	109.73248	6462.52246
458	49.17916	114.69263	5640.48682	458	54.05861	112.17161	6063.84033	458	59.42102	109.74931	6521.41553
459	49.59923	114.71278	5689.66602	459	54.53162	112.18994	6117.89893	459	59.95333	109.76595	6580.84375
460	50.02289	114.73277	5739.26514	460	55.00877	112.20812	6172.43066	460	60.49041	109.78262	6640.79004
461	50.45017	114.75260	5789.28809	461	55.49009	112.22614	6227.43945	461	61.03230	109.79890	6701.28027
462	50.88110	114.77225	5839.74121	462	55.97563	112.24401	6282.98969	462	61.57905	109.81515	6762.31299
463	51.31571	114.79174	5890.61963	463	56.46542	112.26172	6338.90527	463	62.13070	109.83125	6823.89160
464	51.75403	114.81106	5941.93506	464	56.95948	112.27927	6395.37061	464	62.68729	109.84719	6886.02246
465	52.19609	114.83022	5993.68896	465	57.45789	112.29668	6452.33008	465	63.24886	109.86301	6948.70396
466	52.64194	114.84921	6045.88525	466	57.96064	112.31393	6509.78809	466	63.81546	109.87868	7011.96560
467	53.09159	114.86805	6098.52734	467	58.46780	112.33103	6567.74854	467	64.38714	109.89420	7075.77393
468	53.54508	114.88672	6151.62695	468	58.97939	112.34799	6626.21631	468	64.96394	109.90960	7140.16113
469	54.00244	114.90524	6205.16406	469	59.49546	112.36480	6685.19580	469	65.54591	109.92486	7205.12500
470	54.46371	114.92361	6259.16650	470	60.01605	112.38146	6744.69141	470	66.13309	109.93998	7270.67090
471	54.92892	114.94181	6313.62988	471	60.54119	112.39798	6804.70752	471	66.72553	109.95496	7336.80420
472	55.39811	114.95996	6368.55908	472	61.07092	112.41435	6865.24854	472	67.32329	109.96982	7403.52979
473	55.87130	114.97776	6423.96703	473	61.60529	112.43058	6926.31934	473	67.92639	109.98454	7470.85303
474	56.34853	114.99551	6479.82861	474	62.14424	112.44668	6987.92490	474	68.53490	109.99913	7538.77360
475	56.82985	115.01311	6536.17676	475	62.68810	112.46263	7050.06934	475	69.14886	110.01359	7607.31445

idx					idx			idx			
476	57.31527	115.03055	6593.00684	63.23663	476	112.47844	7112.75732	476	69.76831	110.02792	7676.46338
477	57.90483	115.04785	6650.32227	63.78994	477	112.49412	7175.99065	477	70.30332	110.04213	7746.23145
478	58.29858	115.06500	6708.12695	64.34811	478	112.50966	7239.78969	478	71.02333	110.05621	7816.62500
478	58.78655	115.08201	6766.42529	64.9115	478	112.52506	7304.13184	478	71.66019	110.07017	7887.64899
480	59.29877	115.09888	6825.22217	65.47913	480	112.54034	7369.04297	480	72.30214	110.08400	7959.30900
481	59.60528	115.11559	6884.52100	66.06206	481	112.55547	7434.52197	481	72.94984	110.09770	8031.61133
482	60.31612	115.13217	6944.32617	66.63002	482	112.57048	7500.57422	482	73.60336	110.11129	8104.56104
483	60.83132	115.14861	7004.64209	67.20115	483	112.58537	7567.20410	483	74.26272	110.12476	8178.16455
484	61.35092	115.16492	7065.47363	67.60115	484	112.60011	7634.41748	484	74.92799	110.13810	8252.42676
485	61.87496	115.18108	7126.82422	68.39441	485	112.61473	7702.21826	485	75.59922	110.15133	8327.35449
486	62.40347	115.19710	7188.69922	68.99296	486	112.62923	7770.61279	486	76.27647	110.16444	8402.96410
487	62.58650	115.21250	7251.10303	69.59655	487	112.64359	7839.60596	487	76.95977	110.17744	8479.23047
488	63.47409	115.22874	7314.03955	70.20552	488	112.65764	7909.20015	488	77.64920	110.19032	8556.19043
489	64.01628	115.24436	7377.51367	71.41982	489	112.67196	7979.40771	489	78.34481	110.20308	8633.83984
490	64.56306	115.25966	7441.52979	71.42949	490	112.68515	8050.10555	490	79.05635	110.21605	8712.21455
491	65.11454	115.27521	7506.09277	72.06458	491	112.69964	8121.66699	491	79.75478	110.22826	8791.23047
492	65.67072	115.29044	7571.20752	72.63615	492	112.71359	8193.73145	492	80.46925	110.24069	8870.98535
493	66.22187	115.30553	7636.87798	73.33123	493	112.72723	8266.42676	493	81.19012	110.25301	8951.45508
494	66.79739	115.32051	7703.10966	73.97288	494	112.74075	8339.75781	494	81.91744	110.26522	9032.64551
495	67.36796	115.33535	7769.90723	74.62014	495	112.75414	8413.73047	495	82.65129	110.27731	9114.56250
496	67.94339	115.35007	7837.27490	75.27307	496	112.76743	8488.35059	496	83.39171	110.28931	9197.21387
497	68.52374	115.36466	7905.21826	75.93171	497	112.78060	8563.52402	497	84.13876	110.30119	9280.60547
498	69.10905	115.37914	7973.74219	76.58612	498	112.79366	8639.55566	498	84.89250	110.31297	9364.74414
499	69.69835	115.39348	8042.86017	77.26633	499	112.80659	8716.15137	499	85.66239	110.32465	9449.63672
500	70.28470	115.40771	8112.55078	77.94241	500	112.81943	8793.41797	500	86.42030	110.33622	9535.29004

Table 1. (continued) Annuities

M	C(11.00,M,12)	A(11.00,M,12)	S(11.00,M,12)	M	C(11.25,M,12)	A(11.25,M,12)	S(11.25,M,12)	M	C(11.50,M,12)	A(11.50,M,12)	S(11.50,M,12)
1	1.00917	0.99092	1.00000	1	1.00937	0.99071	1.00000	1	1.00958	0.99051	1.00000
2	1.01842	1.97283	2.00917	2	1.01884	1.97222	2.00937	2	1.01926	1.97161	2.00958
3	1.02775	2.94583	3.02758	3	1.02839	2.94462	3.02821	3	1.02903	2.94341	3.02884
4	1.03717	3.90999	4.05534	4	1.03803	3.90798	4.05660	4	1.03889	3.90597	4.05787
5	1.04668	4.86539	5.09251	5	1.04776	4.86239	5.09463	5	1.04884	4.85940	5.09676
6	1.05628	5.81211	6.13919	6	1.05758	5.80794	6.14240	6	1.05890	5.80378	6.14560
7	1.06596	6.75023	7.19547	7	1.06750	6.74471	7.19998	7	1.06904	6.73920	7.20449
8	1.07573	7.67983	8.26143	8	1.07751	7.87278	8.26748	8	1.07929	7.66574	8.27354
9	1.08559	8.60099	9.33718	9	1.08761	8.59223	9.34499	9	1.08963	8.58348	9.35283
10	1.09554	9.51378	10.42275	10	1.09781	9.50314	10.43260	10	1.10007	9.49251	10.44246
11	1.10558	10.41828	11.51829	11	1.10810	10.40558	11.53040	11	1.11062	10.39291	11.54253
12	1.11572	11.31456	12.62387	12	1.11849	11.29965	12.63850	12	1.12126	11.28476	12.65315
13	1.12595	12.20271	13.73959	13	1.12897	12.18541	13.75699	13	1.13200	12.16815	13.77441
14	1.13627	13.08278	14.86554	14	1.13956	13.06295	14.88596	14	1.14285	13.04316	14.90641
15	1.14668	13.95486	16.00190	15	1.15024	13.93233	16.02551	15	1.15381	13.90985	16.04926
16	1.15719	14.81902	17.14849	16	1.16102	14.78364	17.17575	16	1.16486	14.76832	17.20307
17	1.16780	15.67533	18.30568	17	1.17191	15.64695	18.33677	17	1.17603	15.61864	18.36793
18	1.17851	16.52386	19.47348	18	1.18289	16.49233	19.50868	18	1.18730	16.46089	19.54396
19	1.18931	17.36468	20.65199	19	1.19398	17.32967	20.69158	19	1.19867	17.29515	20.73125
20	1.20021	18.19787	21.84130	20	1.20518	18.15962	21.88556	20	1.21016	18.12148	21.92993
21	1.21121	19.02349	23.04151	21	1.21648	18.98167	23.09074	21	1.22176	18.93998	23.14009
22	1.22232	19.84161	24.25273	22	1.22788	19.79608	24.30721	22	1.23347	19.75070	24.36185
23	1.23352	20.65229	25.47504	23	1.23939	20.60293	25.53509	23	1.24529	20.55373	25.59532
24	1.24483	21.45562	26.70856	24	1.25101	21.40228	26.77448	24	1.25722	21.34913	26.84061
25	1.25624	22.25164	27.95339	25	1.26274	22.19421	28.02549	25	1.26927	22.13696	28.09788

n				n				n			
26	1.26775	23.04044	28.20963	26	1.27458	22.97878	29.28823	26	1.28143	22.91736	29.36710
27	1.27998	23.82207	30.47739	27	1.28653	23.75607	30.56281	27	1.28372	23.69033	30.64853
28	1.29110	24.59660	31.75676	28	1.29859	24.52614	31.84934	28	1.30611	24.45596	31.94225
29	1.30294	25.36410	33.04787	29	1.31076	25.28905	33.14792	29	1.31863	25.21432	33.24836
30	1.31488	26.12462	34.35081	30	1.32305	26.04488	34.45869	30	1.33127	25.96548	34.56699
31	1.32694	26.87824	35.66569	31	1.33545	26.79369	35.78173	31	1.34402	26.70952	35.89626
32	1.33910	27.62501	36.99262	32	1.34797	27.53555	37.11719	32	1.35691	27.44649	37.24228
33	1.35137	28.36500	38.33172	33	1.36061	28.27051	38.46516	33	1.36991	28.17646	38.59919
34	1.36376	29.09626	39.68310	34	1.37337	28.99465	39.82578	34	1.38304	28.89951	39.96910
35	1.37626	29.82487	41.04686	35	1.38624	29.72002	41.19914	35	1.39629	29.61569	41.35213
36	1.38888	30.54487	42.42312	36	1.39924	30.43470	42.58538	36	1.40967	30.32508	42.74842
37	1.40161	31.25834	43.81200	37	1.41236	31.14273	43.98462	37	1.42318	31.02773	44.15810
38	1.41446	31.96532	45.21361	38	1.42560	31.84419	45.39598	38	1.43682	31.72371	45.58128
39	1.42742	32.66589	46.62807	39	1.43896	32.53914	46.82257	39	1.45059	32.41308	47.01810
40	1.44051	33.36008	48.05549	40	1.45245	33.22763	48.26154	40	1.46449	33.09591	48.46869
41	1.45371	34.04798	49.49600	41	1.46607	33.90973	49.71399	41	1.47853	33.77226	49.93318
42	1.46704	34.72962	50.94971	42	1.47981	34.58549	51.18005	42	1.49270	34.44219	51.41171
43	1.48049	35.40508	52.41675	43	1.49369	35.25497	52.65987	43	1.50700	35.10576	52.90440
44	1.49406	36.07439	53.89724	44	1.50769	35.91824	54.15355	44	1.52144	35.76303	54.41140
45	1.50775	36.73763	55.39130	45	1.52182	36.57534	55.66124	45	1.53602	36.41407	55.93285
46	1.52157	37.39485	56.89905	46	1.53609	37.22635	57.18307	46	1.55074	37.05892	57.46887
47	1.53552	38.04609	58.42063	47	1.55049	37.87130	58.71916	47	1.56560	37.69765	59.01962
48	1.54960	38.69142	59.95615	48	1.56503	38.51027	60.26985	48	1.58061	38.33031	60.58522
49	1.56380	39.33089	61.50570	49	1.57970	39.14300	61.83468	49	1.59576	38.96699	62.16583
50	1.57814	39.96455	63.06955	50	1.59451	39.77045	63.41438	50	1.61105	39.57769	63.78158

Table 1. (continued) Annuities

M	C(11.00,M,12)	A(11.00,M,12)	S(11.00,M,12)	M	C(11.25,M,12)	A(11.25,M,12)	S(11.25,M,12)	M	C(11.50,M,12)	A(11.50,M,12)	S(11.50,M,12)
51	1.59260	40.50245	64.64768	51	1.60946	40.39178	65.00889	51	1.62649	40.19251	65.37263
52	1.60720	41.21465	66.24029	52	1.62455	41.00734	66.81835	52	1.64207	40.80150	66.99911
53	1.62194	41.83119	67.84749	53	1.63978	41.61778	68.24289	53	1.65781	41.40471	68.64119
54	1.63680	42.44214	69.46943	54	1.65515	42.22135	69.88267	54	1.67370	42.00218	70.29900
55	1.65181	43.04754	71.10623	55	1.67067	42.81991	71.53792	55	1.68974	42.59399	71.97270
56	1.66695	43.64744	72.75803	56	1.68633	43.41292	73.20849	56	1.70593	43.18018	73.66244
57	1.68223	44.24189	74.42499	57	1.70214	44.00041	74.89481	57	1.72228	43.76081	75.36837
58	1.69765	44.83094	76.10722	58	1.71810	44.58245	76.59695	58	1.73879	44.33592	77.09065
59	1.71321	45.41463	77.80046	59	1.73420	45.15929	78.31506	59	1.75545	44.90557	78.82944
60	1.72892	45.99303	79.51807	60	1.75046	45.73037	80.04926	60	1.77227	45.46992	80.58488
61	1.74476	46.56617	81.24699	61	1.76687	46.29634	81.79972	61	1.78926	46.02871	82.35718
62	1.76076	47.13411	82.99175	62	1.78344	46.85705	83.56659	62	1.80640	46.58230	84.14642
63	1.77690	47.69689	84.75251	63	1.80016	47.41256	85.35003	63	1.82371	47.13063	85.96282
64	1.79319	48.25456	86.52941	64	1.81703	47.96291	87.15018	64	1.84119	47.67376	87.77654
65	1.80962	48.80716	88.32260	65	1.83407	48.50814	88.96722	65	1.85884	48.21173	89.61772
66	1.82621	49.35474	90.13223	66	1.85126	49.04831	90.60128	66	1.87665	48.74459	91.47656
67	1.84295	49.89735	91.95844	67	1.86862	49.58347	92.65255	67	1.89463	49.27240	93.35321
68	1.85986	50.43503	93.80138	68	1.88614	50.11366	94.52116	68	1.91279	49.79620	95.24795
69	1.87689	50.96782	95.66123	69	1.90382	50.63892	96.40730	69	1.93112	50.31303	97.16064
70	1.89410	51.49578	97.53812	70	1.92167	51.15929	98.31112	70	1.94963	50.82595	99.09976
71	1.91146	52.01894	99.43223	71	1.93968	51.67484	100.23277	71	1.96831	51.33400	101.04970
72	1.92898	52.53735	101.34369	72	1.95787	52.18560	102.17247	72	1.98718	51.83722	103.00970
73	1.94667	53.05104	103.27267	73	1.97622	52.69194	104.13033	73	2.00622	52.33567	104.98668
74	1.96451	53.56008	105.21334	74	1.99475	53.19294	106.10656	74	2.02545	52.82939	107.00310
75	1.98252	54.06448	107.18385	75	2.01345	53.68960	108.10130	75	2.04486	53.31842	109.02855

n				n				n			
76	2.00069	54.56431	109.16637	76	2.03233	54.19164	110.11475	76	2.06445	53.80281	111.07340
77	2.01903	55.05960	111.16706	77	2.05138	54.66912	112.14708	77	2.08424	54.28260	113.13796
78	2.03754	55.55039	113.18105	78	2.07061	55.15207	114.19946	78	2.10421	54.75784	115.22210
79	2.05622	56.03672	115.22363	79	2.09002	55.63054	116.26907	79	2.12438	55.22857	117.32631
80	2.07507	56.51663	117.27985	80	2.10962	56.10455	118.35509	80	2.14474	55.69482	119.45068
81	2.09409	56.99617	119.35491	81	2.12939	56.57417	120.46871	81	2.16529	56.15666	121.59542
82	2.11328	57.46836	121.44903	82	2.14936	57.03942	122.59911	82	2.18604	56.61411	123.76071
83	2.13265	57.93826	123.56228	83	2.16951	57.50036	124.74746	83	2.20699	57.06721	125.94675
84	2.15220	58.40230	125.69494	84	2.18985	57.95701	126.91697	84	2.22814	57.51602	128.15373
85	2.17193	58.86332	127.84714	85	2.21038	58.40942	129.10681	85	2.24949	57.96056	130.38168
86	2.19184	59.31956	130.01907	86	2.23110	58.85764	131.31718	86	2.27105	58.40089	132.63136
87	2.21193	59.77165	132.21091	87	2.25202	59.30168	133.54829	87	2.29281	58.83703	134.90242
88	2.23221	60.21964	134.42284	88	2.27313	59.74160	135.80031	88	2.31479	59.26904	137.19524
89	2.25267	60.66356	136.65504	89	2.29444	60.17744	138.07343	89	2.33697	59.69694	139.51003
90	2.27332	61.10344	138.90773	90	2.31595	60.60923	140.36787	90	2.35937	60.12078	141.84700
91	2.29416	61.53933	141.18105	91	2.33766	61.03701	142.68382	91	2.38198	60.54060	144.20636
92	2.31519	61.97126	143.47520	92	2.35958	61.46081	145.02148	92	2.40480	60.96644	146.58833
93	2.33641	62.39927	145.79039	93	2.38170	61.88068	147.38106	93	2.42785	61.36832	148.99315
94	2.35783	62.82339	148.12690	94	2.40403	62.29665	149.76276	94	2.45112	61.77630	151.42099
95	2.37944	63.24365	150.48463	95	2.42656	62.70876	152.16678	95	2.47461	62.18040	153.87212
96	2.40125	63.66010	152.86407	96	2.44531	63.11703	154.53334	96	2.49832	62.58067	156.34673
97	2.42327	64.07277	155.26534	97	2.47227	63.52152	157.04265	97	2.52226	62.97714	158.84505
98	2.44548	64.48168	157.68860	98	2.49545	63.92225	159.51492	98	2.54644	63.36985	161.36731
99	2.46790	64.88689	160.13408	99	2.51885	64.31925	162.01038	99	2.57084	63.75883	163.91374
100	**2.49052**	**65.28841**	**162.60197**	**100**	**2.54246**	**64.71257**	**164.52924**	**100**	**2.59548**	**64.14411**	**166.48459**

Table 1. (continued) Annuities

M	C(11.00,M,12)	A(11.00,M,12)	S(11.00,M,12)	M	C(11.25,M,12)	A(11.25,M,12)	S(11.25,M,12)	M	C(11.50,M,12)	A(11.50,M,12)	S(11.50,M,12)
101	2.51335	65.68629	165.09248	101	2.56830	65.10223	167.07169	101	2.62035	64.52573	169.09006
102	2.53639	66.08054	167.60583	102	2.59036	65.48828	169.63799	102	2.64548	64.90374	171.70041
103	2.55964	66.47123	170.14223	103	2.61464	65.87075	172.22835	103	2.67081	65.27876	174.34587
104	2.58310	66.85836	172.70196	104	2.63915	66.24966	174.84299	104	2.69641	65.64082	177.01669
105	2.60678	67.24197	175.28456	105	2.66389	66.62505	177.48213	105	2.72225	66.01637	179.71310
106	2.63067	67.62211	177.89074	106	2.68887	66.99695	180.14603	106	2.74834	66.38023	182.43535
107	2.65479	67.99878	180.52242	107	2.71408	67.36540	182.83490	107	2.77468	66.74062	185.18369
108	2.67912	68.37204	183.17720	108	2.73952	67.73042	185.54898	108	2.80127	67.09761	187.95837
109	2.70368	68.74191	185.85632	109	2.76520	68.09206	188.28850	109	2.82811	67.45120	190.75963
110	2.72847	69.10841	188.56001	110	2.79113	68.45034	191.05371	110	2.85522	67.80144	193.58775
111	2.75348	69.47159	191.28848	111	2.81730	68.80528	193.84483	111	2.88258	68.14835	196.44296
112	2.77872	69.83147	194.04196	112	2.84371	69.15694	196.66212	112	2.91020	68.49197	199.32555
113	2.80419	70.16807	196.82068	113	2.87037	69.50533	199.50584	113	2.93809	68.83232	202.23575
114	2.82989	70.54144	199.62486	114	2.89728	69.85049	202.37621	114	2.96625	69.16945	205.17384
115	2.85584	70.89161	202.45476	115	2.92444	70.19243	205.27348	115	2.99468	69.50337	208.14009
116	2.88201	71.23859	205.31059	116	2.95186	70.53120	208.19792	116	3.02337	69.83413	211.13477
117	2.90843	71.58241	208.19261	117	2.97953	70.86682	211.14978	117	3.05235	70.16175	214.15814
118	2.93509	71.92312	211.10104	118	3.00746	71.19933	214.12930	118	3.08160	70.48625	217.21048
119	2.96200	72.26073	214.03613	119	3.03566	71.52875	217.13676	119	3.11113	70.80768	220.29208
120	2.98915	72.59527	216.99814	120	3.06412	71.85510	220.17242	120	3.14095	71.12605	223.40321
121	3.01655	72.92677	219.98727	121	3.09284	72.17844	223.23654	121	3.17105	71.44141	226.54417
122	3.04420	73.25527	223.00383	122	3.12184	72.49876	226.32939	122	3.20144	71.75377	229.71521
123	3.07211	73.58078	226.04803	123	3.15111	72.81611	229.45122	123	3.23212	72.06316	232.91666
124	3.10027	73.90333	229.12013	124	3.18065	73.13051	232.60233	124	3.26309	72.36962	236.14877
125	3.12869	74.22295	232.22041	125	3.21047	73.44199	235.78297	125	3.29436	72.67317	239.41187

126	3.15737	74.53967	235.34909	126	3.24056	73.75058	238.99344	126	3.32593	72.97384	242.70622
127	3.16631	74.85352	238.50645	127	3.27094	74.06630	242.23401	127	3.35781	73.27165	246.03217
128	3.21552	75.16451	241.69276	128	3.30161	74.35918	245.50494	128	3.38999	73.56664	249.38997
129	3.24499	75.47268	244.90829	129	3.33256	74.65925	248.80655	129	3.42247	73.85883	252.77995
130	3.27474	75.77805	248.15327	130	3.36380	74.95654	252.13911	130	3.45527	74.14824	256.20242
131	3.30476	76.08064	251.42802	131	3.39534	75.25105	255.50291	131	3.48839	74.43490	259.65768
132	3.33505	76.38049	254.73277	132	3.42717	75.54284	258.89825	132	3.52182	74.71885	263.14609
133	3.36562	76.67760	258.06781	133	3.45930	75.83192	262.32544	133	3.55557	75.00009	266.66791
134	3.39647	76.97203	261.43344	134	3.49173	76.11831	265.78473	134	3.58964	75.27967	270.22348
135	3.42761	77.26378	264.82993	135	3.52447	76.40204	269.27646	135	3.62404	75.55461	273.81311
136	3.45903	77.55288	268.25751	136	3.55751	76.68314	272.80093	136	3.65877	75.82793	277.43716
137	3.49074	77.83935	271.71655	137	3.59086	76.96162	276.35843	137	3.69384	76.09865	281.09592
138	3.52273	78.12322	275.20728	138	3.62452	77.23752	279.94928	138	3.72924	76.36680	284.78976
139	3.55503	78.40451	278.73001	139	3.65850	77.51086	283.57382	139	3.76497	76.63240	288.51901
140	3.58761	78.68325	282.28503	140	3.69280	77.78165	287.23233	140	3.80105	76.89549	292.28397
141	3.62050	78.95945	285.87265	141	3.72742	78.04933	290.92514	141	3.83748	77.15607	296.08502
142	3.65369	79.23315	289.49316	142	3.76237	78.31572	294.65256	142	3.87426	77.41419	299.92292
143	3.68718	79.50436	293.14685	143	3.79764	78.57904	298.41492	143	3.91139	77.66985	303.70875
144	3.72098	79.77310	296.83401	144	3.83324	78.83992	302.21255	144	3.94887	77.92009	307.70816
145	3.75509	80.03941	300.55499	145	3.86918	79.09837	306.04581	145	3.98671	78.17393	311.65701
146	3.78951	80.30330	304.31009	146	3.90545	79.35442	309.91498	146	4.02492	78.42238	315.64374
147	3.82425	80.56479	308.09961	147	3.94207	79.60910	313.82043	147	4.06349	78.66847	319.66864
148	3.85930	80.82390	311.92390	148	3.97902	79.85941	317.76251	148	4.10243	78.91223	323.73215
149	3.89468	81.08066	315.79314	149	4.01633	80.10840	321.74152	149	4.14175	79.15367	327.83456
150	3.93038	81.33509	319.67783	150	4.05398	80.35507	325.75784	150	4.18144	79.39282	331.97632

Table 1. (continued) Annuities

M	C(11.00,M,12)	A(11.00,M,12)	S(11.00,M,12)	M	C(11.25,M,12)	A(11.25,M,12)	S(11.25,M,12)	M	C(11.50,M,12)	A(11.50,M,12)	S(11.50,M,12)
151	3.96641	81.58720	323.60822	151	4.09199	80.59945	329.81183	151	4.22151	79.82971	336.15778
152	4.00277	81.83704	327.57462	152	4.13035	80.84156	333.90381	152	4.26197	79.86434	340.37927
153	4.03946	82.08459	331.57739	153	4.16907	81.08142	338.03418	153	4.30281	80.06675	344.64124
154	4.07649	82.32990	335.61685	154	4.20816	81.31905	342.20325	154	4.34405	80.32634	348.94406
155	4.11386	82.57298	339.61833	155	4.24761	81.55448	346.41138	155	4.38568	80.55436	353.28812
156	4.15157	82.81386	343.00719	156	4.28743	81.78773	350.65900	156	4.42771	80.78081	357.67380
157	4.18962	83.05254	347.95874	157	4.32762	82.01880	354.94644	157	4.47014	81.00452	362.10150
158	4.22803	83.28905	352.14838	158	4.36819	82.24773	359.27405	158	4.51298	81.22610	366.57162
159	4.26678	83.52342	356.37640	159	4.40915	82.47453	363.64224	159	4.55623	81.44558	371.08459
160	4.30590	83.75567	360.64319	160	4.45048	82.69922	368.05139	160	4.59989	81.66298	375.64084
161	4.34537	83.98579	364.94907	161	4.49221	82.92183	372.50196	161	4.64397	81.87831	380.24072
162	4.38520	84.21384	369.29443	162	4.53432	83.14237	376.99408	162	4.68848	82.09160	384.88470
163	4.42540	84.43980	373.67966	163	4.57683	83.36086	381.52841	163	4.73341	82.30286	389.57318
164	4.46596	84.66372	378.10504	164	4.61974	83.57732	386.10522	164	4.77877	82.51212	394.30658
165	4.50690	84.88560	382.57101	165	4.66305	83.79177	390.72498	165	4.82457	82.71939	399.08536
166	4.54821	85.10547	387.07791	166	4.70676	84.00423	395.38800	166	4.87090	82.92470	403.90994
167	4.58991	85.32333	391.62613	167	4.75089	84.21472	400.09476	167	4.91748	83.12805	408.78073
168	4.63198	85.53923	396.21603	168	4.79543	84.42326	404.84567	168	4.96461	83.32948	413.69821
169	4.67444	85.75316	400.84802	169	4.84038	84.62985	409.64108	169	5.01219	83.52899	418.66281
170	4.71729	85.96514	405.52246	170	4.88576	84.83453	414.48148	170	5.06022	83.72662	423.67502
171	4.76053	86.17520	410.23975	171	4.93157	85.03730	419.36725	171	5.10871	83.92236	428.73523
172	4.80417	86.38335	415.00027	172	4.97780	85.23819	424.29880	172	5.15767	84.11624	433.84393
173	4.84821	86.58961	419.80444	173	5.02447	85.43722	429.27661	173	5.20710	84.30829	439.00162
174	4.89265	86.79401	424.65265	174	5.07157	85.63440	434.30109	174	5.25700	84.49851	444.20871
175	4.93750	86.99654	429.54529	175	5.11912	85.82974	439.37285	175	5.30738	84.68693	449.46570

176	4.98276	87.19723	434.48279	176	5.16711	86.03328	444.49176	176	5.35824	84.87356	454.77310
177	5.02843	87.39610	439.46555	177	5.21555	86.21501	449.65887	177	5.40959	85.05842	460.13135
178	5.07453	87.53316	444.43399	178	5.26445	86.40496	454.87442	178	5.46143	85.24152	465.54092
179	5.12104	87.78844	449.56851	179	5.31380	86.53315	460.13889	179	5.51377	85.42288	471.00235
180	5.16799	87.98193	454.43984	180	5.36362	86.77969	465.45267	180	5.56661	85.60252	476.51614
181	5.21536	88.17368	459.85754	181	5.41390	86.96430	470.81628	181	5.61996	85.78046	482.08273
182	5.26317	88.36368	465.07291	182	5.46466	87.14729	476.23019	182	5.67382	85.95671	487.70270
183	5.31141	88.55195	470.33609	183	5.51589	87.32859	481.69485	183	5.72819	86.13129	493.37653
184	5.36010	88.73851	475.64749	184	5.56760	87.50820	487.21075	184	5.78309	86.30420	498.10471
185	5.40924	88.92338	481.00760	185	5.61980	87.68614	492.77835	185	5.83851	86.47548	504.88782
186	5.45882	89.10657	486.41694	186	5.67248	87.86243	498.39818	186	5.89446	86.64513	510.72632
187	5.50886	89.28809	491.87564	187	5.72566	88.03709	504.07062	187	5.95095	86.81317	516.62073
188	5.55936	89.46797	497.38452	188	5.77934	88.21011	509.79630	188	6.00798	86.97961	522.57172
189	5.61032	89.64622	502.94388	189	5.83352	88.38154	515.57562	189	6.06556	87.14448	528.57971
190	5.66175	89.82284	508.55420	190	5.88821	88.55137	521.40912	190	6.12368	87.30778	534.64526
191	5.71365	89.99786	514.21594	191	5.94341	88.71962	527.29736	191	6.18237	87.46963	540.76892
192	5.76602	90.17129	519.92957	192	5.99913	88.86631	533.24078	192	6.24162	87.62975	546.96129
193	5.81888	90.34315	525.69956	193	6.05537	89.05146	539.23967	193	6.30143	87.78844	553.19293
194	5.87222	90.51344	531.51447	194	6.11214	89.21507	545.29529	194	6.36182	87.94563	559.49432
195	5.92604	90.68218	537.38666	195	6.16944	89.38715	551.40741	195	6.42279	88.10133	565.85614
196	5.99037	90.84940	543.31274	196	6.22728	89.53773	557.57694	196	6.48434	88.25554	572.27893
197	6.03519	91.01509	549.23809	197	6.28566	89.80414	563.80414	197	6.54648	88.40829	578.76331
198	6.09051	91.17928	555.32831	198	6.34459	89.85445	570.08978	198	6.60922	88.55960	585.30975
199	6.14634	91.34198	561.41876	199	6.40407	90.08978	576.43439	199	6.67256	88.70947	591.91901
200	6.20268	91.50320	567.56512	200	6.46411	90.16530	582.83850	200	6.73650	88.85791	598.59155

Table 1. (continued) Annuities

M	C(11.00,M,12)	A(11.00,M,12)	S(11.00,M,12)	M	C(11.25,M,12)	A(11.25,M,12)	S(11.25,M,12)	M	C(11.50,M,12)	A(11.50,M,12)	S(11.50,M,12)
201	6.25954	91.68296	573.76782	201	6.52471	90.31856	589.30261	201	6.80106	89.00494	605.32906
202	6.31692	91.8127	580.02734	202	6.58588	90.47040	595.82727	202	6.86624	89.15059	612.12909
203	6.37482	91.97813	586.34424	203	6.64762	90.62083	602.41315	203	6.93204	89.29485	618.99536
204	6.43326	92.13358	592.71912	204	6.70995	90.76996	609.06079	204	6.99847	89.43774	625.92737
205	6.49223	92.28761	599.15234	205	6.77285	90.91751	615.77075	205	7.06554	89.57926	632.92584
206	6.55174	92.44023	605.64459	206	6.83635	91.06379	622.54358	206	7.13325	89.71945	639.99139
207	6.61180	92.59148	612.19629	207	6.90044	91.20870	629.37994	207	7.20161	89.85831	647.12463
208	6.67241	92.74135	618.80811	208	6.96513	91.35228	636.28040	208	7.27063	89.99585	654.32629
209	6.73357	92.88986	625.48053	209	7.03043	91.49451	643.24548	209	7.34030	90.13209	661.59686
210	6.79530	93.03702	632.21411	210	7.09634	91.63544	650.27594	210	7.41065	90.26703	668.93719
211	6.85759	93.18285	639.00940	211	7.16287	91.77504	657.37225	211	7.48167	90.40069	676.34784
212	6.92045	93.32734	645.86700	212	7.23002	91.91335	664.53516	212	7.55337	90.53308	683.82953
213	6.98388	93.47053	652.78741	213	7.29780	92.05038	671.76514	213	7.62575	90.66422	691.38287
214	7.04790	93.61242	659.77130	214	7.36622	92.18613	679.06293	214	7.69883	90.79411	699.00861
215	7.11251	93.75301	666.81921	215	7.43527	92.32063	686.42914	215	7.77261	90.92276	706.70746
216	7.17771	93.89233	673.93170	216	7.50498	92.45388	693.86444	216	7.84710	91.05019	714.48010
217	7.24350	94.03039	681.10944	217	7.57534	92.58588	701.36945	217	7.92230	91.17642	722.32715
218	7.30990	94.16719	688.35297	218	7.64636	92.71667	708.94476	218	7.99822	91.30145	730.24945
219	7.37691	94.30275	695.66284	219	7.71804	92.84623	716.59113	219	8.07487	91.42529	738.24768
220	7.44453	94.43707	703.03973	220	7.79040	92.97459	724.30914	220	8.15226	91.54796	746.32257
221	7.51277	94.57018	710.48425	221	7.86343	93.10177	732.09955	221	8.23038	91.66946	754.47485
222	7.58164	94.70208	717.99707	222	7.93715	93.22775	739.96301	222	8.30926	91.78980	762.70520
223	7.65114	94.83278	725.57867	223	8.01156	93.35258	747.90015	223	8.38889	91.90901	771.01447
224	7.72127	94.96229	733.22966	224	8.08667	93.47623	755.91168	224	8.46928	92.02708	779.40338
225	7.79205	95.09062	740.95111	225	8.16248	93.59875	763.99835	225	8.55045	92.14404	787.87268

n				
226	7.86348	95.21790	748.74316	8.23901
227	7.93556	95.34381	756.60663	8.31625
228	8.00830	95.46868	764.54218	8.39421
229	8.08171	95.59241	772.55048	8.47291
230	8.15590	95.71503	780.63220	8.55234
231	8.23056	95.83652	788.78902	8.63252
232	8.30600	95.96692	797.01855	8.71345
233	8.38214	96.07623	805.32458	8.79614
234	8.45898	96.19444	813.70673	8.87759
235	8.53652	96.31158	822.16571	8.96082
236	8.61477	96.42767	830.70221	9.04483
237	8.69374	96.54269	839.31656	9.12962
238	8.77343	96.65667	848.01074	9.21521
239	8.85385	96.76962	856.79418	9.30161
240	8.93501	96.88154	865.63800	9.38881
241	9.01692	96.99244	874.57300	9.47683
242	9.09957	97.10233	883.58997	9.56567
243	9.18299	97.21123	892.68951	9.65535
244	9.26716	97.31914	901.87250	9.74587
245	9.35211	97.42606	911.13965	9.83724
246	9.43784	97.53202	920.49176	9.92946
247	9.52435	97.63702	929.92963	10.02255
248	9.61166	97.74106	939.45398	10.11651
249	9.69977	97.84415	949.06561	10.21136
250	9.78868	97.94631	958.76538	10.30709

n					
226	93.72012	8.63239	92.25988	772.16089	796.42310
227	93.84037	8.71511	92.37462	780.39990	805.05548
228	93.95960	8.79963	92.48827	788.71613	813.77063
229	94.07752	8.88295	92.60085	797.11035	822.56921
230	94.19445	8.96908	92.71236	805.58325	831.45221
231	94.31029	9.05403	92.82281	814.13562	840.42029
232	94.42506	9.14090	92.93457	822.76813	849.47430
233	94.53875	9.22869	93.04057	831.48157	858.61511
234	94.65140	9.31683	93.14790	840.27873	867.84351
235	94.76299	9.40612	93.25421	849.15430	877.16034
236	94.87355	9.49626	93.35952	858.11511	886.56647
237	94.98309	9.58727	93.46382	867.15997	896.06268
238	95.09161	9.67915	93.56714	876.28965	905.64996
239	95.19911	9.77190	93.66947	885.50476	915.32910
240	95.30562	9.86555	93.77084	894.80640	925.10101
241	95.41114	9.96010	93.87123	904.19619	934.96655
242	95.51568	10.05555	93.97068	913.67206	944.92670
243	95.61926	10.15191	94.06918	923.23773	954.98224
244	95.72186	10.24920	94.16676	932.83307	965.13416
245	95.82352	10.34742	94.26340	942.63892	975.38338
246	95.92402	10.44659	94.35912	952.47620	985.73077
247	96.02400	10.54670	94.45394	962.40564	996.17737
248	96.12285	10.64777	94.54785	972.42822	1006.72406
249	96.22078	10.74901	94.64088	982.54474	1017.37183
250	96.31779	10.85283	94.73302	992.75604	1028.12158

Table 1. (continued) Annuities

M	C(11.00,M,12)	A(11.00,M,12)	S(11.00,M,12)
251	9.87841	98.04754	968.55408
252	9.96896	98.14785	978.43250
253	10.06035	98.24725	988.40149
254	10.15257	98.34575	998.46179
255	10.24563	98.44335	1008.61438
256	10.33955	98.54007	1018.86005
257	10.43433	98.63590	1029.19968
258	10.52998	98.73087	1039.63391
259	10.62650	98.82497	1050.16382
260	10.72391	98.91823	1060.79041
261	10.82221	99.01063	1071.51428
262	10.92142	99.10220	1082.33643
263	11.02153	99.19292	1093.25788
264	11.12256	99.28283	1104.27942
265	11.22452	99.37198	1115.40198
266	11.32741	99.46021	1126.62646
267	11.43124	99.54768	1137.95386
268	11.53603	99.63437	1149.38513
269	11.64178	99.72027	1160.92114
270	11.74849	99.80538	1172.56299
271	11.85619	99.88972	1184.31152
272	11.96487	99.97330	1196.16760
273	12.07455	100.05612	1208.13257
274	12.18523	100.13819	1220.20703
275	12.29693	100.21951	1232.39233

M	C(11.25,M,12)	A(11.25,M,12)	S(11.25,M,12)
251	10.40372	96.41392	1003.06317
252	10.50125	96.50915	1013.46686
253	10.59970	96.60349	1023.96814
254	10.69907	96.69695	1034.56775
255	10.79938	96.78955	1045.26686
256	10.90062	96.88129	1056.06628
257	11.00281	96.97218	1066.96692
258	11.10597	97.06222	1077.96973
259	11.21008	97.15142	1089.07568
260	11.31518	97.23980	1100.28577
261	11.42126	97.32735	1111.60095
262	11.52833	97.41409	1123.02222
263	11.63641	97.50003	1134.55054
264	11.74550	97.58517	1146.19689
265	11.85562	97.66952	1157.93237
266	11.96676	97.75308	1169.78809
267	12.07896	97.83588	1181.75476
268	12.19219	97.91789	1193.83374
269	12.30649	97.99915	1206.02600
270	12.42187	98.07966	1218.33240
271	12.53832	98.15941	1230.75427
272	12.65587	98.23843	1243.29260
273	12.77452	98.31670	1255.94849
274	12.89428	98.39426	1268.72302
275	13.01516	98.47109	1281.61731

M	C(11.50,M,12)	A(11.50,M,12)	S(11.50,M,12)
251	10.95684	94.82429	1038.97449
252	11.06184	94.91469	1049.83127
253	11.16785	95.00423	1060.93316
254	11.27488	95.09293	1072.16101
255	11.38283	95.18078	1083.43579
256	11.49201	95.26779	1094.81873
257	11.60215	95.35398	1106.31079
258	11.71333	95.43935	1117.91296
259	11.82559	95.52392	1129.62622
260	11.93891	95.60768	1141.45190
261	12.05333	95.69064	1153.39075
262	12.16884	95.77282	1165.44409
263	12.28546	95.85422	1177.61292
264	12.40319	95.93484	1189.89844
265	12.52206	96.01470	1202.30164
266	12.64206	96.09380	1214.82361
267	12.76321	96.17215	1227.46570
268	12.88553	96.24976	1240.22888
269	13.00901	96.32663	1253.11450
270	13.13368	96.40277	1266.12341
271	13.25955	96.47819	1279.25720
272	13.38662	96.55289	1292.51672
273	13.51491	96.62688	1305.90332
274	13.64442	96.70017	1319.41821
275	13.77518	96.77277	1333.06262

n			n			n			n			
276	12.40965	100.30009	276	1244.68921	13.13718	276	1294.63245	98.54721	276	13.90720	96.84467	1346.83789
277	12.52341	100.37994	277	1257.09888	13.26034	277	1307.76965	98.62263	277	14.04047	96.91589	1360.74500
278	12.63820	100.45907	278	1269.62231	13.38466	278	1321.03003	98.69734	278	14.17503	96.98643	1374.78552
279	12.75406	100.53748	279	1282.26050	13.51014	279	1334.41467	98.77135	279	14.31087	97.05631	1388.96057
280	12.87097	100.61517	280	1295.01453	13.63680	280	1347.92480	98.84469	280	14.44802	97.12553	1403.27198
281	12.98895	100.69216	281	1307.88550	13.76464	281	1361.56152	98.91734	281	14.59648	97.19408	1417.71306
282	13.10802	100.76845	282	1320.87451	13.89301	282	1375.28617	98.98301	282	14.72626	97.26199	1432.30591
283	13.22817	100.84405	283	1333.98254	14.02094	283	1389.21985	99.06062	283	14.86739	97.32925	1447.03210
284	13.34943	100.91896	284	1347.21069	14.15541	284	1403.24377	99.13126	284	15.00987	97.39587	1461.89954
285	13.47180	100.99318	285	1360.56006	14.28812	285	1417.39929	99.20126	285	15.15372	97.46187	1476.90942
286	13.59529	101.06673	286	1374.03196	14.42207	286	1431.68738	99.27059	286	15.29894	97.52723	1492.06311
287	13.71992	101.13963	287	1387.62720	14.55728	287	1446.10398	99.33929	287	15.44555	97.59197	1507.36206
288	13.84568	101.21185	288	1401.34705	14.69375	288	1460.66675	99.40734	288	15.59357	97.65611	1522.80782
289	13.97260	101.28342	289	1415.19275	14.83150	289	1475.36047	99.47476	289	15.74301	97.71962	1538.40125
290	14.10068	101.35434	290	1429.16541	14.97055	290	1490.19802	99.54156	290	15.89388	97.78254	1554.14417
291	14.22994	101.42461	291	1443.26611	15.11090	291	1505.16248	99.60774	291	16.04620	97.84486	1570.03809
292	14.36038	101.49425	292	1457.49597	15.25256	292	1520.27344	99.67330	292	16.19997	97.90659	1586.08435
293	14.49202	101.56325	293	1471.85325	15.39556	293	1535.52800	99.73826	293	16.35522	97.96773	1602.28430
294	14.62486	101.63163	294	1486.34839	15.53989	294	1550.90151	99.80260	294	16.51196	98.02829	1618.63963
295	14.75892	101.69938	295	1500.69538	15.68558	295	1566.46143	99.86636	295	16.67020	98.08828	1635.15149
296	14.89421	101.76653	296	1515.73218	15.83263	296	1582.14697	99.92962	296	16.82996	98.14770	1651.82166
297	15.03074	101.83305	297	1530.62634	15.98106	297	1597.97961	99.99350	297	16.99125	98.20655	1668.65161
298	15.16852	101.89898	298	1545.65710	16.13088	298	1613.96069	100.05408	298	17.15408	98.26485	1685.64282
299	15.30757	101.96431	299	1560.82568	16.28211	299	1630.09155	100.11758	299	17.31847	98.32259	1702.79700
300	15.44789	102.02904	300	1576.13318	16.43475	300	1646.37366	100.17635	300	17.48444	98.37978	1720.11548

Table 1. (continued) Annuities

M	C(11.00,M,12)	A(11.00,M,12)	S(11.00,M,12)	C(11.25,M,12)	A(11.25,M,12)	S(11.25,M,12)	C(11.50,M,12)	A(11.50,M,12)	S(11.50,M,12)
301	15.58949	102.03319	1591.58118	16.58883	100.20663	1662.90847	17.65200	99.43643	1737.59985
302	15.73240	102.15675	1607.17065	16.74435	100.28636	1679.39732	17.82116	99.49255	1755.25183
303	15.87661	102.21973	1622.90308	16.90133	100.35552	1696.14160	17.99195	99.54813	1773.07300
304	16.02215	102.28215	1638.77966	17.05978	100.41454	1713.04297	18.16437	99.60318	1791.06494
305	16.16902	102.34399	1654.80176	17.21971	100.47221	1730.10268	18.33845	99.65771	1809.22837
306	16.31723	102.40528	1670.97083	17.38115	100.52975	1747.32239	18.51419	99.71172	1827.56775
307	16.46681	102.46601	1687.28809	17.54410	100.59675	1764.70361	18.69162	99.76522	1846.08203
308	16.61775	102.52618	1703.75488	17.70857	100.64321	1782.24768	18.87075	99.81821	1864.77356
309	16.77008	102.58582	1720.37256	17.87459	100.69916	1799.96630	19.05159	99.87070	1883.64441
310	16.92381	102.64491	1737.14270	18.04216	100.75459	1817.83081	19.23417	99.92269	1902.69592
311	17.07894	102.70345	1754.06653	18.21131	100.80949	1835.87305	19.41850	99.97419	1921.93018
312	17.23550	102.76147	1771.14563	18.38204	100.86390	1854.08435	19.60459	100.02520	1941.34963
313	17.39349	102.81894	1788.38098	18.55437	100.91779	1872.46631	19.79247	100.07572	1960.96325
314	17.55293	102.87594	1805.77441	18.72832	100.97119	1891.02075	19.98215	100.12577	1980.74573
315	17.71383	102.93239	1823.32739	18.90390	101.02409	1909.74902	20.17364	100.17534	2000.72778
316	17.87621	102.98833	1841.04114	19.08112	101.07649	1928.65295	20.36697	100.22444	2020.90149
317	18.04008	103.04376	1858.91736	19.26001	101.12842	1947.73413	20.56215	100.27307	2041.26948
318	18.20544	103.09869	1876.95792	19.44057	101.17996	1966.99402	20.75921	100.32124	2061.83057
319	18.37233	103.15312	1895.16296	19.62282	101.23082	1986.43469	20.95815	100.36896	2082.58984
320	18.54074	103.20704	1913.53528	19.80679	101.28130	2006.05750	21.15900	100.41622	2103.54788
321	18.71070	103.26051	1932.07593	19.99248	101.33132	2025.86426	21.36177	100.46303	2124.70679
322	18.88221	103.31346	1950.78662	20.17991	101.38087	2045.85669	21.56649	100.50940	2146.06860
323	19.05530	103.36594	1969.66895	20.36909	101.42997	2066.03662	21.73117	100.55533	2167.63525
324	19.22997	103.41795	1988.72424	20.56005	101.47861	2086.40576	21.98183	100.60082	2189.40845
325	19.40625	103.46947	2007.96422	20.75280	101.52679	2106.96582	22.19249	100.64588	2211.39014

326	19.58414	103.52053	2027.36035	326	20.94736	101.57453	2127.71951	326	22.40517	99.69051	2233.58275
327	19.76366	103.57113	2046.94458	327	21.14374	101.62183	2148.66602	327	22.61988	99.73472	2255.98779
328	19.94492	103.62127	2066.70825	328	21.34136	101.66869	2169.80957	328	22.83668	99.77851	2278.60767
329	20.12765	103.67095	2086.15018	329	21.54205	101.71510	2191.15161	329	23.05551	99.82188	2301.44434
330	20.31216	103.72018	2106.78052	330	21.74400	101.76109	2212.69360	330	23.27646	99.86485	2324.50000
331	20.49835	103.76897	2127.09277	331	21.94785	101.80666	2234.43774	331	23.49952	99.90740	2347.77637
332	20.68625	103.81731	2147.59106	332	22.15361	101.85180	2256.38550	332	23.72473	99.94955	2371.27598
333	20.87588	103.86521	2168.27734	333	22.36131	101.89651	2278.53906	333	23.96209	99.99130	2395.00049
334	21.06724	103.91268	2189.15332	334	22.57094	101.94083	2300.90039	334	24.18163	100.03265	2418.96264
335	21.26035	103.95972	2210.22046	335	22.78255	101.98472	2323.47144	335	24.41337	100.07362	2443.13428
336	21.45524	104.00632	2231.49096	336	22.99613	102.02820	2346.25391	336	24.64733	100.11419	2467.54761
337	21.65191	104.05251	2252.93604	337	23.21172	102.07128	2369.25000	337	24.88354	100.15437	2492.19607
338	21.85039	104.09827	2274.58813	338	23.42933	102.11397	2392.46167	338	25.12200	100.19418	2517.07861
339	22.05069	104.14362	2296.43848	339	23.64898	102.15625	2415.89111	339	25.36275	100.23360	2542.20044
340	22.25282	104.18856	2318.48901	340	23.87069	102.19814	2439.54004	340	25.60582	100.27266	2567.56323
341	22.45690	104.23309	2340.74194	341	24.09448	102.23965	2463.41089	341	25.85120	100.31134	2593.16919
342	22.66265	104.27722	2363.19873	342	24.32036	102.28076	2487.50537	342	26.09895	100.34966	2619.02026
343	22.87040	104.32095	2385.86133	343	24.54836	102.32150	2511.82568	343	26.34906	100.38761	2645.11938
344	23.08004	104.36427	2408.73169	344	24.77851	102.36185	2536.37402	344	26.60157	100.42520	2671.46828
345	23.29161	104.40720	2431.81177	345	25.01081	102.40184	2561.15259	345	26.85650	100.46244	2698.06982
346	23.50512	104.44975	2455.10352	346	25.24528	102.44145	2586.16333	346	27.11388	100.49932	2724.92651
347	23.72058	104.49191	2478.60864	347	25.48196	102.48070	2611.40969	347	27.37372	100.53585	2752.04028
348	23.93802	104.53368	2502.32910	348	25.72085	102.51958	2636.89063	348	27.63605	100.57204	2779.41406
349	24.15745	104.57507	2526.26709	349	25.96198	102.55809	2662.61133	349	27.90090	100.60788	2807.05005
350	24.37889	104.61610	2550.42456	350	26.20538	102.59625	2688.57349	350	28.16828	100.64338	2834.95038

Table 1. (continued) Annuities

M	C(11.00,M,12)	A(11.00,M,12)	S(11.00,M,12)	M	C(11.25,M,12)	A(11.25,M,12)	S(11.25,M,12)	M	C(11.50,M,12)	A(11.50,M,12)	S(11.50,M,12)
351	24.60237	104.65674	2574.80347	351	26.45105	102.63406	2714.77801	351	28.43823	100.67854	2863.11974
352	24.82789	104.69702	2599.40576	352	26.69903	102.67151	2741.22974	352	28.71076	100.71137	2891.55737
353	25.05048	104.73639	2624.23364	353	26.94933	102.70962	2767.92871	353	28.98590	100.74787	2920.26831
354	25.28515	104.77648	2649.28931	354	27.20198	102.74538	2794.87817	354	29.26369	100.78204	2949.25415
355	25.51693	104.81567	2674.57446	355	27.45700	102.78180	2822.09008	355	29.54413	100.81580	2978.51782
356	25.75084	104.85450	2700.09131	356	27.71441	102.81789	2849.53711	356	29.82726	100.84942	3008.06201
357	25.99689	104.89298	2725.84229	357	27.97423	102.85363	2877.25146	357	30.11311	100.88263	3037.88916
358	26.22510	104.93111	2751.82910	358	28.23649	102.88905	2905.22568	358	30.40169	100.91552	3068.00244
359	26.46550	104.96890	2778.05420	359	28.50121	102.92413	2933.46240	359	30.69304	100.94810	3098.40405
360	26.70810	105.00634	2804.51963	360	28.76841	102.95889	2961.96362	360	30.98718	100.98037	3129.09717
361	26.95292	105.04344	2831.22778	361	29.03811	102.99333	2990.73193	361	31.28414	101.01234	3160.08423
362	27.19999	105.08021	2858.18066	362	29.31034	103.02745	3019.77002	362	31.58395	101.04400	3191.36841
363	27.44332	105.11664	2885.38066	363	29.58513	103.06125	3049.08032	363	31.88663	101.07536	3222.95239
364	27.70094	105.15274	2912.82983	364	29.86249	103.09473	3078.66553	364	32.19221	101.10642	3254.83887
365	27.95487	105.18851	2940.53101	365	30.14245	103.12791	3108.52808	365	32.50071	101.13719	3287.03125
366	28.21112	105.22396	2968.48584	366	30.42504	103.16078	3138.67041	366	32.81218	101.16766	3319.53198
367	28.46972	105.25909	2996.69678	367	30.71027	103.19334	3169.09546	367	33.12663	101.19785	3352.34399
368	28.73069	105.29389	3025.16650	368	30.99818	103.22560	3199.80566	368	33.44409	101.22775	3385.47070
369	28.99406	105.32838	3053.89722	369	31.28879	103.25756	3230.80396	369	33.76460	101.25737	3418.91479
370	29.25984	105.36256	3082.89136	370	31.58212	103.28922	3262.09277	370	34.08818	101.28671	3452.67944
371	29.52805	105.39642	3112.15112	371	31.87820	103.32059	3293.67480	371	34.41486	101.31577	3486.76758
372	29.79873	105.42998	3141.67920	372	32.17706	103.35167	3325.55298	372	34.74466	101.34454	3521.18237
373	30.07188	105.46323	3171.47603	373	32.47872	103.38246	3357.72998	373	35.07763	101.37305	3555.92700
374	30.34754	105.49619	3201.54960	374	32.78321	103.41296	3390.20874	374	35.41360	101.40129	3591.00464
375	30.62573	105.52884	3231.89746	375	33.09055	103.44318	3422.99194	375	35.75318	101.42926	3626.41846

n				n				n			
376	30.50646	105.56120	3262.52319	376	33.40077	3456.08252	103.47312	376	36.05981	101.45696	3662.17163
377	31.18977	105.59325	3293.42969	377	33.71391	3489.48340	103.50278	377	36.44173	101.48441	3698.26758
378	31.47568	105.62502	3324.61938	378	34.02997	3523.19727	103.53217	378	36.79096	101.51159	3734.70923
379	31.76420	105.65651	3356.09497	379	34.34900	3557.22729	103.56129	379	37.14354	101.53851	3771.50024
380	32.05537	105.68771	3387.85913	380	34.67103	3591.57617	103.59013	380	37.49950	101.56518	3808.64350
381	32.34962	105.71861	3419.91455	381	34.99607	3626.24731	103.61870	381	37.85887	101.59159	3846.14331
382	32.64575	105.74924	3452.26392	382	35.32415	3661.24341	103.64701	382	38.22169	101.61775	3884.00220
383	32.94500	105.77960	3484.90967	383	35.65532	3696.56738	103.67506	383	38.58798	101.64367	3922.22388
384	33.24700	105.80968	3517.85449	384	35.98959	3732.22290	103.70284	384	38.95778	101.66933	3960.81177
385	33.55177	105.83949	3551.10156	385	36.32699	3768.21240	103.73037	385	39.33112	101.69476	3999.76963
386	33.85932	105.86902	3584.65332	386	36.66756	3804.53931	103.75764	386	39.70905	101.71995	4039.10083
387	34.16970	105.89828	3618.51270	387	37.01131	3841.20703	103.78466	387	40.08858	101.74489	4078.80884
388	34.48292	105.92728	3652.68237	388	37.35830	3878.21826	103.81143	388	40.47277	101.76960	4118.89746
389	34.79902	105.95602	3687.16528	389	37.70853	3915.57666	103.83795	389	40.86063	101.79408	4159.37012
390	35.11800	105.98450	3721.96436	390	38.06205	3953.28516	103.86422	390	41.25221	101.81831	4200.23047
391	35.43992	106.01271	3757.08228	391	38.41888	3991.34717	103.89025	391	41.64754	101.84232	4241.48291
392	35.76479	106.04067	3792.52222	392	38.77906	4029.76611	103.91604	392	42.04667	101.86610	4283.13037
393	36.09263	106.06838	3828.28222	393	39.14261	4068.54517	103.94158	393	42.44962	101.88966	4325.17725
394	36.42348	106.09583	3864.37964	394	39.50957	4107.68750	103.96690	394	42.85642	101.91300	4367.62646
395	36.75736	106.12304	3900.80322	395	39.87997	4147.17727	103.99197	395	43.26713	101.93613	4410.48291
396	37.09430	106.15000	3937.56055	396	40.25386	4187.09727	104.01682	396	43.68177	101.95901	4453.75000
397	37.43433	106.17671	3974.65479	397	40.63123	4227.33105	104.04143	397	44.10039	101.98168	4497.43213
398	37.77748	106.20319	4012.08911	398	41.01215	4267.96240	104.06581	398	44.52302	102.00414	4541.53223
399	38.12378	106.22942	4049.86670	399	41.39663	4308.97412	104.08997	399	44.94970	102.02633	4586.05518
400	38.47324	106.25540	4087.99048	400	41.78473	4350.37109	104.11390	400	45.38047	102.04842	4631.00488

Table 1. (continued) Annuities

M	C(11.00,M,12)	A(11.00,M,12)	S(11.00,M,12)		M	C(11.25,M,12)	A(11.25,M,12)	S(11.25,M,12)		M	C(11.50,M,12)	A(11.50,M,12)	S(11.50,M,12)
401	38.82592	106.28116	4126.46338		401	42.17646	104.13760	4392.15576		401	45.81536	102.07025	4676.38574
402	39.18108	106.30669	4165.28955		402	42.57187	104.16109	4434.33203		402	46.25443	102.09187	4722.20117
403	39.54099	106.33197	4204.47119		403	42.97098	104.18436	4476.90430		403	46.69770	102.11328	4768.45557
404	39.90345	106.35703	4244.01221		404	43.37383	104.20742	4519.87500		404	47.14522	102.13449	4815.15288
405	40.26923	106.38187	4283.78046		405	43.78046	104.23026	4563.24902		405	47.59703	102.15550	4862.29834
406	40.63836	106.40647	4324.18506		406	44.19090	104.25289	4607.02930		406	48.05317	102.17632	4909.89551
407	41.01088	106.43085	4364.82324		407	44.60519	104.27531	4651.22021		407	48.51367	102.19693	4957.94824
408	41.38681	106.45502	4405.83398		408	45.02337	104.29752	4695.82520		408	48.97860	102.21735	5006.46240
409	41.76619	106.47897	4447.22119		409	45.44546	104.31953	4740.84863		409	49.44798	102.23756	5055.44092
410	42.14905	106.50269	4488.98730		410	45.87151	104.34132	4786.29443		410	49.92185	102.25760	5104.88867
411	42.53542	106.52620	4531.13623		411	46.30156	104.36292	4832.16553		411	50.40027	102.27744	5154.81055
412	42.92532	106.54949	4573.67188		412	46.73563	104.38432	4878.46729		412	50.88327	102.29710	5205.21094
413	43.31881	106.57258	4616.59717		413	47.17378	104.40552	4925.20313		413	51.37090	102.31656	5256.09424
414	43.71590	106.59545	4659.91602		414	47.61603	104.42652	4972.37695		414	51.86321	102.33584	5307.46484
415	44.11662	106.61812	4703.63184		415	48.06243	104.44733	5019.99268		415	52.36023	102.35494	5359.32813
416	44.52103	106.64058	4747.74854		416	48.51302	104.46794	5068.05518		416	52.86201	102.37386	5411.68848
417	44.92914	106.66284	4792.26953		417	48.96783	104.48837	5116.56836		417	53.36861	102.39259	5464.55029
418	45.34099	106.68489	4837.19873		418	49.42690	104.50859	5165.53613		418	53.88006	102.41116	5517.91895
419	45.75661	106.70675	4882.53965		419	49.89028	104.52864	5214.96289		419	54.39641	102.42953	5571.79932
420	46.17605	106.72841	4928.29590		420	50.35800	104.54849	5264.85303		420	54.91771	102.44775	5626.19580
421	46.59933	106.74986	4974.47217		421	50.83010	104.56817	5315.21143		421	55.44400	102.46578	5681.11328
422	47.02649	106.77113	5021.07129		422	51.30664	104.58766	5366.04150		422	55.97534	102.48365	5736.55713
423	47.45757	106.79220	5068.09814		423	51.78764	104.60697	5417.34814		423	56.51177	102.50134	5792.53271
424	47.89258	106.81308	5115.55566		424	52.27315	104.62610	5469.13574		424	57.05334	102.51887	5849.04448
425	48.33161	106.83377	5163.44824		425	52.76321	104.64505	5521.40869		425	57.60011	102.53623	5906.09766

n			n			n			n			
426	48.77465	106.85427	426	5211.77979	53.25786	426	104.66383	5574.17198	426	58.15210	102.55348	5993.89775
427	49.22175	106.87459	427	5260.55420	53.75716	427	104.68243	5627.42969	427	58.70940	102.57046	6021.85010
428	49.67295	106.89472	428	5309.77637	54.26113	428	104.70086	5681.18701	428	59.27203	102.58733	6080.55957
429	50.12828	106.91467	429	5359.44922	54.76992	429	104.71912	5735.44824	429	59.84005	102.60404	6139.83154
430	50.58779	106.93444	430	5409.57764	55.28329	430	104.73721	5790.21777	430	60.41352	102.62060	6199.67139
431	51.05151	106.95403	431	5460.16504	55.80157	431	104.75513	5845.50146	431	60.99248	102.63699	6260.08496
432	51.51949	106.97343	432	5511.21680	56.32471	432	104.77288	5901.30273	432	61.57699	102.65323	6321.07764
433	51.99175	106.99267	433	5562.73633	56.85276	433	104.79047	5957.62744	433	62.16711	102.66932	6382.65430
434	52.46834	107.01173	434	5614.72803	57.38575	434	104.80790	6014.48047	434	62.76287	102.68525	6444.82178
435	52.94930	107.03062	435	5667.19829	57.92374	435	104.82516	6071.86621	435	63.36435	102.70103	6507.58447
436	53.43467	107.04933	436	5720.14551	58.46678	436	104.84226	6129.79004	436	63.97159	102.71667	6570.94873
437	53.92448	107.06787	437	5773.58008	59.01490	437	104.85921	6198.25635	437	64.58466	102.73215	6634.92041
438	54.41879	107.08625	438	5827.50488	59.56817	438	104.87600	6247.27148	438	65.20359	102.74748	6699.50488
439	54.91763	107.10446	439	5881.92334	60.12662	439	104.89263	6306.83984	439	65.82845	102.76267	6764.70850
440	55.42104	107.12251	440	5936.84131	60.69031	440	104.90910	6366.96631	440	66.45831	102.77773	6830.53711
441	55.92907	107.14038	441	5992.26221	61.25928	441	104.92543	6427.65674	441	67.09621	102.79263	6896.98658
442	56.44175	107.15810	442	6048.19141	61.83359	442	104.94160	6488.91602	442	67.73922	102.80739	6964.03277
443	56.96914	107.17566	443	6104.63330	62.41328	443	104.95763	6550.74961	443	68.38839	102.82201	7031.82203
444	57.48126	107.19305	444	6161.59229	62.99840	444	104.97350	6613.16260	444	69.04378	102.83649	7100.22021
445	58.00917	107.21029	445	6219.07344	63.58901	445	104.98923	6676.16113	445	69.70544	102.85044	7169.26416
446	58.53992	107.22737	446	6277.08734	64.18516	446	105.00481	6739.75000	446	70.37346	102.86505	7238.96924
447	59.07653	107.24430	447	6335.62158	64.78690	447	105.02024	6803.93555	447	71.04787	102.87913	7309.34277
448	59.61806	107.26108	448	6394.68924	65.39427	448	105.03553	6868.72217	448	71.72874	102.89307	7380.63063
449	60.16457	107.27769	449	6454.31592	66.00734	449	105.05068	6934.11670	449	72.41615	102.90688	7452.11963
450	60.71607	107.29417	450	6514.46096	66.62616	450	105.06569	7000.12402	450	73.11013	102.92056	7524.53564

Table 1. (continued) Annuities

M	C(11.00,M,12)	A(11.00,M,12)	S(11.00,M,12)	M	C(11.25,M,12)	A(11.25,M,12)	S(11.25,M,12)	M	C(11.50,M,12)	A(11.50,M,12)	S(11.50,M,12)
451	81.27264	107.31049	6575.19678	451	87.25078	105.08056	7066.75000	451	73.81077	102.93410	7597.84600
452	81.83430	107.32666	6636.46924	452	87.88126	105.09529	7134.00098	452	74.51813	102.94752	7671.45654
453	82.40112	107.34268	6698.30219	453	68.51764	105.10989	7201.88184	453	75.23225	102.96082	7745.97461
454	62.97313	107.35857	6760.70508	454	89.16000	105.12434	7270.39990	454	75.95323	102.97398	7821.20703
455	63.55038	107.37430	6823.67822	455	89.80837	105.13867	7339.55957	455	76.68111	102.98702	7897.16018
456	64.13283	107.38989	6887.22852	456	70.46282	105.15296	7409.36816	456	77.41598	102.99994	7973.84131
457	64.72081	107.40534	6961.36133	457	71.12341	105.16692	7479.83105	457	78.15788	103.01273	8051.25732
458	65.31409	107.42065	7016.08203	458	71.79019	105.18065	7550.96410	458	78.90689	103.02541	8129.41504
459	65.91280	107.43583	7081.39600	459	72.46323	105.19465	7622.74463	459	79.66309	103.03796	8208.32227
460	66.51700	107.45086	7147.30908	460	73.14257	105.20832	7695.20752	460	80.42652	103.05039	8287.98535
461	67.12674	107.46576	7213.82617	461	73.82829	105.22187	7768.35010	461	81.19728	103.06271	8368.41113
462	67.74207	107.48052	7280.96264	462	74.52042	105.23529	7842.17871	462	81.97542	103.07491	8449.60840
463	68.36304	107.49515	7348.69482	463	75.21740	105.24858	7916.69922	463	82.76102	103.08699	8531.58398
464	68.98969	107.50964	7417.05811	464	75.92423	105.26176	7991.97797	464	83.55415	103.09896	8614.34473
465	69.62210	107.52400	7486.04736	465	76.63602	105.27460	8067.84029	465	84.35487	103.11081	8697.89941
466	70.26031	107.53824	7555.66943	466	77.35448	105.28773	8144.47852	466	86.16327	103.12255	8782.25391
467	70.90438	107.55234	7625.93018	467	78.07568	105.30054	8221.83301	467	85.97942	103.13419	8867.41797
468	71.55431	107.56631	7696.83447	468	78.81168	105.31322	8299.91211	468	86.80339	103.14571	8953.39648
469	72.27023	107.58016	7768.38867	469	79.55054	105.32580	8378.72363	469	87.63525	103.15712	9040.20020
470	72.87015	107.59389	7840.59912	470	80.29313	105.33825	8458.27441	470	88.47517	103.16842	9127.83594
471	73.54015	107.60748	7913.47119	471	81.04910	105.35059	8538.57129	471	89.32596	103.17961	9216.31055
472	74.21427	107.62096	7987.01123	472	81.80194	105.36281	8619.62012	472	90.17899	103.19070	9305.63379
473	74.89456	107.63432	8061.12549	473	82.57580	105.37492	8701.42871	473	91.04321	103.20169	9395.81250
474	75.58110	107.64754	8136.12012	474	83.35004	105.38692	8784.00488	474	91.91570	103.21257	9486.85547
475	76.27393	107.66065	8211.70117	475	84.13145	105.39880	8867.35449	475	92.78656	103.22334	9578.77148

n				n				n			
476	76.97311	107.67365	8287.97461	476	84.90018	105.41058	8961.48633	476	98.68596	103.23402	9671.56836
477	77.67969	107.68652	8364.94824	477	85.71631	105.42225	9036.40625	477	94.58369	103.24459	9785.25391
478	78.3075	107.69927	8442.62696	478	86.51991	105.43391	9122.12305	478	96.40523	103.25506	9859.83789
479	79.10933	107.71191	8521.01758	479	87.33102	105.44526	9208.64258	479	96.49011	103.26543	9955.32813
480	79.83450	107.72444	8600.12696	480	88.14976	105.45660	9296.97363	480	97.32971	103.27571	10051.73340
481	80.56631	107.73685	8679.96094	481	88.97616	105.46784	9384.12305	481	98.26185	103.28589	10149.08250
482	81.30484	107.74915	8760.52734	482	89.81031	105.47897	9473.09961	482	99.20352	103.29597	10247.32422
483	82.05013	107.76134	8841.83203	483	90.65228	105.49001	9562.91016	483	100.15422	103.30595	10346.52734
484	82.80225	107.77341	8923.88281	484	91.50214	105.50093	9653.56250	484	101.11404	103.31584	10446.68164
485	83.56128	107.78539	9006.69457	485	92.35698	105.51176	9745.06445	485	102.08305	103.32564	10547.79590
486	84.32726	107.79724	9090.24609	486	93.22585	105.52249	9837.42480	486	103.06134	103.33534	10649.87891
487	85.10026	107.80900	9174.57324	487	94.09985	105.53311	9930.65039	487	104.04901	103.34495	10752.94043
488	85.88034	107.82064	9259.67383	488	94.98203	105.54364	10024.75000	488	105.04615	103.35447	10856.99926
489	86.66758	107.83218	9345.55371	489	95.87249	105.55408	10119.73242	489	106.05284	103.36390	10962.03516
490	87.46203	107.84361	9432.22168	490	96.77129	105.56441	10215.60449	490	107.06918	103.37324	11068.08789
491	88.26376	107.85494	9519.68359	491	97.67853	105.57465	10312.37598	491	108.09526	103.38249	11175.15723
492	89.07285	107.86617	9607.94727	492	98.59426	105.58479	10410.05469	492	109.13177	103.39165	11283.25293
493	89.88935	107.87729	9697.02051	493	99.51859	105.59483	10508.64644	493	110.17701	103.40073	11392.38879
494	90.71334	107.88831	9786.90918	494	100.45157	105.60479	10608.16699	494	111.23287	103.40972	11502.56055
495	91.54488	107.89924	9877.62305	495	101.39330	105.61465	10708.61914	495	112.29896	103.41862	11613.73996
496	92.38404	107.91006	9969.16797	496	102.34386	105.62443	10810.01172	496	113.37505	103.42744	11726.09277
497	93.23089	107.92079	10061.55176	497	103.30334	105.63410	10912.35645	497	114.46156	103.43618	11839.46777
498	94.08551	107.93142	10154.78223	498	104.27180	105.64369	11015.65918	498	115.55849	103.44483	11953.92871
499	94.94796	107.94195	10248.86816	499	105.24336	105.65320	11119.93164	499	116.66592	103.45341	12069.48730
500	96.81831	107.95238	10343.81641	500	106.23607	105.66261	11225.18066	500	117.78397	103.46190	12186.15332

Table 1. (continued) Annuities

W	C(11.75,M,12)	A(11.75,M,12)	S(11.75,M,12)	W	C(12.00,M,12)	A(12.00,M,12)	S(12.00,M,12)	W	C(12.25,M,12)	A(12.25,M,12)	S(12.25,M,12)
1	1.00979	0.99030	1.00000	1	1.01000	0.99010	1.00000	1	1.01021	0.98989	1.00000
2	1.01968	1.97100	2.00979	2	1.02010	1.97039	2.01000	2	1.02052	1.96979	2.01021
3	1.02966	2.94219	3.02947	3	1.03030	2.94099	3.03010	3	1.03094	2.93978	3.03073
4	1.03975	3.90397	4.05913	4	1.04060	3.90197	4.06040	4	1.04146	3.89996	4.06167
5	1.04993	4.85642	5.09888	5	1.05101	4.85343	5.10100	5	1.05209	4.85045	5.10313
6	1.06021	5.79963	6.14881	6	1.06152	5.79548	6.15201	6	1.06283	5.79133	6.15522
7	1.07059	6.73369	7.20901	7	1.07214	6.72819	7.21353	7	1.07368	6.72270	7.21806
8	1.08107	7.65870	8.27960	8	1.08286	7.65168	8.28567	8	1.08464	7.64466	8.29174
9	1.09166	8.57474	9.36067	9	1.09369	8.56602	9.36853	9	1.09572	8.55731	9.37639
10	1.10235	9.48190	10.45233	10	1.10462	9.47130	10.46221	10	1.10690	9.46073	10.47211
11	1.11314	10.38026	11.55468	11	1.11567	10.36763	11.56683	11	1.11820	10.35502	11.57301
12	1.12404	11.26991	12.66781	12	1.12682	11.25508	12.68250	12	1.12962	11.24028	12.69221
13	1.13505	12.15093	13.79185	13	1.13809	12.13374	13.80933	13	1.14115	12.11659	13.82683
14	1.14616	13.02341	14.92690	14	1.14947	13.00370	14.94742	14	1.15280	12.98404	14.96798
15	1.15738	13.88743	16.07306	15	1.16097	13.86505	16.09690	15	1.16457	13.84273	16.12078
16	1.16871	14.74307	17.23044	16	1.17258	14.71787	17.25786	16	1.17645	14.69274	17.28534
17	1.18016	15.59041	18.39915	17	1.18430	15.56225	18.43044	17	1.18846	15.53416	18.46180
18	1.19171	16.42954	19.57931	18	1.19615	16.39827	19.61475	18	1.20060	16.36708	19.65026
19	1.20338	17.26053	20.77103	19	1.20811	17.22601	20.81089	19	1.21285	17.19158	20.85086
20	1.21517	18.08346	21.97441	20	1.22019	18.04555	22.01900	20	1.22523	18.00776	22.06371
21	1.22706	18.89841	23.18958	21	1.23239	18.85698	23.23919	21	1.23774	18.81568	23.28894
22	1.23908	19.70547	24.41664	22	1.24472	19.66038	24.47158	22	1.25038	19.61544	24.52668
23	1.25121	20.50469	25.65572	23	1.25716	20.45582	25.71630	23	1.26314	20.40711	25.77706
24	1.26346	21.29617	26.90693	24	1.26973	21.24339	26.97346	24	1.27604	21.19079	27.04020
25	1.27584	22.07997	28.17040	25	1.28243	22.02316	28.24320	25	1.28906	21.96655	28.31624

n				n				n			
26	1.28833	22.85616	29.44623	26	1.29526	22.75620	29.52563	26	1.30222	22.73447	29.60530
27	1.30094	23.62484	30.73456	27	1.30821	23.55961	30.82089	27	1.31551	23.49463	30.90752
28	1.31368	24.36606	32.03550	28	1.32129	24.31644	32.12909	28	1.32894	24.24711	32.22303
29	1.32654	25.13990	33.34918	29	1.33450	25.06578	33.45039	29	1.34251	24.99198	33.55198
30	1.33953	25.86643	34.67572	30	1.34785	25.80771	34.78489	30	1.35621	25.72633	34.89449
31	1.35265	26.62572	36.01536	31	1.36133	26.54228	36.13274	31	1.37006	26.45922	36.25070
32	1.36589	27.35784	37.36791	32	1.37494	27.26959	37.49406	32	1.38405	27.18174	37.62076
33	1.37927	28.08286	38.73380	33	1.38869	27.98969	38.86901	33	1.39817	27.89636	39.00490
34	1.39277	28.80085	40.11307	34	1.40258	28.70267	40.25770	34	1.41245	28.60495	40.40298
35	1.40641	29.51188	41.50584	35	1.41660	29.40858	41.66027	35	1.42687	29.30579	41.81543
36	1.42018	30.21601	42.91225	36	1.43077	30.10750	43.07688	36	1.44143	29.99954	43.24229
37	1.43409	30.91332	44.33244	37	1.44508	30.79951	44.50764	37	1.45615	30.68629	44.68372
38	1.44813	31.60387	45.76653	38	1.45953	31.48466	45.95272	38	1.47101	31.36609	46.13987
39	1.46231	32.28772	47.21466	39	1.47412	32.18503	47.41225	39	1.48603	32.03902	47.61088
40	1.47663	32.96494	48.67697	40	1.48886	32.83468	48.88637	40	1.50120	32.70516	49.03691
41	1.49109	33.63559	50.15359	41	1.50375	33.49969	50.37524	41	1.51652	33.36456	50.59811
42	1.50569	34.29974	51.64468	42	1.51879	34.15811	51.87899	42	1.53200	34.01730	52.11463
43	1.52043	34.95744	53.15037	43	1.53398	34.81001	53.39778	43	1.54764	34.66345	53.64683
44	1.53532	35.60877	54.67080	44	1.54932	35.45545	54.93176	44	1.56344	35.30306	55.19427
45	1.55035	36.25379	56.20612	45	1.56481	36.09451	56.48107	45	1.57940	35.93621	56.75772
46	1.56553	36.89255	57.75647	46	1.58046	36.72723	58.04588	46	1.59552	36.56297	58.33712
47	1.58086	37.52512	59.32200	47	1.59626	37.35370	59.62634	47	1.61181	37.18338	59.93264
48	1.59634	38.15155	60.90287	48	1.61223	37.97936	61.22261	48	1.62827	37.79753	61.54446
49	1.61197	38.77191	62.49921	49	1.62835	38.59808	62.83483	49	1.64489	38.40548	63.17272
50	1.62776	39.38625	64.11118	50	1.64463	39.15612	64.46318	50	1.66168	39.00728	64.81751

Table 1. (continued) Annuities

M	C(11.75,M,12)	A(11.75,M,12)	S(11.75,M,12)		M	C(12.00,M,12)	A(12.00,M,12)	S(12.00,M,12)		M	C(12.25,M,12)	A(12.25,M,12)	S(12.25,M,12)
51	1.64369	39.99464	65.73939		51	1.66108	39.79913	66.10761		51	1.67964	39.60300	66.47329
52	1.65979	40.59712	67.38262		52	1.67769	40.34019	67.76889		52	1.68578	40.19270	68.15798
53	1.67604	41.18377	69.04241		53	1.69447	40.99435	69.44658		53	1.71309	40.77644	69.85371
54	1.69245	41.78463	70.71845		54	1.71141	41.56866	71.14104		54	1.73058	41.35428	71.56680
55	1.70902	42.36975	72.41090		55	1.72852	42.14719	72.85246		55	1.74824	41.92628	73.29738
56	1.72576	42.94921	74.11993		56	1.74581	42.71999	74.58098		56	1.76609	42.49250	75.04562
57	1.74266	43.52305	75.84569		57	1.76327	43.28772	76.32679		57	1.78412	43.05301	76.81171
58	1.75972	44.09132	77.58834		58	1.78090	43.84963	78.09006		58	1.80233	43.60784	78.59583
59	1.77695	44.65408	79.34806		59	1.79871	44.40459	79.87096		59	1.82073	44.15707	80.39816
60	1.79435	45.21139	81.12501		60	1.81670	44.95504	81.66966		60	1.83932	44.70075	82.21889
61	1.81192	45.76329	82.91936		61	1.83486	45.50003	83.49637		61	1.85809	45.23894	84.05821
62	1.82966	46.30984	84.73128		62	1.85321	46.03964	85.32123		62	1.87706	45.77169	85.91631
63	1.84758	46.85109	86.56094		63	1.87174	46.57390	87.17444		63	1.89622	46.29905	87.79337
64	1.86567	47.38709	88.40852		64	1.89046	47.10287	89.04618		64	1.91558	46.82108	89.68959
65	1.88393	47.91789	90.27419		65	1.90937	47.62661	90.93665		65	1.93514	47.33784	91.60518
66	1.90238	48.44355	92.15812		66	1.92846	48.14515	92.84601		66	1.95489	47.84938	93.54031
67	1.92101	48.96411	94.06050		67	1.94774	48.65057	94.77448		67	1.97485	48.35575	95.49920
68	1.93982	49.47962	95.98151		68	1.96722	49.16690	96.72221		68	1.99501	48.85700	97.47005
69	1.95881	49.99014	97.92133		69	1.98689	49.67020	98.68944		69	2.01537	49.35319	99.46506
70	1.97799	50.49570	99.88014		70	2.00676	50.16851	100.67633		70	2.03595	49.84436	101.48043
71	1.99736	50.99636	101.85813		71	2.02683	50.66310	102.68310		71	2.05673	50.33057	103.51637
72	2.01692	51.49216	103.85549		72	2.04710	51.15039	104.70993		72	2.07773	50.81186	105.57310
73	2.03667	51.98316	105.87241		73	2.06757	51.63405	106.75703		73	2.09894	51.28830	107.65083
74	2.05661	52.46940	107.90908		74	2.08825	52.11292	108.82460		74	2.12036	51.75991	109.74976
75	2.07675	52.95082	109.96569		75	2.10913	52.58705	110.91284		75	2.14201	52.22676	111.87012

76	112.04243	53.42777	2.09708
77	114.13952	53.90000	2.11762
78	116.25713	54.36765	2.13835
79	118.39648	54.83077	2.15929
80	120.55477	55.28939	2.18043
81	122.73521	55.74357	2.20178
82	124.93699	56.19334	2.22334
83	127.16033	56.63876	2.24511
84	129.40544	57.07985	2.26709
85	131.67253	57.51667	2.28929
86	133.96182	57.94925	2.31171
87	136.27353	58.37763	2.33435
88	138.60788	58.80186	2.35720
89	140.96509	59.22198	2.38028
90	143.34537	59.63903	2.40359
91	145.74896	60.05004	2.42713
92	148.17609	60.45805	2.45089
93	150.62697	60.86211	2.47489
94	153.10187	61.26225	2.49912
95	155.60098	61.65851	2.52359
96	158.12457	62.05093	2.54830
97	160.67288	62.43954	2.57326
98	163.24614	62.82439	2.59845
99	165.84519	63.20550	2.62389
100	168.46849	63.58292	2.64969

76	113.02197	53.05648	2.13022
77	115.15219	53.52127	2.15152
78	117.30371	53.98146	2.17304
79	119.47675	54.43709	2.19477
80	121.67152	54.88820	2.21672
81	123.88823	55.33485	2.23888
82	126.12711	55.77708	2.26127
83	128.38838	56.21494	2.28388
84	130.67227	56.64845	2.30672
85	132.97899	57.07767	2.32979
86	135.30878	57.50265	2.35309
87	137.66187	57.92341	2.37662
88	140.03848	58.34001	2.40038
89	142.43887	58.75249	2.42439
90	144.86327	59.16088	2.44863
91	147.31189	59.56523	2.47312
92	149.78502	59.96557	2.49785
93	152.28287	60.36196	2.52283
94	154.80569	60.75441	2.54806
95	157.35374	61.14298	2.57354
96	159.92729	61.52770	2.59927
97	162.52655	61.90802	2.62527
98	165.15182	62.28576	2.65152
99	167.80334	62.65916	2.67803
100	170.48137	63.02888	2.70481

76	114.01214	52.68890	2.16387
77	116.17601	53.14636	2.18596
78	118.36197	53.59921	2.20828
79	120.57025	54.04747	2.23082
80	122.80107	54.49121	2.25359
81	125.05466	54.93046	2.27660
82	127.33127	55.36527	2.29984
83	129.63110	55.79569	2.32332
84	131.95442	56.22176	2.34703
85	134.30145	56.64352	2.37099
86	136.67245	57.06102	2.39520
87	139.06764	57.47431	2.41965
88	141.48729	57.88342	2.44435
89	143.93164	58.28839	2.46930
90	146.40098	58.68927	2.49451
91	148.89546	59.08610	2.51997
92	151.41544	59.47890	2.54570
93	153.96114	59.86777	2.57169
94	156.53282	60.25269	2.59794
95	159.13075	60.63372	2.62446
96	161.75522	61.01090	2.65125
97	164.40646	61.38427	2.67832
98	167.08478	61.75396	2.70566
99	169.79044	62.11972	2.73328
100	172.52371	62.48189	2.76118

Table 1. (continued) Annuities

M	C(11.75,M,12)	A(11.75,M,12)	S(11.75,M,12)	M	C(12.00,M,12)	A(12.00,M,12)	S(12.00,M,12)	M	C(12.25,M,12)	A(12.25,M,12)	S(12.25,M,12)
101	2.67553	63.95667	171.11907	101	2.73186	63.39493	173.18619	101	2.78937	62.84039	175.28490
102	2.70173	64.32681	173.79959	102	2.75918	63.75735	175.91805	102	2.81784	63.19827	178.07428
103	2.72818	64.68335	176.49633	103	2.78677	64.11619	178.67723	103	2.84661	63.54657	180.89211
104	2.75490	65.05634	179.22351	104	2.81464	64.47147	181.46400	104	2.87567	63.89431	183.73871
105	2.78187	65.41581	181.97841	105	2.84279	64.82324	184.27864	105	2.90502	64.23854	186.61438
106	2.80911	65.77190	184.76028	106	2.87121	65.17152	187.12143	106	2.93468	64.57930	189.51941
107	2.83662	66.12433	187.56940	107	2.89993	65.51637	189.99265	107	2.96464	64.91661	192.45409
108	2.86439	66.47344	190.40601	108	2.92893	65.85779	192.89258	108	2.99490	65.25051	195.41872
109	2.89244	66.81917	193.27040	109	2.95821	66.19583	195.82150	109	3.02547	65.58103	198.41362
110	2.92076	67.16154	196.16284	110	2.98780	66.53053	198.77971	110	3.05636	65.90822	201.43909
111	2.94936	67.50060	199.08360	111	3.01768	66.86190	201.76752	111	3.08756	66.23210	204.49544
112	2.97824	67.83637	202.03296	112	3.04785	67.19000	204.78519	112	3.11908	66.55271	207.58301
113	3.00740	68.16888	205.01120	113	3.07833	67.51485	207.83304	113	3.15092	66.87008	210.70207
114	3.03685	68.49817	208.01860	114	3.10911	67.83649	210.91136	114	3.18308	67.18424	213.85300
115	3.06658	68.82427	211.05545	115	3.14020	68.15494	214.02048	115	3.21558	67.49522	217.03607
116	3.09661	69.14720	214.12204	116	3.17161	68.47024	217.16069	116	3.24840	67.80307	220.25165
117	3.12693	69.46700	217.21866	117	3.20332	68.78242	220.33229	117	3.28156	68.10780	223.50006
118	3.15755	69.78371	220.34558	118	3.23536	69.09152	223.53561	118	3.31506	68.40945	226.78162
119	3.18847	70.09734	223.50313	119	3.26771	69.39752	226.77097	119	3.34890	68.70806	230.09668
120	3.21969	70.40792	226.69160	120	3.30039	69.70052	230.03868	120	3.38309	69.00365	233.44559
121	3.25121	70.71550	229.91129	121	3.33339	70.00051	233.33907	121	3.41763	69.29625	236.82867
122	3.28305	71.02010	233.16251	122	3.36672	70.29754	236.67245	122	3.45251	69.58589	240.24631
123	3.31520	71.32174	236.44556	123	3.40039	70.59162	240.03918	123	3.48776	69.87261	243.69882
124	3.34766	71.62045	239.76076	124	3.43440	70.88279	243.43958	124	3.52336	70.15643	247.16658
125	3.38044	71.91628	243.10841	125	3.46874	71.17108	246.87398	125	3.55933	70.43738	250.70995

n			n				n				n	
126	3.41354	72.20923	126	246.48885	3.50343	71.45652	126	250.34271	3.59567	70.71549	126	254.26927
127	3.44695	72.49934	127	249.90239	3.53846	71.73913	127	253.84615	3.63237	70.99080	127	257.86433
128	3.48071	72.79064	128	253.34335	3.57385	72.01894	128	257.39458	3.66945	71.26331	128	261.49731
129	3.51479	73.07114	129	256.83005	3.60968	72.29597	129	260.96844	3.70691	71.53308	129	265.16675
130	3.54921	73.35290	130	260.34485	3.64568	72.57027	130	264.56902	3.74475	71.80013	130	268.87366
131	3.58398	73.63192	131	263.89404	3.68214	72.84186	131	268.21371	3.78298	72.06447	131	272.61841
132	3.61906	73.90823	132	267.47603	3.71896	73.11075	132	271.89584	3.82160	72.32613	132	276.40140
133	3.65449	74.18187	133	271.07708	3.75615	73.37698	133	275.61481	3.86061	72.58516	133	280.22299
134	3.69028	74.45285	134	274.75156	3.79371	73.64057	134	279.37094	3.90002	72.84157	134	284.03359
135	3.72641	74.72121	135	278.44183	3.83165	73.90156	135	283.16464	3.93983	73.09539	135	287.90361
136	3.76290	74.96696	136	282.16824	3.86996	74.15996	136	286.99631	3.98005	73.34664	136	291.92346
137	3.79974	75.25014	137	285.93115	3.90966	74.41580	137	290.86627	4.02068	73.59635	137	295.90350
138	3.83695	75.51076	138	289.73090	3.94775	74.66911	138	294.77433	4.06173	73.84156	138	299.92419
139	3.87452	75.76885	139	293.56784	3.98723	74.91991	139	298.72269	4.10319	74.08527	139	303.98590
140	3.91246	76.02445	140	297.44235	4.02710	75.16823	140	302.70990	4.14508	74.32652	140	308.08911
141	3.95077	76.27757	141	301.35483	4.06737	75.41409	141	306.73700	4.18739	74.56533	141	312.23419
142	3.98945	76.52823	142	305.30557	4.10904	75.65751	142	310.80438	4.23014	74.80173	142	316.42157
143	4.02851	76.77646	143	309.29504	4.14912	75.89852	143	314.91241	4.27332	75.03574	143	320.65170
144	4.06796	77.02228	144	313.32355	4.19062	76.13715	144	319.06155	4.31694	75.26739	144	324.92502
145	4.10779	77.26572	145	317.39151	4.23252	76.37342	145	323.25217	4.36101	75.49669	145	329.24197
146	4.14801	77.50680	146	321.49930	4.27485	76.60735	146	327.48468	4.40553	75.72368	146	333.60300
147	4.18863	77.74554	147	325.64731	4.31760	76.83896	147	331.75952	4.45050	75.94837	147	338.00851
148	4.22964	77.98196	148	329.83594	4.36077	77.06828	148	336.07712	4.49594	76.17079	148	342.45901
149	4.27106	78.21610	149	334.06558	4.40438	77.29532	149	340.43790	4.54183	76.39097	149	346.95496
150	4.31288	78.44797	150	338.33664	4.44842	77.52012	150	344.84229	4.58820	76.60892	150	351.49880

Table 1. (continued) Annuities

M	C(11.75,M,12)	A(11.75,M,12)	S(11.75,M,12)	M	C(12.00,M,12)	A(12.00,M,12)	S(12.00,M,12)	M	C(12.25,M,12)	A(12.25,M,12)	S(12.25,M,12)
151	4.35511	78.87759	342.64964	151	4.49991	77.74269	349.29071	151	4.63503	76.82467	356.08499
152	4.39775	79.90497	347.00464	152	4.53784	77.96306	353.78860	152	4.68235	77.03924	360.72003
153	4.44081	79.13015	351.40237	153	4.59281	78.18325	358.32744	153	4.73015	77.24965	365.40237
154	4.48430	79.35316	355.84320	154	4.62905	78.39728	362.90466	154	4.77844	77.45892	370.13251
155	4.52821	79.57399	360.32751	155	4.67534	78.61117	367.53369	155	4.82722	77.66608	374.91095
156	4.57255	79.79269	364.85571	156	4.72209	78.82294	372.20905	156	4.87649	77.87115	379.73818
157	4.61732	80.00926	369.42825	157	4.76931	79.03261	376.93112	157	4.92627	78.07413	384.61465
158	4.66253	80.22374	374.04556	158	4.81700	79.24020	381.70044	158	4.97656	78.27508	389.54092
159	4.70818	80.43613	378.70810	159	4.86517	79.44575	386.51746	159	5.02737	78.47399	394.51752
160	4.75428	80.64647	383.41629	160	4.91383	79.64925	391.38263	160	5.07969	78.67089	399.54496
161	4.80084	80.85477	388.17056	161	4.96296	79.85075	396.29645	161	5.13053	78.86581	404.62357
162	4.84785	81.06104	392.97141	162	5.01259	80.05025	401.25940	162	5.18291	79.05875	409.75409
163	4.89531	81.26532	397.81924	163	5.06272	80.24777	406.27200	163	5.23582	79.24974	414.86698
164	4.94325	81.46762	402.71457	164	5.11335	80.44334	411.33472	164	5.28926	79.43880	420.17282
165	4.99165	81.66795	407.65781	165	5.16448	80.63696	416.44806	165	5.34326	79.62595	425.46207
166	5.04053	81.86635	412.64948	166	5.21613	80.82868	421.61255	166	5.39790	79.81121	430.80533
167	5.08988	82.06281	417.68997	167	5.26829	81.01849	426.82867	167	5.45291	79.99460	436.20313
168	5.13972	82.25738	422.77988	168	5.32097	81.20643	432.09695	168	5.50857	80.17613	441.65604
169	5.19005	82.45006	427.91959	169	5.37418	81.39250	437.41794	169	5.56481	80.35583	447.16461
170	5.24087	82.64086	433.10962	170	5.42792	81.57674	442.78211	170	5.62161	80.53372	452.72943
171	5.29218	82.82982	438.35049	171	5.48220	81.75915	448.22003	171	5.67900	80.70981	458.35104
172	5.34400	83.01694	443.64267	172	5.53702	81.93975	453.70224	172	5.73697	80.88412	464.03003
173	5.39633	83.20226	448.98669	173	5.59239	82.11856	459.23926	173	5.79554	81.05668	469.76700
174	5.44917	83.38577	454.38303	174	5.64832	82.29561	464.83167	174	5.85470	81.22746	475.56256
175	5.50252	83.56750	459.83218	175	5.70480	82.47089	470.47998	175	5.91447	81.39655	481.41724

n				n				n			
176	465.33472	83.74748	5.55640	176	5.76186	82.64445	476.19478	176	5.97484	81.56391	487.33173
177	470.89111	83.92570	5.61081	177	5.81947	82.81629	481.94662	177	6.03584	81.72959	493.30655
178	476.50192	84.10220	5.66575	178	5.87766	82.98843	487.76608	178	6.09745	81.88359	499.34241
179	482.16766	84.27699	5.72122	179	5.93644	83.15488	493.64374	179	6.15970	82.05594	505.43965
180	487.88889	84.45009	5.77725	180	5.99580	83.32166	499.58017	180	6.22258	82.21664	511.59955
181	493.66614	84.62150	5.83381	181	6.05576	83.48679	505.57599	181	6.28610	82.37572	517.82214
182	499.49994	84.79125	5.89094	182	6.11632	83.65029	511.63174	182	6.35027	82.53320	524.10822
183	505.39087	84.95936	5.94662	183	6.17748	83.81216	517.74805	183	6.41510	82.68908	530.45850
184	511.33961	85.12583	6.00687	184	6.23926	83.97244	523.92554	184	6.49058	82.84338	536.87360
185	517.34637	85.29070	6.06568	185	6.30165	84.13113	530.16479	185	6.54674	82.99613	543.35419
186	523.41205	85.45396	6.12508	186	6.36466	84.28825	536.46643	186	6.61357	83.14734	549.90094
187	529.53711	85.61564	6.18505	187	6.42831	84.44381	542.83112	187	6.68109	83.29701	556.51447
188	535.72217	85.77575	6.24561	188	6.49259	84.59788	549.25940	188	6.74929	83.44518	563.19556
189	541.96777	85.93431	6.30677	189	6.55752	84.75033	555.75201	189	6.81819	83.59184	569.94489
190	548.27454	86.09133	6.36852	190	6.62310	84.90131	562.30961	190	6.88779	83.73703	576.76306
191	554.64307	86.24683	6.43088	191	6.68933	85.05081	568.93262	191	6.95810	83.88074	583.65082
192	561.07397	86.40088	6.49385	192	6.75622	85.19982	575.62196	192	7.02913	84.02301	590.60895
193	567.56781	86.55332	6.55743	193	6.82378	85.34537	582.37817	193	7.10089	84.16394	597.63903
194	574.12524	86.70435	6.62164	194	6.89202	85.49046	589.20197	194	7.17338	84.30325	604.73896
195	580.74689	86.85390	6.68648	195	6.96094	85.63412	596.03099	195	7.24661	84.44124	611.91235
196	587.43335	87.00201	6.75195	196	7.03055	85.77636	603.05498	196	7.32058	84.57784	619.15894
197	594.18530	87.14867	6.81806	197	7.10086	85.91718	610.08545	197	7.39531	84.71306	626.47965
198	601.00336	87.29392	6.88482	198	7.17186	86.05662	617.19628	198	7.47081	84.84692	633.87482
199	607.88818	87.43776	6.95224	199	7.24358	86.19467	624.35815	199	7.54707	84.97942	641.34564
200	614.84045	87.58021	7.02031	200	7.31602	86.33136	631.60175	200	7.62411	85.11058	648.88270

Table 1. (continued) Annuities

M	C(11.75,M,12)	A(11.75,M,12)	S(11.75,M,12)	M	C(12.00,M,12)	A(12.00,M,12)	S(12.00,M,12)	M	C(12.25,M,12)	A(12.25,M,12)	S(12.25,M,12)
201	7.08905	87.72127	621.06078	201	7.38918	86.46669	638.91779	201	7.70194	85.24042	656.51685
202	7.15847	87.86096	628.94983	202	7.46307	86.60069	646.30695	202	7.78057	85.36894	664.21875
203	7.22856	87.99831	636.10828	203	7.53770	86.73335	653.77002	203	7.85999	85.49617	671.99933
204	7.29934	88.13630	643.33685	204	7.61308	86.86470	661.30774	204	7.94023	85.62211	679.85931
205	7.37081	88.27197	650.63617	205	7.68921	86.99426	668.92078	205	8.02129	85.74678	687.79956
206	7.44299	88.40633	658.00696	206	7.76610	87.12352	676.60989	206	8.10317	85.87019	695.82086
207	7.51586	88.53938	665.44995	207	7.84376	87.25101	684.37670	207	8.18589	85.99235	703.92401
208	7.58946	88.67114	672.96582	208	7.92220	87.37724	692.21965	208	8.26945	86.11327	712.10992
209	7.66377	88.80162	680.55530	209	8.00142	87.50221	700.14209	209	8.35387	86.23296	720.37939
210	7.73881	88.93084	688.21906	210	8.08143	87.62595	708.14349	210	8.43915	86.35148	728.73322
211	7.81459	89.05881	695.95789	211	8.16225	87.74847	716.22491	211	8.52530	86.46877	737.17236
212	7.89111	89.18553	703.77248	212	8.24387	87.86977	724.38715	212	8.61233	86.58488	745.69769
213	7.96837	89.31103	711.66357	213	8.32631	87.98988	732.63104	213	8.70025	86.69982	754.31000
214	8.04640	89.43531	719.63196	214	8.40957	88.10879	740.95734	214	8.78906	86.81361	763.01025
215	8.12518	89.55838	727.67834	215	8.49367	88.22652	749.36694	215	8.87879	86.92623	771.79932
216	8.20474	89.68026	735.80353	216	8.57861	88.34309	757.86060	216	8.96942	87.03772	780.67810
217	8.28508	89.80096	744.00824	217	8.66439	88.45850	766.43921	217	9.06099	87.14809	789.64752
218	8.36621	89.92049	752.28933	218	8.75104	88.57278	775.10358	218	9.15348	87.25733	798.70856
219	8.44812	90.03886	760.65965	219	8.83855	88.68592	783.85461	219	9.24692	87.36548	807.96200
220	8.53085	90.15608	769.10767	220	8.92693	88.79794	792.69318	220	9.34132	87.47253	817.10895
221	8.61438	90.27216	777.63855	221	9.01620	88.90885	801.62012	221	9.43668	87.57850	826.45028
222	8.69873	90.38712	786.25287	222	9.10636	89.01866	810.63629	222	9.53301	87.68340	835.88698
223	8.78390	90.50097	794.95160	223	9.19743	89.12739	819.74268	223	9.63033	87.78723	845.41992
224	8.86991	90.61371	803.73553	224	9.28940	89.23503	828.94012	224	9.72864	87.89002	855.05029
225	8.96676	90.72536	812.60541	225	9.38229	89.34162	838.22949	225	9.82795	87.99176	864.77893

n				n				n			
226	9.04446	90.83592	821.56219	226	9.47612	89.44715	847.61182	226	9.99828	88.03250	874.60687
227	9.13302	90.94542	830.60669	227	9.57088	89.55164	857.08789	227	10.12363	88.13220	894.53516
228	9.22245	91.05385	839.73969	228	9.66658	89.65508	866.65881	228	10.13202	88.29090	894.56476
229	9.31275	91.16122	848.56216	229	9.76325	89.75751	876.32539	229	10.23545	88.38960	904.69678
230	9.40394	91.26756	858.27490	230	9.86089	89.85892	886.08862	230	10.33933	88.48531	914.93225
231	9.49602	91.37287	867.67863	231	9.95950	89.95933	895.94952	231	10.44549	88.58105	925.27216
232	9.58900	91.47716	877.17487	232	10.05909	90.05874	905.90900	232	10.55212	88.67581	935.71765
233	9.68290	91.58044	886.76385	233	10.15968	90.15717	915.96814	233	10.65984	88.76962	946.26978
234	9.77771	91.68271	896.44678	234	10.26128	90.25462	926.12781	234	10.76966	88.86249	956.92963
235	9.87345	91.78399	906.22449	235	10.36389	90.35111	936.38910	235	10.87859	88.95441	967.69830
236	9.97013	91.88428	916.09790	236	10.46753	90.44665	946.75299	236	10.98964	89.04540	978.57684
237	10.06775	91.98361	926.06905	237	10.57220	90.54123	957.22052	237	11.10182	89.13548	989.56653
238	10.16633	92.08198	936.13590	238	10.67793	90.63488	967.79272	238	11.21516	89.22465	1000.66833
239	10.26587	92.17939	946.30212	239	10.78471	90.72761	978.47064	239	11.32964	89.31290	1011.88348
240	10.36639	92.27586	956.56799	240	10.89255	90.81941	989.25531	240	11.44530	89.40028	1023.21313
241	10.46793	92.37138	966.93439	241	11.00148	90.91031	1000.14789	241	11.56214	89.49677	1034.65845
242	10.57040	92.46599	977.40228	242	11.11149	91.00031	1011.14435	242	11.68017	89.57239	1046.22058
243	10.67390	92.55968	987.97272	243	11.22261	91.08941	1022.26086	243	11.79940	89.65714	1057.90076
244	10.77841	92.65245	998.64661	244	11.33483	91.17764	1033.48340	244	11.91986	89.74103	1069.70007
245	10.88395	92.74433	1009.42499	245	11.44818	91.26498	1044.81824	245	12.04154	89.82407	1081.62000
246	10.99053	92.83532	1020.30896	246	11.56266	91.35147	1056.26648	246	12.16446	89.90628	1093.66150
247	11.09814	92.92542	1031.29944	247	11.67839	91.43710	1067.82910	247	12.28864	89.98786	1105.82583
248	11.20681	93.01466	1042.39758	248	11.79607	91.52188	1079.50745	248	12.41409	90.06821	1118.11462
249	11.31654	93.10302	1053.60437	249	11.91302	91.60582	1091.30249	249	12.54081	90.14795	1130.52869
250	11.42735	93.19053	1064.92090	250	12.03216	91.68883	1103.21558	250	12.66883	90.22688	1143.06946

Table 1. (continued) Annuities

M	C(11.75,M,12)	A(11.75,M,12)	S(11.75,M,12)	M	C(12.00,M,12)	A(12.00,M,12)	S(12.00,M,12)	M	C(12.25,M,12)	A(12.25,M,12)	S(12.25,M,12)
251	11.53924	93.27719	1076.34827	251	12.15248	91.77122	1115.24768	251	12.79916	90.30502	1155.73828
252	11.65223	93.36301	1087.88757	252	12.27400	91.85269	1127.40015	252	12.92881	90.38237	1168.53650
253	11.76633	93.44900	1099.53979	253	12.39674	91.93336	1139.67419	253	13.06079	90.45893	1181.46533
254	11.88154	93.53217	1111.30615	254	12.52071	92.01323	1152.07092	254	13.19412	90.53472	1194.52612
255	11.99788	93.61552	1123.18762	255	12.64592	92.09231	1164.59155	255	13.32881	90.60975	1207.72021
256	12.11536	93.69805	1135.18555	256	12.77238	92.17060	1177.23755	256	13.46488	90.68401	1221.04907
257	12.23399	93.77979	1147.30090	257	12.90010	92.24812	1190.00989	257	13.60233	90.75753	1234.51392
258	12.35378	93.86074	1159.53491	258	13.02910	92.32487	1202.91003	258	13.74119	90.83031	1248.11621
259	12.47474	93.94090	1171.88867	259	13.15939	92.40086	1215.93909	259	13.88146	90.90234	1261.85742
260	12.59689	94.02029	1184.36340	260	13.29099	92.47610	1229.09851	260	14.02317	90.97366	1275.73889
261	12.72024	94.09890	1196.96033	261	13.42389	92.55059	1242.38953	261	14.16632	91.04424	1289.76208
262	12.84479	94.17675	1209.68054	262	13.55813	92.62435	1255.81335	262	14.31094	91.11412	1303.92834
263	12.97056	94.25385	1222.52527	263	13.69372	92.69738	1269.37146	263	14.45703	91.18330	1318.23938
264	13.09756	94.33020	1235.49685	264	13.83065	92.76968	1283.06519	264	14.60461	91.25176	1332.69629
265	13.22581	94.40581	1248.59338	265	13.96896	92.84127	1296.89587	265	14.75370	91.31964	1347.30090
266	13.35531	94.48069	1261.81921	266	14.10865	92.91215	1310.86487	266	14.90431	91.38663	1362.05469
267	13.48608	94.55484	1275.17456	267	14.24973	92.98233	1324.97351	267	15.05646	91.45306	1376.95898
268	13.61814	94.62827	1288.66064	268	14.39223	93.05180	1339.22327	268	15.21016	91.51880	1392.01538
269	13.75148	94.70099	1302.27801	269	14.53615	93.12060	1353.61548	269	15.36543	91.58389	1407.22559
270	13.88613	94.77300	1316.03027	270	14.68152	93.18871	1368.15161	270	15.52228	91.64831	1422.59106
271	14.02210	94.84432	1329.91638	271	14.82833	93.25615	1382.83313	271	15.69074	91.71207	1438.11328
272	14.15940	94.91495	1343.93848	272	14.97661	93.32292	1397.66150	272	15.84081	91.77521	1453.79407
273	14.29804	94.98489	1358.09790	273	15.12638	93.38903	1412.63806	273	16.00252	91.83770	1469.63489
274	14.43804	95.05415	1372.39687	274	15.27764	93.45448	1427.76440	274	16.16588	91.89955	1485.63733
275	14.57942	95.12273	1386.83398	275	15.43042	93.51929	1443.04211	275	16.33091	91.96078	1501.80322

n									
276	14.72217	95.19066	1401.41333	15.58473	93.58346	1458.47253	16.49762	92.02140	1518.13416
277	14.66633	95.25793	1416.13562	15.74057	93.64699	1474.05725	16.66603	92.08141	1534.63184
278	15.01189	95.32454	1431.00183	15.89798	93.70988	1489.79785	16.83616	92.14090	1551.29785
279	15.15889	95.39051	1446.01379	16.05696	93.77216	1505.69680	17.00903	92.19960	1568.13403
280	15.30732	95.45583	1461.17273	16.21753	93.83383	1521.75281	17.18166	92.25780	1585.14197
281	15.45720	95.52053	1476.47998	16.37970	93.89488	1537.97034	17.35705	92.31541	1602.32373
282	15.60855	95.58459	1491.93713	16.54350	93.95533	1554.34998	17.53424	92.37244	1619.68079
283	15.76139	95.64804	1507.54578	16.70893	94.01517	1570.83343	17.71324	92.42890	1637.21497
284	15.91572	95.71088	1523.30713	16.87602	94.07443	1587.60242	17.89406	92.48478	1654.92822
285	16.07156	95.77309	1539.22290	17.04478	94.13310	1604.47839	18.07673	92.54010	1672.82227
286	16.22892	95.83472	1555.29443	17.21523	94.19118	1621.52319	18.26126	92.59496	1690.89905
287	16.38783	95.89574	1571.52332	17.38738	94.24870	1638.73840	18.44768	92.64907	1709.16028
288	16.54830	95.96616	1587.91113	17.56126	94.30564	1656.12585	18.63600	92.70273	1727.60791
289	16.71033	96.01601	1604.45947	17.73687	94.36202	1673.68713	18.82624	92.75584	1746.24350
290	16.87395	96.07527	1621.16960	17.91424	94.41785	1691.42396	19.01842	92.80843	1765.07019
291	17.03918	96.13396	1638.04370	18.09338	94.47311	1709.33826	19.21257	92.86048	1784.08662
292	17.20602	96.19208	1655.08289	18.27431	94.52783	1727.43164	19.40870	92.91200	1803.30115
293	17.37450	96.24963	1672.28894	18.45706	94.58202	1745.70593	19.60683	92.96301	1822.70984
294	17.54462	96.30663	1689.66345	18.64163	94.63566	1764.16296	19.80698	93.01349	1842.31665
295	17.71641	96.36308	1707.20901	18.82804	94.68877	1782.80457	20.00918	93.06347	1862.12366
296	17.88988	96.41898	1724.92444	19.01633	94.74136	1801.63269	20.21344	93.11294	1882.13281
297	18.06506	96.47433	1742.81433	19.20649	94.79343	1820.64893	20.41978	93.16191	1902.34631
298	18.24194	96.52915	1760.87939	19.39855	94.84497	1839.85547	20.62824	93.21039	1922.76611
299	18.42056	96.58344	1779.12134	19.58254	94.89601	1859.25403	20.83882	93.25808	1943.39429
300	18.60093	96.63720	1797.54187	19.78847	94.94655	1878.84856	21.05155	93.30588	1964.23315

Table 1. (continued) Annuities

M	C(11.75,M,12)	A(11.75,M,12)	S(11.75,M,12)	M	C(12.00,M,12)	A(12.00,M,12)	S(12.00,M,12)	M	C(12.25,M,12)	A(12.25,M,12)	S(12.25,M,12)
301	18.78807	96.69044	1816.14282	301	19.99635	94.99658	1899.63501	301	21.26645	93.35290	1985.28467
302	18.96698	96.74316	1834.92590	302	20.18621	95.04612	1918.62134	302	21.48354	93.39945	2006.55115
303	19.15270	96.79537	1853.89294	303	20.38807	95.09517	1938.80762	303	21.70285	93.44553	2028.03467
304	19.34024	96.84708	1873.04565	304	20.59196	95.14373	1959.19568	304	21.92440	93.49113	2049.73755
305	19.52961	96.89828	1892.38596	305	20.79788	95.19181	1979.78760	305	22.14822	93.53629	2071.66187
306	19.72084	96.94899	1911.91541	306	21.00586	95.23942	2000.58545	306	22.37431	93.58098	2093.81006
307	19.91394	96.99921	1931.63635	307	21.21591	95.28655	2021.59131	307	22.60272	93.62522	2116.18433
308	20.10893	97.04893	1951.55029	308	21.42807	95.33322	2042.60725	308	22.83345	93.66902	2138.78711
309	20.30583	97.09818	1971.65918	309	21.64235	95.37943	2064.23535	309	23.06654	93.71237	2161.62061
310	20.50466	97.14695	1991.96497	310	21.85878	95.42518	2085.87769	310	23.30202	93.75529	2184.68701
311	20.70543	97.19524	2012.46960	311	22.07736	95.47047	2107.73633	311	23.53989	93.79777	2207.98926
312	20.90817	97.24307	2033.17505	312	22.29814	95.51532	2129.81372	312	23.78019	93.83982	2231.52905
313	21.11290	97.29044	2054.08325	313	22.52112	95.55972	2152.11182	313	24.02295	93.88145	2255.30933
314	21.31963	97.33734	2075.19604	314	22.74633	95.60368	2174.63306	314	24.26818	93.92265	2279.33228
315	21.52838	97.38380	2096.51563	315	22.97379	95.64721	2197.37939	315	24.51592	93.96344	2303.60034
316	21.73918	97.42979	2118.04419	316	23.20353	95.69031	2220.35327	316	24.76619	94.00382	2328.11621
317	21.95205	97.47535	2139.78320	317	23.43557	95.73298	2243.55664	317	25.01901	94.04379	2352.88257
318	22.16699	97.52046	2161.73535	318	23.66992	95.77522	2266.99219	318	25.27401	94.08336	2377.90137
319	22.38404	97.56513	2183.90234	319	23.90662	95.81705	2290.66211	319	25.53242	94.12252	2403.17578
320	22.60322	97.60938	2206.28638	320	24.14569	95.85847	2314.56885	320	25.79306	94.16129	2428.70825
321	22.82454	97.65319	2228.88965	321	24.38715	95.89948	2338.71460	321	26.05637	94.19967	2454.50146
322	23.04803	97.69658	2251.71411	322	24.63102	95.94007	2363.10156	322	26.32236	94.23766	2480.55786
323	23.27371	97.73955	2274.76221	323	24.87733	95.98027	2387.73267	323	26.59107	94.27527	2506.88013
324	23.50160	97.78210	2298.03589	324	25.12610	96.02007	2412.61011	324	26.86252	94.31249	2533.47119
325	23.73172	97.82423	2321.53760	325	25.37736	96.05948	2437.73608	325	27.13674	94.34934	2560.33374

326	22.18419	97.18596	2340.26196	326	25.63113	326	96.09849	2463.11353	326	27.41376	326	94.38592	2587.47046
327	24.19874	97.30729	2369.23340	327	25.87745	327	96.13712	2488.74463	327	27.63961	327	94.42193	2614.88428
328	24.43569	97.94821	2393.43213	328	26.14632	328	96.17537	2514.63208	328	27.97631	328	94.45767	2642.57788
329	24.67496	97.98874	2417.06768	329	26.40778	329	96.21323	2540.77832	329	28.26191	329	94.43306	2670.55420
330	24.91656	98.02887	2442.54272	330	26.67196	330	96.25072	2567.10604	330	28.55041	330	94.52808	2698.81592
331	25.16054	98.06861	2467.45923	331	26.93858	331	96.28785	2593.85791	331	28.84187	331	94.56276	2727.36646
332	25.40690	98.10797	2492.61987	332	27.20797	332	96.32460	2620.79963	332	29.13629	332	94.59708	2756.20825
333	25.65568	98.14695	2518.02661	333	27.49005	333	96.36099	2648.00464	333	29.43373	333	94.66468	2785.34473
334	25.90689	98.18555	2543.68237	334	27.75485	334	96.39702	2675.48462	334	29.73420	334	94.69799	2814.77832
335	26.16056	98.22378	2569.58936	335	28.03239	335	96.43269	2703.23950	335	30.03773	335	94.73093	2844.51245
336	26.41672	98.26163	2596.74976	336	28.31272	336	96.46802	2731.27197	336	30.34437	336	94.76355	2874.55029
337	26.67538	98.29912	2622.16650	337	28.59585	337	96.50298	2759.58447	337	30.65413	337	94.79685	2904.89453
338	26.93658	98.33624	2648.84204	338	28.88181	338	96.53761	2788.19042	338	30.96706	338	94.82781	2935.54883
339	27.20033	98.37301	2675.77856	339	29.17062	339	96.57189	2817.06226	339	31.28318	339	94.86945	2966.51587
340	27.46667	98.40942	2702.97876	340	29.46233	340	96.60583	2846.23291	340	31.60253	340	94.90078	2997.79907
341	27.73561	98.44547	2730.44556	341	29.75696	341	96.63943	2875.69507	341	31.92514	341	94.92178	3029.40161
342	28.00719	98.48118	2758.18115	342	30.05452	342	96.67271	2905.45215	342	32.25104	342	94.96248	3061.32666
343	28.28143	98.51653	2786.18823	343	30.35507	343	96.70565	2935.50659	343	32.58027	343	94.98298	3093.57764
344	28.55835	98.55155	2814.46973	344	30.65862	344	96.73827	2965.86182	344	32.91286	344	95.01294	3126.15796
345	28.83798	98.58623	2843.02808	345	30.96520	345	96.77056	2996.52026	345	33.24885	345	95.04271	3159.07080
346	29.12036	98.62057	2871.06621	346	31.27486	346	96.80254	3027.48560	346	33.58928	346	95.07218	3192.31982
347	29.40549	98.65457	2900.98657	347	31.58760	347	96.83420	3058.76050	347	33.93114	347	95.10136	3225.90796
348	29.69342	98.68826	2930.39185	348	31.90348	348	96.86554	3090.34750	348	34.27752	348	95.13023	3259.83911
349	29.98417	98.72160	2960.08545	349	32.22252	349	96.89658	3122.05146	349	34.62744	349	95.15982	3294.11670
350	30.27777	98.75463	2990.06968	350	32.54474	350	96.92730	3154.47412	350	34.96098	350		3328.74414

Table 1. (continued) Annuities

M	C(11.75,M,12)	A(11.75,M,12)	S(11.75,M,12)	M	C(12.00,M,12)	A(12.00,M,12)	S(12.00,M,12)	M	C(12.25,M,12)	A(12.25,M,12)	S(12.25,M,12)
351	30.57423	96.78734	3020.34741	351	32.87019	96.96773	3187.01880	351	35.33902	96.18712	3363.72510
352	30.87361	96.81973	3050.92163	352	33.19889	96.98785	3219.88892	352	35.69677	96.21513	3399.06299
353	31.17591	96.85157	3081.79617	353	33.53088	97.01767	3253.08789	353	36.04134	96.24286	3434.76172
354	31.48117	96.88357	3112.97119	354	33.86619	97.04720	3286.61965	354	36.43134	96.27031	3470.82495
355	31.78943	96.91502	3144.45215	355	34.20485	97.07642	3320.48496	355	36.80324	96.29748	3507.25635
356	32.10070	96.94617	3176.24170	356	34.54690	97.10538	3354.68970	356	37.17894	96.32438	3544.05957
357	32.41502	96.97703	3208.34229	357	34.89236	97.13404	3389.23657	357	37.55848	96.35101	3581.23853
358	32.73241	99.00758	3240.75732	358	35.24129	97.16241	3424.12891	358	37.94189	96.37736	3618.79712
359	33.05292	99.03783	3273.48975	359	35.59370	97.19051	3459.37036	359	38.32921	96.40345	3656.73901
360	33.37656	99.06779	3306.54272	360	35.94964	97.21833	3494.96411	360	38.72049	96.42928	3695.06812
361	33.70338	99.09747	3339.91919	361	36.30914	97.24586	3530.91357	361	39.11576	96.45484	3733.78857
362	34.03339	99.12685	3373.62256	362	36.67223	97.27314	3567.22290	362	39.51506	96.48015	3772.90430
363	34.36663	99.15594	3407.65601	363	37.03895	97.30013	3603.89502	363	39.91845	96.50520	3812.41943
364	34.70314	99.18476	3442.02271	364	37.40934	97.32687	3640.93408	364	40.32595	96.53000	3852.33789
365	35.04294	99.21329	3476.72583	365	37.78343	97.35333	3678.34326	365	40.73761	96.55454	3892.66382
366	35.38607	99.24155	3511.76880	366	38.16127	97.37954	3716.12671	366	41.15347	96.57864	3933.40137
367	35.73256	99.26955	3547.15479	367	38.54288	97.40549	3754.26909	367	41.57358	96.60290	3974.55493
368	36.08244	99.29726	3582.88745	368	38.92831	97.43118	3792.63081	368	41.99798	96.62671	4016.12842
369	36.43575	99.32471	3618.96997	369	39.31759	97.45660	3831.75928	369	42.42671	96.65028	4058.12646
370	36.79251	99.35188	3655.40552	370	39.71077	97.48179	3871.07690	370	42.85984	96.67361	4100.55322
371	37.15277	99.37880	3692.19800	371	40.10788	97.50672	3910.78760	371	43.29734	96.69670	4143.41309
372	37.51656	99.40546	3729.35083	372	40.50896	97.53140	3950.40551	372	43.73933	96.71957	4186.71045
373	37.88391	99.43185	3766.86743	373	40.91404	97.55585	3991.40430	373	44.18584	96.74220	4230.44971
374	38.25486	99.45799	3804.75146	374	41.32318	97.58005	4032.31836	374	44.63691	96.76460	4274.63525
375	38.62944	99.48388	3843.00610	375	41.73642	97.60400	4073.64160	375	45.09257	96.78678	4319.27246

376	39.00768	99.50951	3881.63574	42.15378	376	97.62773	4115.37793	376	45.55289	95.80873	4364.36475
377	39.38963	99.53490	3920.64331	42.57532	377	97.65121	4157.53174	377	46.01791	95.83046	4409.97797
378	39.77532	99.56004	3960.03296	43.00107	378	97.67447	4200.10693	378	46.48768	95.85197	4455.93555
379	40.16479	99.58494	3998.80835	43.43108	379	97.69749	4243.10791	379	46.96224	95.87327	4502.42334
380	40.55807	99.60960	4039.97314	43.86539	380	97.72029	4286.53906	380	47.44165	95.89435	4549.38574
381	40.95520	99.63401	4080.53125	44.30405	381	97.74287	4330.40479	381	47.92596	95.91521	4596.82715
382	41.35622	99.65820	4121.49633	44.74709	382	97.76521	4374.70850	382	48.41519	95.93587	4644.75342
383	41.76117	99.68214	4162.84229	45.19456	383	97.78734	4419.45557	383	48.90943	95.95631	4693.16946
384	42.17008	99.70585	4204.60352	45.64650	384	97.80925	4464.65039	384	49.40871	95.97655	4742.07764
385	42.58299	99.72933	4246.77393	46.10297	385	97.83094	4510.29688	385	49.91309	95.99658	4791.40633
386	42.99995	99.75259	4289.35693	46.56400	386	97.85242	4556.39990	386	50.42262	96.01642	4841.39941
387	43.42099	99.77562	4332.35645	47.02964	387	97.87368	4602.96387	387	50.93735	96.03605	4891.82227
388	43.84616	99.79843	4375.77783	47.49994	388	97.89473	4649.99316	388	51.45734	96.05548	4942.75977
389	44.27548	99.82101	4419.62402	47.97493	389	97.91557	4697.49316	389	51.98263	96.07472	4994.21680
390	44.70901	99.84338	4463.89941	48.45468	390	97.93621	4745.46826	390	52.51329	96.09377	5046.19971
391	45.14679	99.86553	4508.60840	48.93923	391	97.95664	4793.92285	391	53.04386	96.11261	5098.71289
392	45.58885	99.88747	4553.75488	49.42862	392	97.97688	4842.86230	392	53.59091	96.13127	5151.76221
393	46.03524	99.90919	4599.34375	49.92291	393	97.99691	4892.29102	393	54.13798	96.14974	5205.35303
394	46.48600	99.93070	4645.37939	50.42214	394	98.01674	4942.21387	394	54.69064	96.16803	5259.45121
395	46.94118	99.95200	4691.86523	50.92636	395	98.03638	4992.63574	395	55.24894	96.18613	5314.18164
396	47.40081	99.97310	4738.80664	51.43562	396	98.05582	5043.56201	396	55.81294	96.20405	5369.43066
397	47.86494	99.99400	4786.20703	51.94998	397	98.07507	5094.99805	397	56.38270	96.22178	5425.24365
398	48.33362	100.01468	4834.07227	52.46948	398	98.09412	5146.94775	398	56.95827	96.23934	5481.62646
399	48.80689	100.03517	4882.43579	52.99417	399	98.11300	5199.41748	399	57.53972	96.25672	5538.58447
400	49.28479	100.05546	4931.21289	53.52412	400	98.13168	5252.41162	400	58.12710	96.27392	5598.12451

Table 1. (continued) Annuities

N	C(11.75,M,12)	A(11.75,M,12)	S(11.75,M,12)	N	C(12.00,M,12)	A(12.00,M,12)	S(12.00,M,12)	N	C(12.25,M,12)	A(12.25,M,12)	S(12.25,M,12)
401	49.76737	100.07555	4980.49756	401	54.05936	98.15018	5305.93555	401	58.72049	96.29095	5654.25146
402	50.25468	100.08545	5030.26465	402	54.59995	98.16860	5359.99612	402	59.31992	96.30781	5712.97217
403	50.74675	100.11516	5080.51963	403	55.14596	98.18663	5414.59473	403	59.92548	96.32449	5772.29199
404	51.24365	100.13487	5131.26611	404	55.69741	98.20458	5469.74072	404	60.53722	96.34112	5832.21729
405	51.74541	100.15400	5182.50977	405	56.25438	98.22236	5525.43848	405	61.15520	96.35737	5892.75439
406	52.25208	100.17313	5234.25537	406	56.81693	98.23996	5581.69897	406	61.77950	96.37355	5953.90967
407	52.76372	100.19209	5286.50732	407	57.38510	98.25739	5638.50977	407	62.41016	96.38958	6015.68945
408	53.28036	100.21106	5339.27100	408	57.95895	98.27464	5696.89453	408	63.04726	96.40544	6078.09961
409	53.80207	100.22945	5392.55178	409	58.53854	98.29172	5755.85352	409	63.69087	96.42113	6141.14648
410	54.32888	100.24785	5446.35352	410	59.12392	98.30863	5812.39209	410	64.34105	96.43668	6204.83740
411	54.86085	100.26608	5500.68262	411	59.71516	98.32538	5871.51611	411	64.99786	96.45206	6269.17871
412	55.39803	100.28413	5555.54385	412	60.31231	98.34196	5931.23145	412	65.66138	96.46728	6334.17627
413	55.94047	100.30201	5610.94141	413	60.91544	98.35838	5991.54346	413	66.33168	96.48237	6399.83789
414	56.48822	100.31971	5666.88184	414	61.52459	98.37463	6052.45898	414	67.00881	96.49729	6466.16943
415	57.04133	100.33724	5723.37012	415	62.13984	98.39072	6113.98340	415	67.69286	96.51207	6533.17822
416	57.59986	100.35460	5780.41162	416	62.76123	98.40665	6176.12354	416	68.38390	96.52669	6600.87109
417	58.16386	100.37180	5838.01123	417	63.38885	98.42243	6238.88477	417	69.08199	96.54117	6669.25537
418	58.73338	100.38882	5896.17529	418	64.02274	98.43805	6302.27344	418	69.78719	96.55550	6738.33691
419	59.30848	100.40569	5954.90869	419	64.66296	98.45351	6366.29639	419	70.49960	96.56968	6808.12451
420	59.88921	100.42238	6014.21690	420	65.30959	98.46883	6430.96899	420	71.21928	96.58372	6878.62402
421	60.47562	100.43891	6074.10596	421	65.96268	98.48399	6496.26304	421	71.94631	96.59762	6949.84326
422	61.06778	100.45529	6134.58203	422	66.62231	98.49900	6562.23145	422	72.58076	96.61138	7021.78955
423	61.66574	100.47150	6195.64941	423	67.28854	98.51386	6628.85400	423	73.42271	96.62500	7094.47021
424	62.26955	100.48756	6257.31543	424	67.96143	98.52857	6696.14258	424	74.17224	96.63848	7167.89307
425	62.87927	100.50347	6319.58496	425	68.64104	98.54314	6764.10400	425	74.92941	96.65182	7242.06543

426	63.49496	100.51922	6382.46436	426	69.32745	98.55756	6832.74463	426	75.69432	96.66504	7316.99463
427	64.11668	100.53481	6445.95898	427	70.02072	98.57165	6902.07227	427	76.46703	96.67812	7392.66896
428	64.74449	100.55026	6510.07568	428	70.72093	98.58599	6972.09277	428	77.24763	96.69106	7469.15625
429	65.37845	100.56556	6574.82031	429	71.42814	98.59999	7042.81396	429	78.03620	96.70387	7546.40381
430	66.01861	100.58070	6640.19873	430	72.14242	98.61385	7114.24219	430	78.83282	96.71656	7624.43994
431	66.66505	100.59570	6706.21729	431	72.86385	98.62757	7186.38428	431	79.63757	96.72912	7703.27295
432	67.31760	100.61056	6772.88232	432	73.59248	98.64116	7259.24854	432	80.45054	96.74155	7782.91016
433	67.97696	100.62527	6840.20020	433	74.32841	98.65462	7332.84082	433	81.27160	96.75385	7863.36084
434	68.64257	100.63984	6908.17725	434	75.07169	98.66794	7407.16943	434	82.10148	96.76603	7944.63281
435	69.31469	100.65427	6976.81982	435	75.82241	98.68112	7482.24072	435	82.93568	96.77809	8026.73389
436	69.99340	100.66855	7046.13428	436	76.58064	98.69418	7558.06348	436	83.78625	96.79002	8109.67383
437	70.67875	100.68270	7116.12793	437	77.34644	98.70712	7634.64404	437	84.64157	96.80164	8193.45996
438	71.37081	100.69671	7186.80664	438	78.11990	98.71991	7711.98023	438	85.50562	96.81353	8278.10156
439	72.06965	100.71059	7258.17725	439	78.90110	98.73259	7789.11035	439	86.37849	96.82511	8363.60645
440	72.77534	100.72433	7330.24707	440	79.69012	98.74513	7869.01123	440	87.26027	96.83657	8449.96535
441	73.48792	100.73794	7403.02246	441	80.48701	98.75756	7948.70166	441	88.15105	96.84792	8537.24609
442	74.20750	100.75141	7476.51025	442	81.29189	98.76986	8029.18848	442	89.05033	96.85915	8625.39648
443	74.93411	100.76478	7550.71777	443	82.10480	98.78204	8110.48047	443	89.95999	96.87026	8714.44727
444	75.66784	100.77797	7625.65186	444	82.92585	98.79410	8192.58496	444	90.87833	96.88126	8804.40723
445	76.40875	100.79108	7701.31982	445	83.75511	98.80604	8275.51074	445	91.80605	96.89216	8895.28613
446	77.15692	100.80402	7777.72852	446	84.59266	98.81786	8359.26563	446	92.74323	96.90294	8987.09160
447	77.91242	100.81686	7854.88525	447	85.43859	98.82957	8443.85040	447	93.68999	96.91361	9079.83436
448	78.67531	100.82957	7932.79785	448	86.29298	98.84116	8529.29688	448	94.64641	96.92418	9173.52539
449	79.44567	100.84216	8011.47314	449	87.15591	98.85263	8615.58984	449	95.61259	96.93464	9268.17188
450	80.22358	100.85461	8090.91895	450	88.02747	98.86399	8702.74609	450	96.58963	96.94499	9363.78418

Table 1. (continued) Annuities

M	C(11.75,M,12)	A(11.75,M,12)	S(11.75,M,12)	C(12.00,M,12)	A(12.00,M,12)	S(12.00,M,12)	C(12.25,M,12)	A(12.25,M,12)	S(12.25,M,12)
451	81.00910	100.86606	8171.14258	88.90774	98.87524	8790.77344	97.57464	96.95524	9460.37305
452	81.80231	100.87919	8252.15137	89.73681	98.88637	8879.61864	98.57072	96.96593	9557.94727
453	82.60329	100.89130	8333.95410	90.64079	98.89740	8969.47852	99.57636	96.97543	9656.51755
454	83.41212	100.90328	8416.55664	91.60173	98.90832	9060.17285	100.59348	96.98537	9756.09570
455	84.22887	100.91515	8499.96875	92.51775	98.91912	9151.77441	101.62036	96.99521	9856.68848
456	85.05360	100.92691	8584.19824	93.44090	98.92982	9244.29199	102.65774	97.00496	9958.30859
457	85.88642	100.93855	8669.25195	94.37736	98.94042	9337.73535	103.70570	97.01460	10060.96980
458	86.72739	100.95009	8755.13770	95.32113	98.95091	9432.11230	104.76437	97.02414	10164.67285
459	87.57660	100.96150	8841.86523	96.27434	98.96130	9527.43359	105.83384	97.03358	10269.43652
460	88.43412	100.97281	8929.44238	97.23708	98.97158	9623.70801	106.91422	97.04294	10375.27051
461	89.30004	100.98401	9017.87598	98.20946	98.98177	9720.94531	108.00564	97.05220	10482.18457
462	90.17443	100.99510	9107.17578	99.19155	98.99184	9819.15430	109.10820	97.06136	10590.19043
463	91.05740	101.00608	9197.35059	100.18346	99.00183	9918.34668	110.22201	97.07043	10699.29883
464	91.94900	101.01696	9288.40820	101.18530	99.01171	10018.52930	111.34719	97.07941	10809.52051
465	92.84933	101.02773	9380.35742	102.19715	99.02149	10119.71484	112.48386	97.08831	10920.86016
466	93.75848	101.03839	9473.20605	103.21912	99.03118	10221.91211	113.63213	97.09711	11033.35156
467	94.67653	101.04896	9566.96484	104.25131	99.04078	10325.13184	114.79213	97.10582	11146.98438
468	95.60357	101.05942	9661.64160	105.28383	99.05027	10429.38281	115.96397	97.11444	11261.77637
469	96.53969	101.06977	9757.24512	106.34676	99.05968	10534.67676	117.14777	97.12298	11377.74023
470	97.48498	101.08003	9853.78418	107.41023	99.06899	10641.02344	118.34365	97.13143	11494.88770
471	98.43951	101.09019	9951.26953	108.48434	99.07820	10748.43359	119.55174	97.13979	11613.23145
472	99.40340	101.10025	10049.70898	109.56918	99.08733	10856.91797	120.77216	97.14807	11732.78320
473	100.37672	101.11021	10149.11230	110.66487	99.09637	10966.48730	122.00564	97.15627	11853.55566
474	101.35958	101.12008	10249.48926	111.77152	99.10532	11077.15234	123.25051	97.16438	11975.56055
475	102.35207	101.12984	10350.84863	112.88924	99.11417	11188.92383	124.50870	97.17242	12098.81055

idx				idx			idx			idx		
476	103.35426	101.13953	10453.20117	476	114.01813	99.12294	476	11301.81250	97.18037	476	125.77972	12223.31384
477	104.36627	101.14911	10556.55469	477	115.15831	99.13163	477	11415.83105	97.18823	477	127.06373	12349.09961
478	105.38819	101.15859	10660.98188	478	116.30989	99.14022	478	11530.98826	97.19602	478	128.36082	12476.16309
479	106.42011	101.16799	10766.30967	479	117.47289	99.14874	479	11647.29883	97.20374	479	129.67117	12604.52441
480	107.46214	101.17730	10872.72949	480	118.64772	99.15717	480	11764.77246	97.21137	480	130.99430	12734.19531
481	108.51438	101.18651	10980.19838	481	119.83420	99.16551	481	11883.41992	97.21893	481	132.33215	12865.19043
482	109.57692	101.19564	11088.70605	482	121.03254	99.17377	482	12003.25391	97.22641	482	133.68304	12997.52246
483	110.64986	101.20467	11198.28320	483	122.24287	99.18195	483	12124.29613	97.23381	483	135.04771	13131.20508
484	111.73331	101.21362	11308.93262	484	123.46529	99.19005	484	12246.52300	97.24114	484	136.42633	13266.25293
485	112.82736	101.22249	11420.66602	485	124.69995	99.19807	485	12369.99512	97.24840	485	137.81902	13402.67969
486	113.93213	101.23126	11533.49414	486	125.94695	99.20601	486	12494.89434	97.25558	486	139.22592	13540.49905
487	115.04771	101.23996	11647.42578	487	127.20641	99.21387	487	12620.64160	97.26269	487	140.64719	13679.72461
488	116.17422	101.24857	11762.47363	488	128.47847	99.22166	488	12747.84766	97.26973	488	142.08236	13820.37109
489	117.31176	101.25709	11878.64746	489	129.76326	99.22936	489	12876.32617	97.27670	489	143.53339	13962.45410
490	118.46044	101.26553	11995.95996	490	131.06090	99.23699	490	13006.08984	97.28359	490	144.99863	14105.99828
491	119.62036	101.27389	12114.41992	491	132.37151	99.24454	491	13137.15039	97.29042	491	146.47882	14250.99633
492	120.79165	101.28217	12234.04004	492	133.69522	99.25203	492	13269.52246	97.29718	492	147.97412	14397.46582
493	121.97440	101.29037	12354.83203	493	135.03217	99.25945	493	13403.21777	97.30387	493	149.48470	14545.43945
494	123.16873	101.29848	12476.80664	494	136.38249	99.26676	494	13538.25000	97.31049	494	151.01068	14694.92383
495	124.37476	101.30653	12599.89746	495	137.74632	99.27402	495	13674.63164	97.31705	495	152.55225	14845.33457
496	125.59260	101.31449	12724.34961	496	139.12378	99.28121	496	13812.37793	97.32353	496	154.10956	14998.48730
497	126.82236	101.32237	12849.94238	497	140.51501	99.28833	497	13961.50196	97.32996	497	155.68275	15152.59868
498	128.06415	101.33018	12976.76465	498	141.92017	99.29537	498	14092.01758	97.33632	498	157.27202	15308.27300
499	129.31812	101.33791	13104.80249	499	143.33937	99.30235	499	14233.35750	97.34261	499	158.87750	15465.55176
500	130.58435	101.34557	13234.14746	500	144.77277	99.30926	500	14377.27637	97.34884	500	160.49937	15624.42871

Table 1. (continued) Annuities

M	C(12.50,M,12)	A(12.50,M,12)	S(12.50,M,12)	M	C(12.75,M,12)	A(12.75,M,12)	S(12.75,M,12)	M	C(13.00,M,12)	A(13.00,M,12)	S(13.00,M,12)
1	1.01042	0.98969	1.00000	1	1.01062	0.98949	1.00000	1	1.01083	0.98928	1.00000
2	1.02094	1.96918	2.01042	2	1.02136	1.96787	2.01062	2	1.02178	1.96796	2.01083
3	1.03158	2.93857	3.03136	3	1.03221	2.93736	3.03199	3	1.03285	2.93615	3.03262
4	1.04232	3.89796	4.06293	4	1.04318	3.89597	4.06420	4	1.04404	3.89397	4.06547
5	1.05318	4.84747	5.10526	5	1.05427	4.84449	5.10738	5	1.05535	4.84152	5.10951
6	1.06415	5.78719	6.15844	6	1.06547	5.78305	6.16165	6	1.06679	5.77892	6.16487
7	1.07524	6.71722	7.22259	7	1.07679	6.71174	7.22712	7	1.07834	6.70626	7.23165
8	1.08644	7.63766	8.29782	8	1.08823	7.63066	8.30391	8	1.09002	7.62367	8.30999
9	1.09775	8.54861	9.38426	9	1.09979	8.53992	9.39213	9	1.10183	8.53125	9.40002
10	1.10919	9.45017	10.48201	10	1.11148	9.43963	10.49193	10	1.11377	9.42910	10.50185
11	1.12074	10.34244	11.59120	11	1.12329	10.32987	11.60340	11	1.12584	10.31733	11.61562
12	1.13242	11.22550	12.71194	12	1.13522	11.21076	12.72669	12	1.13803	11.19604	12.74146
13	1.14421	12.09947	13.84436	13	1.14728	12.08238	13.86191	13	1.15036	12.06533	13.87949
14	1.15613	12.96442	14.98857	14	1.15947	12.94484	15.00919	14	1.16282	12.92531	15.02986
15	1.16817	13.82046	16.14470	15	1.17179	13.79824	16.16866	15	1.17542	13.77607	16.19268
16	1.18034	14.66767	17.31287	16	1.18424	14.64266	17.34046	16	1.18815	14.61771	17.36810
17	1.19264	15.50615	18.49322	17	1.19682	15.47820	18.52470	17	1.20103	15.45033	18.55625
18	1.20506	16.33598	19.68585	18	1.20954	16.30496	19.72153	18	1.21404	16.27403	19.75728
19	1.21761	17.15726	20.89091	19	1.22239	17.12303	20.93107	19	1.22719	17.08890	20.97131
20	1.23030	17.97007	22.10853	20	1.23538	17.93250	22.15346	20	1.24048	17.89504	22.19850
21	1.24311	18.77450	23.33883	21	1.24851	18.73346	23.38884	21	1.25392	18.69253	23.43899
22	1.25606	19.57064	24.58194	22	1.26177	19.52599	24.63735	22	1.26751	19.48149	24.69291
23	1.26915	20.35857	25.83800	23	1.27518	20.31020	25.89912	23	1.28124	20.26198	25.96042
24	1.28237	21.13838	27.10715	24	1.28873	21.08620	27.17430	24	1.29512	21.03411	27.24165
25	1.29572	21.91015	28.38951	25	1.30242	21.85896	28.46302	25	1.30915	21.79797	28.53677

n				n				n			
26	1.30922	22.67396	29.68524	26	1.31626	22.61969	29.76544	26	1.32333	22.55363	29.84592
27	1.32296	23.42990	30.99446	27	1.33024	23.36543	31.08170	27	1.33767	23.30120	31.16925
28	1.33664	24.17805	32.31731	28	1.34438	24.10927	32.41194	28	1.35216	24.04076	32.50692
29	1.35056	24.91848	33.65395	29	1.35866	24.84929	33.75632	29	1.36681	24.77240	33.85907
30	1.36463	25.65128	35.00452	30	1.37310	25.57357	35.11498	30	1.38161	25.49619	35.22588
31	1.37885	26.37652	36.36914	31	1.38769	26.29419	36.48808	31	1.39658	26.21222	36.60748
32	1.39321	27.09429	37.74799	32	1.40243	27.00724	37.87576	32	1.41171	26.92058	38.00408
33	1.40772	27.80466	39.14120	33	1.41733	27.71279	39.27819	33	1.42700	27.62135	39.41579
34	1.42238	28.50771	40.54892	34	1.43239	28.41092	40.69552	34	1.44246	28.31461	40.84279
35	1.43720	29.20350	41.97131	35	1.44761	29.10172	42.12791	35	1.45809	29.00044	42.28526
36	1.45217	29.89213	43.40850	36	1.46299	29.78525	43.57552	36	1.47389	29.67892	43.74335
37	1.46730	30.57365	44.86068	37	1.47853	30.46160	45.03851	37	1.48986	30.35012	45.21723
38	1.48258	31.24815	46.32798	38	1.49424	31.13083	46.51705	38	1.50599	31.01414	46.70708
39	1.49803	31.91569	47.81056	39	1.51012	31.79303	48.01129	39	1.52231	31.67103	48.21308
40	1.51363	32.57635	49.30859	40	1.52616	32.44827	49.52141	40	1.53880	32.32089	49.73539
41	1.52940	33.23021	50.82822	41	1.54238	33.09661	51.04758	41	1.55547	32.96378	51.27419
42	1.54533	33.87732	52.35162	42	1.55877	33.73815	52.58996	42	1.57232	33.59978	52.82966
43	1.56143	34.51778	53.89695	43	1.57533	34.37294	54.14872	43	1.58935	34.22897	54.40198
44	1.57769	35.15160	55.45837	44	1.59207	35.00105	55.72405	44	1.60657	34.85141	55.99133
45	1.59413	35.77890	57.03606	45	1.60898	35.62256	57.31612	45	1.62398	35.46719	57.59791
46	1.61073	36.39973	58.63019	46	1.62608	36.23753	58.92511	46	1.64157	36.07636	59.22189
47	1.62751	37.01417	60.24092	47	1.64336	36.84605	60.55119	47	1.65535	36.67900	60.86345
48	1.64446	37.62227	61.86843	48	1.66082	37.44816	62.19454	48	1.67733	37.27519	62.52281
49	1.66159	38.22411	63.51289	49	1.67846	38.04394	63.85536	49	1.69650	37.86498	64.20013
50	1.67880	38.81973	65.17448	50	1.69630	38.63346	65.53382	50	1.71387	38.44846	65.89564

Table 1. (continued) Annuities

M	C(12.50,M,12)	A(12.50,M,12)	S(12.50,M,12)	M	C(12.75,M,12)	A(12.75,M,12)	S(12.75,M,12)	M	C(13.00,M,12)	A(13.00,M,12)	S(13.00,M,12)
51	1.69639	39.40922	66.85339	51	1.71432	39.21678	67.23012	51	1.73244	39.02568	67.60950
52	1.71406	39.99263	68.54977	52	1.73253	39.73897	68.94444	52	1.75120	39.58672	69.34194
53	1.73191	40.57003	70.26383	53	1.75094	40.30021	70.67637	53	1.77018	40.16163	71.03015
54	1.74996	41.14147	71.99575	54	1.76955	40.50049	72.42792	54	1.78974	40.72049	72.86333
55	1.76818	41.70702	73.74570	55	1.78835	41.48938	74.19746	55	1.80674	41.27337	74.65268
56	1.78660	42.26674	75.51389	56	1.80735	42.04268	75.98581	56	1.82633	41.82031	76.46142
57	1.80521	42.82069	77.30049	57	1.82655	42.59016	77.79316	57	1.84814	42.36140	78.28975
58	1.82402	43.36898	79.10571	58	1.84596	43.13189	79.61971	58	1.86816	42.89668	80.13789
59	1.84302	43.91152	80.92973	59	1.86557	43.66791	81.46567	59	1.88840	43.42623	82.00605
60	1.86222	44.44852	82.77274	60	1.88539	44.19831	83.33125	60	1.90886	43.95010	83.89445
61	1.88161	44.97997	84.63496	61	1.90543	44.72312	85.21664	61	1.92954	44.46836	85.80330
62	1.90121	45.50595	86.51657	62	1.92567	45.24242	87.12206	62	1.95044	44.98107	87.73284
63	1.92102	46.02651	88.41779	63	1.94613	45.75626	89.04774	63	1.97157	45.48828	89.68327
64	1.94103	46.54170	90.33881	64	1.96681	46.26470	90.99387	64	1.99298	45.99006	91.65485
65	1.96125	47.05158	92.27983	65	1.98771	46.76779	92.96068	65	2.01452	46.48645	93.64777
66	1.98168	47.55620	94.24108	66	2.00883	47.26559	94.94839	66	2.03634	46.97733	95.66229
67	2.00232	48.05563	96.22276	67	2.03017	47.75616	96.95721	67	2.05840	47.46334	97.69963
68	2.02318	48.54990	98.22508	68	2.05174	48.24556	98.98738	68	2.08070	47.94395	99.75703
69	2.04425	49.03907	100.24826	69	2.07354	48.72782	101.03912	69	2.10324	48.41941	101.83774
70	2.06555	49.52320	102.29251	70	2.09557	49.20502	103.11266	70	2.12603	48.88977	103.94098
71	2.08706	50.00235	104.35906	71	2.11784	49.67912	105.20824	71	2.14906	49.35509	106.06701
72	2.10880	50.47655	106.44512	72	2.14034	50.14441	107.32607	72	2.17234	49.81542	108.21606
73	2.13077	50.94587	108.55392	73	2.16308	50.60623	109.46642	73	2.19587	50.27082	110.38840
74	2.15297	51.41034	110.68469	74	2.18606	51.06416	111.62949	74	2.21966	50.72134	112.58428
75	2.17539	51.87003	112.83766	75	2.20929	51.51680	113.81556	75	2.24371	51.16703	114.80394

n			n				n				n	
76	2.19805	52.32437	76	115.01305	2.23276	51.98467	76	116.02485	2.26802	51.60794	76	117.04785
77	2.22095	52.77523	77	117.21111	2.25649	52.40784	77	118.25761	2.29259	52.04413	77	119.31567
78	2.24408	53.22085	78	119.43205	2.28046	52.84634	78	120.51410	2.31742	52.47564	78	121.60825
79	2.26746	53.66187	79	121.67614	2.30469	53.28024	79	122.79456	2.34253	52.90253	79	123.92567
80	2.29108	54.09835	80	123.94360	2.32918	53.70958	80	125.09925	2.36791	53.32485	80	126.26820
81	2.31494	54.53032	81	126.23467	2.35393	54.13440	81	127.42844	2.39356	53.74263	81	128.63611
82	2.33906	54.95784	82	128.54962	2.37894	54.55478	82	129.78236	2.41949	54.15594	82	131.02966
83	2.36342	55.38096	83	130.88867	2.40421	54.97069	83	132.16130	2.44570	54.56483	83	133.44916
84	2.38804	55.79971	84	133.25211	2.42976	55.38226	84	134.56551	2.47219	54.96933	84	135.89485
85	2.41292	56.21415	85	135.64014	2.45557	55.78949	85	136.99527	2.49898	55.36949	85	138.36705
86	2.43805	56.62431	86	138.05305	2.48167	56.19245	86	139.45084	2.52605	55.76537	86	140.86603
87	2.46345	57.03025	87	140.49112	2.50803	56.59117	87	141.93251	2.55341	56.15700	87	143.39207
88	2.48911	57.43200	88	142.95456	2.53468	56.98569	88	144.44054	2.58108	56.54443	88	145.94548
89	2.51504	57.82961	89	145.44368	2.56161	57.37607	89	146.97522	2.60904	56.92772	89	148.52657
90	2.54124	58.22311	90	147.95871	2.58883	57.76235	90	149.53683	2.63730	57.30689	90	151.13560
91	2.56771	58.61257	91	150.49995	2.61634	58.14456	91	152.12566	2.66587	57.68200	91	153.77290
92	2.59445	58.99800	92	153.06766	2.64413	58.52276	92	154.74199	2.69475	58.05309	92	156.43878
93	2.62148	59.37947	93	155.66211	2.67223	58.89698	93	157.38612	2.72395	58.42021	93	159.13353
94	2.64879	59.75700	94	158.28356	2.70062	59.26728	94	160.05836	2.75346	58.78839	94	161.86748
95	2.67638	60.13064	95	160.93237	2.72931	59.63366	95	162.75897	2.78329	59.14268	95	164.61039
96	2.70426	60.50043	96	163.60876	2.75831	59.99619	96	165.48830	2.81344	59.49811	96	167.39421
97	2.73243	60.86640	97	166.31302	2.78762	60.35492	97	168.24681	2.84392	59.84974	97	170.20766
98	2.76089	61.22860	98	169.04544	2.81724	60.70988	98	171.03423	2.87473	60.19760	98	173.05157
99	2.78965	61.58707	99	171.80634	2.84717	61.06127	99	173.86147	2.90587	60.54173	99	175.98630
100	2.81871	61.94184	100	174.55698	2.87742	61.40864	100	176.69664	2.93735	60.88218	100	178.83217

Table 1. (continued) Annuities

M	C(12.50,M,12)	A(12.50,M,12)	S(12.50,M,12)
101	2.84907	62.29296	177.41469
102	2.87774	62.64045	180.26276
103	2.90771	62.99437	183.14050
104	2.93800	63.32473	186.04822
105	2.96961	63.66159	188.9621
106	2.99953	63.99498	191.95482
107	3.03077	64.32439	194.95435
108	3.06235	64.85147	197.98512
109	3.09424	64.97466	201.04747
110	3.12648	65.29450	204.14171
111	3.15904	65.61105	207.26819
112	3.19195	65.92434	210.42723
113	3.22520	66.23440	213.61919
114	3.25880	66.54126	216.84439
115	3.29274	66.84496	220.10318
116	3.32704	67.14553	223.39592
117	3.36170	67.44299	226.72286
118	3.39672	67.73740	230.08466
119	3.43210	68.02876	233.48137
120	3.46785	68.31713	236.91347
121	3.50397	68.60252	240.38132
122	3.54047	68.88496	243.88530
123	3.57735	69.16451	247.42577
124	3.61462	69.44115	251.00311
125	3.65227	69.71496	254.61774

M	C(12.75,M,12)	A(12.75,M,12)	S(12.75,M,12)
101	2.90800	61.75252	179.57607
102	2.93889	62.09278	182.48405
103	2.97012	62.42947	185.42294
104	3.00168	62.76262	188.33307
105	3.03357	63.09226	191.39474
106	3.06580	63.41844	194.42831
107	3.09837	63.74119	197.41941
108	3.13130	64.06055	200.59248
109	3.16457	64.37655	203.72379
110	3.19819	64.68922	206.88835
111	3.23217	64.99961	210.09653
112	3.26651	65.30475	213.31871
113	3.30122	65.60767	216.58522
114	3.33629	65.90740	219.88644
115	3.37174	66.20399	223.22273
116	3.40757	66.49745	226.59447
117	3.44377	66.78783	230.00204
118	3.48036	67.07516	233.44582
119	3.51734	67.35946	236.92618
120	3.55471	67.64078	240.44351
121	3.59248	67.91914	243.99823
122	3.63065	68.19456	247.59071
123	3.66923	68.46710	251.22136
124	3.70821	68.73678	254.89058
125	3.74761	69.00362	258.59879

M	C(13.00,M,12)	A(13.00,M,12)	S(13.00,M,12)
101	2.96917	61.21997	191.76952
102	3.00134	61.55215	194.73868
103	3.03385	61.88177	187.74002
104	3.06672	62.20785	190.77386
105	3.09994	62.53044	193.84059
106	3.13352	62.84957	196.94052
107	3.16747	63.16528	200.07405
108	3.20178	63.47760	203.24152
109	3.23647	63.78658	206.44330
110	3.27153	64.09225	209.67976
111	3.30697	64.39464	212.96129
112	3.34280	64.69379	216.25827
113	3.37901	64.98973	219.60107
114	3.41562	65.28251	222.98009
115	3.45262	65.57214	226.39571
116	3.49002	65.85867	229.84833
117	3.52783	66.14213	233.33835
118	3.56605	66.42255	236.86618
119	3.60468	66.69997	240.43222
120	3.64373	66.97441	244.03691
121	3.68321	67.24592	247.68065
122	3.72311	67.51451	251.36386
123	3.76344	67.78023	255.09696
124	3.80421	68.04309	258.85040
125	3.84542	68.30314	262.65460

126	3.69031	69.98594	259.26999	126	3.78743	69.26765	262.34641	126	3.88708	68.56040	266.50003
127	3.72875	70.25413	261.96030	127	3.82767	69.52690	266.13382	127	3.92919	68.81491	270.38712
128	3.76759	70.51955	265.68906	128	3.86834	69.78741	269.96152	128	3.97176	69.06669	274.31631
129	3.80684	70.78223	269.45667	129	3.90944	70.04920	273.82983	129	4.01479	69.31577	278.28806
130	3.84649	71.04221	273.26349	130	3.95098	70.29630	277.73929	130	4.05828	69.56217	282.30286
131	3.88656	71.29951	277.10999	131	3.99296	70.54675	281.69028	131	4.10225	69.80595	286.36115
132	3.92705	71.55415	280.99655	132	4.03538	70.79455	285.68323	132	4.14669	70.04710	290.46338
133	3.96796	71.80617	284.92358	133	4.07826	71.03975	289.71860	133	4.19161	70.28567	294.61008
134	4.00929	72.05559	288.89154	134	4.12159	71.28238	293.79688	134	4.23702	70.52168	298.80167
135	4.05105	72.30244	292.90086	135	4.16538	71.52245	297.91846	135	4.28292	70.75517	303.03870
136	4.09325	72.54675	296.96190	136	4.20964	71.76000	302.08386	136	4.32832	70.99615	307.32162
137	4.13589	72.78853	301.04514	137	4.25437	71.99506	306.28349	137	4.37622	71.21466	311.65094
138	4.17897	73.02792	305.18103	138	4.29957	72.22764	310.54786	138	4.42363	71.44072	316.02716
139	4.22250	73.26465	309.35999	139	4.34525	72.45777	314.84744	139	4.47155	71.66436	320.45078
140	4.26648	73.49904	313.58249	140	4.39142	72.68549	319.19269	140	4.51989	71.88560	324.92233
141	4.31093	73.73100	317.84897	141	4.43808	72.91081	323.58411	141	4.56896	72.10446	329.44232
142	4.35583	73.96058	322.15991	142	4.48524	73.13377	328.00219	142	4.61846	72.32099	334.01129
143	4.40121	74.18779	326.51575	143	4.53289	73.35438	332.50742	143	4.66849	72.53519	338.62973
144	4.44705	74.41266	330.85693	144	4.58105	73.57266	337.04031	144	4.71906	72.74709	343.29822
145	4.49337	74.63521	335.36398	145	4.62973	73.78866	341.62137	145	4.77019	72.95673	349.01730
146	4.54018	74.85547	339.85736	146	4.67892	74.00239	346.25110	146	4.82186	73.16412	352.78748
147	4.58747	75.07345	344.39755	147	4.72863	74.21386	350.93002	147	4.87410	73.36929	357.60934
148	4.63526	75.28916	348.98502	148	4.77887	74.42312	355.65963	148	4.92690	73.57225	362.48346
149	4.68354	75.50270	353.62030	149	4.82965	74.63017	360.43753	149	4.98028	73.77305	367.41034
150	4.73233	75.71401	356.30388	150	4.88096	74.83504	365.26718	150	5.03423	73.97169	372.39063

Table 1. (continued) Annuities

M	C(12.50,M,12)	A(12.50,M,12)	S(12.50,M,12)	M	C(12.75,M,12)	A(12.75,M,12)	S(12.75,M,12)	M	C(13.00,M,12)	A(13.00,M,12)	S(13.00,M,12)
151	4.78163	75.92315	363.03616	151	4.93282	75.03777	370.14813	151	5.08877	74.16820	377.42487
152	4.83144	76.13013	367.81778	152	4.98524	75.23837	375.08096	152	5.14330	74.36260	382.51364
153	4.88176	76.33497	372.64923	153	5.03820	75.43685	380.06619	153	5.19802	74.55492	387.65753
154	4.93261	76.53770	377.53101	154	5.09173	75.63325	385.10440	154	5.25595	74.74519	392.85715
155	4.98400	76.73834	382.46359	155	5.14583	75.82758	390.19614	155	5.31289	74.93340	398.11310
156	5.03591	76.93692	387.44760	156	5.20051	76.01987	395.34195	156	5.37045	75.11961	403.42599
157	5.08837	77.13345	392.48352	157	5.25576	76.21014	400.54248	157	5.42863	75.30382	408.79645
158	5.14137	77.32794	397.57190	158	5.31161	76.39840	405.79825	158	5.48744	75.49605	414.22507
159	5.19493	77.52044	402.71326	159	5.36804	76.58469	411.10983	159	5.54689	75.66634	419.71252
160	5.24904	77.71095	407.90820	160	5.42508	76.76902	416.47787	160	5.60698	75.84468	425.25940
161	5.30372	77.89950	413.15723	161	5.48272	76.95141	421.90295	161	5.66772	76.02112	430.86636
162	5.35897	78.08610	418.46097	162	5.54097	77.13188	427.38568	162	5.72912	76.19567	436.53409
163	5.41479	78.27078	423.81998	163	5.59985	77.31046	432.92667	163	5.79118	76.36835	442.26321
164	5.47119	78.45355	429.23471	164	5.65934	77.48716	438.52649	164	5.85392	76.53917	448.05438
165	5.52819	78.63445	434.70590	165	5.71947	77.66199	444.18585	165	5.91734	76.70817	453.90833
166	5.58577	78.81348	440.23410	166	5.78024	77.83500	449.90530	166	5.98144	76.87535	459.82565
167	5.64396	78.99065	445.81985	167	5.84166	78.00619	455.68555	167	6.04624	77.04074	465.80710
168	5.70275	79.16601	451.46384	168	5.90373	78.17557	461.52722	168	6.11174	77.20436	471.85336
169	5.76215	79.33955	457.16656	169	5.96645	78.34317	467.43094	169	6.17796	77.36623	477.96509
170	5.82217	79.51131	462.92871	170	6.02985	78.50902	473.39740	170	6.24488	77.52636	484.14304
171	5.88282	79.68130	468.75089	171	6.09391	78.67311	479.42725	171	6.31254	77.68477	490.38794
172	5.94410	79.84953	474.63373	172	6.15866	78.83549	485.52118	172	6.38092	77.84149	496.70047
173	6.00602	80.01603	480.57782	173	6.22410	78.99615	491.67984	173	6.45005	77.99653	503.08139
174	6.06858	80.18082	486.58383	174	6.29023	79.15513	497.90393	174	6.51992	78.14590	509.53143
175	6.13180	80.34389	492.65244	175	6.35706	79.31243	504.19415	175	6.58056	78.30164	516.05133

176	6.19567	80.50530	498.78421	176	6.42461	79.46809	510.55121	176	6.66195	78.45174	522.64191
177	6.26021	80.66504	504.97989	177	6.49287	79.62210	516.97563	177	6.73413	78.60023	529.30383
178	6.32542	80.82314	511.24008	178	6.56185	79.77450	523.46869	178	6.80708	78.74715	536.03796
179	6.39131	80.97960	517.56549	179	6.63157	79.92529	530.03052	179	6.88082	78.89248	542.84503
180	6.45788	81.13445	523.96679	180	6.70203	80.07450	536.66211	180	6.95536	79.03625	549.72589
181	6.52515	81.28770	530.41467	181	6.77324	80.22214	543.36414	181	7.03071	79.17848	556.68127
182	6.59312	81.43937	536.93982	182	6.84521	80.36823	550.13739	182	7.10688	79.31919	563.71198
183	6.66180	81.58948	543.53296	183	6.91794	80.51278	556.98260	183	7.18387	79.45839	570.81885
184	6.73120	81.73804	550.19476	184	6.99144	80.65581	563.90051	184	7.26170	79.59610	578.00269
185	6.80131	81.88507	556.92596	185	7.06573	80.79734	570.89997	185	7.34036	79.73233	585.26440
186	6.87216	82.03059	563.72729	186	7.14080	80.93738	577.96770	186	7.41989	79.86710	592.60480
187	6.94374	82.17461	570.59943	187	7.21667	81.07594	585.09851	187	7.50027	80.00043	600.02466
188	7.01607	82.31713	577.54315	188	7.29335	81.21306	592.31519	188	7.58152	80.13233	607.52490
189	7.08916	82.45819	584.55551	189	7.37084	81.34972	599.60852	189	7.66365	80.26282	615.10645
190	7.16300	82.59780	591.64844	190	7.44916	81.48297	606.97937	190	7.74668	80.39191	622.77008
191	7.23762	82.73597	598.81140	191	7.52830	81.61581	614.42853	191	7.83060	80.51962	630.51678
192	7.31301	82.87271	606.04901	192	7.60829	81.74724	621.96696	192	7.91543	80.64595	638.34735
193	7.38919	83.00804	613.36206	193	7.68913	81.87729	629.56512	193	8.00118	80.77093	646.26282
194	7.46616	83.14198	620.75122	194	7.77083	82.00598	637.25427	194	8.08786	80.89457	654.26398
195	7.54393	83.27454	628.21741	195	7.85319	82.13331	645.02509	195	8.17548	81.01689	662.35187
196	7.62251	83.40572	635.76135	196	7.93683	82.25931	652.87848	196	8.26405	81.13789	670.52734
197	7.70192	83.53556	643.38385	197	8.02116	82.38398	660.81531	197	8.35357	81.25761	678.79938
198	7.78214	83.66406	651.08575	198	8.10639	82.50734	668.83649	198	8.44407	81.37603	687.14436
199	7.86321	83.79124	658.86792	199	8.19252	82.62940	676.94287	199	8.53555	81.43319	695.58899
200	7.94512	83.91710	666.73114	200	8.27966	82.75018	685.13538	200	8.62802	81.60909	704.12457

504

Table 1. (continued) Annuities

M	C(12.50,M,12)	A(12.50,M,12)	S(12.50,M,12)	C(12.75,M,12)	A(12.75,M,12)	S(12.75,M,12)	C(13.00,M,12)	A(13.00,M,12)	S(13.00,M,12)
201	8.02788	84.04166	674.67621	8.36753	82.86969	693.41492	8.72149	81.72375	712.75256
202	8.11150	84.16495	682.70410	8.45644	82.98794	701.78247	8.81597	81.83718	721.47406
203	8.19600	84.28696	690.81561	8.54629	83.10495	710.23889	8.91148	81.94939	730.29004
204	8.28137	84.40771	699.01160	8.63709	83.22073	718.78522	9.00802	82.06041	739.20154
205	8.36763	84.52722	707.29297	8.72886	83.33530	727.42230	9.10560	82.17023	748.20953
206	8.45490	84.64550	715.66058	8.82161	83.44865	736.15118	9.20425	82.27888	757.31512
207	8.54287	84.76255	724.11542	8.91534	83.56081	744.97278	9.30396	82.38635	766.51941
208	8.63106	84.87840	732.65826	9.01006	83.67181	753.88812	9.40475	82.49268	775.82336
209	8.72177	84.99306	741.28916	9.10579	83.78162	762.89813	9.50664	82.59788	785.22809
210	8.81262	85.10653	750.01190	9.20254	83.89029	772.00397	9.60963	82.70193	794.73474
211	8.90442	85.21883	758.82452	9.30032	83.99781	781.20648	9.71373	82.80489	804.34436
212	8.99718	85.32998	767.72894	9.39913	84.10421	790.50684	9.81896	82.90673	814.05811
213	9.09090	85.43998	776.72614	9.49900	84.20948	799.90594	9.92533	83.00748	823.87708
214	9.18559	85.54885	785.81702	9.59993	84.31364	809.40497	10.03286	83.10715	833.60237
215	9.28128	85.65659	796.00262	9.70193	84.41672	819.00488	10.14155	83.20576	843.63527
216	9.37756	85.76323	804.28367	9.80501	84.51871	828.70679	10.25142	83.30331	853.97681
217	9.47564	85.86876	813.66136	9.90919	84.61963	838.51164	10.36247	83.39980	864.22821
218	9.57435	85.97321	823.13751	10.01447	84.71948	848.42102	10.47473	83.49522	874.59370
219	9.67403	86.07658	833.71186	10.12088	84.81828	858.43549	10.58821	83.58972	885.06543
220	9.77495	86.17888	842.38593	10.22841	84.91605	868.55634	10.70291	83.68315	895.65363
221	9.87667	86.28013	852.16077	10.33709	85.01279	878.78479	10.81886	83.77558	906.35657
222	9.97966	86.38033	862.03748	10.44692	85.10851	889.12183	10.93607	83.86702	917.17542
223	10.08351	86.47950	872.01703	10.55792	85.20323	899.56879	11.05454	83.95748	928.11145
224	10.18855	86.57765	882.10052	10.67010	85.29695	910.12671	11.17430	84.04697	939.16602
225	10.29468	86.67478	892.28906	10.78347	85.38969	920.79681	11.29635	84.13551	950.34033

n									
226	10.40191	902.58374	86.77003	10.89904	85.48145	891.59026	11.41772	84.22309	981.63568
227	10.51027	912.98566	86.86607	11.01383	85.57224	942.47827	11.54141	84.30973	973.05341
228	10.61975	923.49591	86.96024	11.13085	85.66208	953.49213	11.66644	84.39545	984.59479
229	10.73037	934.11566	87.05343	11.24912	85.75098	964.62299	11.79283	84.48025	996.26123
230	10.84215	944.84607	87.14566	11.36864	85.83894	975.87207	11.90059	84.56413	1008.05408
231	10.95509	955.68823	87.23695	11.48943	85.92597	987.24072	12.04973	84.64713	1019.97467
232	11.06900	966.64331	87.32729	11.61151	86.01209	998.73016	12.19026	84.72923	1032.02429
233	11.18450	977.71246	87.41669	11.73488	86.09731	1010.34167	12.31222	84.81045	1044.20459
234	11.30101	988.89697	87.50518	11.85956	86.18163	1022.07654	12.44560	84.89079	1056.51685
235	11.41873	1000.19800	87.59278	11.98557	86.26507	1033.58616	12.59043	84.97028	1068.96240
236	11.53767	1011.61676	87.67943	12.11292	86.34762	1045.92163	12.71671	85.04892	1081.54285
237	11.65786	1023.15442	87.76521	12.24162	86.42331	1058.03455	12.85448	85.12672	1094.25962
238	11.77929	1034.81226	87.85010	12.37169	86.51014	1070.27625	12.99374	85.20367	1107.11401
239	11.90200	1046.59155		12.50313	86.59317	1082.64795	13.13450	85.27981	1120.10778
240	12.02597	1058.49353	88.01727	12.63598	86.66926	1095.15100	13.27679	85.35513	1133.24231
241	12.15125	1070.51963	88.09957	12.77024	86.74757	1107.78699	13.42062	85.42964	1146.51904
242	12.27782	1082.67078	88.18102	12.90592	86.82505	1120.55725	13.56601	85.50336	1159.93970
243	12.40571	1094.94861	88.26163	13.04305	86.90287	1133.46313	13.71298	85.57628	1173.50574
244	12.53494	1107.35425	88.34141	13.18163	86.97758	1146.50623	13.86154	85.64842	1187.21875
245	12.66551	1119.88928	88.42036	13.32168	87.05265	1159.68787	14.01170	85.71979	1201.08020
246	12.79745	1132.55469	88.49850	13.46323	87.12692	1173.00962	14.16350	85.79039	1215.09192
247	12.93075	1145.35217	88.57584	13.60627	87.20042	1186.47278	14.31693	85.86024	1229.28549
248	13.06545	1158.28296	88.65237	13.75084	87.27314	1200.07898	14.47203	85.92934	1243.57239
249	13.20155	1171.34839	88.72812	13.89694	87.34510	1213.82983	14.62881	85.99770	1258.04443
250	13.33906	1184.54993	88.80309	14.04460	87.41631	1227.72681	14.78729	86.06532	1272.87322

Table 1. (continued) Annuities

M	C(12.50,M,12)	A(12.50,M,12)	S(12.50,M,12)	M	C(12.75,M,12)	A(12.75,M,12)	S(12.75,M,12)	M	C(13.00,M,12)	A(13.00,M,12)	S(13.00,M,12)
251	13.47801	88.87728	1197.88904	251	14.13982	87.49676	1241.77196	251	14.94749	86.13223	1287.46057
252	13.61841	88.95071	1211.36707	252	14.34463	87.55647	1255.96521	252	15.10942	86.19841	1302.40796
253	13.76027	89.02338	1224.98547	253	14.49704	87.62545	1270.30981	253	15.27311	86.26389	1317.51748
254	13.90360	89.09531	1238.74573	254	14.65107	87.69370	1284.80698	254	15.43856	86.32865	1332.79053
255	14.04843	89.16650	1252.64929	255	14.80674	87.76124	1299.45801	255	15.60581	86.39273	1348.22913
256	14.19477	89.23694	1266.69775	256	14.96406	87.82806	1314.26477	256	15.77488	86.45612	1363.83496
257	14.34263	89.30666	1280.89246	257	15.12306	87.89419	1329.22876	257	15.94577	86.51884	1379.60974
258	14.49203	89.37566	1295.23511	258	15.28374	87.95962	1344.35181	258	16.11852	86.58088	1395.55554
259	14.64299	89.44398	1309.72717	259	15.44613	88.02436	1359.63562	259	16.29313	86.64226	1411.67407
260	14.79552	89.51154	1324.37012	260	15.61024	88.08842	1375.08167	260	16.46964	86.70297	1427.96716
261	14.94964	89.57844	1339.16565	261	15.77610	88.15181	1390.69188	261	16.64807	86.76304	1444.43689
262	15.10537	89.64464	1354.11536	262	15.94372	88.21453	1406.46802	262	16.82842	86.82246	1461.08496
263	15.26272	89.71016	1369.22070	263	16.11312	88.27659	1422.41174	263	17.01073	86.88125	1477.91333
264	15.42170	89.77500	1384.48340	264	16.28433	88.33800	1438.52490	264	17.19501	86.93941	1494.92407
265	15.58235	89.83918	1399.90515	265	16.45735	88.39876	1454.80920	265	17.38129	86.99694	1512.11914
266	15.74466	89.90269	1415.48743	266	16.63221	88.45889	1471.26660	266	17.56959	87.05386	1529.50037
267	15.90867	89.96555	1431.23206	267	16.80892	88.51838	1487.89880	267	17.75992	87.11016	1547.06995
268	16.07438	90.02776	1447.14075	268	16.98752	88.57724	1504.70776	268	17.95232	87.16586	1564.82996
269	16.24183	90.08933	1463.21521	269	17.16801	88.63549	1521.69619	269	18.14681	87.22097	1582.78223
270	16.41101	90.15027	1479.45703	270	17.35042	88.69313	1538.86328	270	18.34340	87.27549	1600.92908
271	16.58196	90.21057	1496.06604	271	17.53477	88.75016	1556.21362	271	18.54212	87.32941	1619.27246
272	16.75469	90.27026	1512.44996	272	17.72108	88.80659	1573.74841	272	18.74299	87.38277	1637.81458
273	16.92921	90.32932	1529.20459	273	17.90936	88.86243	1591.46948	273	18.94604	87.43555	1656.55750
274	17.10556	90.38779	1546.13379	274	18.09365	88.91767	1609.37891	274	19.15129	87.48777	1675.50354
275	17.28374	90.44564	1563.23938	275	18.29196	88.97234	1627.47852	275	19.35876	87.53942	1694.65491

276	17.48378	90.50291	1580.52319	276	18.48631	89.02644	1645.77051	276	19.56848	87.59053	1714.01367
277	17.64570	90.55968	1597.98694	277	18.68273	89.07996	1664.25684	277	19.78047	87.64108	1733.58215
278	17.82951	90.61566	1615.63269	278	18.88123	89.13293	1682.93968	278	19.99476	87.69109	1753.36255
279	18.01523	90.67117	1633.46216	279	19.08165	89.18533	1701.82090	279	20.21137	87.74057	1773.35730
280	18.20289	90.74048	1651.47742	280	19.28459	89.23718	1720.90259	280	20.43033	87.78952	1793.56873
281	18.39250	90.78048	1669.68030	281	19.48949	89.28850	1740.18726	281	20.65166	87.83794	1813.99902
282	18.58409	90.83429	1688.07275	282	19.61656	89.33926	1759.67664	282	20.87338	87.88584	1834.65076
283	18.77768	90.88754	1706.65686	283	19.90584	89.38950	1779.37329	283	21.10153	87.93324	1855.52612
284	18.97328	90.94025	1725.43457	284	20.11734	89.43921	1799.27305	284	21.33013	87.98012	1876.62756
285	19.17091	90.99241	1744.40794	285	20.33109	89.48840	1819.39648	285	21.56121	88.02650	1897.95776
286	19.37061	91.04404	1763.57674	286	20.54710	89.53706	1839.72754	286	21.79479	88.07238	1919.51892
287	19.57239	91.09513	1782.94934	287	20.76542	89.58522	1860.27466	287	22.03090	88.11777	1941.31372
288	19.77627	91.14569	1802.52173	288	20.99605	89.63287	1881.04004	288	22.26957	88.16267	1963.34460
289	19.98227	91.19574	1822.29797	289	21.20903	89.68002	1902.02612	289	22.51082	88.20710	1985.61426
290	20.19042	91.24527	1842.28027	290	21.43437	89.72668	1923.23511	290	22.75469	88.25105	2008.12500
291	20.40074	91.29428	1862.47070	291	21.66211	89.77284	1944.66966	291	23.00120	88.29452	2030.87976
292	20.61324	91.34290	1882.87146	292	21.89227	89.81852	1966.33167	292	23.25038	88.33753	2053.88086
293	20.82796	91.39081	1903.48462	293	22.12488	89.86522	1988.22388	293	23.50226	88.38008	2077.13135
294	21.04492	91.43832	1924.31262	294	22.35995	89.90844	2010.34975	294	23.75686	88.42217	2100.63354
295	21.26414	91.48535	1945.35754	295	22.59753	89.95269	2032.70874	295	24.01423	88.46381	2124.39038
296	21.48564	91.53190	1966.62170	296	22.83763	89.99648	2055.30615	296	24.27438	88.50501	2148.40454
297	21.70945	91.57796	1988.10730	297	23.08028	90.03980	2078.14380	297	24.53736	88.54576	2172.67896
298	21.93559	91.62355	2009.81677	298	23.32551	90.08268	2101.22412	298	24.80318	88.58608	2197.21631
299	22.16409	91.66866	2031.75244	299	23.57334	90.12510	2124.54966	299	25.07188	88.62597	2222.01953
300	22.34496	91.71332	2053.91650	300	23.82381	90.16707	2148.12305	300	25.34349	88.66542	2247.09131

508

Table 1. (continued) Annuities

M	C(12.50,M,12)	A(12.50,M,12)	S(12.50,M,12)	M	C(12.75,M,12)	A(12.75,M,12)	S(12.75,M,12)	M	C(13.00,M,12)	A(13.00,M,12)	S(13.00,M,12)
301	22.62824	91.75751	2076.31128	301	24.07693	90.20860	2171.94678	301	25.61805	88.70446	2272.43481
302	22.86395	91.80125	2098.93970	302	24.33275	90.24970	2196.02368	302	25.89557	88.74307	2298.05298
303	23.10212	91.84454	2121.80347	303	24.59129	90.29037	2220.35645	303	26.17611	88.78128	2323.94849
304	23.34277	91.88737	2144.90576	304	24.85257	90.33060	2244.94775	304	26.45968	88.81907	2350.12451
305	23.58592	91.92977	2168.24864	305	25.11663	90.37042	2269.80029	305	26.74633	88.85646	2376.58423
306	23.83161	91.97173	2191.83447	306	25.38349	90.40981	2294.91699	306	27.03608	88.89345	2403.33057
307	24.07985	92.01326	2215.66602	307	25.65319	90.44880	2320.30054	307	27.32897	88.93004	2430.36670
308	24.33069	92.05436	2239.74585	308	25.92576	90.48737	2345.95361	308	27.62504	88.96624	2457.69580
309	24.58413	92.09504	2264.07666	309	26.20122	90.52554	2371.87939	309	27.92431	89.00205	2485.32080
310	24.84022	92.13529	2288.66064	310	26.47961	90.56330	2398.08057	310	28.22682	89.03748	2513.24512
311	25.09897	92.17514	2313.50098	311	26.76095	90.60067	2424.56030	311	28.53261	89.07253	2541.47192
312	25.36042	92.21457	2338.59985	312	27.04529	90.63764	2451.32129	312	28.84171	89.10719	2570.00439
313	25.62459	92.25359	2363.96021	313	27.33264	90.67422	2478.36646	313	29.15417	89.14149	2598.84619
314	25.89151	92.29221	2389.58496	314	27.62305	90.71043	2505.69922	314	29.47001	89.17543	2628.00024
315	26.16121	92.33044	2415.47632	315	27.91655	90.74625	2533.23227	315	29.78926	89.20900	2657.47046
316	26.43373	92.36862	2441.63770	316	28.21316	90.78169	2561.23977	316	30.11198	89.24221	2687.25952
317	26.70908	92.40572	2468.07129	317	28.51293	90.81676	2589.45190	317	30.43819	89.27506	2717.37158
318	26.98730	92.44276	2494.78052	318	28.81588	90.85147	2617.96484	318	30.76794	89.30756	2747.80981
319	27.26841	92.47944	2521.76758	319	29.12205	90.88581	2646.79076	319	31.10126	89.33971	2778.57764
320	27.55246	92.51573	2549.03613	320	29.43147	90.91978	2675.90083	320	31.43819	89.37152	2809.87896
321	27.83946	92.55165	2576.58862	321	29.74418	90.95341	2705.33423	321	31.77877	89.40299	2841.11719
322	28.12946	92.58720	2604.42798	322	30.06021	90.98667	2735.07837	322	32.12304	89.43412	2872.89600
323	28.42247	92.62239	2632.55762	323	30.37960	91.01959	2765.13867	323	32.47104	89.46492	2905.01904
324	28.71854	92.65721	2660.97998	324	30.70218	91.05216	2796.51907	324	32.82281	89.49538	2937.48999
325	29.01769	92.69167	2689.69849	325	31.02859	91.08439	2828.22046	325	33.17839	89.52553	2970.31274

326	29.31996	92.72578	2718.71631	31.35827	326	91.11628	2857.24927	326	33.53782	89.55534	3003.49121
327	29.62538	92.75953	2748.03613	31.69745	327	91.14768	2888.60742	327	33.90115	89.58484	3037.02905
328	29.93398	92.79294	2777.66162	32.02818	328	91.17905	2920.29883	328	34.26841	89.61402	3070.93018
329	30.24579	92.82600	2807.59546	32.36847	329	91.20995	2952.32715	329	34.63565	89.64289	3105.19673
330	30.56085	92.85872	2837.84131	32.71239	330	91.24052	2984.69656	330	35.01492	89.67145	3139.83838
331	30.87919	92.89111	2868.40210	33.05996	331	91.27077	3017.40796	331	35.39424	89.69970	3174.85327
332	31.20085	92.92316	2899.28125	33.41122	332	91.30070	3050.46777	332	35.77768	89.72765	3210.24756
333	31.52598	92.95488	2930.48218	33.76622	333	91.33031	3083.87915	333	36.16527	89.75530	3246.02515
334	31.85425	92.98627	2962.00806	34.12498	334	91.35962	3117.64526	334	36.55706	89.78266	3282.19043
335	32.19607	93.01734	2993.86230	34.48756	335	91.38861	3151.77026	335	36.95310	89.80972	3318.74756
336	32.52134	93.04809	3026.04834	34.85399	336	91.41730	3186.25781	336	37.35342	89.83649	3355.70068
337	32.86010	93.07852	3058.56982	35.22431	337	91.44569	3221.11182	337	37.75808	89.86298	3393.05396
338	33.20239	93.10863	3091.42983	35.59857	338	91.47379	3256.33618	338	38.16713	89.88918	3430.81201
339	33.54825	93.13844	3124.63232	35.97681	339	91.50158	3291.93481	339	38.58061	89.91509	3468.97925
340	33.89771	93.16795	3158.18042	36.35906	340	91.52908	3327.91162	340	38.99857	89.94073	3507.55981
341	34.25007	93.19714	3192.07813	36.74537	341	91.55630	3364.27051	341	39.42105	89.96610	3546.55835
342	34.60759	93.22604	3226.32910	37.13580	342	91.58322	3401.01587	342	39.84811	89.99120	3585.97949
343	34.96809	93.25464	3260.93052	37.53036	343	91.60987	3438.15166	343	40.27980	90.01603	3625.82764
344	35.33234	93.28294	3296.90479	37.92912	344	91.63624	3475.68213	344	40.71616	90.04059	3666.10742
345	35.70039	93.31095	3331.23706	38.33212	345	91.66232	3513.61133	345	41.15725	90.06488	3706.82349
346	36.07227	93.33867	3366.83750	38.73940	346	91.68813	3551.94336	346	41.60312	90.08892	3747.98047
347	36.44802	93.36611	3403.00977	39.15100	347	91.71368	3590.68286	347	42.05383	90.11270	3789.58398
348	36.82768	93.39326	3439.45776	39.56698	348	91.73895	3629.83374	348	42.50941	90.13622	3831.63770
349	37.21130	93.42014	3476.28540	39.98738	349	91.76396	3669.40008	349	42.96992	90.15949	3874.14722
350	37.59892	93.44673	3513.49658	40.41225	350	91.78870	3709.38818	350	43.43543	90.18252	3917.11694

Table 1. (continued) Annuities

M	C(12.50,M,12)	A(12.50,M,12)	S(12.50,M,12)	M	C(12.75,M,12)	A(12.75,M,12)	S(12.75,M,12)	M	C(13.00,M,12)	A(13.00,M,12)	S(13.00,M,12)
351	37.99058	93.47305	3551.09670	351	40.84163	91.81319	3749.00054	351	43.90598	90.20529	3960.55249
352	38.38631	93.49911	3589.08618	352	41.27557	91.83742	3790.64209	352	44.38163	90.22783	4004.45850
353	38.78617	93.52489	3627.47241	353	41.71412	91.86139	3831.91772	353	44.86243	90.25011	4048.84009
354	39.19019	93.55041	3666.25879	354	42.15734	91.88511	3873.63164	354	45.34844	90.27217	4093.70264
355	39.59843	93.57566	3705.44897	355	42.60526	91.90858	3915.78906	355	45.83972	90.29398	4139.05078
356	40.01091	93.60065	3745.04736	356	43.05794	91.93181	3958.39429	356	46.33632	90.31557	4184.89063
357	40.42769	93.62539	3785.05811	357	43.51543	91.95479	4001.45239	357	46.83829	90.33691	4231.22705
358	40.84881	93.64986	3825.48684	358	43.97778	91.97752	4044.96777	358	47.34571	90.35803	4278.06543
359	41.27432	93.67410	3866.33472	359	44.44505	92.00002	4088.94556	359	47.85862	90.37893	4325.41113
360	41.70426	93.69807	3907.60913	360	44.91727	92.02229	4133.39063	360	48.37709	90.39960	4373.26953
361	42.13868	93.72180	3949.31323	361	45.39452	92.04432	4178.30762	361	48.90117	90.42005	4421.64648
362	42.57763	93.74529	3991.45190	362	45.87684	92.06612	4223.70215	362	49.43093	90.44028	4470.54785
363	43.02114	93.76853	4034.03003	363	46.36428	92.08768	4269.57910	363	49.96644	90.46030	4519.97852
364	43.46928	93.79154	4077.05078	364	46.85690	92.10902	4315.94336	364	50.50774	90.48009	4569.94531
365	43.92208	93.81431	4120.52002	365	47.35475	92.13014	4362.80029	365	51.05491	90.49968	4620.45313
366	44.37960	93.83684	4164.44189	366	47.85790	92.15104	4410.15479	366	51.60800	90.51906	4671.50781
367	44.84189	93.85914	4208.82178	367	48.36639	92.17171	4458.01270	367	52.16709	90.53822	4723.11572
368	45.30899	93.88121	4253.66357	368	48.88028	92.19217	4506.37939	368	52.73223	90.55719	4775.28271
369	45.78096	93.90305	4298.96191	369	49.39964	92.21241	4555.25977	369	53.30350	90.57595	4828.01514
370	46.25785	93.92467	4344.75342	370	49.92450	92.23244	4604.65918	370	53.88095	90.59451	4881.31885
371	46.73970	93.94607	4391.01123	371	50.45495	92.25227	4654.58350	371	54.46466	90.61287	4935.19971
372	47.22657	93.96724	4437.75098	372	50.99104	92.27188	4705.03857	372	55.05470	90.63103	4989.66406
373	47.71852	93.98820	4484.97754	373	51.53282	92.29128	4756.02979	373	55.65112	90.64900	5044.71875
374	48.21558	94.00894	4532.69629	374	52.08035	92.31048	4807.56250	374	56.25401	90.66678	5100.37012
375	48.71788	94.02946	4580.91162	375	52.63371	92.32948	4859.64307	375	56.86343	90.68436	5156.62402

376	49.22531	94.04978	4629.68939	376	53.19294	92.34828	4912.27637	57.47945	376	90.70177	5213.48730
377	49.73807	94.06989	4678.86498	377	53.75811	92.36688	4965.46973	58.10214	377	90.71897	5270.96680
378	50.25618	94.08978	4728.59277	378	54.32930	92.38528	5019.22754	58.73158	378	90.73600	5329.06934
379	50.77796	94.10947	4778.90912	379	54.90654	92.40350	5073.55713	59.36784	379	90.75285	5387.80078
380	51.30363	94.12897	4829.62891	380	55.48993	92.42152	5128.46338	60.01099	380	90.76951	5447.16846
381	51.84310	94.14825	4880.93750	381	56.07961	92.43935	5183.95981	60.66111	381	90.78601	5507.17069
382	52.38313	94.16734	4932.78027	382	56.67535	92.45700	5240.03271	61.31028	382	90.80230	5567.84082
383	52.92879	94.18624	4985.16357	383	57.27753	92.47446	5296.70850	61.96256	383	90.81844	5629.15918
384	53.48013	94.20494	5038.09229	384	57.89610	92.49173	5353.98584	62.65403	384	90.83440	5691.14160
385	54.03722	94.22344	5091.57275	385	58.50114	92.50883	5411.87207	63.33279	385	90.85019	5753.79541
386	54.60010	94.24176	5145.60986	386	59.12271	92.52574	5470.37305	64.01889	386	90.86581	5817.12842
387	55.16885	94.25989	5200.20996	387	59.75009	92.54247	5529.49661	64.71243	387	90.88126	5881.14746
388	55.74353	94.27782	5255.37891	388	60.38575	92.55904	5589.24658	65.41348	388	90.89655	5945.85986
389	56.32419	94.29558	5311.12207	389	61.02734	92.57542	5649.63232	66.12212	389	90.91167	6011.27295
390	56.91090	94.31315	5367.44629	390	61.67576	92.59164	5710.65967	66.83845	390	90.92663	6077.39551
391	57.50372	94.33054	5424.35742	391	62.33107	92.60768	5772.33545	67.56253	391	90.94143	6144.23389
392	58.10272	94.34775	5491.06133	392	62.98333	92.62356	5834.66650	68.29446	392	90.95608	6211.79639
393	58.70796	94.36478	5539.96387	393	63.66264	92.63926	5897.66016	69.03432	393	90.97056	6280.09082
394	59.31950	94.38164	5596.67188	394	64.33905	92.65481	5961.32275	69.78219	394	90.98489	6349.12500
395	59.93741	94.39832	5657.99121	395	65.02265	92.67018	6025.66162	70.53816	395	90.99907	6418.90723
396	60.56176	94.41484	5717.92871	396	65.71352	92.68540	6090.68408	71.30232	396	91.01309	6489.44531
397	61.19261	94.43118	5778.49023	397	66.41173	92.70046	6156.39796	72.07477	397	91.02697	6560.74756
398	61.83003	94.44735	5839.68311	398	67.11735	92.71535	6222.80957	72.85558	398	91.04070	6632.82227
399	62.47409	94.46336	5901.53718	399	67.83047	92.73010	6289.92676	73.64484	399	91.05427	6705.87822
400	63.12487	94.47920	5963.98730	400	68.55117	92.74469	6357.75732	74.44267	400	91.06770	6779.32275

Table 1. (continued) Annuities

N	C(12.50,M,12)	A(12.50,M,12)	S(12.50,M,12)	N	C(12.75,M,12)	A(12.75,M,12)	S(12.75,M,12)	N	C(13.00,M,12)	A(13.00,M,12)	S(13.00,M,12)
401	63.78242	94.49488	6027.11182	401	69.27963	92.75912	6426.30859	401	75.24912	91.08099	6853.76563
402	84.44692	94.51040	6090.89453	402	70.01563	92.77341	6495.58789	402	76.06432	91.09414	6929.01465
403	85.11813	94.52575	6155.34131	403	70.75954	92.78754	6565.60352	403	76.88835	91.10715	7005.07910
404	65.79645	94.54096	6220.45947	404	71.51136	92.90152	6636.36328	404	77.72131	91.12001	7081.96729
405	66.48183	94.55599	6286.25586	405	72.27116	92.81536	6707.87451	405	78.56328	91.13274	7159.68896
406	67.17435	94.57088	6352.73779	406	73.03905	92.82905	6790.14600	406	79.41440	91.14533	7238.25195
407	67.87408	94.58561	6419.91211	407	73.81509	92.84260	6853.18457	407	80.27472	91.15579	7317.66650
408	68.58111	94.60020	6487.78613	408	74.59937	92.85600	6927.00000	408	81.14436	91.17011	7397.94092
409	69.29549	94.61462	6556.38719	409	75.39199	92.86926	7001.59912	409	82.02342	91.18230	7479.08545
410	70.01732	94.62891	6625.66260	410	76.11303	92.88239	7076.99121	410	82.91201	91.19437	7561.10889
411	70.74667	94.64304	6695.68018	411	77.00258	92.89538	7153.18408	411	83.81023	91.20630	7644.02100
412	71.48361	94.65703	6766.42676	412	77.82073	92.90823	7230.18701	412	84.71817	91.21810	7727.83105
413	72.22823	94.67088	6837.91016	413	78.64758	92.92094	7308.00781	413	85.63595	91.22978	7812.54932
414	72.98061	94.68458	6910.13987	414	79.48321	92.93353	7386.65527	414	86.56367	91.24133	7898.18555
415	73.74082	94.69814	6983.11914	415	80.32772	92.94598	7466.13867	415	87.50145	91.25276	7984.74902
416	74.50896	94.71156	7056.85986	416	81.18120	92.95829	7546.46631	416	88.44433	91.26407	8072.25049
417	75.28510	94.72485	7131.36914	417	82.04375	92.97048	7627.64746	417	89.40758	91.27525	8160.6971
418	76.06931	94.73799	7206.65430	418	82.91547	92.98254	7709.69092	418	90.37616	91.28632	8250.10742
419	76.86170	94.75100	7282.72363	419	83.79644	92.99448	7792.60645	419	91.35524	91.29726	8340.48340
420	77.66235	94.76388	7359.58496	420	84.68678	93.00628	7876.40283	420	92.34492	91.30809	8431.83887
421	78.47133	94.77662	7437.24756	421	85.58658	93.01797	7961.08984	421	93.34532	91.31880	8524.18359
422	79.28873	94.78923	7515.71875	422	86.49538	93.02953	8046.67627	422	94.35657	91.32940	8617.52380
423	80.11466	94.80171	7595.00732	423	87.41496	93.04097	8133.17236	423	95.37876	91.33989	8711.88574
424	80.94919	94.81406	7675.12207	424	88.34374	93.05228	8220.58691	424	96.41203	91.35026	8807.26367
425	81.79241	94.82629	7756.07129	425	89.28239	93.06348	8308.93066	425	97.45650	91.36052	8903.67578

n		n			n			n				
426	82.64442	426	94.83839	7837.86377	426	90.23102	93.07457	426	8398.21289	98.51228	91.37067	9001.13291
427	83.50529	427	94.86037	7920.50830	427	91.18972	93.10553	427	8488.44434	99.57949	91.38071	9099.64453
428	84.37514	428	94.86222	8004.01367	428	92.13962	93.10619	428	8579.63379	100.65826	91.39065	9198.22461
429	85.25405	429	94.87395	8088.18867	429	93.13779	93.10712	429	8671.73097	101.74873	91.40047	9298.88281
430	86.14211	430	94.88556	8173.64258	430	94.12739	93.11774	430	8764.93066	102.85101	91.41020	9401.63184
431	87.03942	431	94.89705	8259.78418	431	95.12749	93.12826	431	8859.05762	103.96523	91.41982	9504.48242
432	87.94608	432	94.90842	8346.82422	432	96.13622	93.13966	432	8964.18555	105.09151	91.42934	9608.44727
433	88.86219	433	94.91987	8434.77051	433	97.15969	93.14896	433	9050.32324	106.23001	91.43874	9713.53906
434	89.78788	434	94.93081	8523.63184	434	98.19201	93.15913	434	9147.48340	107.38084	91.44906	9819.76953
435	90.72313	435	94.94183	8613.41992	435	99.23530	93.16921	435	9245.67490	108.54413	91.45728	9927.15039
436	91.66816	436	94.95274	8704.14355	436	100.28967	93.17918	436	9344.91016	109.72002	91.46638	10035.69434
437	92.62304	437	94.96354	8796.81152	437	101.35526	93.18905	437	9445.20020	110.90865	91.47540	10145.41406
438	93.58706	438	94.97422	8888.43457	438	102.43215	93.19881	438	9546.55566	112.11017	91.48432	10256.32324
439	94.56274	439	94.98479	8982.02246	439	103.52049	93.20847	439	9648.98730	113.32469	91.49315	10368.43262
440	95.54776	440	94.99526	9076.58496	440	104.62040	93.21803	440	9752.50781	114.55238	91.50188	10481.75781
441	96.54305	441	95.00562	9172.13281	441	105.73199	93.22749	441	9857.12891	115.78336	91.51051	10536.31055
442	97.54871	442	95.01587	9268.67578	442	106.85539	93.23686	442	9962.06035	117.04779	91.51906	10712.10352
443	98.56484	443	95.02602	9366.22461	443	107.99073	93.24611	443	10069.71582	118.31580	91.52751	10829.15137
444	99.59156	444	95.03606	9464.78906	444	109.13813	93.25527	444	10177.70703	119.59756	91.53587	10947.46690
445	100.62897	445	95.04600	9564.38096	445	110.29773	93.26434	445	10286.84473	120.89320	91.54414	11067.06445
446	101.74718	446	95.05583	9665.00197	446	111.46964	93.27331	446	10397.14258	122.20288	91.55232	11187.95801
447	102.73633	447	95.06557	9766.68750	447	112.65401	93.28219	447	10508.81203	123.52674	91.56042	11310.16113
448	103.80650	448	95.07520	9869.42883	448	113.85095	93.29397	448	10621.26660	124.86495	91.56843	11433.68750
449	104.88702	449	95.08473	9973.23047	449	115.06062	93.29966	449	10735.11719	126.21765	91.57635	11558.55273
450	105.96039	450	95.09417	10078.11816	450	116.28314	93.30826	450	10850.17773	127.58501	91.58419	11684.77051

Table 1. (continued) Annuities

M	C(12.50,M,12)	A(12.50,M,12)	S(12.50,M,12)	C(12.75,M,12)	A(12.75,M,12)	S(12.75,M,12)	C(13.00,M,12)	A(13.00,M,12)	S(13.00,M,12)
451	107.08436	96.10351	10184.09963	117.51965	93.31677	10966.46094	128.96718	91.59194	11812.35547
452	108.19982	96.11275	10291.18262	118.76728	93.32519	11083.97949	130.36432	91.59962	11941.32227
453	109.32690	96.12169	10399.38201	120.02918	93.33352	11202.74707	131.77660	91.60722	12071.68652
454	110.46572	96.13095	10508.70898	121.30450	93.34177	11322.77637	133.20418	91.61471	12203.46289
455	111.61641	96.13991	10619.17400	122.59335	93.34992	11444.09008	134.64723	91.62214	12336.66699
456	112.77908	96.14877	10730.79102	123.89591	93.35799	11566.67383	136.10591	91.62949	12471.31445
457	113.95387	96.15756	10843.57031	125.21230	93.36598	11690.56934	137.58038	91.63675	12607.42030
458	115.14088	96.16624	10967.52441	126.54269	93.37388	11815.78223	139.07085	91.64394	12745.00098
459	116.34026	96.17483	11072.66504	127.88720	93.38170	11942.32820	140.57744	91.65105	12884.07227
460	117.55214	96.18333	11189.00586	129.24600	93.38943	12070.21191	142.10037	91.65810	13024.64941
461	118.77664	96.19176	11306.55762	130.61923	93.39709	12199.45801	143.63979	91.66505	13166.75000
462	120.01390	96.20009	11425.33398	132.00706	93.40467	12330.07715	145.19588	91.67194	13310.18965
463	121.26405	96.20834	11545.34963	133.40964	93.41216	12462.08398	146.76884	91.67876	13455.56496
464	122.52721	96.21650	11666.61230	134.82712	93.41958	12596.49414	148.35884	91.68549	13602.35449
465	123.80354	96.22457	11789.13965	136.25966	93.42692	12730.32129	149.96605	91.69216	13750.71289
466	125.03815	96.23257	11912.94336	137.70741	93.43418	12866.58105	151.59068	91.69976	13900.67871
467	126.39621	96.24048	12038.03613	139.17056	93.44137	13004.28809	153.23283	91.70528	14052.26963
468	127.71284	96.24831	12164.43262	140.64925	93.44848	13143.45898	154.89294	91.71175	14205.50208
469	129.04318	96.25606	12292.14551	142.14365	93.45551	13284.10840	156.57095	91.71813	14360.39551
470	130.38737	96.26373	12421.18848	143.65392	93.46247	13426.25196	158.26714	91.72445	14516.96680
471	131.74557	96.27132	12551.57617	145.18024	93.46936	13569.90527	159.98169	91.73070	14675.23340
472	133.11794	96.27883	12683.32129	146.72278	93.47618	13715.08594	161.71483	91.73689	14835.21582
473	134.50458	96.28626	12816.43945	148.28171	93.48292	13861.80859	163.46674	91.74300	14996.93066
474	135.90567	96.29362	12950.94434	149.85721	93.48959	14010.08984	165.23763	91.74905	15160.39746
475	137.32135	96.30090	13086.84961	151.44945	93.49620	14159.94727	167.02771	91.75504	15325.63477

476	96.30811	138.75179	13224.17090	476	153.05859	93.50273	14311.39746	476	91.76096	168.83717	15492.86211
477	96.31525	140.19711	13362.92285	477	154.64844	93.50919	14464.45605	477	91.76682	170.66624	15661.50000
478	96.32230	141.65750	13503.12012	478	156.32837	93.51559	14619.14063	478	91.77262	172.51512	15832.16602
479	96.32929	143.13310	13644.77734	479	157.98935	93.52192	14775.46875	479	91.77835	174.38405	16004.68066
480	96.33620	144.62407	13787.91016	480	159.66798	93.52818	14933.45901	480	91.78403	176.27321	16179.06543
481	96.34305	146.13057	13932.53418	481	161.36446	93.53439	15093.12598	481	91.78963	178.18283	16355.33789
482	96.34982	147.65276	14078.66504	482	163.07896	93.54051	15254.49023	482	91.79519	180.11314	16533.52148
483	96.35652	149.19081	14226.31836	483	164.81168	93.54659	15417.56534	483	91.80068	182.06436	16713.63281
484	96.36316	150.74487	14375.50879	484	166.56281	93.55258	15582.30096	484	91.80611	184.03673	16895.69727
485	96.36972	152.31514	14526.25391	485	168.33253	93.55853	15748.94434	485	91.81148	186.03046	17079.73438
486	96.37622	153.90175	14678.56836	486	170.12106	93.56441	15917.27637	486	91.81681	188.04579	17265.76563
487	96.38265	155.50490	14832.47070	487	171.92860	93.57022	16087.39746	487	91.82207	190.08296	17453.81055
488	96.38902	157.12474	14987.97559	488	173.75534	93.57597	16259.32617	488	91.82728	192.14220	17643.89453
489	96.39532	158.74146	15145.10059	489	175.60149	93.58167	16433.08203	489	91.83242	194.22372	17836.03711
490	96.40155	160.41522	15303.86133	490	177.46725	93.58730	16608.68359	490	91.83752	196.32782	18030.25977
491	96.40772	162.09621	15464.27734	491	179.35284	93.59288	16786.15039	491	91.84256	198.45471	18226.58789
492	96.41383	163.77461	15626.36328	492	181.25847	93.59840	16965.50195	492	91.84754	200.60463	18425.04297
493	96.41987	165.46061	15790.13770	493	183.19434	93.60386	17146.76172	493	91.85247	202.77786	18625.64648
494	96.42585	167.20436	15955.61016	494	185.13068	93.60926	17329.94531	494	91.85735	204.97461	18828.42578
495	96.43177	168.94606	16123.02227	495	187.07959	93.61460	17515.07617	495	91.86217	207.19616	19033.40039
496	96.43762	170.70592	16291.76855	496	189.08560	93.61989	17702.17383	496	91.86696	209.43977	19240.59570
497	96.44342	172.48512	16462.47461	497	191.09464	93.62512	17891.25977	497	91.87167	211.70871	19450.03516
498	96.44916	174.28032	16634.95898	498	193.12502	93.63030	18082.35352	498	91.87635	214.00223	19661.74414
499	96.45484	176.09624	16809.23828	499	195.17697	93.63543	18275.47852	499	91.88097	216.32059	19875.74609
500	96.46046	177.93057	16985.33594	500	197.25073	93.64050	18470.65625	500	91.88554	218.66405	20092.06641

Table 1. (continued) Annuities

N	C(13.25,M,12)	A(13.25,M,12)	S(13.25,M,12)	M	C(13.50,M,12)	A(13.50,M,12)	S(13.50,M,12)	M	C(13.75,M,12)	A(13.75,M,12)	S(13.75,M,12)
1	1.01104	0.98908	1.00000	1	1.01125	0.98888	1.00000	1	1.01146	0.98867	1.00000
2	1.02221	1.96736	2.01104	2	1.02263	1.96575	2.01125	2	1.02305	1.96614	2.01146
3	1.03349	2.93495	3.03325	3	1.03413	2.93374	3.03388	3	1.03477	2.93254	3.03451
4	1.04490	3.89198	4.06674	4	1.04577	3.88990	4.06801	4	1.04663	3.88799	4.06928
5	1.05644	4.83855	5.11164	5	1.05753	4.83558	5.11377	5	1.05862	4.83262	5.11590
6	1.06811	5.77479	6.16808	6	1.06943	5.77060	6.17130	6	1.07075	5.76654	6.17452
7	1.07990	6.70080	7.23619	7	1.08146	6.69534	7.24073	7	1.08302	6.68989	7.24527
8	1.09182	7.61670	8.31609	8	1.09362	7.60973	8.32219	8	1.09543	7.60277	8.32829
9	1.10388	8.52259	9.40791	9	1.10593	8.51396	9.41581	9	1.10796	8.50531	9.42372
10	1.11607	9.41860	10.51179	10	1.11837	9.40811	10.52174	10	1.12068	9.39763	10.53170
11	1.12839	10.30481	11.62786	11	1.13095	10.29232	11.64011	11	1.13352	10.27964	11.65238
12	1.14086	11.18135	12.75625	12	1.14367	11.16669	12.77106	12	1.14650	11.15206	12.78589
13	1.15345	12.04832	13.89710	13	1.15654	12.03134	13.91474	13	1.15964	12.01439	13.93240
14	1.16618	12.90582	15.05055	14	1.16955	12.88637	15.07128	14	1.17293	12.86696	15.09204
15	1.17906	13.75396	16.21673	15	1.18271	13.73188	16.24083	15	1.18637	13.70987	16.26497
16	1.19208	14.59282	17.39579	16	1.19601	14.56800	17.42354	16	1.19996	14.54323	17.45134
17	1.20524	15.42253	18.58787	17	1.20947	15.39480	18.61955	17	1.21371	15.36715	18.65130
18	1.21855	16.24318	19.79311	18	1.22308	16.21241	19.82902	18	1.22762	16.18173	19.86502
19	1.23200	17.05486	21.01166	19	1.23684	17.02093	21.05210	19	1.24169	16.98709	21.09263
20	1.24561	17.85769	22.24366	20	1.25075	17.82045	22.28893	20	1.25591	17.78332	22.33432
21	1.25936	18.65174	23.48927	21	1.26482	18.61107	23.53968	21	1.27030	18.57053	23.59023
22	1.27327	19.43712	24.74863	22	1.27905	19.39290	24.80451	22	1.28486	19.34883	24.86054
23	1.28733	20.21393	26.02190	23	1.29344	20.16603	26.08356	23	1.29958	20.11830	26.14540
24	1.30154	20.98225	27.30922	24	1.30799	20.93057	27.37700	24	1.31447	20.87906	27.44498
25	1.31591	21.74218	28.61076	25	1.32271	21.68659	28.68499	25	1.32954	21.63121	28.75946

n				n				n			
26	1.33044	22.43381	29.92667	26	1.33759	22.43421	30.00769	26	1.34477	22.37483	30.08899
27	1.34513	23.23723	31.25711	27	1.35263	23.17351	31.34528	27	1.36018	23.11003	31.43378
28	1.35998	23.97283	32.60224	28	1.36785	23.90458	32.69791	28	1.37576	23.83689	32.78194
29	1.37500	24.69981	33.96222	29	1.38324	24.62752	34.06577	29	1.39153	24.55553	34.16970
30	1.39018	25.41914	35.33722	30	1.39880	25.34242	35.44901	30	1.40747	25.26602	35.56123
31	1.40553	26.13061	36.72741	31	1.41454	26.04936	36.84781	31	1.42360	25.96847	36.96870
32	1.42105	26.83432	38.12294	32	1.43045	26.74844	38.26234	32	1.43991	26.66295	38.38230
33	1.43674	27.53034	39.55399	33	1.44654	27.43974	39.69927	33	1.45641	27.34957	39.83221
34	1.45261	28.21875	40.99073	34	1.46282	28.12336	41.13934	34	1.47310	28.02842	41.28863
35	1.46865	28.89965	42.44334	35	1.47927	28.79938	42.60216	35	1.48998	28.69957	42.76173
36	1.48486	29.57312	43.91198	36	1.49592	29.46785	44.08143	36	1.50705	29.36311	44.25170
37	1.50126	30.23923	45.33684	37	1.51275	30.12880	45.57735	37	1.52432	30.01914	45.75675
38	1.51783	30.89906	46.89910	38	1.52976	30.78260	47.09009	38	1.54179	30.66774	47.28307
39	1.53459	31.54970	48.41593	39	1.54697	31.42902	48.61996	39	1.55945	31.30899	48.82486
40	1.55154	32.19422	49.95053	40	1.56438	32.06825	50.16683	40	1.57732	31.94298	50.38431
41	1.56867	32.83170	51.50206	41	1.58198	32.70037	51.73121	41	1.59639	32.56979	51.96163
42	1.58599	33.46222	53.07073	42	1.59977	33.32546	53.31318	42	1.61387	33.18949	53.55702
43	1.60350	34.08586	54.65672	43	1.61777	33.94360	54.91236	43	1.63216	33.80217	55.17070
44	1.62121	34.70268	56.26022	44	1.63597	34.55485	56.52073	44	1.65087	34.40791	56.80286
45	1.63911	35.31277	57.88143	45	1.65438	35.15931	58.16670	45	1.66978	35.00679	58.45373
46	1.65721	35.91303	59.52053	46	1.67299	35.75704	59.82108	46	1.68892	35.59889	60.12351
47	1.67550	36.51303	61.17774	47	1.69181	36.34813	61.49406	47	1.70827	36.18428	61.81243
48	1.69400	37.10335	62.85324	48	1.71084	36.93471	63.18587	48	1.72784	36.76303	63.52069
49	1.71271	37.68722	64.54725	49	1.73009	37.51064	64.89671	49	1.74764	37.33524	65.24854
50	1.73162	38.26471	66.25996	50	1.74955	38.08221	66.62679	50	1.76766	37.90036	66.99817

Table 1. (continued) Annuities

M	C(13.25,M,12)	A(13.25,M,12)	S(13.25,M,12)	M	C(13.50,M,12)	A(13.50,M,12)	S(13.50,M,12)	M	C(13.75,M,12)	A(13.75,M,12)	S(13.75,M,12)
51	1.75074	38.86590	67.99158	51	1.76923	38.64743	68.37635	51	1.78792	38.46026	68.76384
52	1.77007	39.05085	69.74232	52	1.78914	39.20636	70.14558	52	1.80841	39.01324	70.55176
53	1.78962	39.25069	71.51239	53	1.80927	39.75907	71.93472	53	1.82913	39.55995	72.36016
54	1.80938	40.51281	73.30201	54	1.82962	40.30563	73.74399	54	1.85009	40.10046	74.18929
55	1.82935	41.05894	75.11138	55	1.85020	40.84612	75.57361	55	1.87128	40.63485	76.03838
56	1.84955	41.59962	76.94073	56	1.87102	41.38058	77.42381	56	1.89273	41.16319	77.91066
57	1.86998	42.13428	78.79029	57	1.89207	41.90910	79.29482	57	1.91441	41.68555	79.80338
58	1.89062	42.66331	80.66027	58	1.91335	42.43175	81.18689	58	1.93635	42.20196	81.71760
59	1.91150	43.18646	82.55089	59	1.93488	42.94857	83.10024	59	1.95854	42.71257	83.65414
60	1.93261	43.70390	84.46239	60	1.95665	43.45966	85.03513	60	1.98098	43.21737	85.61269
61	1.95394	44.21568	86.39500	61	1.97866	43.96505	86.99177	61	2.00368	43.71645	87.59367
62	1.97552	44.72187	88.34894	62	2.00092	44.46482	88.97043	62	2.02664	44.20988	89.59734
63	1.99733	45.22254	90.32446	63	2.02343	44.95903	90.97134	63	2.04986	44.69772	91.62398
64	2.01939	45.71774	92.32179	64	2.04619	45.44774	92.99477	64	2.07335	45.18003	93.87384
65	2.04168	46.20753	94.34118	65	2.06921	45.93102	95.04096	65	2.09710	45.65688	95.74718
66	2.06423	46.69198	96.38287	66	2.09249	46.40892	97.11018	66	2.12113	46.12832	97.84428
67	2.08702	47.17113	98.44709	67	2.11603	46.88150	99.20266	67	2.14544	46.59443	99.96542
68	2.11006	47.64505	100.53411	68	2.13984	47.34883	101.31870	68	2.17002	47.05526	102.11086
69	2.13336	48.11379	102.64417	69	2.16391	47.81096	103.45853	69	2.19489	47.51096	104.28088
70	2.15692	48.57742	104.77754	70	2.18825	48.26794	105.62244	70	2.22003	47.96130	106.47576
71	2.18073	49.03598	106.93466	71	2.21287	48.71984	107.81069	71	2.24547	48.40664	108.69579
72	2.20481	49.48953	109.11519	72	2.23777	49.16671	110.02356	72	2.27120	48.84694	110.94127
73	2.22916	49.93813	111.32001	73	2.26294	49.60862	112.26132	73	2.29723	49.28225	113.21247
74	2.25377	50.38183	113.54916	74	2.28840	50.04560	114.52426	74	2.32355	49.71262	115.50970
75	2.27866	50.82069	115.80293	75	2.31414	50.47773	116.81266	75	2.35017	50.13812	117.83324

n									
76	2.30392	51.25475	118.08160	2.34018	50.90505	119.12681	2.37710	50.55880	120.18342
77	2.32926	51.48407	120.38541	2.36650	51.32761	121.46698	2.40434	50.97472	122.56052
78	2.35497	52.10870	122.71467	2.39313	51.74548	123.83348	2.43189	51.38592	124.96496
79	2.38098	52.52870	125.06964	2.42005	52.15869	126.22661	2.45975	51.79247	127.39574
80	2.40727	52.94411	127.45062	2.44727	52.56731	128.64665	2.48794	52.19440	129.85649
81	2.43386	53.35498	129.85788	2.47481	52.97138	131.09393	2.51645	52.59979	132.34444
82	2.46072	53.76136	132.29973	2.50265	53.37096	133.56874	2.54528	52.98467	134.66089
83	2.48789	54.16331	134.75246	2.53080	53.76609	136.07138	2.57445	53.37311	137.40616
84	2.51536	54.56087	137.24034	2.55927	54.15683	138.60219	2.60394	53.75714	139.99061
85	2.54314	54.96408	139.75571	2.58807	54.54321	141.16147	2.63378	54.13682	142.58455
86	2.57122	55.34301	142.29864	2.61718	54.92530	143.74963	2.66396	54.51220	145.21834
87	2.59961	55.72768	144.87006	2.64663	55.30314	146.36671	2.69448	54.88333	147.88229
88	2.62831	56.10815	147.46967	2.67640	55.67678	149.01334	2.72536	55.25026	150.57678
89	2.65733	56.48447	150.09799	2.70651	56.04628	151.68974	2.75659	55.61302	153.33224
90	2.68667	56.85667	152.75531	2.73696	56.41163	154.39628	2.78817	55.97168	156.05873
91	2.71634	57.22482	155.44199	2.76775	56.77293	157.13321	2.82012	56.32627	158.84699
92	2.74633	57.58894	158.15833	2.79889	57.13022	159.90096	2.85243	56.67685	161.66702
93	2.77666	57.94909	160.90465	2.83037	57.48353	162.69904	2.88512	57.02346	164.51945
94	2.80731	58.30530	163.68162	2.86221	57.83291	165.53021	2.91818	57.36614	167.40457
95	2.83831	58.65762	166.48962	2.89441	58.17840	168.39243	2.95161	57.70494	170.32275
96	2.86965	59.00612	169.32693	2.92698	58.52005	171.28685	2.98544	58.03990	173.27437
97	2.90134	59.35076	172.19658	2.95991	58.85730	174.21382	3.01964	58.37106	176.25980
98	2.93337	59.69167	175.09792	2.99320	59.19199	177.17372	3.05424	58.69947	179.27945
99	2.96576	60.02885	178.03130	3.02688	59.52236	180.16639	3.08924	59.02218	182.33389
100	2.99851	60.36235	180.99706	3.06093	59.84906	183.19982	3.12464	59.34222	186.42298

Table 1. (continued) Annuities

M	C(13.25,M,12)	A(13.25,M,12)	S(13.25,M,12)	M	C(13.50,M,12)	A(13.50,M,12)	S(13.50,M,12)	M	C(13.75,M,12)	A(13.75,M,12)	S(13.75,M,12)
101	3.03162	60.69220	183.99556	101	3.09537	60.17212	186.25475	101	3.16044	59.65963	188.54756
102	3.06509	61.01846	187.02719	102	3.13019	60.49159	189.35011	102	3.19665	59.97145	191.70801
103	3.09994	61.34115	190.09227	103	3.16540	60.80751	192.48030	103	3.23328	60.28074	194.90466
104	3.13315	61.66032	193.19121	104	3.20101	61.11991	195.64571	104	3.27033	60.58652	198.13794
105	3.16775	61.97600	196.32437	105	3.23703	61.42884	198.84671	105	3.30780	60.88883	201.40828
106	3.20273	62.28823	199.49211	106	3.27344	61.73433	202.08374	106	3.34571	61.18772	204.71608
107	3.23809	62.59706	202.69484	107	3.31027	62.03642	205.35718	107	3.38404	61.48333	208.06178
108	3.27384	62.90251	205.93292	108	3.34751	62.33514	208.66745	108	3.42282	61.77538	211.44583
109	3.30999	63.20462	209.20662	109	3.38517	62.63055	212.01495	109	3.46204	62.06423	214.86864
110	3.34654	63.50344	212.51677	110	3.42325	62.92267	215.40013	110	3.50171	62.34981	218.33067
111	3.38349	63.79899	215.86330	111	3.46176	63.21154	218.82338	111	3.54183	62.63215	221.83238
112	3.42085	64.09132	219.24680	112	3.50071	63.49720	222.28514	112	3.58241	62.91129	225.37422
113	3.45862	64.39045	222.66765	113	3.54009	63.77967	225.78584	113	3.62346	63.18727	228.96663
114	3.49681	64.66643	226.12627	114	3.57992	64.05901	229.32594	114	3.66498	63.46012	232.59009
115	3.53542	64.94927	229.62308	115	3.62019	64.33524	232.90585	115	3.70697	63.72988	236.24507
116	3.57446	65.22504	233.15849	116	3.66092	64.60839	236.52605	116	3.74945	63.99659	239.93044
117	3.61393	65.50504	236.73296	117	3.70210	64.87851	240.18697	117	3.79241	64.26027	243.70143
118	3.65383	65.77943	240.34688	118	3.74375	65.14562	243.88907	118	3.83587	64.52097	247.49391
119	3.69417	66.05013	244.00072	119	3.78587	65.40976	247.63283	119	3.87982	64.77871	251.32977
120	3.73496	66.31787	247.69489	120	3.82846	65.67097	251.41969	120	3.92428	65.03354	255.20969
121	3.77620	66.58269	251.42986	121	3.87153	65.92926	255.24715	121	3.96924	65.28547	259.13398
122	3.81790	66.84460	255.20605	122	3.91509	66.18468	259.11868	122	4.01472	65.53455	263.10312
123	3.86006	67.10367	259.02396	123	3.95914	66.43726	263.03375	123	4.06073	65.78082	267.11783
124	3.90268	67.35991	262.88400	124	4.00367	66.68703	266.99289	124	4.10725	66.02429	271.17666
125	3.94577	67.61334	266.78668	125	4.04871	66.93403	270.99655	125	4.15432	66.26500	275.28560

n				n				n			
126	3.98934	67.86401	270.73245	126	4.09426	67.17827	275.04526	126	4.20192	66.50299	279.44012
127	4.03339	68.11194	274.72100	127	4.14032	67.41900	279.13953	127	4.25006	66.73828	283.64206
128	4.07792	68.35716	278.75519	128	4.18690	67.65864	283.27965	128	4.29676	66.97090	287.89212
129	4.12295	68.59971	282.83310	129	4.23400	67.89482	287.46674	129	4.34802	67.20090	292.19089
130	4.16847	68.83961	286.95605	130	4.28163	68.12838	291.70074	130	4.39784	67.42828	296.53891
131	4.21450	69.07688	291.12451	131	4.32960	68.35934	295.98039	131	4.44823	67.65308	300.93674
132	4.26103	69.31157	295.33902	132	4.37851	68.58772	300.31219	132	4.49920	67.87535	305.39498
133	4.30908	69.54369	299.60007	133	4.42777	68.81357	304.69070	133	4.55076	68.09609	309.88418
134	4.35565	69.77328	303.90814	134	4.47758	69.03690	309.11847	134	4.60290	68.31235	314.43494
135	4.40375	70.00035	308.26379	135	4.52796	69.25775	313.59604	135	4.65564	68.52714	319.03784
136	4.45237	70.22495	312.66754	136	4.57890	69.47615	318.12399	136	4.70899	68.73950	323.61948
137	4.50153	70.44710	317.11990	137	4.63041	69.69211	322.70291	137	4.76294	68.94946	328.40247
138	4.55124	70.66682	321.62143	138	4.68250	69.90567	327.33331	138	4.81752	69.15703	333.16541
139	4.60149	70.88414	326.17267	139	4.73518	70.11686	332.01581	139	4.87272	69.36225	337.98294
140	4.65230	71.09909	330.77417	140	4.78845	70.32571	336.75096	140	4.92855	69.56516	342.85565
141	4.70367	71.31169	335.42645	141	4.84232	70.53220	341.53943	141	4.98503	69.76575	347.78421
142	4.75560	71.52197	340.13013	142	4.89679	70.73642	346.38174	142	5.04215	69.96408	352.76923
143	4.80811	71.72996	344.88574	143	4.95188	70.93836	351.27856	143	5.09992	70.16016	357.81137
144	4.86120	71.93566	349.69385	144	5.00759	71.13806	356.23044	144	5.15836	70.35403	362.91129
145	4.91488	72.13912	354.55505	145	5.06393	71.33554	361.23804	145	5.21746	70.54568	368.06867
146	4.96915	72.34036	359.46994	146	5.12090	71.53082	366.30194	146	5.27725	70.73518	373.28711
147	5.02401	72.53941	364.43909	147	5.17851	71.72392	371.42285	147	5.33772	70.92252	378.56436
148	5.07949	72.73628	369.46310	148	5.23677	71.91488	376.60135	148	5.39888	71.10775	383.90210
149	5.13557	72.93100	374.54257	149	5.29568	72.10371	381.83813	149	5.46074	71.29088	389.30096
150	5.18228	73.12359	379.67016	150	5.35526	72.29044	387.13379	150	5.52331	71.47192	394.76172

Table 1. (continued) Annuities

M	C(13.25,M,12)	A(13.25,M,12)	S(13.25,M,12)	M	C(13.50,M,12)	A(13.50,M,12)	S(13.50,M,12)	M	C(13.75,M,12)	A(13.75,M,12)	S(13.75,M,12)
151	5.24961	73.31408	384.87045	151	5.41550	72.47510	392.48904	151	5.59860	71.85092	400.28503
152	5.30758	73.50249	390.12006	152	5.47643	72.65770	397.90457	152	5.65061	71.92790	405.87181
153	5.36618	73.68884	395.42761	153	5.53804	72.83827	403.39098	153	5.71536	72.00286	411.52222
154	5.42543	73.87316	400.73379	154	5.60034	73.01683	408.91904	154	5.79085	72.17585	417.23758
155	5.48534	74.05547	406.21924	155	5.66334	73.19341	414.51935	155	5.84709	72.34688	423.01843
156	5.54590	74.23578	411.70459	156	5.72706	73.36801	420.18271	156	5.91408	72.51596	428.86554
157	5.60714	74.41412	417.25049	157	5.79148	73.54068	425.90976	157	5.99185	72.68314	434.77960
158	5.66905	74.59052	422.85764	158	5.85664	73.71143	431.70123	158	6.05039	72.84841	440.76144
159	5.73165	74.76499	428.52667	159	5.92253	73.88027	437.55789	159	6.11972	73.01182	446.81196
160	5.79494	74.93755	434.25833	160	5.98915	74.04724	443.49041	160	6.18994	73.17338	452.93158
161	5.85892	75.10823	440.05325	161	6.05653	74.21236	449.46957	161	6.26077	73.33310	459.12140
162	5.92361	75.27705	445.91217	162	6.12467	74.37563	455.52609	162	6.33250	73.49101	465.38217
163	5.98902	75.44402	451.83578	163	6.19357	74.53709	461.65076	163	6.40506	73.64714	471.71469
164	6.05515	75.60917	457.82483	164	6.26325	74.69675	467.84433	164	6.47946	73.80150	478.11975
165	6.12201	75.77251	463.87997	165	6.33371	74.85463	474.10757	165	6.55269	73.95411	484.59821
166	6.18961	75.93407	470.00198	166	6.40496	75.01077	480.44131	166	6.62777	74.10499	491.15088
167	6.25795	76.09387	476.19159	167	6.47702	75.16515	486.84625	167	6.70371	74.25418	497.77866
168	6.32705	76.25192	482.44962	168	6.54989	75.31783	493.32327	168	6.79053	74.40164	504.48236
169	6.39691	76.40825	488.77658	169	6.62357	75.46880	499.87317	169	6.85822	74.54745	511.26291
170	6.46754	76.56287	495.17349	170	6.69809	75.61810	506.49673	170	6.93690	74.69161	518.12109
171	6.53896	76.71580	501.64102	171	6.77344	75.76574	513.19482	171	7.01629	74.83414	525.05792
172	6.61115	76.86706	508.17996	172	6.84964	75.91173	519.96826	172	7.09668	74.97504	532.07422
173	6.68415	77.01666	514.77914	173	6.92670	76.05610	526.81793	173	7.17600	75.11436	539.17090
174	6.75796	77.16464	521.47528	174	7.00463	76.19886	533.74463	174	7.26025	75.25210	546.34888
175	6.83258	77.31100	528.23322	175	7.08343	76.34003	540.74921	175	7.34344	75.38828	553.60913

n									
176	6.90802	77.45576	535.06580	7.16312	76.47964	547.83264	7.42758	75.52290	560.96258
177	6.98429	77.59894	541.97392	7.24370	76.61769	554.99679	7.51269	75.65601	568.39013
178	7.06141	77.74055	548.95813	7.32519	76.75420	562.23960	7.59877	75.78761	575.89282
179	7.13938	77.88062	556.01953	7.40760	76.88900	569.56470	7.68584	75.91772	583.49164
180	7.21821	78.01916	563.15894	7.49094	77.02270	576.97229	7.77390	76.04636	591.17743
181	7.29791	78.15618	570.37714	7.57521	77.15471	584.46320	7.86298	76.17354	596.96135
182	7.37850	78.29171	577.87505	7.66043	77.28525	592.03845	7.96308	76.29928	606.81433
183	7.45997	78.42576	585.05353	7.74661	77.41434	599.69885	8.04421	76.42359	614.76746
184	7.54234	78.55834	592.51349	7.83376	77.54198	607.44550	8.13638	76.54649	622.81165
185	7.62562	78.68948	600.05585	7.92189	77.66822	615.27924	8.22961	76.66801	630.94800
186	7.70982	78.81918	607.68146	8.01101	77.79305	623.20111	8.32391	76.78814	639.17761
187	7.79495	78.94747	615.39130	8.10114	77.91649	631.21216	8.41929	76.90691	647.50153
188	7.88101	79.07436	623.18622	8.19227	78.03855	639.31329	8.51576	77.02435	655.92084
189	7.96803	79.19986	631.06720	8.28444	78.15926	647.50555	8.61334	77.14044	664.43658
190	8.05601	79.32400	639.03528	8.37764	78.27863	655.78998	8.71203	77.25523	673.04993
191	8.14497	79.44677	647.09125	8.47189	78.39667	664.18760	8.81186	77.36871	681.76196
192	8.23490	79.56821	655.23627	8.56719	78.51339	672.63963	8.91282	77.48091	690.57385
193	8.32583	79.68831	663.47113	8.66358	78.62881	681.20673	9.01496	77.59184	699.48663
194	8.41776	79.80711	671.79700	8.76104	78.74236	689.87030	9.11825	77.70151	708.50159
195	8.51070	79.92461	680.21472	8.85960	78.85583	698.63135	9.22273	77.80994	717.61987
196	8.60468	80.04082	688.72540	8.95927	78.96745	707.49091	9.32840	77.91714	726.74259
197	8.69675	80.15577	697.33014	9.06006	79.07782	716.45020	9.43529	78.02312	736.17036
198	8.79675	80.26946	706.02979	9.16199	79.18697	725.51025	9.54341	78.12791	745.60626
199	8.88287	80.38197	714.82556	9.26506	79.29490	734.67224	9.65276	78.23150	755.14966
200	8.99106	80.43313	723.71838	9.36930	79.40163	743.93732	9.76336	78.33392	764.80243

Table 1. (continued) Annuities

M	C(13.25,M,12)	A(13.25,M,12)	S(13.25,M,12)	M	C(13.50,M,12)	A(13.50,M,12)	S(13.50,M,12)	M	C(13.75,M,12)	A(13.75,M,12)	S(13.75,M,12)
201	9.09033	80.60314	732.70947	201	9.47470	79.50717	753.30664	201	9.87523	78.43519	774.56560
202	9.19071	80.71194	741.79990	202	9.58129	79.61154	762.78131	202	9.98839	78.53580	784.44104
203	9.28219	80.81956	750.93048	203	9.68908	79.71475	772.36261	203	10.10284	78.63428	794.42944
204	9.39479	80.92600	760.28271	204	9.79808	79.81682	782.05170	204	10.21860	78.73215	804.53223
205	9.49852	81.03128	769.67749	205	9.90831	79.91774	791.84979	205	10.33569	78.82890	814.75085
206	9.60340	81.13541	779.17603	206	10.01978	80.01754	801.75806	206	10.45412	78.92455	825.08655
207	9.70944	81.23840	788.77942	207	10.13250	80.11623	811.77783	207	10.57390	79.01913	835.54065
208	9.81665	81.34027	798.48883	208	10.24649	80.21383	821.91034	208	10.69506	79.11263	846.11456
209	9.92504	81.44103	808.30548	209	10.36176	80.31034	832.15686	209	10.81761	79.20507	856.80963
210	10.03463	81.54069	818.23053	210	10.47833	80.40577	842.51862	210	10.94156	79.29646	867.62726
211	10.14543	81.63925	828.26514	211	10.59622	80.50014	852.99595	211	11.06693	79.38683	878.56879
212	10.25745	81.73674	838.41058	212	10.71542	80.59347	863.59314	212	11.19374	79.47616	889.63574
213	10.37071	81.83314	848.66803	213	10.83597	80.68575	874.30859	213	11.32200	79.56448	900.82947
214	10.48522	81.92854	859.03874	214	10.95788	80.77702	885.14459	214	11.45174	79.65181	912.15149
215	10.60099	82.02287	869.52399	215	11.08115	80.86726	896.10242	215	11.58295	79.73814	923.60321
216	10.71805	82.11617	880.12494	216	11.20582	80.95650	907.18359	216	11.71567	79.82349	935.18618
217	10.83639	82.20845	890.84302	217	11.33188	81.04475	918.38940	217	11.84992	79.90788	946.90186
218	10.95604	82.29973	901.67948	218	11.45936	81.13201	929.72131	218	11.98570	79.99132	958.75177
219	11.07702	82.39000	912.63544	219	11.58828	81.21830	941.18066	219	12.12303	80.07381	970.73749
220	11.19932	82.47929	923.71246	220	11.71865	81.30363	952.76892	220	12.26194	80.15536	982.86047
221	11.32298	82.56761	934.91180	221	11.85049	81.38802	964.48761	221	12.40244	80.23590	995.12244
222	11.44801	82.65496	946.23480	222	11.98380	81.47147	976.33607	222	12.54456	80.31570	1007.52480
223	11.57441	82.74136	957.68280	223	12.11862	81.55398	988.32190	223	12.68830	80.39452	1020.06946
224	11.70222	82.82681	969.25720	224	12.25496	81.63558	1000.44049	224	12.83368	80.47243	1032.75769
225	11.83143	82.91133	980.95941	225	12.39282	81.71628	1012.69543	225	12.98073	80.54948	1045.59143

n			
226	11.96207	82.99493	992.79083
227	12.09415	83.07761	1004.75233
228	12.22679	83.15939	1016.84705
229	12.36270	83.24029	1029.07471
230	12.49920	83.32029	1041.43738
231	12.63722	83.39942	1053.93665
232	12.77675	83.47769	1066.57385
233	12.91783	83.55510	1079.35059
234	13.06046	83.63167	1092.26843
235	13.20467	83.70740	1105.32896
236	13.35048	83.78230	1118.53357
237	13.49789	83.85639	1131.88403
238	13.64683	83.92966	1145.38196
239	13.79761	84.00214	1159.02881
240	13.94996	84.07383	1172.82642
241	14.10399	84.14473	1186.77637
242	14.25972	84.21486	1200.80037
243	14.41717	84.28422	1215.14014
244	14.57636	84.35282	1229.55725
245	14.73731	84.42068	1244.13367
246	14.90033	84.48779	1258.70097
247	15.06456	84.55417	1273.77100
248	15.23089	84.61983	1288.83557
249	15.39907	84.68477	1304.06641
250	15.56910	84.74899	1319.46558

n			
226	12.53224	81.79607	1025.08826
227	12.67323	81.87498	1037.62048
228	12.81590	81.95300	1050.29370
229	12.95998	82.03017	1063.10950
230	13.10578	82.10647	1076.06946
231	13.25322	82.18192	1089.17529
232	13.40232	82.25654	1102.42847
233	13.55310	82.33032	1115.83081
234	13.70557	82.40328	1129.38391
235	13.85976	82.47543	1143.08948
236	14.01568	82.54678	1156.94922
237	14.17336	82.61734	1170.96437
238	14.33281	82.68710	1185.13831
239	14.49405	82.75610	1199.47107
240	14.65711	82.82433	1213.9621
241	14.82200	82.89179	1228.62231
242	14.98975	82.95851	1243.4421
243	15.15737	83.02448	1258.43298
244	15.32789	83.08973	1273.59033
245	15.50033	83.15424	1288.91833
246	15.67471	83.21904	1304.41958
247	15.85105	83.28113	1320.09326
248	16.02937	83.34351	1335.94434
249	16.20970	83.40520	1351.97375
250	16.39206	83.46621	1368.18347

n			
226	13.12947	80.62564	1058.57214
227	13.27991	80.70094	1071.70154
228	13.43208	80.77539	1084.90157
229	13.58599	80.84899	1098.41357
230	13.74166	80.92177	1111.99963
231	13.89912	80.99371	1125.74121
232	14.05838	81.06484	1139.64038
233	14.21947	81.13517	1153.69873
234	14.38240	81.20470	1167.91021
235	14.54719	81.27345	1182.30066
236	14.71388	81.34141	1196.80778
237	14.88248	81.40860	1211.50165
238	15.05301	81.47503	1226.44421
239	15.22549	81.54071	1241.49719
240	15.39995	81.60564	1256.72266
241	15.57640	81.66985	1272.12256
242	15.75488	81.73331	1287.69697
243	15.93541	81.79607	1303.45386
244	16.11900	81.85811	1319.38928
245	16.30269	81.91945	1335.50732
246	16.48949	81.98009	1351.80994
247	16.67643	82.04005	1368.29944
248	16.86954	82.09933	1384.97791
249	17.06284	82.15794	1401.84741
250	17.25835	82.21588	1418.91028

Table 1. (continued) Annuities

M	C(13.25,M,12)	A(13.25,M,12)	S(13.25,M,12)	M	C(13.50,M,12)	A(13.50,M,12)	S(13.50,M,12)	M	C(13.75,M,12)	A(13.75,M,12)	S(13.75,M,12)
251	15.74101	84.81252	1335.03467	251	16.57648	83.52654	1384.57556	251	17.45610	82.27317	1436.16870
252	15.91481	84.87536	1350.77563	252	16.76296	83.58619	1401.15198	252	17.65612	82.32980	1453.82476
253	16.09054	84.93751	1366.69043	253	16.95154	83.64518	1417.91492	253	17.85943	82.38580	1471.28088
254	16.26821	84.99898	1382.78101	254	17.14225	83.70351	1434.86646	254	18.06305	82.44116	1489.13928
255	16.44783	85.05978	1399.04919	255	17.33510	83.76120	1452.00879	255	18.27003	82.49590	1507.20239
256	16.62945	85.11991	1415.49707	256	17.53012	83.81824	1469.34387	256	18.47937	82.55001	1525.47241
257	16.81306	85.17939	1432.12646	257	17.72733	83.87466	1486.87402	257	18.69110	82.60352	1543.95178
258	16.99871	85.23821	1448.93958	258	17.92676	83.93044	1504.60132	258	18.90528	82.65641	1562.64282
259	17.18640	85.29640	1465.93823	259	18.12844	83.98560	1522.52808	259	19.12191	82.70870	1581.54810
260	17.37617	85.35395	1483.12463	260	18.33239	84.04015	1540.65649	260	19.34101	82.76041	1600.67004
261	17.56803	85.41087	1500.50085	261	18.53862	84.09408	1558.98889	261	19.56263	82.81152	1620.01111
262	17.76201	85.46717	1518.06885	262	18.74718	84.14743	1577.52747	262	19.78678	82.86207	1639.57373
263	17.95810	85.52286	1535.83081	263	18.95809	84.20018	1596.27466	263	20.01351	82.91203	1659.36047
264	18.15642	85.57798	1553.78894	264	19.17137	84.25235	1615.23279	264	20.24283	82.96143	1679.37402
265	18.35690	85.63241	1571.94543	265	19.38705	84.30392	1634.40417	265	20.47478	83.01027	1699.61682
266	18.55959	85.68629	1590.30237	266	19.60515	84.35493	1653.79126	266	20.70938	83.05856	1720.09155
267	18.76452	85.73959	1608.86194	267	19.82571	84.40537	1673.39636	267	20.94668	83.10630	1740.80090
268	18.97171	85.79229	1627.62646	268	20.04875	84.45525	1693.22205	268	21.18669	83.15350	1761.74768
269	19.18119	85.84443	1646.59814	269	20.27420	84.50456	1713.27087	269	21.42945	83.20016	1782.93433
270	19.39298	85.89599	1665.77930	270	20.50238	84.55334	1733.54517	270	21.67500	83.24630	1804.36377
271	19.60711	85.94699	1685.17224	271	20.73303	84.60150	1754.04749	271	21.92336	83.29192	1826.03882
272	19.82361	85.99744	1704.77942	272	20.96828	84.64928	1774.78052	272	22.17457	83.33701	1847.96216
273	20.04249	86.04733	1724.60303	273	21.20215	84.69644	1796.74683	273	22.42865	83.38160	1870.13672
274	20.26379	86.09668	1744.64551	274	21.44068	84.74308	1816.94897	274	22.68564	83.42567	1892.56531
275	20.48754	86.14549	1764.90330	275	21.68188	84.78920	1838.38965	275	22.94558	83.46926	1915.25098

Index	Col1	Col2	Col3	Col4	Col5	Col6	Col7	Col8	Col9
276	20.71376	1785.36885	86.13377	21.92580	1960.07153	84.83491	23.20850	1938.19666	83.51234
277	20.94247	1806.11060	86.24152	22.17247	1981.99731	84.87991	23.47443	1961.40515	83.55495
278	21.17371	1827.05310	86.28875	22.42291	1904.16990	84.92451	23.74341	1984.87952	83.59706
279	21.40750	1848.20610	86.33546	22.67416	1926.59167	84.96861	24.01547	2008.62292	83.63870
280	21.64388	1869.63428	86.38166	22.92924	1949.26587	85.01222	24.29065	2032.63843	83.67987
281	21.88286	1891.27820	86.42738	23.18719	1972.19507	85.05535	24.56898	2056.92896	83.72057
282	22.12449	1913.16101	86.47256	23.44905	1995.38232	85.09900	24.85050	2081.49905	83.76081
283	22.36878	1935.28552	86.51727	23.71184	2018.80032	85.14017	25.13524	2106.34839	83.80060
284	22.61577	1957.65430	86.56148	23.97860	2042.54224	85.18108	25.42325	2131.48364	83.83994
285	22.86548	1980.27002	86.60522	24.24836	2066.52075	85.23311	25.71456	2156.90698	83.87882
286	23.11796	2003.13550	86.64847	24.52115	2090.76904	85.28390	26.00920	2182.62158	83.91727
287	23.37321	2026.25354	86.69125	24.79702	2115.29028	85.30422	26.30723	2208.63086	83.95528
288	23.63129	2049.62671	86.73357	25.07598	2140.08716	85.34410	26.60867	2234.93799	83.99286
289	23.89222	2073.25606	86.77543	25.35809	2165.16333	85.38354	26.91356	2261.54663	84.03002
290	24.15603	2097.15015	86.81683	25.64337	2190.52124	85.42253	27.22194	2288.46021	84.06676
291	24.42276	2121.30615	86.85777	25.93185	2216.16479	85.46110	27.53386	2315.68213	84.10307
292	24.69242	2145.72900	86.89827	26.22359	2242.03668	85.49823	27.84835	2343.21606	84.13898
293	24.96507	2170.42139	86.93832	26.51860	2268.32007	85.53694	28.16846	2371.06543	84.17448
294	25.24073	2195.36647	86.97794	26.81694	2294.83887	85.57423	28.49122	2399.23389	84.20356
295	25.51943	2220.62720	87.01713	27.11863	2321.65576	85.61111	28.81768	2427.72510	84.24428
296	25.80120	2246.14673	87.05589	27.42371	2348.77441	85.64757	29.14789	2456.54272	84.27859
297	26.09609	2271.73223	87.09422	27.73223	2376.19800	85.68363	29.48187	2485.69067	84.31251
298	26.37412	2298.03394	87.13213	28.04422	2403.93018	85.71928	29.81868	2515.17236	84.34604
299	26.66534	2324.40796	87.16964	28.35971	2431.97437	85.75455	30.16137	2544.99219	84.37920
300	26.95977	2351.07349	87.20673	28.67876	2460.33423	85.78942	30.50697	2575.15356	84.41198

Table 1. (continued) Annuities

M	C(13.25,M,12)	A(13.25,M,12)	S(13.25,M,12)	M	C(13.50,M,12)	A(13.50,M,12)	S(13.50,M,12)	M	C(13.75,M,12)	A(13.75,M,12)	S(13.75,M,12)
301	27.25745	87.24342	2378.03320	301	29.00140	85.82390	2489.01294	301	30.85553	84.44438	2605.66040
302	27.55842	87.27970	2405.29053	302	29.32766	85.85799	2518.01440	302	31.21009	84.47643	2636.51709
303	27.86271	87.31560	2432.84912	303	29.65760	85.89172	2547.34204	303	31.56771	84.50810	2667.72705
304	28.17036	87.35109	2460.71167	304	29.99125	85.92506	2576.99951	304	31.92942	84.53942	2699.29492
305	28.48141	87.38621	2488.88208	305	30.32865	85.95803	2606.99097	305	32.29528	84.57039	2731.22437
306	28.79589	87.42093	2517.36353	306	30.66985	85.99063	2637.31958	306	32.66533	84.60100	2763.51953
307	29.11384	87.45528	2546.15942	307	31.01488	86.02288	2667.98926	307	33.03962	84.63126	2796.18491
308	29.43531	87.48925	2575.27319	308	31.36380	86.05478	2699.00415	308	33.41820	84.66119	2829.22437
309	29.76032	87.52285	2604.70850	309	31.71664	86.08629	2730.36792	309	33.80111	84.69077	2862.64258
310	30.08893	87.55609	2634.46875	310	32.07345	86.11747	2762.08472	310	34.18842	84.72002	2896.44385
311	30.42116	87.58896	2664.55786	311	32.43428	86.14830	2794.15820	311	34.58016	84.74894	2930.63232
312	30.75706	87.62148	2694.97900	312	32.79916	86.17879	2826.59253	312	34.97639	84.77753	2965.21240
313	31.09667	87.65363	2725.73608	313	33.16816	86.20894	2859.39160	313	35.37718	84.80580	3000.18872
314	31.44003	87.68544	2756.83276	314	33.54130	86.23875	2892.55981	314	35.78252	84.83375	3035.56592
315	31.78718	87.71690	2788.27271	315	33.91864	86.26823	2926.10107	315	36.19254	84.86137	3071.34839
316	32.13816	87.74801	2820.05981	316	34.30022	86.29739	2960.01978	316	36.60724	84.88869	3107.54102
317	32.49302	87.77879	2852.19800	317	34.68610	86.32622	2994.31982	317	37.02670	84.91570	3144.14819
318	32.85180	87.80923	2884.69116	318	35.07632	86.35473	3029.00610	318	37.45096	84.94241	3181.17505
319	33.21453	87.83933	2917.54297	319	35.47092	86.38292	3064.08228	319	37.88009	84.96880	3218.62598
320	33.58128	87.86911	2950.75732	320	35.86997	86.41080	3099.55322	320	38.31413	84.99490	3256.50610
321	33.95207	87.89857	2984.33862	321	36.27351	86.43837	3135.42334	321	38.75315	85.02071	3294.82007
322	34.32696	87.92770	3018.29004	322	36.68159	86.46563	3171.61678	322	39.19719	85.04622	3333.57324
323	34.70599	87.95651	3052.61768	323	37.09426	86.49258	3208.37642	323	39.64633	85.07144	3372.77051
324	35.08920	87.98501	3087.32373	324	37.51157	86.51925	3245.47266	324	40.10061	85.09638	3412.41675
325	35.47664	88.01320	3122.41284	325	37.93357	86.54561	3282.98413	325	40.56010	85.12103	3452.51733

n				n				n			
326	35.86838	88.04108	3157.88935	326	38.36032	86.57168	3320.91772	326	41.02485	85.14541	3489.07739
327	36.26441	88.06866	3190.75781	327	38.79188	86.59746	3359.27808	327	41.49492	85.18961	3534.10229
328	36.66433	88.09592	3223.82846	328	39.22828	86.62295	3396.06982	328	41.97039	85.19334	3575.59717
329	37.06967	88.12290	3256.68726	329	39.66961	86.64816	3437.29810	329	42.45129	85.21689	3617.56763
330	37.47898	88.14958	3303.75684	330	40.11589	86.67308	3476.96777	330	42.93722	85.24018	3660.01904
331	37.89281	88.17597	3341.25384	331	40.56719	86.69773	3517.08374	331	43.42971	85.26321	3702.96679
332	38.31121	88.20208	3379.12866	332	41.02357	86.72211	3557.85088	332	43.92735	85.28597	3746.38647
333	38.73423	88.22790	3417.43994	333	41.48509	86.74622	3596.67456	333	44.43068	85.30848	3790.31372
334	39.16192	88.25343	3456.17407	334	41.95179	86.77005	3640.15967	334	44.93978	85.33073	3834.74438
335	39.59433	88.27869	3496.33594	335	42.42375	86.79362	3682.11133	335	45.45472	85.35273	3879.68433
336	40.03152	88.30367	3534.93042	336	42.90102	86.81693	3724.53516	336	45.97555	85.37448	3925.13892
337	40.47354	88.32838	3574.96191	337	43.38366	86.83998	3767.43604	337	46.50235	85.39599	3971.11450
338	40.90043	88.35281	3615.43530	338	43.87172	86.86278	3810.81982	338	47.03519	85.41724	4017.61694
339	41.37226	88.37698	3656.35596	339	44.36528	86.88531	3854.69141	339	47.57414	85.43826	4064.65210
340	41.82030	88.40089	3697.72603	340	44.86439	86.90761	3899.05688	340	48.11926	85.45905	4112.22607
341	42.29094	88.42454	3739.55713	341	45.36911	86.92965	3943.92114	341	48.67062	85.47959	4160.34521
342	42.75791	88.44792	3781.84814	342	45.87952	86.95145	3989.29028	342	49.22831	85.49991	4209.01611
343	43.23003	88.47105	3824.60596	343	46.39566	86.97300	4035.16992	343	49.79838	85.51999	4258.24414
344	43.70736	88.49393	3867.83618	344	46.91761	86.99431	4082.56543	344	50.36292	85.53985	4308.03662
345	44.18996	88.51656	3911.54346	345	47.44543	87.01539	4128.48291	345	50.93999	85.55948	4358.39941
346	44.67789	88.53895	3965.73340	346	47.97919	87.03623	4175.92822	346	51.52368	85.57889	4409.33336
347	45.17121	88.56108	4000.41138	347	48.51896	87.05684	4223.90771	347	52.11406	85.59808	4460.06328
348	45.66997	88.58298	4045.58252	348	49.06490	87.07722	4272.42676	348	52.71120	85.61705	4512.97705
349	46.17424	88.60464	4091.25244	349	49.61678	87.09737	4321.49121	349	53.31518	85.63580	4565.68948
350	46.68409	88.62606	4137.42676	350	50.17487	87.11731	4371.10840	350	53.92609	85.65435	4619.00391

Table 1. (continued) Annuities

M	C(13.25,M,12)	A(13.25,M,12)	S(13.25,M,12)	M	C(13.50,M,12)	A(13.50,M,12)	S(13.50,M,12)	M	C(13.75,M,12)	A(13.75,M,12)	S(13.75,M,12)
351	47.19955	88.64725	4184.11084	351	50.73944	87.13702	4421.28320	351	54.54398	85.67268	4672.92989
352	47.72072	88.66820	4231.31006	352	51.31025	87.15650	4472.02246	352	55.16897	85.69080	4727.47363
353	48.24763	88.68893	4279.03076	353	51.88750	87.17577	4523.33301	353	55.80112	85.70972	4782.64258
354	48.79037	88.70943	4327.27881	354	52.47123	87.19483	4575.22021	354	56.44050	85.72645	4838.44385
355	49.31898	88.72970	4376.05908	355	53.06153	87.21368	4627.69141	355	57.08722	85.74397	4894.88428
356	49.86355	88.74976	4425.37793	356	53.65847	87.23232	4680.75293	356	57.74134	85.76128	4951.97168
357	50.41413	88.76959	4475.24170	357	54.26213	87.25075	4734.41162	357	58.40296	85.77840	5009.71289
358	50.97078	88.78922	4525.65576	358	54.87258	87.26897	4788.67383	358	59.07216	85.79633	5068.11572
359	51.53358	88.80862	4576.62646	359	55.48989	87.28699	4843.54639	359	59.74903	85.81207	5127.18799
360	52.10260	88.82781	4628.16016	360	56.11416	87.30481	4899.03613	360	60.43365	85.82961	5186.93701
361	52.67790	88.84679	4680.26270	361	56.74544	87.32243	4955.15039	361	61.12613	85.84498	5247.37061
362	53.25965	88.86557	4732.94043	362	57.38383	87.33996	5011.89600	362	61.82653	85.86115	5308.49707
363	53.84763	88.88414	4786.20020	363	58.02940	87.35709	5069.27979	363	62.53496	85.87740	5370.32324
364	54.44220	88.90250	4840.04785	364	58.68223	87.37414	5127.30908	364	63.25150	85.89295	5432.85840
365	55.04333	88.92068	4894.48975	365	59.34240	87.39098	5185.99121	365	63.97626	85.90858	5496.10996
366	55.65110	88.93864	4949.53320	366	60.01001	87.40765	5245.33350	366	64.70932	85.92403	5560.08594
367	56.26558	88.95641	5005.18408	367	60.68512	87.42413	5305.34375	367	65.45078	85.93932	5624.79641
368	56.88684	88.97400	5061.44971	368	61.36782	87.44042	5366.02881	368	66.20074	85.95442	5690.24609
369	57.51497	88.99138	5118.33691	369	62.05821	87.45654	5427.39648	369	66.96929	85.96935	5756.44678
370	58.15003	89.00858	5175.85156	370	62.75637	87.47247	5489.45459	370	67.72653	85.98412	5823.40625
371	58.79210	89.02559	5234.00195	371	63.46238	87.48801	5552.21094	371	68.50256	85.99872	5891.13281
372	59.44127	89.04241	5292.79395	372	64.17632	87.50381	5615.67334	372	69.28749	86.01315	5959.63525
373	60.09760	89.05905	5352.23535	373	64.89831	87.51922	5679.85010	373	70.08141	86.02742	6028.92285
374	60.76117	89.07551	5412.33252	374	65.62842	87.53446	5744.74805	374	70.88442	86.04153	6099.00439
375	61.43208	89.09179	5473.03375	375	66.36674	87.54962	5810.37646	375	71.65664	86.05547	6169.88867

idx								
376	62.11039	89.10789	5534.52588	67.11337	87.56442	5876.74316	72.51817	86.06996	6241.58545
377	62.78619	89.12381	5596.63623	67.66839	87.57916	5943.85693	73.34910	86.08289	6314.10352
378	63.48957	89.13966	5659.43262	68.63190	87.59373	6011.72510	74.18956	86.09637	6387.45264
379	64.19060	89.15514	5722.98236	69.40401	87.60814	6080.36593	75.03965	86.10970	6461.64209
380		89.17055	5787.11279	70.18481	87.62239	6149.78123	75.89948	86.12268	6536.68164
381	65.61597	89.18579	5852.01221	70.97439	87.63647	6219.94590	76.76916	86.13590	6612.58105
382	66.34048	89.20097	5917.62788	71.77285	87.65041	6290.92041	77.64690	86.14878	6689.35059
383	67.07298	89.21577	5983.96875	72.56030	87.66418	6362.69287	78.53853	86.16151	6766.99902
384	67.81358	89.23052	6051.04150	73.35683	87.67781	6435.27344	79.43845	86.17410	6845.53760
385	68.56236	89.24510	6118.85498	74.22254	87.69128	6508.67041	80.34069	86.18655	6924.97607
386	69.31940	89.25953	6187.41748	75.05794	87.70461	6582.89058	81.26935	86.19885	7005.32471
387	70.08490	89.27380	6256.73682	75.90194	87.71778	6657.96020	82.20056	86.21102	7096.59424
388	70.85966	89.28791	6326.82178	76.75584	87.73081	6733.85205	83.14244	86.22305	7168.79492
389	71.64105	89.30187	6397.68018	77.61934	87.74370	6810.60791	84.09512	86.23494	7251.93750
390	72.43029	89.31567	6469.32129	78.49256	87.75643	6888.22754	85.05870	86.24670	7336.03223
391	73.23186	89.32933	6541.75342	79.37560	87.76904	6966.72021	86.03333	86.25832	7421.09131
392	74.04046	89.34283	6614.98535	80.26858	87.78149	7046.09670	87.01913	86.26981	7507.12451
393	74.85799	89.35619	6689.02588	81.17159	87.79381	7126.36428	88.01623	86.28117	7594.14355
394	75.68455	89.36941	6763.88379	82.08478	87.80599	7207.53564	89.02475	86.29240	7682.14355
395	76.52023	89.38248	6839.56836	83.00823	87.81804	7289.62061	90.04482	86.30351	7771.18457
396	77.36514	89.39540	6916.08838	83.94207	87.82996	7372.62891	91.07658	86.31449	7861.22949
397	78.21938	89.40819	6993.45361	84.80642	87.84174	7456.57080	92.12017	86.32535	7952.30615
398	79.08005	89.42083	7071.87334	85.84139	87.85339	7541.45752	93.17571	86.33607	8044.42627
399	79.95627	89.43334	7150.75635	86.80711	87.86711	7627.29683	94.24335	86.34669	8137.60205
400	80.83912	89.44571	7230.71240	87.78369	87.87630	7714.10596	95.32323	86.35718	8231.84473

Table 1. (continued) Annuities

N	C(13.25,M,12)	A(13.25,M,12)	S(13.25,M,12)
401	81.73171	89.45795	7311.55176
402	82.63417	89.47005	7393.28320
403	83.54659	89.48202	7475.91748
404	84.46908	89.49386	7559.46387
405	85.40176	89.50556	7643.93311
406	86.34474	89.51714	7729.33496
407	87.29813	89.52860	7815.67969
408	88.26205	89.53993	7902.97803
409	89.23660	89.55114	7991.23975
410	90.22192	89.56222	8080.47656
411	91.21812	89.57318	8170.69824
412	92.22533	89.58402	8261.91602
413	93.24365	89.59475	8354.14160
414	94.27322	89.60535	8447.38574
415	95.31415	89.61586	8541.65820
416	96.36658	89.62623	8636.97266
417	97.43063	89.63649	8733.33887
418	98.50642	89.64664	8830.76953
419	99.59409	89.65668	8929.27637
420	100.69378	89.66661	9028.87012
421	101.80560	89.67644	9129.56445
422	102.92971	89.68615	9231.37012
423	104.06622	89.69576	9334.28990
424	105.21528	89.70527	9438.36523
425	106.37704	89.71467	9543.58105

N	C(13.50,M,12)	A(13.50,M,12)	S(13.50,M,12)
401	88.77126	87.86756	7801.88965
402	89.76994	87.89070	7890.66064
403	90.77965	87.90971	7980.43066
404	91.90112	87.92661	8071.21045
405	92.83388	87.93138	8163.01172
406	93.87826	87.94203	8255.84570
407	94.93439	87.95257	8349.72363
408	96.00240	87.96298	8444.65820
409	97.08243	87.97328	8540.66016
410	98.17461	87.96347	8637.74316
411	99.27908	87.99354	8735.91699
412	100.39597	88.00350	8835.19629
413	101.52541	88.01335	8935.59277
414	102.66758	88.02309	9037.11816
415	103.82259	88.03272	9139.78516
416	104.99059	88.04225	9243.60840
417	106.17174	88.05167	9348.59863
418	107.36617	88.06098	9454.77051
419	108.57404	88.07019	9562.13672
420	109.79549	88.07930	9670.71094
421	111.03069	88.08830	9790.50596
422	112.27979	88.09721	9891.53711
423	113.54294	88.10602	10003.81641
424	114.82030	88.11473	10117.35938
425	116.11202	88.12334	10232.17969

N	C(13.75,M,12)	A(13.75,M,12)	S(13.75,M,12)
401	95.41547	86.36755	8327.16797
402	97.52023	86.37781	8423.58398
403	98.63765	86.38794	8521.10352
404	99.76788	86.39739	8619.74121
405	100.91105	86.40788	8719.50977
406	102.06732	86.41767	8820.42090
407	103.23684	86.42736	8922.48828
408	104.41976	86.43694	9025.72461
409	105.61624	86.44640	9130.14453
410	106.82642	86.45576	9235.76074
411	108.05048	86.46502	9342.58691
412	109.28856	86.47417	9450.63770
413	110.54082	86.48322	9559.92578
414	111.80743	86.49216	9670.46680
415	113.08856	86.50101	9782.27441
416	114.38437	86.50974	9896.36328
417	115.69502	86.51839	10009.74707
418	117.02070	86.52693	10125.44238
419	118.36156	86.53539	10242.46289
420	119.71778	86.54374	10360.82422
421	121.08965	86.55199	10480.54199
422	122.47704	86.56016	10601.63184
423	123.88042	86.56823	10724.10938
424	125.29988	86.57621	10847.98926
425	126.73561	86.58411	10973.28906

426	107.55162	89.72316	9640.95901	426	117.41828	88.13196	10348.29196	426	128.1877	86.5919	11100.02539
427	108.73917	89.73316	9757.50977	427	118.73924	88.14028	10465.70398	427	129.65660	86.59362	11228.21288
428	109.95393	89.74226	9866.24302	428	120.07506	88.14861	10584.44922	428	131.14226	86.60724	11357.86914
429	111.15376	89.75125	9976.18948	429	121.42590	88.15685	10704.52441	429	132.64433	86.61478	11489.01172
430	112.38107	89.76015	10087.34277	430	122.79196	88.16499	10825.96020	430	134.16	86.62224	11621.65625
431	113.62195	89.76895	10199.72363	431	124.17336	88.17304	10948.74219	431	135.70212	86.62960	11755.82128
432	114.87653	89.77768	10313.34570	432	125.57030	88.18101	11072.91602	432	137.25708	86.63689	11891.53344
433	116.14496	89.78633	10428.22168	433	126.98297	88.18888	11196.49633	433	138.8977	86.64409	12028.79027
434	117.42738	89.79478	10544.36719	434	128.41153	88.19666	11325.46875	434	140.42058	86.65121	12167.61035
435	118.72398	89.80320	10661.79195	435	129.85616	88.20437	11453.86006	435	142.02963	86.65826	12308.03125
436	120.03489	89.81154	10780.51855	436	131.31703	88.21198	11583.78633	436	143.65694	86.66521	12450.06055
437	121.36028	89.81978	10900.55273	437	132.79436	88.21951	11715.05371	437	145.30301	86.67210	12539.71777
438	122.70029	89.82798	11021.91309	438	134.28828	88.22696	11847.84766	438	146.96794	86.67890	12739.02051
439	124.05511	89.83598	11144.61426	439	135.79903	88.23432	11982.13672	439	148.65196	86.68563	12886.96828
440	125.42489	89.84396	11268.66895	440	137.32677	88.24161	12117.90555	440	150.35526	86.69228	13034.64063
441	126.80978	89.85184	11394.03075	441	138.87170	88.24880	12255.26172	441	152.07808	86.69865	13184.99512
442	128.20998	89.85964	11520.90332	442	140.43401	88.25593	12394.13379	442	153.82663	86.70536	13337.07324
443	129.62563	89.86738	11649.11328	443	142.01389	88.26297	12534.56836	443	155.58316	86.71178	13490.89453
444	131.05692	89.87499	11778.73926	444	143.61154	88.26993	12676.58203	444	157.36589	86.71814	13646.47754
445	132.50400	89.88254	11909.79560	445	145.22717	88.27682	12820.19336	445	159.16104	86.72442	13803.84375
446	133.96706	89.89000	12042.29960	446	146.86098	88.28362	12965.42090	446	160.99284	86.73063	13963.01270
447	135.44629	89.89738	12176.26758	447	148.51317	88.29036	13112.28125	447	162.83755	86.73677	14124.00488
448	136.94183	89.90469	12311.71387	448	150.18394	88.29702	13260.?	448	164.70340	86.74284	14286.84277
449	138.45390	89.91191	12448.65527	449	151.87350	88.30360	13410.97852	449	166.59064	86.74885	14451.54590
450	139.96287	89.91905	12587.10938	450	153.58208	88.31011	13562.86254	450	168.49940	86.75478	14618.13672

Table 1. (continued) Annuities

M	C(13.25,M,12)	A(13.25,M,12)	S(13.25,M,12)	C(13.50,M,12)	A(13.50,M,12)	S(13.50,M,12)	C(13.75,M,12)	A(13.75,M,12)	S(13.75,M,12)
451	141.52831	89.92612	12727.09180	155.30988	88.31655	13716.43457	170.43021	86.76065	14786.63672
452	143.09102	89.93311	12868.62012	157.05711	88.32292	13871.74414	172.38306	86.76645	14957.06641
453	144.67037	89.94002	13011.71094	158.82401	88.32822	14028.60078	174.35828	86.77219	15129.44922
454	146.26839	89.94686	13156.38184	160.61078	88.33544	14187.62500	176.35612	86.77785	15303.80762
455	147.88344	89.95360	13302.65039	162.41765	88.34160	14348.26633	178.37688	86.78346	15480.16406
456	149.51631	89.96030	13450.53418	164.24486	88.34769	14510.65332	180.42078	86.78901	15658.54102
457	151.16722	89.96690	13600.05078	166.09261	88.35371	14674.89944	182.48810	86.79449	15838.96191
458	152.83636	89.97346	13751.21777	167.96115	88.35966	14840.99121	184.57912	86.79990	16021.45020
459	154.52398	89.97993	13904.05371	169.85071	88.36555	15008.95215	186.69408	86.80526	16206.02930
460	156.23013	89.98634	14058.57813	171.76154	88.37137	15178.80273	188.83328	86.81055	16392.72266
461	157.95517	89.99267	14214.80762	173.69385	88.37713	15350.56445	190.99699	86.81579	16581.55664
462	159.69926	89.99893	14372.76367	175.64730	88.38282	15524.25879	193.18550	86.82097	16772.55273
463	161.46260	90.00513	14532.46289	177.62395	88.38845	15699.90625	195.39909	86.82609	16965.73828
464	163.24542	90.01125	14693.92490	179.62221	88.39402	15877.53027	197.69803	86.83115	17161.13672
465	165.04789	90.01731	14857.17090	181.64296	88.39952	16057.15234	199.90263	86.83615	17358.77539
466	166.87033	90.02330	15022.21875	183.68645	88.40497	16238.79590	202.13319	86.84109	17558.67773
467	168.71286	90.02923	15189.08887	185.75291	88.41035	16422.48242	204.50999	86.84599	17760.87109
468	170.57573	90.03509	15357.80176	187.84264	88.41567	16608.23438	206.85333	86.85081	17965.39096
469	172.45917	90.04089	15528.37695	189.95587	88.42094	16796.07617	209.22353	86.85560	18172.23438
470	174.36340	90.04662	15700.83691	192.09288	88.42615	16986.03320	211.62008	86.86032	18381.45898
471	176.28867	90.05230	15875.20020	194.25392	88.43130	17178.12500	214.04570	86.86498	18593.07813
472	178.23518	90.05791	16051.48828	196.43927	88.43639	17372.37891	216.49831	86.86961	18807.12500
473	180.20320	90.06345	16229.72363	198.64922	88.44142	17568.81836	218.97902	86.87418	19023.62305
474	182.19295	90.06895	16409.92578	200.88402	88.44640	17767.46875	221.48816	86.87869	19242.60156
475	184.20465	90.07437	16592.11914	203.14397	88.45132	17968.35156	224.02603	86.88316	19464.08984

476	186.23859	90.07974	16776.32422	205.42934	476	88.45618	18171.43609	226.53100	476	86.88757	19688.11719
477	188.29497	90.08505	16862.56250	207.74042	477	88.46100	18376.92578	229.18938	477	86.89194	19914.70898
478	190.37405	90.09031	17150.85742	210.07750	478	88.46576	18584.66602	231.81551	478	86.89625	20143.89844
479	192.47610	90.09550	17341.23242	212.44087	479	88.47047	18794.74414	234.47173	479	86.90051	20375.71484
480	194.60136	90.10064	17533.70703	214.83083	480	88.47512	19007.18359	237.15839	480	86.90473	20610.18555
481	196.75009	90.10572	17728.30859	217.24768	481	88.47973	19222.01563	239.87582	481	86.90890	20847.34375
482	198.92253	90.11075	17925.05859	219.69711	482	88.48428	19439.26367	242.62440	482	86.91302	21087.22070
483	201.11897	90.11572	18123.98242	222.16324	483	88.48878	19658.96508	245.40448	483	86.91710	21329.84375
484	203.33966	90.12064	18325.10156	224.66258	484	88.49323	19881.11719	248.21640	484	86.92113	21575.25000
485	205.58487	90.12550	18528.44141	227.19003	485	88.49763	20105.78125	251.06055	485	86.92511	21823.46484
486	207.85487	90.13032	18734.02539	229.74593	486	88.50198	20332.97070	253.53729	486	86.92905	22074.52539
487	210.14933	90.13508	18941.88086	232.33057	487	88.50629	20562.71690	256.84698	487	86.93294	22328.46289
488	212.47034	90.13978	19152.02930	234.94427	488	88.51054	20795.04688	259.73001	488	86.93679	22585.31055
489	214.81636	90.14444	19364.50000	237.58740	489	88.51475	21029.99819	262.76678	489	86.94059	22845.09961
490	217.18829	90.14904	19579.31641	240.26027	490	88.51891	21267.57813	265.77765	490	86.94436	23107.86719
491	219.58641	90.15359	19796.50586	242.96320	491	88.52303	21507.83984	268.82300	491	86.94807	23373.64453
492	222.01102	90.15810	20016.09180	245.69653	492	88.52710	21750.80273	271.90326	492	86.95175	23642.46875
493	224.46239	90.16255	20238.10352	248.46062	493	88.53113	21996.49905	275.01883	493	86.95539	23914.37109
494	226.94083	90.16696	20462.56445	251.25590	494	88.53510	22244.96890	278.17007	494	86.95899	24189.39063
495	229.44662	90.17132	20689.50586	254.08243	495	88.53904	22496.21484	281.35745	495	86.96254	24467.56055
496	231.98010	90.17563	20918.95313	256.94096	496	88.54293	22750.23688	284.58133	496	86.96605	24748.97197
497	234.54155	90.17989	21150.33359	259.83142	497	88.54678	23007.23828	287.84216	497	86.96953	25033.49905
498	237.13129	90.18411	21385.47461	262.75455	498	88.55059	23267.07031	291.14035	498	86.97296	25321.34180
499	239.74960	90.18828	21622.60547	265.71051	499	88.55435	23529.82422	294.47635	499	86.97636	25612.48047
500	242.36684	90.19241	21862.35547	268.69977	500	88.55807	23795.53516	297.85056	500	86.97971	25906.95703

INDEX

A

Abandonment, as lease provision, 225
Acceleration clause, as mortgage provision, 209–10
Acceptance
  as lease validity requirement, 228
  mortgages, 206
Accrued depreciation, 42–46
  measures of, 43–46
    comparable income method, 43
    comparable sales method, 43
    formula method, 44–46
  sources of, 42–43
    economic obsolescene, 43
    functional obsolescence, 43
    physical deterioration, 42
Acknowledgment, as lease validity requirement, 228
Actual eviction, 229
Agents, construction mortgages, designation of, 108
Alternation/destruction, as mortgage provision, 209
Annual mortgage constant, 144–46
Annuities
  exponential annuity, 269
  future value of, 267, 269–73
  linear annuity, 269
  present value of, 267, 274–81
  sum of, 266–67
  table, 284–522
  types of, 268–69
    annuity due, 268
    deferred annuity, 268–69
    ordinary annuity, 268
Annuity due, definition of, 268

Appraisals, 37–79
  approaches to
    cost approach, 37, 39, 40–46
    income approach, 37, 39, 46–59
    market approach, 37, 39, 59–71
  direct capitalization, 53–54
  formulas, 53–59
  property description/location, 71–76
    government survey, 74–76
    lot and block number, 71–72
    metes and bounds, 72–74
  residual techniques, 54–59
    building residual technique, 56–58
    land residual technique, 58–59
    property residual technique, 59
  See also Real estate valuation
Arbitration, as lease provision, 226
Area of lot
  determination of, 76–79
  polygonal lot, 78–79
  quadrilateral lot having two parallel sides, 77–78
  triangular lot, 76–77
Asking price
  varying balloon payment date and, 17–19
  varying down payment and, 22–23
Assessment lien, 237
Assessments, installment land contracts, 113
Assignment
  installment land contracts, 110, 113
  as lease provision, 224
  mechanic's lien, 244
  mortgages, 199–200
Attachment lien, 237–40